THE USAF IN THE PERSIAN GULF WAR

Airpower Advantage

Planning the Gulf War Air Campaign 1989–1991

Diane T. Putney

Air Force History and Museums Program
United States Air Force
Washington, D.C., 2004

Opinions, conclusions, and recommendations expressed or implied within are solely those of the author and do not necessarily represent the views of the Air Force History and Museums Program, the U.S. Air Force, the Department of Defense, or any other U.S. government agency.

Photographs on pages 26 and 220 appear here courtesy of the George Bush Presidential Library.

The maps shown on the cover of this book were created by air campaign planners in Riyadh in preparation for the 1990–1991 Persian Gulf War.

Library of Congress Cataloging-in-Publication Data

Putney, Diane T. (Diane Therese), 1949–
Airpower advantage : planning the Gulf War air campaign, 1989–1991 / Diane T. Putney.
p. cm. — (The USAF in the Persian Gulf War)
Includes bibliographical references and index.
1. Persian Gulf War, 1991 — Aerial operations, American. 2. Military planning — United States. 3. United States. Air Force — History. I. Title. II. Series.

Foreword

American air power is a dominant force in today's world. Its ascendancy, evolving in the half century since the end of World War II, became evident during the first Gulf War. Although a great deal has been written about military operations in Desert Shield and Desert Storm, this deeply researched volume by Dr. Diane Putney probes the little-known story of how the Gulf War air campaign plan came to fruition.

Based on archival documentation and interviews with USAF planners, this work takes the reader into the planning cells where the difficult work of building an air campaign plan was accomplished on an around-the-clock basis. The tension among air planners is palpable as Dr. Putney traces the incremental progress and friction along the way.

The author places the complexities of the planning process within the context of coalition objectives. All the major players are here: President George H. W. Bush, General H. Norman Schwarzkopf, General Colin Powell, General Chuck Horner, and Secretary of Defense Richard Cheney.

The air planning process generated much debate and friction, but resulted in great success — a 43-day conflict with minimum casualties. Dr. Putney's rendering of this behind-the-scenes evolution of the planning process, in its complexity and even suspense, provides a fascinating window into how wars are planned and fought today and what might be the implications for the future.

C. R. ANDEREGG
Director of Air Force History

Preface

Planning air campaigns is crucially important to airmen, notably to those planning the 1991 Desert Storm campaign. Their air plan emerged, expanded, and evolved as individuals from Florida and South Carolina military bases, from Saudi Arabia, the Pentagon, and the White House all contributed to the process. That the officers responsible for crafting the Gulf War air plan found the ordeal to be arduous, complicated, and contentious is undeniable, but we have now a documented, close look at the collaborative, intellectual effort that went into producing their war plan. Although *planning* is seemingly less exciting than *combat*, the Desert Storm undertaking included strong-willed officers, bold thinking, and the clash and melding of ideas. Planners knew that if their ideas were not sound and shrewd, they doomed the pilots and the war's outcome. Many key participants generously shared their experiences, and their vivid words enliven this account.

When Iraq invaded Kuwait in August 1990, the unified combatant command responsible for Southwest Asia, the U.S. Central Command, had no *offensive* plan ready to execute in response to Iraqi aggression. The U.S. Central Command Commander, General H. Norman Schwarzkopf, USA, directed and participated in the offensive planning process that lasted throughout Desert Shield and continued even as the air war commenced on January 17, 1991. He described the enterprise: "It is a tortuous process coming up with the decisions that involve the lives of hundreds of thousands of people. It's not simple. . . . You agonize over your decisions. You agonize over your plan." Because the Central Command commander would execute air operations in all phases of his offensive plan, the air campaign was the dominant feature in the Gulf War of 1991. As early as August 25, 1990, the basic framework of the war plan had emerged, with Phase I, Strategic Air Campaign; Phase II, Air Supremacy in Kuwait; Phase III, Attrition of Ground Combat Power (later, Preparation of the Battlefield); and Phase IV, Ground Attack.

Schwarzkopf appointed as his Joint Force Air Component Commander Lt. Gen. Charles A. Horner, the U.S. Central Command Air Forces Commander. This study shows that Horner had to defend the existence of the JFACC function, often countering complaints from other component commands. His experiences in the Vietnam War affected how he carried out his JFACC responsibilities and operated the Tactical Air Control System. The Commander, U.S. Central Command heeded his advice to think in terms of target sets and objectives when wielding the aerial weapon, and throughout Desert Shield Schwarzkopf said little about apportionment and allocation and much about what he expected air power to accomplish.

Air Force, Navy, Marine Corps, and Army forces executed the air campaign, and war preparations were joint, with Coalition partners participating, before and during the war. Numerous issues involving air tasking authority, procedures and policies, weapon systems and missions, and targets had to be aired and resolved. Concepts from two sets of defensive plans worked their way into Desert Storm products. Before the Iraqis invaded Kuwait, the Central Command concentrated its efforts on producing Operations Plan 1002–90 to defend Saudi Arabia against an Iraqi invasion, and from this document emerged the idea that air power had to attrit enemy ground forces to the extent that force ratios changed in favor of Coalition troops launching a counterattack.

The Air Staff, through its Deputy Directorate for Warfighting Concepts (usually called Checkmate, shortened form of the name of one of the directorate divisions) led by Col. John A. Warden III, made important contributions to air campaign planning. Warden turned a request for an air retaliation option into a strategic air campaign and sold it to Schwarzkopf, which, in the words of General Colin L. Powell, former Chairman of the Joint Chiefs of Staff, "remained the heart of the Desert Storm air war."

After the conflict, Horner observed, "In wartime, it all starts and ends with intelligence." CENTAF's chief intelligence officer, Col. Christopher Christon, thought the war would inflict on the intelligence function "two sucking chest wounds," referring to difficulties in disseminating target material and in assessing bomb damage. His prediction proved to be correct, and this study attempts to untangle problems and accomplishments with intelligence-related personalities, procedures, and technology. In October 1990 the planning emphasis shifted from the strategic campaign to the air counterland phase to attrit the enemy fielded army down to the 50 percent level. This was an extraordinary task that the Central Command commander levied on airmen, who confidently accepted the historic mission.

The Air Force History Support Office (AFHSO) has produced three other Persian Gulf War studies complementary to this one, covering the Desert Shield deployment and logistics, the execution of the strategic air campaign, and the air war in the Kuwaiti theater of operations, by William T. Y'Blood, Richard G. Davis, and Perry D. Jamieson, respectively.

Special thanks go to the Air Force leaders and planners who produced the air campaign and generously gave their time for interviews, some in several sessions, and then helped again by reading and critiquing the manuscript and answering follow-up questions: General Charles A. "Chuck" Horner, Col. John A. Warden III, Lt. Gen. Buster C. Glosson, Maj. Gen. David A. Deptula, Col. Samuel J. Baptiste, Brig. Gen. Richard B. H. "Rick" Lewis, Lt. Col. John R.

Glock, and CMSgt John Burton. General Deptula took time from his enormously busy schedule to provide documents and photographs.

Others who carefully reviewed the manuscript and offered valuable comments were Col. George K. Williams, Herman S. Wolk, Wayne W. Thompson, Perry D. Jamieson, and Richard G. Davis from AFHSO; Col. Allan W. Howey, Col. Richard T. Reynolds, and Col. Edward C. Mann from Air University; and Jeffery S. Underwood and James M. George from the Air Combat Command. Herman Wolk also directed the book through the lengthy declassification and policy review processes. Wayne Thompson, the historian from AFHSO temporarily assigned to Checkmate before and during the war, patiently answered my many questions about the planning effort, offered good counsel, and unstintingly helped with the book in a variety of ways from start to finish.

Many officers gave interviews, most in person and some over the telephone, with the complete list included in the bibliography. Special acknowledgment goes to Vice Adm. John M. McConnell, Lt. Gen. Robert M. Alexander, Maj. Gen. Larry L. Henry, Col. James R. Blackburn, Col. Christopher L. Christon, Col. Bernard E. "Ben" Harvey, Col. John Leonardo, Col. Mark B. "Buck" Rogers, Col. Roy "Mac" Sikes, Col. William Bruner, and Col. Gary Ware.

Richard H. Kohn, the Air Force Historian during the Gulf War, strongly advocated the view that the Center for Air Force History should produce Air Force history books, and his deputy, Col. David A. Tretler, assigned historians to write the set of Gulf War books and got the project off to a superb start. Robert P. Smith approved my assignment to the project, and Richard P. Hallion, the subsequent Air Force Historian, enthusiastically endorsed the project and included me as a team member in his Gulf War "road show" briefing circuit. Expert assistance acquiring microfilm, articles, books, and photos came from William C. Heimdahl, Sheldon A. Goldberg, Yvonne Kinkaid, Vicky Crone, and William T. "Tom" Y'Blood. Sheldon Goldberg helped with security procedures.

Personnel at the Air Force Historical Research Agency (AFHRA) and at the command history offices greatly assisted with the search for documents and other tasks: Frederick Shaw, Timothy Warnock, Joseph Caver, Archangelo "Archie" DiFante, MSgt. Barry Spink, and Lt. Col. Richard Sergeant, USAFR, at AFHRA; Grant M. Hales at Air Combat Command; David L. Rosmer at Ninth Air Force; George W. "Skip" Bradley at Air Force Space Command; Donald W. Klinko at Air Logistics Command; MSgt. Theodore J. "Jackie" Turner at Air Intelligence Agency; Herbert A. Mason at Air Force Special Operations Command; Robert L. Mandler at Air Warfare Center; and Robert B. Sligh at Third Air Force. A history involving a unified command requires research outside the Air Force and most helpful were Ronald H. Cole and Wayne M. Dzwonchyk from the Joint History Office; Hans S. Pawlisch from Central Command; Edward J. Marolda from the Naval Historical Center; Deane Allen from the Defense Intelligence Agency; and Dale Steinhauer from the Center for Army Lessons Learned.

The chief of the editing section at AFHSO, Richard I. Wolf, assisted with computer equipment and software programs, simple and complex. Barbara Wittig expertly functioned as the lead editor, and in her capable, experienced hands the manuscript became a book.

The Author

The author, Diane T. Putney, is a historian with the Historical Office of the Office of the Secretary of Defense. From 1982 to 1983 she served as the historian for the 1100th Air Base Wing, Military Airlift Command. From 1983 to 1989 she was the historian for the Air Force Intelligence Agency. She then assumed responsibilities as the Assistant Deputy Chief Historian for Readiness and Field Programs, Office of the Air Force Historian. From 1992 to 2000 she was a historian with the Air Force History Support Office, Bolling AFB, serving as the office's Pentagon Team Chief, 1999–2000. Dr. Putney has written unit histories, articles, book reviews, and reports for special projects, lectured on airpower and intelligence history, and edited the book, *ULTRA and the Army Air Forces in World War II.*

Contents

Illustrations

Chapter One

OPLAN 1002–90

When Lt. Gen. Charles A. "Chuck" Horner, USAF, directed and coordinated the Desert Storm air campaign, he formally functioned as the nation's first Joint Force Air Component Commander (JFACC) in a major regional conflict. Under the authority of the Goldwater-Nichols Department of Defense (DoD) Reorganization Act of 1986, he had spent over three years preparing to be the JFACC in Southwest Asia (SWA) in case war broke out there, involving aircraft and weapons systems from the Air Force, Army, Navy, and Marine Corps and from other nations. Deployments to the region, exercises, and training gave him and his staff valuable experience in carrying out his JFACC responsibilities. Military service viewpoints always surfaced and sometimes threatened the centralized control of air power, the essence of the JFACC function, but Horner held firm to the value of applying the unity of command principle to the control of air assets. As a commander who had spent his career in the Tactical Air Command (TAC), he understood well the Army's AirLand Battle doctrine and strove to integrate Army representatives fully into his Tactical Air Control Center (TACC). As the Cold War ended, Iraq emerged as the major threat to peace in the Middle East, and Horner planned to employ air power to defend the Arabian peninsula against the Iraqis, according to the U.S. Central Command's (CENTCOM's) Operations Plan (OPLAN) 1002–90.

U.S. Central Command Air Forces

In March 1987, General Horner assumed command of the Ninth Air Force and U.S. Central Command Air Forces (CENTAF) headquartered at Shaw Air Force Base (AFB), South Carolina. Two months later, he pinned on his third star as a lieutenant general. This 51-year-old pilot had attended the University of Iowa and earned a bachelor of arts degree in 1958. After receiving a commission as a second lieutenant in the U.S. Air Force, he earned his pilot wings in 1959.

He served two tours of duty in Southeast Asia during the Vietnam War, flying more than a hundred F–105 missions, many as a Wild Weasel, killing surface-to-air missile (SAM) radars. In the late 1970s he commanded training and fighter wings and in 1983 became commander of the Air Force's Air Defense Weapons Center. Two years later he assumed the duties of deputy chief of staff (DCS) for plans at TAC headquarters.[1]

Arriving at Shaw just six months after President Ronald W. Reagan signed the Goldwater-Nichols DoD Reorganization Act of 1986, Horner discovered he liked how the legislation increased the authority of the Chairman of the Joint Chiefs of Staff (CJCS) and the commanders of the unified and specified combatant commands, and he liked how it emphasized the joint conduct of military operations. (Joint operations and organizations are those in which elements of more than one military service participate. Unified commands are composed of forces from two or more military services, under a single commander.)[2]

The Goldwater-Nichols Act clearly delineated a chain of command that ran from the President to the Secretary of Defense (SecDef) to the commander of a unified command, unless the President directed otherwise. The President could require the CJCS to transmit messages from him and the SecDef — by definition, the National Command Authorities (NCA) — to a unified command, and the President could assign duties to the CJCS to assist him perform his command functions. The CJCS gained power at the expense of the service chiefs. He could now advise the President by virtue of his office; his counsel did not require consensus or a unanimous Joint Chiefs of Staff (JCS) position. The legislation also clarified the responsibilities of the unified commanders and increased their authority. In 1989, the CENTCOM commander (the CINCCENT) exercised his newly mandated authority to clarify the responsibilities of the component commanders. For example, he issued a regulation clearly stating that the Air Force component commander, the CENTAF commander, had operational control (OPCON) over all Air Force forces assigned to the CINCCENT, who himself held combatant command.[3]

Horner had two bosses in 1987. The CINCCENT, General George B. Crist, USMC, directed him as he functioned as CENTAF commander; and the TAC commander, General Robert D. Russ, USAF, directed him as he led the Ninth Air Force. As one of TAC's three numbered air forces, the Ninth served both as a supporting command within TAC and as a supported command within CENTCOM. Depending on the wartime scenario, it sent resources and personnel to other commands, or it received them. By increasing the authority and highlighting the importance of the unified commands, Goldwater-Nichols emphasized that Congress expected commanders to prepare for combat. If the President ordered CENTCOM to military action, CENTAF, not the Ninth Air Force, would deploy and fight as the component entity. Excluded from the warfighting chain of command were the TAC commander and the Air Force Chief of Staff (CSAF). (The Department of the Air Force functions to organize, train, equip, sustain, and provide operationally ready forces to the combatant commands, which employ them.)

CENTOM's mandate was to counter threats with force projection in the Middle East and the Horn of Africa. Established in 1983, it traced its lineage to the Rapid Deployment Joint Task Force which had evolved from a worldwide deployable force to a de facto regional unified command. Horner appreciated that General Russ at TAC headquarters understood the Goldwater-Nichols legislation and allowed him to fulfill his responsibilities as CENTAF commander within CENTCOM. Horner welcomed the freedom to concentrate on his warfighting role.[4]

CENTAF existed as one of CENTCOM's four service component commands. (The unified command itself was one of eight in the DoD.) The other three CENTCOM components were U.S. Army Forces Central Command (ARCENT) headquartered at Fort McPherson, Georgia; U.S. Naval Forces Central Command (NAVCENT), at Pearl Harbor, Hawaii; and U.S. Marine Forces Central Command (MARCENT), at Camp Pendleton, California. The Special Operations Command Central Command (SOCCENT), headquartered at MacDill AFB was a subunified command that provided forces for CENTCOM. CENTCOM's mission — to protect friendly nations, deter aggression, and counter hostile forces in its area of responsibility (AOR) — covered nineteen countries in SWA and Africa. Ensuring the readiness and employment of air resources in support of CENTCOM comprised CENTAF's mission.[5]

Horner Meets Schwarzkopf, February 1989

General Horner served under two CINCCENTs, General Crist and his successor, General H. Norman Schwarzkopf, USA, who arrived as commander in November 1988. Horner met with Schwarzkopf for the first time on February 21, 1989, at Shaw AFB.[6] Their daylong visit passed cordially, although the temperaments of the two commanders varied sharply. Horner was usually laid-back, conveying a casual ease, even when events turned chaotic and anger swelled within him. He gritted his teeth and seethed at times, but rarely did he become demonstrative and shout or pound the desk. Schwarzkopf, by contrast, was outspoken and excitable, prone to volcanic tirades, which soon subsided, and he nourished no persistent anger. His tempests occurred so frequently that they earned him the nickname, "Stormin' Norman."[7]

During their meeting, Horner asked two questions, prompting Schwarzkopf to state or clarify his intentions. The new CINCCENT communicated two crucial decisions that months later influenced the course of Desert Shield and Desert Storm. The airman had carefully considered his queries, knowing their grave importance to the CENTAF and CENTCOM missions. Horner never met with a commander without having first determined what he wanted to accomplish during the encounter.[8]

After briefing Schwarzkopf on the status of planning initiatives, Horner posed his first question. He pointed out that in CENTCOM under General Crist,

Lt. Gen. Charles A. Horner

the NAVCENT commander served as the CINCCENT's naval boss. The CENT-AF commander operated as his air chief — the JFACC. Horner stated that he would like to continue as the JFACC. Was that what General Schwarzkopf had in mind? The CINCCENT replied positively; he wanted Horner as his air commander. He responded exactly as Horner had hoped.[9] As commander of a unified command, Schwarzkopf functioned as the Joint Force Commander (JFC) of the component commands' forces, and he had the option, but not the obligation, to appoint a JFACC for the centralized, unified control of air assets. If the JFC exercised that option, he could appoint someone other than the CENTAF commander to operate as the air component commander; for example, he could appoint the CENTCOM director of operations (CENTCOM J–3) or the leader of MAR-CENT's aviation wing to be the JFACC.[10]

The CINCCENT also could appoint the JFACC to be both the theater Airspace Control Authority (ACA), a functional responsibility all four services had endorsed in 1975, and the Area Air Defense Commander (AADC), affirmed by the Army and the Air Force in 1976. The basic Air Force doctrine manual of 1984 explained that the theater air commander, functioning as the authority for airspace control and for air defense, facilitated gaining and maintaining control of the aerospace environment. Schwarzkopf assigned these two functions to Horner when he made him his JFACC. As the ACA, the air component commander established a joint airspace management system for the coordination, integration, and regulation of the use of airspace in the AOR; as the AADC, he integrated the operations of all available air defense weapon systems of all components and allied forces.[11]

In talking about using air resources effectively, Schwarzkopf said that, as

CINCCENT, he *apportioned* air, while the JFACC *allotted* it to meet the apportionment requirement. Schwarzkopf admitted that he did not really know how to apportion air. Horner replied that neither did he nor anyone else. These were surprising admissions, because the Army and Air Force had been formally discussing these concepts since 1981 when plans and operations officers from the Army and Air Force, assigned to the Pentagon, signed an agreement on apportionment and allocation for offensive air support. In 1984, the Army and Air Force chiefs of staff signed a joint agreement about these procedures, and the Air Force doctrine manual discussed them.[12] The JCS in 1989 defined *apportionment* as "The determination and assignment of the total expected effort by percentage and/or by priority that should be devoted to the various air operations and/or geographic areas for a given period of time." They also defined *allocation* as "The translation of the apportionment into total numbers of sorties by aircraft type available for each operation/task."[13]

Horner, a pragmatic, skilled airman, suggested to the CINCCENT a practical way to think about employing air power. He advised Schwarzkopf simply to tell him what he wanted done, and he, Horner, would choose targets to achieve the CENTCOM commander's goals. He would assign aircraft on the basis of payload, range, and capability. Aircraft flying to targets located within the fire support coordination line (FSCL) comprised close air support (CAS) missions.[14] Aircraft flying to shoot down enemy planes and hit airfields, radars, air defense sites, and command and control (C^2) positions, and aircraft patrolling to defend friendly forces constituted counterair missions. Aircraft sent against enemy resupply operations produced interdiction missions. Apportionment occurred as the CINCCENT told the airmen what he wanted done; allotment occurred as the airmen did it. "It really comes to targeting, not level of effort," Horner explained. The CINCCENT agreed to apportion air as suggested, by explaining his intentions and identifying the results desired.[15] This distillation of responsibility influenced Horner's thinking about the use of air power and his conviction that the JFACC managed, controlled, and deconflicted air resources best through the air tasking order (ATO). A document sent to air units, the ATO assigned missions, targets, target coordinates, time over targets, tanker and refueling requirements, and airspace, as well as communicating other essential information. Horner would expertly produce the ATO and generate sorties to achieve the CINCCENT's aims and intended outcomes.

Horner believed passionately in the value of the JFACC's selecting targets for the JFC in the theater of war, in sharp contrast with the failed policy of the Vietnam era when targets were chosen in Washington, D.C. Horner explained,

> That is the lesson of Vietnam. Remember our great President saying, "They don't bomb a shit house in North Vietnam if I don't approve it." Well, I was the guy bombing the shit houses, and I was never going to let that happen if I ever got in charge, because it is not right. If you want

> to know whether war is going to be successful or not, just ask where the targets are being picked. If they say, "We picked them in Washington," get out of the country. Go to Canada until the war is over because it is a loser.[16]

Horner then asked Schwarzkopf his second question. Now that the CINCCENT had air and naval bosses, who was the *land* boss, the Joint Force Land Component Commander (JFLCC)? The JFACC suggested that the ARCENT commander could assume the JFLCC responsibility and represent Army and Marine interests. While he waited for the CINCCENT's reply, Horner thought his hesitation stemmed from Schwarzkopf's knowledge that the Marines would prefer not having the Third Army commander, who was the ARCENT commander, as the land boss. Schwarzkopf stated that he himself would be the land component commander. Acknowledging the CINCCENT's reply, Horner respectfully told him that the JFACC sometimes disagreed with the JFLCC and would debate and argue courses of action. Horner hoped Schwarzkopf would welcome legitimate, frank discussion of contentious issues, but then step back and, as the CINCCENT/JFC, decide. Schwarzkopf chuckled at that scenario.[17] Throughout Desert Shield and Desert Storm, Horner remained the JFACC, and the CINCCENT remained the JFLCC. This latter arrangement eliminated for the ground-force commanders a single boss representing and prioritizing their interests. Confusion and misunderstanding would result.

Controlling Air Power: TACS and TACC

Horner and key members of his staff in 1989 — Maj. Gen. Thomas R. Olsen, CENTAF vice commander; Col. James C. Crigger, Jr., DCS for operations; and Col. Richard B. Bennett, director of tactical exercise operations and plans — took special interest in command-and-control exercises because they allowed CENTAF to establish and operate the TACC and develop the ATO, two vital JFACC functions. The TACC, the hub of the Tactical Air Control System (TACS), facilitated the command and control of air power, including airspace control and area air defense. Each of the Air Force components of the unified commands established some form of the TACS and TACC for air operations. During Desert Shield and Desert Storm, Schwarzkopf and Horner would manage the Coalition air assets through the TACS and TACC. The establishment and operation of these entities fundamentally affected the employment of air power.[18]

The TACS consisted of ten parts: TACC, the system's nerve center; Control and Reporting Center (CRC), a mobile or fixed radar site; Control and Reporting Post (CRP), a radar surveillance control site subordinate to the CRC; Forward Air Control Post, a highly flexible, mobile radar unit subordinate to the CRC or CRP to fill gaps in radar coverage; Message Processing Center, for the automated communications among the TACS components; Airborne Warning and Control System (AWACS), an airborne radar warning and control platform; Airborne

Battlefield Command and Control Center, an airborne command platform, lacking radar, for control beyond the communications range of ground TACS elements; Air Support Operations Center (ASOC), an air unit normally assigned to the corps command post; Tactical Air Control Party, an air unit assigned to a corps, division, brigade, or battalion, subordinate to the ASOC; and Wing Operations Center, a wing unit for managing and controlling sorties.[19]

Representatives from the Strategic Air Command (SAC), Military Airlift Command (MAC), and CENTCOM component commands also functioned within the TACS through the TACC. Because of its nuclear, as opposed to conventional, mission, SAC was a specified combatant command as well as a USAF major command. Horner never forgot that during the Vietnam War, SAC's control of the B–52s caused a serious unity of command problem, which he did not wish repeated in the CENTCOM AOR. Neither did the SAC commander (CINCSAC) in 1988, General John T. Chain, Jr., USAF, wish the situation repeated. He advocated transferring OPCON for conventional SAC bombers to the theater commanders who would, in turn, transfer OPCON to their respective JFACCs. Early that year, Chain adopted the policy of giving OPCON for B–52G aircraft dedicated to conventional operations to a supported theater commander during contingencies or war. Horner incorporated the SAC commander's policy into a CENTAF regulation published in June 1990. SAC and CENTCOM negotiated a command arrangement agreement to effect this transfer policy. The document awaited Schwarzkopf's signature just before Iraq invaded Kuwait, but it remained unsigned as Desert Shield commenced. The CINCSAC initially retained OPCON for tanker and reconnaissance aircraft.[20]

At the end of the 1980s, SAC participated in CENTCOM, TAC, and CENTAF exercises such as Bright Star, Gallant Eagle/Knight, and the flag exercises. In a 1989 Blue Flag C^2 exercise, SAC, for the first time, sent a planning cadre known as Strategic Forces (STRATFOR) Advisor to Horner's TACC. The JFACC's chain of command incorporated the STRATFOR commander, who advised Horner on the efficient use of SAC bombers, tankers, and reconnaissance aircraft.[21]

For management of CENTCOM's assigned airlift forces, the MAC commander designated a Commander, Airlift Forces who established an Airlift Control Center to collocate and interface with the TACC. The JFACC exercised command and control of intratheater airlift through the Airlift Forces commander, who monitored and coordinated airlift coming into the theater. Liaison officers in the TACC from ARCENT, NAVCENT, MARCENT, and SOCCENT represented their respective commands to the JFACC. Army personnel formed the battlefield coordination element (BCE), while the NAVCENT and MARCENT officers staffed the Navy and amphibious liaison element.[22]

Colonel Crigger believed that formation and integration of the BCE into the TACC marked the most important innovation in a decade for improving the ability of the Air Force and Army to synchronize operations. Horner saw it as the Army's means to directly influence the development of the ATO, and he urged ground force commanders to use it. The Army and the Air Force had approved the BCE concept in 1982 as the land component commander's liaison cell within the TACC. As ARCENT's coordination agency, the BCE exchanged operational and intelligence information with the other elements of the TACC; processed ARCENT's requests for tactical air support; monitored and explained the ARCENT battle situation; updated the ground commanders' prioritized interdiction target list; and coordinated ARCENT's fire support coordination measures. Although the BCE was an ARCENT entity on paper, the command owned no operational forces during peacetime, so the XVIII Airborne Corps staffed it.[23]

AirLand Battle and Air Power

The Army defined AirLand Battle doctrine in its 1982 revision of Field Manual (FM) 100–5 as the basic operational concept for how it would fight. Despite the provocative name, "AirLand Battle," the new doctrine slighted the role of air power in combat and failed to discuss the critical interaction among the air commander, corps commanders, component commanders, land component commander, and the JFC. The doctrine introduced the reader to the operational level of warfare in conjunction with the strategic and tactical levels, but throughout the manual the text failed to sustain any discussion of the operational level.[24] The authors could not overcome the dilemma of the Army having previously abolished the field army echelon, the operational-level entity, leaving the corps as the largest field organization. As AirLand Battle repeatedly indicated, the corps was a tactical-level, not an operational-level entity. The doctrine focused on the Army organizations in-being, the corps and the echelons below the corps, and gave only lip service to the operational level of warfare at the fielded army and JFACC levels.[25] It also neglected to mention TACS and TACC in terms of the Army's command and control structure, although the ground commander depended on these entities for timely and massive air power.

A subsequent revision of FM 100–5 discussed air operations at greater length, and the Army included a section that took text verbatim from the Air Force's basic doctrine manual of 1984. It covered the tactical missions — counterair, air interdiction, CAS, special operations, airlift, and surveillance and reconnaissance. It defined battlefield air interdiction (BAI) as "air interdiction attacks against targets which have a near-term effect on the operations or scheme of maneuver of friendly forces, but are not in close proximity to friendly forces." It noted that BAI required joint coordination at the component level during planning and might require the same coordination during execution. It asserted that the air component commander executed BAI as part of the total air interdiction effort.[26]

General Wilbur L. Creech, USAF, an officer whom General Horner admired, commanded TAC from 1978 to 1984 and enthusiastically assisted the Army in developing its AirLand Battle doctrine. He valued the enterprise for "getting us back to our roots of supporting the Army" and for radically expanding the

Army's field of vision, from including just the traditional close-in, set-piece battle and CAS to encompassing the deep battle against follow-on forces and including air superiority and air interdiction. In addition, Creech strongly believed that TAC had to support the Army or risk losing its tactical aircraft, as he had seen nearly occur in 1962 when the Howze Board (named for its president, Lt. Gen. Hamilton H. Howze, USA) recommended that Army aviation include not only helicopters, but attack, reconnaissance, cargo, and utility aircraft.[27] Creech's successor at TAC from 1985 to 1991, General Robert D. Russ, continued forging a close relationship between TAC and the Army. Writing in 1988, Russ asserted:

> Everything that tactical air does directly supports Army operations. Whether it's shooting down enemy airplanes, destroying a tank factory, attacking reinforcements or killing armor on the frontline, tactical air's objective is to give friendly ground forces the advantage on the battlefield....The Army tells us their scheme of maneuver and what effect upon the enemy they want us to create, we then provide the appropriate tactical air to achieve their objective. Most recently, our discussions have focused on the need for both close air support and air interdiction/battlefield air interdiction on the lethal, dynamic battlefield of the 1990s as described in AirLand Battle Doctrine.[28]

As did Generals Creech and Russ, Horner recognized the value of AirLand Battle ideas in stimulating Army officers to expand their thinking about modern warfare, and he understood that a CINCCENT with an Army background, such as General Schwarzkopf, would be thoroughly immersed in the AirLand Battle frame of mind. He believed, however, that the doctrine overemphasized the role of the corps commanders, parceled up the battlefield by their sectors, and imposed their limited vision on war planning. Although the 1986 version of FM 100–5 did mention the importance of the operational or theater perspective, it still focused on the tactical viewpoint by highlighting the corps in warfare and neglecting the roles of the echelon above the corps, the land component commander, and the JFC. By 1990 Army doctrine had not yet come to terms with the implications of the Goldwater-Nichols legislation and its emphasis on joint operations as well as with the authority of the unified commander in warfare. As JFACC, Horner lived constantly with the fact that the CINCCENT was the boss and chief strategist. The Army was not in charge of the modern battlefield, the CINCCENT was. Despite Air Force officers assisting its evolution, the CENTAF commander viewed AirLand Battle as most certainly Army doctrine, not Air Force or joint doctrine. He cooperated with the Army, but he did not work for it.[29]

Concepts that emerged during the development and implementation of AirLand Battle and which appeared in offensive war planning included battlefield air interdiction, shape and isolate the battlefield, center of gravity, servicing targets, scheme of maneuver, air superiority over the battlefield, and intelligence preparation of the battlefield. Sometimes the notions surfaced only to be argued away. The Army's AirLand Battle doctrine would not influence the basic phasing and structure of the Gulf War air campaign and war plan, but it would greatly affect the planning for and execution of the ground war.

Emphasis on War Planning

General Colin L. Powell, USA, the newly installed CJCS, summoned Schwarzkopf to the Pentagon in October 1989 to discuss contingency planning for CENTCOM's AOR. Following SecDef guidance, the CJCS directed the CINCCENT to shift his command's focus from the Soviet Union as the primary threat to Iraq as the major menace to peace in the Middle East. Schwarzkopf readily agreed with Powell's emphasis because it guaranteed CENTCOM's status as a unified command. For months, Schwarzkopf had pondered events signaling the end of the Cold War between the two superpowers. In July 1988, while serving a tour of duty in Washington, the CJCS, Admiral William J. Crowe, Jr., had hosted a cordial visit to the Pentagon by the highest ranking military officer in the Soviet Union, Marshal Sergei Akhromeyev. Crowe afterward confidently told Schwarzkopf that the United States would not have to fight the Russians. The CINCCENT had received many briefings about the positive changes occurring in the Soviet empire and could readily see the progress made in American-Soviet arms-control talks. Newspapers presented fascinating stories about the easing of the hard-line Communist stranglehold on the Soviet nation.[30]

In the summer and fall of 1989, as Under Secretary of Defense for Policy Paul D. Wolfowitz developed the planning guidance document for fiscal years 1992–1997, he conferred with the CINCCENT and the CJCS about issues concerning SWA. He eventually recommended to the SecDef, Richard B. Cheney, that the United States continue to view SWA as an important region for American interests, but it should shift its focus from the Soviet Union as the most likely threat to peace there to intraregional instability as the primary menace. He did not discount the capability of the Soviet Union to disrupt the flow of oil from the region and invade Iran, but he significantly downplayed the Soviet threat in comparison with dangers posited in DoD strategy papers presented over the past forty years. His assessment accounted for the withdrawal of Soviet troops from Afghanistan, the demise of the Warsaw Pact, and the Soviet Union's cooperative stance on nuclear arms issues.[31] Secretary Cheney signed the planning document in January 1990, formally stating the national defense policy and highlighting the importance of SWA and the defense of the Arabian peninsula against regional threats.[32]

Updating OPLAN 1002–88 to focus on conflict in the Gulf region, absent Soviet military intervention, received top priority at CENTCOM headquarters in November 1989. The CINCCENT's staff concentrated on transforming the older plan into OPLAN 1002–90, focusing on intraregional threats and identifying Iraq instead of Iran as a primary AOR adversary. Concurrently, the 1988 OPLAN, which addressed Soviet armed conflict in the AOR, remained on the shelf. Because CENTCOM's AOR comprised nineteen nations, the command had a series of plans or planning concepts covering various countries and scenarios, but 1002–90 dominated planning in the latter part of 1989 and first half of 1990, and its assumptions most closely reflected the crisis precipitated by Iraq's invasion of Kuwait.[33]

OPLAN 1002–90 Outline

In April 1990, the CINCCENT issued a draft outline for OPLAN 1002–90 which provided direction on how U.S. forces would aid friendly countries on the Arabian peninsula and ensure the flow of oil from there to the United States and its allies. The CINCCENT intended to publish a fully developed draft plan in time for the testing of its concept of operations (CONOPS) and logistics assumptions at the JCS-sponsored exercise Internal Look in July 1990. The outline identified Iraq as the belligerent that would attack Kuwait and Saudi Arabia. Phase I produced deterrent measures, and Phase II consisted of counterair operations and an interdiction campaign to gain control of the air, protect U.S. forces, and delay, disrupt, or destroy attacking enemy forces. U.S. troops would also defend critical port, air, and oil facilities during these periods. Phase III placed forces on the counteroffensive when attrition reduced enemy troops to a force ratio favorable to the United States.[34]

The responsibility the CINCCENT levied on the JFACC and his airmen in Phase II of OPLAN 1002–90 would profoundly influence the Desert Storm war strategy. In both plans, Schwarzkopf mandated that air power attrit enemy ground forces to the point that force ratios shifted to favor the offensive land campaign. The counterattack would commence only when air power had destroyed significant portions of the Iraqi army. The air forces, therefore, had to accomplish a major counterland mission in advance of offensive land operations. The idea of air pounding, degrading, and destroying the enemy army as an essential prelude to the ground counterattack would steadily grow in significance as Desert Storm approached, and it formed the basis of Phase III of the CINCCENT's war plan.[35]

CENTCOM identified Iraq as the probable aggressor in the region and adopted the axiom that planning should address a potential enemy's capabilities rather than his intentions. A CENTCOM intelligence estimate described Iraq as the most formidable Arab military force, with its nearly million-man army vastly outnumbering all others on the Arabian peninsula. The eight-year Iran-Iraq War produced for Saddam Hussein an experienced, battle-tested officer corps. His nation had the capability to damage oil facilities throughout the region. It had acquired the latest weapons from the USSR and Western Europe, and it strained to develop a formidable arsenal of nuclear, biological, and chemical (NBC) weapons and ballistic missiles. Saudi Arabia could not militarily match Iraq. The Saudi kingdom could, however, abundantly produce oil, and, as Schwarzkopf observed, "Mideast oil is the West's lifeblood."[36]

Iraq As Friend and Foe

As CENTCOM revised its planning concepts, assumptions, and scenarios, so did its component commands. The choice of Iraq as the principal threat to peace on the Arabian peninsula stirred controversy, as Horner learned from February 28 to March 1, 1990, when he and his intelligence officers, led by Col. John A. Leonardo, DCS, CENTAF Directorate of Intelligence (CENTAF/IN), hosted a symposium, "Conflict and Instability in Southwest Asia, 1990–1995." SWA experts and scholars from government and academia attended at Shaw AFB. A CENTAF staff member informed the participants:

> The major thrust of USCENTCOM planning for SWA has changed; instead of concentrating on the Soviet threat to Iran, the new emphasis is on regional conflicts within SWA (i.e., intraregional rather than interregional). The major U.S. objective continues to be to protect the free flow of oil. The major USCENTCOM planning document now is OPLAN 1002, which will counteract an Iraqi invasion of Kuwait and Saudi Arabia.[37]

Many of the attendees disagreed with the view that Iraq was a powerful aggressor and posed a near-term threat in SWA. Col. Randy Witt, the CENTAF communications officer, admitted that it looked to him as if Iraq was the new bête noire to justify maintaining the same U.S. force structure for the region, now that the Soviet empire had collapsed and Cold War tensions had eased. One participant from the Department of State telephoned his office in Washington, and reported CENTAF's characterization of Iraq as a Middle East belligerent. An official from the State Department subsequently telephoned and complained to Schwarzkopf at MacDill AFB, who in turn called Horner and vehemently berated him.[38] The State Department also objected to the conference's openness to individuals who had security clearances but who lacked a need to know with regard to contingency planning. Shortly afterward, CENTAF sent a message to the command's wings and groups giving this guidance:

> The identification of any nation as the focus of U.S. planning efforts, especially in the Middle East, is an extremely sensitive matter and should not be a topic of discussion in unrestricted meetings or gatherings. The slightest misperception of our plans or intentions could cause extensive problems. The use of Iraq as the threat for USCINCCENT OPLAN 1002–90 does not, repeat, does not, imply that the US considers Iraq a threat to our interests or to regional stability.[39]

Concurrently, the administration of President George H. W. Bush pursued a policy, disclosed in the secret National Security Directive (NSD) 26 dated October 2, 1989, which attempted to influence and moderate Iraqi behavior regarding terrorism, human rights, and the use of chemical weapons (CW) and biological weapons (BW). This policy was designed to help U.S. corporations invest in Iraq to facilitate the reconstruction of its economy, wrecked by its war with Iran. The exportation of agricultural products to Iraq, an important aspect of American-Iraqi financial relations in 1989, made Iraq the ninth-largest purchaser of U.S. farm produce. The Department of Agriculture's Commodity Credit Corporation extended credit guarantees to the country valued at $1 billion a year. On January 17, 1990, President Bush authorized an Export-Import Bank line of credit for Iraq worth approximately $200 million for the purchase of grain, which Secretary of State James A. Baker III called the "high-water mark of our efforts to moderate Iraqi behavior." The Bush administration continued the policies of the Reagan administration, which had tilted toward Iraq during the Iran-Iraq War, by offering credit guarantees and by supplying Saddam Hussein with military intelligence to enable his forces to check the expansionist aspirations of the revolutionary government in Tehran. If Iraq accepted U.S. financial carrots but failed to alter its conduct, NSD 26 called for using sticks in the form of economic and political sanctions.[40] A CENTCOM report noted in May 1990 that improved U.S.-Iraqi relations, including low-level military talks, should be a command regional objective to ease the worries about Iraq that moderate Arab states harbored and promote a "calming dialogue" in the region.[41]

Horner Meets Schwarzkopf, April 1990

In April 1990 Horner flew to Tampa, Florida, to meet with Schwarzkopf at CENTCOM headquarters and discuss the upcoming Internal Look command-post exercise in July 1990, which would test the developing CENTCOM 1002–90 plan. Not unexpectedly, the plan failed to designate a JFLCC, so the responsibility remained with the CINCCENT. As the JFACC, Horner wanted to avoid service doctrine battles in July, and he thought it prudent to have a preliminary discussion with Schwarzkopf about his ideas for using air power and secure the CINCCENT's approval for them.[42]

Horner's briefing in April addressed the plan's scenario of Iraq invading Kuwait and Saudi Arabia, and of the nations of the Gulf Cooperation Council (GCC) allying themselves with the United States, contributing forces, and making available basing sites.[43] The briefing consisted of three parts, matching the three phases of OPLAN 1002–90. For Phase I, Deterrence, Horner discussed the availability and arrival of aircraft in-theater over a 22-day period; basing sites and support; communications; airspace requirements; and air operations. As the ACA, he assumed responsibility for the operation of a control system promoting the safe, efficient, and flexible use of airspace, and he explained to the CINC-

CENT how new military air routes would mesh with the civilian ones over the entire Arabian peninsula and incorporate military liaison teams at various sites. In Phase I, Iraq had not yet invaded, so air operations would focus on intelligence collection, which Horner described as "intelligence preparation of the battlefield," a term he borrowed from AirLand Battle doctrine.[44]

For Phase II, Defend, Delay, and Attrit, Horner addressed Iraq's attack into Kuwait and Saudi Arabia. The defense of U.S. forces arriving at ports and airfields and the protection of GCC military and political personnel and facilities received top priority. As AADC, Horner discussed at length the existing Saudi and GCC air defense system, divided into sectors, with radar, fighter, and AWACS coverage. He knew the structure well from CENTAF's involvement in Elf One during the 1980s when the Air Force provided continuous AWACS coverage for Saudi Arabia's eastern air defense sector, and he advised that U.S. forces graft onto it. He saw no reason to force the Arab forces to change the system, creating ill-will instead of engendering cooperation; moreover, it lent itself to immediate use in operations and precluded the Marine Corps from establishing its own air sector.[45]

Horner suggested incorporating the Army's Patriot missiles into the air defense system to defend against Iraqi ballistic missiles, rather than against aircraft. He showed the CINCCENT a map of the Arabian peninsula overlaid with the ranges of Iraqi Soviet-made SS–1C Scud B missiles, ranging more than 186 miles, and the al-Hussein missiles, Iraqi-modified Scuds, ranging nearly 373 miles and capable of striking as far as Riyadh in Saudi Arabia, the site of Saudi C^2 facilities. The Scuds worried Horner because Iraq fired them during the war of the cities in the Iran-Iraq War. Furthermore, during the Gallant Eagle/Knight exercise in 1988, an Army brigadier general, during the free-play scenario, lobbed numerous Soviet-made SS–12 Scaleboard missiles with chemical warheads against Horner's airfields, drastically disrupting his air operations. These simulated attacks prompted the JFACC to address countering the missile threat, knowing he could provide an adequate counterair defense against aircraft.[46]

Before briefing General Schwarzkopf, Horner had discussed the use of Patriots with the Third Army and ARCENT commander, Lt. Gen. John J. Yeosock, who readily agreed to provide Patriot missile batteries for Internal Look. Yeosock explained, though, that when the Patriot was first fielded in 1983, the U.S. Army had directed that the missile shoot down aircraft. To become a tactical antiballistic missile system, its software had to be reprogrammed, permitting its radar to look for missiles at higher altitudes and velocities and to launch missiles with special fuzing and warheads. The Patriot missile's contractor had barely begun to manufacture the antimissile version when Desert Shield began. New Army orders subsequently led the contractor to dramatically accelerate production of the newer system.[47]

Horner introduced his analysis of offensive counterair operations in Phase II by advising Schwarzkopf that the way to win is to go on the offense even while defending. He noted that without border-crossing authority into Iraq, the air forces would be largely limited to the suppression of enemy air defenses (SEAD). With such authority, air power could strike seven offensive counterair targets in Iraq, three of which were in high-risk locations. A formidable air force existed for round-the-clock interdiction, and his staff was building target folders for seventeen targets in Kuwait and for enemy interdiction in an area there. He also identified interdiction targets in Iraq, once border-crossing authority was granted. Horner cautioned the CINCCENT, however, that much of the Iraqi invading force would mass before their D-day, and by Phase II, they would have dispersed. He did not address air power attriting the Iraqi forces to a level favorable to a U.S. counteroffensive, so he did not discuss criteria for measuring it.[48] The air attrition mandate would dominate the third phase of Desert Storm planning, and the problem of tracking its rate would confound planners and decisionmakers during the war, but it was not a concern during Internal Look.

Knowing that Iraqi CW preyed upon Schwarzkopf's mind and incessantly worried him, Horner presented the CINCCENT with a twofold strategy. First, strike at Iraq's two CW storage and production centers and five fixed Scud sites. He admitted that these attacks would probably not prevent the delivery of CW, except in the long run so, second, he proposed a "chemical retaliation" targeting strategy whereby the United States would "hold hostage" valuable targets in Iraq by warning Saddam Hussein that if he used CW, Coalition air power would destroy his high-value facilities. Horner listed two oil refineries, three electrical power plants, and the Baghdad Nuclear Research Center as the "hostage" targets, bringing his target list total to thirteen. He explained later, "The way I would have implemented it if he had used chemicals, I would have taken out all his oil refineries and said, 'Okay, now do you want to use chemicals again?'" After Desert Storm, the general realized that his strategy of coercion through targeting was naive because he applied his values and logic to a vicious, brutal despot who seemed to care little for what Horner and his staff had viewed as high-value assets.[49]

As Horner discussed his CW retaliation plan with the CINCCENT, he referred to punishment, deterrent, and quid-pro-quo targeting and inadvertently called the Iraqi high-value assets *strategic* targets. As soon as he said the word *strategic*, he regretted it. He disliked the word for many reasons.[50] The words *strategic* and *tactical* had become interchangeable, ambiguous, and even meaningless terms. As JFACC, he avoided using both words when describing types of aircraft and targets. "Air is air," he often lectured. "It's not strategic air; it's not tactical air. It's air!"[51] As the planning for Desert Storm progressed, Horner thought that the idea for the CINCCENT's offensive strategic air campaign originated in April 1990, when he and Schwarzkopf had talked about strategic targeting to deter Iraq's use of CW.[52] The meeting may have sparked the idea of strategic air operations in the CINCCENT's mind, but the idea did not consume him, which it would later for other reasons.[53]

Airpower Advantage

When Horner briefed the CINCCENT on Phase III, Counteroffensive, to recapture critical port and oil facilities and end the conflict on favorable terms, he noted that Coalition air and land forces simultaneously conducting operations would be crammed into a small geographic area, mandating extremely close integration of all operations. The air forces had to adjust to a rapidly changing, dense, unpredictable battleground and avoid fratricide. He proposed flowing air sorties steadily toward the battlefield on the basis of the previous day's planning, but if ground commanders asked for immediate, unplanned air support, the TACC would retask and retarget pilots while in flight, taking advantage of air power's flexibility. Horner explained that with planned missions and retargeting as required, he would "build a hose and point it where the ground commander sees that it's needed."[54]

For the next few months, and during Desert Shield, he continued to develop and explain his "air" hose concept, eventually calling it Push CAS. He emphasized the concept to ensure that the allies used air power efficiently and effectively. His idea for it originated when he was a young officer. He explained:

> It started in working with the Army over the years. This is from a pilot sitting in Vietnam. We used to have a thing called Whiplash Bango where we would sit alert to go fly if the long-range patrols that were being inserted into Laos and North Vietnam — that nobody ever could talk about because they were so secret — might need CAS if they got into trouble; so we used to sit alert for that. Well, you would sit there all day, and meantime, your friends are going up and getting combat sorties, and you're sitting there. Finally, the TACC at Saigon realized you hadn't been launched, and you had come to the end of the period, so they would launch you, and you would go hit some just *dumb* target. They would just want to fly you! I swore that I would never be a part of that again, any kind of alert CAS.[55]

Horner also knew that in desert warfare, engagements would happen quickly, and Army commanders could not predict when and where they would need air support. The commanders understood that as well, so they would try to bank air, that is, to request, acquire, and save it until needed. They would have aircraft at bases on alert, waiting for calls for CAS. Horner lamented:

> The trouble is any time you have an airplane that is not being loaded, flown to a target, flown from a target, or being turned around, then you have a wasted asset. Airplanes sitting on alert are wasted assets. The Army understands that with artillery. They say you never hold artillery in reserve. You never hold air in reserve.[56]

Schwarzkopf agreed with Horner's recommendations. Horner sent copies of his briefing to the other components to keep them apprised of his thoughts and those of the CINCCENT.[57]

OPLAN 1002–90 Second Draft

On July 18, 1990, the CINCCENT issued the second draft OPLAN 1002–90 in time for the Internal Look exercise. The plan's schedule called for the commander to send the final version to the JCS, complete with annexes and time-phased force deployment data, in August 1991.[58] The new version contained no major changes from the outline issued in April, and it mainly discussed the deployment, not the employment, of forces. CENTCOM continued to design the plan around an intraregional conflict on the Arabian peninsula to protect U.S. and allied access to key oil resources. CENTCOM explained the strategic importance of its AOR by stating that the area contained approximately two-thirds of the world's proven oil reserves, half of which was on the peninsula. U.S. dependence on oil from this region was expected to grow from 10 percent to 25 percent of U.S. total consumption by the year 2000. Also, important waterways existed in the area, enabling global commerce.[59]

CENTCOM continued to structure OPLAN 1002–90 in three phases.[60] The timing for the start of Phase III still depended on the attrition of enemy troops until the combat force ratio shifted to favor theater offensive operations. The plan, however, did not specify an optimum ratio. At CENTCOM headquarters, the Combat Analysis Group (CAG) used computer war-gaming and tactical warfare (TACWAR) modeling to produce risk and feasibility assessments for various courses of action and troop-strength scenarios. Shortly after Iraq invaded Kuwait in August 1990, the CAG determined that attriting attacking Iraqi forces by air to the 50 percent level prevented them from pushing U.S. forces off the Arabian peninsula. This percentage originally pertained to an operational, theaterwide view of opposing ground forces, not accounting for the level of destruction required to render each individual unit ineffective. This 50 percent objective would pervade Desert Storm Phase III planning, confusing and perplexing officers attempting to track progress in achieving it, but in July 1990, OPLAN 1002–90 offered no such precise attrition figure.[61]

OPLAN 1002–90 assumed that Iraq might use CW and BW.[62] It did not, however, discuss or offer options to prevent such use, nor did it include Horner's concept of deterring their employment by means of strategic targeting. The plan did not include the concepts of strategic targeting, strategic attacks, or a strategic air campaign, which later comprised a crucial part of Phase I of Desert Storm.

A Joint Target List for CENTCOM's AOR accompanied OPLAN 1002–90. In part, the list consisted of more than 300 fixed targets in Iraq considered to have military significance and to be potential candidates for attack. The plan defined a target as "A geographical area, complex, or installation planned for capture, destruction, or disruption by military forces."[63] The list comprised fixed installations and objects such as bridges, tunnels, railroad yards, and storage facilities for petroleum, oil, and lubricant (POL) products which if denied, neutralized, or destroyed, would impede the operations of hostile forces. The staff and command components of CENTCOM nominated targets for the list. CENTCOM's small targeting section validated their selections, which meant it took actions to ensure that critical data about the nominations were correct and current and that they supported the CINCCENT's OPLAN objectives. CENTAF's 9th Tactical Intelligence Squadron used the Joint Target List and other documents in its library to develop CENTAF's own target compilation and to initiate the collection and production of imagery in preparation for Internal Look.[64]

Internal Look Exercise

To test OPLAN 1002–90, CENTCOM and the JCS sponsored the Internal Look joint exercise at Duke and Hurlburt Fields in Florida and at Ft. Bragg, North Carolina, in July 1990, with a command-post component July 23–28 at Hurlburt Field. CENTCOM and component commanders and senior staff attended. The scenario called for Iraqi forces to attack Kuwait, consolidate their hold there, and invade Saudi Arabia along two routes. The Saudi government would give the CENTCOM commander responsibility for protecting the critical coastal area from al-Jubail to Dhahran and would call on U.S. forces deployed along the Persian Gulf to defend against its invaders. U.S. forces were to deploy to the region before Iraq attacked the Saudi kingdom.[65]

CENTAF began compiling its Internal Look target list in February 1990 after conclusion of the Blue Flag 90 exercise, which was predicated on OPLAN 1021 with the Soviets pushing through Iran. In this scenario, interdiction would have been more effective, given Iran's many geographic choke points in the Zagros mountains. Targeteers and other intelligence officers now had to learn and quickly become experts on a new country, Iraq, while nominating targets for CENTCOM's 1002 Joint Target List. In June the targeteers briefed Horner on their recently completed study on targets in Iraq. They identified lines of communication (LOC), roads, highways, and expressways in southern Iraq, Kuwait, and northern Saudi Arabia, and they selected twenty-five bridges for their list. For Kuwait, they chose targets in the following categories: offensive counterair, airfields, communications, power plants, refined POL storage, and desalinization plants. For Iraq, they selected targets in these categories: airfields (operational, forward operating bases, and under construction); command, control, and communications (C^3); early warning radar (EWR) and ground-controlled interception (GCI) sites; POL facilities; ammunition storage areas; fixed Scud sites; and miscellaneous high-value targets. High-value targets included the Baghdad Nuclear Research Center; two CW production and storage facilities; three power plants; and eight port or naval facilities.[66]

The exercise identified Horner as the JFACC, AADC, and ACA; his TACC generated the ATO and oversaw the execution of the air war. During the first two days, aircraft delivered munitions against troop concentrations, tanks, armored personnel carriers (APCs), convoys, logistical sites, and C^2 nodes in northeastern

Saudi Arabia and Kuwait. During the final two days, the President and the SecDef (the NCA) allowed cross-border strikes, permitting attacks against Iraq itself. Horner directed that aircraft hit C^2 and leadership facilities in Baghdad. His air guidance letter for the attacks characterized them as "deep interdiction strikes against high-impact targets in the Baghdad area." CENTAF did not call them strategic targets. The JFACC viewed missions against all targets beyond the FSCL as interdiction. Later he explained that air power was most effective "halfway between CAS and Dresden firestorm."[67]

The Internal Look exercise produced bleak results. The scenario sent six heavy Iraqi divisions into Saudi Arabia against forces of the XVIII Airborne Corps, the 82d Airborne Division and the 24th Infantry Division, Mechanized, already in northeastern Saudi Arabia and positioned to defend. The helicopters of the Corps's 101st Airborne Division provided air cover, as did fixed-wing assets. The Americans held the Dhahran airfield and the Dammam port and defended the Abquaiq oil refineries, but at a staggering cost: the XVIII Corps lost half its fighting strength. An Army study in 1993 reported, "The main tactical lesson from the exercise was that no matter how much Air Force and attack helicopter reinforcement the allotted forces had, they would have a tough time confronting Iraqi armored formations."[68] Horner knew these sobering results.

Internal Look had relied on TACWAR, the JCS's theater-level force-on-force model adopted in 1988 to assess the ability of armored forces to move forward against firepower from air, land, and sea forces. After the Persian Gulf War, Air Force leaders criticized TACWAR for failing to accurately account for the effectiveness of modern air power in warfare and for producing distorted outcomes, just as it had in Internal Look.[69]

Crisis Brews in the AOR

In July 1990 real-world events disclosed an eerie resemblance to the Internal Look scenario. Seven weeks before the exercise, at an Arab League meeting in Baghdad, Saddam Hussein denounced Kuwait and its emir for waging economic warfare against his homeland, and he demanded territorial concessions and billions of dollars in reparations for Iraq's devastation during the war with Iran. Saddam argued that since his country suffered terribly in the long, bloody conflict against revolutionary, fundamentalist Iran, Kuwait should compensate it more generously than it already had. The war, which Iraq had callously started, left the country with an $80 billion debt and a staggering $320 billion reconstruction requirement. The emir rejected Iraq's demands. On July 16, Tariq Aziz, the Iraqi foreign minister, wrote a letter to the Arab League denouncing Kuwait and the United Arab Emirates (UAE) for "direct aggression" against his country by having exceeded agreed-upon oil production quotas. The Iraqis believed that overproduction caused depressed oil prices, depriving them of billions of dollars in oil revenues. The next day in a radio speech, Saddam publicly continued his tirade against the two Arab nations and accused the United States of encouraging them and other enemies of Iraq. He warned that if policies failed to change, "something effective must be done." On July 21, American satellite imagery confirmed the movement of Iraqi troops and equipment toward the Kuwaiti border; CENTCOM assessed additional intelligence and increased its regional alert status.[70]

Over the next week, Iraq improved its air defenses at a few bases as well as along the Kuwaiti border, and began a new pattern of flying activity. On July 22 President Bush approved a request from the UAE for two air refueling tankers to support UAE combat patrols. SAC sent KC–135 aircraft ostensibly to participate with the UAE air force in a training exercise, code named Operation Ivory Justice. On July 24 CENTCOM further increased its alert status, and Saddam met with the President of Egypt, Hosni Mubarak, and assured him that while Kuwait and Iraq discussed Iraq's demands, he would take no action, but if a solution did not materialize, he would act rather than allow a postwar economic burden to crush his nation.[71]

On July 25 Saddam hastily summoned the U.S. Ambassador to Iraq, April Glaspie, to a rare meeting and delivered a rambling, two-hour speech to her, becoming emotional while criticizing Kuwait for not easing Iraq's financial troubles, which would soon force him, he claimed, to cut pensions for war widows and orphans. He stated that Iraq had suffered thousands of casualties in the war against Iran, and that American public opinion would never allow the United States to accept 10,000 dead in a single battle, as his nation had endured.[72] Glaspie, who spoke Arabic fluently, went into the meeting following guidance provided in a cable on the Iraq-Kuwait dispute which the Department of State had sent to embassies in SWA on July 19, stating that the United States wished to see the disagreement resolved peacefully and that the American government had no position on the substance and points of the Iraq-Kuwait dispute. The United States was committed to the free flow of oil from the region, supported the sovereignty of the Gulf states, and would defend vital interests in the region. She reported that Saddam knew about the Ivory Justice operation and expressed concern that the Americans encouraged Kuwait and the UAE in their "intransigence" and would adopt a hard line toward his nation, which he did not welcome. She commented that Saddam would not allow himself "to be perceived as caving in to superpower bullying."[73]

During the July 26–27 meeting of the Organization of Petroleum Exporting Countries in Geneva, Switzerland, Kuwait and the UAE agreed to raise oil prices and lower production rates, but this did not appease Saddam. At a meeting arranged by the Saudi king, Fahd bin Abd al-Aziz, in Jeddah, Saudi Arabia, July 31–August 1, the Iraqis asked for new concessions from Kuwait: cancellation of Iraq's wartime debt; ceding part of the Rumaila oil field; and payments for oil which Kuwait took from the Rumaila field. Kuwait refused the demands.[74]

Response to Iraq's Invasion

When Schwarzkopf and his staff returned to CENTCOM headquarters, July 28th, at the end of Internal Look, they maintained a close watch on the unfolding crisis in the Middle East and continued to develop OPLAN 1002–90 and began to plan retaliatory options for a quick military reaction against aggression by Saddam Hussein. The CJCS and the CINCCENT had discussed the need for military ripostes as early as July 24. The CENTCOM commander clearly remembered similar swift reactive strikes against Iran during Operation Earnest Will, when U.S. forces attacked two oil platforms after Iran fired a cruise missile into an American-flagged tanker, and then again when the Americans struck three warships after an Iranian mine severely damaged the frigate USS *Samuel B. Roberts*. On July 29, the UAE requested an extension of the Ivory Justice operation, whereby SAC KC–135 tankers refueled Mirage 2000 fighters flying combat air patrols (CAPs) over UAE oil facilities, and Schwarzkopf recommended to the NCA that the refueling assistance continue until August 8, which they approved.[75]

On July 31, the CJCS told the CINCCENT to fly to Washington the next day and brief the SecDef and the JCS on the situation in the CENTCOM AOR and on CENTCOM's contingency plans. On August 1, Maj. Gen. Burton R. Moore, USAF, the CENTCOM J–3, accompanied Schwarzkopf to the meeting at 1400 in the Tank, the formal JCS briefing room. The CJCS had not requested that any of the component commanders attend, so Horner remained at Shaw AFB. When Moore first heard about the briefing requirement, he wrote in his notes that the CINCCENT would discuss surgical strikes and full-scale strikes. He recorded that Schwarzkopf wanted his staff to expand the CENTCOM retaliatory strike list to include more military targets, that is, facilities directly related to the deployment and sustainment of armed forces, as opposed to economic and political targets. Moore recalled that about twenty or thirty targets comprised the list at this time and that the CINCCENT's request for additional military targets gave CENTCOM an expanded menu of targets to choose from, not necessarily more targets to actually strike.[76]

Schwarzkopf spent about ninety minutes in the Tank. He stated that the Iraqis would probably invade Kuwait, seizing not the entire country, but only the Kuwaiti portion of the Rumaila oil field and Bubiyan Island, the island dominating the route to Iraq's new port, Umm Qasr. He discussed air and sea strikes against high-value targets in Iraq, which could be destroyed quickly, and he explained the OPLAN 1002–90 deployment to defend Saudi Arabia. Both the CINCCENT and his J–3 remembered the meeting as going well and their instructions being to continue planning along the courses outlined. Schwarzkopf recalled, "The meeting ended with no sense of urgency."[77]

Without warning, on August 2 at 0100 local time in Kuwait, Iraq launched the invasion of its small, southern, oil-rich neighbor. Two divisions, armored and mechanized infantry of the Republican Guard Forces Command, launched the main attack along the axis from Safwan to Abdali into Kuwait. A third Republican Guard armored division conducted a supporting thrust farther west. The Guard constituted Iraq's elite forces and fielded the formidable Soviet-made T–72 tanks. Aircraft accompanied the invaders as they initially met no resistance and linked up at al-Jahra, less than forty miles west of Kuwait City. At 0130, heliborne special operations troops and amphibious commando forces stormed government buildings in the city, including palaces. The emir escaped to Saudi Arabia; his brother perished. The soldiers of the main attacking force met resistance as they seized control of and secured the capital while their supporting division established defensive lines south of the city. Tank forces then pushed on to assault and control Kuwaiti ports. By noon on August 3 the Iraqis had overrun two main Kuwaiti air bases and positioned themselves near the Kuwaiti-Saudi border.[78]

On August 1 at 2100 local time in Washington, D.C., President Bush reacted to the invasion by issuing a public statement condemning Iraqi aggression and calling for an immediate and unconditional withdrawal of Iraqi troops. President Bush, through Secretary Cheney, authorized Chairman Powell to issue a deployment order and a warning order. The first directed that selected U.S. forces remain at stations or deploy to the CENTCOM AOR. This message called for the USS *Independence* carrier battle group to proceed from the area of Diego Garcia in the Indian Ocean to the North Arabian Sea, and for the USS *Vandergrift* and USS *Reid* to remain with the Joint Task Force Middle East (JTFME) in the Persian Gulf.[79] In addition, the CJCS directed SAC to retain two KC–135 tankers at Diego Garcia and to deploy two additional KC–10s there.[80]

The second message, issued an hour and a half after the first, contained a warning order for Schwarzkopf to plan for the deployment of forces in accordance with CENTAF's Rapid Reaction Plan 1307–88, which enabled the quick deployment anywhere in the CENTCOM AOR of a small, initial force package of twelve F–16s or eight F–15Cs, two E–3 AWACS, one RC–135 Rivet Joint, and three KC–10s.[81] The purpose of the deployment ranged from a show of force to limited counterair and/or air-to-ground operations. The reaction plan included follow-on forces consisting of twelve F–16s or eight F–15Cs, two E–3s, one RC–135, and three KC–10s. Forces in the reaction plan served as a building block for a subsequent, larger buildup, as outlined in OPLAN 1002–90.[82]

The CINCCENT passed the warning order on to Horner at Shaw AFB and directed him to reply within a few hours, describing how the deployment specified in the reaction plan would proceed according to three courses of action. The first two courses of action focused on the packages the plan had already specified as the initial and follow-on forces. The third course required the deployment of five additional tactical fighter squadrons. The mission of the force modules encompassed show of force, defensive counterair, air-to-ground, and surveillance–signals intelligence operations. The CENTAF commander responded by describing the three courses of action in terms of aircraft, bases from which they would operate, and missions they would undertake, among other considerations.[83]

Early on August 2, at 0500 in Washington, Bush signed two executive orders freezing Iraqi and Kuwaiti financial assets in the United States. That same day, the United Nations Security Council condemned the invasion and demanded a withdrawal. Later that morning, at 0800, the President convened a meeting of the National Security Council (NSC) in the White House Cabinet Room, with Powell and Schwarzkopf in attendance. Powell earlier had described for the CENTCOM commander the protocol for such a meeting — don't speak until invited to do so — and Powell told him to address only the military options that could be executed quickly, which meant that the CINCCENT would not thoroughly discuss OPLAN 1002–90. Much of the discussion focused on diplomatic and economic questions that Iraq's dominance of Kuwait now raised.[84]

Robert Kimmit, representing the State Department while Secretary Baker traveled abroad, reported that 3,800 American citizens and 130 embassy personnel were unharmed in Kuwait, and 500 Americans and 42 embassy staff were unharmed in Baghdad. He also reported that the State Department was considering evacuating all of the Americans. Schwarzkopf recalled the President instructing that if Iraq took American embassy staff hostage, "be prepared to fight."[85]

The CINCCENT described the fighting in Kuwait City, and because William H. Webster, head of the Central Intelligence Agency (CIA) and Director of Central Intelligence, had just reported that his agency had lost contact with the American embassy in the capital, Schwarzkopf, using military communications, explained that the Iraqis had not attacked the embassy. He then described naval air strikes against targets in Iraq, which could be launched immediately. U.S. Air Force F–15s and F–16s stood alert to be deployed to the region, but Saudi Arabia had not approved their basing in the Saudi kingdom. Schwarzkopf then briefly discussed CENTCOM's "rehearsed" 1002–90 plan to defend Saudi Arabia.[86] Secretary Cheney felt "a little unprepared" for the meeting because he had no other "practical military options to lay before the President."[87]

"Options, options, options" emerged as the mantra of the NCA over the next few days as they groped to develop a coherent and effective American response to Iraqi aggression. The courses of action they wanted to consider encompassed foreign policy; economic strategy; plans for noncombatant evacuation operations to remove U.S. civilians from Kuwait City and Baghdad; and military actions ranging from a few limited, punitive air strikes to a full deployment of troops, as outlined in OPLAN 1002–90. Officials scrutinized reconnaissance satellite photographs and pondered intelligence reports to learn about the disposition of Iraqi troops and determine if Saddam Hussein would order them south into Saudi Arabia. President Bush consulted with King Fahd of Saudi Arabia, who severely criticized Saddam Hussein but suggested no joint course of action with the United States, and with President Mubarek of Egypt and King Hussein I of Jordan, who suggested that an Arab solution to the crisis might be possible over the next forty-eight hours. Bush told Mubarek about U.S. economic sanctions, but he emphasized that if there were threats against Americans, "That would be a whole new ball game" — much more than economic measures would be necessary.[88]

On the afternoon of August 2, a meeting convened at the Pentagon, producing discussions which soon would lead to the initiation of planning that served as the basis for the first phase of the Desert Storm air campaign. Lt. Gen. Thomas W. Kelly, USA, Joint Staff J–3, began the session by describing how the Iraqis carried out their offensive operations. The discussion soon focused on what the United States could do militarily in response to the assault and further Iraqi provocation. Cheney expressed the view that he still needed a set of military options he could present to the President. He wanted to know how the United States could "hurt" Iraq. The briefing Schwarzkopf had presented that morning about a few air strikes against targets in Iraq had not satisfied Cheney's requirements. Powell answered that the JCS and CENTCOM were working on options. He then suggested that a "few, pinprick, surgical strikes" against Iraq would have little effect on Saddam, would swiftly escalate American involvement in the crisis, and would require further action if the Iraqis ignored the bombing or retaliated against it. If the United States did not respond again, it would highlight American timidity and weakness. Discussion ensued about hitting Iraqi pipelines and CW and nuclear weapons sites and whether such bombing would provoke Saddam to attack Saudi Arabia. As the meeting wore on, Cheney received advice about the dangers and risks of military action, but no specific plans for possible military responses, as he had requested. Afterward, alone with Powell, Cheney emphasized the need for options, and bluntly, caustically told the CJCS to refrain from giving him political advice — he wanted military advice and plans for military action.[89]

At 0700 the next day, August 3, General Kelly attended a meeting with Powell, at which Powell reported Cheney's frustration of the day before at not having more military options. Kelly recorded Powell's comments and then wrote in his notes the CJCS's remark: "More serious air campaign to punish — CENTCOM working."[90] Cheney's prodding and dissatisfaction with the dearth of military options provided the catalyst for Powell and Schwarzkopf to begin thinking about and planning for the "serious air campaign to punish" Iraq. By the morning of August 3, the concept of an air campaign had emerged, implying a comprehensive, coordinated, intense offensive against Iraq, not just a few air strikes. Cheney and Powell now looked for a broad, punishing, stunning use of power — a *serious* air campaign — as an option in response to Iraq's further aggression.[91]

Also on the morning of August 3 the President convened another meeting of the NSC in the White House Cabinet Room, at which the CJCS told the President that military force could be used to deter Iraqi action toward Saudi Arabia and then to engage Iraqi troops in Kuwait and attack Iraq itself. Brent Scowcroft, the National Security Advisor, kept the meeting tightly focused and later warned that Iraq might take Americans as hostages. The State Department representative Lawrence Eagleburger reported that the Iraqi foreign minister had failed to assure that no Americans would be harmed. The President quickly interjected, "We should tell Saddam this would be a new ball game and give him our bottom line…American deaths and hostages will not be tolerated." The President requested a briefing the next morning on military options.[92] Powell later telephoned Schwarzkopf and told him to deliver the main presentation the next day. Bush's determination to disallow hostage-taking infused new urgency into the planning for a retaliatory air campaign.

CENTCOM headquarters, already operating at an accelerated pace, plunged into preparing Schwarzkopf to brief at Camp David within twenty-four hours. Meanwhile, planners at SAC headquarters in Omaha, Nebraska, and Navy planners aboard ships also labored furiously to ready special weapon systems in case retaliatory strikes required their use.[93] Targeteers and operations officers at SAC coordinated with officers at the JCS and CENTCOM J–3 to prepare strikes for B–52s carrying and firing conventional air-launched cruise missiles (CALCMs). Only personnel with special security clearances dealt with these stand-off missiles and black programs. Unfortunately, recent testing of the CALCMs failed to convince SAC's leaders of their reliability and accuracy, rendering their immediate employment questionable.[94] Navy officers at the Cruise Missile Support Activities offices in the Atlantic and Pacific Commands also coordinated with CENTCOM J–3 to plan launches of the nearly ten-year-old Tomahawk land-attack missiles (TLAMs). As of August 3, the JTFME had TLAMs aboard vessels in the Persian Gulf, but they were not immediately ready for firing because their terrain contour-matching guidance system had not been programmed to hit targets deep within Iraq, and they lacked other navigational and targeting data. At that time, the TLAMs functioned as antiship missiles or against interdiction targets in Phase II of OPLAN 1002–90. Even with mission planners working frantically round-the-clock, days passed before the missiles could be accurately programmed and launched.[95]

After receiving word about the Camp David briefing on August 4, Schwarzkopf drove his staff "mercilessly" and turned CENTCOM headquarters into a "pressure cooker" as personnel produced the information, assessments, and papers he needed to explain how air, ground, and naval forces would flow to the theater according to concepts outlined in OPLAN 1002–90.[96] Planners had not finalized the time-phased force deployment document, so the staff struggled to accurately state the deployment flow. The CINCCENT turned to General Moore to supply material about the movement of aircraft, but the J–3 lacked the necessary data and had trouble presenting it to Schwarzkopf, who bitterly complained that he did not understand it.[97]

Early in the afternoon, the CINCCENT called for General Horner, who was on a training mission in his F–16, to come to CENTCOM headquarters immediately. Since the invasion, Schwarzkopf had not contacted his JFACC. CENTAF officers rushed to provide their boss with up-to-date briefings as he prepared to fly to MacDill AFB. Throughout the evening and night in Florida, Horner, J–3 officers, and the CENTAF staff, communicating by telephone and fax machine, prepared the air portion of the CENTCOM briefing. At about 0300 Horner, the CINCCENT, and the CENTCOM director of plans and policy (J–5), Rear Adm. Grant A. Sharp, left MacDill on their multilegged trip to Camp David.[98]

Camp David Meeting, August 4, 1990

At 0830 the President convened his meeting. In attendance in the large conference room were Schwarzkopf, Horner, and Sharp from CENTCOM; Secretary Cheney; Under Secretary Wolfowitz; Chairman Powell; Brent Scowcroft; William Webster; James Danforth "Dan" Quayle, vice president; Secretary Baker; John H. Sununu, chief of staff; Richard Haass, special assistant for Middle Eastern affairs; Marlin Fitzwater, press secretary; General Kelly, Joint Staff J–3; and Capt. John M. "Mike" McConnell, USN, Joint Staff director of intelligence (J–2). Webster led off with a CIA briefing. Cheney then spoke about the importance of having military options and defining military objectives. Powell made a few remarks, explaining that the regional war plan had deterrent and war-fighting pieces, and turned over the briefing to Schwarzkopf.[99]

The CINCCENT described the Iraqi order of battle and how the invaders conquered Kuwait, highlighted the strengths and weaknesses of Iraqi military forces, and explained how American forces would flow to the theater over a seventeen-week period for the defense of Saudi Arabia. Land- and sea-based air power would protect the ground forces as they arrived in the AOR. To go on the offensive and expel the Iraqis from Kuwait would require additional forces and require from eight to ten months for their arrival in theater.[100]

One slide with the CINCCENT's "back-of-the-envelope calculation" carried over from OPLAN 1002–90 to Desert Shield/Storm an extremely important air-

Lt. Gen. Charles A. Horner (center, rear) waits to brief Secretary of Defense Richard Cheney and President George H. W. Bush (left to right), among others, on August 4, 1990, at Camp David in Maryland.

power mission: significantly attrit the enemy army to a force ratio conducive to a successful friendly ground attack.[101] This same airpower requirement appeared in Phase II of OPLAN 1002–90; now the CINCCENT repeated it as a requirement in the real-world crisis of Iraq's invasion of Kuwait. His calculations disclosed that for U.S. defensive operations, CENTCOM required 5⅓ friendly divisions in theater. For offensive operations an additional 6⅔ divisions were available for deployment, totaling 12. Twelve friendly divisions would be insufficient, however, because the Iraqis had deployed about 9 divisions. Schwarzkopf explained that a friendly attacker-to-defender ratio should be about 3:1, 4:1, or 5:1. At a minimum of 3:1, he needed 27 divisions to attack; at a maximum of 5:1, he needed 45. His 12 American to 9 Iraqi divisions would produce an unacceptable attacker-to-defender ratio of only 1⅓:1. The CINCCENT thus looked to the strength of air power to make up the difference in missing divisions. His slide proclaimed:

> THEREFORE MUST HAVE HEAVY AIR ATTRITION PRIOR TO ABILITY TO WAGE SUCCESSFUL OFFENSE[102]

An underlying precept in war planning emerged: the successful ground offensive requires air power's attrition and destruction of the enemy ground forces in a powerful counterland mission.

Horner followed the CINCCENT and spoke about Navy, Air Force, and Saudi air power in defense of the kingdom. He recalled,

> I think basically I said, "We have these kinds of airplanes. We could put these kinds of sortie rates up each day, using these kinds of weapons that are prepositioned in the theater, and we would probably be flying out of these bases here; and if they got overrun, we would go back to these bases here."[103]

His comments complemented the CINCCENT's and described how air power would hit the lead elements of the attacking enemy forces and concentrate on their logistics and sustaining components, their vulnerable points. The Saudis stationed ground forces close to the Kuwaiti-Saudi border, which would be the first, albeit tenuous, roadblock confronting the invaders. As OPLAN 1002–90 outlined, the main body of U.S. troops would trade space for time as it prepared to defend key ports and facilities well south of the Saudi frontline defenders. Air power would support the Army's scheme of maneuver.[104] As CENTAF commander, Horner also discussed how the United States could wage a campaign to conduct "punitive air strikes against Iraq" and hit nine high-value military, one political, and thirteen economic targets should the NCA "decide to do that because of [Iraq's use of] Scuds with chemical warheads."[105]

Secretary Cheney asked whether air power could achieve goals set for it, because it had not always done so in the past. Schwarzkopf responded that the situation in the region would enhance air power's effectiveness because the desert made targets easy to see and thus produced a target-rich environment; Iraqi forces would suffer a heavy, sustained air attack for the first time, generating confusion and degrading their effectiveness; precision-guided munitions (PGMs) would take their toll; and Iraqis in the rear of the theater would now be subjected to attacks, affecting their morale.[106] The President leaned toward sending troops to defend the kingdom, but he needed to know King Fahd's current view of the crisis, his willingness to receive American forces, and his level of determination to use force to confront Saddam's aggression. After the meeting, a few advisors remained behind and continued their discussion, which led to Bush's later telephoning the King and sending a team to Saudi Arabia to give an intelligence briefing to the monarch, replete with satellite photographs revealing the disposition of Iraqi troops in Kuwait and near the Saudi border, and to explain and offer the OPLAN 1002–90 troop deployment for defensive purposes.[107]

Start of Desert Shield

On Sunday August 5, Generals Schwarzkopf and Horner accompanied Secretary Cheney on his trip to meet with the Saudi king. Other team members were Under Secretary of Defense Wolfowitz; Robert Gates, National Security Council member; Pete Williams, Assistant Secretary of Defense for Public Affairs; Charles W. Freeman, Jr., American ambassador to Saudi Arabia; General Yeosock, ARCENT commander; Maj. Gen. Dane Starling, USA, CENTCOM director of logistics (J–4); Admiral Sharp, CENTCOM director of plans (J–5); Col. William R. Rider, CENTAF DCS for logistics; and a representative from the CIA. After their arrival in Jeddah on Monday August 6, Cheney, Wolfowitz, Gates, Freeman, and Schwarzkopf met with the king, the crown prince, and Saudi officials at the royal palace, while Horner and Yeosock waited nearby in an outer chamber. During the nearly two-hour conference, they discussed intelligence, U.S. diplomatic initiatives to impose economic and political sanctions against Iraq, and the size and timetable for a deployment of U.S. defensive forces.[108]

As they drove to their quarters in Jeddah, Horner asked Wolfowitz how the meeting went. Wolfowitz replied, "They have invited us! They want us to come!" Cheney telephoned the President and relayed the king's request for U.S. forces. President Bush authorized Secretary Cheney to deploy them, and Cheney informed Chairman Powell and General Schwarzkopf of the President's decision. That night in Jeddah, Horner slept very little. "You are kind of overwhelmed with the magnitude of what might go on," he mused.[109]

In a meeting among Horner, Cheney, and Schwarzkopf early the next morning, Schwarzkopf told Cheney that Horner would remain in Saudi Arabia as the CENTCOM Forward commander, while he, Schwarzkopf, would return to CENTCOM headquarters to manage the initial deployment flow. Horner later met with Cheney, Schwarzkopf, and Prince Sultan bin Abd al-Aziz bin Abd al-

Rahman al-Saud, the Saudi defense minister. Secretary Cheney and the prince discussed terms and arrangements for food, fuel, and housing for the troops. Shortly afterward, Cheney and Schwarzkopf departed the country, leaving Horner in charge.[110]

The military officers remaining behind in Jeddah with Horner were Yeosock, Sharp, Starling, and Rider. They flew to Riyadh to meet with Saudi military leaders and prepare to receive deployment forces and defend Saudi Arabia. The date August 7, 1990, marked the official start of the OPLAN 1002–90 deployment, which the JCS named Desert Shield on August 9.[111] Originally expecting to make only a short trip to Saudi Arabia, Horner would remain in the AOR throughout Desert Shield and Desert Storm and not return to the United States until April 1991. He first functioned in the theater, not as the JFACC, but as the CENTCOM Forward commander.

Chapter Two

Instant Thunder

General Schwarzkopf needed an air campaign option, and he telephoned the Air Staff for it on August 8, 1990, despite objections from his JFACC and the Goldwater-Nichols legislation placing war planning in the CINCCENT's hands. He did not ask General Horner for the plan because, in an unexpected turn of events, he had just left the lieutenant general in Saudi Arabia with major new responsibilities as the CENTCOM Forward commander. Horner's own CENTAF staff was en route to the theater and, once there, would focus on defensive, not offensive, planning and the Desert Shield deployment. In the Pentagon on the Air Staff, the deputy director for warfighting concepts led the effort to produce the air plan for the CINCCENT, titled, "Instant Thunder." The airmen presented Schwarzkopf with a stand-alone, war-winning strategic air plan — more than he had requested when he called for an air option for retaliatory purposes. Nonetheless, the CINCCENT enthusiastically accepted it.

CENTAF's Aborted Punishment ATO

At Shaw AFB early Sunday morning, August 5, 1990, right before Horner flew his F–16 to Washington to join Secretary Cheney's group traveling to Saudi Arabia to confer with King Fahd, Horner briefly met with his staff. He told them to continue preparations for the execution of CENTAF Plan 1307 and development of an Iraqi target list. As he had told Colonel Crigger, his director of operations, the previous day, they needed targets in three categories: political, economic, and military. The list and accompanying ATO would provide the CINCCENT with a strong retaliatory strike if needed. The CENTAF staff dubbed the air tasking order requirement the "Punishment ATO."[1]

Desert Shield cut short the CENTAF planning effort. The headquarters staff began to leave for Riyadh on August 7, the first day of the deployment. Once in the AOR, they focused continuously on the deployment and the defense of Saudi Arabia. As they departed Shaw AFB, their Iraqi "punishment" list consisted of seventeen targets, which if struck would have destroyed: Iraq's only known nuclear research facility, one of Saddam Hussein's presidential palaces, the ministry of defense and air force headquarters, the army headquarters, the only known space and missile test launch facility, five POL facilities, and seven electric power sites. Time ran out, though, and the staff deployed before they could produce the list's accompanying ATO, which at the time would have been premised on the CENTAF 1307 and OPLAN 1002 deployment options.[2]

CINCCENT's Request to Air Staff

When Schwarzkopf departed Saudi Arabia on August 7, he told Horner that his primary jobs were to receive and base the deploying troops and develop the detailed plan to defend Saudi Arabia against invading Iraqi troops, according to the concepts in OPLAN 1002–90. Schwarzkopf knew that all of Horner's CENTAF staff were preparing to leave Shaw AFB or were already en route to the theater to organize and manage the air assets to defend key oil and port facilities and defend the troops arriving on ships and aircraft. He clearly understood that Horner, as the newly designated in-theater commander, had his hands full with scores of tasks to accomplish, including such basic jobs as locating space for and establishing a CENTCOM headquarters.[3] He also knew that the NCA wanted a "serious air campaign" option to use against Iraq.

On the airport ramp at Jeddah, Schwarzkopf told Horner he would call the Joint Staff to request assistance with producing a list of strategic targets.[4] Horner immediately cautioned the CINCCENT to keep the planning and targeting in theater and not repeat the serious mistake of the Vietnam War by allowing people in Washington to select the targets. Horner and his staff would produce the list and accompanying ATO. He was angry, not because Schwarzkopf wanted a strategic target list, but because the CINCCENT was calling the Pentagon for it. Horner knew that Schwarzkopf was a Vietnam veteran and believed that Schwarzkopf should have known better than to give responsibility for target selection to an organization outside the theater of war. Nonetheless, as distasteful as the action was, Schwarzkopf had to pull in more help with targeting because Horner was now the acting CINCCENT in the AOR, he no longer functioned as the JFACC, and he faced a tremendous, nearly overwhelming workload. Schwarzkopf trusted Horner's judgment and experience — that was why he was leaving him in charge — and he consoled the airman by telling him he would assume full responsibility for the strategic air planning once the preliminary work was complete.[5]

Immediately upon returning to his headquarters at MacDill AFB on August 8, Schwarzkopf telephoned Powell, conferred with him about Desert Shield, and discussed the idea of asking the Joint Staff (or the Air Staff) for assistance with building a strategic targets list. The idea of having the Joint Staff build the list was quickly abandoned, and at approximately 0800 the CINCCENT telephoned

USAF Chief of Staff General Michael J. Dugan to request that the Air Staff develop the strategic list and an accompanying air plan. Dugan was out of town, so Vice Chief of Staff General John M. "Mike" Loh spoke with Schwarzkopf.[6]

General John M. Loh

The telephone call from the CINCCENT to the vice chief would lead to a planning effort that would have an enormous influence on the development of the Gulf War air campaign. During their ten-minute conversation, the CINCCENT explained that if the Iraqis took hostages or used CW, President Bush and Secretary Cheney would immediately ask for military options for retaliation, so he needed to be ready to brief them, especially on a spectrum of targets by which to punish Iraq. Loh remembered Schwarzkopf specifically talking about an "air campaign" or a "campaign plan" and that he needed it fast in case Saddam launched a CW attack. He also recalled that the CINCCENT requested a "strategic air campaign." "I need broader planning, Mike; I need broader planning," he remembered the commander saying, explaining that he could not turn to his CENTCOM staff at MacDill AFB because they lacked expertise to do strategic targeting. Schwarzkopf recalled that he had asked for a "strategic bombing campaign," a "retaliatory air campaign," and a "retaliatory package."[7]

Thus, on August 8, Schwarzkopf directly involved the Air Staff in war planning even though the Goldwater-Nichols legislation had placed such responsibility with the unified commanders and the JCS. The crisis in the CENTCOM AOR and requirements of the NCA overrode the CINCCENT's reluctance to turn for help to a service headquarters in the Pentagon. He requested a plan with three important characteristics: retaliatory purpose, strategic targeting, and a campaign, a series of interrelated operations as opposed to a few surgical tit-for-tat strikes. Its purpose was to punish Iraq if Saddam began murdering hostages or launching CW attacks. The targeting of Saddam's homeland had to be severe in retaliation against such acts. Strategic strikes against Saddam's country comprised the appropriate, harsh response.

That the CENTCOM commander called the Air Staff for a retaliatory air campaign option would be misunderstood by some Air Staff planners, but Schwarzkopf had no doubt about why he called the Air Staff. In his autobiography he explained:

> The taking of American hostages could be cause for war and I felt sick to my stomach at the news. By the time we'd opted for Desert Shield, we'd completed our planning for symbolic air strikes, but symbolic is all they were. If the Iraqis started executing U.S. embassy employees, say, and the President wanted to retaliate, Central Command had little to offer short of a nuclear strike on Baghdad. I would never have recommended such a course of action, and even if I had, I am certain the President would never have approved it.
>
> The following morning I called Colin Powell and asked that the Air Force put planners to work on a strategic bombing campaign aimed at Iraq's military, which would provide the retaliatory options we needed.[8]

Having suddenly received the planning baton, General Loh told Schwarzkopf that, yes, the Air Staff could help him and that, in fact, a small planning cell had already begun to look at a strategic set of targets: leadership and industrial sites, and facilities that sustain a war.[9] The vice chief recollected, "my reaction was, 'I know *exactly* what he is talking about. He is talking about a broader campaign, the same thing that Minter Alexander talked about the day or two days before.'"[10] Maj. Gen. R. Minter Alexander was the director of plans at Air Force headquarters, and the cell he had told Loh about was under the direction of the deputy director for warfighting concepts, Col. John A. Warden III. Loh told Schwarzkopf that he would acquire support from TAC and SAC and develop an air campaign framework, showing required forces, and bring it to him within the week. The CENTCOM commander mentioned that he would let the CJCS know of the Air Staff planning, and vice chief said that he would also keep the CJCS informed.[11]

Immediately after his telephone conversation with Schwarzkopf, Loh telephoned General Russ at TAC headquarters and told him about the CINCCENT's request for assistance with an air option and for broader, strategic targeting. Russ was upbeat and said he would direct the planning cell he used with the Atlantic Command, which dealt primarily with B–52 issues and long-range missions, to develop targets in Iraq. Loh hesitated before he had contacted Russ, who was more senior, because he did not want the TAC commander to push the entire planning effort to Langley AFB from the Pentagon and change the orientation of the campaign from strategic targets to targets more associated with AirLand Battle and battlefield air interdiction. Russ, however, made no such suggestions. Loh then called General Chain at SAC who expressed optimism and said his staff would contact the Air Staff planners and provide whatever support they needed.[12]

The vice chief of staff next summoned General Alexander to his office, in the absence of Alexander's boss, Lt. Gen. Jimmie V. Adams, DCS, Plans and Operations, who was out of town at the time. Alexander, in turn, called for Colonel Warden. In telling them about the CINCENT's request, Loh recalled saying,

> Okay, go into high gear. If you need any help from SAC or TAC, let me know. You might need some planners from SAC to help with this. We need to develop a target set of all the categories of targets. We need to bring the CIA in. We need to get Warden working with all of the folks that he knows. We need to really find all the sources of information about the critical targets that make Iraq run as a country.

Warden remembered Loh stating that Schwarzkopf wanted a strategic air campaign. The colonel immediately recognized that the CINCCENT's "wonderful telephone call," as he later described it, offered an incredibly real, crucial opportunity for him and his staff to directly influence unified command war planning, and he was supremely confident and ready to seize and exploit the opportunity.[13]

Uninvited and missing from the meeting was Maj. Gen. James R. Clapper, Jr., Assistant Chief of Staff for Intelligence, even though Loh recognized that intelligence played an essential role in identifying targets. Loh may not have remembered at this early stage of planning the great extent that intelligence also plays in disclosing critical nodes in target systems, the relationship between target systems and objectives, the array of weapons defending critical sites, and the effectiveness of strikes. Intelligence officers specialize in discovering, verifying, and studying targets. Loh did not think it necessary at the outset to involve Clapper at such a high level of command or explain to him the purpose of the planning and make him an integral part of the team. Nor did the vice chief impress upon his intelligence officer the importance of this project vis-à-vis others, or direct him to use Air Force intelligence resources and conduits throughout the national intelligence community in support of Colonel Warden's initiative. Intelligence would emerge as a major problem during the offensive air campaign planning enterprise, in part because of a lack of face-to-face, hour-to-hour, day-to-day contact between the operators and planners and the intelligence staff, all of whose responsibilities intimately intertwine. Planners communicate requirements and intentions so intelligence officers can attempt to meet their articulated needs, as well as anticipate new ones. Without accurate, timely intelligence, an air campaign would fail. General Loh initially envisioned Warden tapping his informal intelligence sources to identify key Iraqi targets. At this time, Warden's conduits into the huge, complex, secretive intelligence community in Washington were through the section in the warfighting concepts cell that specialized in camouflage, concealment, and deception led by Col. Richard Stimer and Capt. Steven Hedger, an Air force officer assigned to the directorate.[14]

Colonel Warden, a graduate of the Air Force Academy in 1965, served two tours in Vietnam, flying OV–10s and F–4Ds. At age 47 in 1990, he was of average height, lean, intense, and devoted to thinking about how to turn a collection of aircraft into a decisive force in warfare. Under Warden's direction, his staff in the Deputy Directorate for Warfighting Concepts had begun on August 7 to formulate an operational air campaign for Iraq, even before Loh received Schwarzkopf's telephone call. Indeed, since 1988, his staffers had been catalysts on the Air Staff for thinking about and discussing the effective use of air power and the requirements of an air campaign. Warden had assumed responsibilities as deputy director in 1988 after his return from Europe, where he had flown the F–15 Eagle and briefly served as the commander of the prestigious 36th Tactical Fighter Wing at Bitburg Air Base (AB) in Germany.[15]

Warden left Bitburg and came to the Pentagon in January 1988 to plan for the Constant Demo air base operability exercise scheduled for 1991. In March 1988 when General Dugan, then a lieutenant general serving as DCS, Plans and Operations, asked Warden what initiatives the Air Force should undertake concerning concepts of warfare, Warden prepared a paper. He presented his ideas about reshaping the curriculum at the Air War College, developing an air counterpart to the Navy's new maritime strategy, and providing more publicity about what air power could do for the nation. Dugan responded positively, saying he would have Maj. Gen. Charles G. Boyd, the new USAF Director of Plans, read it and decide how to apply the ideas suggested. Dugan made Warden his special assistant and in July 1988 appointed him to head the Deputy Directorate for Warfighting Concepts, which originally consisted of four divisions: Doctrine, Strategy, Long-Range Plans, and Concepts.[16]

Warden's Air Power Concepts

Warden had definite ideas about the effective use of air power and its doctrinal implications for the Air Force and the DoD. The academic environment helped him to think about the nature of warfare and air power and to formulate his concepts. In 1974–1975 he earned his master's degree in political science at Texas Tech University where Frederick H. Hartmann directed his thesis research and introduced him to grand strategy, the level at which heads of state operated as they set war objectives, built coalitions, and committed national resources to achieve victory.[17] At the university, Warden became "enamored" with the British "indirect approach" strategy and developed a strong skepticism of the famous Prussian theorist Carl von Clausewitz.[18] Warden read the works of B. H. Liddell Hart, the British military correspondent, strategist, and leading proponent of the indirect approach to war, which advocated the avoidance of direct, frontal attacks against the main army of the enemy.[19]

In his book, *Strategy,* published in 1954 and used by Warden in his thesis, Liddell Hart criticized military leaders who conducted wars believing that the destruction of the enemy's forces in battle was the primary aim of warfare.[20] He urged strategists keep in mind constantly three concepts: identify and strike at the enemy's Achilles' heel, or weakness; aim to compel the enemy to capitulate and undermine his will to resist; and conduct war to shape the kind of peace desired.[21] The British author proclaimed that the "immemorial lesson" of warfare is that the true aim in conflict is "the mind of the hostile rulers, not the bodies of their troops."[22] Warden incorporated Liddell Hart's ideas into his own views about warfare.

In 1986 Warden attended the National War College at Fort Lesley J. McNair in Washington, D.C., at a time when the director of the college infused the curriculum with emphasis on the operational art.[23] Warden produced a study on the operational art as applied to airmen, titled *The Air Campaign: Planning for Combat*, which the National Defense University published in 1988. The book discussed conventional air warfare at the operational level, which he described as that dimension of warfare below the grand strategic and strategic levels and above the tactical level. The theater commander focused on the level corresponding to the responsibility exercised in World War II by General Dwight D. Eisenhower in Europe, General Douglas MacArthur in the Southwest Pacific, and Admiral Chester W. Nimitz in the Pacific Ocean area.[24]

Presenting a key idea, Warden wrote that, given appropriate circumstances, the commander should use air forces as the primary means to achieve political and military objectives, with ground and naval forces supporting the air effort. He acknowledged that air power would not always be the appropriate leading force, and in some cases would play a supporting role to land or naval forces, but, nonetheless, the theater commander clearly possessed a third means for decisively waging war, a viable air option. He proclaimed the idea that, in most cases of warfare, the commander should employ air power first to attain air superiority in the operational theater because the absence of air dominance would seriously jeopardize or doom other military operations. The colonel repeated Air Force doctrine in advocating the attainment of air superiority as the first and primary airpower role in warfare.[25]

Warden suggested guidelines for expending effort on air superiority, interdiction, and close air support.[26] He urged that after attaining air superiority, the commander should focus air power on distant, intermediate, and close interdiction, and only then on close air support for ground forces, barring no major, decisive land offensive by the enemy. In weighing the priorities between interdiction and close air support, he concluded that logic and the "weight of history" consistently leaned toward interdiction.[27] He did not discuss *strategic* attacks, per se, in his book, nor the air counterland mission, as required in CENTCOM's OPLAN 1002–90. Like most fighter pilots at the time, he thought of strategic air attacks as deep, or distant, interdiction.[28]

Just as the Army planners did in 1986 when they revised the AirLand Battle doctrine in FM 100–5, Warden borrowed the term *center of gravity* from Clausewitz and applied it prominently in his book. He judged it a useful term for planning war operations because it described "that point where the enemy is most vulnerable and the point where an attack will have the best chance of being decisive." He noted, "The term is borrowed from mechanics, indicating a point against which a level of effort, such as a push, will accomplish more than that same level of effort could accomplish if applied elsewhere. Clausewitz called it the 'hub of all power and movement.'"[29]

Warden agreed with Clausewitz (and Army planners) about the importance of reflecting upon and identifying the enemy's centers of gravity. Clausewitz wrote, "The first task, then, in planning for war is to identify the enemy's centers of gravity."[30] Warden wrote, "Perhaps the most important responsibility of a commander is to identify correctly and strike appropriately every center of gravity."[31] In two chapters of his long masterpiece, Clausewitz offered examples of the center of gravity, but Warden rejected the first, narrow identification, which offered that it was "that area where the greatest concentration of enemy troops can be found."[32] The colonel agreed with Clausewitz's second explanation of the concept which offered more examples: a nation's army, a nation's capital, an alliance's cohesion, leaders, or public opinion.[33]

Warden's book also emphasized that an air campaign often required time to achieve objectives and, depending on the scenario, might not be executed quickly. He wrote: "In the very short term, air cannot stop large bodies of men. Interdiction takes time to work; and attacks on war production take even more time. Ground must be the key force if time is of the essence, and it is agreed that ground action can lead to the political objective significantly faster than could air action."[34] The colonel's air concepts evolved and changed from 1986 to 1991, and he continued to refine them in the postwar period.

Warden's Ring Models

Warden built his deputy directorate into an exciting, heady place to work in the Pentagon, patterning it after the organization as led by Maj. Gen. Richard L. Lawson (1975–1977) and Maj. Gen. James H. Ahmann (1977–1979) during the time he himself worked in the Middle East Plans Division (1977–1978). Warden recalled his early Pentagon tour:

> I came into plans at a perfect time because Lawson was the guy that was all over Washington. He'd go over and had lunch once a week with the director of political/military affairs in the State Department, he'd go over to the White House, and so on, and he'd instill this feeling that, "Hey, literally if you're in [the directorate], you're in the most influential, most important organization in Washington. You can do anything you want from [the directorate of plans]."[35]

Addressing his staff in 1988, he exhorted, "Our charter is to think, and we can think any kind of thoughts that we want to think, and it's okay. In fact, that is what we are supposed to be doing." He challenged his eighty people to contemplate air power in terms of what it was, reasons for using it, how and when to employ it, and how to sell it. His people were not beholden to any command or agency. The colonel saw himself as a coach or cheerleader who gave people directions and basic ideas and allowed them the freedom to develop, explain, and justify airpower rationales. He explained, "We were going to bring the Air Force back into prominence. To bring it back into prominence we have got to develop the concepts that will work in the real world, and we want to win wars for the country, so it was very clear where we needed to go."[36]

Col. John A. Warden III

Warden significantly contributed to the mix of ideas between the Deputy Directorate for Warfighting Concepts and Gulf War planners by identifying centers of gravity of potential enemies of the United States. He conceptualized them as a nation-state's five strategic rings. In a paper he wrote and revised a number of times, changing its title from "Global Strategy Outline" to "Centers of Gravity — The Key to Success in War," he asserted that the best way to wage war was *not* to have armies clash on the battlefield. He stated:

> Too frequently, our vision of war concentrates almost exclusively on its most obvious manifestation — the clash of the fielded military forces of the contestants. Indeed, Clausewitz identified the battle as the essence of war....Clausewitz may have been right for the technological time and place in which he lived, but it is not clear today that the actual clash of men on the front is the only way or the best way to wage war. We will suggest, to the contrary, that it may be the most costly and least productive approach in perhaps the majority of cases.[37]

Colonel Warden presented a model of a nation's centers of gravity, consisting of five concentric rings in a bull's-eye format. The most important centers of gravity occupied the center of the strategic ring model. He labeled the crucially important, innermost circle the *command* ring. Warden viewed command, or leadership, as paramount because that was the element of a nation-state that empowered it to make concessions. He acknowledged the difficulty in modern times of seizing and killing the commander and his support element, so he advised applying sufficient pressure against the other four rings to force leaders to capitulate. He asserted, "The essence of war is applying pressure against the enemy's innermost strategic ring — its command structure."[38]

The colonel explained that J. F. C. Fuller's *The Generalship of Alexander the Great* influenced his thinking about the primacy of the command ring representing the key center of gravity in a nation-state and the importance of riveting attention on this center as the primary target. He first encountered Fuller's book while he was a student at the Air Force Academy, and he considered it not only an important work in military history, but in world history as well. Fuller, a strategist and military historian, published the volume in 1957. In one section he emphasized the courage and wisdom of Alexander at the Battle of Arbela in 331 B.C.E. when he thrust directly for Darius the Third of Persia on the field of battle instead of reinforcing his right and left flanks which Darius's troops threatened. Warden explained,

> Alexander, when he saw an opening in the lines, took his companion cavalry and headed straight for Darius the Third, even though in theory that was pretty dangerous and probably a risky thing to do. Because Darius was so clearly the center of gravity, Alexander knew that plunging into this great horde of Persians was well worth the risk, so that was a key concept.[39]

The use of air power in 1972 in Linebacker II during the Vietnam War and in 1986 in Operation El Dorado Canyon against Muammar al-Qaddafi of Libya also impressed Warden who saw, as a result of American strategic air attacks, enemy leaders bending to the will of the United States.[40]

Warden designated the second-most important ring of his model *essential industry*. This could be the industry of the nation itself or that of an allied nation. If essential industry was destroyed or if the nation-state was denied access to its allies' industrial output, the state could not employ modern weapons and would thus be forced to make concessions.[41] In the third ring, labeled *transportation system,* Warden included "rail lines, airlines, highways, bridges, airfields, ports, telegraph lines, satellite uplinks, radio stations, and a number of other similar systems."[42] *The population and its food sources* constituted the fourth ring. Warden suggested that two types of indirect attack on the population may be necessary: first, propaganda or psychological operations (PSYOPS), "such as North Vietnam used against the United States," and second, a scorched-earth policy, such as "Sherman used against the South by marching through Georgia."[43]

Warden designated *fielded military forces of the state* as the fifth, outermost, and least important of the five rings. He noted, "Although we tend to think of military forces as being the most vital in war, in fact, they are means to an end. That is, their only function is to protect their own inner rings or to threaten those of an enemy." Air forces could overfly the fielded military force to hit leadership and destroy a nation's ability to command and control its troops. In addition, they could render a fielded force incapable of fighting effectively by destroying its essential industries and its logistics supplies.[44]

Explaining his model, he posited that ground forces have to fight from the "outside in," that is, to attack first through the outermost ring, the fielded force, and then through the interior rings to cause the leadership to surrender, but air forces can fight wars "inside out," hitting the innermost ring first, the leadership, where concessions originate, and then throughout the other rings, as necessary, to force capitulation.[45] He emphasized the primacy of the command ring, instructing:

> It is imperative to remember that all actions are aimed against the mind of the enemy command; thus, an attack against industry or infrastructure not only has some ultimate effect on fielded forces, but has a direct effect on commanders who must assess the cost of rebuilding, the effect on the state's economic position in the post war period, and whether the cost is worth the potential gain from continuing the war.... Military forces are a means to an end. It is pointless to deal with enemy forces if they can be bypassed, by strategy or technology, either in the defense or offense.[46]

Warden observed that centers of gravity existed not only at the nation-state or strategic level, but also at the operational level involving the enemy's fielded force. He admitted that sometimes a theater commander had to target operational centers of gravity in lieu of strategic ones, explaining that the combat leader "may be forced to deal with the enemy's fielded military forces because he cannot reach strategic centers without first removing enemy defenses or because his political masters will not permit him to attack strategic centers." If restraints prevented him from targeting strategic sites, compelling him to attack the enemy fielded force, he must still focus on centers of gravity.[47]

At the operational level, Warden again identified five centers of gravity, or rings. *The military commander himself and his C^3 system* created the first, innermost, and most important ring. The leader emerged as the primary target because he could make concessions to the attacker.[48] *Logistics* formed the second operational ring and included ammunition, fuel, and food.[49]

Infrastructure constituted the third operational ring and consisted of roads, air-sea-rail routes, communication lines, and pipelines. *Support personnel* who operated the logistics and infrastructure systems comprised the fourth ring. Again, Warden placed *fielded forces,* including aircraft, ships, and troops, in the outermost ring. "The fifth ring is toughest to reduce, simply because it is designed to be tough," Warden observed. "As a general rule, a campaign that focuses on the fifth ring (either by choice or because no alternatives exist) is likely to be the longest and bloodiest for both sides."[50]

Warden distilled his thinking about both the strategic and operational rings with the summary:

> We may not have to find and destroy thirty thousand tanks if we can destroy the few hundred fuel or ammunition distribution points. We may not have to destroy the few hundred fuel distribution points if we can immobilize an entire society by destroying dozens of electrical generation systems. And we may not need to destroy dozens of electrical generation systems if we can capture or kill the enemy leader.[51]

The colonel freely shared his thoughts with members of his staff, encouraged them to develop his concepts further, and adopted their ideas as he saw merit in them. He lectured to diverse audiences, always provoking discussion. While presenting the five strategic rings model at the School of Advanced Military Science at Fort Leavenworth, Kansas, he maintained that, unlike Clausewitz, he did not see an enemy's army as the primary center of gravity of a nation-state. Echoing Liddell Hart, he told a roomful of skeptical Army officers, "It's time to move beyond Clausewitz." His dismissal of the Prussian theorist, though, rejected a portion of his thought, not his entire corpus of ideas. Warden thought eclectically, frequently choosing and discarding ideas from a variety of sources and people.[52] His lectures about the five strategic rings also reflected the thoughts of the well-known American airpower theorist of the 1920s and 1930s, Brig. Gen. William "Billy" Mitchell, who wrote in *Skyways*:

> The advent of air power which can go straight to the vital centers and entirely neutralize or destroy them has put a completely new complexion on the old system of making war. It is now realized that the hostile main army in the field is a false objective and the real objectives are the vital centers. The old theory, that victory meant the destruction of the hostile main army, is untenable. Armies themselves can be disregarded by air power if a rapid stroke is made against the opposing centers, because a greatly superior army numerically is at the mercy of an air force inferior in numbers.[53]

Warden's concepts also derived from ideas generated at the Air Corps Tactical School (ACTS) during the interwar years. By 1926 many members of the school's faculty advocated the strategic role of bombardment aircraft acting independently of surface forces. By 1935 the school advocated high-altitude daylight precision bombing as the operational mission of an independent, strategic air force, striking vital points of a nation's economic structure.[54] Warden differed from most of the ACTS faculty, however, who thought that breaking the will of the enemy nation and people was the proper objective of strategic air warfare.[55] The colonel focused on breaking the will of the enemy leadership as the primary objective.

Checkmate

A 1989 reorganization of the Air Staff in the Directorate of Plans and Operations resulted in Warden's assuming responsibility for additional divisions and the merging of the Checkmate Division and the Mission Area Analysis Division into the Force Assessment Division. The Checkmate unit had achieved renown throughout the Pentagon for two functions. It first earned fame in 1976 when CSAF General David C. Jones, established it to study U.S. and allied conventional warfighting against the Soviet Union and to identify attendant requirements, problems, and limitations. Checkmate developed a Red team, patterned on Soviet strategy, operations, and tactics, to pose realistic threats to a Blue team, which was to counter Red team challenges. The Checkmate staff did war-gaming and often gave briefings to senior military and congressional leaders.[56] Recognition reappeared in 1983 when CSAF General Charles A. Gabriel established a joint cell within Checkmate to develop proposals by which the Army's AirLand Battle doctrine could be implemented in conjunction with Air Force assistance. The Army and the Air Force agreed in 1984 on a set of thirty-one initiatives to achieve this goal.[57] Because of the popularity of the Checkmate name, and since the new Force Assessment Division that had absorbed Checkmate occupied its old war-gaming center in the Pentagon basement, the "Checkmate" appellation continued to be informally used. Indeed, "Checkmate" was used to describe the source of Air Staff war planning throughout Desert Shield and Desert Storm although all of the warfighting divisions participated, not just the original Checkmate personnel.[58]

In 1989 and 1990, the ideas of Colonel Warden and his staff about air power and national defense continued to develop, under the rubrics "Air Option" and "Global Reach, Global Power." The former reflected the theme in Warden's *Air Campaign* book and highlighted how land-based air power contributed to America's security and why such force should be considered along with maritime and land operations in national strategic thinking. Through his lectures on the subject, Warden touted air power in economic and military terms. From an economic viewpoint in an era of diminishing defense budgets, the air option was affordable, and it strengthened the American economic and technological base. From a military perspective, air power benefited the nation because of its employability within hours or days, whereas ground forces might take as long as a month before they could be employed in sufficient numbers and strength to achieve national objectives. Air power "pits U.S. strength against enemy weakness" and offered the possibility of a short conflict, resulting in relatively few casualties, for both the "casualty-intolerant America" and the enemy.[59] The dual concept of air power as the nation's preeminent strength vis-à-vis other countries and air power as a force capable of quickly achieving objectives would later emerge in Phase I of the Gulf War air campaign.

Iraqi Air Campaign

When General Loh summoned General Alexander and Colonel Warden to his office the morning of August 8, 1990, just after receiving Schwarzkopf's telephone request, the group in Checkmate had already been developing an air campaign against Iraq, independently initiated by Warden the day before. The colonel, on vacation with his wife when the crisis erupted in SWA, flew home immediately and reported back to work to monitor the events and look for an opportunity to "sell" his ideas. He judged that, because sometimes the JCS asked service chiefs for inputs, this could be the means to interject his concepts about the air option into unified command planning. He would first deliver an air plan to General Dugan.[60] On Tuesday, August 7, the official start of Desert Shield, he ordered his deputy, Col. Emery M. Kiraly, to the basement Checkmate area to use the five-ring model and begin selecting target sets for an Iraqi air campaign.[61] Warden later told his staff that the situation in the CENTCOM AOR presented tremendous opportunities and they should think about the effective use of air power in the contingency and be proactive in offering suggestions.[62]

By midday on August 7, the Checkmate staff had laid out the five strategic ring categories in columns across the top of a large board and were brainstorming to suggest target sets, debating about which set belonged in which category. In addition, the staff divided themselves into groups and began formulating a basic outline for a campaign. For the next seven months, Warden's staff formed an extraordinarily energized and creative group of officers forging what they thought could be a significant chapter in the history of air power.[63]

During the evening of August 7, Lt. Col. David A. Deptula of the Secretary of the Air Force's (SecAF's) Special Staff Group (previously assigned to Warden's deputy directorate) met with Warden, Lt. Col. Bernard E. Harvey, acting Chief of the Deputy Directorate's Strategy Division, and others to discuss the deployment.[64] Deptula recalled that the flow of troops, weapon systems, and equipment looked solely defensive in nature, which it was.[65] The group was rightly perplexed about why CENTCOM sent F–111Ds instead of F–111Fs which were PGM-capable.[66] Warden invited Deptula back the next day to discuss using air power to force Saddam Hussein to withdraw his troops from Kuwait.[67]

Around noon on August 8, just four hours after the CINCCENT's telephone call, Warden briefed the plan titled "Iraqi Air Campaign" to Alexander. Then, with Alexander and Maj. Gen. Charles A. May, Jr., assistant DCS, Plans and Operations, he explained it to Loh. The plan included military objectives; strategy; assumptions; five strategic rings and their corresponding strategic target categories; five operational rings and corresponding operational target categories; and Air Force weapon systems.[68]

The staff included a statement of Presidential objectives, pieced together from listening to Bush's morning address to the nation announcing the deployment of forces. In abbreviated and paraphrased form, the plan listed four goals: withdrawal of Iraqi forces from Kuwait; restoration of Kuwaiti sovereignty; unimpeded flow of oil; and protection of American lives. It also listed four military objectives: forced withdrawal of Iraqis from Kuwait; degradation of the offensive capability of Iraq; protection of oil facilities; and damage to Saddam's effectiveness as an Arab leader.[69]

The military strategy employed air power against Iraqi centers of gravity to prevent Iraq from launching offensive operations against Saudi Arabia and defensive operations in Kuwait. The plan asserted the campaign would be directed against Saddam Hussein, not the Iraqi people; would be an offensive air operation (the Instant Thunder plan, in contrast with the Rolling Thunder approach during the Vietnam War); would employ U.S. strength against Iraqi weakness;

and would preclude force on force, which meant that air power would provide an alternative to U.S. ground forces' engaging the Iraqi army.[70]

The planners assumed that Iraq would act unilaterally with no military allies; that selective, not massive, destruction of Iraq would occur, which would psychologically affect the Iraqis; that civilian casualties and collateral damage would be minimized; and that U.S. losses would be minimal, even zero.[71] Collateral damage referred to unintended destruction as a result of bomb strikes. The plan presented the five strategic ring categories as concentric circles on one page and as columns across another page, with the corresponding target sets listed beneath each column head. The plan listed the following target categories and their respective target sets: under leadership were Saddam Hussein and military and civilian C^2 systems; under essential industry were oil, electricity, chemical plants, and a nuclear research facility; under infrastructure were railroads, ports, highways, and civilian and military airfields; under population were the Iraqi people and foreign workers, targeted only with PSYOPS; and under fielded force appeared strategic air defensive and offensive capabilities associated with Iraqi missiles carrying CW warheads.[72]

"Iraqi Air Campaign" presented not only strategic target categories and sets, but operational ones as well, as described in Warden's "Centers of Gravity" paper. The planners displayed Iraq's operational centers of gravity, from the core to the periphery, as joint commander, war supplies, infrastructure, support personnel, and fielded combat forces. The leadership set encompassed field generals, administration, and C^3. War supplies included POL, water, ammunition, and food. Under infrastructure were railroads, highways, seaports, airports, and LOC. The staff identified no targets sets for the support personnel. Under fielded force, the lethal weapon sets were Iraqi air defensive and air offensive capabilities, with only PSYOPS for the remainder of the force.[73] Even at the operational level, Warden's staff did not employ force on force or air power directly against the mass of the Iraqi army and their artillery and tanks. The plan lacked a counterland air attrition mission comparable to that specified in CENTCOM's OPLAN 1002–90.

U.S. Air Force and Saudi aircraft comprised the weapon systems: 14 to 32 B–52Gs for area and mining operations; 48 F–15s to complement the Royal Saudi Air Force (RSAF) fighters; unspecified numbers of stealth F–117As, F–111Fs, F–15Es, and F–16s; Volant Solo EC–130E aircraft for PSYOPS; and unspecified aircraft for unconventional operations.[74] At this point, Warden planned the campaign using only Air Force forces and excluded systems from the Navy and Marine Corps. He commented, "I have got to admit that I had more than a little bit of a thought in the back of my mind that we might be able to do the whole thing from the Air Force standpoint and that would be a very desirable thing to make happen."[75]

General Loh approved the thrust of the briefing and directed the planners to press on with its development so that, in two days, the basic concepts and outline of the product would be complete. Later in the day General Alexander received word that the CINCCENT would be briefed at MacDill AFB on Friday morning, the 10th.[76] To ensure that the Air Staff did, indeed, have the outline of the strategic air campaign ready to brief Schwarzkopf, calls for planning assistance went to SAC and TAC. By the night of August 8, four SAC augmentees had arrived in Washington, but TAC, on the other hand, requested that the Air Staff send a draft to TAC headquarters at Langley AFB where the document would be given a thorough and comprehensive review and critique. The draft went to Langley, and TAC delayed sending augmentees to the Pentagon.[77]

Intelligence Support

Misunderstanding between Generals Alexander and Clapper marred the formal entry of the intelligence function into the Instant Thunder planning process. This miscommunication got the operator-intelligence team off to a shaky start, contributing to Alexander's perception that intelligence officers focused too narrowly on their own specialty and discipline in an isolated intelligence chain of command, and expressed an unwillingness to meet the needs of their customers. For targeting support, Alexander telephoned Clapper and asked him to help Warden and the Checkmate staff develop a strategic air campaign — at General Loh's request. Alexander did not mention Schwarzkopf's call to Loh. Clapper questioned why the Air Staff undertook campaign planning in light of Goldwater-Nichols legislation and stated that he was "thinly manned," making detailed targeting difficult. He also related that he had recently visited Shaw AFB where the intelligence officers had shown him the Iraqi targeting they had accomplished. Clapper asked if what the officers had produced at Shaw correlated with Checkmate's task. Alexander definitely did not hear an upbeat, enthusiastic reply about the help that Clapper would provide; instead, it seemed he heard excuses why the assistance would not be forthcoming. Clapper later explained, "I simply did not appreciate then the pressure he was under." Alexander misinterpreted Clapper's comments about the analysis at Shaw as saying that an Iraqi strategic air campaign already existed and doubting the value of Warden's doing a second one.[78]

The two generals conversed cordially, but Clapper had not given total commitment to the Checkmate effort, although he may have stated he would send one of his colonels to see Warden. Alexander called Loh and complained, and Loh told him to tell Clapper that he *must* support the planning. Only much later did Clapper learn about the vice chief's displeasure with him. Eventually it was arranged that Air Staff's chief targeteer, Col. James R. Blackburn, Jr., director of the Air Force Intelligence Agency (AFIA) Directorate of Targets, assist Warden.[79] This action, representing the beginning of the intelligence community's formal involvement with the war planning, probably mollified Loh's initial irritation with Clapper.

Blackburn met with Warden on August 9 and learned that Schwarzkopf had requested a strategic air campaign. Remembering the Vietnam War when target selection was done outside the theater of war, and knowing the responsibilities levied by the Goldwater-Nichols Act, Blackburn thought it unwise for the Air Staff to get directly involved in war planning, and he expressed his concern to Warden and his staff. Blackburn's lack of enthusiasm for the enterprise annoyed the Checkmate group, which gratefully and eagerly welcomed the opportunity to show the nation how to wield air power effectively. Nonetheless, the chief targeteer and thirteen staff members began the supportive targeting process. The Checkmate planners immediately asked for imagery, but the targeteer first wanted to know the objectives and guidance the planners had devised to direct the planning and targeting process. Warden discussed with Blackburn the Presidential and military objectives, the plan's strategy and assumptions, and the five strategic rings.[80]

Blackburn recognized the ring model from an earlier briefing Warden had presented to the targeting staff. To Blackburn, the strategic rings represented neither an unorthodox nor revolutionary approach; they simply reflected the three basic target types — military, command, and economic — familiar to all targeteers and explained not only in their introductory targeting pamphlet but also in Air Force doctrine.[81]

When told the plan had to be executable, Blackburn explained to Warden that his intelligence staff would have to do weaponeering and aim-point selection for each target, working directly with weapon systems operators. Warden immediately asked which and how many operators were needed, and Blackburn said at least one for each Air Force system. Blackburn marveled, when, within hours, operators began flowing into Checkmate. "Warden got things done," he noted.[82]

Even while analyzing target sets, the intelligence officers had to jump ahead in the target development process and begin identifying Iraqi facilities and acquiring imagery on them. They defined a target as "a geographic area, complex, or installation planned for capture or destruction by military forces." A target system or set included "all the targets...situated in a particular geographic area and...functionally related." A country's POL system formed a typical target set, as did a country's air defense system. Targeteers further divided a target set into its components. The components of an air defense system, for example, would be C^2 units, EWR, target acquisition radar, antiaircraft artillery (AAA), SAM batteries, airfields, and missile support facilities. Further comprising target components were target elements. Examples of elements of the airfield component were runways, aircrew facilities, maintenance areas, munitions storage, POL storage, and operations areas.[83]

To select individual targets, targeteers studied current intelligence reports and databases focused on installations and systems with efforts to identify sites that would support the stated objectives and guidance they had received. They attempted to understand target characteristics, functions, and interrelations. In particular they looked for critical nodes of system components and target elements. Unfortunately, the databases on Iraq were out of date, incomplete, and erroneous, and available data failed to meet the needs of the targeteers.[84]

When Colonel Blackburn requested, through official channels at the Defense Intelligence Agency (DIA), targeting and intelligence support for the project he was working on for the CENTCOM commander and the Air Staff, his request was initially met with disbelief because the DIA was already addressing imagery and intelligence requirements submitted directly by CENTCOM headquarters. He was told to "get in line" and wait until the DIA completed the CENTCOM taskings. Blackburn submitted through the DIA's Joint Intelligence Center a work order that became lost and remained unfilled. He had an unpleasant encounter with the Joint Staff J–2 director, Captain McConnell, over nonresponse to his requests for assistance. McConnell would later play a prominent role in supplying intelligence for the air campaign, and Blackburn's tiff with him disclosed that even intelligence officers experienced frustration and roadblocks, inadvertent though they were, within their own community. Rather than functioning as a stovepiped system, McConnell found himself in a pipe-organ entity, separated from other intelligence components by bureaucracy, security requirements, and mission. DIA officials viewed Blackburn and the Air Staff's project as a service tasking, not a CENTCOM, war-related one, thus having lower priority under the unified command structure, especially in time of crisis.[85]

With the CENTCOM briefing date bearing down on him, Blackburn sent one of the targeteers to the DIA facility at Bolling AFB to "roam the halls, begging, borrowing, and stealing" intelligence studies and imagery related to the Iraqi targets. Much of what they collected were merely photocopies of studies and prints. At Blackburn's request, the small remnant intelligence staff at CENTAF sent him a list of the targets (now numbering forty-eight) still under development at Shaw AFB. Blackburn also requested intelligence support from the few analysts in the AFIA who had Middle East intelligence specialties. By combing through studies and reports, the analysts, targeteers, and operators began to identify targets to form sets under each category. In the process, however, information lapses and contradictions appeared that required more research to determine the correct information.[86]

After a couple of days, Warden requested that Blackburn and the targeteers move from their offices at Bolling AFB across the Potomac River to the Pentagon to work closely with the Checkmate operators and augmentees. The targeteers with their dozens of boxes of materials occupied the Checkmate lounge area.[87] As initiated by Warden, this collocation of targeteers and analysts with the operators facilitated an understanding of planning objectives and requirements and encouraged a beneficial working arrangement between the groups. Eventually, in theater, the targeteers remained isolated, unfortunately handicapping planning efforts.

Identifying targets, the targeteers next acquired imagery for them, assisted by the small AFIA section at the Navy Yard in Washington, D.C., as well as through the informal beg, borrow, and steal method of targeteers visiting DIA. Old microfiche of the Automated Tactical Target Graphics system comprised the first imagery acquired. For each targeted installation, the graphics provided annotated photographs and a textual description. As with other material, however, the collection method was out of date and incomplete.[88]

The targeteers and intelligence officers, like everyone else in Checkmate, were putting in hectic, fifteen-hour workdays. When submitting production orders to the unit at the Navy Yard, they did not ask for new imagery; they merely sought archival material. Sometimes photographs sent to the targeteers in Checkmate bore no resemblance to the old Automated Tactical Target Graphics imagery or to images in studies and reports, so the discrepancies had to be resolved. Sometimes a target appearing in a photograph was not the major focus of the print, so an enlargement was required. Pentagon targeteers and the photo interpreters at the Navy Yard communicated extensively. In one instance, Blackburn, who had photo interpretation experience, found a water distillation plant misidentified as a petroleum plant.[89]

Once they identified targets and acquired imagery for them, targeteers tried to do analysis in depth, but given the time constraints, they performed only rule-of-thumb weaponeering instead of more precise analysis using data published in the Joint Munitions Effectiveness Manual. The manual, however, had no information on highly secret, black programs for weapons development, like the GBU–27 laser-guided munition dropped by the F–117A stealth aircraft. Targeteers and weapon system operators worked very closely, again selecting aim points, or desired mean points of impact (DMPIs), for each of the targets. The selection process identified the best points for weapon application, precisely located the aim points, and determined the height of the weapons burst.[90]

F–117A Nighthawks

Blackburn had concerns with two target sets under the strategic leadership category: Saddam Hussein, and military and civilian C^2 systems. He thought that Saddam per se should not be identified as the primary target because he believed that Presidential Executive Order 12333 prohibited the targeting of an individual. Sometime later, he obtained a legal opinion that Saddam could be attacked during wartime in his capacity as a military leader who commanded military forces and directed their operations. Others, however, constantly raised the same issue. Warden yielded and changed the wording of the target from *Hussein* to *Hussein regime*. He noted though, "We proceeded to target exactly the same thing that we were going to target anyway. We didn't change any of the physical targeting; we just changed the label on it."[91]

Regarding military and civilian C^2, the planners had wanted to destroy civilian television and radio broadcasting stations throughout Iraq. Blackburn feared the goal of destroying all such broadcasting capability would become a "weapon-sortie sponge" because so many transmitters existed in Iraq and they were relatively easy to replace. He suggested that rather than destroying these targets, degrading them would achieve the objective of isolating Saddam and denying him the means of communicating with the Iraqi population and feeding it propaganda. To a targeteer, target sets had to be identified in relation to objectives and interdependence among them. Each target set itself had to be analyzed to determine its components, characteristics, and complexity. Objectives had to be determined for each set. These objectives helped determine if the set and its components should be destroyed, degraded, neutralized, or exploited. Blackburn explained that degrading, rather than destroying, radio and television broadcasting would require fewer sorties and still prevent the Iraqi leader from using broadcasts to bolster his regime. The operators agreed.[92]

Instant Thunder

On the morning of August 10, General Loh met with Generals May and Alexander, Colonel Warden, and others to receive the version of the strategic air campaign that was to be briefed to General Schwarzkopf. Warden presented the plan, which differed in three ways from the one given to Loh two days earlier. The staff had renamed it and had added and deleted sections.[93]

The revised version now carried the title, "Instant Thunder: A Strategic Air Campaign Proposal for CINCCENT."[94] The new name emphasized the plan as the antithesis to the Vietnam War's Rolling Thunder in which President Lyndon B. Johnson imposed limitations on the air campaign's targets, weaponry, and sorties to ensure that it did not provoke Soviet or Chinese intervention, sidetrack his Great Society program, nor damage America's relations with its allies.[95]

Another revision of the Air Staff plan deleted the sections showing the five operational rings and the target sets under the operational target categories. The new version focused on only strategic target sets and identified the following as target categories for the five strategic rings: leadership, key production, infrastructure, population, and fielded military force. Because Schwarzkopf had requested an air campaign with broad, strategic targeting, Warden dropped the operational rings from the plan. The Air Staff produced solely a strategic air campaign; nonetheless, Warden exuded confidence that strategic power alone could achieve the objectives of the plan.[96]

The staff also expanded the plan with new ideas presented as objectives, course of action, planning considerations, CONOPS, assumptions, and a war-termination scenario. They added a lengthy second part that consisted of a general target list, B–52G representative targets, a key F–117A target, a force summary, campaign deployment flow, execution flow, results, a deception plan, and PSYOPS objectives.[97]

The plan still included four Presidential objectives, slightly differing from the first iteration and taken exactly from the President's address to the nation:

> Immediate, unconditional and complete withdrawal of all Iraqi forces from Kuwait
> Kuwait's legitimate government must be restored to replace the puppet regime
> Committed to the security and stability of the Persian Gulf
> Protect the lives of American citizens abroad.[98]

The planners provided three campaign objectives:

> Raise to unacceptable level the cost to Iraq of remaining in Kuwait
> Isolate forces in Kuwait from an incapacitated regime
> Disarm the Hussein regime.[99]

They presented five planning considerations:

> Pit U.S. strengths against Iraqi weaknesses — avoid employing U.S. weaknesses against Iraqi strengths
> Target is Hussein regime, not Iraqi people
> Selective destruction of key targets [instead of] massive destruction to enable quick rebuilding
> Minimize civilian casualties/collateral damage
> Minimize U.S. losses.[100]

In trying to minimize civilian casualties and collateral damage, the planners followed international law (codified in the laws of armed conflict) and its strictures about discrimination, although nowhere in Instant Thunder did they mention the legal code. According to the law and the just-war tradition, attackers had to distinguish between military and civilian targets, and between combatants, who could intentionally be attacked, and noncombatants, who could not deliberately be struck.[101] J. F. C. Fuller's *The Generalship of Alexander the Great* also directly influenced Warden's thinking and thus influenced the plan with regard to the treatment of the enemy population. Like Alexander, who viewed the enemy population as potential allies and treated them well, Warden wanted to spare the people from direct lethal attacks, try to win them over to the U.S. cause, and encourage them to turn against their leader. He wanted the populace to view the Americans as liberators, not as conquerors.[102]

In the extremely unlikely event that the strategic air campaign did not achieve Presidential and campaign objectives, the staff provided a worst-case scenario. The situation resulted in neither the ouster of Saddam Hussein nor his capitulation under President Bush's terms. Even if he held on, however, his regime would retain no economy. It would be unable to resupply and support Iraqi troops in Kuwait, defend the country from aerial attack, or engage in offensive operations. The status quo that preceded the invasion would not reappear, and the United States would continue, in a limited way, to counter the Iraqi regime. Acting in conjunction with allies, the Americans would continue the naval blockade and provide "U.S. air cover for Arab actions," which would liberate Kuwait. The plan's creators emphasized an Arab ground war without the involvement of U.S. ground troops. At this point in the scenario, the plan stated, "Bulk of U.S. forces withdraw." The Air Staff officers did not envision the United States using American ground forces to militarily coerce the Iraqi forces to withdraw from Kuwait.[103]

The planners deleted Warden's concentric circles illustrating the strategic rings; instead, they showed the target categories linearly across the briefing page and identified corresponding target sets beneath each column. As General Alexander recalled, they eliminated the rings in response to feedback from TAC headquarters indicating that the slide was "an academic bunch of crap."[104] They placed the Hussein regime, telecommunications, and C^3 target sets under the leadership category, basically the same target sets of the first plan. (They used the term *telecommunications* to denote civilian communications, distinguishing them from military C^3).[105]

Under key production, they listed oil as a target set in both plans, but in the new strategic plan, the oil components differed. The planners originally targeted oil export and civilian and military internal consumption facilities; in the new version, they identified only oil distribution and storage facilities. Electricity remained a system in both plans, with no components identified. The Baghdad Nuclear Research Center was now described as an NBC research facility. They entered the chemical industrial target set of the first plan as military production and storage in the new set.[106]

In the infrastructure category, the planners deleted three target sets: ports, highways, and civilian and military airfields. They retained railroads.[107] For the population category, they added "soldiers in Kuwait" to the sets "Iraqis" and "foreign workers." They would employ only PSYOPS, not lethal weapons, against each of these sets.[108] The strategic campaign was to be so effective, and the price to Saddam of allowing the strategic air campaign to continue to be too high, that the regime would pull the Iraqi troops out of Kuwait. Therefore, dropping bombs on soldiers there would be unnecessary; leaflet drops would suffice to encourage their surrender and return home. Under the fielded force category, the sets remained the same: strategic air defensive and strategic air offensive capabilities. Under the latter set, bombers now appeared as a component with missiles.[109]

Changes to the Instant Thunder weapon system array gave the plan a faint joint character. Planners included naval air assets "in excess of fleet defense," and marine air "as available." They also included RSAF aircraft.[110] The Air Force aircraft, primarily combat platforms, consisted of the following:

Aircraft	No. of Squadrons	No. of Aircraft
F–15	2	48
F–4G	1	24
F–117A	2	30
F–111F	1	24
F–111F		8 carrying GBU–15s
F–15E	1	24
OA–10	1	18
F–16	4	72
EF–111	1	6
B–52	1	20
F–111D/E	2	36
A–10	3	72
AWACS		5
B–52	an unspecified number from the continental U.S.[111]	

The revised plan highlighted two weapon systems, the B–52G and the F–117A. The B–52G would employ three types of munitions: long-range stand-off munitions, the Have Nap missile, and general-purpose bombs. The Air Force controlled the first type of munition in a black, supersecret program to protect information about the AGM–86C CALCMs. Have Nap was an Israeli 3,000-pound missile with a television guidance system for day and an infrared seeker for night operations. Planners intended to employ the F–117A carrying a GBU–27, the munition consisting of a BLU–109 (I–2000) penetrating bomb guided by a Paveway III laser kit and specially configured for the radar-evading aircraft, against the Iraqi southern air defense sector operations center (SOC). Eight F–117s would attack the SOC at night and hit it at four different points, two bombs per aim point. Later in theater, Colonel Deptula would reduce the number of F–117s attacking the SOC and develop a strategy of "targeting for effects," which did not originally appear in the Instant Thunder plan.[112]

In a section about strategic environment, the planners offered six assertions,

Delivered by B-52s, CALCMs used the global positioning system.

two of which suggested executing the air plan as quickly as possible: "time works against the U.S. presence in SWA," and "initiative, surprise, and deception make it important to strike before Hussein acts."[113] The plan's deployment-flow section presented the scheduled movement for combat aircraft, day by day, from August 8 to 24. It then proposed an alternative flow, which would place sufficient numbers of appropriate combat aircraft in theater to allow launching the strategic air campaign on August 18. The decision to change the deployment flow had to be made on or by August 12 to allow enough time for the necessary combat aircraft to arrive in theater for the August 18 execution date.[114]

The plan briefly sketched how the strategic air campaign would unfold over the first two days, with attacks in three waves over 24-hour periods. Targets during the first two days would be from the general target-set list, with aircraft on alert for interdiction if Saudi Arabia were attacked. Defensive counterair operations would be undertaken as required. After the morning of the second day, air superiority would be attained. During the third through the sixth days, target sets would be leadership, railroads, electricity, POL, and the NBC research facility. F–16 and A–10 aircraft would be on call and, as required, sent against Iraqi ground forces, LOCs, and supply lines.[115] The planners predicted the air campaign results: in six to nine days, all targets, estimated to be about seventy-five, would be destroyed.[116]

The lengthy PSYOPS section of the plan presented assumptions, objectives, and a CONOPS. The assumptions suggested that overt PSYOPS would be essentially truthful, openly associated with the United States, and coordinated with other governmental agencies, and would heed national policy directives. Two objectives separated Saddam Hussein from domestic and international support and from "broad sectors" of the Iraqi armed forces. In addition, PSYOPS would undermine the propaganda the regime churned out. Planners targeted foreign workers in Iraq, to "neutralize" their support of Saddam's military initiatives, and certain unspecified "Iraqi audiences," to lessen their opposition to U.S. actions. The operations would increase support for U.S. actions among other Arabs in the region. The CONOPS stated that PSYOPS messages would support "each military strike"; U.S. broadcasts would replace Iraqi ones knocked off the air; PSYOPS would accompany military actions undertaken to protect hostages; and the PSYOPS campaign would cease when the Iraqi government complied with standards of the international community.[117]

Fear of TAC Veto

At the conclusion of the briefing, Loh telephoned Dugan to inquire if he wished to receive the briefing before its presentation to the JCS and Schwarzkopf. The vice chief kept the CSAF apprised of all that transpired on the Air Staff in producing the strategic air campaign, and the CSAF discussed developments with other Air Force leaders. The evening of August 9, for example, Dugan had a discussion with General Russ about TAC's participation in forming the plan. Dugan declined Warden's offer of flying to Massachusetts to meet with him, recommended against presenting the plan first at TAC or to the JCS, and directed the planners to fly directly to MacDill AFB and brief Schwarzkopf that Friday, August 10.[118]

Alexander and Warden considered Dugan's decision to take Instant Thunder directly to the CENTCOM commander, bypassing General Russ at TAC, to be a considerable victory. Alexander believed that the TAC commander and his staff were too committed to using air power according to the Army's AirLand Battle doctrine and adverse to using it in a conventional strategic air campaign, and that the TAC commander and his staff would have ordered changes in Instant Thunder that would have destroyed its strategic emphasis.

General Russ's Critique of Instant Thunder

At TAC headquarters, General Russ reviewed Instant Thunder, and after the war he sharply criticized it. None of his objections, however, corroborated the views of Warden and Alexander that he disliked Instant Thunder because he was too wedded to the Army's AirLand Battle doctrine to appreciate a strategic air campaign and he wanted the plan to be more supportive of the Army. First, Russ worried that the air campaign was being developed without the input of General Horner, the JFACC, the commander responsible for executing it. The Air Staff repeated the mistakes of the Vietnam War by selecting targets and planning operations in Washington instead of allowing warriors in theater to perform these critical functions. Russ explained:

> The Pentagon is the one that developed the initial plan. They were telling them how to fight the war. Had the war failed, you would not see anyone in the Pentagon out in front taking the blame because the plan wasn't any good. Horner is the one who would get chewed. Warden wouldn't be anywhere around. Horner is the one who would get the heat. What I'm saying is that he has the responsibility to fight the war; then by god let him fight the war, and let him ask for what he needs and tell us what he doesn't need. What starts as a little bit of help from the Pentagon soon leads to more and more "help" and pretty soon you get the President in on it....Then you have people in the White House sitting on the floor trying to figure out what targets they are going to hit. That is *just the wrong way to fight a war!*[119]

The Vietnam War still seared some airmen who had fought it, strongly influencing their judgment. The CINCCENT himself had telephoned the Air Staff and requested the air campaign. The Air Staff had to respond to Schwarzkopf's request, so the first criticism was unfair, but understandable, for even the CINCCENT admitted discomfort with the Pentagon doing war planning.

Russ next disagreed with Instant Thunder's contention that the Air Force alone would achieve Presidential and CENTCOM objectives — win the war — without the Army and Navy. He stated:

> One of the things you learn as TAC commander is to be sensitive with the Army and other services. I had been criticized because I said tactical air power's primary role is to support the Army. I had a gut feeling that there was a group of hair-on-fire majors in Washington that were going to win the war all by themselves. They were going to have the Air Force win the war.
>
> Now, I didn't doubt that we could probably do that if taken to the final conclusion, but I also was very dubious of the fact that anybody would ever allow the Air Force to do it all by themselves. I have been in the Joint arena too long watching these things, and everybody has got to do something.[120]

It is unclear whether Russ thought the air campaign itself had to be more joint in character, with many more aircraft from the other services participating, making Instant Thunder less of an Air Force–only show, or whether he meant that the war itself had to be planned to include ground and maritime campaign phases, rendering it less of an airpower show. Even the Air Staff moved toward the former position. From the strategic perspective, the Navy would then enforce the naval embargo on Iraq, and premises from OPLAN 1002–90 indicated that CENTCOM would use massive numbers of American ground forces to defend Saudi Arabia and restore lost territory. Russ worried that the plan would be rejected for not being joint enough, but the CENTCOM commander seemed to know that no single service would or could shoulder all the wartime responsibilities, and he was not as bothered as the TAC commander about Warden's claims for what Instant Thunder could accomplish. Schwarzkopf had called for the plan as a retaliatory option, not as the offensive war plan to eject the Iraqis from Kuwait. It provided an acceptable response if the Iraqis were to kill hostages.

Russ correctly saw a major flaw in Instant Thunder in its failure to include an electronic countermeasures (ECM) plan. This, indeed, created a serious shortcoming because the Air Staff's product was supposed to have been executable, and attaining air superiority required ECM and electronic combat (EC). To correct the ECM deficiency, Russ sent Brig. Gen. Larry L. Henry, USAF, an EC specialist, to the JFACC in Saudi Arabia to help with planning to defeat the Iraqi air defense system.[121]

After General Loh had initially telephoned Russ and discussed with him broad planning and target options against Iraq, Russ directed Brig. Gen. Thomas R. Griffith, his DCS for plans, to lead the effort to develop air campaign options to assist Loh and Dugan in responding to General Schwarzkopf's request. The TAC plan, however, was not yet completed when the Air Staff planners traveled to MacDill AFB to meet with the CENTCOM commander.

CINCCENT's Briefing — August 10

For about forty minutes on August 10th, Air Staff planners briefed Instant Thunder to the CINCCENT at MacDill AFB. Assisted by General Alexander and Colonel Harvey, Colonel Warden briefed the plan to General Schwarzkopf, Lt. Gen. Craven C. Rogers, USAF, CENTCOM deputy commander, and General Moore, CENTCOM J–3.[122] Most of Schwarzkopf's questions plus much of the general discussion focused on when the plan would be executable and what changes in the deployment flow were necessary to support its execution. When the CINCCENT heard that, with some changes in the flow, the plan would be ready to execute on August 18, he stated that if Saddam Hussein decided to attack on that day, "We'd be in dire straits; I'd say I can't hold out if you don't execute air attacks." At one point, Alexander stated that the planners would focus on deployment-flow changes, doing "in-depth work, real quick." Schwarzkopf suggested they focus on August 22 as D-day.[123]

The CINCCENT readily accepted Warden's Clausewitzian "center of gravity" terminology. Indeed, he was quite familiar with it; it permeated the Army's FM 100–5 AirLand Battle doctrine manual. The general emphasized three target sets: Saddam Hussein's regime, military production and storage, and the NBC facility. With respect to leadership, Schwarzkopf referred to remarks recently made by the Egyptian president indicating that the Iraqis had to withdraw from Kuwait and that Saddam had to be removed from power. Regarding the military support facilities, Schwarzkopf emphasized CW production and storage; concerning the weapons of mass destruction, he wanted all key components of the vast NBC research facility identified and targeted.[124]

At the end of the presentation, he instructed the airmen to explain the plan to the CJCS. He stated that he had already briefed the President on many of its elements. He told the airmen, "You've restored my confidence in the United States Air Force." He pointed out that CENTAF could not do such a plan, because its commander was already in Saudi Arabia and his staff focused on the Desert Shield deployment. "Do it where you want. It's up to the Air Force.... Shit, I love it," he exclaimed.[125]

With an important revelation, Schwarzkopf explained why he wanted and needed the Air Staff plan. He stated that Saddam Hussein was a "crazy man," who could "lash out" and attack Saudi Arabia, do something "nasty" to the hostages, or drop CW on Israel. The general needed a plan to "fall back on" in response to such "crazy" acts.[126] To Schwarzkopf, therefore, the strategic air campaign plan was a retaliation plan, just as he had requested, in case Saddam committed more acts of aggression. This differed significantly from the planners' view that the strategic air campaign plan was the best means to achieve the President's and their objectives, including forcing the Iraqis to withdraw from Kuwait.

The CINCCENT offered intriguing remarks about the PSYOPS directed against Iraqi troops in Kuwait. "This is where America has the edge," he stated.

"After you do this, we'll drop leaflets on his frontline forces and tell them they're out of business."[127] To Schwarzkopf, the strategic air campaign plan was not expected to, nor did it, direct lethal air power against the Iraqi ground forces. Likewise, to the planners, the strategic air campaign, synonymous with the entire air campaign plan, excluded the use of air power against Iraqi troops and their tanks and artillery.

The general told the planners he would telephone the CJCS that day to request that he issue directives for detailed planning on Instant Thunder. "I will tell [Powell], what do you lose by planning [?] So what if it leaks. It took us a long time to do this in Vietnam, and we never did it in the Iranian hostage crisis." The general viewed Instant Thunder in terms of history — the Linebacker strategic air campaign against North Vietnam in 1972, and the crisis in 1979–1981 when the Iranians seized the American embassy in Tehran and took hostages. Alexander said, "We'll throw everything at him." Schwarzkopf replied, "I'm with you. This will lower losses."[128]

Warden returned to the issue briefly raised during the presentation about launching the campaign from bases in Saudi Arabia. Schwarzkopf had asked for a "Plan B" to accomodate launching from Turkey if the Saudis declined approval for Instant Thunder. "Our agreement is for the defense of Saudi Arabia, not to go against [a] third country without prior consultation," he reminded them.[129] The airmen knew that a campaign against Iraq without the use of Saudi air bases posed complicated, serious problems.

At the conclusion of the session, Warden departed the room with the CINCCENT and, as he later recounted, told the commander, "General, you have the opportunity now to carry off the most brilliant operation that any American general has executed since Douglas MacArthur went ashore at Inchon."[130] The planners then met with General Moore, who thought well of Instant Thunder and knew it had positively impressed the CINCCENT.[131] They continued discussing the air campaign, noting that sending aircraft and support materiel to the theater to execute the plan would necessitate that shipment of other supplies would have to stop, but noting also that changing the flow generated great difficulties. Within the theater, too, a base-saturation problem had emerged.[132]

On the return flight to Andrews AFB, the excited planners brimmed with ideas about what they yet had to accomplish to make Instant Thunder an executable plan. Later that evening at the Pentagon, Alexander met with the Checkmate staff and told them that the next day they would brief their plan to Chairman Powell, and that TAC representatives would arrive to assist with the effort.[133]

The following morning, Warden met with his staff, who knew well the seriousness and significance of their planning mission. The colonel told them they were to produce an "executable" product that would be a "strategic, political-military campaign — pure Clausewitz" and proclaiming that "every bomb is political," since the air war was being waged against Saddam Hussein, not the Iraqi people. He cautioned them not to get "bogged down in tactical details" but to plan as necessary to reach "strategic levels." He told them they were putting together a campaign their comrades would execute, with friends dying. If they planned properly, the result would be a "classical strategic victory" to "go down in the history books." The plan had to be completed for Schwarzkopf on Wednesday, August 15, five days hence.[134]

Warden did not explain to his staff that the CINCCENT approved of Instant Thunder for reasons different from those that were driving him, because he himself did not fully understand the commander's rationale. He assumed that Schwarzkopf was a "bright guy" and therefore saw the merits of the Air Staff plan and accepted it just as he had explained it. If the CINCCENT had to execute military action soon, he had no other options.[135] Comparing five basic characteristics of Instant Thunder with the features that Schwarzkopf had in mind for his retaliation plan, two important differences appeared. The purpose of the Air Staff's Instant Thunder was to achieve Presidential and self-defined campaign objectives, which included forcing the Iraqi army from Kuwait. The Air Staff plan was a military *solution* in contrast to the purpose of the retaliation plan the commander sought — a military *option* to strike at the Iraqi nation if Saddam used CW or killed hostages. The targets of the two plans, the one on paper as Instant Thunder and the other in Schwarzkopf's mind, were the same — strategic, high-value, political, economic, and military targets in Iraq. Nor did the intensity of the two plans differ — both were air campaigns, a series of related military operations, not just surgical, pinprick strikes. The CINCCENT had sought a "serious air campaign" against Iraq. The duration of the campaigns was also similar. On August 10, Warden's plan would last from six to nine days; later it would last only six days, conforming with the construct of *instant.* The CINCCENT approved of a short campaign. Finally, for the Air Staff, Instant Thunder could and should be executed even if Saddam refrained from additional aggressive actions, such as harming hostages. Warden wanted Instant Thunder executed soon because he believed time worked against U.S. presence in the region. His plan proclaimed, "Important to strike before Hussein acts."[136] In contrast, the cause for initiating the CINCCENT's air retaliation plan was Saddam Hussein's commission of additional heinous acts, requiring a superpower to make an appropriate response.

The CINCCENT did not agree with Warden's purpose for Instant Thunder nor with the rationale for quickly executing the plan even if Iraq committed no further aggression. Nonetheless, the commander embraced the Air Staff draft plan because it had other characteristics he sought, and he could reformulate its purpose easily enough and implement it if the NCA directed him to use military force. He enthusiastically received the plan knowing that he and his JFACC could adapt it to their requirements.

TAC's Plan

TAC's plan finally arrived at the Pentagon a few minutes after midnight, August 10/11. General Griffith sent it by fax to General Alexander.[137] Arriving too late to influence the Instant Thunder briefing for Schwarzkopf earlier in the afternoon, it nevertheless inspired the Checkmate planners to incorporate a statement into their material refuting its concepts. Produced at General Russ's direction in response to the Air Force vice chief's telephone call to him on August 8, the plan carried the title, "CENTCOM Air Campaign Plan." The TAC commander later described its origin and selectivity:

> They came to me for an input on what options were available to apply air power to help solve the problem. I submitted an input. I could have easily said, "Take everything we have and go downtown and wipe everybody out." This is an easy input to make, but I didn't. I tried to provide a selective way in which we could judiciously apply air power and not simply apply overwhelming force, because you have public opinion and other things to worry about.[138]

The plan contained sections on the President's and the CINCCENT's objectives, assumptions, planning factors, expected outcomes, air strategy, target priorities, nuclear reactor targeting, and targeted key installations.[139] It included a three-part air strategy. The first placed air power in a deterrent posture while a quick buildup of forces occurred.[140] The second explained how to use air power based on the scenario that Iraqi forces still occupied Kuwait but that they had not attacked Saudi Arabia. Airmen would employ air power to "demonstrate our ability to conduct offensive operations against Iraqi targets of our choosing."[141] They would then "escalate as required until all significant targets are destroyed." Finally they would "keep up the pressure until Iraqi power has diminished to the point that regional stability has been restored." The three functions, according to the plan, allowed Saddam time and the opportunity to "reevaluate his situation and back out while there is something to save."[142]

Explaining the rationale behind the second part, General Griffith stated that he and General Russ thought they should "do some selective things first," just to get Saddam Hussein's attention. They considered hitting the nuclear research center; pause for twelve hours or so, then hit two more high-value targets, and pause again before striking three more key facilities. If Iraq did not respond in Kuwait or elsewhere, then "go for the gusto" and bomb extensively.[143]

The third and final part of the strategy explained how to use air power if Iraq attacked Saudi Arabia. Initially, it specified using air power to establish air superiority, destroy the capability to employ CW, support the ground commander's scheme of maneuver, and interdict Iraqi resupply operations to fielded forces.[144] Secondly, it specified expanding air superiority over Kuwait and Iraq, widening the scope of the interdiction operations, and conducting CAS and BAI operations.[145] Finally, the effort would "demonstrate air supremacy over the entire region," execute strategic strikes against military targets, and, upon order, extend such attacks to economic targets, while continuing support for the ground commander's scheme of maneuver.[146]

TAC planners had developed their air campaign in response to multiple scenarios, providing numerous options to the CINCCENT, whereas the Air Staff focused Instant Thunder on just a strategic air campaign executed to deny Saddam more opportunity for aggression. Alexander gave the TAC product to Warden, who shared it with his Checkmate staff.[147] When members saw its call for gradualism, they derided it as a misguided use of air power, likening it to the failed policies of the Vietnam War, a rehash of the Rolling Thunder campaign. To counter that kind of thinking, they included in their plan the glaring, negative statement about Instant Thunder: "What it is not — a graduated, long-term campaign designed to provide escalation options to counter Iraqi moves."[148] Warden judged the TAC plan inconsequential and discarded it. He knew Schwarzkopf had affirmed and bought the Instant Thunder draft; now he had to sell it to Chairman Powell.

On August 9, 1990, General Loh had attended a JCS meeting in the Tank, substituting for General Dugan who was still out of town. It was then that Chairman Powell told Loh he had discussed the Air Staff planning effort with Schwarzkopf, and he asked the Air Force Vice Chief of Staff to make it joint. Loh responded that he would brief it to the Joint Staff Director and Joint Staff J–3 as soon as the planners had developed something firm. CENTCOM, however, had scheduled a presentation for the CINCCENT on August 10, before Loh could send his planners to the JCS. While General Alexander and Colonel Warden feared having to brief Instant Thunder to General Russ at TAC before giving it to the CINCCENT, Loh worried about failing to present it to the JCS before the CENTCOM commander saw it. On the morning of the 10th, when Loh telephoned Dugan and inquired if he should send the planners to TAC and the JCS before they traveled to MacDill AFB, Dugan told him to send them directly to the CINCCENT without delay. Loh subsequently called Lt. Gen. Michael P. C. Carns, the Joint Staff Director, and arranged for a presentation to the CJCS for the next day. Later on the 10th, Schwarzkopf also called Powell and discussed the Air Staff plan that Loh would bring to the CJCS.[149]

CJCS's Briefing — August 11

Instant Thunder won the CJCS's approval when Warden and others briefed him on the 11th.[150] Powell told them it was a "good plan, very fine piece of work." He asked many practical questions about the logistics necessary to support an air campaign launched, if necessary, in eleven days, on August 22. He wanted to know if the fuel and munitions would be available in sufficient quantities, observing that the Air Force looked weaker in available ordnance than in numbers of aircraft. He asked about the deployment flow and necessary changes to meet the requirements of the plan. He inquired about which equipment would have to be put on hold in the deployment flow to allow space for Instant Thunder assets, what were the tradeoffs. He did not want to change the deployment flow, and he asked when the plan would be ready to execute without alterations. The colonel said his staff would require about a day and a half to determine detailed deployment information. Powell suggested they return in a few days and talk over logistics.[151] He also questioned if the targeting supported the plan's execution. Colonel Blackburn did not attend, but Loh answered that fifty targeteers were working the issues (mistakenly tripling the actual number). Warden offered to send some sample target folders to the Chairman the next day. Powell also questioned Schwarzkopf's contention that Turkey would allow the United States to launch the air campaign from Turkish air bases.[152]

After the initial presentation, discussion commenced about the strategic air campaign's excluding targets in Kuwait, and then Powell dropped his bombshell question. "OK, it's day 6," he asked, and the strategic air campaign is finished. "Now what?"[153] Warden expressed confidence that Instant Thunder would induce the Iraqis to withdraw from Kuwait. The colonel later explained, "I made the statement that I thought there was a high probability that the war could be concluded just with the strategic operations; that after the strategic operations we could tell Saddam, 'Hey, you have got to withdraw your forces from Kuwait,' and they would march home." He also stated that he clearly told Powell that he thought Saddam Hussein would withdraw his army from Kuwait after six to nine days of Instant Thunder.[154] Alexander remembered, "Warden was of the opinion that the strategic air campaign would end the war."[155] In the ensuing discussion, the CJCS remarked, "I won't be happy until I see those tanks destroyed."[156] He explained that if massive air attacks were launched against Iraq, the United States might as well finish the job and destroy the Iraqi army. He wanted the airmen to undertake the counterland mission. "I don't want them to go home — I want to leave smoking tanks as kilometer posts all the way to Baghdad," Powell insisted.[157]

The group then discussed the execution of a strategic air campaign and attacks against Iraqi ground troops. Alexander observed that attacking tanks was tremendously difficult, but Loh and Warden said it could be done. Powell stated, "Once you've done the strategic air campaign, [we] don't want to just sit and wait for results like we had to do after Hiroshima." Alexander emphasized that they needed to ensure that achieving tactical level objectives did not compromise the success of the strategic campaign. The CJCS replied, "Right, but I can't recommend only the strategic air campaign to the President."[158]

Powell rejected a fundamental idea upon which Instant Thunder was based, namely, that the air campaign should *not* use air power directly against the Iraqi military forces in Kuwait and southern Iraq. Compared with Warden, Powell had a more comprehensive view of the air operations required to achieve national objectives and force the Iraqis from Kuwait. He envisioned a campaign with phasing. The first phase comprised Instant Thunder's strategic strikes; the second, lethal air attacks directly against the enemy's fielded army.

Reflecting after the war on the meeting, Alexander correctly concluded that the CJCS had merely humored the airmen by not openly disagreeing with their contention that the Iraqi army would leave Kuwait as the result of Instant Thunder.[159] Indeed, on August 4 at Camp David, Powell had agreed with Schwarzkopf's telling the President that to eject the Iraqis from Kuwait more U.S. ground troops would be needed than were called for in OPLAN 1002–90 and that the additional deployment would require 8 to 10 months for completion. On August 15 Powell would tell the President that by the third week of October enough forces would be in the theater to successfully defend Saudi Arabia, but to go on the offensive, even more troops would be needed. He wrote after the war, "Warden's approach could destroy or severely cripple the Iraqi regime. But we also needed an air plan to help drive Saddam out of Kuwait, if it came to that." He referred to Instant Thunder as an "air option" should Saddam Hussein "attempt another provocation requiring our instant response." Powell directed the airmen to do more with air power than just a strategic air campaign.[160] Instant Thunder was a partial solution, not the entire answer to achieving the President's objectives. Early on, Powell thought beyond retaliation to offensive operations to liberate Kuwait.

Later, back in Checkmate, the pace and scope of activity on Saturday, August 11 increased enormously, prompting Colonel Deptula and Lt. Col. Ronnie A. Stanfill to organize the rapidly expanding, hectic effort. The officers established campaign plans and applications teams to address each target set and weapon system, including tankers and Volant Solo aircraft; munitions and logistics; strategy and doctrine; search and rescue; foreign aircraft; and SEAD. They formed no intelligence team, although the targeteers diligently labored on their portion of the plan.[161] The Checkmate area overflowed with personnel from the deputy directorate and representatives from a variety of organizations, including other Air Staff offices, SAC, TAC, the Fighter Weapons School at Nellis AFB, and the other services.[162]

Copies of excerpts from the Air War Plan Division's Plan No. 1 of 1941 (the air plan that defeated Hitler) and reproductions of the Normandy invasion plan of 1944 and the invasion plan against Japan of 1945 circulated among the planners.[163] The staff tried to draw ideas from history even as they sensed they were making history. Alexander told key personnel to record in notebooks what they were doing so they could later explain how they shaped the history of air power. At Warden's request, the Air Force historian sent one of his staff historians to Checkmate to assist with the planning, and he stayed throughout Desert Shield and Desert Storm.[164]

Chapter Three

Desert Storm Phase I

Throughout the week of August 11–17, 1990, the Air Staff planners continued to develop Instant Thunder, and the discrepancy of viewpoint between General Schwarzkopf and Colonel Warden about the plan's purpose and immediate cause never resolved itself, but neither did it pose any obstacles. The planning enterprise assumed joint aspects, although it fundamentally created an Air Force product. Supported by the SecAF, Donald B. Rice, and Generals Dugan and Loh, Warden explained the plan to leaders of the other services, whose representatives reported to Checkmate to assist with its development. On August 17, Schwarzkopf received his second and final Instant Thunder briefing and again responded favorably, instructing Warden to deliver the retaliation option to General Horner in Riyadh. Unbeknownst to the Air Staff, Instant Thunder profoundly influenced the CINCCENT's offensive strategy, which encompassed strategic and counterland phases. Instant Thunder formed the basis of Phase I of Schwarzkopf's Desert Storm war plan.

J–3 for Air

On Sunday, August 12, General Adams, DCS for plans and operations, the officer in the Air Staff chain of command between Generals Loh and Alexander, returned to the Pentagon after a short leave in Florida. He had kept apprised of the Desert Shield deployment and Checkmate's activity by talking with his deputy, Maj. Gen. Charles A. May, and he now believed the time had come to head back to Washington to become involved directly in the development of Instant Thunder. At some point he had also talked with General Russ at TAC headquarters before arriving at the Pentagon. He started Sunday morning irritated and angry that the Air Staff involved itself in war planning, which (just as Horner had told the CINCCENT) was the responsibility of the unified and component commands. The Vietnam War had taught him — and Horner and Russ —

that the warfighters in theater, whose lives were at stake and who knew the combat situation best, should do the war planning. That Warden led the effort worsened the problem because Adams saw him as a "zealot" and "visionary" who believed that he had the only answer for employing air power. The colonel and his officers in the Deputy Directorate for Warfighting Concepts, his "disciples," constantly looked for a way to show what air power could do. The general thought the colonel would antagonize the other services by claiming that the Air Force on its own would win the war.[1] Recalling Warden's early planning, General Adams stated:

> I felt my job was to fly top cover for him but to keep him corralled so that he didn't get way out in front of the process because what we really had was an Air Force staff office doing operators' business for a joint organization, and I expressed great nervousness about that from the very beginning, and I didn't want them out on the street beating their chests about how great air power is and how we could bring the guys to their knees if they would just leave us alone and we didn't need those other services. It was not a time for us to make that speech.[2]

Adams had an extremely busy morning, filling it with an acerbic discussion with Alexander at the Pentagon's river entrance; a breakfast meeting at Loh's house; a briefing from Warden and others in Checkmate; a briefing about the deployment, and a meeting with General Kelly, Joint Staff J–3, and other Joint Staff officers in a conference room near the Tank.[3]

By early afternoon Adams's anger had dissipated, and he formed two distinct, important ideas about Checkmate's planning, one of which was inaccurate. First, he knew that the reason for the Air Staff's involvement stemmed from the CINCCENT's telephone call and his explanation that he could not turn to CENTAF for the planning because Horner was now the CENTCOM Forward commander, with other duties, and his staff was working the deployment flow. Adams's second, and mistaken, idea was that the CINCCENT wanted the Air Staff to produce an offensive air campaign to eject the Iraqis from Kuwait. The many people talking to him that morning had jumbled Schwarzkopf's reason for requesting Air Staff help. The CINCCENT had called for a strategic air campaign as an option for use if Saddam escalated the level of terror, like taking and harming hostages. Adams recalled the meeting with General Kelly that Sunday morning and related, "We were in Kelly's office, and that is when they asked me to put together the air plan for if we had to force Saddam Hussein out of Kuwait — how would [we] do it? What would be the air role in doing that?"[4] Loh had told Adams about the CINCCENT's telephone call, emphasizing *what* Schwarzkopf wanted, not *why* he wanted it.[5] The purpose of the air campaign as a strategic *retaliatory* option did not distinctly register in Adams's mind.

At General Kelly's meeting, Adams expressed concern that the Air Staff would be seen as interfering in the CENTAF and CENTCOM planning process.

Lt. Gen. Jimmie V. Adams

Lt. Gen. Lee Butler, USAF, Joint Staff J–5, plainly stated that he did not have the resources and expertise within his staff to respond to the CINCCENT's request for an air campaign. Hearing Adams's discomfort about interjecting the Air Staff into unified command planning, contravening the intention of the Goldwater-Nichols Act, Kelly informally deputized Adams the Joint Staff J–3 for Air. The title conveyed no authority, but it did help allay Adams's fear that he would be accused of usurping the CINCCENT's and CJCS's planning prerogatives. Knowing that Powell wanted the effort to be joint, Adams that afternoon telephoned each of his counterparts in the other services, the deputy chiefs of staff for operations, and asked them to send representatives to Checkmate.[6]

When Warden had briefed Instant Thunder to Adams, the colonel primarily remembered the general asking questions about radio frequencies and ingress altitudes, queries essential for the execution of air missions. Warden interpreted the line of inquiry to mean that the general had no appreciation of the big picture because he was too immersed in the tactical, not the strategic or operational, approach to planning, and that he also was trying to expose Checkmate planners as unrealistic theoreticians.[7] Adams, however, understood that Warden touted the plan as "executable" and wanted to make the point that Instant Thunder was far from completion, "superficial" in some aspects, especially with regard to targeting and weaponeering. In fact, information about radio frequencies was a key item in the ATO, and Adams refused to allow Checkmate to write the ATO in the Pentagon. He clearly recognized that details at that level of planning must be done in theater.[8] Following Warden's presentation, Colonel Blackburn discussed the targeting analysis his intelligence officers had accomplished for Instant Thunder, and Adams became more comfortable with the Checkmate plan.[9] Warden often defended his strategic air campaign by suggesting that its critics were too tactically minded and focused exclusively on using air power in support of the Army's AirLand Battle doctrine.[10] Adams, however, was initially skeptical of the plan because he believed it lacked essential information to make it executable and it was too optimistic about what Air Force air power could accomplish. He explained, "We don't have to go out and tell people we are going to win the war. What we have to do is go out and do something that brings results."[11]

Adams offered two critical suggestions to improve Instant Thunder. The first was either to make the timetable longer or to leave it open-ended. He told Warden to delete the slide showing the six- to nine-day allotment. He could not offer a better estimate; he just thought it made the Air Force look "too tall."[12] Second, and more important, he suggested that Warden add phases to the air campaign to first attack the Iraqi army, and then, with leftover air power, execute the strategic phase. He raised this point without any reference to the AirLand Battle doctrine. Warden immediately countered that Adams had just reversed the order of the phases that Powell had wanted the day before. Adams answered that the plan was not yet firmly established. A discussion ensued about phasing, during which Warden interjected, "[We] don't want to do a half-assed strategic campaign." Adams retorted, "Right, but [we] don't want to leave those Iraqi forces in place to kill 200,000 soldiers." The general directed that the planners come up with aircraft and munitions deployment numbers to see if the two phases could be executed simultaneously.[13]

By the conclusion of the briefing, Adams had instructed the planners to meet with him the next day with information about the phase to "take down" the Iraqi army; incorporating allies and the other services into the air campaign; tanker support; logistics flow; sortie rate assumptions; and limiting factors (LIMFACs) if the plan had to be executed soon. Recognizing that the planners had an enormous workload, he told them he would leave so they could continue. As he departed, he admitted to them that they had already gotten much of the job done without him. "Good work," he told them.[14]

Reserve Forces in Lieu of Phase II

On August 13, Warden briefed General Adams again, and in just twenty-four hours the Instant Thunder plan had doubled in size, with new material focused on targets and target sets, deployment flow, logistics, and Phase II, An Operational Air Campaign Against Iraqi Forces in Kuwait, developed in response to Chairman Powell's directive to destroy tanks and General Adams's concerns about the Iraqi army. Colonel Kiraly initially led the development of Phase II; then the responsibility for it fell to Lt. Col. Phillip S. Meilinger, Lt. Col. Michael W. Luers, and Maj. Terry New. They developed a fourfold CONOPS for Phase II: gain air superiority in Kuwait; target Iraqi systems designed to deliver CW; attack Iraqi C^3 and military support systems in Kuwait; and target Iraqi armored forces in Kuwait. The Phase II target sets were Iraqi air defenses, corps and division C^3 nodes in Kuwait, corps and division military support structure, LOC, and armored forces.[15]

Warden viewed Instant Thunder Phase II with disdain and ignored it. He told Kiraly that Powell thought like a "typical army guy" because he wanted to go kill tanks and did not understand the full potential of air power.[16] Lt. Col. Daniel T. Kuehl recalled, "Warden was loath to take effort away from the strat[egic] plan."[17] Colonel Harvey viewed as one of his primary jobs in Checkmate helping Warden to maintain the "strategic purity" of Instant Thunder.[18] Warden was supremely confident in his five strategic rings model and its underlying assumption that air forces should overfly the fielded enemy ground forces and attack the most important target, leadership. Direct attacks against the innermost ring and strikes against the enemy nation-state's key production and infrastructure would pressure the leadership to sue for peace.[19] As Warden saw it, the Iraqi head of state was especially vulnerable and likely to capitulate if confronted with strategic attacks. He explained:

> From what we knew about Saddam Hussein, which was not as extensive as it later became, he had a reputation for pragmatism. After all, he had just signed a peace treaty with Iran and given up the gains that he had made from the long war with Iran. He had a history of making tactically appropriate retreats when necessary, and it seemed like that under this particular circumstance he would be quite likely to do exactly the same thing because he would recognize that he was in an impossible position; and to save himself, he would agree to terms which we assumed were not going to be overly onerous.[20]

Iraqi missiles and bombers constituted the entire set of fifth-ring targets in Instant Thunder; the Air Staff planners had not directed lethal air strikes against the Republican Guard and the regular army in Kuwait.

From a military standpoint, Warden thought Instant Thunder Phase II unnecessary because not only would strategic attacks force leaders to bend to the will of the United States, they would render a nation-state incapable of launching operations. He stated after the war:

> At a strategic level, there is less difference between one country and another than [there is], say, at a tactical level, and if you succeed in taking away the enemy's strategically important things, you can just plain prevent him from having the ability to do subsequent things, especially offensive things. As a general principle, you are very confident that good strategic attack will just plain impose — we were not using that word then, but we are using it now — strategic paralysis on the enemy.[21]

For Warden, striking at the "strategic" base of a nation state and its air defense system would eliminate the country's offensive capability.[22] Furthermore, Warden had a vague idea before the war, which later manifested itself during the conflict, that the United States could, with PSYOPS, literally turn the conscript Iraqi troops in Kuwait and march them north against Iraqi leaders. He expounded, "My own vision of how the war ought to be conducted was one that deliberately avoided destroying the Army in Kuwait because I wanted to use the Army in Kuwait to go after Saddam Hussein."[23] Finally, in addition to believing he had the correct assumptions supporting his strategic plan, the colonel knew that General Schwarzkopf liked Instant Thunder. Why change and ruin it when not necessary?

Colonel Meilinger also thought Phase II caused a "diversion of effort" from the strategic air campaign. He described the original Instant Thunder as an "aerial Schlieffen Plan" and told Warden, "We must not weaken the right!"[24] That is,

Lt. Col. Phillip S. Meilinger (foreground) and Lt. Col. Allan Howey (left rear)

planners must not weaken the strategic air campaign against Iraq by diverting air assets to attack Saddam's fielded forces in the Kuwaiti Theater of Operations (KTO). Warden agreed with Meilinger's aerial Schlieffen Plan metaphor.[25]

On August 14 Warden and Adams discussed Phases I and II of Instant Thunder, and Adams still urged simultaneous execution. Warden, believing that the success of Phase I would preclude the necessity for Phase II, countered with the suggestion that Phase I be initiated first and independently. He emphasized that three squadrons of F–16s, however, would be held in operational reserve and, assisted by ground attack aircraft from all the services, would strike the Iraqi army if it invaded Saudi Arabia.[26] This suggestion finally mollified the general's insistence on simultaneous execution.[27] Adams described how he came to believe in Warden's air campaign:

> As the guys would brief me we would have lots of discussions down there in XOXW [the Deputy Directorate for Warfighting Concepts] with Warden and his guys. Lots of dialogue about whether we were on the right track, how critical are these kinds of targets, and do we need to concentrate more on the forces that are in Kuwait, is that a better thing to do. The guys convinced me that we were on the right track, and we put together what I thought was a credi[ble] plan.[28]

Warden had sold Adams, the reluctant buyer, on the merits of Instant Thunder as a short, independent strategic air campaign. Lacking Warden's absolute faith in it, though, Adams counted on Horner's and Schwarzkopf's passing judgment on it and reworking sections, as necessary, to meet theater requirements.[29] To Warden, Instant Thunder was a strategic air campaign, and he continued to ignore its Phase II.

As the week wore on, Instant Thunder addressed the uncertainty about the execution of the plan inducing the Iraqi forces to move south against the Saudi and American troops. A briefing slide posed and answered the question, "What If: Iraq attacks Saudi Arabia in response to Instant Thunder?" The planners gave reassurances that sufficient air power would be available to defend against attack by enemy ground forces and that the rollback of Iraqi troops would have only minimal impact on the strategic air campaign. The air power immediately available to counter invading troops and tanks consisted of the following fixed-wing and rotary wing aircraft:

Aircraft	No. of Squadrons	No. of Aircraft
A–10	4	96 airplanes
AV–8B	2	40 airplanes
F/A–18	3	36 airplanes
AH–1W	2	30 helicopters
AH–64	4	75 helicopters[30]

Planners noted that Instant Thunder had target systems in common with a CAS and BAI campaign, such as systems to achieve air superiority, destroy C^2 networks, and interdict supply lines.[31] Warden believed the reserve aircraft striking the invading force would ensure that airplanes flying against strategic targets would not be diverted, avoiding the mistake of World War II when commanders disallowed unrelenting and undeviating strategic air attacks in favor of diverting the air effort to tactical, close support of ground troops and nonstrategic targets.[32]

In his book, *The Air Campaign,* Warden had discussed the idea of holding aircraft in reserve, which ran counter to the conventional air wisdom that a sortie not flown was a sortie lost. He had presented his thoughts about reserves as a hypothesis.[33] Chairman Powell's and General Adams's concerns about the Iraqi army prompted him to highlight operational reserves in the Air Staff plan. What he had written as a hypothesis, he now spoke of as fact: air reserves sprang from a fundamentally sound concept and would produce desired results — halting the invading Iraqi army — if coupled with Instant Thunder. The Air Staff plan failed to provide, however, any discussion of the invasion scenario and the strategy of the air defense and counterattack to include probable invasion routes, enemy order of battle, chokepoints, center of gravity targets, and other crucial aspects of employing the operational reserves. The reserves were an afterthought and presented as such in Instant Thunder.

General Griffith from TAC headquarters, who had sent the TAC plan to Alexander, spent time at Checkmate August 11–17 and argued passionately that U.S. Army ground forces were necessary to control and halt an Iraqi invasion of Saudi Arabia. Air power alone was insufficient: the U.S. Army had an important role to play in halting the Iraqi assault. He argued against executing Instant Thunder until sufficient numbers of Army troops were in place to repel the invasion that could be triggered by the plan's execution. Griffith explained,

> The initial thing that I was concerned about, and I know that General Russ and General Horner were too, is if, number one, we drop the first bomb, we had better have enough Army up there to prevent Hussein from driving to Riyadh and picking up General Horner and throwing him in the back of the pick-up truck.[34]

Griffith recalled Warden's reaction to his viewpoint:

> He says, "Who gives a shit about the Army." I said, "John…if we could go in there and drop a bomb right tonight, if you were Saddam Hussein,

> wouldn't you take an armored division and if you looked across and all you see is a Saudi Arabian brigade sitting over there, say, 'Hey, I'm taking out Horner right now.'" I said, "If I was Hussein that is what I would do." He didn't agree with me on that.[35]

Warden expressed his unshakable confidence that Instant Thunder's execution would prevent an Iraqi invasion of Saudi Arabia. He stated after the war:

> I made the point that it is highly unlikely that anybody is going to be able to organize themselves and to launch any kind of dangerous offensive with little or no notice when the home front is falling apart behind them. People just don't do that. It is *just not done,* never has been done, and there is no reason to think that it is going to be [done] now. Physically it is very difficult to do because of the lack of communications support, logistics support, opportunity to practice, etc.[36]

Warden's reserve air force would provide enough power to halt and repulse an Iraqi invasion of Saudi Arabia, precipitated by the implementation of Instant Thunder. He reasoned, however, that the reserve force was hardly necessary because the strategic air campaign's intensity and scope would prevent Saddam from launching the massive ground assault in the first place. The reasoning all fit together neatly, logically for him. He had even tried to shape Instant Thunder so it could be executed in the near term to preclude the possibility of it being turned into "mere" AirLand Battle interdiction and CAS operations at the expense of the mighty strategic campaign he envisioned.[37]

"Joint" Planning

Throughout the week after the briefing to Chairman Powell, other actions occurred to give Instant Thunder a joint character in addition to General Adams being designated J–3 for Air: personnel from the other military services joined Air Staff planning teams; Air Staff members reported to CENTCOM and Joint Staff offices as liaison officers; Instant Thunder briefings were given to leaders in the Joint Staff and the other services; and Maj. Gen. James W. Meier, USAF, Joint Staff deputy director for operations, National Military Command System, became the JCS point of contact for the Air Staff enterprise.

Responding to the call for weapon system operators and planners from the other services to come to Checkmate, more than a dozen officers soon arrived and joined teams focusing on weapon systems and target sets. Capt. William H. Switzer III headed the Navy's contingent and Lt. Col. Slade A. Brewer led the Marine's. The Army sent only a representative or two who intermittently participated in the planning effort.[38] On August 11 Lt. Col. William Lucyshyn from the Concepts Division and Maj. Mark C. Christian from the Directorate of Targets traveled to MacDill AFB to be the Air Staff liaison officers at CENTCOM headquarters. Col. J. C. Wilson from CENTCOM J–3, became Checkmate's primary point of contact on the CENTCOM staff.[39] At mid-week, General Meier was appointed to head the delegation of officers who were to take the plan to Schwarzkopf the second time.[40]

The Chief of Naval Operations (CNO) and the Commandant of the Marine Corps agreed to receive the Instant Thunder briefing, but the Army Chief of Staff had to decline the offer. On August 14 Warden and Captain Switzer briefed Adm. Frank B. Kelso II, the CNO, and approximately a dozen other naval officers. In the half-hour session, the CNO asked only a few questions, two of which concerned SEAD and the expected role of carrier air power. He observed that to be executable, the plan still required much detailed planning.[41] Warden, Switzer, and Brewer briefed the plan to General Alfred M. Gray, the Marine Corps Commandant, and his key staff. The general was called away for most of the briefing, but he did ask when the plan would be executable. Warden answered, the first week in September, unless the deployment flow changed, giving priority to the strategic air campaign. The commandant said the plan reflected "a hell of a good effort."[42]

After General Alexander explained the plan to him, Lt. Gen. Henry Viccellio, Jr., USAF, DCS, Logistics and Engineering, began immediately to try to speed the flow to theater of logistics supplies necessary to sustain the execution of Instant Thunder in the near future. General Boyd, now the Air University Commander and a former prisoner of war in North Vietnam, enthusiastically approved of the Air Staff plan. In 1988, as the Air Staff's Director of Plans, he had encouraged Warden in the Deputy Directorate for Warfighting Concepts to think boldly about independent air campaigns. "Right on, right on, right on," was how Alexander recalled Boyd's response to the strategic air campaign plan.[43]

CSAF's and SecAF's Briefings — August 14 and 15

On August 14 the CSAF, General Dugan, received his first formal briefing on the plan, and he requested four changes as improvements. First, he wanted more study done on Saddam Hussein. He believed that economic targets such as oil and electricity would fail to induce the tyrant to make concessions because Saddam did not care about those assets. The general believed that the Iraqi leader valued only things with personal significance, and those kinds of targets had to be hit to force him to make concessions.[44] Although Dugan's view on the importance of enemy leaders agreed with the primary importance Warden placed on the leadership ring of his strategic model, the CSAF disagreed with Warden's assumption that attacks against the key production and infrastructure categories, the second and third rings, would necessarily coerce a head of state to sue for peace.

Second, Dugan directed that the planners study all aspects of the Iraqi CW chain of production — transportation, storage, air base distribution, and delivery — and target the system's components and elements. Third, he wanted a Red team formed to study the Iraqi air force's capability to inflict damage on U.S. assets in theater.[45] Fourth, he asked planners to think of ways to "induce" the Iraqi troops in Kuwait to "head north." He did not want to use air power directly against the Iraqi troops there, fearing that the Americans would end up destroying Kuwait to "save it." Warden pointed out that Chairman Powell had specifically asked for a plan to destroy tanks in Kuwait so the Iraqi troops could not leave with them. He explained Phase II of the plan to meet the CJCS's requirement. Like Warden, the CSAF believed the strategic emphasis represented the real value of the air campaign, not strikes against the Iraqi army.[46]

The SecAF received the Instant Thunder briefing the morning of Wednesday, August 15, wedged between discussion of the President's option of calling up Reserve forces and a briefing on the cost of the Desert Shield deployment. Since August 7 Loh had been keeping Secretary Rice informed of the deployment flow and air campaign planning, but this was Rice's first formal, complete briefing. Warden presented it, and Generals Dugan, Loh, and Adams endorsed it. Secretary Rice asked questions about PSYOPS; methods for destroying NBC facilities; naval involvement in the planning process and the air campaign; attacks against Iraqi forces moving along highways; Have Nap missiles; and the availability of PGMs. Answers satisfied him. Adams told Rice the plan would be ready to execute from approximately September 6th to 9th. According to the SecAF, the planning process and deployment looked far enough along to allow the plan's execution on August 20. He told the planners to present the briefing to Under Secretary Wolfowitz, who was responsible for overseeing DoD war planning.[47]

In the afternoon of August 15, Secretary Rice attended a meeting at the Pentagon with President Bush, Secretary Cheney, the JCS, and General Schwarzkopf, among others. The thrust of the meeting was the progress of the Desert Shield deployment and milestone dates identifying when sufficient forces capable of defending Saudi Arabia would arrive in theater. Cheney asked the President to think about issuing additional guidance about other missions that the military would be required to perform, in addition to defending Saudi Arabia, so that an adequate flow of forces could be effected. Word later filtered back to the Air Staff planners that a few slides on the air campaign that were prepared for Powell were used at the meeting, but Warden never felt certain they were.[48] While waiting for the President to address personnel assembled in the Pentagon courtyard, Schwarzkopf chatted with Secretary Rice and told him how pleased he was with the air campaign being planned for CENTCOM.[49] Bush thanked the Pentagon audience for their efforts and support for the massive deployment underway, and he repeated his four objectives of August 8, which the planners had incorporated into Instant Thunder.[50]

Wednesday, August 15, marked the day the planners were scheduled to brief the air campaign plan to Schwarzkopf for the second time, but the previous day Adams told Warden the session had been postponed. Then, late in the afternoon on Wednesday, General Moore, from CENTCOM, telephoned Warden directly and requested that the Air Staff planners present the air plan to the CINCCENT on Friday morning, August 17. In discussing its status with Moore, Warden told him that if the deployment flow remained unchanged, the plan could be executed the third week of September, with most of the necessary forces in theater the first week of that month. To execute earlier, in the first days of September, some changes in the flow would have to be made, but nothing would be "extraordinary." After his discussion with Moore, Warden immediately called Alexander, who shortly thereafter met with him and the team chiefs to discuss the plan and the personnel who would take it to MacDill AFB on Friday morning.[51]

CENTCOM Coordination

While Checkmate developed Instant Thunder, the CENTCOM staff at MacDill AFB labored with the deployment and war planning. Late in the afternoon of August 16, CENTCOM sent a message to the JCS, the Air Staff Directorate of Plans and Operations, the Office of the Assistant Chief of Staff, Intelligence, and to more than forty other DoD organizations identifying target sets, objectives, and 109 targets for "intelligence production and operational planning."[52]

CENTCOM had worked on its target list since mid-July; by August 11 it had identified 83 installations. At CENTCOM headquarters, Major Christian, the Air Staff targeting liaison officer, had merged the Instant Thunder target list with the CENTCOM list. When Colonels Blackburn and Warden had sent Major Christian to MacDill on August 11, he augmented the minuscule CENTCOM target development branch which consisted of only three officers, one of whom, the chief of targets, a lieutenant colonel, had just been hospitalized. The division chief, Col. Roger Cannon, appointed Christian to head of the CENTCOM targeting branch, working with the two other officers from the Navy and the Air Force.[53] As Blackburn had told General Adams during the latter's first Instant Thunder briefing, he coordinated the Checkmate targeting process with CENTCOM, that is, with Colonel Cannon. Blackburn sent the Instant Thunder list to Christian on August 11, and comparing the two lists, Christian found 31 common installations. On August 12 he sent Blackburn a highly classified list of targets and a Navy intelligence list.[54]

Because of its unified command structure, CENTCOM received far more direct support from the DIA than Checkmate did. Intelligence liaison personnel at CENTCOM headquarters officially tapped into DIA's databases and analytical capability and nominated and validated targets. Other DoD organizations around the world also nominated Iraqi targets to CENTCOM. Nonetheless, the lack of complete, current installation databases, target materials, and current intelligence studies on Iraq hampered the target development process at CENTCOM as it had at the Air Staff. At CENTCOM, as at CENTAF, intelligence officers were still in the process of reorienting to Iraq as the primary threat in the AOR, not a Soviet Union invasion of Iran.[55] CENTCOM could not even determine or verify some

Basic Encyclopedia numbers for targets on its list.[56]

By August 16 the CENTCOM list of 109 targets consisted of 9 target sets, which corresponded to 9 of the 10 sets now identified for Instant Thunder. Airfields were not included as a set on the CENTCOM list, although a few appeared as targets under the CW category. Airfields were CENTCOM targets simply because they were associated with storage and delivery of CW. In contrast, the Air Staff included them in association with CW and air superiority.[57]

Comparing the CENTCOM list of 109 targets and the Instant Thunder list of 84, the officers found that the lists had 76 targets in common. Because the CENTCOM message directed that production and planning efforts focus on the CENTCOM list, Blackburn telephoned Cannon at MacDill AFB, and they discussed the briefing that the Air Staff would present to the CINCCENT the next morning and the commonality of targets. Blackburn told his counterpart that he had planned to send images of the Instant Thunder targets to the Defense Mapping Agency Aerospace Center (DMAAC) in St. Louis, Missouri, and request that DMAAC mensurate — precisely determine and measure the coordinates — for the aim points, or the DMPIs. Blackburn asked if he should send all 84 targets or just the 76 common to both lists. Without consulting Warden, Blackburn decided that if CENTCOM was not going to use the other eight targets, he would not ask DMAAC to address them.[58]

Cannon asked Blackburn to do two things: first, direct DMAAC to provide DMPIs for multiple weapon systems, not just one system per target, as in Instant Thunder, and second, request DMAAC to provide mensurated points for the 109 targets. Blackburn agreed and countered with a request that CENTCOM send a message delegating imagery production tasking authority to the AFIA Directorate of Targets, so that he could get the DIA to officially work his requirements for imagery. CENTCOM's message, sent August 16, delighted Blackburn.[59]

General Meier of the Joint Staff was to accompany the briefers to CENTCOM headquarters on Friday morning, August 17, and sponsor the Instant Thunder presentation on behalf of the Joint Staff. At a dry run of the briefing on Thursday afternoon, the general directed the planners to add more operational detail to their slides. He wanted them to return to him later for a second session. During the tense, two-hour evening meeting, he raised numerous questions about logistics, the briefers, and order of slides, even musing aloud that he might do the presentation himself. Exasperated, Colonels Warden and Blackburn bluntly recommended that they themselves should brief the operational concepts and targeting sections. The general eventually agreed with them.[60] Throughout the night of August 16/17, the planners labored to complete the Instant Thunder Operation Order (OPORD) and slides.

Instant Thunder Finalized

The Instant Thunder material prepared for Schwarzkopf consisted of two documents. The first was a packet of 30 briefing slides bearing the JCS seal. The second was the Instant Thunder OPORD, 180 pages long. Because of the lack of preparation time, the OPORD was neither finished nor uniformly edited, and some annexes consisted of project officers' point papers and slides with handwritten notes. The OPORD came with a three-page overview, wherein the planners discussed objectives, assumptions, the mission, and CONOPS, plus seventeen annexes.[61] The Instant Thunder material did not discuss phases or phasing. Warden would not present Instant Thunder Phase II unless the CINCCENT asked for it, which he did not.

On its first full page, the OPORD proclaimed Instant Thunder the "proposed Iraq air campaign" and a "strategic air campaign," implying that the strategic operations would comprise the entire, comprehensive campaign, with no phasing necessary.[62] It further stated that the campaign was designed to accomplish the NCA's objectives, which were then listed as the objectives President Bush had announced on August 8. The OPORD thus presented the strategic air campaign as the instrument to achieve Presidential objectives, including the first one, the immediate, unconditional, and complete withdrawal of all Iraqi forces from Kuwait.[63]

The five Instant Thunder target categories still related directly to the five strategic rings: leadership, key production, infrastructure, population, and fielded force. Nowhere in the briefing slides or in the OPORD, however, did the graphic showing five concentric rings appear, having been permanently deleted from the plan by August 10. The addition of naval ports and the clarification of some target set components and elements slightly modified the targets section.[64]

Instant Thunder presented 84 targets. Each was identified with name, geographic coordinates, Basic Encyclopedia number, and functional description. Noting that the target list was being continually refined, planners and targeteers believed they had found the targets to achieve the objectives. No targets existed in Kuwait, although officers would soon include one air defense site there.[65] Instant Thunder listed ten target sets, and specified the intended results:

Instant Thunder Target Set	Result	No. of Targets
Strategic air defense	Destroyed	10
Strategic CW	Long term setback	8
National leadership	Incapacitated	5
Telecommunications	Disrupted/degraded	19
Electricity	Cut 60% Baghdad, 35% in Iraq	10
Oil (Internal)	Cut consumption 70%	6
Railroads	Disrupted/degraded	3
Airfields	Disrupted/degraded	7

Ports	Disrupted	1
Military production and storage depots	Disrupted/degraded	15
Total[66]		84

Two waves of attacks would occur the first night, the first coming an hour after sunset, and the second, an hour before sunrise. These would be followed by attacks the following afternoon and the next night. Pilots would fly 1,200 sorties the first full day of the campaign and 900 each of the succeeding five days.[67] During the initial nighttime attack, approximately 75 to 100 sorties would be held in reserve to hit Scud sites and other contingency targets. The plan did not explain how the reserve aircraft would operate against the Scuds, which were associated with CW. An annex provided an assessment of the status of Iraq's NBC weapons capability after the attacks of the first day, concluding that Iraq could still launch surface-to-surface missiles carrying CW if all sites were not attacked and the Iraqis could continue to transmit and receive launch orders.[68]

Iraq's Scuds caused the planners serious difficulty. One slide stated, "Chemical-capable long-range Scuds present real problem."[69] The target list in the OPORD included only fixed Scud-related sites, and they appeared under both the strategic CW target set and the military research, production, and storage set. At the bottom of the OPORD's strategic CW target list, a planner typed the phrases, "mobile Scud TELs [transporter-erector-launchers]" and "mobile missiles," but offered no explanation nor operational concept for eliminating the mobile Scuds.[70] Instant Thunder presented no solution to what would become one of the most difficult problems in Desert Storm war planning.

The final version of Instant Thunder focused on employing Air Force, Navy, and Marine Corps aircraft. Allied air forces would be integrated, where possible, with Saudi aircraft flying CAPs and with British aircraft in striking airfields. To deconflict airspace, the Air Force would fly in western Baghdad and south-central Iraq; the Navy, in eastern Baghdad and southeastern Iraq; and the Marines, in south-central Iraq, establishing, in effect, route packs.[71]

Colonel Deptula produced a unique, extraordinary section of the Instant Thunder OPORD and slides and called it the attack flow plan. He updated it the evening of August 16, so it was one of the most current sections in the briefing presented to Schwarzkopf. The flow plan covered the first two days of the strategic air campaign, when air power hit the 84 targets, and it was divided according to the first two waves of attack during the first night, and then the daytime and nighttime waves of the second day.[72] It showed the timing and order of attacks. Deptula presented the plan on pieces of typing paper, each divided into eight columns. Above the left-hand column was the indicator designating the day. From left to right, he labeled the columns, some in abbreviated form, as wave, target Basic Encyclopedia number, target type, target description, aircraft quantity, aircraft type, type of mission, and flow. Looking down the list, one could learn what the targets were, where they were located, when they were to be struck in relation to other targets, and which aircraft would fly against them in what type of mission.[73] Later, in theater, Deptula would develop his flow plan into the master attack plan (MAP), an integral and crucial part of Gulf War planning.

Planners had two significant logistics concerns, based on the assumption that the Desert Shield deployment flow would not change to meet Instant Thunder requirements. The first involved munitions readiness. In addition to weapons awaiting airlift from Europe, munitions had to be properly distributed to bases, and components, such as bomb bodies, fuzes, and tail fins, required proper matching. Airbase refueling capability caused the second concern, but it posed too many detailed questions for the Air Staff planners to answer. They concluded that refueling on the ground might fall short of sortie surge requirements and suggested that the problem had to be studied and solutions arrived at in theater.[74] They determined that ninety-four was the minimum complement of tankers required for operations covering six days.[75]

In the reconnaissance section, the planners addressed only airborne, in-theater assets: RC–135 Rivet Joint, U–2 Senior Year, U–2 Senior Span, U–2/TR–1 Advanced Synthetic Aperture Radar System (ASARS), and RF–4. They did not discuss national overhead reconnaissance systems, assigning that responsibility to CENTCOM. They acknowledged that satellite coverage depended on the weather and the orbital mechanics of the systems.[76] They made a colossal assumption that all necessary equipment would be in place, with all required communication links available, prior to the plan's execution.[77] No discussion mentioned how electronic images could, would, or should be disseminated directly to combat units. This would soon mushroom in theater and become a gigantic problem.

CINCCENT's Briefing — August 17

On August 17 the huge Air Staff team that had been selected to take Instant Thunder to the CINCCENT Schwarzkopf flew to MacDill AFB. The group consisted of General Meier and Capt. George Johnson, USN, both from the Joint Staff, and Colonels Warden and Blackburn, plus about thirty others — Air Staff officers and representatives from SAC, TAC, and the other services. Warden included as many people as possible who had prepared the plan to allow them to participate in what he viewed as a historic presentation to the CINCCENT and to have their expertise readily available if detailed questions arose.[78] The briefing for Schwarzkopf took place at 1000 in his command conference room, which accommodated only a few of the Washington group and a large number of CENTCOM staff. It lasted nearly two hours. Meier introduced Warden, who spoke first, using his slides. Early on, he talked about minimizing civilian casualties and collateral damage, and Schwarzkopf questioned him if indeed there would be civilian casualties. Warden assented, saying that the PSYOPS would emphasize Saddam Hussein's responsibility for the casualties and that the United States had no choice in the matter.[79] Referring to the target sets, he explained that the strategic attacks would inflict "paralysis and shock" upon the Iraqi nation.[80]

After Warden's section on operational concepts, Blackburn discussed target sets and focused in detail on a few representative installations, although he was prepared to brief them all. When discussing Iraq's only nuclear research center, he explained that one option was to use four Have Nap missiles launched from B–52s against one building. Schwarzkopf questioned whether the other structures in the complex would be hit. The planners answered that they concentrated on one building and were considering others. Schwarzkopf also asked about the location of the Abu Ghurayb presidential grounds, and when told it was fifteen miles west of Baghdad, he replied, "Very good." Blackburn's other two targets were the Ajaji thermal power plant, the largest electrical facility in Iraq, and the Basrah petroleum refinery. Halfway through his briefing, Colonel Harvey from Checkmate wrote a note that Blackburn's portion was "outstanding...with purposes very clear."[81] The targeteer was a hero now, but by month's end, many in Checkmate would view him quite differently.

Before concluding, Blackburn explained to Schwarzkopf how, the previous day, the focus of the Air Staff targeteers had changed from directly supporting target development for the Air Staff's list of 84 targets to now supporting CENTCOM's list of 109 targets. He told the general about the arrangement he had made with Col. Roger Cannon at CENTCOM to acquire mensurated points from the DMAAC for the unified command's list.[82] The colonel thought it extremely important to tell Schwarzkopf how he and the Air Staff targeteers would be supporting CENTCOM, which to him meant less assistance to Checkmate and Warden. Blackburn recalled:

> I told him, We have been working this closely with your staff. In fact, your staff has just promulgated the CENTCOM list. I viewed our list as a conceptual list, and now the definitive list was CENTCOM's. I made that point not only for their benefit but for John Warden's. See, I could see it coming. The Checkmate effort — they weren't going to let go; 84 was the gospel. For one thing, initially they were concerned as we made the list get bigger and bigger that would make the air campaign plan take longer and longer, and they already had a time line, about a 7-day window. John Warden had concern with that target list growing. He didn't want to see it grow.[83]

Schwarzkopf did not say anything directly in response to what Blackburn had said, not placing the same significance on it as Blackburn had. Blackburn thought the CINCCENT nodded to him in agreement. The CENTCOM commander followed with a question about the special targeting requirements for the TLAMs. When told that the Navy folks were working them, the discussion led to missiles.[84]

Warden continued the session, highlighting Instant Thunder's execution. Responding to a Schwarzkopf question about thirty-two fighter/attack squadrons, the colonel replied that that number would be in theater by the end of September if the priority of the deployment flow did not change.[85] Discussing air superiority, Warden stated that by the first morning, the Iraqi air force would be driven into "autonomous actions." On PSYOPS and deception, he offered that there was a "good chance" that "somebody reasonable would take over," replacing Saddam Hussein, but he identified no candidates.[86] A slide proclaimed:

PSYOPS CRITICAL ELEMENT OF CAMPAIGN

DESTROY IRAQ TV & BROADCAST STATIONS

SUBSTITUTE U.S. BROADCASTS

SEPARATE HUSSEIN REGIME FROM SUPPORT OF PEOPLE AND MILITARY[87]

When Warden showed Schwarzkopf the slide, "What If: Iraq attacks Saudi Arabia in response to Instant Thunder?" he explained that the reserve forces — A–10s, AV–8Bs, F/A–18s, and helicopters — would be in theater by the end of September but would not be used in the strategic campaign, so they would be available to attack invading Iraqi troops. If these reserve forces could not stop the assault, they could slow it down and prevent the Iraqi army from reaching "anything significant." The colonel, however, emphasized the primacy of the strategic campaign and called it an aerial Schlieffen plan, to which the CINCCENT immediately countered, "Don't call it a Schlieffen plan." Schwarzkopf probably rejected the analogy because the original plan carried the stigma of illegality when it led Germany to violate Belgian neutrality, which expanded the war in Europe in 1914, and more importantly, it failed. Warden unhesitatingly replied, "But it is a Schlieffen plan rotated into the third dimension."[88] The CINCCENT observed that if Instant Thunder was executed at the end of September, he was confident, but an early execution worried him. Meier added that the CSAF thought the plan was executable in mid-September and that the risks of doing it earlier were acceptable. General Moore observed that the plan included only the forces assigned to CENTCOM at that time and excluded the forces based in Turkey.[89]

The reference to Turkey reminded Schwarzkopf that on August 10 he had directed Warden to develop Plan B, which the colonel had not done, but the CINCCENT now admitted that, as of August 17, the attitude of the Saudis was that Iraq must be destroyed as a military power. With respect to the LIMFACs, Warden told the CINCCENT that Scuds were a difficult problem and suggested the possibility of using AC–130s to destroy them. To Schwarzkopf's query about the "cost in human life to us," Warden answered that he thought ten to fifteen aircraft would be lost the first day, and fewer after that, for a total of from fifteen to twenty. General Rogers, the CENTCOM deputy commander, disagreed, saying it would be higher. Warden replied with an explanation for his numbers. The massive attack would overwhelm the Iraqis and suppress their air defense system.[90]

Rogers commented that Warden had thoroughly discussed Iraq but had ignored Kuwait. During the ensuing discussion, Warden mentioned that Chairman Powell had directed him to kill tanks in Kuwait, and that, in response, his staff had developed an Instant Thunder Phase II plan.[91] Schwarzkopf, however, said that Kuwait did not concern him. He even asked if the single target there, a ground-to-air-assets building, could be spared from attack. Moore interjected that radars could be rendered ineffective with lethal or nonlethal ECM. Warden noted that with good deception, the Iraqis could be persuaded to put even more SAMs in Kuwait, which would be a "good place for them" while U.S. aircraft were flying over Iraq. Thus, Warden did not brief the CINCCENT on his Instant Thunder Phase II, produced at the direction of Chairman Powell and targeting Iraqi forces in Kuwait. Schwarzkopf did not want to hear it; he focused on his retaliation option, the strategic air campaign. Rogers brought up two other issues: munitions and base saturation. Schwarzkopf admitted, "Ninety-four tankers just about blew my mind."[92] (The night the air war started in January 1991, 160 tankers would be airborne.)

During a discussion about SEAD, a Marine officer suggested that, to strengthen electronic warfare support on missions, the air operations could be extended. Schwarzkopf firmly disagreed with the idea of protracting the strategic air campaign. He stated that the United Nations Security Council would "scream" about such an operation, but if the United States could accomplish the strikes quickly, in six days, the Americans could "apologize" and end them, having struck all the targets before too much opposition mobilized. The United States must complete the retaliation swiftly before international pressure stopped it. Warden had kept the campaign short to market and sell it. Schwarzkopf bought it, in part because of its quickness. This characteristic of the strategic air campaign — brevity — would stick even when the CINCCENT changed the purpose of the campaign and adopted it as part of his four-phased offensive war plan. Planners in theater would have to grapple later with the limited time span.

The CINCCENT continued by emphasizing that the United States had a smaller army than Iraq's, and thus an American ground campaign unwisely played to Saddam's strength instead of his weakness. Captain Johnson paraphrased Schwarzkopf's comment: "the one area where we have an overwhelming advantage that can be brought to bear in the near term is strike warfare (TACAIR [tactical aircraft] and conventional cruise missiles)."[93] The CINCCENT agreed that air power pitted U.S. strength against Iraqi weakness, as Instant Thunder proclaimed, and he intended to exploit the overwhelming airpower advantage.

When General Meier asked Schwarzkopf what else could be done for him, the CINCCENT pointed to Warden and said that he wanted the colonel and at least one other person to go to Riyadh to brief the material to General Horner and "hand the plan off to him." He told them not to leave it at CENTCOM, but to carry and deliver it, the sooner the better. He said that the group had done its job, and now "we must turn [it] into [a] real-world plan."[94] The CINCCENT was true to his word to Horner, having told him that once officers in Washington had accomplished the initial work, Horner would assume control of the product. Warden had originally thought that the CINCCENT might ask him to join the CENTCOM staff and complete Instant Thunder, still believing it would be executed in a matter of days, not weeks. He thought, "Now we are at the point of tying up and putting the final details so we can pull the lanyard and launch."[95]

General Rogers cautioned that the material must stay "close hold," to which Schwarzkopf replied that it will probably "leak out" and in fact, he cynically stated, would probably appear soon in the *Early Bird,* the daily package of newspaper articles distributed throughout the Pentagon. The execution day absolutely had to remain secret, which had not been discussed during the briefing and which depended on Saddam's further provocation.[96] Warden's estimates of when the plan would be ready varied depending on the latest information about the deployment flow. Right before the session ended, Warden told Schwarzkopf that they needed to discuss the deception phase, and he and only a few others talked with the general about those requirements.[97]

The warm, positive reception the CINCCENT had given Instant Thunder sent the spirits of the Checkmate officers soaring. After the group returned to Washington, members assembled in the Pentagon to assess how far the planning effort had come and where it headed. Warden told them Schwarzkopf's understanding of strength against weakness and his positive impression that American strength was air power. Warden told his staff to take the day off and come back to work on Sunday. Instant Thunder was not perfected yet because they had to pound airfields to ensure air superiority. Colonel Blackburn pointed out that the CENTCOM target list of 109 targets, the list he now focused on, did not emphasize airfields. After other comments, Warden stated that Checkmate's continued work on Instant Thunder was "strictly an operation thing, an assessment to provide as requested or required." The next evening Warden, accompanied by Colonels Deptula, Harvey, and Stanfill, departed from Andrews AFB for Riyadh to deliver the Instant Thunder briefing to General Horner.[98]

Targeting Imagery

On Saturday, August 18, while Checkmate members enjoyed a rare day off, Blackburn's targeteers worked on both the Instant Thunder target list to select aim points for multiple weapon systems and the additional twenty-five installations from the CENTCOM list to develop materials and select DMPIs. The colonel's delight at receiving the CENTCOM message delegating imagery production tasking authority to him was short-lived, for he soon realized that it conferred on him far less clout with the DIA than he had expected because CENTCOM's direct requests to DIA enjoyed precedence. CENTCOM had identified

66 priority targets and 43 secondary targets from the list of 109 and tasked DIA to produce operational support packages (OSPs) for the primary ones. OSPs were 22- by18-inch bound imagery and textual sheets focused on groups of targets by geography or function, and they provided very detailed analysis. DIA did not pull people from working OSPs to assist Blackburn's targeteers to acquire the imagery they needed for selecting aim points on the additional targets. The targeteers, therefore, were back to relying on the small unit at the Navy Yard and continued to "roam the halls of the DIA begging, borrowing, and stealing" any relevant imagery they could lay their hands on.[99]

A full week later, on August 22, the targeteers completed their labor on the 109 targets. The next day, a targeteer carried the images, pinpricked to show aim points, and worksheets to St. Louis, where DMAAC would mensurate the points. Blackburn sent a similar package to CENTCOM in Florida. Finally, more than another week later on August 31, DMAAC began to send the first of five long messages to fifty recipients, including CENTAF in Saudi Arabia. Sadly, without the accompanying imagery, Horner's targeteers in Riyadh could not use the DMAAC data. Blackburn had not sent a set of the images to the CENTAF staff in theater, causing much of the hard work the targeteers did in Washington to go to waste.[100]

CENTCOM's Desert Storm Phase I

Shortly after Warden had departed CENTCOM headquarters at the conclusion of his Instant Thunder briefing on August 17, Schwarzkopf had an inspiration that profoundly affected the Gulf War planning. The Air Staff had given him an excellent strategic retaliation plan. Horner would soon receive it, turn it into a real-world plan, and execute it if necessary. The CINCCENT, by now however, needed an offensive war plan to expel the Iraqis from Kuwait and achieve Presidential objectives, which he believed necessitated a ground campaign. From the very beginning of the crisis, Schwarzkopf thought that the expulsion of the Iraqis from Kuwait required major land operations. His staff, under his direction, had already begun to develop a phased war plan. Now he realized he could use Instant Thunder for two purposes: retaliation *and* offensive warfare.[101] The idea that the Air Force's strategic air campaign should be an integral part of his offensive operations and precede his ground campaign excited him.

John Warden had fired up the CENTCOM commander about the value of a strategic campaign beyond its worth as a retaliation operation. The CINCCENT now saw it as a prelude to the ground offensive. He did not view it as a standalone, war-winning, independent air campaign as Warden did, but as the first phase of a multiphased war plan. After the war, Schwarzkopf was asked if he ever saw Warden's strategic air campaign as "the total way of getting Iraqis out of Kuwait." He replied, "It was an option but I have never felt that it was a complete option. I always felt that it would take ground forces on the ground to, in fact, eject the ground forces that were over there."[102] The CINCCENT would now take the concepts from the airmen and incorporate them into his CENTCOM offensive planning. He would utilize strategic strikes to precede attacks against the enemy fielded forces. CENTCOM OPLAN 1002–90 had not called for sustained strategic bombardment prior to the ground counteroffensive. Schwarzkopf introduced a new framework into CENTCOM planning.

Schwarzkopf's vision for fighting the war against Iraq, his Desert Storm strategy, comprised four phases:

Phase I	Strategic Air Campaign (6 days)
Phase II	Kuwait Air Campaign (2 days)
Phase III	Ground Combat Power Attrition (5–6 days)
Phase IV	Ground Attack (2–3 days)[103]

The CINCCENT clearly acknowledged the connection between Instant Thunder and Phase I. He wrote after the war,

> I called...and asked that the Air Force put planners to work on a strategic bombing campaign aimed at Iraq's military, which would provide the retaliatory options we needed. The plan they came up with was code-named Instant Thunder; it would ultimately become the first phase of Desert Storm.[104]

Maj. Gen. Robert B. Johnston, USMC, the CINCCENT's chief of staff to whom the commander explained his framework for the CENTCOM offensive plan, recalled that the Air Staff essentially developed the strategic plan briefed to Schwarzkopf at MacDill AFB and sent it to Horner, which became Phase I. Johnston remembered that the CINCCENT talked about the plan in terms of Iraq's strategic weaknesses and centers of gravity.[105]

On Saturday, August 25th at the Pentagon, a week after the MacDill briefing and the day before he left the United States for Saudi Arabia, Schwarzkopf presented to Secretary Cheney and Chairman Powell his offensive campaign plan for Desert Storm. By this early date, the CINCCENT had chosen the name "Desert Storm" for offensive operations, and the CJCS approved the appellation. Powell related, "As we started to develop an offensive option alongside the defensive stance, Norm and I talked about how to differentiate the two. Desert Shield, Phase II? Norm suggested 'Desert Storm.' Stormin' Norman's storm. It was a natural, and we all went for it."[106]

Schwarzkopf's own CENTCOM staff developed the first version of the four-phased Desert Storm plan. The commander's presentation began with his statement of intent:

> We will offset the imbalance of ground combat power by using our strength against his weakness. Initially execute deception operations to focus his attention on defense and cause incorrect organization of

> forces. We will initially attack into the Iraqi homeland using air power to decapitate his leadership, command and control, and eliminate his ability to reinforce Iraqi forces in Kuwait and southern Iraq. We will then gain undisputed air superiority over Kuwait so that we can subsequently and selectively attack Iraqi ground forces with air power in order to reduce his combat power and destroy reinforcing units. Finally, we will fix Iraqi forces in place by feints and limited objective attacks followed by armored force penetration and exploitation to seize key lines of communication nodes, which will put us in a position to interdict resupply and remaining reinforcements from Iraq and eliminate forces in Kuwait.[107]

He identified air power's strategic projection as one of the strengths of the United States, and the "limited amount of combat ground power" as a weakness.[108]

The objectives of the CINCCENT's Phase I, Strategic Air Campaign were destroying the regime's command and control of military operations, preventing reinforcement of Iraqi forces in Kuwait, and demoralizing the troops in Kuwait.[109] The forces executing this phase numbered 720 aircraft and 125 TLAMs. The aircraft surge capability would be 1,200. Average daily sorties would be 900, plus those for ground alert.[110] The Desert Storm Phase I strategic target sets, which the targeteers from Checkmate and CENTCOM had compared and discussed, replicated those from Instant Thunder, except for airfields. The nine Phase I strategic target sets encompassed air defense; chemical; leadership; electric power; oil; railroads and bridges; naval forces; military support, production, and storage; and telecommunications.[111] On August 25 the status of planning on Phase I was "partially complete."[112] Because of the Air Staff intense effort on it, the strategic campaign was the most fleshed out of all the phases.

The objectives of CENTCOM's Desert Storm Phase II were to achieve air superiority over Kuwait and freedom of the skies for airplane and helicopter operations. The CONOPS required eliminating the Iraqi air force over Kuwait, and lethal and nonlethal SEAD there.[113]

The objectives of Phase III were to diminish Iraqi ground combat capability, to "soften" the ground forces as a prelude to attack, to lessen the ability of the enemy to use CW, and to prevent the Republican Guard reinforcing into Kuwait. The concepts of Phase III encompassed "neutralizing" the Republican Guard and "isolating" the battle area in Kuwait. The execution of this phase would involve air, naval, and ground special operations forces (SOF).[114]

The objectives of Phase IV were the expulsion of the Iraqi troops from Kuwait, absolute control over Iraqi LOC, and isolation of remaining Iraqi forces. The concepts of the phase required an amphibious deception and limited attack in daytime, and a nighttime, main attack of a mechanized and armor thrust by allied forces. The execution of this phase would involve ground, air, and naval forces.[115] Analysis showed that a direct frontal assault to destroy and drive out

Iraqi forces was not feasible. A slight flank attack, however, to isolate and fix enemy troops in their positions was recommended.[116]

Comparing Instant Thunder and Desert Storm Phase I from the CINC-CENT's perspective on August 25, 1990, and later, Instant Thunder retaliated, whereas Desert Storm initiated offensive operations to liberate Kuwait, differences mostly of intent, not of action. The targets of the two plans began to diverge as Phase I numbered 109 and Instant Thunder numbered 84. The intensity of both plans remained severe and high. Six days comprised the optimum time for each. Saddam's carrying out an act of terror would cause authorities to pull the trigger on Instant Thunder. In contrast, the readiness of the United States and the Coalition to execute an air and ground war to achieve Presidential and U.N. objectives and to expel the Iraqis from Kuwait would be the trigger to initiate Desert Storm Phase I and the follow-on phases.

Desert Storm Phase III incorporated the airpower counterland mission, carried over from Phase II of CENTCOM OPLAN 1002–90. Desert Storm's Phase III, however, now identified a specific attrition percentage that air power had to attain: 50 percent attrition of the Iraqi ground combat strength. After the war, Schwarzkopf wrote about conceiving the four Desert Storm phases in August 1990, and in specifically explaining Phase III, he stated, "Pulling a number out of the air, I said I'd need fifty percent of the Iraqi occupying forces destroyed before launching whatever ground offensive we might eventually plan." He described Phase III as "attrition of enemy force by fifty percent."[117] Just as OPLAN 1002–90 had mandated, the friendly ground-attack phase would not commence until air power in the preceding phase had attrited the Iraqi army to produce force ratios favorable to the attackers.[118]

The CINCCENT did not actually pull the 50 percent attrition figure from the air because his CAG at CENTCOM headquarters had produced this percentage as early as August 14 in relation to offensive operations. The CAG's function was to conduct operations research for the entire CENTCOM staff and analyze courses of action and theater plans using computer war-gaming and simulation models. Its postwar chronology indicated, "On 14 August 1990, [CAG] completes first offensive campaign study for [CENTCOM J–5]. Results show 50% reduction in enemy strength required to achieve desired objectives. CINC briefs CJCS — code named Desert Storm — on 25 August." The CAG's postwar report recorded that air power was to achieve the 50 percent reduction in enemy ground strength. Its close-hold analysis disclosed the feasibility of a single corps offensive strategy if an aggressive air campaign accompanied it.[119] The CINCCENT depended heavily on air power as he began to formulate his offensive war plan.

Chapter Four

Desert Shield Planning

General Schwarzkopf returned to Florida on August 7, 1990, after accompanying Secretary Cheney to Saudi Arabia to offer U.S. military assistance to King Fahd, resulting in the start of Desert Shield. From his headquarters at MacDill AFB, the CINCCENT managed the deployment and left General Horner in the theater as the CENTCOM Forward commander to receive and base incoming troops and develop a plan to counter an Iraqi invasion of Saudi territory. The CENTAF staff in the AOR devised a defensive air campaign dependent on the daily logistics flow, involving Coalition forces, and incorporating EC. At CENTCOM headquarters, computer simulation analyses indicated that air power had to attrit Iraqi army divisions to 50 percent of their combat strength to prevent them from pushing the Americans off the Arabian peninsula, again highlighting the airpower counterland mission. While focusing on defensive planning and operations, CENTAF built the networks and established the procedures and communication links to execute a defensive — or an offensive — air campaign.

CENTCOM Forward Commander

At Jeddah, Saudi Arabia, on Tuesday morning August 7, 1990, the day Desert Shield commenced, Secretary Cheney called together the group of people who had traveled with him to the theater, inviting also Maj. Gen. Donald L. Kaufman, USAF, head of the U.S. Military Training Mission (USMTM) to Saudi Arabia.[1] The delegation met in the government guest hotel, a palace, where they had spent the previous night. Cheney stated that Admiral Sharp, CENTCOM J–5, would accompany Under Secretary Wolfowitz who would visit countries in the GCC to seek their assistance and ask permission to deploy military forces, especially aircraft, to the member states. Secretary Cheney himself would travel to Egypt and Morocco to explain the deployment and solicit support for it. The

United States quickly needed Egypt's authorization for the carrier USS *Dwight D. Eisenhower* and other ships to move through the Suez Canal into the Red Sea.[2]

Shortly after the meeting, Schwarzkopf and Horner drove to Prince Abdallah AB where, on the ramp, the CINCCENT told the airman he would call on the Joint Staff for assistance with developing strategic targeting. Horner strongly urged Schwarzkopf to reconsider involving officers in the Pentagon in war planning because it would repeat a serious mistake of the Vietnam War. Knowing that Horner now assumed tremendous new responsibilities as the CENTCOM Forward commander and that his CENTAF staff had just received deployment orders, the CINCCENT stuck to his decision to call Washington for help, but he promised Horner that he would regain control of the planning at the completion of the initial work. Schwarzkopf then departed the AOR, not to return until August 26.

Horner flew to Riyadh with Ambassador Freeman, Generals Yeosock, Kaufman, and Starling, and Colonel Rider. He appointed Kaufman his chief of staff who, with his USMTM staff, would provide valuable assistance throughout Desert Shield. The ambassador also gave generous and effective support. Like Horner, General Yeosock, the ARCENT and Third Army commander, had considerable experience working in the theater with Saudi military officials. A few years earlier he had advised the Saudi Arabian National Guard and developed a friendship with Crown Prince Abdallah bin Abd al-Aziz al-Saud, who helped smooth the way for the Americans.[4] Yeosock's wry humor had come through a few hours earlier when Horner asked him, "John, what have you got to defend us?" In reply, Yeosock reached deep into his pocket and pulled out his small knife.[5] The reality behind the response explains, in part, why the CENTCOM Forward commander had slept very little the previous night, pondering the defense burden the Americans had undertaken, the enormity of the operation about to unfold, and the amount of work ahead to implement the massive deployment.[6]

In Riyadh the evening of August 7, in the Ministry of Defense and Aviation (MODA) building, Horner attended a meeting chaired by General Muhammad bin Salih al-Hammad, head of the Saudi military forces. Lt. Gen. Ahmad al-Buhairi, chief of the RSAF, attended, as did the commanders of the navy and army and a member of the royal family, Lt. Gen. Prince Khalid bin Sultan bin Abd al-Aziz al-Saud, the son of Prince Sultan and the nephew of the king. Horner arranged for the Saudis to receive the same CIA intelligence briefing presented to the monarch that included reconnaissance satellite images revealing the disposition of Iraqi troops in Kuwait. He then described the American deployment and answered questions.[7]

From his experience in the region during Earnest Will, Elf One, and the flag exercises, Horner dealt with the Saudis forthrightly and as equals, and he wanted to avoid the legacy of the Vietnam War, when Americas often pushed aside their South Vietnamese allies. He reflected, too, on the perception conveyed by President Bush at Camp David that he was determined to involve the Saudis directly in the defense of their country. Therefore, General al-Hammad's polite but firm resistance in response to Horner's request that the Saudis and Americans establish a coalition headquarters in the MODA building surprised him. After discussion and phone calls by General Khalid and General al-Hammad, the Saudis did open up rooms in the MODA for a combined headquarters and for the CENTCOM headquarters. Horner temporarily worked out of the USMTM space in the building.[8]

General Khalid emerged as the chief Saudi military official, and King Fahd placed him in charge of the newly established Joint Forces Command on August 10, 1990. Khalid had commanded the Royal Saudi Air Defense Forces, including the CSS–2 missiles he had secretly acquired from China in 1986 and 1987. He had attended the Royal Military Academy at Sandhurst in the United Kingdom, the U.S. Army Command and General Staff College at Fort Leavenworth, the Air War College at Maxwell AFB, and the Naval Postgraduate School at Monterey, California. As commander of the Joint Forces Command, he led the Saudi, Egyptian, and Syrian forces, the troops from the GCC countries, and the small contingents such as those from Poland, Czechoslovakia, Senegal, Morocco, Nigeria, and other nations. He commanded the French until the start of Desert Storm when OPCON passed to Schwarzkopf. General Khalid considered one of his main responsibilities to be keeping the Coalition together, and he believed that Saddam Hussein would try desperately to destroy it. In mid-August he feared an Iraqi invasion and wondered about the level of commitment of the Americans arriving in the heart of Islam. He wrote after the war:

> Studying my charts and trying to put myself in [Saddam's] shoes, I thought he would make a frontal attack on our oil fields and our ports, and perhaps use special forces in our rear. We could throw our air force at him, and we would no doubt have to sacrifice it in doing so. We could also expect some immediate help from the U.S. Air Force, seeing that some American wings had already arrived and two U.S. carrier battle groups had deployed to the region. But once Saddam seized control of more than 40 percent of world oil reserves, the West might think twice before challenging him.[9]

General Khalid's Joint Forces Command staff played an extremely important role in facilitating the beddown, the basing, of forces arriving in the kingdom and keeping them supplied with basic necessities.[10]

Horner sent Colonel Rider, his logistician, to General al-Buhairi in the RSAF headquarters building, located a few miles away from the MODA facility, and the Saudi officer helped the logistician select space for the CENTAF headquarters. Behind the structure, CENTAF would soon set up its air-conditioned bubble-tent for the TACC. Air leaders from both the RSAF and USAF built a cordial and effective working relationship during Desert Shield and Desert Storm because of their prewar experience with exercises and operations and their similar thinking about air roles and missions. Horner had first met al-Buhairi during his visit to Nellis AFB when he was wing commander there, and a friendship between the two developed over the years. General Kaufman noted that of all the Saudi military officials, only al-Buhairi had warned that the Iraqi intimidation of Kuwait was not an extortionary bluff and that Saddam Hussein did, indeed, intend to invade its small neighbor.[11]

Desert Shield Mission OPORD

On August 10, 1990, from his headquarters in Florida, Schwarzkopf issued a CENTCOM OPORD which defined the mission of the Desert Shield forces: "Deploy to the area of operations and take actions in concert with host nation forces, friendly regional forces, and other allies to defend against an Iraqi attack into Saudi Arabia and be prepared to conduct other operations as directed." The deployment's CONOPS consisted of three phases consistent with those outlined in CENTCOM OPLAN 1002–90: deterrence, to include operations for protecting the kingdom and combined training with allied forces; interdiction of invading troops and defense of key installations on the Arabian peninsula; and restoration of international borders.[12]

The OPORD provided a threat assessment that concluded, despite Iraq's claims it would soon begin troop withdrawals from Kuwait, that no indicators pointed to such action. Indeed, Iraqi forces in that country greatly surpassed those required for the occupation. Although noting that troops occupied hastily built defensive positions near oil fields and refineries in southern Kuwait, the OPORD warned that the Iraqis could attack Saudi Arabia in forty-eight hours, possibly seizing the Saudi port town of Khafji and its surrounding oil fields. At Iraq's airfields, personnel loaded aircraft with external fuel tanks and armed them with munitions. Along Iraq's southern border with Saudi Arabia, one Iraqi armor brigade and one mechanized infantry brigade assumed positions.[13]

According to the OPORD, the Iraqi air force posed a significant threat, comprising MiG–29 Fulcrums, MiG–21 Fishbeds, MiG–23 Floggers, MiG–25 Foxbats, and Mirage F1Es. The Iraqis would fly these aircraft in counterair roles primarily in support of strike aircraft. The air defense order of battle consisted of SAMs and air defense artillery. The SAMs included Roland Is and IIs, both French-built, and SA–2s, –3s, –6s, –8s, –7/14s, –9s, and –13s. Air defense artillery included self-propelled air defense guns — the S–60 (57mm) and ZSU–23–4 (23mm) — and towed guns — the M1939 (37mm) and ZU–23 (23mm). The OPORD stated that the Iraqis had captured and activated Kuwaiti SA–8 and I-Hawk missile sites.[14]

Not surprisingly, Schwarzkopf's OPORD designated the CENTAF commander the JFACC and delineated his responsibilities, heeding the command prerogatives of the component commanders and stipulating that the JFACC would function under the authority of the JFC, the CINCCENT. The JFACC would plan, coordinate, allocate, and task air missions based on the CINCCENT's apportionment guidance. He received authorization to directly coordinate with the commanders of ARCENT, MARCENT, NAVCENT, SOCCENT, the JTFME, and supporting forces to ensure unity of effort.[15] The OPORD also assigned the JFACC two broad, related responsibilities. As AADC, he would establish and operate an integrated, combined air defense and airspace control system; as ACA, he would facilitate the safe effective use of airspace.[16]

One section of the OPORD surprised and disappointed Horner; the CINCSAC, General Chain; and the STRATFOR commander to CENTAF, Brig. Gen. Patrick P. Caruana, who had arrived in Riyadh on August 9. It directed that B–52 assets based in the AOR remain under the OPCON of the SAC commander, even though Chain expected to transfer OPCON of the B–52s in theater to the CENTCOM commander. OPCON specified that command functions over subordinate forces include organizing, tasking, providing objectives, and employing them to accomplish assigned missions.[17] Since 1988, SAC had developed a policy to transfer OPCON of B–52s to a supported theater commander to correct a command and control problem that had been experienced in the Vietnam War and to provide the war-fighting commander with fully responsive bomber assets. A SAC OPCON policy statement had been prepared for inclusion in the draft of the revised CENTCOM OPLAN 1002–90. In 1990 Schwarzkopf and Chain had drawn up an agreement about the transfer, but it awaited the CINCCENT's signature when Iraq invaded Kuwait.[18]

Upon receiving the OPORD on August 10, Brig. Gen. Kenneth F. Keller, SAC's director of command control, telephoned General Moore, CENTCOM J–3, and explained SAC's desire to transfer the B–52s for deployment and employment purposes. Moore requested that Keller put the statement in writing to Schwarzkopf, which he did by message on August 16. As a result, CENTCOM issued an amendment to its OPORD reflecting the CENTCOM commander's OPCON of the B–52s.[19]

Forward basing of the Cold War bombers presented an extremely sensitive issue, handled by STRATFOR, CENTAF, CENTCOM, SAC, and the Department of State. CENTAF preferred basing the bombers at Cairo and Jeddah New, but the Egyptians and Saudis viewed the aircraft as blatantly offensive, not defensive, weapons, and they prohibited the aircraft from entering their countries. They would bar the B–52s from landing on their soil until the war began. Spain, too, rejected bombers at Moron AB, only allowing them there when offensive warfare loomed.[20] The first B–52s to deploy in Desert Shield arrived August 12 at Diego Garcia, a British-owned island in the Indian Ocean, and they remained there, where SAC had built facilities and stored supplies and munitions. These aircraft flew from Loring AFB, Maine, and had no preplanned nuclear mission under the Single Integrated Operational Plan (SIOP). By the end of Desert Storm, seventy-four B–52Gs deployed, including SIOP-capable aircraft. The Gulf War directly affected over 65 percent of the SIOP bomber force, in part because of the large number of tankers sent to the Middle East which degraded SIOP bomber operations.[21]

SAC's OPCON transferral message pertained only to B–52s. The SAC commander retained OPCON of his command's deployed tankers and reconnaissance aircraft. Soon, however, General Chain did delegate OPCON for the KC–10 and KC–135 tankers to the STRATFOR commander, General Caruana, who also commanded the 17th Air Division (Provisional) of CENTAF and reported to the CENTAF commander. Chain also delegated to Caruana OPCON for reconnaissance aircraft (RC–135s, TR–1s, U–2s), which flew as U.S. national reconnaissance assets.[22]

Introducing the ATO

Horner in the MODA building relied on his CENTAF staff in the RSAF facility to fulfill the JFACC responsibilities in the first few weeks of Desert Shield. Approximately fifteen members of the staff arrived in Riyadh on the morning of August 8, led by CENTAF deputy commander General Olsen. One of their first tasks comprised establishing secure communications with Ninth Air Force at Shaw AFB to learn the sequence and schedule of aircraft flying to the theater and to identify and secure suitable bases for deploying air assets. The requirements of Desert Shield led the JCS and CENTCOM to deploy more forces to the AOR than were planned for in CENTAF Rapid Reaction Plan 1307 and CENTCOM OPLAN 1002–90, and to send them without adhering to a fully developed time-phased force deployment list, generating great confusion on both sides of the Atlantic.[23] Only a skeletal staff remained at Ninth Air Force–CENTAF headquarters in the United States, so General Russ discussed the situation with Horner. TAC at Langley AFB assumed responsibilities as CENTAF Rear on August 12. At TAC, the DCS for operations Brig. Gen. Michael E. Ryan immersed himself in Desert Shield logistics to provide the support for forces in theater to fight as long as necessary at any level of intensity. He explained:

> I worried food first. Then once we kind of got a handle on that, I worried munitions because the last thing in the world we needed to do was to run out of munitions. My theory is, you figure out what you need and at least double it. So I pushed very hard right in the beginning to get a handle on munitions requirements.[24]

Horner formally charged the tiny CENTAF staff with two missions: facilitate the deployment of air forces to the CENTCOM AOR, and prepare concepts of air operations for the defense of Saudi Arabia. During the early days of August, the defense of the Saudi kingdom dominated everyone's thoughts. Col. George L. Getchell, CENTAF Chief of Staff, recalled, "We thought any minute Saddam's [troops] would come rolling across the border." Colonel Crigger, CENTAF DCS for operations, explained, "Iraqi forces were less than 150 n[autical] miles from key oil fields, military installations, and port cities with no significant ground forces to oppose their advance into Saudi Arabia." Continued Iraqi aggression so concerned General Olsen that he tasked Maj. Harry L. Heintzelman IV of the Judge Advocate's Office to draft a headquarters evacuation plan executable with twelve hours of warning and requiring air and surface transportation from Riyadh westward across the peninsula to Jeddah. Indeed, Olsen did not unpack his suitcase. Describing the days of August 8–12, Horner stated, "It was just a wild time. We were working eighteen to twenty hours a day. During that time we never knew if the Iraqis would attack Saudi Arabia or not."[25] The general admitted, "Those were some of the worst nights in my life, because I had good information as to what the Iraqi threat was."[26]

On August 9, CENTAF flew its first defensive sorties: U.S. AWACS, RC–135s, and F–15s in high-value air asset CAPs. The staff at headquarters planned and coordinated these flights which were flown in conjunction with Saudi AWACS aircraft and fighters. On August 10, CENTAF issued its first air guidance letter for sorties flown August 11 and 12. On August 12, an eight-page guidance letter, accompanied by a 42-page ATO issued for August 14, identified interdiction and defensive counterair as the first two priorities.[27]

Throughout August, a key function of the CENTAF staff in Riyadh was the generation of the JFACC's ATO. Lt. Col. Samuel J. Baptiste, chief of combat plans, later explained, "The whole reason for the CENTAF headquarters to be there was to act as a JFACC and produce the ATO and be the center of the tasking."[28] Ordinarily, TACC's Combat Plans Division prepared the tasking order, but the TACC, with its computer and communications equipment, generators, bubble-tent housing, and operational staff of about seventy personnel, would not deploy from Shaw AFB until August 16. In the meantime, key, experienced members of the CENTAF staff in Riyadh prepared and disseminated the daily ATOs and monitored air operations. Later, flight-duty officers from the wings assisted them in the TACC, contributing current and weaponeering knowledge to the ATO planning process and maintaining continual contact with the wings to help them execute the required sorties.[29]

Lt. Col. Samuel J. Baptiste

CENTAF's early ATOs focused on the defense of Saudi Arabia. Caruana observed,

> We were there [to fight a war] from the very minute we landed. Even though we really were not sure, we were postured. My staff was pos-

> tured, and I know General Horner's position was to be prepared to defend ourselves and our allies. We needed to be prepared to fight from the minute we got to the ground.[30]

The number of air assets flowing to theater affected the sorties in the earliest ATOs. "Every day we had to make a new strategy based on how many forces we received that day," Horner stated. He continued,

> Yeosock and I would sit down and figure out where we were going to bed them down and then what we would have them do if we got attacked. We normally did that every evening with the new opportunities of being attacked. During the day we would work out what we would do, while we were doing all the other beddown things and coordinate this with what we thought we could hold.[31]

Horner knew that the JFACC quickly had to assert control over the flying done by the massive numbers of aircraft arriving in theater. He and General Olsen understood that to establish the authority of the JFACC they had to implement the ATO process. He believed that without the ATO, no viable JFACC existed.[32] The Saudis' prohibition against flying through their airspace unless the sorties appeared in the ATO rendered the ATO legitimate and the JFACC's authority real. The host nationals insisted on the rule, bluntly asserted, that if a sortie was not in the ATO, it didn't fly. By means of the ATO, the Saudis could control the Americans and quell fears that pilots would fly wildly about the kingdom and buzz villages, animal herds, and the sacred city of Mecca. Over many days and weeks, the CENTAF staff coordinated with RSAF officers to produce a countrywide ATO, and the staff emphasized the importance of centralized control of air operations. Saudis daily participated in developing the ATOs. A corollary rule permitting aerial refueling only for missions in the ATO reinforced the JFACC's authority and span of control, a stricture particularly affecting Navy flights.[33]

The British readily agreed to incorporate their flying into the RSAF–JFACC ATO. On August 9 twelve Tornados arrived at the King Abd al-Aziz Royal Saudi Air Base (RSAB) at Dhahran, and the following day Olsen met with Air Vice Marshal "Sandy" Wilson, Commander of the British Air and Naval Task Force, and discussed British deployment plans. Olsen offered as much support as possible for Tornados going to Dhahran; Jaguars going to Thumrait, Oman; and tankers going to Seeb, Oman.[34]

As the daily ATO grew from forty to hundreds of pages of taskings and instructions, the CENTAF combat plans staff grappled with computer and communication problems associated with producing and disseminating the order. Not surprisingly, the staff created it on a computer, but not by using an ATO-design software program. During Internal Look, the staff operated Templar software created specifically for ATO production, but because it was such a new program and so few people knew how to use it, planners decided not to rely on it in Desert

Shield. The possibility that Templar would malfunction without anyone being able to fix the system outweighed the speed it offered. In addition, in August and September, CENTAF lacked the time and Templar experts to train people to operate the system. Thus, the staff generated the ATO on off-the-shelf software, requiring many hours of program adjustment and repetitive proofreading.[35]

Disseminating the ATO quickly and securely to Coalition air units presented an even more formidable challenge. On August 12, CENTAF sent the ATO electronically to Air Force units in Saudi Arabia via secure fax machines loaned by the RSAF. The staff issued instructions to the wing operations centers over Secure Telephone Units (STU IIIs), which encrypted voice and data signals and transmitted them over commercial telephone lines. Later, the CENTAF staff members also used the Saudis' secure wide-area logistics communications network. Where no telecommunication links yet existed, C–21 Learjets delivered the ATO; four or sometimes five small jets would cover the Arabian peninsula in a period of nine to ten hours. The Navy initially received the ATO via personal computers connected to STU IIIs, connecting Riyadh with the NAVCENT command ship. Carrier-based aircraft then made courier flights to deliver the ATO in hard copy and on disk.[36]

CENTAF eventually relied on the Computer-Assisted Force Management System (CAFMS) to transmit the ATO to Air Force units. TAC had developed it, allowing remote computer terminals to access the tasking order via a host computer. CAFMS enabled two-way, real-time communication between host terminals in Riyadh and remote ones in wing operations centers. System equipment began to be deployed August 14, but it would take weeks before terminals operated at many bases.[37] Since CAFMS was not a standard, Air Force–wide design, when SAC units received their CAFMS equipment, CENTAF had to send teams to train operators. Because one CAFMS host computer could communicate with only eleven remote terminals, CENTAF augmented its two hosts with the three used in Blue Flag exercises and by the purchase of two more. The Navy also lacked familiarity with CAFMS and had no hardware to receive the ATO via the system. By the end of September, to supplement communication via STU IIIs and courier flights, NAVCENT received portions of the ATO or the entire document by satellite communication links, which routed ATO messages through Guam.[38]

Desert Shield Defensive Planning

In addition to producing daily ATOs to task sorties for operational missions (flying CAPs, AWACS, and reconnaissance) and, later, to schedule training flights, the CENTAF staff also produced ATOs to respond directly to an Iraqi invasion and to defend Saudi Arabia. They produced two versions of the defensive ATOs intended to halt an Iraqi assault into the Saudi kingdom. They called their first version the D-day ATO. They completed it on August 23, 1990, built it to cover a 48-hour period, and focused it on thwarting the invasion. In mid-September, after additional air assets had arrived in theater, CENTAF produced the second version, known as the D-day ATO Bravo, or simply ATO Bravo, which over a 24-hour period directed air strikes against the invaders and a great variety of interdiction targets in Kuwait and Iraq. CENTAF planners expected the defensive air campaigns to last for days as air power delayed, attrited, and halted the invaders, even though the ATOs covered no more than forty-eight hours. The fluid situation and objectives would influence and guide the development of subsequent ATOs.[39] Three aspects of the Desert Shield defensive planning would carry over to the Desert Storm air campaign: selecting interdiction targets; assigning aircraft to air sectors, or boxes, to hunt and destroy targets; and pursuing electronic warfare objectives.

Colonels Crigger and Baptiste led the effort on the defensive, reactive plans and ATOs. Relying on air-to-air and air-to-ground strikes, the D-day plan's overall objectives were to maintain air superiority over the Arabian peninsula, establish air superiority over the KTO, and attack invading Iraqi forces. The KTO comprised Kuwait and portions of Iraq from Basra northwest to Nasiriyah and southward to the Neutral Zone on the Iraqi-Saudi border.[40]

By August 23, the D-day ATO consisted of two phases: the first was a "hard initial thrust" against invading Iraqi forces; the second was the application of "continuous pressure" against the aggressors. The plan initially relied upon U.S. Air Force, U.S. Navy, Saudi, and British air assets. Over a seven-hour period, alert aircraft from three bases, Dhahran, Dhafra, and Thumrait, would make the hard, initial thrust against the attacking troops to demonstrate resolve and produce significant attrition and demoralization. During the continuous pressure phase, fourteen waves of aircraft from the *Eisenhower* carrier group in the Red Sea and the *Independence* group in the Gulf of Oman would strike over a 36-hour period. This phase required a large fleet of tankers, with preplanned orbits used for the initial response and a follow-on tanker flow to sustain the pressure. Because the Navy fueled their aircraft with JP–5 and the Air Force used JP–4 with a lower flash point than that considered safe by the Navy for use on carriers, planners faced the complex challenge of sending tankers airborne with appropriate fuel and refueling equipment to service a variety of aircraft with differing fuel requirements. The main objective of the D-day ATO was to send fighters and tankers to "inflict maximum damage" and then return them to bases as soon as possible for follow-on tasking.[41]

On a map, the CENTAF planners identified the probable Iraqi invasion routes into the northeastern part of Saudi Arabia and drew over them air sectors or boxes. Their plan called for the airborne command element (ACE) on the AWACS to vector coalition aircraft to the blocks of airspace over territory where Iraqi forces concentrated. Once there, pilots would strike ground targets of opportunity. CENTAF assigned arbitrary boundaries and identifiers to the invasion boxes. During Desert Storm, CENTAF would again establish sectors, dubbed "kill boxes," and send pilots to them to find and hit targets. The boxes in the offensive campaign would correspond to the grid system the Saudis used in their national air defense system and would encompass the entire KTO.[42]

By the third week of August, the CENTAF staff had coordinated D-day strategy with Army, Navy, Marine Corps, and Saudi air representatives. The joint coordination proceeded smoothly; in fact, as early as August 14, the Army had only to identify the FSCL and the fallback line. The CENTAF staff worked closely with RSAF representatives in the TACC to develop the plan, and the Saudis, in turn, fully supported it. Horner and Maj. Clinton D. Null, USAF, briefed the D-day operations to General al-Buhairi on August 23, who approved them that day. Shortly thereafter, Null traveled to Saudi air bases and briefed the plan to commanders.[43]

The ARCENT defensive strategy followed the concepts in CENTCOM OPLAN 1002–90. The Army established enclaves around the port of al-Jubail, 160 miles from the Kuwaiti border, and farther south around the port of Dammam and the air base at Dhahran. The ports served as the main points of debarkation for arriving Marine Corps and Army forces. Early on, the light infantry troops of the 82d Airborne Division of the XVIII Airborne Corps provided the bulk of ARCENT's defensive power. Considering these paratroopers vis-à-vis the heavy Iraqi armor divisions they would confront, Horner thought of the airborne soldiers as "prisoners of war waiting to be captured."[44] The 2d Mechanized Brigade of the Saudi Arabian National Guard occupied territory closest to the Kuwaiti-Saudi border, in front of the Americans, and formed the Eastern Area Command. To the west, thirty miles from King Khalid Military City (KKMC), near the Iraqi-Saudi border, the Peninsula Shield forces held defensive positions and formed the Northern Area Command.[45] They consisted of a Saudi brigade group and a few companies and battalions from the GCC countries. Forces from all parts of the kingdom rushed to reinforce the two commands.[46]

The commander of the XVIII Airborne Corps, Lt. Gen. Gary E. Luck, believed that until his Corps's 24th Infantry Division, Mechanized, arrived in theater, with its 1,600 armored and 3,500 wheeled vehicles and 90 helicopters, the danger from an Iraqi invasion remained great.[47] Horner believed that when the 24th Division arrived, the Coalition would then have a chance of fighting an effective delaying defense. Flying to Jeddah on August 17, Horner briefed Secretary Cheney on the D-day air plan, the enclave strategy (which he likened to the Pusan Perimeter defense of the Korean War), and the importance of the swift arrival of the heavy armor of the 24th Infantry Division. The first of the ten ships necessary to transport the division had departed Savannah, Georgia, on August 13 and arrived at Dammam on August 27. Another ship, the *Antares,* carrying elements of the division's aviation brigade and support command, developed boiler trouble, broke down, and drifted in the Atlantic for two days before being towed to Spain, where handlers reloaded the cargo to the *Altair* to continue its transport to the theater. Not until September 12 did major elements of the division arrive in Saudi Arabia. On September 3, however, enough units had disembarked at Dhahran so that, with the Marines and 101st Airborne Division, American ground forces moved into positions to defend Saudi Arabia by sectors.[48]

In early August, Col. Gary Ware's CAG employed the TACWAR computer model and tried to determine to what extent air power had to attrit the Iraqis invading Saudi Arabia to prevent U.S. forces from suffering heavy casualties or to prevent Saddam's army from pushing the Americans off the peninsula. The J–2 intelligence staff supplied up-to-date threat assessments and possible enemy courses of action. Computer simulation showed that air power had to destroy 50 percent of the tanks, artillery, APCs, and light weapons of the invading forces. These results impressed Schwarzkopf, who ordered an acceleration of the deployment of A–10 Thunderbolt IIs and other assets capable of killing tanks and vehicles. On August 14 the CAG ran a simulation of a friendly ground attack into Kuwait 120 days after the deployment began, accounting for additional units in the AOR. Again the CAG's analysis generated the 50 percent attrition requirement to produce force ratios of greater than 3:1 favoring the counterattack. Thus, as early as August, defensive and offensive planning required an airpower, counterland mission with the goal of attriting Iraqi ground forces 50 percent.[49]

To fully coordinate the Army's strategy and operations with CENTAF, ARCENT formed and staffed the BCE in CENTAF's TACC by the end of August. As expected, the Navy and Marine Corps sent liaison officers to the air control center. The components also sent representatives to the JFACC's Joint Targets Board. Chaired by Capt. John Heidrick, a CENTAF targeteer, the board consisted of personnel from CENTAF, the CENTAF Judge Advocate's Office, ARCENT, MARCENT, and NAVCENT. Infrequently, representatives from the RSAF, RAF, Royal Saudi Land Forces, and Kuwaiti, Italian, and French air forces attended the meetings, but only RAF and RSAF personnel nominated targets.[50] Officers holding the rank of captain, major, or lieutenant colonel served on the board, which had convened at CENTAF headquarters through many exercises over the years, including Internal Look. During Desert Storm a targeting controversy would lead Schwarzkopf to convene a Joint Targets Coordination Board at CENTCOM headquarters, chaired by his deputy commander, but the change in locale and participation of higher ranking officers did not alleviate the problem.

The JFACC's Joint Targets Board nominated targets for the KTO. Marine Corps members nominated some of the first ones placed on the list: Iraqi Frog surface-to-surface rocket sites. Elements of two Iraqi Frog–7 brigades had been noted in Kuwait since the invasion, and the Iraqis were suspected of operating captured Kuwaiti equipment. Early target sets for the ATO Bravo plan would include Frog rocket and Silkworm missile sites, C^2 sites associated with air defense and corps headquarters, primary and forward operating airfields, logistics sites, bridges in Kuwait, and the Ras al-Qulayah naval port. In October, the list also included fixed Scud sites in Western Iraq. CENTAF produced detailed target planning worksheets (with DMPIs) and imagery for ATO Bravo targets.[51] It would use this material in Phases II and III of the Desert Storm campaign.[52]

On August 25 Capt. Thomas Kniffen of the Judge Advocate's Office met with Capt. Steve Devours and Capt. Patrick Hannafin of the TACC and discussed the JFACC's defensive target list in terms of its adherence to the law of armed conflict. The operators raised questions about hitting chemical plants, supplies, and systems. Devours explained that strikes against such targets would probably release CW into the air and could cause many unintended casualties and deaths. The discussion raised more questions than it provided answers, and the officers noted that CENTAF intelligence had not yet confirmed the presence of any CW in Kuwait. ARCENT representatives had wanted to target a desalinization plant, but this was prohibited because Kuwaiti civilians relied on the facility for fresh water.[53] This suggestion to defeat the Iraqi army by curtailing its water supply offered a promising target strategy against a desert-based army.

The ATO Bravo of September 14, 1990, provided targeting guidance that called for the counterair mission to give priority to enemy bombers and threats to AWACS and tankers; disrupt and attrit enemy air operations; and conduct SEAD to aid battlefield air operations in support of ground forces. Objectives required aircraft to destroy armor, delay and attrit Iraqi assault forces, and strike battlefield targets of opportunity. Airmen would also target follow-on enemy forces and strike supplies and facilities that directly sustained the enemy's offensive.[54]

Because an Iraqi invasion of Saudi Arabia would trigger the execution of the ATO Bravo, the first allied strike sorties would react to the Iraqi attack and could occur anytime, day or night. Not all aircraft, however, were both day- and night-capable. Most of the F–16s lacked low-altitude navigation and targeting infrared for night (LANTIRN) pods and operated best in daylight. Normally the ATO cycle began at 0400, but Desert Shield required a flexible response time in reaction to Iraqi initiatives. Horner suggested a merry-go-round concept to match airframe capabilities with day and night requirements. He tasked targeteers to identify sites and facilities requiring initial attack, regardless of clock time. He then requested two mini-ATOs for these key targets, geared by the appropriate type of airframe to night and to day missions. Each tasked unit knew what sorties were to be flown, depending on the time of day, and each would then jump on the merry-go-round to continue and complete the ATO cycle.[55]

After the CENTAF staff distributed the ATO Bravo to Coalition units in September, they updated its target list continuously, and several times over the next three months they published updated versions. By the end of September, however, the threat of Saddam Hussein's sending his army south to meet the formidable Coalition forces arrayed against him had greatly diminished, compared with the danger present in early August. The defensive plan then became a cover to disguise training in support of an offensive air campaign.[56] Fortunately the defensive plan never had to be executed because, in September, a Saudi F–15 pilot defected to Sudan. Assuming the Iraqis would acquire information from him, planners changed call signs, altitudes, routes, and procedures, but otherwise did not fundamentally alter the ATO.[57]

EC and Defensive Planning

Plans to defend Saudi Arabia incorporated EC components to protect friendly electromagnetic assets and to neutralize or destroy those of the enemy.[58] The objectives underlying the EC aspects of the defense would carry over to the EC portion of the Desert Storm offensive air war. For defense and offense, planners designed the EC component to be crucial for gaining air superiority and in keeping aircraft losses to a minimum. The architect of the EC campaign, Brig. Gen. Larry L. Henry, arrived at CENTAF headquarters August 13. He had been the inspector general at TAC at Langley AFB, but General Russ knew that Henry had commanded an F–4G Wild Weasel wing, which trained to shoot AGM–88 high-speed antiradiation missiles (HARMs) against the control radars of enemy SAMs. Russ also knew that Henry had extensive EC experience, so when the TAC commander talked with Horner, he offered Henry to lead the CENTAF EC effort. Horner immediately accepted. During the Vietnam War, Henry had flown as a weapon systems officer (WSO) in the F–4 Phantom and had served four tours as a WSO and fast forward air controller. While at George AFB from 1985 to 1990, as a wing and then an air division commander, he belonged to the Ninth Air Force and served under Horner. From George AFB, Henry's F–4G Wild Weasel units had participated in three CENTCOM Bright Star exercises in Egypt where he had acquired valuable experience flying against Soviet-built Egyptian air defense systems similar to those that the Iraqis employed. The Bright Stars offered greater realism than the TAC Green Flag EC exercises in the United States.[59]

Brig. Gen. Larry L. Henry

At RSAF headquarters building in Riyadh, Henry reported to General Olsen, the acting CENTAF commander, and he received instructions to develop an EC plan in case the Iraqis invaded Saudi Arabia. The defense of the kingdom against an Iraqi assault comprised his first and primary responsibility. The next day, Horner met with him, when they discussed SEAD.[60] Horner had flown the F–105F Wild Weasel on SEAD missions during his second tour in Vietnam, and he knew well the capabilities and limitations of aircraft flying to neutralize or destroy air defense systems.[61] Flying above 10,000 feet put pilots beyond the lethally effective range of AAA and infrared-directed SAMs, although it still rendered them vulnerable to long-range, radar-directed SAMs, like the SA–2.[62] If the radar-directed SAMs, however, could be neutralized and destroyed, pilots would fly in safe airspace. The Air Force had accelerated its program to develop the Wild Weasel systems to home in on the emissions from SAM radars and to launch missiles against them. Horner and Henry discussed the importance of reducing the SAM threat to free up medium-altitude levels.[63]

F–4G Wild Weasel

On the flight to the theater, Henry studied intelligence maps and data that Col. Kenneth A. Minihan, deputy director for intelligence at TAC headquarters, had given him just before his departure from Langley AFB. He also reread Air Force Manuals 1–1 and 1–2, the basic and operational doctrine publications, respectively, to ensure that his planning reflected sound Air Force concepts. He reflected, too, upon how the Israelis fought. In 1983, during his studies at the National War College at Fort Lesley J. McNair, Washington, D.C., he and a few other students received an award for writing a paper they produced on the Israeli operation Peace for Galilee, when the Israel Defense Forces entered Lebanon in 1982 and the Israeli air force, flying against a formidable Russian-built Syrian air defense system in the Bekka Valley, dismantled it by destroying 16 of 19 SAM sites in just over eight minutes. This extraordinary success contrasted with the disaster the Israelis experienced in 1973 during the Yom Kippur War, when enemy SAMs and AAA shot down 150 of their aircraft, 25 percent of their combat planes, even though Israeli pilots flew effectively against the enemy in air-to-air engagements. The Israeli combat experiences in 1973 and 1982 influenced Henry's concept of operations.[64]

Like all airmen, the general firmly believed that an air campaign — defensive *or* offensive — first required the gaining of air superiority. Achieving that goal, however, came not only from shooting down enemy aircraft and closing airfields but also by destroying or neutralizing the enemy's radars, missiles, AAA, and the C^3 systems linking them. The Iraqi air force concerned him less than Iraqi SAMs and the integrated air defense system (IADS) directing them. Air Force, Navy, Marine Corps, and RSAF pilots would handle the enemy aircraft the Iraqis vectored to their targets with EWR and the GCI system, also a part of the IADS. Henry worried about the SAMs blowing the nonstealthy Coalition aircraft to pieces as they interdicted invading forces. He would therefore initially focus the Coalition's EC air assets against the Iraqi missiles and C^3, which would then free up the medium-altitude regime.[65]

"Will they attack?" formed the key question in the minds of everyone in CENTAF. Henry's EC cell, initially occupying space near Olsen's office on the third floor of the RSAF building, struggled to find an answer. Studying everything he could lay his hands on that explained how the Iraqis fought wars, Henry concluded that the Republican Guard would spearhead the invasion into Saudi Arabia, as many officers had already concluded. He explained further, however, that the Republican Guard would not move until they could do so under a mobile SA–6 air defense, SAM umbrella. The SA–2 and SA–3 fixed SAM sites the Iraqis had prepared in Kuwait did not augur an invasion so much as the movement of the SA–6 units in front of the lead, assault formations. EC air assets would focus on destroying and neutralizing the SAM umbrella formed by SA–6s supported by SA–8s, SA–9s, Rolands, and AAA.[66]

Henry arrived in the theater before many of the CENTCOM EC air assets did. F–4Gs had not yet touched down in the AOR, and the EC–130H Compass Call electronic signal jammers waited in Lajes in the Azores while dysentery contracted from an impure water supply ravaged personnel at their assigned base in the UAE. Munitions, too, lagged behind. A few times a week, Horner met with Henry and other key staff and discussed the availability of aircraft, missiles, bombs, fuel, and supplies and how they would employ them in air defense operations, knowing that sustainability could make or break the defense once battle commenced. Henry recalled:

> It was not just the aircraft that I was concerned about. We did not have the munitions to prosecute the campaign nor did we have the munitions in theater in specific quantities to really pound them when they came across the border. The A–10s...were going to be very important because of the cannons. But we didn't have a lot of bombs — not good ones. We didn't have that much precision capability yet.... I watched daily, counted, kissed, felt, touched, jealously guarded the HARMs that came into theater. I watch[ed] them everyday. Munitions were a *big* concern.[67]

The defensive plan changed and matured as additional aircraft and munitions flowed to the AOR. While both defensive and offensive air campaign plans evolved, the daily status of air assets arriving in theater directly and continuously affected the defensive effort.[68]

With Horner's encouragement, Henry crafted a CONOPS to integrate all EC air assets into a unified SEAD effort as an integral part of the JFACC's D-day air plan. He sent a message on August 21, 1990, to NAVCENT, MARCENT, and ARCENT, among others, addressing an EC campaign. The ideas he conveyed emphasizing jointness, integration of systems, attacks against C^3 facilities and radars, and exploitation or jamming of battlefield communications would undergird the EC component of the Desert Storm air campaign as well. Henry explained that the tasking for the defensive campaign would appear in the EC portion of the ATO, planned by a joint EC planning cell which, exploiting intelligence from a variety of sources, would nominate C^3 nodes, radars, SAMs, and other related targets. His message stated that the priority of the SEAD campaign was to neutralize or kill the air defenses protecting invading troops. EC objectives were to destroy or cut C^3, kill or neutralize fixed SAM targets, sever or suppress mobile SAMs and AAA, and jam or collect intelligence from communication networks.[69] Henry explained that destruction of the enemy air defense umbrella was the main thrust of the defense to expose the invading forces to air attacks and allow their attrition.

Henry visited 3d Marine Air Wing Commander Maj. Gen. Royal N. Moore, Jr., at Shaikh Isa in Bahrain to convince him to provide the EC campaign with F/A–18 Hornet HARM shooters and EA–6B Prowlers, which could jam signals and shoot missiles. The EA–6Bs would function primarily as jammers against EWR, GCI sites, and acquisition radars and emitters on aircraft identification–friend-or-foe (IFF) systems. For being a "crusty fellow," as Henry remembered him, Moore cooperated, as long as Henry did not request too many assets to fly missions not directly related to Marines engaged in combat. Since MARCENT had no HARMs at Shaikh Isa, Henry's offer to share those he possessed mellowed Moore. Scarcity of aircraft and munitions forced cooperation as F–4G HARM shooters began to fly training missions with EA–6B jammers. The Marine air commander agreed that his component's EC missions would be tasked in the ATO after Marine representatives to the joint EC planning group coordinated with the MARCENT commander.[70]

Henry also visited Navy aircraft carriers and flew EA–6B missions with personnel from the USS *John F. Kennedy*, which arrived in the Red Sea in September. He worked out agreements whereby Navy carriers would make available EA–6B and other HARM-capable aircraft, like A–6 Intruders and A–7 Corsair IIs, to support SEAD taskings. The EA–6Bs would have the same job as the EF–111As had: jam EWR, GCI, and acquisition radars. Again, Henry carefully avoided demanding too many aircraft for the EC campaign, and he agreed not to task all the assets from any one carrier battle group. He also requested that the Navy provide tactical air-launched decoys (TALDs) for the defensive campaign and promised to send HARMs to Jeddah for the Navy to use with carriers in the Red Sea.[71]

Once Henry assembled a joint EC air force, he knew the aircrews flying a variety of aircraft had to train together to learn how to operate in congested airspace, integrate communications, and avoid jamming friendly systems in electronic fratricide. He therefore quickly established a training area in Saudi Arabia, west of Kuwait and south of Iraq, dubbed the "Junkyard," and he tasked EC assets through the ATO generated and executed by CENTAF's TACC. Here, once

EF–111A Ravens being refueled

a week, planners sent EA–6B Prowlers, EF–111A Ravens, EC–130H Compass Calls, F–4G Wild Weasels, F/A–18 Hornets, Tornado GR–1s with air-launched antiradiation missiles (ALARMs), E–3 AWACS, and RC–135 Rivet Joints in coordination exercises, after which Henry held detailed debriefings to critique the missions. The RC–135s collected intelligence, and Henry forced them to establish communication links directly to the EC–130s, which specialized in jamming communications. (During Desert Storm, Rivet Joint and Compass Call aircraft working in concert would help a Saudi F–15 pilot shoot down two Iraqi aircraft.) In the training exercises, aircraft flying close to the Iraqi border enabled data collection as the Iraqis watched the aircraft flights.[72]

With his training program in place, Henry felt confident that EC assets for the initial D-day air campaign would eliminate the C^3 and missile umbrella protecting Iraqi forces pushing into Saudi Arabia. Responding to an armored assault, the JFACC would use jamming and lethal munitions against the "V" SOC in Kuwait (the fifth SOC which the Iraqis had hastily constructed at al-Salem), and thus destroy a key C^3 facility. EA–6Bs and EF–111As would jam EWR and GCI radars to disorient the Iraqi air forces and operate in conjunction with Compass Call to jam battlefield communications and aircraft IFF and navigational systems. The versatile EA–6Bs would also jam in support of F–4Gs and F/A–18s. Navy HARM shooters would attack the fixed SAM sites. F–4G Wild Weasels would go after the mobile SAMs. An EC specialist would fly aboard the AWACS to assist in battlefield management. Rivet Joint would collect and communicate signals intelligence. EC would render the skies safe for the allied air forces flying in their sector boxes to strike the invaders' armor and logistics.[73]

By September Henry had moved his EC cell to the basement of the RSAF building, and it continued to expand to include representatives from all of the SEAD aircraft — NAVCENT, MARCENT, the original CENTAF EC division, the Air Force Electronic Warfare Center, the Joint Electronic Warfare Center, the Air Force Electronic Security Command, and CENTAF/IN. Colonel Leonardo, the CENTAF/IN director sent an intelligence officer to the EC shop, Lt. Col. Sarah L. Cunningham, who became one of Henry's key aides during Desert

Shield and Desert Storm, along with a young officer from the Electronic Security Command, Lt. Eric Holdaway.[74]

Henry and his EC cell undertook four key tasks during the early weeks and months of Desert Shield. First, they studied intelligence flowing to them about the computerized C^3 system for the Iraqi IADS, called Kari, which the French had produced for tracking airborne threats and assigning tracks to aircraft or missiles. (*Kari* is the French word for Iraq spelled backwards.) When he first arrived in theater, Henry and a few of his staff had visited the MODA building searching for data relating to Kari. They came away with two books that Henry and Lieutenant Holdaway nearly memorized, along with updated intelligence reports, to find vulnerabilities in Kari's connectivity linking the components of the IADS. As Henry began to support Horner with development of the offensive air campaign, he would, indeed, focus on major weaknesses in Kari and fully exploit them.[75]

Second, they prepared overlays for U.S., British, Saudi, and French forces showing the coverage of SAMs with relation to EWR and GCI, and produced threat studies for the theater. An enormous problem confronted them, which they could never completely solve: establish a single electronic order of battle database for use throughout the theater. Databases proliferated, and so did the extent of the SAM threat. The DIA, Navy, CENTCOM, CENTAF, and other commands maintained their own electronic orders of battle, and since each included data from different collectors at various times on separate orbits using inconsistent collection procedures, a single stationary SAM site, for example, might be assigned multiple locations. Additionally, the cell coordinated with intelligence organizations to ensure that Coalition partners, especially the Arabs, would receive data necessary to fly missions safely, but not enough to reveal sources and methods of electronic order of battle intelligence collection. Henry favored sharing essential data with the Arabs, believing it unconscionable to withhold it for security reasons. Arabs could not work in his cell, but he did receive authorization to share sanitized information with them.[76]

Third, the cell coordinated with wings to receive visits from teams of specialists from the Tactical Air Warfare Center to test, recalibrate, and reprogram jamming pods and radar-warning receivers on aircraft to ensure they accurately detected and responded to enemy radar lock-ons. Nearly every unit required reprogramming after the deployment, and training in the Junkyard enabled pilots to test the effectiveness of and gain confidence in their EC equipment. Last, the cell coordinated with wings and the TACC to arrange for EC aggressors from Eglin AFB to fly against Coalition aircraft in training exercises.[77]

Air Defense and Air Traffic Control

The Desert Shield OPORD on August 10 had designated the JFACC the AADC, so CENTAF immediately began to undertake AADC responsibilities. The OPORD delineated two basic requirements: to establish the air defense system and integrate forces into it in accordance with the CINCCENT's priorities; and to establish and adjust procedures for weapons and fire-control and airspace coordination. The purpose of air defense comprised the detection and identification of any airborne object intruding into protected airspace and, if determined hostile, the destruction of the object according to rules of engagement. While preparing for the Internal Look exercise, Horner had planned to integrate U.S. air assets into the Saudi air defense system rather than develop a separate American architecture, and CENTAF followed this strategy during Desert Shield. The Saudis had developed a reliable system, especially in the northeastern part of the country, to protect oil fields and ports, and the Elf One and Earnest Will operations had given CENTAF valuable experience in working with it. Grafting onto the host nation's organization precluded other CENTCOM components, notably the Marines, from establishing their own area air defense system.

The Saudi network incorporated the airspace of the GCC countries and consisted of seven air defense–airspace control sectors: Eastern, Central, Northwest, Western, Southern, Oman, and UAE. It incorporated control centers, radar sites, missile and artillery systems, fighter-interceptor aircraft on alert and patrol, and AWACS. Since August 2, the RSAF had flown their AWACS twenty-four hours a day, and their morale remained high, their professionalism evident. CENTAF would augment the Saudi system with U.S. AWACS, CAPs, tanker and air intelligence operations, and communication networks.[78] AWACS initially provided the major communications link between the Saudi and American systems. With its deep-looking radar and its ability to reduce terrain-masking effects, AWACS provided low-altitude coverage beyond ground-system capabilities. It also provided aircraft-tracking identification, surveillance, weapons control of friendly aircraft, air refueling and navigational assistance, and threat detection and warning from its own capabilities and those of signals intelligence assets.[79]

Horner intended to control all of the Coalition's missiles in the AOR to insure that none accidentally shot down friendly aircraft. CENTAF acted quickly to pull the Marine, Army, and Saudi Hawk weapons and other surface-to-air systems into the air defense network. The JFACC's view of the missiles differed fundamentally from the view of the units employing them. Horner relied not on missiles, but on Coalition aircraft, especially F–15 Eagles on CAPs with AWACS, as the first line of defense in the AOR. He wanted to destroy Iraqi aircraft well before they flew into range of cities, bases, and facilities. Given the friendly-fire issues and the reliance on air-to-air defense, CENTAF issued rules restricting missile firings.[80] During air defense training, however, the TACC sent aircraft against missiles to test detection and tracking, and operators simulated launches.[81]

The French, Syrian, and Egyptian missiles also came into the air defense system, and CENTAF relied on its tactical air control parties to accomplish the integration, which consisted of two- or three-man teams with equipment allowing communication to coordinate air support. The CENTAF teams, however, had difficulty working with the Syrians and Egyptians, whose governments contributed no aircraft to the Coalition. In early October at an air defense meeting at the Saudi Air Defense headquarters in KKMC, the Egyptian representatives stated that they would shoot any target that flew toward them. One American attending the meeting reported that the Egyptians posed a greater danger to allied pilots than the Iraqis did. Not until November did the situation change when Generals Schwarzkopf and Khalid al-Saud arranged for a meeting with the Egyptians and Syrians in the MODA building, where Horner explained weapon control requirements to them. They then visited CENTAF's newly established control and reporting center at KKMC and viewed the display from the AWACS to see for themselves the picture of flying activity in the theater and the protection that aircraft on patrol and alert provided against Iraqi air attacks. The center served a new subsector, linked to the older, larger sector controlled from Dhahran, to cover the northern area of Saudi Arabia and Coalition forces if they moved into Iraq. CENTCOM sent Hawk and Patriot missile batteries to the subsector, and C–5s brought radars and C^2 equipment from the United States, which Americans and Coalition representatives operated. CENTAF also flew aircraft over national contingents in training exercises to allow the ground troops to see friendly planes overhead.[82]

The first battery of Patriot missiles to arrive in theater protected the air base at Dhahran. Horner and Yeosock agreed that, because of the Scud threat, technicians set the Patriots in the antimissile, not the antiaircraft mode.[83] Planners knew that Iraq had demonstrated a willingness and capability to launch Scud missiles in the War of the Cities during the Iran-Iraq War. Iraq had fired nearly 200 modified Scuds against urban areas in Iran, including Tehran. In February 1990, U.S. intelligence revealed that Iraq had built five fixed launch sites in the western part of the country, placing launches within reach of Israel. Scuds fired from southern Iraq could also hit Saudi Arabia. The Iraqis could fire missiles from fixed sites and mobile launch vehicles, the latter of which consisted of Soviet-built MAZ–534 TELs and locally produced mobile erector-launchers. Planners worried that Scuds could carry BW or CW warheads as well as relatively small high-explosive ones.[84]

Before the Iraqi invasion of Kuwait, the DoD had just begun to develop a system to provide deployed forces with the earliest possible warning of tactical ballistic missiles. As a Scud launched, it produced a visible, very hot plume which sensors on the Defense Support Program satellites could detect. These satellites could provide U.S. space organizations with early warning of a Scud attack, and the missile's heat signature could allow calculations that revealed the approximate location of the launch site. A warning system could then be established to alert a Patriot battery whose phased-array radar system, set in the antimissile mode, would begin to detect and track an incoming missile within its range. The Scud net took weeks to activate.[85]

Rules of engagement (ROE) governed the employment of weapons in the JFACC's air defense system. CENTCOM issued them after approval by the JCS, and they primarily delineated the circumstances and limitations under which forces would commence and continue combat with other forces. The CENTCOM staff relied heavily on CENTAF for help in formulating changes to the peacetime rules already in effect for air-to-air engagements. CENTAF issued its own rules and interpretations as supplements to the CENTCOM directives. CENTCOM and CENTAF issued two ROE sets, one for peacetime and the other for wartime implementation. On August 9, CENTAF's air defense specialists, in close consultation with the lawyer, Major Heintzelman, began to write peacetime ROE for operations in response to Iraqi aircraft entering Saudi airspace or threatening Coalition forces. Within a few days, they also began to develop wartime ROE. To formulate the rules, they referred to the draft CENTCOM 1002–90 OPLAN; CENTCOM regulations; ROE that CENTAF had drawn up for the Internal Look exercise; and ROE guidance received in a CJCS message of August 9, 1990.[86]

The CJCS indicated that the NCA authorized U.S. forces to attack units that used weapon-system or fire-control radars against them or that otherwise showed hostile intent. The NCA also authorized use of electronic support measures, nondestructive ECM, and electronic counter-countermeasures, as well as decoys and tactical deception. U.S. forces that accidentally entered Iraqi or Kuwaiti territory or airspace could use force in self-defense as they withdrew. The CJCS's message provided very brief operational ROE if the CINCCENT or his designated subordinate commanders declared Iraqi forces hostile or if the NCA ordered operations against Iraqi forces. The message concluded by stating, "Nothing in these rules negates a commander's obligation to take all necessary and appropriate action for his unit's self-defense."[87]

On August 16 CENTAF sent an eleven-page ROE to coalition units, summarizing CENTCOM and JCS guidance and establishing policies and procedures for the interception, identification, and engagement of "airborne objects" by CENTAF forces not operating in support of U.S. naval forces. Foreign nationals received summaries of the regulation, not the original text.[88]

The ROE of August 16 provided beyond visual range (BVR) rules which required double-checking the target for friendly and enemy attributes and checking to ensure that no friendly aircraft flew in the area. "The essence of the BVR ROE is that the shooter must be convinced that he is shooting at an enemy aircraft and that no friendly aircraft can inadvertently be hit," the message explained. "The basic rule for firing air-to-air missiles is that it is better to let an enemy aircraft get away than to take a chance on shooting a friendly aircraft."[89] From August 18 to 30, Heintzelman worked to simplify the August 16 ROE, eliminating legal jargon and presenting rules in simple, direct language for pilots who quickly had to make life and death decisions and for the Coalition partners who did not speak or read English fluently. On September 2, CENTAF issued two basic instructions that pertained to Iraqi aircraft penetrating Saudi airspace and engaging targets BVR. The Saudis and British concurred with these instructions.[90]

In early October the CENTCOM staff began their review of CENTAF's draft wartime ROE, and on the 17th they sent it to Coalition units for review and approval. From October through December, the Navy presented the main obstacles to finalizing the ROE by its slowness in responding; the Navy objected to CENTAF issuing ROE and to BVR procedures. The main problem centered on the use of the Navy's Phoenix air-to-air missile and IFF requirements.[91]

The Desert Shield OPORD of August 10 assigned another major responsibility to the JFACC interwoven with air defense: ACA. The CENTAF staff formulated and published airspace control procedures, which involved civilian air traffic systems and combat airspace management. The Saudis allowed many Coalition aircraft to fly from civilian airports throughout the kingdom, and the Desert Shield deployment produced a tenfold increase in the number of aircraft flying through the Saudi air control system, which could not easily handle the enormous volume of traffic. The crowded northwest area quickly became hazardous airspace, especially as swifter planes overtook slower aircraft. The quality of the Saudi radar facilities ranged from new and excellent, like those at Jeddah and Riyadh, to antiquated and less capable ones, like those at Khamis Mushait, Taif, and Tabuk. Communications did not always link radar sites, and large radar and radio gaps existed across the peninsula.[92]

Over many weeks, CENTAF personnel assisted the Saudis with improving their air traffic system by providing and installing radio equipment, training controllers, supervising operations, and performing control functions. Using the computerized Combat Airspace Deconfliction System (CADS), CENTAF eventually assumed management over the entire airspace control process in Saudi Arabia. A versatile system, CADS plotted and reserved airspace for refueling tracks, air transit routes, CAPs, missile engagement zones, restricted operating zones, strike and other corridors, Patriot missile zones, minimum-risk routes, restricted-fire areas, and no-fire areas.[93]

The CENTAF staff clearly understood that it had to painstakingly coordinate with the governments of allied countries as they based aircraft, built an air defense system, assisted with air traffic control, and generated ATOs, which included an airspace control order. They made their first international contacts with Egypt and members of the GCC. Because CENTCOM had not submitted its OPLAN 1002–90 to any of these nations, the staff negotiated everything from scratch during the early days of Desert Shield.[94] While GCC nations promptly gave permission for the first U.S. aircraft to land at bases and airports, follow-on sorties and activity required careful, detailed negotiation by CENTCOM and CENTAF representatives, U.S. embassy personnel, and host-nation authorities. In theory, the Saudi air defense system tied into the GCC system, but in fact the

GCC countries had not initiated standard, allied air defense operations, nor had they established effective communication links between national systems. CENTCOM and CENTAF staff members spent many hours and days addressing issues and solving problems associated with Coalition air operations.[95] For air traffic control, CENTAF liaison teams traveled to host nations to answer questions about operations, clarify jargon and language problems, and solve problems concerning flight clearances, routes, and plans. At some sites where they found inadequate host-nation air traffic control capability, they established elaborate field-control facilities.[96]

CENTAF–Component Interaction

The wide scope of the JFACC's responsibilities in planning the defense of Saudi Arabia required that the CENTAF staff coordinate constantly with the CENTCOM component commands. CENTAF secured the Navy's participation in the ATO process even as NAVCENT made its first attempts to enforce United Nations Security Council Resolution 661 approved on August 6, 1990, imposing an embargo on Iraq. By August 7 the Navy had increased its presence in the region when the USS *Independence* carrier battle group arrived in the Gulf of Oman, having sailed from the Indian Ocean a few days earlier. The *Independence* operated closely with the ships in the Persian Gulf in the JTFME, commanded by Rear Adm. William M. Fogarty. The USS *Dwight D. Eisenhower* carrier group then sailed from the eastern Mediterranean through the Suez Canal to the Red Sea.[97]

The Desert Shield OPORD had tasked the commander of the JTFME with operational and tactical control of all U.S. naval forces entering the AOR, except Navy special operations forces.[98] Usually, the commander of the Middle East Force served as the NAVCENT commander; however, the Navy did not follow this arrangement for Desert Shield. It selected a more senior officer, Vice Adm. Henry H. Mauz, Jr., Commander of the Seventh Fleet in Hawaii, for the position. Mauz deployed by air to the Gulf with key members of his Seventh Fleet staff on August 15. They set up NAVCENT headquarters on the USS *LaSalle*, the flagship of the JTFME, until the Seventh Fleet command ship, USS *Blue Ridge*, arrived in the Gulf on September 1.[99] When he first visited Horner in Riyadh, Mauz, a surface warfare officer, asked that CENTAF adopt air route packages similar to those used in the Vietnam War. Horner passionately replied, "Don't ever talk to me about it again because we're not going to do it! I'll resign first." Noting the air leader's strong feeling about the route packs, the admiral dropped the request.[100]

On August 11 Chairman Powell issued an alert order that announced, "The Secretary of Defense has authorized execution planning for a maritime interdiction operation to enforce an economic quarantine of Iraq/Kuwait in support of Operation Desert Shield." On August 16 President Bush ordered the embargo enforced. Forces in the AOR went on alert on August 17 when the USS *Reid*, a frigate, fired warning shots across the bow of a fully loaded Iraqi oil tanker heading south in the Persian Gulf. The tanker's captain communicated with Baghdad and radioed a message of defiance to the *Reid*. U.S. naval authorities in the Gulf directly communicated with Schwarzkopf in Florida, who talked with Powell in the Pentagon. The CINCCENT telephoned Horner to warn him that the Iraqis might attack and that naval and air forces should be ready to launch retaliatory strikes. Horner and Olsen worked to ensure that adequate force could strike with minimal warning.

At CENTCOM headquarters at MacDill AFB, tension ran high, and Maj. Gen. Robert B. Johnston, USMC, CENTCOM Chief of Staff, thought war with Iraq imminent. An officer on watch duty at the time recalled, "When we fired across bows, many thought the balloon was going up, and we didn't want it to, because [there was] not en[ough] strength on [the] ground." Col. Ervin C. Sharpe, commander of the 354th Tactical Fighter Wing, whose A–10s were near the Iraqi border at King Fahd International Airport, received a call from Horner. "You are in a very tight situation. Be prepared to fight or evacuate," the general told him. The 354th readied itself to fly and fight.[101] As the crisis unfolded, the Joint Staff ordered NAVCENT not to sink the oil tanker without permission from the President. The immediate crisis passed when Powell relayed word from Bush to break off the engagement and continue only to track the ship as the Security Council debated another resolution authorizing the use of force to implement the first one related to the embargo. The second resolution, 665, passed August 25.[102]

The embargo moved to the forefront during JFACC–Navy discussions of numerous questions about air support for naval operations and the location of CAPs, coordination and ownership of airspace, location and number of air tanker tracks, and C^2 procedures. At Horner's urging, General Olsen pressed the Navy for more information on its embargo plans and operations so that if the JFACC had to support it with CAPs and tankers, he would have as much advanced planning time as possible. Olsen talked frequently with Brig. Gen. Buster C. Glosson, USAF, JTFME deputy commander, whom, within a few days, Horner would call to Riyadh to plan the JFACC's offensive campaign.[103]

During the night of August 19, Rear Adm. Timothy W. Wright arrived in Saudi Arabia to be the NAVCENT's personal representative in Riyadh, and he initiated steps to provide regular briefings to CENTAF about embargo operations.[104] On August 21 the Navy flew its first sorties through Saudi airspace from the Red Sea, and these were officially in the JFACC's ATO, scrutinized and approved by RSAF authorities. During Desert Shield, Navy flights off the carriers in the Red Sea appeared in the ATO, while those from carriers in the Gulf of Oman, and later from those in the Persian Gulf, generally did not. This was so because Red Sea sorties usually involved flying over Saudi territory, whereas those from the Gulf carriers overflew water. Consequently, the Red Sea naval airmen gained valuable experience with the ATO process, which their counterparts in the Gulf of Oman–Persian Gulf area lacked.[105]

MARCENT's concerns about the JFACC's span of control centered on the number of Marine aircraft tasked in the ATO. On August 8, the same day he pinned on his third star, Lt. Gen. Walter E. Boomer assumed command of the I Marine Expeditionary Force, comprising MARCENT, the Marine Corps' CENTCOM component.[106] Boomer espoused the view that the JFACC would never *command* Marine air but would and should *coordinate* air assets. He stated, "Someone must coordinate all of that aviation, and 99 times out of 100 he will — and should — come from the U.S. Air Force. Marines don't, or they should not, have a problem with JFACC." Horner did not debate whether the JFACC functioned as a commander or coordinator of Marine air: rather, he focused on getting that air power into the ATO and acquiring the sorties from the Marines consistent with the CINCCENT's guidance. When Boomer first met with the CENTCOM Forward commander in theater he recalled Horner telling him, "I don't want to take OPCON of your airplanes. All I want to do is work together and win this war." Boomer observed that Marines hate to give up any fixed air, because, unlike the Army, they had no tactical missile systems or massive fleets of helicopters. His staff had urged him to negotiate for the route pack system, but because Horner firmly opposed it, he conceded on the ATO. Throughout Desert Shield, at the component command level, the JFACC–MARCENT interaction remained cordial. Persistent quibbling occurred at the level where staffs hammered out air defense, airspace control, and ATO agreements; however, Boomer noted that the trust between himself and Horner kept the quibbling to a minimum.[107]

Lacking squadrons of fixed-wing aircraft, ARCENT's first encounter in theater with the JFACC's planning process involved coordination on air defenses and identification of missile engagement zones. The coordination on the use of Hawks and Patriots went smoothly, with the primary discussion centering on where to locate the Patriot batteries. During Desert Shield, the Army selected as the FSCL the international boundary line between Saudi Arabia and Kuwait, formed by a continuous 8- to 10-foot-high sand berm, easily seen from the air. According to joint doctrine, the ground commander chose the FSCL after coordination with the JFACC. Horner concurred with the political boundary as the coordination line because it was a recognizable geographic feature. It also ensured that he would know of any Army movements north of the boundary. He believed that once in battle, the corps commander should avoid establishing the FSCL too much farther beyond the forward line of troops than the range of his artillery. He also thought ARCENT should include its helicopters in the ATO if they flew beyond the FSCL, but knowing the Army's opposition to this idea, he never made an issue of their inclusion, and the helicopters stayed out of the tasking order throughout Desert Shield and Desert Storm.[108] The JFACC explained his view about the helicopters, especially the AH–64 Apache tank killers:

> Basically, if it's inside the fire support coordination line, don't bother to tell me. If it's over the fire support coordination line, put it in the ATO.

> Get the air cover; get the ECM support; get the TOT [time over target]; get the coordination; get all the benefits from that — and the Army aviation guys understand it — but the trouble is, the ground Army is afraid they are going to have an Army Air Corps that is going to want to be a separate service, which is exactly right because air power should not be run by ground guys, any more than ground ought to be run by air guys. Is that parochial? Sure. Is it common sense? Yes. Does history tell us that's the way we do it? Yes.[109]

ARCENT did include fixed-wing aircraft in the ATO, and when Horner asked one Army controller in the TACC about the level of cooperation from Army pilots flying airplanes, the answer delighted him. Horner remembered the crusty older major explaining to him that he simply assigned embarrassing call signs, like Yellow Belly or Coward, to anyone not following airspace management procedures. He rewarded cooperation with call signs such as Courageous, Bayonet, and Charger. He experienced no trouble in obtaining compliance.[110]

CENTAF staff coordinated with personnel from SOCCENT about search and rescue (SAR) and combat search and rescue (CSAR). CENTCOM had dispersed responsibility for these functions among the component commands, and the commanders with partial responsibility held differing views on how they should train for and execute rescue operations. CENTCOM specifically delegated major SAR and CSAR responsibilities to both CENTAF and SOCCENT without stipulating chain-of-command relationships nor providing the mechanisms to facilitate a reconciliation of differing command procedures.

The CENTCOM OPORD of August 10 designated the CENTAF commander as the CSAR coordinator for CENTCOM, stating,

> He may direct components to conduct CSAR operations on a mission-priority basis and has authority to use assets from any component for CSAR operations assuring that assets required for CSAR are not diverted from component commander missions with a higher USCINCCENT established priority.

The order specifically directed that the CENTAF commander assume responsibility for CSAR operations, and it stipulated that the JFACC assume command, less OPCON, of Air Force SOF upon their entry into the AOR. The four components of SOCCENT provided the command its personnel: Army Special Operations Forces Task Force; the Naval Special Weapons Task Group; the Air Force Special Operations Command, Central; and a special forces group. The OPORD also levied CSAR responsibilities on the commander of SOCCENT.[111]

SOCCENT controlled the aircraft best suited for performing CSAR in a very hostile environment with its all-weather radar-evading, combat- and night-capable helicopters equipped with sophisticated communication systems: MH–53s, MH–60s, and MH–47s. The CENTAF commander depended on SOCCENT assets for rescues, but SOCCENT did not consistently make its aircraft available to the JFACC nor allow its flights to appear in the ATO. CSAR was not the only mission SOCCENT had to execute. During Desert Shield, for example, SOCCENT's forces were tasked to plan a direct-action mission to rescue personnel in the U.S. and British embassies in Kuwait City. The command planned and conducted twenty-three rehearsals involving all forces included in the operation. The Air Force SOF firmly declined to participate in the ATO process for these exercises, in part, for fear of compromising a highly secret, dangerous mission.[112]

Air Force SOF tried to plan CSAR around nighttime pickups of downed crew members; maintain autonomy of SOCCENT to decide which CSAR missions it could conduct, based on the threat; and adhere to strict secrecy about mission planning, withholding information requested by the rescue specialists in the TACC and the ATO builders. Some CENTAF staff thought that SOCCENT tended to plan CSAR missions as if they were recovery operations to retrieve commandos from reconnaissance and covert missions behind enemy lines. CENTAF, on the other hand, wanted SOCCENT to conduct *rescue* operations, which would entail picking up crews at all times of the day and night, closely coordinating with the CSAR specialists in the TACC, positioning SOF aircraft close to the combat areas and having them on ground alert, and providing relevant data to ATO builders and TACC operators to preclude friendly fire and airspace control accidents.[113]

By August 28 Maj. Thomas J. Stilwell, one of CENTAF's rescue experts, arrived in Riyadh, and following directives in CENTCOM regulations and a joint CSAR document recently produced by Air Force and Army through the Air-Land Forces Application Agency at Langley AFB, Virginia, he requested that component commands send representatives to augment CENTCOM's Joint Rescue Coordination Center (JRCC), located within the TACC. Because of staff shortages, ARCENT and NAVCENT did not immediately comply with the request, but MARCENT and SOCCENT did. The SOCCENT representatives, however, were pararescue personnel, not controllers, so their ability to facilitate the launching of rescue missions was limited.[114]

The Air Force's Air Rescue Service (ARS), located at McClellan AFB, California, sent personnel to augment the JRCC, and they arrived on September 4, led by Lt. Col. Joseph Hampton, who assumed command of the JRCC. Throughout Desert Shield, ARS deployed pilots, flight engineers, pararescue specialists, intelligence officers, administrative staff, and rescue controllers to the theater, but no aircraft. An Air Staff decision prevented the call-up of ARS National Guard and Reserve personnel. Most people staffing the JRCC understood peacetime SAR, but did not understand CSAR operations. Indeed, personnel in component Rescue Coordination Centers and crews manning AWACS, who coordinated searches and assets and provided communication relays to the JRCC, had to quickly learn CSAR procedures.[115]

From September through early November, the JRCC drafted and coordinated the theater air rescue plan. Generals Horner and al-Buhairi approved and signed it November 1, 1990. It defined the CSAR area of operations, assigned and described organizational responsibilities, identified the capabilities of Coalition forces, described operating procedures, discussed missions for medical evacuation and for locating emergency transmitters, and provided reporting and documentation forms. The Saudis, British, and French provided inputs. By the start of Desert Storm, nineteen people manned the JRCC. Included were individuals from the Coalition forces and those forming the JRCC's intelligence cell and the element for survival, evasion, resistance, and escape. As JRCC commander, Colonel Hampton reported to two bosses, to Colonel Crigger on the CENTAF staff and to the CSAR point-of-contact in the CENTCOM Joint Operations Center in the MODA building.[116]

Desert Shield Training

Over the 5½ months of Desert Shield, Coalition air forces flew massive numbers of training sorties in the AOR, and the daily ATOs incorporated the flights. Eventually, exercises corresponded to the types of missions the units would fly in offensive combat operations, but initially, training simply enabled pilots to adjust to the desert environment. Col. David A. Sawyer, commander of the 23d Tactical Fighter Wing flying A–10s recalled:

> The real danger while operating at lower altitudes out here was that you cannot perceive the horizon.... We needed to religiously fly our altitude on instruments, and we couldn't depend on going lower and estimating our altitudes above the ground. As a result, we started out flying at a higher altitude from the very beginning. We had a 1,000-foot minimum on our operations to start here. We then went down to 500 feet. That is OK, but there is no shrubbery, nothing to estimate your height above the ground.[117]

Unit training developed from simple training regimens to more complex ones, taking into account host-nation restrictions. On August 18, in response to Saudi concerns about excessive flying activity alarming the Saudi population, Horner formally prohibited low-level and supersonic flying; in addition, he disallowed CENTAF aircraft from dropping live ordnance during training operations. Units had not anticipated the long Desert Shield buildup of forces and had deployed ready to fight; thus, they arrived in theater with no training ordnance, only live munitions, necessitating simulated weapons delivery.[118]

On August 21 Major General Olsen reached agreement with the RSAF's director of operations, whereby they established training areas in Saudi Arabia south of the 27th parallel. By September the units clamoring to fly in the northeast airspace grew so numerous that the Saudi commander there ordered his staff to establish additional training areas, and he scheduled flights by weekly blocks of time. In October CENTAF commenced live-weapons training. It also created a new organization within the TACC, a peacetime operational planning staff, to negotiate and develop procedures for using ranges, acquiring training munitions, and accomplishing exercise objectives.[119]

On September 8, CENTAF commenced package training in which aircraft with various missions, like air-to-air and air-to-ground, and support flew together. Planners also put sorties in the ATO to simulate attacking enemy aircraft. On September 12 the training expanded to include Coalition aircraft. The ATO included B–52s from Diego Garcia for battlefield air interdiction, but they also received tasking to strike two Iraqi main operating bases, in coordination with carrier naval aircraft. For these attacks, the Navy acted as the package commander, which meant that the naval officers studied the targets and threats and planned the attack using all assets assigned to the mission. To lessen confusion, STRATFOR representatives visited planners aboard carriers and developed tactics for the joint strike operations. When a carrier swap-out occurred, however, STRATFOR planners had to renegotiate tactics with Navy planners aboard replacement carriers. Commencing October 24, Initial Hack, the largest exercise to date, ostensibly tested D-day missions and tactics, but it actually flew operations required for the offensive air campaign, focusing on C^2 and air refueling and involving 282 fighter sorties, 48 CAP flights, and 88 tanker and 13 AWACS missions.[120]

The CENTAF staff built the foundation for the Gulf War air campaign by establishing and testing the operational systems and procedures required to successfully execute air operations. Early on, they focused on uniting Coalition forces in a defensive mode while setting in place the people, equipment, procedures, and orders that would support an offensive air campaign.

Chapter Five

JFACC and Instant Thunder

While General Horner functioned as the CENTCOM Forward commander in Saudi Arabia, the CINCCENT in Florida turned to the Air Staff for an air option in case Saddam Hussein's forces committed further aggression. Under Colonel Warden's leadership, Checkmate produced Instant Thunder, and Schwarzkopf told the colonel to travel to Saudi Arabia to present the strategic air campaign briefing to Horner, who would turn it into a real-world plan. In Riyadh, when Warden discussed his ideas with the CENTAF staff, key officers welcomed him and hoped he would remain in theater and continue the offensive planning effort. Horner, however, disagreed with major assertions in Instant Thunder and thought that the Air Staff colonel presented only a partial answer to the requirement for an offensive air campaign. The lieutenant general then summoned General Glosson to Riyadh to head the Special Planning Group.

CENTAF Staff and Instant Thunder

On Sunday, August 19, the Air Staff Instant Thunder planners, Colonels Warden, Deptula, Harvey, and Stanfill, landed in Riyadh at 1730 after an 18-hour flight. During the trip, the planners reviewed the Instant Thunder briefing slides and discussed their strategy for presenting their air campaign plan to Horner. Some of the officers catnapped, but none slept soundly, though they had put in eighteen-hour days during the previous week and had gotten no sleep the night of August 16/17 as they finalized their briefing to meet General Meier's specifications before making their second and final presentation to the CINCCENT on Friday, August 17, at MacDill AFB.[1]

The Air Staff officers briefed Instant Thunder to key members of the CENTAF staff prior to Warden's major presentation to Horner, and the initial sessions proceeded cordially. Warden and his deputies explained the plan to General Olsen, who functioned as CENTAF commander while Horner assumed the re-

Lt. Col. Bernard E. Harvey, Col. John A. Warden III, Lt. Col. David A. Deptula, and Lt. Col. Ronnie A. Stanfill (left to right) en route to Riyadh, Saudi Arabia, to brief the Instant Thunder plan to Lt. Gen. Charles A. Horner.

sponsibilities of CENTCOM Forward commander; General Caruana, STRATFOR commander; General Henry, director of CENTAF's EC cell; Colonel Crigger, director of CENTAF operations; Colonel Leonardo, director of CENTAF/IN; Colonel Baptiste, director of CENTAF combat plans; and Lt. Col. Steven G. Wilson, an Air Staff officer recently arrived in theater.[2]

Key officers at CENTAF headquarters already knew quite a bit about Instant Thunder. Caruana, Leonardo, and Baptiste had been prebriefed on the concepts before the arrival of the Checkmate team. Caruana had heard about it from SAC headquarters. Baptiste had attended a briefing on Instant Thunder which Colonel Wilson had presented to Horner the previous week. General Adams had sent Wilson and a very early draft of the document to keep Horner fully apprised of the Air Staff's progress with developing the strategic air campaign that Schwarzkopf had requested. Adams explained, "What I was trying to do is give Horner a heads-up on what his boss was seeing, because his boss got enthusiastic about the plan." Leonardo had first learned of the effort shortly before he deployed, when Colonel Blackburn, director of the AFIA Directorate of Targets, telephoned him at Shaw AFB and asked him to send CENTAF's target lists to Checkmate for use in developing a target base. The CENTAF material had supported the CENTCOM 1002–90 OPLAN and the Punishment ATO, the retaliatory targeting that General Horner had requested of his staff in early August.[3]

Warden began his briefing to Olsen and the others by explaining that the CINCCENT had requested the plan, that Checkmate had been part of a joint effort to produce it, and that he offered it in the spirit, "If it makes sense, use it; if not, chuck it." The colonel's presentation generated a blend of questions and comments and progressed smoothly.[4]

Olsen asked for more details about telecommunications targets, pointing out that they were often sheltered in hardened, underground facilities. Warden acknowledged this but noted that the emphasis was on "creating and exploiting confusion," not on destroying those sites. The general raised the problem of the Iraqi ground forces advancing into Saudi Arabia, and Warden responded that CIA, DIA, and Checkmate assessments indicated that air forces could stop the Iraqi offense.[5] General Caruana queried whether Instant Thunder could be launched earlier than October 7, the date by which the Army said it could stop an Iraqi ground assault. Warden's answer got everyone's undivided attention: Instant Thunder could be executed in mid-September. He explained that by August 19, CENTCOM already had enough aircraft and weapons in theater to execute the plan, even with the problem of "mixing, matching, and moving" assets to the appropriate bases. He did call attention to the number of HARMs in the AOR comprising one of the strategic campaign's LIMFACs. Olsen explained that CENTAF expected the arrival of about 130 missiles within four days, and Warden noted that the total number would then reach approximately 600, which would be "more than enough" to execute the plan. Another LIMFAC focused on deploying sufficient aircraft and weapons for precision strikes, which led to a discussion of laser-guided munition–capable F–111Fs, in contrast with F–111Ds which lacked precision delivery capability. Colonel Crigger noted that Horner had already instructed the staff to acquire F–111Fs from RAF Lakenheath, United Kingdom.[6]

Caruana inquired if officials in Washington expressed concern about the balance of power in the Middle East after the destruction of Iraq. Warden answered affirmatively, noting that Chairman Powell had observed that Iran was too weak to fill the power vacuum. Caruana also questioned whether the Navy had a separate planning group for the air campaign. The answer given was that the Air Force functioned as the "executive agent" for Instant Thunder and that Navy personnel had assisted in developing the plan.[7] When Caruana queried if a basic assumption of the plan was "no ground war," Warden explained that Schwarzkopf and Powell saw no need to weaken the strategic campaign by diverting air power to attack ground forces, and he then described the "aerial Schlieffen" concept.[8] Olsen stated that the Saudis were beginning to realize that they would have to hold some forces in reserve and "give up some sand" to prevent a breakthrough. Warden pointed out that a "huge number" of Air Force, Marine Corps, Navy, and Saudi aircraft, in excess of Instant Thunder requirements, was available to check an Iraqi ground advance.[9]

General Henry raised the issue of SEAD and suggested that if Iraq put any more SAMs into Kuwait, the small nation would sink. He expressed some concern about what he termed "route packs" assigned to the Air Force, Navy, and Marine Corps. He asked, too, about Turkey and its role in the campaign. Warden responded that Turkey and the second front it represented presented a nasty problem for Iraq but that, at present, Turkey refrained from actively supporting the Coalition. The ensuing discussion led the colonel to state his view that if Iraq pulled its troops from Kuwait, the political will in the United States and international community to punish Iraq's aggression would dissipate. Most in the room seemed to agree that time was on Saddam Hussein's side in terms of the Coalition's cohesiveness.[10]

Warden offered the view that bringing allied members into the strategic air campaign would be "difficult." Olsen replied that just that day he had been talking with British officials about sending into the theater GR–1 Tornados, which employed mines and cratering bomblets against air bases. This led to discussion about hitting airfields, during which Warden and Caruana strongly agreed that airfields comprised an essential target set. Crigger and Wilson noted that hitting some airfields would prevent the Iraqis from delivering CW.[11] Warden described mobile Scuds as a "real problem." Sharing information from SAC relating to mobile and fixed Scud launchers, he suggested using AC–130s against the mobile missile targets.[12]

During the briefing, Olsen and Crigger responded favorably to the planners and their product. Olsen asked Warden if he had brought more than three days' worth of clothing because he wanted the colonel and his deputies to remain in Riyadh and further develop their plan, which was a "good start." Otherwise, he would have to pull CENTAF people from other jobs to work it. Olsen, as Deptula recalled, "mentioned that this was exactly what they would have liked to have done, too, but they simply ran out of time and became focused on the near-term." Deptula also remembered Olsen saying, "We purposely have not taken anything deep. To do this we'd have to pull people out of what they're currently doing — planning for defense — to make this happen. When we get done with the support of the ground war, then we can do some thinking about a deep war." Crigger stated that after the strategic campaign's execution, "lots of [Iraqi] ground power" would be "left over." He thought Instant Thunder would "operate well" with the defensive campaign. Near the end of the session, he offered the comment that Horner had stated that he wanted to turn the Air Staff plan into an ATO. Olsen told Warden that "we" and "you" need to work together. He would arrange for the colonel to meet with Horner sometime the next morning. Until then, the Air Staff team should get some rest.[13]

Leaving the RSAF building shortly after midnight, the group drove to the White Palace Hotel, but not before getting lost and driving around Riyadh for well over an hour. Eventually arriving at their destination, the men were dismayed to hear that the hotel had given away their rooms. With some cajoling, the clerk offered them cots in the main ballroom, where about 300 GIs were already billeted. After about three hours' sleep, the planners arose and met for breakfast and a discussion of the objectives for briefing Horner. They hoped to obtain his acceptance of the Instant Thunder concept, secure the order to have F–111Fs arrive in theater instead of F–111Ds, and have the deployment flow expedited so that air forces would be in place and ready to execute Instant Thunder as soon as possible.[14]

The group drove to the RSAF building where they met with Colonel Wilson. Five days earlier, accompanied by Baptiste, Wilson had given the Instant Thunder briefing slides to Horner in his office in the MODA building. Right from the start, the general severely lectured Wilson on the responsibilities of the Air Staff and those of the JFACC. Planning and war fighting comprised JFACC duties, and the officers in Washington were not the war fighters and should not plan an air campaign and select targets. It was the problem of the Vietnam War all over again: officials in Washington interfering with theater operations.[15] While the general flipped through the slides, Wilson talked about the plan, which at that time presented an early formulation of the Instant Thunder concepts, and he repeated what he could remember from the tutorials Deptula and others had given him on it. Wilson remembered the general belittling the plan's "college-boy" terms, such as "center of gravity" (which appeared prominently in Army doctrine). Baptiste remembered Horner throwing the briefing across the room.[16]

On August 20, Wilson cautioned Warden and his Air Staff colleagues to expect a negative reaction from Horner as they briefed their ideas to him. As Deptula remembered his meeting with Wilson that morning, he recounted:

> Steve was extremely frustrated and irritated, because he was getting slow rolled and ignored, I guess, and had been for about the past week. His bottom line was that there was no leadership, that the [CEN]TAF staff was wandering adrift with no focus. The combat operations staff is working on an immediate problem: what if the Iraqis cross the line with tanks, but nobody was thinking of the long term. The total effort was directed at tactical level details and no strategic plan or thought on how to employ air power offensively.[17]

Wilson also remembered Horner saying that Instant Thunder "wouldn't work," that it would force the Iraqis to attack Saudi Arabia.[18]

Wilson correctly stated that the CENTAF staff focused on a defensive plan, not an offensive one. Olsen and Crigger believed that time and manpower prevented them from developing plans simultaneously for offensive and defensive contingencies. In their minds, the offensive effort required more deep, high-value, strategic targeting than a defensive campaign required. Their objection to such targeting was not that it did not conform to the Army's AirLand Battle doctrine or support the Army's scheme of maneuver. They, in fact, agreed with Instant Thunder's strategic targeting. They lacked the means and time to develop the offensive approach and thought the Air Staff effort would complement their defensive preparations against the Iraqi ground forces. The CENTCOM mission OPORD of August 10, 1990, under which they deployed, required them to produce a defensive plan, which constituted their primary mission as of August 20. After hearing Warden's evening presentation on August 19, the CENTAF staff members welcomed the Air Staff officers to undertake offensive planning. Warden recalled, "We went through the Schwarzkopf briefing with the guys. They all seemed very enthusiastic, very positive; no negatives. The reception was good."[19]

In the morning of August 20, the Air Staff officers met with Maj. Horst A. Roehler, who discussed the D-day game plan. Warden asked many questions, starting with CENTAF's assessment of how the Iraqis would array themselves if they attacked Saudi Arabia and what would be their expected rate of advance. The major stated that they would march in columns. During the Iran-Iraq War, the Iraqis had failed to meet their objective of 45 kilometers a day, thus CENTAF concluded that their best rate would be 20 to 30 kilometers per day. Warden queried about air superiority. Roehler noted that they had none but added that they were increasing the number of defensive SAM sites around their deployed troops. The colonel inquired about SAM altitude ranges, CENTAF sortie and tank-killing rates, and the mobile SAM umbrella. After more discussion, Warden concluded that the D-day plan looked "pretty solid, you've got 'em."[20] His final questions concerned whether CENTAF had any "preemptive considerations" and if the command had any attrition modeling capabilities. Roehler answered both questions negatively.[21]

The Air Staff planners met early in the afternoon in General Olsen's office and discussed requirements for executing Instant Thunder with Colonels Crigger and Rider. After a short discussion about logistics, Warden suggested that he brief the plan to the CENTAF wing and squadron commanders. Crigger disapproved of the idea, wanting the wings, as Deptula recalled, "to be concentrating on what they're doing now, flying their CAPs for the AWACS and setting up their own individual areas and getting used to where they are."[22] Rider noted that CENTAF not only executed air operations, but it also supported the Army's deployment and buildup in theater. Warden asked if they had any suggestions for improving Instant Thunder, and Crigger did. He explained that he thought the capability of the air forces to operate at night was "very limited" and that instead of two attack waves the first night, there ought to be one just before dawn and then a second in daylight, and a redeployment of A–10s and F–16s to repel a possible Iraqi counterattack. Crigger also suggested that Warden scrub his plan with CENTAF/IN, reach agreement on targets, refine the target list, and freeze the list by the following week. Again, the session had gone amicably and smoothly, with no one objecting to Instant Thunder because of its strategic focus.[23]

Colonel Warden Briefs General Horner

Olsen scheduled the Instant Thunder briefing for General Horner in the afternoon of Monday, August 20. Previously, the CENTCOM Forward commander had learned quite a bit about the Air Staff plan from telephone calls from Generals Schwarzkopf, Dugan, Adams, Russ, and Ryan; from the personal briefing on its concepts from Colonel Wilson; and from a message about it from General Griffith, the TAC DCS for plans, who offered TAC's comments on Instant Thunder and the command's alternative strategy. Horner had forwarded the message and the TAC plan to Olsen, with the written comment, "Do with this what you wish. How can a person in an ivory tower far from the front not knowing what needs to be done (guidance) write such a message? Wonders never cease."[24] Horner disliked officers at TAC headquarters' developing war plans as much as he disapproved of the Air Staff's direct involvement in such activity.

Warden's Instant Thunder briefing to Horner began at 1355 in a conference room next to Olsen's office in the RSAF building. Those in attendance included Generals Olsen, Caruana, and Henry; Colonels Crigger, Leonardo, Rider, Baptiste, and Wilson; Maj. John Turk, a CENTAF officer who had assisted in Checkmate as the plan developed; and the four Air Staff officers.[25] Although Wilson had cautioned Warden to expect a negative reaction from Horner, the key Instant Thunder planner considered that the CENTAF staff the night before and that morning had given his plan a good hearing. He thought it probable that the general would ask him to remain in theater to finalize the strategic air campaign.[26] He desired that outcome.[27]

When Horner arrived from the MODA building, came into the conference room, and sat down, two viewpoints conflicted him. First, he was still annoyed and angry at the Air Staff for, from his perspective, usurping the JFACC's responsibility for air war planning. The specter of Lyndon Johnson picking targets and the unreasonable rules of engagement during the Vietnam War haunted him, as did the disastrous raid he had flown in July 1965 against fake SAM sites — a mission planned, in part, in Washington, without more input from the pilots whose lives were at stake. He wanted to use the briefing to send a message to the Air Staff leaders, "Don't do any more planning. Stay out of CENTAF's business." He wanted to reject the plan and the planners.[28]

On the other hand, as Horner's deputy, General Olsen, had clearly pointed out, Warden and his team should stay in Riyadh to continue developing the plan they had brought to the theater. The CENTAF staff was overwhelmed with work, stretched to the breaking point, and needed the help the Air Staff officers could provide. The CINCCENT himself had sent the plan. Horner knew the Air Staff officers could beneficially augment the CENTAF planning staff at this critical time. Therefore, the briefing would include Horner "interviewing" Warden, whom he did not know, to see if he could work with him.[29]

To begin the session, Warden placed a couple of boxes of candy on the table in front of Horner. "What is this shit?" the general inquired. The colonel explained that General Adams had sent the boxes and a bag full of lip balm, razor blades, and suntan lotion for the use of CENTAF personnel because these were scarce items in theater. Horner spurned the offering and ordered, "Proceed."[30] Warden thought the gifts' icy reception gave his presentation a "bad start."[31] To Deptula, "very tense" best described the atmosphere in the room.[32]

Warden rapidly delivered the briefing in its entirety.[33] He described Instant Thunder as a war-winning plan.[34] General Henry clearly remembered him characterizing it as a six-day bombing campaign that would force the Iraqis to capitulate.[35] The colonel did not explain that Instant Thunder was a retaliatory option for use if Saddam Hussein executed hostages or used CW, as Schwarzkopf viewed the situation. Neither did he indicate that the CINCCENT wanted Horner to turn the Air Staff effort into a real-world plan, as the CENTCOM commander had expressed it on August 17. Warden described his campaign as he understood it, and he presented it just as he had in the briefing to Schwarzkopf three days earlier.[36]

Looking through the pages, Horner's first comment noted that Saddam Hussein was "bunkered up" and that time was on "our side strategically," not on Saddam's, as the briefing stated. When discussion led to the use of PGMs, the general corrected Warden by explaining the importance of precision *delivery* of weapons; he alluded to the difficulty of hitting radio towers in Vietnam. The colonel agreed but also said that the Vietnam experience highlighted the need for sophisticated *weapons*. With the mention of precision delivery, Deptula remembered hearing other Air Force leaders — especially those from TAC — espouse the value of precision delivery of weapons instead of precision weapons per se. They explained that it was cheaper to have specially configured platforms, such as F–16s, deliver nonprecision, or "dumb," bombs, than to have aircraft deliver "smart," or guided, weapons.[37] Throughout Desert Storm, most F–16s, the Air Force's most numerous aircraft, would fly without PGM capability.

Horner next stated that he had "a little trouble" with Instant Thunder's basic premise of "severing the head from the body." He believed that in the short term, the plan might work, but over the long term, say, in twenty years, it would prove disastrous, creating "hatred against America." He then asked if the planners had done any analysis on "neutralizing" instead of directly "taking out" the air defense system. To Deptula, the general suggested that "perhaps this was too much directed at the destruction of the air defense network, and we didn't necessarily have to do all that." As discussion proceeded, Warden stated that a 35 percent to 40 percent level of effort attacked aircraft on the ground, and Horner suggested that that "may be a poor way" to dedicate assets, and he directed Colonel Crigger to examine that problem.[38]

The general returned to the issue that seemed to bother him the most — targeting Saddam Hussein. He asked about the level of effort trying to "kill him" and asked if the planners had studied Saddam's C^2 systems, because, failing to kill the Iraqi leader, the campaign must "destroy" his C^2. Warden acknowledged that the studies used in Checkmate were not that good, and Horner immediately tasked Colonel Leonardo to "study his C^2." Warden explained that the plan assumed "we would not totally isolate" Saddam. The general replied that the C^2 *must* be destroyed. Warden cautioned him about the difficulty of trying to completely destroy such a system and guaranteeing its destruction. Horner told him it was not his job to do that; it was CENTAF's responsibility. He stated that Warden had produced an "academic study," but that he would "make it a reality."[39]

The general then asked a series of questions that Warden answered: What's the goal of attacking railroads? Why attack ports? Why use TLAMs — they lacked a powerful warhead — for initial strikes in highly defended areas?[40] Why Volant Solo?[41] He directed Colonel Leonardo to study military storage versus production facilities.[42] The briefing item about using multinational forces interested him, and Warden explained that Chairman Powell had commented that non-Americans had "to bleed and die" too, if American lives were at risk.[43] When Horner observed the availability of three carrier battle groups, he noted, the "budget battle must be getting tough."[44] Deptula recalled that during the ensuing discussion, Warden referred often to strategic perspective, and the general interrupted, saying, "Well look, let's not use the terms 'strategic' and 'tactical.' Targets are targets."[45] The questions continued: What does night buy you? Why use cruise missiles? "Let's be honest," he said, "[their use is] an attempt to sell a weapon."[46] When Horner saw Instant Thunder's partitioning of airspace to the Air Force, Marine Corps, and Navy on the basis of geographic sectors, he sternly directed, "Don't deconflict by route packages. We did that in Vietnam; we'll never do that again."[47] He observed that the plan was unclear and "faulty" on the concepts of trying to overwhelm the enemy versus applying continuous pressure against him. He directed Crigger and Leonardo to "wrestle" with the ideas of "overwhelm" versus "sustain."[48]

Next came discussion of PSYOPS, a "critical element" in Instant Thunder, but not developed by the planners. Horner inquired about who would develop the PSYOPS campaign. Deptula recalled, "Warden's response was not really a clean answer: the Army, the Air Force, and whoever else you want." The general also asked about the extent the plan depended on PSYOPS and if Warden attempted to change the Iraqi government, to which the colonel replied, "Yes."[49] Horner doubted that the planners understood "the Iraqi mind." Warden agreed but did offer that in Checkmate they had studied information from an Iraqi defector.[50]

In discussing LIMFACs, the issue of F–111Fs arose. Olsen stated that the deployment now included those aircraft. Horner noted too that the JRCC was also on its way to collocate with the TACC.[51]

Returning to the concepts of the plan, Horner stated his view that the Air Staff planners' "main effort was to do targeting." He suggested that they needed to "rethink" their "targeting philosophy" and "timeline" in the deployment data. Warden asserted that the goal was a mid-September execution and that "everyone" drove toward that time period. Horner replied that an "armored division" (referring to the 24th Infantry Division, Mechanized), would arrive at the end of September, and then the plan could be implemented.[52] The general emphasized that he could not even fully defend until the end of the following week. He explained that a person in theater had a different outlook from the people in Washington.[53] To the "armchair generals" in the Pentagon, things did not look so bad.[54] He likened the Americans' situation in the AOR in early August, threatened by Iraqi divisions, to being prisoners of war. As time passed and the deployment got underway, things improved, and personnel could begin to feed and house themselves, so, by the third week, they could defend themselves.[55] "You've got a different mindset in Washington, D.C., than you've got in theater when your ass is on the line," he observed.[56]

Horner told Warden he would take his "target lists" and "refine them." He tasked Leonardo to do this, warning him to do careful and substantive work: "be able to stand some tough questions — no fluff." Horner directed Leonardo to plan using three scenarios: first, Instant Thunder triggers an Iraqi invasion; second, Instant Thunder accompanies a land campaign; and finally, Instant Thunder is executed but hostages are dispersed to target sites.[57] Horner then asked Warden if he could have the officers who had accompanied him. He requested that the Air Staff lieutenant colonels remain in theater, and each agreed. He pointedly did not ask Warden to stay.[58]

Horner stated that he would take the PSYOPS portion and place it at the CINCCENT's level. He asked if the planners had done any attrition analysis. Stanfill replied that their calculations had estimated a 10 percent loss rate the first day, then a subsequent drop to 1 percent. A question about analysis by weapon systems led Stanfill to describe at an excessive length the retaliatory raid, El Dorado Canyon.[59]

Warden offered the view that they had to improve the targeting against Saddam Hussein, about which Horner expressed skepticism. The colonel countered that it was "not imperative to get him...[but] to isolate him for a while."[60] Horner moved on, saying that the goal was to "build an ATO" to execute the plan, which should be "open-ended, beyond six days," "gut Iraq," but "not necessarily [be] against [the Iraqi] people."[61] He believed the plan's execution would incur a 200-year penalty because non-Arabs attacked Iraq, but he knew he had to have the plan ready to execute because he, as Harvey noted, "must give [the] CINCCENT [the] option in [the] event of unacceptable Iraqi behavior."[62] This idea of retaliation was echoed by Deptula, who recalled Horner saying, "We must give the President this option."[63] Stanfill wrote in his notebook: ". . . if machine-gunning of hostages, then I need an option for President."[64]

Horner told Warden his plan had some good components — leadership and C^2 targets — but he believed that CENTAF did not yet have a really good feel for the defense of Saudi Arabia.[65] He told Colonels Crigger, Leonardo, and Rider that, as they refined the plan, they should not do anything that would "impact negatively on [our] ability to defend."[66] Stanfill noted that they still had the deception plan to discuss, but Warden cautioned that they could not talk about it in the present conference room.[67]

Horner asked if it was Powell's view that the plan must be "multinational." Warden answered, "yes," and Horner suggested that they "build" it in isolation, then explain it to the Saudis.[68] He then returned to the targets, saying, "I'm still uncomfortable about [the] target list" and "decapitate the snake." He did not see it as a "slick plan," but rather as a "hit-him-in-the-face" one. The general was "glad" the planners were in Riyadh, getting a feel for theater concerns.[69] He then swore and exclaimed, "This is not an exercise." The Saudis had only two battalions of armored police cars at the border.[70] Horner never realized how much time it would take to transport ground troops from the United States to the AOR. "You can't do it with air alone," he said.[71] Horner openly expressed his concerns about the threat from the Iraqi divisions and tanks. Doubting that Instant Thunder would force the Iraqis to withdraw from Kuwait, he believed it would provoke them to invade the Saudi kingdom. He wanted to know "what needed to be done if Iraqi ground forces became a player."[72] He held the responsibility, after all, for the defense of Saudi Arabia. The Iraqi army in Kuwait remained a problem even if it did not push farther south.[73]

The general's worries presented an opportunity for Warden to highlight and explain in detail the Instant Thunder briefing slide, "What If: Iraq attacks Saudi Arabia in response to Instant Thunder." The colonel had presented this slide near the end of his initial remarks, but its message was swamped by the theme that strategic attacks would achieve objectives mandated by the NCA, including forcing the Iraqis to withdraw from Kuwait. The slide also proclaimed, "Combined Instant Thunder and battlefield air operations can stop ground advance."[74] As Warden had explained the week before, he believed that a nation under strategic air attack cannot organize and launch a "dangerous offensive," so if Saddam did send forces south, the Instant Thunder reserve aircraft would stop them, or slow them so they could not reach anything of operational or strategic significance.[75]

Warden now had the chance to explain the rationale and strategy for defending against the invaders with the "reserve" aircraft and for his position that the arrival and employment of the 24th Infantry Division, Mechanized, was not necessary to stop the Iraqi push into Saudi territory. He probably would have had to answer questions from General Henry, however, about the EC aspects of defensive air operations and explain whether enough specialized aircraft and munitions would be available in theater for simultaneous execution of Instant Thunder and air operations directly against an invading army protected by its mobile SAM umbrella. Warden could also have pulled out and explained the Instant Thunder Phase II briefing, An Operational Air Campaign Against Iraqi Forces in Kuwait, produced in Checkmate at the behest of Chairman Powell and General Adams. He could have used the material to show Horner that a few Air Staff planners had studied the Iraqi army threat and the means to eliminate it. For Warden, though, the Instant Thunder Phase II plan still weakened the right wing of his aerial Schlieffen plan and unwisely diverted strategic air power. Besides, Schwarzkopf himself had not thought the phase necessary. Warden maintained an absolutely unshakable faith in his rationale of five strategic rings, war from the inside out, and the power of the strategic air campaign to force the leadership to capitulate. Airmen could overfly the fielded ground forces and attack the Hussein regime, the most important center of gravity. The Iraqi army was simply not an essential target set for Warden, and it did not appear among Instant Thunder's eighty-four targets.

Warden was exasperated by Horner's "long spiel."[76] Had Horner not comprehended what the colonel had explained about strategic air power for the last hour? Didn't he understand that the essence of war applied pressure against a nation's command structure to induce it to make concessions?[77] Why couldn't Horner see that if the enemy command element did not act rationally and make concessions in response to strategic attacks, those same attacks against other strategic centers of gravity would render the enemy impotent?[78] Why couldn't he grasp that strategic attacks would inflict "paralysis and shock" upon the Iraqi state?[79] Why didn't he appreciate that if a state's essential industries were destroyed, the state became incapable of employing modern weapons and must make major concessions?[80] Why didn't Horner see it was unlikely that under strategic attack people were going to organize and execute a major offensive while their home front was falling apart around them. "People just don't do that. It is *just not done*, never has been done, and there is no reason to think that it is going to be done now."[81]

At this critical point in his briefing, Colonel Warden bluntly, confidently lectured Horner, "Ground forces aren't important to [the] campaign. I don't believe the [Iraqi tanks] can move under air superiority. You're being overly pessimistic about those tanks."[82] These comments surprised the group. "You could hear a pin drop," Deptula recalled. "Everybody kinda took a breath and held."[83] The general looked at Warden who promptly offered an apology, which was calmly accepted.[84] Horner continued by complaining that Washington was not the place to plan a war. If people there wanted to fight, let them come to the theater.[85] The briefing was drawing to a close. The possibility that Horner would request that Warden remain in theater had long since vanished. Horner directed his staff to plan to attack Iraqi ground forces and chemical weapons capability.[86] He thanked the colonel and departed.[87]

At 1600, shortly after the briefing, the Checkmate planners held their own meeting. Horner's failure to wholeheartedly endorse their campaign terribly disappointed them.[88] They identified what they saw as the two major issues on which Horner's view of Instant Thunder diverged from theirs, Powell's, and Schwarzkopf's. First, the plan did not "just beat up on someone," as they thought Horner saw it with his concern about a "200-year legacy of hatred."[89] Second, Instant

Thunder did not require that U.S. Army ground forces be in theater before its execution.[90] Warden also worried about Horner's understanding of the leadership target objectives. Warden admitted that he himself had to rethink and better explain that portion of the briefing. He mused that it would be "great" if the campaign eliminated Saddam, but even if it did not, it took away his "capability."[91]

The group pinned their hopes on Schwarzkopf's arriving in theater within a few days to keep the strategic flame alive.[92] They believed he, far better than Horner, understood the plan and the use and potency of strategic air power. Unbeknownst to the Air Staff officers, however, the CINCCENT at that time readied his four-phase Desert Storm war plan for his briefing to Chairman Powell on August 25. Schwarzkopf, like Horner, believed that forcing the Iraqis from Kuwait involved far greater application of military power than Instant Thunder provided. The same day that Warden met Horner, Schwarzkopf briefed the Desert Shield deployment flow to Powell and the chiefs of the unified commands, who convened in Washington, D.C., August 20–21. Like Horner, Schwarzkopf relied heavily on both ground and air forces to bolster theater defenses. He told the commanders that CENTCOM would not attain a "high confidence" defense in the Gulf region until September 25, when the forces in theater totaled 146,000 troops comprising Navy, Army, Air Force, Marine Corps, and SOF.[93]

JFACC's Critique of Instant Thunder

General Horner viewed Instant Thunder as a seriously flawed plan. He later stated, "Warden thinks in terms of these concentric circles. He doesn't understand that sometimes there are legitimate, higher priorities than your master air campaign plan. If your army is getting overrun, who gives a shit what you take out deep?"[94] Recalling the briefing, he stated:

> I think Warden felt that he was designing the air campaign, and it didn't bother me. That's fine. We were faced with 27 divisions and no ground forces, so we were busy doing a defensive campaign. When they came over, I was struck by several things. There was a lot of brilliance to the plan. I liked some of the factors. But just as there was genius, there was also no common sense. The thing was not executable. It didn't have the mundaneness of what do you do about the army in Kuwait. Warden's conclusion was that they would all surrender when the first bomb dropped on Baghdad.[95]

In contrast to Warden, Horner did not believe that air power alone could halt an Iraqi invasion of Saudi Arabia, given the air forces in the theater in August and September. Not until the arrival of the 24th Infantry Division, Mechanized, with its heavy tanks, was the general confident that he could defend against an Iraqi onslaught. He explained:

> Quite frankly, we could not have issued speeding tickets to the tanks as they would have come rolling down that interstate highway on the east coast. It was an opportunity the Iraqis did not take, but every night we'd get more forces, and we'd sit down and get a game plan of what we'd do if we came under attack....
>
> Later we were able to add more heavy forces, and the point where the issue is no longer really in doubt was when we got the 24th Infantry Division there with their tanks. Then we knew we could defend the port of Dammam, which is just across from Bahrain, and that would allow us to bring our forces on board; we wouldn't have to fight our way in from Jeddah.[96]

When asked, "At what point did you know that you had enough force to stop an Iraqi invasion?" Horner replied, "When the 24th Infantry Division got there."[97] The Internal Look exercise in July — with air power but without a strategic air campaign — had shown Horner that even with the armored division in place, the Army's XVIII Airborne Corps would lose half its fighting strength against an Iraqi onslaught.

As the general saw it, Instant Thunder was a "larva," with a metamorphosis yet to occur to change it into a "butterfly" and a more fully developed theater air campaign.[98] Warden "gave a partial answer," which was "excellent."[99] Horner explained, "I sat there and listened to it, and I said, 'There are some really good thoughts here,' *but* it was incomplete. It developed the idea that air power was going to smash Iraq, and they were all going to give up and go home. Well, that is pure bull. I mean, anybody could see that."[100]

Warden sold Instant Thunder as a stand-alone, war-winning strategic air campaign that would force the Iraqi army to leave Kuwait — without designating the fielded Iraqi ground forces as a target set unless those troops invaded Saudi Arabia. Horner rejected the proposition that strategic strikes against eighty-four targets in Iraq over six days would induce the Iraqis to leave Kuwait, and he worried that in response to Instant Thunder, the Iraqi army would push south and invade the nation whose defense was his responsibility. In the general's view, Warden failed the interview-cum-briefing, and thus he did not ask the colonel to remain in theater to plan his offensive campaign. "He could have had that job!" the commander admitted. "He had it! But he blew it!"[101]

As Warden departed Riyadh later that evening, his loyal, young deputies, Colonels Deptula, Harvey, and Stanfill, joined by Wilson, said goodbye to their hero, who "tried to be upbeat, but seemed tired, down."[102] The dejected, down-in-the-mouth planners then moved from the White Palace to al-Kazahd Hotel. They splurged on a lavish dinner, raising their flagging spirits somewhat.[103]

That night Generals Horner and Henry dined together, and the EC expert expressed amazement at Horner's patience with Warden. Henry thought of the Air Staff plan as Instant "Blunder," which he described as "this idea to go up and put six days' worth of hell in Baghdad, and the war was going to end....Hitler made this mistake, didn't he? 'We'll go bomb the hell out of London, and they'll quit.' Didn't happen. Instant Blunder would have done the same thing."[104] The generals discussed the need for someone on the CENTAF staff to focus on the plan that Schwarzkopf had sent to the AOR and on offensive planning. Henry stated that it required a full-time effort and pointed out that he could not do it while he developed the EC portion of the D-day plan, which devoured all of his time. The discussion turned to General Glosson's directing the special planning enterprise. As the deputy commander of JTFME, headquartered on the USS *LaSalle,* Glosson had already enthusiastically expressed interest to Horner about moving to Riyadh and working for him. The CENTCOM Forward commander complied, deciding to call Buster Glosson that night to come to CENTAF.[105]

The Exiles and Intelligence Support

The next morning at breakfast, Deptula, Harvey, and Stanfill (dubbed "the Exiles" by Harvey), rekindled and fanned their determination to influence CENTAF's offensive air campaign. They took as their charter Horner's request to each of them to remain in theater to assist with the planning. This seemed reasonable because they perceived the CENTAF staff as focused single-mindedly on defensive planning. They would concentrate on the offensive effort.[106]

A sense of urgency permeated their outlook. When Deptula had debriefed Secretary Rice about the August 17 presentation to Schwarzkopf, General Dugan joined them, and the SecAF and CSAF both discussed the date for the execution of Instant Thunder. Dugan thought the end of September appropriate. Rice emphasized an earlier time, before Saddam Hussein had prepared his defenses. He thought that approximately September 6th would allow enough time to prepare for execution of the strategic campaign. When Warden briefed Horner, they too discussed September execution dates. The Exiles believed Instant Thunder could be executed in the near future; they had no time to waste while finalizing the Air Staff plan.[107]

The group met Wilson at the RSAF building and commenced their labor in the conference room next to General Olsen's office, which Wilson had been using with others over the past several days. Their renewed optimism and self-defined mission aside, the group initially operated in "tremendous uncertainty" and "groped" about trying to build an executable ATO, as Horner had described his requirement the day before. To help maintain security for the planning, they used a cover story that they were conducting a Desert Shield logistics study.[108]

The first planning activity the Exiles undertook consisted of answering the questions Horner had raised during the briefing about Instant Thunder. Deptula sketched an organization chart showing Wilson in charge, because he was the ranking officer in the group; Major Turk as the CENTAF liaison officer; and Deptula, Harvey, and Stanfill as section chiefs handling, respectively, the attack flow plan, assessments, and resources. Deptula specified the objectives for the group, augmented by the CENTAF staff, to produce four products over the next few days: a target list on August 22d; an attack flow plan on the 23d; force packaging on the 24th; and the ATO on the 25th.[109]

The Exiles' optimism soon ebbed as they found themselves unable to convince anyone on the CENTAF staff to provide them with administrative support and computer equipment. No senior officers had yet directed the CENTAF staff to support the Air Staff "logistics" project (and rumors circulated among the personnel that Horner had thrown the three lieutenant colonels' boss out of country).[110] Deptula lamented, "We were getting slow rolled at every turn from the CENTAF staff."[111] One officer from the operations shop recalled that, indeed, "Some guys were 'slow rolling' the Air Staff guys." Their attitude toward the newcomers was "Who are you? You're outsiders."[112] After vainly requesting the loan of some computers, Harvey considered it a victory when the enlisted historians assigned to the headquarters agreed to share their computer with the planners, but only when they were not using it.[113]

Wilson sought out General Olsen about acquiring office space and support, and the general quickly authorized a tent to be set up in the nearby fenced-in soccer field and to be designated and guarded as an area to store sensitive compartmented information (SCI). The well-guarded tent would provide more protection for Instant Thunder, which incorporated special category (SPECAT) information. Learning of the SCI tent initiative, Deptula disapproved of the idea and delayed moving into it, wanting to remain in the conference room with its proximity to the CENTAF commander.[114]

The Exiles had a difficult time, too, acquiring intelligence support for their planning efforts. Intelligence emerged as Deptula's primary concern. He would immediately need two products. First, he sought a master target list, collated from lists the Air Staff, CENTAF, and CENTCOM had developed thus far. Next, he required a large map with Instant Thunder targets identified on it so, as he produced the attack flow, he could design aircraft force packages, relying on common SEAD assets, to strike collocated, interdependent targets.[115] Over the next forty-eight hours, the lack of support that Wilson's planning group received from some intelligence personnel created a rift between planners and intelligence officers that over the next six months fluctuated, but never closed.

Two rebuffs from intelligence officers caused the rift. At midmorning on August 21, the group briefed Instant Thunder and Instant Thunder Phase II to a few officers, including Maj. Walter E. Jordan, the executive officer to the CENTAF/IN, whom Colonel Leonardo designated as the intelligence point of contact for Instant Thunder. The planners discussed the pressing need for imagery and materials, and they explained that photographs existed at the Air Staff for the eighty-four Instant Thunder targets. Jordan agreed that he and Stanfill should contact Colonel Blackburn, the targeteer who had assisted with the development of the plan at Checkmate, and request that he personally carry the photos to

Riyadh and pass them off with full explanations to CENTAF personnel. They telephoned Washington via Checkmate, and Lt. Col. Larry D. Autry later relayed to them Blackburn's firm, negative answer. The targeteer explained that in his briefing to the CINCCENT on August 17 he had told Schwarzkopf that he worked for him and CENTCOM. He told the campaign planners that he would accept tasking only from CENTCOM headquarters.[116] The reply infuriated Stanfill. "I consider this to be criminal!" he complained. "If the Iraqis attack before peacetime...data arrives — aircrews will die."[117] Blackburn expressed reluctance to depart Washington for Riyadh because he felt compelled to remain in the Pentagon to ensure that Warden did not run "roughshod" over the targeteers. "Don't get me wrong," he explained, "John Warden did a whole lot of things, but John Warden was marching to his own agenda sometimes."[118] The targeteer knew that the CINCCENT had told the planners to take Instant Thunder to Riyadh and give it to Horner. The Air Staff colonels who remained in theater and worked the plan required that Blackburn immediately send a set of the target photos to the JFACC. He withheld them, however, even though warfare could break out at any time.

In the meantime, Colonel Leonardo, director of CENTAF/IN who had attended Warden's briefing to Horner, and his deputy, Col. William C. Hubbard, called together five targeteers, some of whom were from CENTAF and some from SAC, and gave them guidance.[119] They received instructions to report to the Air Staff officers and receive the Instant Thunder briefing.[120] They then were to develop CENTAF's target list for an offensive air campaign. The colonels told the targeteers that the Air Staff group was "mucking in CENTAF's business" and would be gone by the end of the week, according to Horner who was "humoring" them for a while before sending them back to Washington, D.C. Nonetheless, CENTAF needed an offensive air plan, and the targeteers had to produce CENTAF's offensive target list.[121]

Deptula and Harvey gave the targeteers an Instant Thunder overview, and the intelligence officers went off to search for secluded space where they could work with the highly classified SPECAT material they now had and develop CENTAF's offensive target list. The only private area they could find was the empty pump room in the basement of the RSAF building, for which they unsuccessfully scrounged for a table and chairs.[122] Sitting on the floor, they began to develop the new compilation by comparing and ranking targets from four lists: the 200 sites CENTAF identified by July 1990 for CENTCOM's OPLAN 1002–90; the targets CENTAF chose after the Internal Look exercise for the Punishment ATO; the 109 targets CENTCOM promulgated August 16, 1990; and the 84 targets from the Air Staff's Instant Thunder. They did not simply consolidate the lists, rather they added or deleted targets as they thought appropriate. Their goal was to prepare and brief the offensive targets to Leonardo, which they did.[123]

Deptula later found the officers in the pump room, and when he learned they had deleted some Instant Thunder targets, he strenuously objected, explaining that the "chief targeteer of the Air Force," meaning Colonel Blackburn, had developed the Instant Thunder list using the best intelligence in Washington, and that all of the targets were valid and important. The officers queried Deptula about who was the "chief targeteer of the Air Force," pointing out that it was not his job on the Air Staff to develop target lists for CENTAF, and besides, he had omitted the crucially important Salman Pak BW site.[124] (One of the targeteer's initial reactions to Instant Thunder was that it was "nothing more than an Air War College paper," produced by amateurs.[125]) When Deptula stated that he had to have a map for the Instant Thunder targets, one captain replied that it was not his job to provide maps; his task was to respond to Colonel Leonardo. Frustrated, Deptula left the area; the next day, however, he received the sorely needed map.[126]

The targeteers' lack of support for the Exiles' requirements crystallized the planners' view that intelligence officers were totally uncooperative, with the worst of the people slow-rolling and undermining the efforts of the operator-planners who were trying to produce an executable ATO. For the intelligence personnel, their resistance stemmed from their understanding of a sanctioned chain of command, outside of which the Air Staff planners functioned.[127]

In contrast, while the intelligence officers seemed uncooperative, Warden and the Checkmate staff eagerly supported the Exiles. On the morning of August 22, Harvey telephoned the colonel, who gladly received the call and explained that Checkmate operated at a normal pace, but that if the CINCCENT required it, they would immediately move to 24-hour operations to supply the campaign planners with any assistance requested. He encouraged Harvey to telephone once or twice a day if he thought Checkmate could render valuable support.[128] A short time later, Harvey sent a fax to Checkmate stating, "We are still woefully, ambitiously short of intel support. Request you attempt to forward any data you deem appropriate."[129] Harvey's telephone call and fax to Warden began an extraordinary intelligence support link between the offensive air campaign planners in Riyadh and the Air Staff's Checkmate staff, which would continue throughout Desert Shield and Desert Storm and significantly affect the development and execution of the air campaign.

Glosson Directs the Special Planning Group

Meanwhile, General Glosson, aboard the USS *LaSalle* in the Persian Gulf near Bahrain, responded to Horner's request that he head the CENTAF Special Planning Project, immediately flying to Riyadh on August 21. Glosson had worked for Horner in previous assignments, and the senior officer knew him as a "go-getter," who "gets the job done."[130] When Glosson commanded the 414th Fighter Weapons Squadron at Nellis AFB, Horner led the 474th Tactical Fighter Wing, also located there, and when Glosson commanded the 1st Tactical Fighter Wing at Langley AFB, Horner assumed command of the Ninth Air Force and CENTAF. Like his boss, Glosson had flown combat missions during the Vietnam

War. He thought of Horner as a leader who did not micromanage but who would assign an officer a job and expect him to do it and ask for help if needed.[131]

Glosson arrived in the Persian Gulf in mid-July 1990, working under Rear Adm. William M. Fogarty, the JTFME director, and spending most of his time focused on Ivory Justice, the operation in which the United States provided tanker support to the UAE before and after Iraq invaded Kuwait. He even traveled to Abu Dhabi for two weeks to direct the operation. He often coordinated naval air missions with the CENTAF staff, with General Olsen in particular. Because the JTFME functioned under the authority of CENTCOM, on July 17, just before flying to his new assignment, Glosson met with Schwarzkopf at MacDill AFB and received the CINCCENT's assessment of the political and military situation in the entire CENTCOM AOR. During the crisis surrounding Iraq's aggression, Schwarzkopf talked with Glosson a few times by telephone. The airman thought the "chemistry" between him and the CINCCENT was "right."[132]

General Henry met Glosson at the airport in Riyadh in the evening of August 21 and provided an overview of CENTAF operations during their ride to General Olsen's office, where the three officers met for an hour. At 1900, Glosson and Henry joined Horner for dinner. The discussion turned tense, stirring Horner's anger and grave concern when the discussion turned to the Air Staff's war planning and Saudi Arabia's vulnerability to an Iraqi attack. Afterward, Horner met privately with Glosson in the CENTAF commander's office in the RSAF building, and he directed Glosson to have Deptula give him the Air Staff briefing; have Crigger give him the D-day briefing; produce a two- or three-day ATO for the CINCCENT and brief it to Horner on Sunday, August 26; and send the "Warden crowd" home in a few days. Glosson asked that the Air Staff lieutenant colonels be allowed to stay for a couple of weeks so he could take advantage of the work they had already accomplished on the air plan and until he could build a staff. Horner agreed.[133]

Horner then offered Glosson the conference room next to the CENTAF commander's office and told him that once the CINCCENT approved the ATO, he could produce an offensive plan. Horner related that he needed help and that he himself did not have time to develop the ATO. He stated that Glosson could start with a "blank sheet" and take what was best from the Air Staff plan and improve upon it and not be "constrained" by it.[134] He stressed the importance of absolute secrecy for the special planning effort because, as the diplomats pursued their negotiations, he wanted to avoid complicating or terminating diplomatic efforts by the leaked fact that the United States was planning offensive strikes against Iraq.[135] Horner ended the session by telling the new arrival to "get out of here" and be prepared to brief on Sunday. In his final remark, he said, "I'm glad you're here."[136]

The next day, Wednesday, August 22, as Glosson toured CENTAF headquarters, he conferred with Colonels Crigger (operations), Rider (logistics), and Leonardo (intelligence), and Baptiste (plans), and Major Heintzelman (legal affairs). Leonardo expressed grave pessimism that he could adequately support Glosson because he lacked targeting intelligence and material. The general mentally noted the sad state of affairs with intelligence support and he concluded that he should try to acquire help directly from the National Security Agency (NSA), CIA, and the Pentagon.[137] Once again, a planner, this time the key operator-planner, concluded that good intelligence support was in short supply. Later that day Colonels Deptula and Harvey briefed Instant Thunder to Glosson, along with Rear Adm. Timothy W. Wright, the NAVCENT commander's personal representative in Riyadh. Before the presentation began, Henry chatted with Glosson and described the Air Staff plan as a grandiose, unexecutable product put together by "academics" and stated that Horner had sent Warden home in a "body bag." The afternoon session lasted nearly an hour and a half, with Glosson asking questions and expressing concern about Saddam Hussein's ability to use CW.[138]

That evening the chief planner met privately with the Air Staff lieutenant colonels and told them that, at Horner's direction, they were to stay and assist him in turning the Air Staff plan into an executable ATO by Friday, August 24, for a briefing to Horner on Sunday. When Deptula heard that they had to produce an executable ATO within hours, he thought, "You gotta be shitting me! We've got a lot of work to do between now and then to turn this thing into reality."[139] Instant Thunder formed the basis of the strategic air campaign which Glosson's Special Planning Group would turn into an executable ATO. Glosson wanted the Air Staff officers to stay with the project because they were already familiar with the plan and had done good work on it, and besides, he liked their patches, pointing to those on Deptula's and Stanfill's flight suits, signifying that they had graduated from the prestigious USAF Fighter Weapons School at Nellis AFB.[140] The general, too, proudly wore the patch.

The night of August 22, Glosson returned to the USS *LaSalle* to pack and tie up loose ends as deputy commander of the JTFME. Since the arrival in theater of Vice Adm. Henry Mauz, Jr., responsibility for JTFME functions shifted to NAVCENT, and Glosson's responsibility had diminished. While he was onboard the ship, Schwarzkopf telephoned for Admiral Fogarty, who was unavailable, so Glosson took the call. The CINCCENT talked about the naval embargo and the importance of everyone staying calm and not "hunting trouble." He related that he had talked with Horner about Glosson's move to CENTAF and said he had okayed it. "Don't forget you're still working for me," the CINCCENT told him. He said he needed something to give to the President "if Saddam acts crazy," something that would last about three or four days, a week maximum, but more than the air operations in Libya. He related that he had the Air Staff "work up a plan" and that it was a "good start." "See if you can use some of it to build what I need," he directed. He told Glosson he would brief Powell and Cheney that week on a "theater campaign — all four phases." He said he would need the airman's help with the theater plan when he got there and he did not want Air Staff involvement.[141]

Glosson penned a note after the telephone conversation indicating that Horner was correct about the CINCCENT wanting an ATO for operations to last only a few days, an expanded El Dorado Canyon in a sense. Horner had not talked with Glosson about four phases, and this was the first time Glosson had heard of a phased theater campaign.[142] He thought that the CINCCENT's view, "No Air Staff," would please Horner.[143]

On the morning of August 23, after returning from the USS *LaSalle* and moving into his new quarters in Riyadh, Glosson arrived at the 40- by 20-foot conference room on the third floor of the RSAF building to perform his duties as director of the Special Planning Group. His initial staff consisted of the three colonels from the Air Staff, whom the general described as "the core of the group that had been loosely gathered for about three days."[144] Personnel from the CENTAF staff, especially those who knew how to develop an ATO, soon augmented the group. Glosson explained,

> The first action that I took was to insure that I had an expert in building ATOs, a person that was very familiar [with] and had built numerous op orders, a person that had been involved in execution planning, to include the entire gamut from the SEAD aspects to munitions, to weapons systems themselves, including the timing, AWACS, tankers, Rivet Joint, and all the support elements.[145]

Generals Caruana and Henry provided planning expertise on SAC aircraft and EC, respectively. Rear Adm. Wright, who had initially received the Instant Thunder briefing with Glosson on August 22, joined the group for a few days.[146]

Throughout August and September, the following officers joined the Special Planning Group and brought with them their individual operational expertise:

Officer	Expertise
Maj. John D. Sweeney, Maj. David L. Waterstreet	ATO process
Maj. Scott Hente, Lt. Col. James Pritchett	Tankers
Lt. Col. Bert Pryor, Maj. Al Vogel	AWACS
Maj. John Kinser	AWACS & ACE
Lt. Col. Robert Kershaw (who replaced Maj. Jordan)	Intelligence
Capt. Jay Bachhuber, Capt. Timothy Carver, Capt. Thomas Clements, Capt. John Glock	Targeting
Maj. John Turk	Air-to-air combat
Maj. Gary Alexander, Maj. Mike Oelrich	EC
Capt. Eric Holdaway	Electronic & signals intelligence
Maj. Robert Eskridge	F–117s
Capt. James R. Hawkins	B–52s
Capt. Kirby Lindsey	Logistics

Capt. Thomas R. O'Boyle	Special operations
Capt. William Bruner	F–111s
Maj. Harry Heintzelman	Law of armed conflict[147]

Lt. Col. Rogers K. Greenawalt functioned as Glosson's executive officer. The other service representatives were

Representative	Service
Cdr. Donald McSwain	Navy, Persian Gulf
Cdr. Maurice Smith	Navy, Red Sea
Maj. Jeffrey Olsen	Marine Corps
Lt. Col. William G. Welch	Army[148]

Secrecy enshrouded the Special Planning Group. The CENTAF staff members who produced the daily ATO and the D-day ATO, as well as operations specialists in the TACC, remained apart from Glosson's Top Secret, SPECAT, limited-distribution planning enterprise. To ensure the security of target imagery and data and to enable the use of SCI material, Glosson pushed others to quickly complete erection of the tent in the well-guarded soccer field, located about a ten-minute walk from the RSAF building and the other special planners. At about 2000 on August 23, Glosson visited the SCI tent and introduced himself to the targeteers assigned to the offensive planning effort.[149] This was the first time the targeteers had heard of or met Glosson. The general saw that they needed more tables and chairs and a telephone and told them he would see that those items were promptly delivered. He told them that they now worked for him and he wanted them to provide imagery and target materials for the offensive campaign. The photos he requested supported a master target list consolidating the Instant Thunder, CENTCOM, and CENTAF lists. He wanted no BW storage sites targeted, but he did ask for pictures of the facilities.[150] He left the targeteers, believing he had clearly stated his intelligence needs, which he did, but the officers could not promptly satisfy the pressing, major targeting requirements of the Special Planning Group, which would emerge as an enormous problem confronting Glosson throughout Desert Shield and Desert Storm.

The night of August 23, when Glosson met with his planners to discuss targeting matters, Lt. Col. John S. Meyer, USAF, the recently arrived key intelligence officer for STRATFOR, attended, as did the targeteers Captains Glock and Carver. The general once again told them to combine the Instant Thunder, CENTAF, and CENTCOM lists and to follow the guidance accompanying the CENTCOM list for prioritizing targets. Questions arose over the whereabouts of the imagery for the eighty-four Instant Thunder sites. Colonel Harvey explained that Colonel Blackburn had sent a set of that imagery to the DMAAC in St. Louis for mensuration of DMPIs and that the DMAAC would soon send a series of messages specifying the precise DMPI coordinates. In addition, efforts were still underway to acquire from Blackburn a set of the Instant Thunder imagery.[151] The planners completely depended on the Air Staff chief targeteer to send the photographs.

After Glosson arranged to have officers from CENTAF headquarters join his group, he next requested that two representatives from each of the operational flying units participate. He explained, "The reason I got two people is I let the unit commander decide whom he sent, and I figured that there would never be a situation where a person would select the exact people that I would — so out of the two people, I would at least get one that I could hang onto for a while." Glosson thought the wing commanders sent "very bright" officers, "top-drawer guys" and "hard workers."[152]

A lack of computer equipment hindered the operations of the Special Planning Group as it expanded. The two laptops that Major Waterstreet provided for the ATO were insufficient to the war-planning task. Because the group had not deployed as a unit from a base, it had no equipment of its own and depended on CENTAF headquarters to supply it. The command staff had, for the most part, deployed on August 8 without its own computers. Although the staff had taken their computers to the Internal Look exercise, most of the officers in early August thought they would deploy for only a short time and could send for their equipment, if needed. They were wrong on the first point and correct on the second, but they had not anticipated the lengthy time it took before their supplies arrived in the AOR.[153]

When a CENTAF staff officer questioned the cost of the special planners' purchasing a computer commercially in Riyadh, an exasperated Glosson instructed his staff to go into the city and buy a Macintosh computer and printer and charge it to his personal credit card, which greatly impressed the group. Although CENTAF was genuinely unable to supply computers to the special planners, as an organization, it was also reluctant to do so. Its own requirements for producing the daily and D-day ATOs and fulfilling other JFACC and deployment responsibilities prevented it from complying with the planners' requests, and some on the CENTAF staff considered members of the Special Planning Group to be "outsiders" who should fend for themselves.[154]

Colonel Baptiste of the Combat Plans Division, however, who had received the Instant Thunder briefing early on, welcomed and tried to support Glosson's group because its members assumed responsibility for the offensive ATO, instead of having the tasking responsibility fall to the regular CENTAF staff, who strained to generate the daily and D-day ATOs. Referring to the special planners, Baptiste noted, "To be quite truthful with you, me and my guys were working our butts off trying to get those other ATOs out. That was a full-time job!...We would have had to split my guys up. That is the only way we could have done it." Most of the CENTAF staff remained together, laboring on the defensive plan and operational and training missions, while the new arrivals in theater and personnel from the flying units comprised Glosson's group.[155]

Master Attack Plan

As the unit expanded around him, Deptula concentrated on producing an updated version of his "attack flow" document, which he would refine into one of the most important planning products of the war. On Saturday, August 18, the day after the second Instant Thunder briefing to Schwarzkopf at MacDill AFB, Deptula had returned to the Pentagon and prepared an improved, revised "campaign flow" plan, whereby he once again identified attacks by day, time, target, Basic Encyclopedia number, target type, target description, aircraft quantity, aircraft type, mission, and flow sequence. This document served as the framework for his development of the flow plans in theater. As he had first calculated in the week of August 12, the attack plan depended on the number of sorties available. His sortie numbers on August 24 were based on only U.S. Air Force, Navy, and Marine Corps aircraft.[156]

Responding to new intelligence and information about additional aircraft arriving in theater, Deptula updated the flow plan on a laptop; consequently, more than one version of the plan circulated within the group. To preclude anyone unwittingly using a draft, he dubbed the latest printout the "MAP," and by August 27, the MAP was certified as being the current, authorized version if

6:48 PM
20 JAN/1600

MASTER ATTACK PLAN
FIFTH 24 HOURS

1/20/91
APPROVED

TOT*	MSN#	BEN	TGT	DESCRIPTION	AC
0115	4401A(U)	[DELETED]	A30	H-3 AFLD SW	10 GR-1
-0130				SEAD (RED SEA GROUP)	
0200	3321A		SAD68	I-HAWK NW BAG	1 F-117
	3322A		SAD67	I-HAWK TNG SITE	1 F-117
	3323A		L06	INTERNAL SECURITY HQ	1 F-117
	3324A	[DELETED]	L08	MINISTRY OF DEFENSE	1 F-117
	3325A		L16	PRESIDENTIAL PALACE	1 F-117
	3326A		L15	TAJI PRESIDENTIAL RETREAT	1 F-117
0200			RG03	MEDINAH CP	4 F-16L
TO		[DELETED]	RG04	HAMURABI CP	4 F-16L
0215					
*388TFW					
~~0210~~			~~SC42~~	3004N 04742E/FROG BATT	4 F-111
				SCUD C2 BKR - KANMALL	
TO			SAD06	314019N 0471434E	4 F-111
				AL AMARAH IOC & GCI SITE	
0230			SAD05	292345N 0473739E	4 F-111
				AL JAHRAH IOC/CP	
		[DELETED]	SAD25	292105N 0473830E	4 F-111
				5TG AD SEC OPS CTR AL SALEM	
			SC31	292105N 0473830E	4 F-111
				AL JAHRAH MISSILE FAC	
			SC32	291902N 0473752E	4 F-111
				AL JAHRAH AMMO STOR (SCUD)	
				SEAD	4 F-4G
				SEAD	4 F-4G
				SWEEP/FORCE PROTECT	8 F-15C
0215	3327A		L04	N TAJI C3 FAC #2	1 F-117
	[illegible]		L19	INTEL SERVICE HQ	
	3331A		C21	ABU GHURAYB BW PT	2 F-117
	3333A		C22	ABU GHURAYB VACCINE PT	1 F-117
	33325A		CCC28	BAG TELECOM CTR	2 F-117
	3377	[DELETED]	~~L34~~ C11	NAT C3 BKR NUC RESEARCH FAC	1 F-117
	~~3340~~		SAD28	AL TAJI IOC	
	3342A		C23	TAJI BW FAC	1 F-117
*DUAL DOOR GBU-10					
0215	4411A(U)		A08	AR RUMAYLAH	8 GA-1*
		[DELETED]		SEAD	
TO	4421A(U)		A31	AN NUMANIYAH	8 GR-1
0230				SEAD	2EF-111
*COORD EF-111 W/MSN 0471X					

A completed and approved master attack plan

Deptula had dated and initialed it and Glosson had signed it. The MAP, a detailed attack plan, formed the basis of the Gulf War ATO, providing a script, in chronological order, of who was to do what. When merged with the air refueling plan, the MAP directly guided the development of the ATO sent to the flying units, which directed the flight of every sortie against the enemy.[157]

A significant change in the Instant Thunder plan eliminated the two attack waves of the first night and substituted only a single wave. Instant Thunder's initial strikes had time over targets at approximately one hour after sunset, and its second wave strikes were scheduled for approximately one hour before sunrise. The two waves had originally been planned to allow the very limited number of F–117s to return to base, rearm, and reattack, remaining under the cover of darkness.[158] The availability in theater of more F–4Gs, in particular, enabled more aircraft to join in a single wave the first night. Colonel Crigger lobbied for the change. On August 19, when he had met with Warden, Crigger first raised the issue of launching only one attack at night, followed by more strikes in the early daylight. He also brought the issue to Glosson's attention, explaining:

> When you looked at the F–16s they were going to send up there without LANTIRN, to go with a "night go" didn't make a whole lot of sense. You had a lot better capability with those airplanes in a "day go"; so to try to optimize the airplanes that you had, it made sense to start out in the night with your 117s. There is a lot to be said of the old gunfighter with the sun-at-your-back type thing coming out of the east, once you have hit them once, and then right back.[159]

Glosson asked Deptula to examine the feasibility of sending only one wave the first night. With the arrival of additional aircraft, Deptula laid out a new sortie flow that produced an effective, single attack wave.[160]

Colonel Crigger's Responsibility

Horner relied on Crigger to rectify what he saw as a major flaw in Instant Thunder's success as a war-winning plan: its failure to offensively and lethally target and strike the Iraqi army. At midmorning on August 24, Glosson called a meeting of the special planners to discuss preparations for the presentation scheduled for Horner on Sunday, August 26. Crigger attended, and he prepared to brief a plan for attacking the Iraqi ground forces on the Kuwaiti-Saudi border. Aircraft available for this effort consisted of A–10s, AV–8s, F–16s, F/A–18s, Saudi F–5s, and Apache helicopters, assets not essential to the Instant Thunder strikes. Some F–4Gs would fly in the KTO, and B–52s would hit enemy troops in the open.[161]

At Horner's direction, Crigger developed the ideas to implement the JFACC's strategy for simultaneous attacks against the Iraqi army as the strategic air campaign commenced. Crigger recalled that Horner had instructed him to look beyond the D-day planning to attacking Iraqi troops concurrently with the strategic operations.[162] At the midmorning meeting, however, Glosson tasked Deptula, not Crigger, to strike the Republican Guard, which had repeated the tactics it had used during the Iran-Iraq War. Equipped with new, Soviet T–72 tanks, the Guard led attacks, seized territory, established strong, defensible positions, and then pulled back for refitting.[163] Colonel Leonardo and his intelligence officers tried to locate exactly where the elite troops had re-deployed in Iraq.[164]

Col. James C. Crigger

As Crigger's staff planned the offensive strikes against the Iraqi army, Colonel Harvey showed some of his staff members the briefing slides for Instant Thunder Phase II which Checkmate had developed in response to Chairman Powell's direction on August 11 to kill Iraqi tanks. Crigger's staff found Checkmate's products useful to their offensive planning and adopted their title, format, and content.[165] Also at the meeting, the planners discussed the need for an OPORD to accompany the executable ATO and to explain offensive planning concepts. Maj. John Kinser from CENTAF headquarters, Maj. Pete Harvell from CENTCOM headquarters, and Harvey formed the core group to write the OPORD. As he had discussed with Deptula previously, Harvey gave the group the 180-page Instant Thunder OPORD and briefing slides for Instant Thunder Phase II, which it adopted as the basis for the new CENTAF OPORD.[166]

The Air Staff colonels continued communicating with Warden and the Checkmate staff as they prepared the MAP, OPORD, and briefing for Glosson to present to Horner. Knowing Horner's disdain for the Pentagon's intrusion into war planning and for armchair generals in Washington, the colonels thought it prudent not to speak of their telephone calls to Warden. Maintaining the secrecy of the Air Staff connection was not easily achieved, however, because the special planners did not yet have a STU III phone readily at their disposal in the third-floor conference room. They cautiously used phones in the CENTAF headquarters area and did not disclose to unindoctrinated CENTAF staff either the party called or the real nature of the planning. They initially relied on the STU III phone in the SCI tent as their link to Checkmate for a source of valuable data and ideas. Glosson soon learned of the connection and allowed it to continue because he needed reliable, timely intelligence from wherever he could acquire it. He thought it wise, however, to keep the Air Staff input hidden from Horner, and even personally cautioned Deptula not to let the general even catch a glimpse of the Air Staff officers. He knew also from his phone conversation with the CINCCENT that Schwarzkopf did not approve of continued Air Staff involvement in offensive planning, so it was just best to keep the link secret.[167]

Glosson's Instant Thunder Briefing

Glosson and the special planners worked through the night of Saturday to Sunday, August 25/26, to prepare for the meeting with Horner at 0800 on Sunday. At the appointed hour, only Generals Horner, Glosson, Olsen, Caruana, and Henry and Colonel Crigger assembled for the presentation. Glosson briefed the offensive attacks into Iraq, and Crigger, the offensive strikes into the Kuwaiti theater. With his boss's approval, Deptula entered the projection room and flipped the briefing slides as he took notes on the session.[168]

"The first time Buster briefed me the strategic plan," Horner recalled, "he got thrown out of the office. It was a terrible briefing."[169] Glosson remembered his new boss "exploding" during it.[170] Henry, who often spun out folksy descriptions for events, summed up the session immediately after as "ill-prepared, poorly presented, and violently received."[171] Of course, the CENTCOM Forward commander did not actually toss the brigadier general from the room or ask him to leave, but he did severely criticize the delivery. Horner explained, "It wasn't the substance of his briefing that caused him to die; it was the presentation."[172] He especially disliked the organization and structure. "I said, 'Buster, what you have got to do is to peel it back like an onion. It has got to tell a story so that people who don't know air can understand this.'"[173] Horner reacted negatively to Glosson's presentation, not the briefing's substance, based on Instant Thunder concepts. Afterward, Glosson would improve the presentation by using large flip charts and maps to better explain how the campaign would unfold and to indicate the location of targets.[174]

Glosson titled his briefing, "Instant Thunder Concept of Operations and Execution," indicative of the fact that the Air Staff plan laid the foundation upon which the general built the strategic air campaign.[175] Horner retitled it, "Offensive Campaign Phase I." When explaining the new name, the lieutenant general cautioned the officers in the room to keep what he was about to tell them absolutely secret. He then described CENTCOM's war plan in four phases, as presented in the slides, "Offensive Campaign Concept of Operations Outline." Surprisingly, Horner's copy of the four CENTCOM phases was not the current Desert Storm version, which the CINCCENT had briefed to Powell and Cheney on August 25 and which presented the four phases: Strategic Air Campaign; Kuwait Air Campaign; Ground Combat Power Attrition; and Ground Attack.[176] Instead, Horner's slides were an early draft of the phases: Strategic Air Campaign; Preparation of the Battlefield; Assault into Kuwait; and End State.[177] Within a day or so, Horner would acquire an up-to-date version of Schwarzkopf's four phases, and Glosson would then use the same phased framework that the CINCCENT had crafted and presented to Powell and Cheney.[178] The "preparation of the battlefield" terminology would stick with Horner, however, and he would later emphasize and use that phrase in lieu of "ground combat power attrition" to describe Desert Storm Phase III.

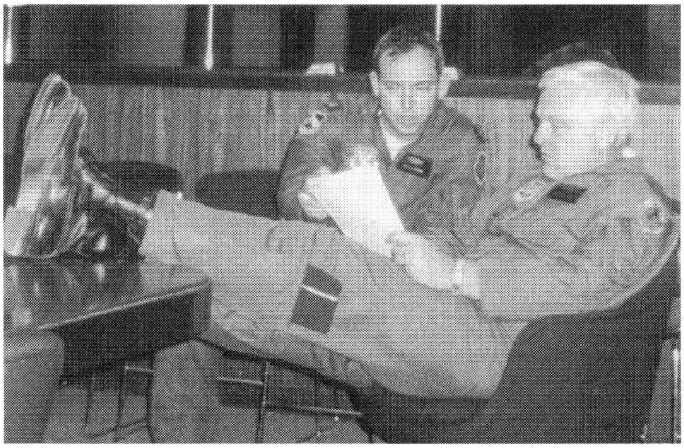

Near midnight on August 25, 1990, Brig. Gen. Buster C. Glosson and Lt. Col. David A. Deptula discuss the air campaign briefing that Glosson will present to General Horner the next day.

Colonel Crigger presented a second, shorter briefing on air operations against the Iraqi ground forces. He described the operations as interdiction, SEAD, and antiarmor. Horner changed the order to SEAD, antiarmor, and interdiction. The general would gain control of the battlefield and then do whatever the Army wanted done.[179]

All day Sunday, Glosson and Deptula reworked their offensive campaign according to Horner's directions. The younger officer called this process the CENTAF-ization of Instant Thunder. In the late afternoon, Horner stopped by to see how they were doing, and passed on to Glosson more information about the CINCCENT's briefing to the CJCS and the SecDef. When Horner again saw some of the Instant Thunder material, he derided it. Ironically, while Schwarzkopf referred to Saddam Hussein as the "crazy man" in Baghdad, Horner referred to John Warden as that "crazy man" in Washington.[180]

Retaliatory Option Becomes Phase I

On Monday, August 27, Glosson informally presented the revised briefing, "Offensive Campaign Phase I," using flip charts to supplement the briefing slides. According to Horner, "Buster doesn't like to be embarrassed, so then he went back and personally really put his thoughts to work and pulled it together the second time. That briefing never really changed, other than the details as new targets were uncovered and new forces deployed. The thrust of the briefing, the plan of the briefing, never changed."[181] The revisions satisfied Horner.

Glosson halved his Phase I briefing to 16 slides, compared with his presentation the day before. The word *strategic* vanished from the pages, replaced by *key,* to accommodate Horner's preference for using the descriptives *key* or *high-value* rather than *strategic* when referring to targets. The campaign presented three objectives, which Horner had passed to Glosson and identified them as the CINCCENT's: "decapitate leadership, destroy command and control, and reduce military capabilities."[182] Because Horner believed that the responsibility for PSYOPS in the CENTCOM AOR resided with the CINCCENT, the plan excluded discussion of PSYOPS, an important part of the original Instant Thunder plan. Later, as he learned of Saudi sensitivities about PSYOPS, he thought it fortunate that Schwarzkopf kept "a strong hand in this effort," eliminating the opportunity for CENTAF to "screw up" on this issue, which greatly concerned and required the coordination of the host nationals.[183]

The duration of Phase I was three to six days. Glosson kept it short after reflecting on his telephone conversation with the CINCCENT on August 22 when Schwarzkopf told him to limit the campaign to three or four days, a week maximum. The quickness of the operations reflected the retaliatory nature of the strategic air campaign. Even though it was now called Phase I, it still served as the serious air campaign against Iraq that Secretary Cheney had requested on August 2 and for which the CINCCENT had telephoned the Air Staff on August 8. It now also formed the basis of the first phase of the CINCCENT's offensive war planning.

The Phase I briefing included four new ideas and corresponding slides and charts. The first presented Glosson's "Concept to Execution," expressed via an engineer's flow chart schematic:[184]

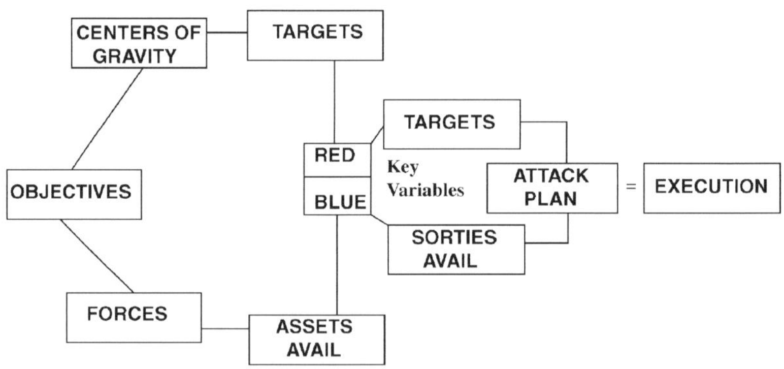

The second slide presented a centers-of-gravity chart listing leadership, infrastructure, and military forces. These three elements served as the Phase I target categories, with military *forces* used interchangeably with military *capabilities.* The targets numbered 127. The military capability category included such sites and equipment as the Baghdad air defense headquarters, Scud TELs, CW bunkers, CW-related airfields, and air defense sites.[185]

Neither the Republican Guard nor the Iraqi army in Kuwait appeared as Phase I targets on August 27, though a Republican Guard regiment had been a high-priority target in Glosson's briefing the previous day. The Guard would reappear in Phase I at a later date, but the elimination of that target set from Phase I on August 27 occurred because CENTAF offensive planning now consisted of Phases II and III, which were now Colonel Crigger's responsibility, not Glosson's. The Republican Guard and the Iraqi army in Kuwait would be destroyed in Phase III.[186]

A chart depicting the number of strike and SEAD sorties occurring in the first twenty-four hours came next, which prompted Horner to introduce a significant concept into the air campaign: continuously hit the Iraqis with air attacks and allow no significant pause. When the general first noted that the chart showed no sorties during certain blocks of time, he suggested distributing the strikes to eliminate some of the gaps. Tackling the problem, Deptula relied heavily on Navy TLAMs as time-fillers.[187] The fourth innovation incorporated a "results" chart. Phase I would "weaken resolve" and "induce fear" among Iraqis which would "generate internal strife." This phase would also "destroy military capability" and "eliminate gov't control" which would "decapitate Saddam regime." The internal strife and decapitated regime would result in "change."[188]

As the special planners prepared the briefings, ATO, and OPORD for Phase I, a message from Schwarzkopf injected urgency into the offensive planning effort. The CINCCENT needed to know how many targets the United States could strike if Saddam Hussein were to put a bullet through the head of the American ambassador in Kuwait. He wanted an "honest feel" for the amount of pounding the Americans could give Saddam. Glosson directed that the answer derive from Phase I targets and the availability of target folders.[189] Intense concern that the "crazy man in Baghdad" would execute Americans kept the planning effort in highest gear should a retaliatory option be needed.

Chapter Six

Special Planning Group

Believing that tension in the Persian Gulf region could rapidly escalate and require an immediate military response, General Glosson drove his Special Planning Group to prepare an executable ATO for the first phase of the Desert Storm air campaign and to include wing commanders and operators in the planning process. A lack of quality targeting material, however, disclosed an inability of intelligence organizations to support the prompt execution of the air campaign. The general developed his own intelligence sources and approved planning innovations: the MAP, a new target identification system, and a "targeting for effects" strategy.

Targeting Imagery Withheld

By the end of August, relations between the United States and Iraq worsened when the Iraqis demanded that all countries close and vacate their embassies in Kuwait. Iraq had annexed the nation it had invaded and declared it the nineteenth Iraqi province. Kuwait could no longer maintain independent, international relations; Baghdad would represent its interests in foreign affairs. The United States and the United Nations condemned Iraq's actions, and American diplomatic representatives and those from eight other nations remained at their posts in Kuwait City. In response, the Iraqis cut off electricity and supplies flowing to the facilities. Worse, Saddam Hussein further ordered the detention of foreigners in Iraq and Kuwait and had some people placed near oil facilities and chemical plants, possible targets in an air raid. President Bush penned his reaction to the Iraqi conduct: "Blatant hostage holding. Another blatant disregard of international law by a cruel and ruthless dictator. I cannot tolerate, nor will I, another Tehran. I am determined in that."[1]

To give the CINCCENT and the President a viable military option against Iraq, Glosson increased the pressure on his staff to produce as soon as possible an executable ATO for Phase I of the offensive air campaign. Referring to Saddam, Glosson commented, "Frankly, we gotta be ready in case that idiot starts putting bullets [through] Americans' heads." He told his planners to prepare for combat, not just a training scenario. "I hear too many people thinking in exercise terms....We're about to go to war, and we're going to be on the pointed edge of the spear," he declared.[2]

Glosson's directive to identify and count the strategic targets for which folders existed intensified the effort by Colonel Stanfill to obtain the Instant Thunder imagery acquired by Colonel Blackburn and his targeteers in Washington. The officer in Riyadh placed urgent telephone calls to Checkmate to track down the photographs and immediately send them to the Special Planning Group. Colonel Deptula had assured Glosson that Blackburn possessed imagery for each of the 84 Instant Thunder targets, and he tried to find out how soon the items would arrive in the AOR. Colonel Harvey informed the general that the DMAAC would send the mensurated coordinates for the imagery's pinpricked DMPIs. To their chagrin, however, they all waited in vain for the Instant Thunder imagery.[3]

Colonel Blackburn did not send the Special Planning Group the set of Instant Thunder photographs or the additional imagery of targets from the list CENTCOM had promulgated August 16.[4] "To this day," Deptula complained, "I don't know where those target packages are, and it caused no end of consternation and frustration that we had to reinvent the wheel with intelligence over here to put together new target folders to give to the units."[5] The officer moaned, "We were going crazy trying to acquire the folders for the Instant Thunder targets!"[6] Blackburn's withholding the imagery equally frustrated the targeteers in theater because it undermined their ability to support General Glosson and further eroded the confidence the planners placed in the targeteers' ability to satisfy operational requirements.[7]

Blackburn knew that in declining to fill the requests for the photographs he angered personnel in Riyadh; he believed, though, that by sending the set to them — images of poor quality — he would jeopardize the success of the air campaign.[8] When he returned from Florida with Warden after briefing Schwarzkopf on August 17, he and his staff of targeteers continued to work in Checkmate eighteen hours a day to locate photos for the 33 additional targets on the CENTCOM list of 109. They already had acquired the imagery for the 84 Instant Thunder targets, 76 of which overlapped with the CENTCOM list. They then had to select DMPIs for each of the 109 targets, based on multiple weapon systems.[9]

Blackburn knew that the DIA would shunt aside his request for imagery because it first responded to orders from the war-fighting commands, not from Air Staff offices, and he was aware that CENTCOM had already tasked the agency to do Desert Shield projects. He therefore negotiated with Colonel Cannon in CENTCOM J–2 to have Schwarzkopf's command send a message to the Air Staff targeteer authorizing him to task DIA on CENTCOM's behalf. Blackburn had told the CENTCOM commander at the briefing on August 17 that henceforward he would work directly for CENTCOM. He now desired and did indeed receive a message giving him DIA production tasking authority.[10]

Responding to the message, however, DIA told the targeteer that it would respond to his requests just as soon as it completed another higher priority job for CENTCOM. The DIA personnel labored twenty-four hours a day, seven days a week, preparing OSPs for CENTCOM's priority targets from the CENTCOM list of 109. DIA prepared the OSPs to be flown in bulk to Saudi Arabia. Unfortunately, most of the targets for which Blackburn needed imagery appeared on CENTCOM's secondary list, not the primary one on which DIA focused. Blackburn had to wait his turn, which could be weeks. Once again, the colonel resorted to acquiring imagery by sending targeteers to the DIA building to informally "beg, borrow, and steal" the required photos from analysts. The targeteer did not request that reconnaissance systems collect new imagery; he merely asked for material already on the shelf, archival products of any sort. As the targeteers had discovered when searching for Instant Thunder photos, sometimes the only available images were photocopies from microfilms of photos published in old studies. Nonetheless, within just a few days, they had acquired an image of some sort for each of the CENTCOM targets. They made three sets.[11]

Blackburn sent the first set of photos, with pinpricks showing DMPIs, to the DMAAC in St. Louis. An officer hand-carried the bundle and stayed at the facility as an adviser on the project. The targeteer had arranged for the DMAAC to mensurate the DMPIs, and the center went into a 24-hour production schedule to complete the task. Blackburn coordinated closely with Cannon at CENTCOM (a message from the CENTCOM chief of staff to the DMAAC on August 24 had formally tasked the center to mensurate DMPI coordinates, which it did).[12] By August 27 and for the next two and a half weeks, DMAAC issued a series of Top Secret messages listing targets, weapon systems, and DMPI coordinates for the targets. One message explained that the DMPI selection provided detailed and precise information for the delivery of weapons, but not the assignment of weapons to targets.[13] DMAAC sent the messages to approximately fifty addresses, including CENTCOM components and units, Air Force major commands, and Colonel Warden's directorate.

The messages flowed to the Special Planning Group's SCI tent where Glosson's targeteers worked. Unfortunately, Captain Glock and the other targeteers found the messages useless without the accompanying photographs because DMAAC described DMPIs for Blackburn's images and provided only narratives describing the location of aim points. It did not send the photos or provide explanations for why the DMPIs were selected, and it stipulated no objectives. Glock went to Colonel Leonardo and explained that the accompanying set of photos remained in Washington and must be acquired, but this did not result in the photos being sent to the theater.[14]

Blackburn sent the second set of photos by courier to Colonel Cannon at CENTCOM because he believed it was crucially important to keep the command informed of what he was doing. He kept the third set of photos for himself, with his staff's targeting material, in case he should need it for "subsequent support."[15] When members of Checkmate, responding to calls from Stanfill, asked Blackburn to send the target photos to Riyadh, they requested that he send target folders. Blackburn denied having any folders because, to him, a folder constituted a formal, substantive product.[16] Explaining a folder's contents, he said, opening one, "I would like to see good imagery. I would like to see enlargements of aim points, specific building dimensions, construct of the building, everything I need to support weaponeering." In contrast, he described the material in his possession as "working folders" or "target workups." Referring to one of his items, he said,

> To me, to call it a target folder implies there is more there than there really is.... To call it something as formal as a target folder implies that there is a lot more meat in there than there was. To me, if someone handed me a target folder, and I opened it up and there was a xerox copy of a piece of imagery, I would be pretty disappointed.

Blackburn thought that many of the images in his folders were pitiful, and then after transmittal to Riyadh, each would be "a fax of a xerox of a fourth generation that is five years old." He lamented, "I didn't want a 'go-to-war' plan based on a five-year-old xeroxed copy of an image from a book, from an old study."[17]

Blackburn knew that as poor as his target materials were, the DIA, as tasked by CENTCOM, produced superb products, "the highest quality...in the world." He believed that by denying Glosson's planners access to his miserable folders, they would naturally turn to CENTCOM and the intelligence system it controlled and would "make the system work." Blackburn wanted them "to invigorate the right procedures and taskings" to get as much targeting material as they needed from the U.S. intelligence community, through the war fighting command. "CENTCOM had to drive target materials," he explained.[18]

Blackburn knew, too, that the planners and intelligence officers in theater had to ensure that the "right conduits," "right tentacles," and adequate communication systems were built to transmit target materials from CENTAF or CENTCOM headquarters to the wings and units.[19] He explained:

> I got the request, and I said, "I don't have target folders," because they were talking about support of the wings. I said, "Guys, I tried to drive that and make that happen from CENTCOM, where that's got to come, and I got a copy to them. It's between you and your higher headquarters, CENTCOM."

The targeteer wanted the operator-planners to activate and tap into the intelligence system. "The system needs to be poked to be worked," he stated. "My getting a copy of a xeroxed image over to them is not going to help that unit execute to fly and bomb the target." The chief Air Staff targeteer did not understand how the system functioned in theater, but he was sure it would. "They needed to task their own lines of communication. Did I specifically lay that out? I wasn't even sure of the lash-up of intel in theater, and I wasn't the guy to work that."[20]

Blackburn's faith in the system and his holding on to the very items the special planners believed they needed so desperately angered them and Colonel Warden. To the Checkmate leader, the intelligence system failed to function, operating so slowly as of August 27–28 that it was useless, just at the very time the planners had to produce an executable plan, should Saddam Hussein assassinate Americans. Warden's view was "get the stuff to the people who needed it and fix the system later."[21] In contrast, Blackburn's view was to operate "by the book" to acquire the best products available. The planners needed targeting materials immediately if the CINCCENT had to execute air strikes immediately. The packages were good enough to send to DMAAC in St. Louis and CENTCOM in Florida and to retain for the targeteer's subsequent use, so they were good enough to send to the theater. To the JFACC's Special Planning Group, something was better than nothing.

Problems Acquiring Target Material and Imagery

The task of acquiring targeting material and imagery for offensive war planning fell directly on the young targeteers in the SCI tent in Riyadh, and the assignment severely tested their faith in the system. *Target material* meant target intelligence in graphic, textual, tabular, or another presentation format.[22] Targeteers faced three daunting problems in trying to make the national intelligence system flow material to them in support of the Special Planning Group and thence from the planners to the units.

Constituting the first was the lack of a CENTAF intelligence architecture, a blueprint, or plan, to explain how the national intelligence community, CENTCOM, and CENTAF would interrelate to activate the flow of intelligence analysis, targeting material and imagery, and battle damage assessments (BDA) to the theater in direct support of the planners and fighters. One intelligence officer explained, "Photos just don't appear, images just don't get taken, and HUMINT [human intelligence] taskings just don't materialize. A whole intelligence management structure had to be activated."[23] No comprehensive plan existed so that people, systems, and sources of data could be quickly integrated to produce timely intelligence. The delineation of responsibilities for the collection, production, and dissemination of intelligence at the national and theater levels and for support for the units was unclear, if stated at all.[24]

Even had a CENTAF intelligence blueprint existed, targeteers still faced a second problem: intelligence units of both CENTCOM and CENTAF were ill-prepared to support the Special Planning Group's offensive war planning. CENTCOM functioned as a have-not unified command, unlike commands such as the European and Pacific Commands which had organizations and numerous forces directly under their own control. CENTCOM, a have-not command, depended on augmentees to increase its ranks during wartime.[25]

To compensate for its small, undernourished size, CENTCOM developed a federated concept of intelligence, whereby it delegated responsibility to its components to specify requirements and develop the intelligence for component warfighting by analyzing both national and theater sources.[26] Under this concept, CENTCOM merely monitored the intelligence activities of its components, it neither directed nor supported them. CENTCOM delegated to CENTAF the responsibility for air order of battle and electronic order of battle; to ARCENT, it delegated responsibility for ground order of battle; and to NAVCENT, responsibility for naval order of battle.[27]

Aside from its small size and its federated structure, CENTCOM J–2 could not support CENTAF/IN, which in turn supported the Special Planning Group, because the J–2 entity was not prepared to go to war. The CINCCENT admitted, "CENTCOM's J–2 was not properly resourced, equipped, manned, trained, or organized to deploy and fight."[28] Aggravating the problem was that Schwarzkopf had established low deployment priorities for flowing equipment and personnel into Saudi Arabia for command, control, communications, and intelligence (C^3I). In the first weeks of Desert Shield, at precisely the time the planners urgently required it, no robust intelligence capability developed in the AOR.[29]

CENTAF/IN also lacked the capability to support the offensive air campaign. It had no effective collection management program until November and no local imagery production capability during the first three months of the deployment. Its own assessment later concluded,

> Basic database and automated processing support was either not available or woefully inadequate for the majority of intelligence functions (targeting, collection management, unit support, production management, [order of battle] maintenance, administration), and there was no connectivity with national data bases. [The] situation improved gradually with introduction of borrowed and bought systems, but these introduced their own problems of standardization and maintainability.[30]

CENTAF/IN was also unprepared to service the intelligence and imagery requirements of the Air Force's PGM systems — F–117As, F–15Es, and F–111Fs — upon which the strategic air campaign heavily depended.[31]

CENTAF did a superb job in generating the ATO, but it lacked the personnel, training, and equipment to support the units to ensure the successful execution of the ATO. The communication conduits and tentacles that Blackburn had worried about were, indeed, missing in theater. The capability to electronically transmit sufficient amounts of high-quality mission-planning and BDA imagery was absent.[32] General Horner mused,

> There is no doubt about it, we were ill-prepared to go to war on the intelligence side. We had a peacetime organization trying to fight war. We never exercised intelligence properly during our ORIs [operational

> readiness inspections]. We blew that. We exercised maintenance, we exercised munitions, we exercised pilots. I'm not down on the people; I'm down on the way we prepared to fight the war.[33]

The targeteers' third problem, though intangible, was real: the intense ill-will between the Air Staff lieutenant colonels and the intelligence officers. Deptula thought that Colonel Leonardo in theater and Colonel Blackburn in Washington undermined the offensive war planning by their lack of support for the enterprise. The outspoken criticism of Instant Thunder from the special planning targeteers — intelligence officers — contributed to Deptula's perception that intelligence was hindering the development of offensive war-planning.[34] Also permeating the atmosphere of the RSAF building was Horner's hostility toward the Air Staff's armchair generals and to Instant Thunder. The negativism spilled over to the CENTAF staff. Shortly after Warden briefed Horner, Leonardo sent the five targeteers to assist the Air Staff lieutenant colonels with instructions that Horner was "humoring" the officers, who would be gone in a week.[35]

Although CENTAF/IN gave the Special Planning Group its own targeteers in the SCI tent, CENTAF/IN provided woefully inadequate support because it remained isolated from the DoD targeting program. The directorate lacked online access to databases that allowed information exchange between the intelligence community and operational users. For example, it could not call up the Basic Encyclopedia, which derived from a compilation of installations and physical areas of potential significance. The encyclopedia contained basic data on the identification, location, and function of each installation. It could be used to select facilities for attack or to identify installations (such as universities and hospitals) to place on a no-strike list. CENTAF/IN had not deployed with online connectivity because, even at Shaw AFB in peacetime, it lacked that capability.[36]

Online access was critical to offensive planning because the intelligence community added, deleted, and upgraded installations in databases, especially after the August 2 Iraqi invasion of Kuwait. Before then, the U.S. collection program had not treated Iraq as a high priority, so now that the special planners needed the most up-to-date information, with accompanying imagery, the intelligence community was scrambling to identify Iraqi targets. Intelligence officers at the Ninth Air Force had been leaders in refocusing collection efforts toward Iraq (starting in spring 1990 when they began supporting target development for CENTCOM's OPLAN 1002–90), but their efforts were just beginning when Iraq seized Kuwait.[37]

The targeteers did have access to the Automated Tactical Target Graphics (ATTG) system, brought to the theater by CENTAF/IN.[38] ATTGs were lacking, however, for many targets on the special planners' target lists.[39] The average production date for the ATTGs was 1982; the oldest dated to 1972.[40]

The targeteers came to rely heavily on the TAC's 480th Tactical Intelligence Group at Langley AFB for the Special Planning Group's target material. Both the

480th Tactical Intelligence Group and 544th Strategic Intelligence Wing at Offutt AFB, Nebraska, functioned as DIA-delegated producers of the material, which meant that as the unified commands tasked the DIA to provide it, DIA, in turn, tasked various intelligence organizations to actually produce the photographic prints and textual data for targets. The 480th served as the DIA's primary delegated producer for CENTCOM. The unit also provided the command with air and defensive missile orders of battle.[41]

DIA kept for itself the responsibility to produce OSPs for CENTCOM, which provided imagery and textual data by target sets. CENTCOM directed the DIA to produce and distribute the OSPs under the JCS SPECAT security system, which further delayed production because few DIA analysts held the security clearance required for handling such material. The SPECAT OSPs would also cause difficulty for CENTAF in their distribution because neither CENTAF headquarters nor the wings and squadrons were sufficiently staffed with personnel authorized to receive the products. The DIA would not complete and send the first OSPs to theater until the first week of September, after having been tasked by CENTCOM in mid-August.[42]

While the DIA produced OSPs, it tasked the 480th Tactical Intelligence Group to create contingency target graphics (CTGs) and basic target graphics (BTGs) for CENTCOM. CTGs consisted of an image and a couple of lines of narrative; BTGs presented a gridded image and textual data about the photo itself and the target. BTGs began to replace ATTG data in 1990; their graphics were simpler than an ATTG's but more elaborate than a CTG's.[43]

CENTAF Rear headquarters, collocated at TAC headquarters, assisted the DIA and 480th Tactical Intelligence Group in sending target materials to theater by using an ancient means of delivery — couriers. An RC–135 Rivet Joint aircraft flew from Langley AFB to Riyadh on a daily, scheduled basis, delivering CTGs, BTGs, and other types of imagery and intelligence reports. The flights made bulk shipments. The 480th Tactical Intelligence Group used an even quicker transmittal means for single-item deliveries — electronic transmissions via satellite link. The first products sent electronically from the 480th to CENTAF came over a system known generically as a secondary imagery dissemination system (SIDS) and specifically as the Tactical Digital Facsimile (TDF). The TDF, a secure fax machine, transmitted and received photographic, printed, and handwritten material. Unfortunately, TDF transmission time was slower and product resolution was poorer than when other secure systems were used.[44]

Photos were required for targets in both Iraq and Kuwait, with the result that the demand for imagery was extraordinary. One officer observed, "The Army want[ed] a photo of every god-damned soldier [in Kuwait]! Everyone wanted pictures of where the hostages were. Everyone wanted pictures of the embassy in Kuwait."[45] CENTAF personnel looked for imagery for all targets in the offensive and defensive ATOs. Navy planners asked for imagery relating to all Iraqi maritime assets.

By the end of August, the 480th Tactical Intelligence Group's CTGs began to flow into the Special Planning Group's SCI tent for use by the targeteers. If the planners needed additional imagery of targets, that is, single prints without textual analysis and data, they contacted the 480th directly and requested that the prints be sent via TDF, followed by the hard copy sent on the EC–135. By early September BTGs began arriving in the tent.[46]

CENTAF had no authority to directly task the DIA or any of its delegated producers to provide new target material. The DIA tasking process required an intelligence officer, Captain Glock, for example, to prepare a written request and give it to the CENTAF/IN production-tasking monitor, who sent it to CENTCOM, which forwarded it to DIA, which tasked a delegated producer for it, which waited its turn to acquire the national overhead system imagery on the target, analyze it, and produce the target material, which then sent the material to the DIA, which sent it to CENTCOM, which sent it to CENTAF/IN, which gave it to the captain, who gave it to Glosson, weeks after the general thought he should have it.[47]

To give the special planners more responsive service, Glock cut through the DIA unified command bureaucracy and telephoned his buddies at SAC headquarters and 544th Strategic Intelligence Wing and requested information from online databases and intelligence studies, using the STU III telephone or secure fax machine. By calling the wing directly, the captain established an ad hoc conduit to the national intelligence community, as responsive to his requirements as Checkmate was to those from Colonels Deptula, Harvey, and Stanfill. Because most of the SAC intelligence personnel held multiple security clearances, the officer could freely converse with his colleagues about Glosson's targeting requirements. The security-access problem had kept the special planning targeteers isolated from the rest of the CENTAF staff.[48]

Glock's informal, effective intelligence conduit was short-lived. At the end of August, Colonel Meyer, the STRATFOR/IN director, arrived in theater and directed that all intelligence-related communication with SAC headquarters cease and be redirected to SAC via STRATFOR/IN. Analyst-to-analyst communication had to stop, which slowed Glock's access to SAC's intelligence systems and cut him and the other targeteers off from his coworkers, who were no longer just a phone call away and available to answer his queries anytime, day or night. His ability to respond quickly to Glosson's targeting queries suffered noticeably. The targeteer lamented that had he left Riyadh and returned to SAC headquarters, he could have provided greater assistance to the Special Planning Group

Capt. John R. Glock

because at Offutt AFB he would have had the tools to do his job and would have used them to send the planners the intelligence products they required.[49]

On the morning of August 27, Glosson held a staff meeting at which he bluntly stated that food in the U.S. embassy in Kuwait was expected to run out on September 5. "Enough said?" he asked. All understood the urgency of the special planning project. Halfway through the meeting, looking around the room, the general asked, "Who's working targeting?" No one from the SCI tent or from CENTAF/IN was present at the group's meeting.[50] The decision to segregate the targeteers in the tent was already denying the planners their expertise at crucial meetings, plus it prevented the targeteers the benefit of associating with their colleagues as Glosson directed their work and discussed problems. Throughout Desert Shield, the targeteers usually worked in the tent, isolated from the regular CENTAF staff and, more detrimentally, from their prime customers, the special planners. Glosson acquiesced to this unwise arrangement.[51] At that time, the targeteers compiled the list that the general had requested, disclosing the targets for which folders existed. For the general's 127 targets, ATTG data were available for only 29. Using the 544th Strategic Intelligence Wing's Digital Imagery Transfer System, the targeteers did acquire imagery for 108 targets. Blackburn's Instant Thunder imagery remained in the Pentagon.[52]

On the afternoon of August 28, after a meeting with wing representatives, Glosson told the targeteers that within twenty-four hours they had to send all the target folders to the wings. They labored all evening and night to respond to the directive, photocopying all ATTG sheets and photos and placing them in folders, with weaponeering sheets and intelligence reports. Because more than one wing would strike some targets, the targeteers made duplicates or triplicates of certain items. Harvey examined the products and thought they were "pitiful excuses for folders." Glock thought that about 80 targets had folders suitable for mission planning. He believed, too, that this would be the first task from Glosson that the targeteers would respond to on time.[53]

At about 0030 local time on August 29 a distressing event occurred. Colonel Leonardo, CENTAF/IN, came to the SCI tent and, as an officer observed, "ranted and raved."[54] He was furious at Glosson's directive to send the target folders to the wings by the next day and at what he said was the general's intention to send original imagery, ATTG sheets included, to the units. Leonardo complained that the wings should not receive the only imagery CENTAF/IN processed. What Glosson wanted was "not doable" and "not necessary."[55] The colonel fumed, "It was not right," and he exited the tent.[56]

Early the next afternoon, Glosson came to the SCI tent and went "ballistic."[57] The targeteers still sorted and packaged target folders and showed the general the bundles already completed, grouped according to wings and carrier groups. He inquired if the material included original imagery. The targeteers explained that, no, the originals would stay behind, while only photocopies went to the wings. Glosson demanded that they send all originals, which presented clearer images than copies. Raising his voice, he angrily stated that they were about to go to war and the pilots needed the best target material available. One captain stepped forward and explained that the defense planners also had to use Automated Tactical Target Graphics, and once they left Riyadh, it would be a long time before the target graphics could be replaced; if other targeting was necessary, no targeting graphics would be available. Glosson insisted that the offensive planning requirements be met. The young officer repeated that others also needed the graphics. The general sternly ordered him to leave the tent and go back to work for CENTAF/IN, which he did. Glosson ordered the other targeteers to send originals, so they unwrapped the bundles and replaced the photocopies with originals.[58] Harvey later noted, "General Glosson is really pushing things into action. [He] has placed his big boots squarely in the middle of the intel tent getting t[arget] folders out to…units."[59]

"Deptula Numbers" in Lieu of Basic Encyclopedia Numbers

Target folders were not the only issue to cause the value of the targeteers' stock to plummet in the special planning enterprise. In Checkmate, when Colonel Deptula worked on Instant Thunder and its flow plan, enthusiastic personnel surrounded him, eager to put together the CINCCENT's air plan. In Riyadh, it seemed everywhere he turned he met pessimism about the strategic air campaign. The targeteers resisted him on two crucially important ideas he conceived for generating the target list and preparing the MAP: Deptula numbers and targeting for effects.

At the time that the special planners had prepared the first briefing for General Horner, Glosson directed the targeteers to merge the Instant Thunder, CENTAF, and CENTCOM target lists. Following standard targeting procedures, they also prioritized the list, merging all targets from the separate Instant Thunder target categories. They matched as many targets as possible with their Basic Encyclopedia numbers. The JCS had mandated that Basic Encyclopedia numbers be used as unique identifiers to reduce confusion and possible errors within the DoD products.[60] When Captain Glock completed the list, Deptula immediately saw that it undermined his ability to work on his MAP because the merged list intermixed targets from all categories and, therefore, changed his Instant Thunder identification numbers, the Deptula numbers, as the targeteers referred to them. The colonel's numbers were now out of order. For example, on the intelligence officer's list, the twelfth strategic air defense target, SAD12, may have been listed ahead of SAD08, depending on the latest intelligence the targeteers had acquired. In addition, targets that had no Deptula numbers at all now appeared on the list.[61]

Deptula had invented his personal target identification system in Checkmate the week of August 8, calling his designators "target category numbers" or "category identification numbers." They constituted a convenient, shorthand, layman's alphanumeric system of identifiers, which functioned superbly for the operator-planners. Each identifier consisted of a letter or letters, signifying the target category, and a number, originally assigned in Checkmate after Blackburn's targeteers had prioritized the target category lists. At a glance, the Deptula numbers revealed a target's Instant Thunder category and its position on the list. For example, SAD10 was the tenth strategic air defense target on the SAD list. The Deptula category letters were A for airfields; C for chemical targets; E for electricity; L for leadership; NP for naval port; CCC for telecommunications; MP or MS for military production and storage; RR for railroads; O for oil; and SAD for strategic air defense. Deptula numbers perfectly suited the colonel's thought process and provided a congenial system for other special planners, as well.[62]

Deptula numbers enabled the colonel to immediately visualize a target, especially if he lacked a photo of it. E11 conjured up for him an image of an electrical power plant; to him, its Basic Encyclopedia number meant nothing. When Deptula numbers were placed on a map, he could quickly refer to target locations and mentally link attacks in adjacent areas. He neither knew of nor used the DoD's functional category codes, which designated targets' functions by five-digit numeric codes. All electrical power plants anywhere in the world carried the same category code. Intelligence officers who worked with the codes on a regular basis soon memorized them and came to know target types just by glancing at the numbers. Category codes, like Basic Encyclopedia numbers, however, conveyed no mnemonic aspect, whereas the Instant Thunder planners could easily remember that SAD meant strategic air defense, E meant electricity, and so on.[63]

Glock encouraged Deptula to abandon his unorthodox numbers and adopt the use of Basic Encyclopedia numbers because throughout DoD they were the standard, recognized target identifiers. Each target had only one Basic Encyclopedia number, whereas, multiple Deptula numbers could be assigned a single site, such as Tallil airfield being C01 and A05, although Deptula readily understood that C01 represented a chemical-related target at Tallil, and A05, a counterair one. The intelligence officers preferred Basic Encyclopedia numbers because they allowed for reshuffling target priorities without distorting the meaning of the number, but if new intelligence disclosed that SAD12 was more important than SAD08, moving SAD12 higher on the prioritized list distorted the original meaning of SAD12 in relation to other SAD targets.[64]

Deptula tried to use the prioritized list, but he found it alien to his way of conceptualizing the attack flow and selecting targets for it. He insisted that the list of targets be separated by Instant Thunder target categories and be reassigned the sequential Deptula numbers. He wanted new targets added to the end of the list under each category in the order of their receipt. He realized and accepted that the targets would not then be listed in priority order, but chronologically as acquired. He wanted each target to permanently retain its original Deptula number because on the MAP he identified it as such. Glock objected to this procedure because it did not reveal the priority of categories or the priority of targets across and within categories. By not prioritizing targets within each category list, it was unclear if SAD12 was more important than SAD 20. When Glock gave the colonel a traditional, standard target list, Deptula said it was "like throwing a hand grenade into the planning process," necessitating a complete revision of the MAP, requiring many hours of his time.[65]

Deptula had no time to debate the merits of his system. He just knew it worked for him and for others in accomplishing their tasks, and Basic Encyclopedia numbers hindered him. He told the captain that, henceforward, the special planners on the third floor of the RSAF building would keep and maintain the target list, not the targeteers in the SCI tent.[66]

The planners basically built the offensive target list according to target categories and Deptula numbers. As new targets emerged, the planners assigned them the alphanumeric designators in chronological order. They did not prioritize the new targets. By mid-December their list included 240 targets, and during the war they added hundreds more. As best they could, they diligently added Basic Encyclopedia numbers to their lists. Glosson approved of their procedures. Before Desert Storm, officers within the Special Planning Group, not the targeteers in the SCI tent, became the experts on the various target categories. Prioritization would occur during the war as Deptula daily crafted the MAP. The planners did not maintain a single prioritized list, mixing targets from all the categories, nor did they prioritize targets within each of the various category lists.[67]

Targeting for Effects

The second of Deptula's new ideas was targeting for effects, which he believed improved the standard Air Force targeting methodology. When Glosson asked the targeteers in the SCI tent to consolidate the Instant Thunder, CENTAF, and CENTCOM lists, they prioritized the targets on a single list and then weaponeered for destruction.[68] Glock recalled that Deptula told them to *destroy* targets and *kill* the air defense facilities. They interpreted his instructions to mean that they should weaponeer for destruction, the highest level of damage in the targeteer's lexicon, although they had other standard options such as attacking to disrupt, delay, neutralize, deceive, or harass.[69] The targeteers defined weaponeering as "The process of determining the quantity of a specific type weapon required to achieve a specified level of damage to a given target, considering target vulnerability, weapon effects, munition delivery errors, damage criteria, probability of kill, weapon reliability, etc."[70] They consulted the DoD's Joint Munitions Effectiveness Manual and, using target worksheets, indicated weapons and aircraft, in optimal combinations, that would destroy each target.[71]

When they gave Deptula their assessments, he realized he had available only a tiny fraction of the aircraft necessary to strike the required targets on the first day of the air campaign. As a glaring example, only eighteen F–117A stealth aircraft had arrived in theater as of August 31, 1990, and eight of them in each of two groups were needed to destroy just two targets, the Taji and the Tallil airfield SOCs.[72] Destruction of the C^2 equipment in the bunkers at the bottom of each hardened facility required eight F–117s delivering GBU–10 and GBU–27 2,000-pound bombs. The weaponeering accomplished in Checkmate for Instant Thunder had also required that eight F–117s deliver laser-guided weapons against a SOC. Deptula mused, "That's a hell of a lot of resources being sucked up."[73] Although the Air Force called the F–117A a fighter, it operated as a single-seat, light bomber, carrying only two weapons internally and delivering only one PGM at a time, necessitating a separate run-in to drop the second bomb. At the start of Desert Storm, the F–117s would hit one target and then fly to a different facility and strike it, minimizing the amount of time over each target.

Struggling to match a limited number of aircraft against a large number of targets, especially critical components of the air defense system about which the planners had just received new intelligence, Deptula formulated the concept he initially described as targeting for effects, and which he much later termed "simultaneity" and "parallel warfare." He realized that to achieve the effects he wanted, he did not have to destroy targets, he had only to disrupt or maim their function.[74] He explained,

> The thought struck me that all you need to do is put one or two bombs on one of these places and that's enough to achieve what we want to do at that time and that frees up all these other assets. Now I don't have to put 8 117s against the operations center, I'll put one or two of them and that frees up 6 or 7 others to use against other targets....So now if I could get this entire base at one time, right off the bat, even though I don't destroy it 100 percent, that is a hell of an impact that you can have.[75]

Targeting for effects focused on damaging or eliminating the function of a facility, not physically destroying the target. This procedure allowed the key planner to dispense with weaponeering as done by targeteers. Rudimentary, rule-of-thumb weaponeering was sufficient, commensurate with the level of knowledge a pilot acquired at the USAF Fighter Weapons School. "I'm not going to weaponeer," Deptula explained, "because of the number of targets we have, combined with the number of assets we have — I'm not going to achieve 80 percent destruction on every single target. It would suck up too many resources."[76] This methodology enabled him to dispense with a single, prioritized target list. Instead, he listed the targets according to their categories, which enabled him to use his unique target identification system and build and constantly modify the MAP.[77] As he saw it, many more targets were Priority 1 than were indicated by a single, prioritized list. He observed, "There's not a 1 through 6 priority. Some of those are all 1s. That kind of mindset is the thing that drove me to just putting one or two bombs on a couple of the targets. That opens up the number of targets that I can hit."[78]

Targeting for effects meant simultaneously striking targets from all categories. This rationale led the colonel to plan attacks against as many targets as possible to achieve the effect of disrupting their military function.[79] Deptula developed a strategy to disrupt and maim, which already existed as a standard Air Force targeting option.[80] His rationale did not flow from theory, but from practical and time-constrained concerns stemming from the lack of a sufficient number of stealth aircraft in theater.

Targeting for effects acted as a force multiplier for Deptula, and the force he most wanted to increase was that of the F–117As. The aircraft had three attributes that made them his weapon of choice. First, their stealthiness gave them "an inherent degree of air superiority."[81] Their missions did not first require force packaging and strikes to take down radars and cripple air defense assets. Cloaked in the night's darkness and evading radar detection, the planes flew to targets and returned as solo, untracked night bombers.[82]

Second, the accuracy of the laser-guided bombs the F–117As delivered was extraordinary.[83] Deptula talked with the 37th Tactical Fighter Wing commander, which flew the stealth aircraft, and with the F–117 representative in the Special Planning Group and heard about the precision of laser-guided weapons, including the GBU–27. The weapons in flight detected laser energy that guided them to targets illuminated by an external laser source, which in the case of the F–117 emanated from the delivery aircraft. Deptula's reliance on the F–117s was based on data the 37th Tactical Fighter Wing compiled, which consistently disclosed bull's-eye hits. Not only could the GBU–27 reliably hit DMPIs, its accuracy minimized collateral damage.[84]

Finally, the F–117's GBU–27 was a hardened, penetrator bomb, capable of passing through four to six feet of concrete, an indispensable capability against numerous targets. As Deptula observed,

> Penetration was a big factor in this conflict: hardened aircraft shelters, bunkers, air defense operations centers, the sector operations centers, and the [intercept operations centers]. This guy really spent a lot of money on hardening his facilities. They have a much harder infrastructure than the United States.[85]

The reinforced concrete in Iraq met its match with the GBU–27.[86]

As a targeteer, Captain Glock worried about Deptula's targeting for effects and spoke to the colonel about it. Dropping only one GBU–27 against a SOC hardened by concrete made little sense to him, because the 2,000-pound PGM contained only about 550 pounds of explosives. The GBU–27 carried a fuze that ticked as the bomb penetrated, but he believed the weapon would detonate before it punched and burrowed deeply enough to arrive at the core of the operations center.[87]

The targeteer thought the BDA imagery would fail to reveal if a SOC was disrupted. He feared the Iraqis might simply cease all operations at the air defense centers until an appointed day, husbanding their resources, and then activate them and swing into full operation at the most inopportune time, like the day the ground war started. Glock knew, too, that some bunkers were both hardened and compartmentalized, and the 550 pounds of explosives detonating in a reinforced compartment would cause only slight damage to the target and not necessarily prevent it from functioning.

He believed that levels of physical destruction correlated with disrupting and eliminating the target's function. As a targeteer, he did not want to physically destroy a target, he wanted to reduce its operation to a level to meet the targeting objective. If one of the air campaign's goals was to eliminate Iraq as a regional threat, the facilities supporting Iraq's ability to threaten its neighbors had to be sufficiently damaged to achieve the desired objective. If the Iraqis waved the white flag in only a few days, and if Saddam Hussein himself was not killed, targeting for effects would leave the despot in power and Iraq as a regional menace. Glock advocated prioritizing the categories and prioritizing all targets within each category. He thought it foolish to "waste" weapons on radio and television transmitters when planners should concentrate on more important and critical targets, many of which were hardened. Targeting for effects would squander air power and produce an unfocused air campaign.[88]

Deptula told the captain that the targeteer's methodology reflected a narrow, service-the-target-list mentality, which overlooked stunning, interrelated results achievable against an entire target base to create widespread disruption in the functions of individual target systems, particularly in the opening night of the air campaign.[89] He explained that he wanted to stun operators and maim all the target sets simultaneously, as opposed to striking one target sct at a time, because the across-the-board effects would be more debilitating to the Iraqi defenders.[90] Although the planner did not explicitly prioritize target sets or targets within sets on a list, he did craft the MAP with priorities and centers of gravity uppermost in his mind.[91] He later explained,

> While attacking all target categories, focus was maintained within the target sets. Eliminating the Iraqi integrated air defense system and rendering their air force ineffective [were] the first priority of the air campaign; however, stealth aircraft allowed us to keep continuous pressure on key leadership and command and control nodes prior to the attainment of air superiority by conventional means.[92]

When Deptula sought Glosson's approval for his targeting strategy, the general asked, "What in the hell do you mean, 'targeting for effects'?" Upon hearing the explanation about hitting the entire target base to achieve widespread, paralyzing blows against the Iraqi defenders and not obliterate targets, Glosson authorized the methodology. He did not see it as revolutionary in any way, but indicative of a commonsense approach, especially since it exploited the accuracy of PGMs. "Don't change a thing, keep doing what you're doing," he told the colonel.[93]

Deptula targeted for functional disruption for the first twenty-four hours of the air campaign. During the war, Glosson's concern that the conflict might end abruptly kept the focus on hitting as many targets as possible before a ceasefire to maintain pressure on the military forces. Targeting for effects, and the effects being functional disruption and kills, became the strategic air campaign's underlying bombardment strategy. The special planners did not, however, develop and apply clear criteria to determine when structural damage was sufficient to produce functional disruption and destruction. Problems with BDA would make evaluations of structural and functional damage very difficult.

Against CW targets, General Glosson ignored the functional approach and demanded absolute physical kills. He wanted these targets destroyed so that the Iraqis could not remove any of their components. Warden in Checkmate weighed in, urging Glosson after the first few days of the war to concentrate his forces on two target categories, aircraft shelters and telecommunications. Receiving target nominations from Checkmate and other sources and reflecting the priorities of Generals Glosson and Horner and target category experts in the Special Planning Group, Deptula continued to build each day's MAP during the conflict. His emphasis on building force packages for nonstealthy aircraft and sending them and the F–117As on separate but mutually supportive missions also influenced the targets selected and effects achieved.[94]

Push–Pull Intelligence and the IADS

In late August, yet another intelligence problem confronted the Special Planning Group: CENTAF/IN's tendency to provide intelligence data only if the planners specifically asked for it. The members had to *pull* intelligence, rather than CENTAF/IN *pushing* it to them.[95] The issue first arose as Glosson and Deptula tried to understand and target the Iraqi IADS. Deptula had brought from the Pentagon the draft, 60-page Operation Proud Flame report produced by the Joint Electronic Warfare Center's (JEWC's) liaison office in Europe. As the two officers waited in Bahrain for a flight to Riyadh, after their meeting with Navy officials on the USS *LaSalle,* Deptula started reading the intelligence product, which analyzed the Iraqi air defense system and electronic order of battle. Glosson joined him, and they both intently studied the report and sketched a diagram of the entire IADS layout. They thought the study conveyed indispensable information.[96]

They were surprised to learn that the IADS consisted of four, not two, SOCs which covered the country in its northern, central, western, and southern regions. A fifth SOC was being established for Kuwait. Each SOC had subordinate intercept operations centers (IOCs), and each IOC had observation and EWR reporting posts. This new information considerably expanded the strategic target base. IOCs vectored Iraqi aircraft against enemy aircraft and provided data for SAM launches. The national air defense operations center (ADOC) was located in Baghdad. Kari linked components of the IADS and functioned as the system's brain. To shoot down incoming enemy aircraft, the IADS relied on intercept aircraft; radar- and infrared-guided SAMs; and AAA, firing in mostly barrage mode. The system's radars were low-frequency, early-warning models and higher frequency tracking and acquisition radars.[97]

The day after he read the IADS study, Glosson asked a lieutenant colonel from CENTAF/IN who was now assigned as the Special Planning Group's chief intelligence officer if he had known about the Proud Flame report. The officer replied that he had. Glosson inquired why he and his staff had not been provided with such information. The colonel replied that they had not asked for it.[98] To the key planners, this was an example of the push-versus-pull intelligence support problem. "You had to ask for the right information. Ask for updates on the order of battle, chemical [weapons] capable airfields, Scuds, location of Republican Guards — all would go unfilled until the second or third requests," Deptula lamented.[99]

The special planners valued the subsequent Proud Flame analysis that JEWC disseminated. Glosson occasionally telephoned Maj. Gen. Gary W. O'Shaughnessy, commander of the Air Force's Electronic Security Command and director of JEWC in San Antonio, Texas, to acquire additional information about the Iraqi air defense system and electronic order of battle. On August 30, another JEWC report disclosed a fifth air defense sector, this one responsible for the airspace over Kuwait.[100] The flood of new information about the IADS and the numerous targets it suggested prompted Deptula to adopt his strategy of targeting for effects, in part, to free up enough aircraft to strike the critical components of the air defense system to swiftly gain air superiority as the air campaign commenced.

Glosson's Personal Intelligence Sources

While the Special Planning Group relied on Checkmate to supplement and supplant the intelligence coming from CENTAF/IN, Glosson tapped his own intelligence sources. In planning against the Iraqi air force, he blended data from official sources with what he acquired from talking with pilots from Egypt, Bahrain, Saudi Arabia, Kuwait, and UAE. He acquired some of the most persuasive information about the Iraqi air force from a Middle Eastern military contact. In reply to a query from Glosson about the number of Iraqi fighter pilots good enough to be in the U.S. Air Force, the officer replied it was 20, maximally 30. The general asked British and French pilots who had trained the Iraqis, and they estimated that there were 50 to 60 good Iraqi pilots.[101] Glosson therefore decided on 50 as the number of really competent pilots. He mandated that the offensive planning be built on the assumption that there were only fifty good Iraqi pilots and that they concentrated at only a few airfields: Tallil, al-Taqaddum, al-Asad, Balad SE, and al-Jarrah.[102]

To further understand the vulnerability of electrical power plants as a target set, Glosson telephoned his friends who worked for a U.S. power company and questioned them about regenerating power at facilities when their major components were damaged. He agreed with the Instant Thunder rationale of striking the electrical plants such that they could be rebuilt in a relatively short period after the conflict. He commented,

> If they were going against a power grid, I wanted them to go against the elements in the power station that would be most easily repairable after the war. You must understand that I had the mindset at that point in time that probably the U.S. government would be instrumental in putting this country back together.[103]

He discussed with his American contacts the components that Iraq had as backups and could utilize to restore power, and those pieces of equipment it had to acquire from abroad, having no spares. He learned that Iraq could rather easily replace transformers and within days build transformer workarounds. Although Iraq could not replace generators, the United States could within weeks or months.[104]

Glosson's research suggested to him that the air campaign should target generators. This directly conflicted with the advice Deptula gave the targeteers whereby he identified the DMPI as the transformers, not the generators, to facilitate their quick repair. The Instant Thunder planners had understood that generators were custom-made, not quickly built, and certainly not readily available in the quantity necessary if they were destroyed at all the targeted Iraqi power plants. The inconsistency and differing conclusions about generators and transformers as targets would remain unresolved during Desert Shield and would plague the planners during Desert Storm.[105] In addition, officers at SAC headquarters who planned the B–52 CALCM strikes against electric power plants in Iraq selected neither generators nor transformers as aim points. To achieve the desired effect of limiting long-term damage to electrical facilities and to capitalize on the limited number of CALCMs and the weapon's highly unusual and secret effects, the planners targeted the middle rows of switches at the power facilities to disrupt the wiring leading to the circuit breakers.[106] In this case, the weapon determined the aim point.

Glosson's estimation of the value of telecommunications targets increased significantly when he consulted with members of the royal families of Coalition nations in the Persian Gulf region. He noted:

> I talked to every royal family, all five. Over a period of a week and a half I asked this question of everyone of them: "Tell me the two things that would bother you most if you didn't have it...." Every one of them gave me the telephone as most important. The second thing that every one of them gave me was a radio or television. Then depending on which nation you talked to, some of them had cars next. Some of them had housing next. Some of them had medical treatment; it was kind of a hodgepodge. But it was very enlightening to me that they all said tele-

> phones, radio, and television. I believed that. It was reinforcing; it wasn't something I didn't expect.[107]

Instant Thunder's emphasis on cutting Saddam's control over the Iraqi population by targeting Iraqi civil telecommunications appealed to the general. He explained:

> I not only wanted to destroy their command and control and the way they function as a nation, but also the way they control their military. I wanted to make it as near impossible as I could for that government to talk to the outside world, to communicate with his own people. I wanted to put every household in an autonomous mode and make them feel that they were isolated. I didn't want them to be able to listen to radio stations and know what was happening.[108]

Glosson's personal intelligence collection system included friends who worked at key agencies in the U.S. national intelligence community and who answered questions that he telephoned to them. The contacts, whom he thought of as his moles, held positions at the NSA, CIA, and NSC. The NSA contact had been a student with him at the National War College; the CIA contact was an ex-fighter pilot; and the NSC contact was an individual whom the general had met when he worked on the Air Staff as a legislative liaison officer.[109] His most lucrative personal intelligence source, Rear Adm. John M. "Mike" McConnell, Joint Staff J–2, would not enter the picture until mid-October, after Glosson's visit to Washington to brief the air campaign to President Bush.[110]

MAP and ATO

As Glosson and the Special Planning Group worked feverishly at the end of August to rework the Instant Thunder plan and develop the target list and materials, they also had to produce an executable ATO. The group completely depended on personnel from the CENTAF Combat Plans Division for knowledge and expertise to accomplish the task. Initially, Major Waterstreet reported to the general to produce the ATO for the group. Major Sweeney joined him shortly thereafter. They carried a heavy workload. They prepared the daily ATO and the D-day ATO, which they attended to in the morning and early afternoons, before progressing to Glosson's ATO in the late afternoon and evening. They could not explain to their colleagues in Combat Plans where they went or what they did. Using a laptop, they clandestinely developed the Desert Storm ATO.[111]

With Glosson's approval, Deptula made his MAP the starting point for the ATO builders, but Waterstreet and Sweeney did not consider it necessary for their work and viewed Deptula as "basically ignorant of the planning and ATO process." They saw him spending prodigious amounts of time choosing targets and then selecting aircraft to support a mission — building force packages — for his MAP. They explained to him CENTAF's established procedures for producing an ATO, which involved teams of targeteers and operator-planners doing weaponeering and force packaging more efficiently and swiftly than he could working alone. Sweeney recalled,

Maj. John D. Sweeney

> In the very beginning of this planning process, Dave Deptula (with only air-to-air background) was obviously struggling with how to balance the target priorities, timing, force packages, etc. I commented to him, "Dave, we have guys on the staff who are trained to do that. Why don't you let them help?" Dave's reply was "No, I have to do it myself."[112]

Waterstreet and Sweeney tried to convince Deptula to adjust his planning method to exploit the expertise of the CENTAF staff. Deptula recollected their telling him he devoted too many hours figuring out strike packages for each target. He should select the targets from the list the intelligence officers provided, based on the commander's objectives, prioritize the targets, and indicate the level of damage required for each. Deptula remembered heavy emphasis on physically destroying targets instead of functionally disrupting them. Targeteers would then weaponeer to determine the type and number of munitions for the desired level of destruction. Planners would then construct the force packages for the strike aircraft.[113] Deptula explained his targeting-for-effects rationale and emphasized that the MAP introduced timing and coherency for strikes which the ATO, built merely from standard procedures, lacked.

Deptula's choice of targets for his attack plan focused on their intrinsic value and a target's proximity to other targets and its function in relationship to them. He grouped facilities and areas for attack on the basis of their interrelated ability to threaten Saudi Arabia or Coalition forces or defend Iraqi forces and sites. A geographical and political map of Iraq showing the location of the strategic targets by their Deptula numbers enabled him to lay out the attack flow because it showed target locations and revealed target types and functions. He mentally processed this information to identify which targets had to be taken out simultaneously and which sequentially to break the functional interdependence of the sites. The location and function of targets suggested to him the force packaging required.[114] He explained:

> It is so important to understand that it's just not a target list that's prioritized, and we match assets to it....If you wanted to hit Latifiya solid fuel propellant factory...we also have a couple of other places up there. We've got al-Asad and al-Taqaddum airfields. If you just use a target list mentality, you don't know when those things will pop up on the ATO. What you have to do is look at a map. Latifiya is right here, al-

> Taqaddum is here, and al-Asad is here....If you leave it to chance or...just to priorities, and put Latifiya first, it may fall out as being attacked first. If you attack it first, you leave your flank open. There's activity over here, and you leave yourself vulnerable to come under attack by these and these places. What I mean by coherency and timing is what I did in this actual example: attack al-Asad at 0700, put together an attack package for al-Taqaddum at 0710 and an attack package for Latifiya at 0720. At 0720...you step across...you cut them off. That's the kind of thought process that goes together in putting together an attack plan. It's not simply matching assets with targets.[115]

Deptula could not see a step to integrate timing and coherency within the standard CENTAF procedures for developing the ATO.[116] To him the generation of the tasking order merely involved a process. The ATO, he stated, "is nothing more than an administrative vehicle to get the plan out to the units, to the executors. We should never associate the term *planning* with the ATO. We should associate processing with the ATO. The plan is something separate and distinct."[117] The MAP was more than the ATO and more than simply serving the target list. To Glosson and Deptula, "servicing the target list was the whoring of air power."[118] The general, too, saw a significant, qualitative difference between the MAP and the ATO. The ATO was merely a "mechanical process."[119] "The brai[n] of an air campaign," said Glosson, "is the master attack plan."[120] The general and the colonel discussed the MAP's format and approach, and because they agreed on its considerable value, the younger officer did not have to worry about anyone going around him to the general to force him to stop using it.[121]

Not only was Deptula's MAP new to the ATO builders, so was his designator "SAT" to identify a type of air mission. Majors Waterstreet and Sweeney queried him about the meaning of SAT on his attack plan, to which he replied "strategic attack." They claimed there was "no such mission" and explained to him that the ATO's CAFMS allowed for only three types of air mission: OCA, offensive counterair; INT, interdiction; and CAS, close air support. Deptula thought the limited air mission designators in CAFMS, and CENTAF's acquiescence to the limitation, absurd, provoking him to launch into a "two-hour lecture on doctrine" and the effective use of air power. Waterstreet and Sweeney were quite right, however; CAFMS could not accept SAT. The CENTAF staff described *strategic* targets as deep interdiction. Deptula had to settle for INT as the designator for the strategic air campaign's sorties. He fumed, asking what *interdiction* had to do with striking such obviously strategic sites as the Ministry of Defense building and radio and television stations in Baghdad.[122] Throughout Desert Shield, Deptula launched into two-hour effective-use-of-air-power lectures so frequently and with such enthusiasm that some members of the Special Planning Group humorously dubbed him the "Prophet of Air Power," facetiously putting him in a category with Douhet, Trenchard, and Mitchell.[123]

Deptula manually produced the MAP, then the administrative staff entered his data into a MacIntosh computer but one that lacked an interactive database program. Deptula had to manually track each change in the flow plan. Revisions occurred constantly as he learned of new targets and assets, creating complex, cascading effects throughout the document, each requiring adjustment. Deptula invented the MAP, so no off-the-shelf software existed for its production. In August and early September he concentrated on writing the MAP for the ATO, and he did not have time to coordinate with a software specialist to develop a computer program to accommodate his needs. During the five months of Desert Shield, he returned to Washington a few times, and in his absence, the Special Planning Group made only slight changes on the first day's MAP (compared with changes in January 1991 and those during Desert Storm, which he made). The absence of an interactive database made MAP production an extraordinarily difficult mental exercise, and because the colonel did not document and record his rationale for selecting specific targets from the categories and for grouping them and timing force packages for coherency, only he intimately understood the MAP. He was the primary person to work on it through Desert Shield, and the only person during Desert Storm.[124] He constantly apprised Glosson of his planning, and the general's directives often led to additional changes.

By General Horner's explicit direction during Desert Shield, Glosson and Deptula could produce ATOs for only the first two days of the air campaign. Horner wanted the third day's ATO to respond to the attacks of the first forty-eight hours and thus avoid inflexibility — the third day's ATO remained a shell. The JFACC explained:

> You see, in SAC they used to plan the war....Everything became very rigid. It got so if you didn't go to the chow hall at a certain time in SAC, then you would lose points. I'm not against that! For nuclear war, that is probably the way to do business. In conventional war, it's action–reaction a lot, and you have got to be able to capitalize on mistakes the enemy makes....I did not want them to become so enthralled with preplanning that they were unable to react when the war started. That is why I would never let them do a full-day, third-day ATO.[125]

In planning tanker missions, a crucially important aspect of ATO building, the Special Planning Group received expert assistance from two "tanker guys," Colonel Pritchett and Major Hente, who received guidance from General Caruana and worked closely with Majors Waterstreet and Sweeney and individual unit representatives in coordinating tanker assets with receiver missions and requirements. They eventually created two products for the offensive ATO: special instructions (SPINS) and mission lines. Tanker SPINS provided a one-line version of each refueling event, showing receiver mission number, number and type of aircraft, package identification, tanker track or orbit, altitude, offload, fuel available, tanker mission number, and base of origin, with perhaps additional remarks as well. When sorted in a particular order, this information facilitated force management and confirmed that refueling needs were met. Major Sweeney explained that SPINS ensured that aircraft receive the required amount of fuel at the correct place and time, with tanker cells aligned at the proper altitudes; that SPINS allowed tanker bases to see their requirements and assisted base personnel to ready the aircraft and execute flow planning; and that SPINS provided a snapshot of all refueling activities for a specific time.[126]

When the Special Planning Group first formed, members placed little emphasis on SPINS because the planners assumed that a quick execution of the offensive ATO would rely on the SPINS used for the daily ATO or the D-day ATO, modified as required. By the end of November, however, the Desert Storm ATO developed its own SPINS. At this time, Major Sweeney negotiated with the tanker, radio frequency, and airspace managers to agree on one format for Desert Storm ATO SPINS, based on the format designed for the Special Planning Group's ATO. The new SPINS did cause some shift in the Desert Storm airspace and tanker locations then in use, but they effectively supported the first two days of the air campaign. The refueling requirements generated during the third through sixth days of the campaign, however, a period for which no finely honed, preplanned MAPs and ATOs existed, would create a wartime planning crisis which Glosson would address and resolve, relying on his Vietnam War experience.[127]

Once the planners completed and checked the SPINS, they used the instructions to create in the CAFMS individual tanker mission lines for the ATO. Maj. Thomas Eaves wrote the computer software program that automatically converted SPINS data to CAFMS lines. His program operated quickly and saved the CENTAF staff hundreds of hours of manual data entry and proofreading. The ATO builders and tanker experts believed Eaves's talent, that of a programming genius, would have saved millions of dollars for a company in the private sector.[128]

Involving the Wings

Glosson harbored strong feelings about involving the wing commanders and units in the planning process, stemming from his experience in Vietnam. He believed the operators would offer valuable suggestions about the best use of their assets. He noted:

> On the receiving end as a captain and a junior major I saw the headquarters send down ATOs which absolutely bordered on being criminally negligent. They sent us to the same targets, or the same route of flight, the same time of day, day in and day out. The people in Haiphong and Hanoi could have set a tea call at 8:00 to 8:30 every morning by the noise of the jets and been very certain that they would have been with-

> in 5 or 10 minutes of exactly the same time. We would do the same thing in the afternoon, and we continued that for years on end. Our loss rate, I think, was significantly higher as a result of that stupidity. So, I made a promise to myself: Not me! I committed myself to individual units having a say in not only the control of their own tactics, but having a say in how we were doing things from an overall perspective...as long as it didn't detract from the overall objectives that were set.[129]

On August 28 at the RSAF headquarters building, Glosson met with representatives from each of the operational units, including Marine Corps and Navy personnel, and briefed them on Phase I of the offensive air campaign. He told them that their units had to prepare their portion of the first day's ATO for a "possible execution" August 31. He explained that target folders would be sent to the units the next day, August 29, after which they would have twenty-four hours to contact the Special Planning Group with their questions and concerns and be ready to execute. He commented that they had to be prepared if Saddam Hussein should start to kill Americans. He called the plan Desert Storm.[130]

Glosson repeated the briefing he had given Horner on August 27, after which Deptula explained the MAP and its attack flow. The operators asked questions and offered suggestions. One comment highlighted the need for a standard time reference, and the colonel responded that they based the MAP on Baghdad time, the same as local time in Riyadh. Glosson emphasized that pilots had to arrive over their targets within three minutes of the planned time, or else go home. When discussing deception, the general explained that the air picture the Iraqis would see on their radars would be the same they had seen throughout Desert Shield, and it would remain unchanged until the initial offensive strikes.[131]

In Glosson's briefing to the operators, he did not use the word *strategic;* he described Phase I as a *deep interdiction* air campaign. Later that evening in the dinner line, Deptula asked him why he avoided the word, and he replied that strategic meant nuclear weapons. The colonel rejoined, as he had with the ATO builders, that attacking the Ministry of Defense in Baghdad was not an interdiction operation, nor were striking the Baath Party Headquarters building and radio and television stations in downtown Baghdad interdiction. The operations comprised strategic strikes and strategic targets. The colonel and general tossed ideas back and forth throughout dinner, as they often would throughout the deployment and war. Afterward, Glosson adopted the word *strategic* to describe the air campaign and its targets. Deptula subsequently told Colonel Harvey, who helped to write the OPORD for the offensive air campaign Phase I, to insert *strategic* into the OPORD wherever appropriate. Harvey gleefully complied.[132]

Flying to each land-based unit on August 29 and 30, Colonel Wilson hand-delivered the ATO and target folders for the offensive air campaign. A letter from Glosson to the commanders stated:

> We need your help in scrubbing the Air Tasking Order and studying target packages to ensure feasibility.... We must be prepared to execute this campaign [no later than 1800L] 31 Aug 90. Although we don't anticipate execution at this time, rapidly changing events in Iraq dictate we prepare for execution should the situation arise. I need your help in preparing your unit and safeguarding the sensitivity of this mission.[133]

The plan's secrecy precluded the special planners from telephoning ahead to give notice of Wilson's mission. Arriving at bases in the middle of the night, commanders did not always greet him, cordially or otherwise. He briefed as many commanders or representatives as possible. The aircrew transported him as quickly as possible through the circuit of bases. Upon his return to Riyadh after his grueling trip, Wilson reported to Glosson that some commanders received neither the briefing nor material. The general hit upon the idea of stimulating the enthusiasm of the commanders to acquire and study the planning packages by telephoning each the next day, telling them he would visit them and that he expected each to explain how his unit would execute its portion of the ATO. The general did indeed visit the units September 6–8 and received the briefings.[134]

Meeting on the USS *LaSalle*

On August 30 Glosson and Deptula flew to the port city of Manama, Bahrain, where they met on the USS *LaSalle* with Vice Adm. Henry H. Mauz, Jr., who had taken command of NAVCENT on August 16; with Rear Adm. Fogarty, Glosson's former boss as commander of JTFME and now NAVCENT's commander of the U.S. Maritime Interception Force; and with General Moore, the 3d Marine Air Wing commander. Just the day before, Wilson had delivered the Phase I ATO to Moore and briefed him on the tasking. Moore's boss, Lt. Gen. Walter E. Boomer, commander of MARCENT, had received the Instant Thunder briefing in Riyadh on August 23. He urged Glosson to brief the 3d Marine Air Wing commander and give him target materials as soon as possible so that the Marines could begin planning their offensive air operations.[135]

Moore did not want to provide F/A–18s for the strategic air campaign; he wanted to keep and use them for tasking by the Marines. He did not wish to see the offensive campaign start before September 15, this to allow enough time for the Marines to practice their missions. He said the television transmitters assigned as targets to his aviators "didn't excite him" and observed that the F–117 stealth aircraft "didn't do shit in Panama." He wanted to split up joint force packages to eliminate complex coordination requirements. That the air campaign planning originated in Washington did not inspire him.[136]

Admiral Mauz emphasized that the Navy units required time to practice their missions, and he questioned the importance of some of the assigned Iraqi naval targets. When Glosson asked him to send one of his two Red Sea carriers closer to Yemen to deter and defend against that country's launching strikes against Coalition forces, especially the F–117As at Khamis Mushait in southwestern Saudi Arabia, Mauz told Glosson he could not do that because two carriers operated in mutual support. The admiral requested that Glosson unmix the force packages, which required, in his view, too much coordination among carrier and land-based units. Mauz preferred that Navy units fly single-service packages. Glosson agreed, and later Deptula spent hours redesigning the attack missions, only to have the Navy representatives in the Special Planning Group a few days afterward ask for mixed-service packages to provide more SEAD support. Deptula accommodated them, again spending hours revising the MAP.[137]

Immediately after the meeting on the *LaSalle*, Mauz and Glosson met privately, and Deptula had an opportunity to chat with General Moore, explaining to him that in Panama, during Just Cause, the F–117As were not supposed to hit a barracks directly, but were to strike a few yards nearby to disorient, not kill, the Panamanian soldiers within the structure. Moore replied, "I sure as hell hope they hit something this time." He expressed the view that the first bombs should drop after the first Marines crossed the line, revealing a sharply divergent view of air power from that held by the Air Force officers.[138] Deptula thought the Marine Corps should have allowed all their aircraft to participate in the offensive air campaign instead of keeping many idle and wasting sorties. He reasoned:

> We could have used the AV–8s up against Tallil. Their concern is so dogmatic that we want to take their air away from them, and that's not true. We Air Force guys understand that that's the way they've built their MAGTF [Marine Air-Ground Task Force]. They built them intentionally light on artillery, because they plan on using air to compensate for that. If they get into a major ground battle, or a ground battle period, we're not going to hold that air away from them. That's the way they act, and that's why they kept their AV–8s, which is fine. We had enough F–16s to compensate.[139]

Glosson, Mauz, and Moore left unresolved the number and types of aircraft that the Marine Corps would provide for Phase I. Not until Glosson again met with Moore on September 7 could he count on the Marines providing for the strategic campaign half of the F/A–18s, all of the A–6Es and EA–6Bs, and two KC–130s, but no AV–8Bs. Schwarzkopf approved of the apportionment and wanted to hold the AV–8s and A–10s in reserve in case the Iraqis invaded Saudi Arabia.[140]

F–117s and Jamming Controversy

At the end of August, Col. Alton C. Whitley, Jr., commander of the 37th Tactical Fighter Wing which flew the F–117A Nighthawks from their base at Khamis Mushait, visited Riyadh and made a controversial request which resonated not only throughout Desert Shield and Desert Storm, but beyond. He asked for direct electronic jamming support from EF–111A Ravens for the first F–117A sorties to Baghdad the first night of the war, where an estimated 550 missiles and 1,300 AAA guns defended the city. By August 28 Glosson had planned to send approximately thirty F–117As against about twenty strategic air defense, leadership, and C^3 targets in the Baghdad area precisely five minutes after the initial H-hour strike by TLAMs against electric power plants.[141] The initial attack sequence and sortie packaging changed frequently over the next few days. On August 29, only ten F–117s were to strike only eight targets in the Baghdad area at H+0005, supported by four EF–111s. Two days later, the Navy representatives in the Special Planning Group informed Glosson that the Navy was unable to launch the TLAMs against electric power plants for the H-hour strikes in Baghdad because they lacked the appropriate imagery to program the missiles for nighttime operations. Stealth aircraft, therefore, would execute the first strikes in Baghdad. By September 1, Glosson and Deptula planned that five F–117s, supported by only two EF–111s, would deliver the first strikes against five leadership and strategic air defense targets in the capital city. Planning for the opening moments of the air campaign continued into September, with new strike packages designed, targets chosen, and additional MAP changes made. By the end of September, the Navy TLAMs would be reinserted into the MAP for nighttime attacks against power plants in Baghdad, but these would occur after the stealth attacks.[142]

The computerized flight planning system, Elvira, that Colonel Whitley and the F–117 pilots used in mission preparation accounted for radar threats against stealth platforms, and it plotted routes to avoid such threats.[143] As Lt. Col. Ralph W. Getchell later explained,

Navy TLAM missile

> From the exhaustive classified test reports available, we knew the aircraft's low observable characteristics would give us a substantial advantage over the Iraqi interceptors, surface-to-air missiles (SAMs), and anti-aircraft artillery (AAA) which were ready to oppose our attacks. But the F–117 is LOW observable, not NO observable. In planning our attack routes, we carefully took advantage of our strengths to minimize the times during which we could possibly be detected and tracked.

The F–117A was low-observable when it was "stealthed-up," but it became more visible if it lost some of its stealth, for example, if a bomb bay door failed to close properly, maintenance access panels fell off, or radio antennas failed to retract. The jamming from EF–111s provided insurance against the F–117's being detected and tracked.[144]

Peacetime Red Flag exercises had taught F–117 pilots that when jamming was used against enemy radars, radar operators lessened the effects of the jamming by reducing the sensitivity, or gain, of their radar receiver. Getchell noted, "Any reduction in gain would cause the small radar blip of a malfunctioning F–117 to disappear from the scope." Another F–117 pilot, Lt. Col. Michael P. Setnor, later observed that when radar operators adjusted their radarscopes to eliminate jamming noise, an F–15E blip on the screen decreased from the size of a dime to a pinhead, while the F–117A blip went from appearing as a pinhead to vanishing from the screen. Jamming would prevent radars from airborne and ground-based sites from finding and tracking the stealth assets.[145]

Glosson strongly opposed direct jamming support for the F–117s on the basis of firsthand experience with the aircraft. As wing commander of the 1st Tactical Fighter Wing, he spent ten days at Nellis AFB flying with his F–15C squadron trying to shoot down F–117As. "I chased those little bastards around over the desert out there in an F–15, and I knew if I couldn't shoot one of them down, [some] Iraqi wasn't going to shoot them down," he concluded.[146] He believed aircraft lacking stealth technology required electronic jamming support more than the F–117s. He thought, too, that the jamming noise would tip off the Iraqis to an imminent raid.[147]

General Horner, on the other hand, deferred to the radar and stealth experts. He explained, "It is using the IMOM [Improved Many-on-Many] model. It's majors talking to majors. Remember, we are decentralized. If Chuck Horner is making decisions on where to put the jamming aircraft, then Chuck Horner isn't doing his job....You've got guys that have PhDs in electronics. Let them use their PhDs. Let them make the decisions."[148] Horner's EC expert, General Henry, favored jamming support for two reasons; one was political, the other, operational. First, to lose an F–117A, a product of sophisticated American aerospace technology, would strike a blow against U.S. national prestige. He stated, "The very first night was where I was really concerned about it, and how I wanted to use them because we did not want to take a chance on losing that national asset.

If we had to lose EF–111s in the process, I was willing to do that."[149] In contrast, Glosson was willing to lose one or two F–117s, expecting losses to come merely from lucky Iraqi shots — golden BBs.[150] Second, Henry believed the jamming would not tip off the Iraqis about the arrival of the F–117s; instead it would ensure their effectiveness and survival. He explained that the EF–111s would fly low and so close in time with the F–117s that the Iraqis would not have time to react to the jamming before the stealth aircraft dropped their guided munitions.[151] (Timing and target complications would prevent Henry's idea from occurring as he envisioned in early September.) Horner did allow jamming for some of the F–117s that flew to Baghdad the first night of the war. As officers during Desert Shield continued to plan and refine the sequence and time of the attacks into Baghdad and environs, concerns about the survivability of the F–117As reemerged.

Chapter Seven

Phase I Triumphant

From late August until mid-October, the JFACC's offensive planning focused on Phase I, the strategic air campaign. During this time, planners added two separate target sets to the strategic list, the Republican Guard and Scuds, and emphasized weapons of mass destruction, airfields, and air defense sites. General Glosson presented milestone briefings to General Schwarzkopf on September 3, Chairman Powell on September 13, and President Bush on October 11, each earning approval for CENTAF's war planning. By mid-October the strike list totaled 218 targets in 12 sets. Checkmate continued to support development of the strategic air plan, while revelations in the press from the Air Force chief of staff infuriated the CINCCENT and accelerated the acquisition of drones for a deception project already underway. The special planners continued to experience shortcomings with intelligence support, although target materials began to flow to the theater.

CINCCENT Arrives in Theater

On August 27 Generals Horner and Yeosock met General Schwarzkopf at Riyadh AB. Immediately afterward, General Khalid welcomed the CENTCOM commander-in-chief and Joint Force commander with a traditional coffee ceremony at the Persian carpeted VIP terminal on the base. For the next few days Schwarzkopf immersed himself in the same type of issues Horner, as CENTCOM Forward commander, had dealt with: establishing smooth, effective working relationships with the Saudis and other Coalition partners; facilitating the deployment and beddown of forces; and ensuring the defense of Saudi Arabia against an Iraqi attack.[1] Horner happily turned over responsibilities to the CINC and assumed full-time duties as CENTAF commander and JFACC. He greatly preferred solving air-related problems rather than grappling with such affairs as international protocol and customs, transshipment of equipment across borders, and Arab sensitivities about military women driving vehicles.[2]

CINCCENT Adds Republican Guard to Phase I

On Friday, August 31, Schwarzkopf altered Phase I by directing the planners to attack the Republican Guard on the initial day of the strategic air campaign. The four-phase Desert Storm plan, which he had briefed to Secretary Cheney and Chairman Powell in the Pentagon on August 25, had included the Guard, but only in Phase III, Ground Combat Power Attrition. Cheney told Schwarzkopf to add the elite forces to Phase I as well because they sustained Saddam's regime and the Iraqi occupation of Kuwait, and they posed a significant offensive threat to other nations in the region. Weakening them would diminish Iraq's postwar position in the Middle East.[3] The Iraqi leader had incorporated his Republican Guard, comprising about 20 percent of his land forces, into his domestic power base and rewarded them with privileges, good pay, and the best equipment and training. As an elite force, they conducted the main offensive assaults and functioned as the powerful defensive strategic reserve.[4]

Earlier, when Glosson briefed Horner on August 26, he had already identified the Republican Guard as a target of high priority in the strategic air campaign and had asked the intelligence officers to determine where the troops who had pulled out of Kuwait and returned to Iraq were located and where their headquarters was.[5] On August 31, Colonel Deptula added F–16 attacks to the MAP against the Guard at H+0600, six hours after H-hour, when the first bombs were to have been dropped on Baghdad. Two days later, he created two other F–16 strike packages against the Guard, at H+0400 and H+0500, and further changed the timing of the F–16 strikes against the elite force.[6]

When Deptula added the strikes at H+0600, he lamented that he had to break apart a large strategic air package against Baghdad to support the attacks on the Republican Guard. He complained, "Air power is subverted by ground force concerns." He feared that a significant diversion of SEAD, counterair, and tankers to support strikes against the Guard would dilute the strategic air campaign. On September 2 he and Glosson discussed where they should place the elite troops among the target categories, and the younger officer argued vigorously against placing them in the leadership set. He referred to Colonel Warden's model of the five strategic rings and pointed out that if the Republican Guard had to enter the strategic campaign's targeting, it should enter via the fifth ring, the fielded forces, not the first ring, leadership. He then elaborated on the ring analogy by sketching a picture of a castle, bridge, moat, village, roads, and knights on horses, to illustrate that the knights, like the Republican Guard, functioned as fielded forces, not as leadership assets. Because the CENTAF MAP included no fielded force category, per se, Deptula suggested the military production and storage group as the logical choice for placement of the troops. Glosson had already discussed this arrangement with the CINCCENT's director of operations, General Moore, and he told Deptula to add them to that category. On September 3 the Republican Guard appeared in the Phase I briefing slides and OPORD under the military production and storage set and in the MAP as "RG."[7]

Adding the Guard to the strategic air campaign's target list, which originated with Instant Thunder, significantly changed the Air Staff plan. Warden had considered attacking the forces in his campaign, but he firmly opposed doing so for multiple reasons. While acknowledging that Saddam Hussein greatly valued the Guard troops, the colonel believed they presented a difficult target set to find and track, necessitating a significant number of reconnaissance aircraft and intelligence assets to constantly search for the tactical mobile force. The target arrays then required a large number of strike aircraft to attack the dispersed troops, tanks, and equipment. Because the Guard had withdrawn into Iraq, it did not pose a direct threat against Coalition forces, and it constituted a less important target than leadership, C^3, and key supply points. Attacking the Guard would produce only minimal results. Sorties against them, at the expense of political and leadership targets, would reduce the effectiveness of the strategic air campaign.[8] Warden did not share Secretary Cheney's view that the Guard represented a strategic target because it directly supported Saddam Hussein and formed the shock troops and backbone of the Iraqi ground forces, thus undergirding the threat to Iraqi's regional neighbors. He viewed sorties against it unfavorably because they diverted assets from the Iraqi strategic centers of gravity. Later in Desert Shield, General Adams would direct Warden to use his staff to analyze the amount of air power required to destroy the Iraqi army, including the Republican Guard, and the colonel complied, but reluctantly.

Over the next few months, the targeting of the Republican Guard underwent many changes.[9] From September through November 20, planners incorporated only F–16s and one F–117 into the MAP to attack Guard targets during the first twenty-four hours. On September 3 Glosson told Schwarzkopf that B–52s would hit the elite forces beginning in the *second* twenty-four hours, but later, F/A–18s and F–16s replaced the B–52s as the aircraft striking the Guard. When Saddam released his hostages in December, planners canceled a special operation to rescue them, thus eliminating an F–117 strike against the Guard's 35th Warning-Control Regiment Bunker. That same month, Glosson intently focused on employing B–52s against the Guard in round-the-clock operations throughout the air campaign, beginning in the first twenty-four hours.

Western Scud Sites

In early September the planners made a second significant change in the strategic air campaign: an emphasis in the opening minutes on striking Scud missiles threatening Israel from the H–2 airfield area in western Iraq. The evening of September 2, Horner summoned Glosson to his office and told him that President Bush and Secretary Cheney had talked with Israeli officials and requested that their military forces refrain from attacking Iraq. The NCA believed that if Israel joined the war, some Arab nations would abandon the Coalition to avoid having to fight alongside their longtime enemy against their Arab neighbors. The Israelis agreed to Bush's request on condition that the United States eliminate the Scud missiles aimed at Israel from the fixed sites on the H–2 airfield. Horner told Glosson to attack those locations early to prevent Saddam from retaliating as Desert Storm commenced.[10]

Glosson had already planned to attack western Scud sites. The MAP for September 1 disclosed five locations, including the H–2 airfield, and intelligence officers still attempted to locate and verify other targets. Glosson had timed the attacks to commence twenty minutes after the initial strikes in Baghdad. The planners did not want to send F–117s against the Scuds, believing their use in the west would detract from the overall impact of the initial strategic attack. Deptula discussed using AC–130 gunships but nixed the idea because F–4G HARM shooters, already in short supply, would have to join the mission packages to kill SA–6s to protect the AC–130s all the time they were near or over their targets. After more discussion, Glosson finally selected F–15Es, accompanied by EF–111 jammers, to strike the western Scud sites, and Horner agreed. Glosson was comfortable with the choice because he did not want to send the F–15Es to Baghdad and against its formidable SAM rings. He was concerned that the aircraft's radar-warning reception would not cover all the frequency bands that the Iraqis used with their IADS in a highly defended area. Deptula changed the time of the attacks against the H–2 Scud sites to H+0005 to coincide with F–117 strikes in Baghdad.[11] These early attacks would preclude Scud launches as bombs struck the Iraqi capital, preventing Saddam's retaliatory missile attacks from drawing the Israelis into the war.

Scuds in the Yemen Arab Republic (North Yemen), in the southwestern corner of the Arabian peninsula, greatly worried King Fahd, who feared that the Yemenis, who did not condemn Iraq's invasion of Kuwait, would exploit the crisis in the northeast to settle a border dispute by seizing the Saudi province of Asir.[12] On August 31 Glosson directed Deptula to include F–15Es in the MAP on five-minute alert status from H-hour to H+2400 to strike Scud launch sites if the Yemenis fired missiles against Saudi Arabia or Coalition forces. After H+2400, the alert status changed from a five-minute to thirty-minute interval. By September 3 the MAP showed Yemeni Scud sites as targets for six F–16s with the new LANTIRN pods. A few days later, the planners added four F–111Fs to the Yemeni mission. On September 9 they assigned eight RAF Jaguars against the Scuds, only to replace them with four F–111Fs three days later. The F–111Fs remained tasked against the Scuds until early October, when international tension involving Yemen eased, the threat from Yemeni Scud strikes drastically diminished, and planners removed the Yemeni targets from the MAP.[13]

Milestone Briefing — CINCCENT, September 3

The first briefing the CINCCENT received in theater on the air campaign occurred Monday, September 3, at the MODA building. The special planners worked to the last minute preparing materials for the presentation, a major event which the officers jokingly titled "Buster and His Boys." Glosson's responsibility encompassed Phase I, and Colonel Crigger's covered Phases II and III. The general concentrated on the first twenty-four hours of the strategic campaign, divided into four six-hour periods, which he presented on two- by three-foot charts with acetate overlays. Horner thought that the charts clearly and sequentially explained the many complicated air attacks throughout Iraq, as laid out in the MAP, and that they peeled like an onion, as he liked to say, to convey complicated planning, step by step. Deptula supervised the drawing of the charts, and Glosson used note cards, each corresponding to a chart.[14]

As he and his staff further developed the air campaign, Glosson briefed General Moore, CENTCOM J–3, on August 29; other key members of the CENTCOM staff on September 1; wing and unit commanders on September 2; and General Olsen and other CENTAF officers on September 3. On Saturday the 1st, CENTCOM general and flag officers and five colonels traveled to the RSAF building to receive briefings from Glosson and Crigger and to pass along insights about Schwarzkopf's key concerns. General Johnston, CENTCOM chief of staff; Admiral Sharp, CENTCOM J–5; and General Moore asked most of the questions. While discussing Glosson's Phase I, they told the planners that the CINCCENT would ask about the percentage of targets from the original Instant Thunder list now included in Phase I; targeting for the Republican Guard; and the date the CENTCOM commander could execute the plan. On the last point, Glosson answered that he would provide a definite reply by about Tuesday or Wednesday, as soon as his staff completed their survey of ordnance in theater and considered the LIMFACs. Crigger briefed that, to defend Saudi Arabia from an invasion or to attack the Iraqis preemptively, the campaign would focus on hitting the Iraqi IADS and then striking armor, C^3 sites, and logistics bases before conducting interdiction operations. The comments again stressed that the CINCCENT would inquire about the execution date.[15]

Admiral Sharp handed Crigger a paper at the meeting that levied on the airmen a mission significant in the history of air warfare, although at the time it was hardly noticed. CENTCOM listed attrition levels against the Iraqi ground forces that the air campaign must achieve in Phases II and III, to precede the land war. He provided the types and quantity of combat equipment the Iraqis possessed and specified how many items of each type the air strikes had to destroy to achieve force levels conducive to mounting a successful ground attack in Phase IV of Desert Storm. The number of required kills reached 50 percent for each target category.

CENTCOM's Attrition Requirements

Iraqi Equipment	Approximate Current Strength	Attrition Goal
Tanks	2,400	1,200
APCs	1,900	950
Artillery	1,700	850
AAA	1,300	650
Multiple-rocket launchers	200	100
FROGs	0	0
SAMs	300	150[16]

The air campaign in Phases II and III would execute a counterland mission to destroy half the enemy's weapons of war before ground combat even commenced. Never in warfare had commanders expected air power to destroy the opposing army to such a degree before the start of ground operations. The attrition requirement, which the CENTCOM CAG had calculated immediately after Iraq invaded Kuwait and which Schwarzkopf referred to when he briefed President Bush at Camp David on August 4, now came to the attention of the CENTAF planners, especially Colonel Crigger. Sharp's list on September 1 provided specific attrition goals for Phase II — air defense artillery, multiple rocket launchers, and missiles — but these would soon fall by the wayside, whereas the target categories for Phase III — tanks, APCs, and artillery — would eventually dominate planning for the preparation of the battlefield portion of the air campaign.

Early the next day, Sunday, September 2, about one hundred Navy, Marine Corps, and Air Force commanders and directors of operations gathered at the RSAF building to hear Glosson's Phase I presentation and give feedback about their sorties in the ATO, which Colonel Wilson had hand-delivered to them. Horner's introduction described the plan as an air campaign and noted that SEAD comprised a vital operation. Glosson briefed quickly. Then the officers raised questions about dozens of tactical problems, many of which they resolved on the spot while others required further coordination and action. The session generated positive, cordial discussion. Navy representatives brought up targeting concerns. They thought ten A–6s attacking SAM sites in the west Baghdad area would not survive, and they requested additional attacks against airfields in the Basra area to counter threats from F1 Mirages firing Exocet missiles and jeopardizing ships in the Gulf of Oman and the Persian Gulf.[17] The issues would be worked.

On September 3 when Glosson and Crigger briefed Generals Olsen and Henry and other members of the CENTAF staff, topics arose that focused on the importance of Phases II and III vis-à-vis Phase I. Crigger again explained the threefold mission of Phases II and III — SEAD, destruction of ground targets, and interdiction. He continued, however, by suggesting that air assets for interdiction would come from Phase I resources. He recommended starting Phase II the first morning of the Phase I offensive. He rationalized such an early start to prevent the Iraqis from moving southward into Saudi Arabia. He wanted eight F–16s from Phase I as well as F–4Gs and a tanker for the strikes. Glosson pointed to the detrimental aspects of executing the strategic air operations on a piecemeal basis. Deptula thought Crigger's ideas totally unacceptable; he relished hearing General Henry say that the Coalition should "wait for [the] Iraqis to cross south." Horner and Crigger, nonetheless, wanted a nearly simultaneous execution of Phases II and III with Phase I. According to Crigger,

> I was directed by Gen Horner to expand the combat plans division planning effort from the "D-day" ATO to look at an offensive plan to attack Iraqi forces in Kuwait/Southern Iraq that would compl[e]ment the strategic air campaign. The objectives of this operation would be to freeze Iraqi forces in place, suppress enemy air defenses, and attrit these forces as the strategic air campaign was launched.[18]

Horner viewed the air campaign differently from Schwarzkopf's four-phased Desert Storm concept. As he had told Warden on August 20, he worried about the Iraqi ground forces invading Saudi Arabia. He believed air power should prevent an assault into the kingdom. He saw CENTAF's D-day plan as the means to make it difficult for the Iraqis to move against the Saudis in reaction to air strikes against Baghdad and to slow their assault, should it commence. For Horner, the air campaign consisted of two major components: the offensive strategic strikes to gain air superiority and hit vital targets like Scuds and NBC sites, and the D-day, defensive strikes to pin the Iraqi ground forces in place.[19] In early September, he wanted to merge the phases, which to some degree would occur in Desert Storm despite the CINCCENT's initial concepts of phased, sequenced air operations and missions.

Horner, Glosson, and Crigger rode together in an automobile to the MODA building at about 1700 on September 3 to brief Schwarzkopf. Deptula and a driver followed in a truck and promptly got lost; Deptula carried the briefing material, including the charts and tripod. With just minutes to spare, he found the facility and conference room, only to learn to his disappointment that a tabletop presentation was expected, so he was not needed to flip slides, a function he eagerly welcomed because it allowed him to attend and listen to the briefing. From CENTAF, only Horner, Glosson, and Crigger remained in the conference room to brief the CINCCENT.[20]

They presented Schwarzkopf slides, charts, the OPORD, MAP, and ATO. In addition to the charts depicting the Phase I attacks over the first twenty-four hours, charts also showed the opening scene with CAPs and the Iraqi IADS and KTO targets. Most of Glosson's briefing concentrated on the material on the charts.[21] Similar to the briefing approved by Horner on August 27, the planners prepared a packet of slides titled "Offensive Campaign Phase I." It included the following pages: Concept to Execution, presenting Glosson's flow chart diagram; Centers of Gravity, listing leadership, infrastructure, and military forces;

Strike and Support Forces, identifying assets available September 3 and 15; Attack Flow Intensity, showing, in bar-graph format, strike and SEAD sorties over the first twenty-four hours; Attack Plan, indicating a three- to six-day duration; and Results, revealing that the campaign would "decapitate Saddam regime" and "generate internal strife" leading to "change."[22]

The target list slide showed the categories and number of targets for the original Instant Thunder list (84 targets); the CENTCOM list (141); and the CENTAF list (174). As of September 3, Phase I included 174 targets in 10 target sets:

Target Set	No. of Targets
Strategic air defense	21
Strategic CW	20
Leadership	15
Telecommunications	26
Electricity	14
Oil	8
Railroads	12
Airfields	13
Ports	4
Military production and storage	41
	174

Included in the military production and storage set were the Republican Guard targets; in strategic CW were the five western Scud sites. The slide, "Original 84 Target List," revealed that in the first twenty-four hours, 71 percent of the original Instant Thunder targets would be struck.[23]

The Attack Plan page for the first day of Phase I showed 637 strike and 749 SEAD sorties. The second day addressed key targets requiring additional attacks and the sites not covered during the first twenty-four hours. Strikes on the third through sixth days would destroy long-term warfighting capabilities associated with military production areas and research and development facilities. Six slides explained the second twenty-four hours of the strategic campaign. They disclosed targets; attack times in predawn, day, and night periods; and numbers and types of aircraft employed.[24]

The short duration of Phase I, from three to six days, reflected the retaliatory nature of the operations and Colonel Warden's faith in strategic air power, and it stemmed from Schwarzkopf's telephone call to the Air Staff on August 8 for an air option against Iraq. Phase I, incorporating 174 targets, doubled the number of Instant Thunder targets but maintained the brevity of the Air Staff plan. At this early date, Glosson did not emphasize Phase I in relation to the other phases nor to the entire Desert Storm offensive war plan and objectives. He knew from his telephone conversation with Schwarzkopf the night of August 22 that the CENTCOM commander wanted a three- to four-day campaign, a week maximum, to respond with if Iraq were to commit further acts of aggression. Unaddressed by the planners, however, was how the first phase of the offensive plan would accomplish the objectives in just six days, especially as the target list grew daily and the military production and storage and the strategic CW categories incorporated scores of new targets associated with maintaining Iraq's power base and its ability to threaten nations in SWA. The airmen did not raise the point with Schwarzkopf that a retaliation campaign could be short, but an offensive strategic campaign would probably be lengthier, especially since intelligence had now begun to flow about numerous military sites in Iraq. Horner understood that the CINCCENT initially wanted a short strategic air campaign, but he also felt confident that, as the air plan developed as an integral component of the effort to dismantle the Iraqi war machine, Schwarzkopf and the NCA would give him the time to accomplish national objectives and allow for difficulties with weather, target acquisition rates, tanker availability, aircraft attrition, and the chaos inherent in the execution of operations.[25]

The slide "Location of Hostages on Target List" disclosed that the Iraqis held "human shields" at nine target sites comprising one power plant, three petroleum refineries, one CW production facility, one superphosphate fertilizer plant, one storage complex, one industrial facility, and one military installation. Saddam had announced on August 19, 1990, that the Iraqis had placed Westerners at sites to deter air strikes. President Bush responded by demanding their release and labeling the people "hostages."[26]

The LIMFACs slide displayed three categories of factors affecting the air campaign by how soon the assets in each category could arrive in theater and be usable. The first category comprised munitions: GBU–27s for F–117s which would arrive, or close, on September 4; GBU–24s, on loan from the Saudis for F–111Fs, would close on September 10; MK–84s and CBU–87s for F–16s would close on September 6–8; and HARMs for F–4Gs and F/A–18s would close on September 10. Aircraft comprised the second LIMFAC category. Twelve F–117s would close forty-eight hours after being requested; twelve F–4Gs had closing dates to be determined, as did four EF–111s; and twenty-two KC–10s would close thirty-six hours after being requested, as would twenty-five KC–135s. The third LIMFAC, the CALCM, closed twenty hours after the execution order.[27]

Glosson considered the F–117s a crucial weapon system and relied heavily on them in the strategic air campaign, but only eighteen F–117s had arrived in theater even though the general had told the special planners that the air campaign execution might be imminent. Deptula found it unfathomable why TAC had not sent all the stealth aircraft to the AOR so that pilots could familiarize themselves with the environment, learn the ATO system, practice tanking operations, and exercise their critically important roles in the air campaign.[28] Because the Air Force inventory included only fifty-nine F–117s, the last few having been delivered to the service in July 1990, some of the pilots and aircraft had to remain in the United States at the Tonapah test range in Nevada to continue training. On

September 20, MAC, SAC, and TAC sent a message to the JCS explaining the deployment staging for twelve additional F–117s. They also identified the aircraft's cargo and refueling requirements. The Nighthawks would arrive at Khamis Mushait between forty-eight and sixty hours after receipt of the deployment order.[29] On December 3, eighteen F–117s deployed to Saudi Arabia, and after Desert Storm commenced, additional aircraft and pilots arrived in the AOR for a total of forty-two F–117s, all in the 37th Tactical Fighter Wing.

Glosson did not mention intelligence as a LIMFAC in his briefing to the CINCCENT. More than any other issue since August 22, intelligence had exasperated him, but he chose not to identify the serious problem in support of the JFACC. Plus, as with Instant Thunder, the CENTAF OPORD failed to include an intelligence annex to address the air campaign's critical intelligence-support issues: target selection and critical-node analysis; production and dissemination of targeting materials; and establishment of a quick-reaction BDA system. The OPORD's intelligence annex merely addressed enemy order of battle — essential but inadequate.[30] In this regard, however, the oversight was not unusual in CENTCOM and CENTAF planning, focused as it usually was on the adversary's order of battle.

Both Horner and Glosson signed the CENTAF Phase I OPORD dated September 2, 1990, that stated:

> When directed by USCINCCENT, the Joint Force Air Component Commander (JFACC) will conduct a strategic air campaign against Iraq to isolate and incapacitate the national leadership, destroy critical control centers, and neutralize Iraqi offensive military capabilities to include Iraqi forces in Kuwait and Southern Iraq.[31]

Whole sections of the document came directly from the Instant Thunder OPORD of August 17, 1990, which the Warden group brought to the theater, thus clearly revealing that the Air Staff plan was the basis for the Desert Storm strategic air campaign.

On September 3, Glosson's Phase I presentation to Schwarzkopf consumed so much time that Colonel Crigger could not brief Phases II and III. A Phase I slide, however, did disclose the number and type of aircraft for Phases II and III closing by September 15: 24 F/A–18s; 96 A–10s; 40 AV–8Bs; and 132 AH–64/AH–1s. The JFACC would employ these aircraft to defend or initiate Phase II/III. Buried in the OPORD in an appendix was a section titled, "Phase II/III Operations," with an execution statement explaining:

> The JFACC will conduct, on order, an air campaign to roll back the Iraqi integrated air defense system (IADS) umbrella in Kuwait by attacking fixed SAM sites and mobile SAM/AAA systems. As battlefield air superiority is achieved the campaign will target enemy positions in Kuwait, concentrating on armored forces, C^{3}I nodes and the

> enemy's logistics base. Phase II/III may be initiated in response to an Iraqi attack out of Kuwait and/or as directed by USCINCCENT.[32]

During the session, the CINCCENT reaffirmed his Desert Storm phasing. He directed that if the Iraqis did not attack Saudi Arabia, Phases II and III would follow Phase I, and not be executed simultaneously with it, as Horner favored.[33]

The CINCCENT reacted positively to Glosson's Phase I briefing. According to Schwarzkopf,

> Instant Thunder had been ready since early September. Brigadier General Buster Glosson, Chuck Horner's top planner, had expanded the retaliatory scheme of the Pentagon Air Staff into the best air campaign I'd ever seen. It gave us a broad range of attack options and could be conducted as a stand-alone operation or as part of a larger war.[34]

He also explained, "I would also tell you that anyone who received a briefing on that plan came away very impressed with the significance of the plan....For the first time we had a capability to focus on military targets and avoid civilian areas."[35] Prior to the session, Deptula pitched practice questions to Glosson, some of which the CINCCENT subsequently asked, so the planner's answers came easily. The CENTCOM commander also raised a few issues requiring additional research on attrition rates, Scuds, and the use of AC–130s and drones.[36]

When Glosson left the conference room, he smiled triumphantly and gave a thumbs-up to Deptula. He related that the CINCCENT had reacted most favorably. When Schwarzkopf inquired when the plan could be executed, he had confidently answered, "September 13th," at which, he observed, Horner "nearly choked."[37] The chief special planner had not cleared the date with the JFACC. Later, as Glosson regaled his staff about the presentation, Horner stopped by. He commented that his special planner was full of bluster, referring to his identifying September 13 as the date the plan could be executed.[38] Horner lacked absolute confidence that enough munitions were on hand if the campaign should last longer than six days and involve an Iraqi invasion, yet he did not disagree that the plan was executable on the 13th.[39] He inquired about the Air Staff colonels and was told all had departed for the United States except Deptula, who was in the room. He asked the MAP builder to stay on and mentioned that he would call Deptula's boss at the Pentagon, if it became necessary to retain him. The CENTAF commander genuinely thanked his special planning staff for a job well done.[40] He believed Glosson had prepared tremendously for the briefing, and he appreciated the effort because he never wanted to present air matters and courses of action to the CINCCENT without first having had them thoroughly studied by professional, experienced airmen.[41]

The briefing on September 3 was a milestone. In twenty-six days, from August 8 to September 3, the CINCCENT had requested and received an offensive air campaign plan which, during its development, elicited from military leaders at least seven different views on the effective use of air power. They recognized the advantage that air power gave the United States, but each held a different view of how best to use it. Schwarzkopf on August 8 thought of offensive air power as a means to retaliate against some horrific act by Saddam Hussein. Warden presented Instant Thunder as a stand-alone, war-winning strategic air campaign. Powell readily agreed with the necessity for the strategic air campaign, but he then wanted air power to directly strike the enemy army. Adams agreed with Powell, but he wanted to attack the army first and then, in sequence, execute the strategic air campaign. General Russ wanted to use air power in an escalating manner to demonstrate its effectiveness. Horner saw the strategic air campaign as necessary, but he wanted it executed simultaneously with strikes against the enemy army. Glosson, like Powell and then Schwarzkopf, wanted air power phased and employed sequentially. The CINCCENT had expanded his thinking about air power and chose to incorporate it into all phases of his Desert Storm war plan.

Glosson Requests Checkmate Help

After his session with Schwarzkopf, Glosson formally requested assistance from Warden and Checkmate to answer questions and finalize Phase I. The officers at the Pentagon could find data and acquire intelligence more quickly than could the regular CENTAF staff and the Special Planning Group representatives. Since August 22, Colonel Harvey and the other Air Staff personnel had regularly called the Pentagon and received information, in push and pull modes. The young officers in Saudi Arabia had initially kept the Checkmate connection secret because, as Deptula noted, "At the very beginning General Horner and General Glosson are very adverse [toward] anything coming out of the Pentagon, anything coming from Checkmate." On August 29, however, Harvey showed Glosson two Checkmate messages about counterair operations and multinational force participation. The general found their content useful, and he directed Harvey to tell Warden to continue sending such inputs but to address them, "Personal for Brigadier General Glosson." On September 1 Warden sent personally addressed messages to Glosson on the following topics: offensive counterair and airfield attack; LIMFACs for the quick execution of Instant Thunder; status of additional GBU–15, GBU–24, and SEAD assets; and Scuds.[42] Colonels Harvey and Stanfill returned to Checkmate and applied their understanding of theater planning needs to help focus Air Staff support for Glosson's group.

On September 4 Glosson telephoned General Adams at the Air Staff and requested that Checkmate assist in answering the CINCCENT's questions from the previous day. He explained that he did not have the resources and personnel in theater to generate the kind of analysis and data collection required for planning. He especially needed targeting materials. Adams agreed that Checkmate could greatly assist, but he cautioned about Warden's enthusiasm for air power and his modus operandi, stating,

> Now I told Buster early on, I said, "John's tendency is to get out in front of the process especially when he believes that the purity has been diluted in what he views as an air campaign, so you are working the real one and he is working the theoretical one, and he is always angry when the theoretical is not executed precisely as he has designed it.... Whenever he gets too heavy for you, you tell me and I will pull him off, shut him down, or whatever you want."

Glosson replied that he would take whatever Warden provided and select the good from the bad.[43] On September 8 Warden sent Glosson messages addressing the Iraqi CW capability and Scud characteristics; the projected Instant Thunder attrition; drone support; telecommunications connectivity; caution concerning key religious sites; targeting CW and BW sites; and PSYOPS objectives in support of the air campaign.[44] Deptula telephoned Checkmate after the messages arrived in Riyadh, praising their usefulness.[45]

Warden had rebounded quickly from his setback in briefing Horner; Glosson's request for support made him jubilant. On his trip from Riyadh, he had planned to fly to Offutt AFB to brief Instant Thunder to the SAC commander, but upon learning of this itinerary, General Adams recalled him to Washington immediately. The activity in Warden's directorate had by then wound down, but on September 5, with Adams's approval, he invited other Air Force and joint personnel to the Checkmate area and began to keep longer hours. He started to read extensively on air power, including two classics, *Victory through Air Power* by Alexander P. DeSeversky and *Winged Defense* by Brig. Gen. William "Billy" Mitchell. He hung a portrait of Mitchell in his office. In mid-September he renamed his organization the Deputy Directorate for War *Winning* Concepts. As he led his staff, he continued to refer to the strategic air campaign as Instant Thunder, not Desert Storm Phase I.[46]

For intelligence, Warden informally contacted, briefed, and asked for and received assistance from individuals from a variety of organizations, including the Armed Forces Electronic Warfare Center; the AFIA, DIA, and CIA, with its National Photographic Interpretation Center; and NSA. He tapped, too, RAND, the Department of State, Air War College, and Office of Air Force History, among other organizations.[47] He acquired intelligence from the CIA primarily through the National Intelligence Officer for Warning, Charles E. Allen, whom he met when he briefed Instant Thunder to the National Intelligence Council. General Alexander asked the head of the Intelligence Community Staff, Lt. Gen. C. Norman Wood, formerly Assistant Chief of Staff for Intelligence on the Air Staff, to smooth the way for Warden and his people to meet the appropriate people in the intelligence community. A RAND expert on the Middle East cooperated with Checkmate, and he urged his colleagues at the State Department, CIA, and DIA to support the Checkmate division. Deptula saw Checkmate as an intelligence "fusion center," acquiring relevant information from a variety of agencies, evaluating it, and passing it to the Special Planning Group in a timely manner. General Adams said of Warden's enterprise, "John had built quite a significant network of experts to really help lay out those details, and Buster Glosson used them almost every day, calling back, faxing back, or sending a message back saying, 'Hey, we need more information about — fill in the blank — as the thing evolved.'"[48]

Alexander talked with Glosson a few times, but he sensed that Glosson was more comfortable talking directly with Warden. As Air Staff director of plans, Alexander did what he could to facilitate Checkmate's support for CENTAF's war planning because he recognized that a strategic air campaign transcended the tactical and operational levels of warfare and reached the national and international levels, involving the power centers and infrastructures of a targeted country. It encompassed the entire economy, political system, and military establishment of a nation, and it required a prodigious amount of detailed information about the adversary to achieve a successful campaign — far beyond the capability of a deployed headquarters of a numbered air force to accumulate and analyze on its own. Strategic warfare necessitated a comprehensive planning effort and involvement of the entire national intelligence community, into which Checkmate had tapped. Alexander understood that the Air Staff's work contributed greatly to the ability of CENTAF and CENTCOM to wage strategic warfare.[49]

In early September Glosson hid from Horner the fact that Warden and his staff provided vital assistance to the CENTAF Special Planning Group. Before showing Horner the material from Checkmate, Glosson first cut off Air Staff identifiers and all references to Instant Thunder. He confided in Deptula that he had to be careful; he was "walking on eggshells" for accepting and requesting Warden's help. He believed that if Horner learned of it, he would order Glosson to cease contact with the Air Staff.[50] Within a few weeks, however, the CENTAF commander did become aware of the Checkmate connection, yet he did not order it terminated, knowing that the center of gravity for the air campaign planning had permanently shifted to the theater, and as long as the JFACC maintained control of the plan, Glosson's group could receive assistance from any source.[51]

From September 6 to 8, 1990, Glosson and Deptula visited the bases and units in the AOR that were directly participating in the strategic air campaign. Back in Riyadh, they again relied heavily on Checkmate to address a few of the numerous questions generated and the problems identified during their trip. A "stewpot" of concerns covered such topics as tanker tracks, training, fuel bladders, munitions, tactics, air deconfliction, divert bases, SOF, alternate targets, CAPs, AWACS orbits, SEAD, and target imagery and intelligence. At each location, the commanders briefed and critiqued their parts assigned in the ATO. Glosson gave each an updated version of the ATO. Complying with Glosson's request to assess the units' readiness for war, Deptula observed them as "leaning forward/positive," "ready and eager," and "good attitude."[52]

Air Campaign's Opening Minutes

On the flights between air bases as Glosson and Deptula visited the commanders whose units would execute Desert Storm Phase I, the two planners talked about the first night's attacks as they struggled to identify the targets and attack sequence and timing necessary to achieve the interrelated objectives of surprise, striking leadership and C^2 sites, preventing the Iraqis from firing Scuds at Israel, and obtaining air superiority. Glosson had already spent many hours talking with General Henry, his EC expert, about achieving air superiority by defeating the Iraqi IADS. For the offensive air campaign, both Glosson and Horner would adopt the strategy Henry articulated for the defensive air campaign. They would not only destroy Iraqi aircraft in air-to-air combat, they would also destroy the air force on the ground (as a component of the IADS) and overwhelm and render ineffective the C^2 system (controlling aircraft, SAMs, and AAA).[53] On August 21, 1990, in his message to the units about the joint EC campaign, Henry had outlined his EC objectives for the air offensive:

Destroy/disrupt C^2 nodes
Disrupt EWR/GCI coverage and communications
Force air defense assets into autonomous modes
Use expendable drones for deception
Employ maximum available HARM shooters[54]

Henry preached that to destroy the IADS, the Coalition had to attack it as a whole and to strike its heart, the Kari C^2 system. With the centralized direction of the IADS destroyed, the SAM site radars would operate autonomously and so stay up longer, rendering them more susceptible to jamming and destruction with EC. Glosson also emphasized overwhelming Kari, which was designed to handle far fewer attacking aircraft than the Coalition could simultaneously send against it. Horner expected his planners to design a campaign to eliminate the radar-guided SAM threat to create a safe regime at medium altitude so pilots could fly above the short-range threat from infrared SAMs and AAA guns.[55]

When Glosson completed his visits to the bases, he gave many questions from the units to Majors Sweeney and Waterstreet and told them to incorporate the answers into the ATO. By this time, the MAP they studied to generate the ATO included an unusual designation: H-hour *minus* time. The negative designator indicated time *preceding* H-hour, prior to when the first bombs dropped on Baghdad. It originated on September 4 when Glosson told Deptula to target the Iraqi AWACS. Saddam Hussein's air force included two aircraft designed to function as AWACS, aircraft code-named Adnan 1 and Baghdad 1. They were modified Soviet Il–76 transport aircraft, less capable than the EWR platforms the Americans and Saudis flew. On September 6, the MAP indicated that two F–15Cs would be on alert for Adnan 1 at H–0030. Deptula therefore incorporated the pre-H-hour concept, which proved useful for other additions to the MAP as well, especially since he lacked an interactive database, without which he would have had to spend too much time manually revising times-over-target to adjust for cascading changes on the attack plan.[56]

During the six days of September 6 through 11, Glosson and Deptula continued to ponder and determine how to execute the opening minutes of the air campaign. General Henry and Major Eskridge, the F–117 representative in the Special Planning Group, assisted them. On September 9, Henry's staff produced a much-needed map showing the key nodes of the Iraqi IADS and important airfields, and Deptula intently studied it to ensure that he targeted key facilities. The colonel's notes and the MAP for September 11 reveal his thinking about timing and coherence. At H–0021, SOF on the ground would strike two border EWR sites. These EWR sites functioned as reporting posts for the Nukhayb IOC. At H–0009, one F–117 would then attack the Nukhayb IOC, in the central sector of the IADS system. At H-hour, two F–117s would strike two communications targets in Baghdad. Effectively striking the border sites and IOC would breach the IADS and open an air corridor for nonstealthy aircraft to pass through. First through the breach was a package of F–15Es and their EF–111 jammers en route to the western Scud sites for strikes at H+0005, and three EF–111 jammers supporting six F–117s on their way to Baghdad and other areas for strikes also at H+0005. The group of F–117s executing the attacks at H+0005 in and around Baghdad received jamming support, while the F–117 striking the IOC at H–0009 and the F–117s hitting the communication sites in Baghdad at H-hour had no electronic jamming. The attacks at H-hour would definitely alert the Iraqis to the start of the air campaign, so the F–117s over Baghdad at H+0005 would be flying near numerous, fully alerted SAM sites, into an air defense system far more dense than the one that protecting Hanoi during Linebacker II. They received jamming support.[57]

The attack flow for the opening minutes of the air campaign, as recorded on September 11, was essentially executed the night the air campaign commenced, with one change: at H–0021, instead of ground SOF attacking the two border EWR posts, Regular Army forces in AH–64 Apache helicopters would strike the sites. The planners intended that the attacks in the opening minutes of the air campaign would destroy Kari key elements to blind and deafen the system. They planned to send the first two F–117s without jamming support to Baghdad, an F–117 without jamming support to the Nukhayb IOC, and a wave of F–117s with jamming support to the Baghdad area, at H+0005. Their intention was to prevent Iraqi Scud strikes against Israel in response to the first strikes against Baghdad.[58]

Henry advised Glosson and Horner on the strengths and weaknesses of the Kari IADS C^2 system and believed that the attacks against the two border EWR sites — a full twenty-one minutes before the first strikes in Baghdad — would not tip off the Iraqis to the start of the air war. He and Lieutenant Holdaway had studied the IADS ad infinitum and noted that sometimes the Iraqi's components went off the air and stopped communicating for brief periods, for no apparent reason, and the disconnects caused no alarm signals within the Iraqi chain of command. Henry thought of the IADS as a "Tinkertoy" and looked for "sprockets" he could break which would cause gaps in their C^3 system. He believed that taking down the two border EWR sites could be done clandestinely without the sites communicating that they were under attack.[59] Unfortunately, personnel at one of the sites on January 17, 1991, did communicate within the IADS that air strikes were underway, even as the Apache gunships destroyed the site.

The MAP of September 11 included a new, important, controversial target in the strategic air defense target category, which could just as well have been in the telecommunications set. In the first week of September, Warden learned that one building in downtown Baghdad functioned as the focal point of the entire Iraqi national telecommunications system. Planners informally dubbed it the "AT&T building." The colonel told his staff that by destroying the facility or by cutting electricity to it, the system throughout Iraq would stop functioning. Intelligence would eventually reveal that the building was not as vital to the national telecommunications system as was initially thought, but it did confirm that the facility comprised a key target. On September 6 Warden tasked Maj. Mark "Buck" Rogers to ensure that the AT&T building was "taken out."[60] It stood approximately fifteen stories tall and was collocated with what Rogers called the "hub of all telecommunications activity into and out of Iraq as well as long distance connectivity within Iraq." Based on the information Rogers sent to Glosson, Deptula placed the AT&T building in the MAP for attack at H-hour.[61]

Targeting C^3 and telecommunications facilities raised the issue among planners and some analysts in the intelligence community about striking sites that could possibly produce information for intelligence. When CENTCOM issued its joint no-fire target list in September, it solicited nominations for additional facilities for the list. One agency's submission conflicted with targets the special planners' wanted to hit. For weeks, discussion occurred among the intelligence community, CENTCOM, CENTAF, and the Air Staff about sorting out targets for strikes and for exploitation.[62] Col. Christopher Christon explained that General Schwarzkopf made the final decisions:

> Ultimately the CINC decides what is on the no-strike target list. It is his call. I often kid my friends...saying, "I always take your no-strike target list, then I start targeting them because I know they are important." (I really didn't do that, even though there are some people that believe we did. That isn't how we did business.) There was a very serious consideration of their recommendations.[63]

The colonel did criticize some experts for not explaining to the planners the importance of targets and the impact of losing various intelligence sources.

In October, planners also added the Baghdad Telecommunications Center, a C^3 target, to the MAP for attack by an F–117A at H-hour. Located in west-central Baghdad, it functioned as a major switching center for international communications and as a regional switching station serving the city. It consisted of an eleven-story control building, a relay tower, two support buildings, and a power-generating structure.[64] Thus the "Baghdad Telecom Ctr" and the "AT&T Tele Ex/Bag Intel TP Ex" comprised the only targets on the MAP slated for F–117A strikes at H-hour.[65]

When they established the sequence of events for the opening minutes of the air campaign, planners agreed upon the stratagem of allowing the Iraqis to grow accustomed to seeing on their radarscopes each night many types of aircraft flying a variety of missions. The images on the screens would desensitize the enemy to seeing CAP, AWACS, reconnaissance, transport, tanker, and other aircraft flying in and out of airspace over Saudi Arabia, just south of Iraq. The Iraqis would not think it unusual to see a nightly air armada so that when the air campaign commenced, they would not view with alarm numerous airborne aircraft. As early as September 6 Glosson and Deptula discussed the ruse, highlighting the KC–135 tanker aircraft moving close to the Iraqi border on a routine basis, conducting refueling operations, and then moving back again. The night the air war would start, the KC–135s would move up and back, but the F–117s they had just refueled would continue toward Baghdad. On September 27 the general tasked units to taxi at 2200 and fly training missions while intelligence officers tried to detect any changes in the Iraqi alert posture. The following week units flew exercises that simulated the execution of 60 percent of the first attacks of the air campaign. Nightly offensive training continued throughout Desert Shield.[66]

Phases I through III Planning Consolidated

On September 12 Horner consolidated all planning for Phases I through III into Glosson's Special Planning Group, and discussion continued on how best to employ air power. Colonel Crigger had been responsible for planning Phases II and III, but he could see that there was much overlap among the campaign phases. "After working with the planning for Phases II and III in parallel with the strategic air campaign (Phase I)," he explained, "it became evident that the phases, from an air campaign perspective, were becoming more and more entwined and [there] were not clear break points when one phase would end and another would begin." Crigger suggested that Horner consolidate all offensive planning for Phases I through III into Glosson's group. The JFACC agreed.[67]

Glosson assumed responsibility for Phases II and III the afternoon of September 12, which required that he brief them to Chairman Powell in Riyadh the next morning. Immediately upon receiving his assignment, Glosson walked with Deptula to the basement of the RSAF building to receive Crigger's Phase II and III presentation.[68] Crigger stressed that Phase II required more SEAD support, especially F–4G HARM shooters to destroy SAM radars. The lack of sufficient numbers of F–4Gs proved a consistent, thorny problem for the planners. Deptula reminded Glosson repeatedly about the need for more F–4Gs, and he quickly came to realize that, in developing the MAP, the first question he had to ask was how many Weasels (F–4Gs) were available. The air campaign's success depended on SEAD support.[69]

Deptula eagerly welcomed the opportunity to assist Glosson in preparing the Phases II and III briefing because it ensured that Phase I would be executed prior to, not simultaneous with, the other phases. He and Glosson could better maintain the "strategic focus" of the offensive air campaign.[70] He expressed great relief that Crigger would not make more claims for Phase I aircraft for use in Phases II and III, thus diluting Phase I. In November, Deptula explained:

> When you accomplish Phase I, what we're doing is isolating the leader, Saddam Hussein, from his forces, in addition to reducing his military production base. We're eliminating his air force by virtually rendering it ineffective by cutting all his critical command and control nodes. We're attacking his entire integrated air defense system and command and control structure throughout his country and for all intents and purposes isolating him from his forces in Kuwait. Now, after that is accomplished, the forces in Kuwait had three options. They could stay in place, and by virtue of the interdiction that's built into the plan, they would end up just wilting, like a [grape on a] vine without water, because they are not getting re-supplied from anywhere. They are not getting reinforcements like they did in Vietnam....The second option is they could climb out of their tanks and go north after they become aware of the destruction that's been quickly rained on Iraq. Or third, they could attack south.[71]

Deptula advocated the Coalition forces' conducting a retrograde movement if the Iraqis invaded Saudi Arabia, as Generals Horner and Yeosock had planned for in early August, and letting the enemy move south and out from beneath their IADS umbrella. As they then waited for their logistics resupply, Coalition air would roll in and hammer them with interdiction assets. The planner saw air power interdicting the enemy forces and not allowing them to engage in close combat with the Coalition ground units. He lectured:

> People misuse the term "CAS." To do CAS, by definition, you have to have friendly troops in close proximity, and we're hoping there won't be any troops in close proximity. If you take those assets associated with doing CAS, A–10s, AV–8s, F/A–18s, F–16s, and you attack their logistics tail, you will basically stop them in their tracks. Attack the leverage targets.[72]

After discussing Phases II and III with Horner, Glosson discussed them with Deptula and Colonel Welch, the Army officer who headed the BCE. Glosson told them that the JFACC had presented a fourth option to the Iraqis — surrender — in addition to Deptula's three options — wilt on the vine, withdraw north, or attack south. Horner emphasized that the CINCCENT and CJCS worried that the enemy troops would surrender with their tanks and equipment intact. Welch pointed out that if the Iraqis did capitulate, the Coalition could dictate the terms and demand that the Iraqis leave Kuwait without their tanks. Deptula readily agreed. "If he surrenders," he later said, "we don't let him take his tanks home with him. You pull them across the line and park them all in columns, put the keys on the dashboard and let them walk north. I'm being a little facetious, but we do control the terms of surrender." Glosson and Deptula adjusted the briefing material for the next day's presentation.[73]

Milestone Briefing — CJCS, September 13

On September 13 Glosson delivered another momentous briefing on the strategic air campaign. In fifty-five minutes at the MODA building, he explained the plan, "Offensive Campaign Phase I," to Chairman Powell, Generals Schwarzkopf and Horner, and the CENTCOM component commanders. Others presented briefings as well, following JCS procedures, that is, one briefer at a time entered the conference room, spoke, answered questions, and exited.[74]

The material Glosson presented essentially repeated the briefing he delivered to Schwarzkopf on September 3: 174 targets and a 3- to 6-day duration. He used the same acetate charts and briefing slides and he presented the MAP and ATO. He eliminated two slides: the Instant Thunder target categories and the location of hostages. He added one slide, "Air Campaign Forces," that listed long-range bombers, land-based fighters, carrier-based fighters, and specialized weapon systems. He streamlined or updated other slides.[75]

As Glosson used the charts, walked the CJCS through the first twenty-four hours, and explained the attacks for the remaining days of the strategic air campaign, Horner studied Powell, with whom he had attended the National War College, and wondered what the CJCS thought about air power. Surely Powell saw how great an advantage it gave a nation and the enormously important role it played in warfare. Horner mused that perhaps he thought the air campaign briefing oversold air power. He recalled,

> I think Powell was concerned that air might be too attractive; that it might make air look too good. I don't know that, and that is mind reading; but you sit there in the meeting and wonder how it's going; what's going on. Don't get me wrong, but he has a predilection towards ground forces. But also understand now, we still don't have a national strategy that involves offensive operations.[76]

During the session, Glosson primarily discussed Phase I of the air campaign and paid little attention to Phases II and III. On the "Strike Forces" slide for the first phase, a small section listed the forces available by September 13 for defending or initiating phases II and III: 24 F/A–18s, 96 A–10s, 40 AV–8Bs, and

132 AH–64/AH–1s.[77] Glosson did not mention nor had he prepared to discuss the Phase III 50 percent counterland requirement, which he would not focus on until late October.

The LIMFACs slide highlighted four issues that affected immediate execution of Phase I: munitions, aircraft, beddown, and execution order. Two types of munitions, GBU–24 and GBU–27, would close on September 15. Twelve additional F–117 aircraft closed sixty hours after being requested, and 27 KC–10 tankers and 40 KC–135s would close thirty-six hours after being requested. With NCA approval, the B–52 CALCMs would close in twenty hours.[78]

Agreement about the date on which the strategic air campaign would be executable comprised a key outcome of the briefing. Powell asked if the employment could occur the day after tomorrow, September 15. Glosson confidently responded, "Yes." In the ensuing discussion, the CJCS noted that he did not want the plan executed for only twenty-four hours, but for a longer time, and that munitions and aircraft would have to be available to support it. The time set for being ready to execute Phase I was set for the evening of September 15.[79] At the end of the session Powell told Glosson that his presentation was "extremely impressive." Schwarzkopf later stated that the CJCS was "very impressed with it."[80]

Once again, however, the airmen boxed themselves in on the duration of the strategic air campaign. They had planned their operations to last three to six days, and decision-makers concurred with that duration, not desiring a shorter campaign, yet more importantly, not offering the airmen more days or weeks if needed. The Instant Thunder time frame continued unchanged, unanalyzed to determine whether it was long enough now that the target list had doubled. The airmen did not even suggest to the CJCS that six days was the minimum time necessary, given the day 3 to day 6 strike objectives: "key targets requiring additional attacks," "targets not covered during first 48 hours," and "destroy long-term warfighting capabilities."[81] The airmen restricted themselves to a time frame that had made Horner uncomfortable when Colonel Warden had presented it on August 20. Horner knew, however, the time constraint did not bother the CINCCENT. Indeed, the September 13 briefing represented a major accomplishment for Glosson's Special Planning Group.

General Dugan's Ouster

Meanwhile, from September 10 to 14, General Michael J. Dugan, the CSAF, traveled to the Gulf region to visit deployed Air Force units, and within two days of his return to Washington, D.C., Secretary Cheney fired him for comments he made to reporters whom he had invited along for the trip: Rick Atkinson of the *Washington Post*, John Broder of the *Los Angeles Times*, and John Morrocco of *Aviation Week & Space Technology*. An officer rarely traveled with news reporters, but Dugan instituted a policy of openness with the press. Four general officers accompanied Dugan: General Adams; Maj. Gen. Philip G. Killey, Direc-

Lt. Gen. Charles A. Horner, CENTAF commander, stands with General Michael J. Dugan, Air Force Chief of Staff, in Saudi Arabia in September 1990

tor of the Air National Guard; Lt. Gen. Thomas R. Ferguson, Jr., Commander of the Aeronautical Systems Division; and Lt. Gen. Henry Viccellio, Jr., DCS, Logistics and Engineering.[82]

Shortly after Adams boarded the aircraft for the long flight to Saudi Arabia, Brig. Gen. (selectee) Hallie E. Robertson, director of public affairs, came on board and told him that the three reporters would be along and that Dugan wanted each of the generals to spend half an hour with them on the flights to and back. Adams reaction was

> [W]hat are we going to do with three reporters!?...I have never been on a trip where you had a reporter, especially when you are going somewhere where the lid had been clamped, and this is just after the big campaign where Dugan has said, "OK, our reputation in the past has been we don't let anybody in; we can't talk, etc., etc.," and now we open the doors wide..., and he gives everybody our telephone numbers, and we are going to spill our guts....We get on the airplane, and I get to meet these guys. We thought it was a mistake for him to take the reporters. To be locked up in an airplane for seventeen hours with three guys [who] you want to be very careful with about what you say...was wrong.

Despite his dislike for the task, Adams and each of the generals at their appointed time spent thirty minutes or so with the reporters.[83]

In Saudi Arabia the reporters were restricted to Riyadh and Dhahran, and Dugan and the officers left them for two days. The CSAF had originally wanted the men to visit Khamis Mushait, the secret F–117 air base, but the Saudis and CENTCOM staff vetoed the idea.[84] In Riyadh, Horner hosted Dugan's visit which included dinner at the American ambassador's residence, meetings with the chief of the RSAF and the CENTCOM commander, and a tour of CENTAF headquarters. Glosson briefed Dugan on the day 1 Desert Storm air operations. Schwarzkopf had initially not wanted Dugan to receive a campaign briefing at all, but he relented when Horner personally requested one for his chief of staff. Dugan visited sites in Saudi Arabia, Oman, and the UAE.[85]

During their stay in theater, the reporters reflected upon the information the officers had given them on their arrival flight and considered their story angle. John Morrocco sent his report to *Aviation Week* to meet a filing deadline. Atkinson and Broder, after consulting with their editors, decided to wait to submit their articles until after their return to Washington. Dugan, the generals, and the reporters rendezvoused in Dhahran September 14 for the flight home. Atkinson concluded he had no focus for his story. He realized, however, that after additional discussion with Dugan, he could frame the story around the use of air power against Iraq in contrast with how the United States employed it during the Vietnam War. He looked forward to meeting with the generals again and posing specific questions: "Could air power alone force Saddam Hussein out of Kuwait, sparing huge losses to U.S. ground forces? How? What targets would be most effective in reversing the Iraqi invasion? Did you have to destroy Kuwait in order to save it? What made the Air Force believe bombing would be more effective against Saddam than it was against Ho Chi Minh?" The interviews on the return flight lasted five hours. "The 16-hour flight home passed amiably," reported Atkinson.[86]

On Sunday September 16, 1990, a headline on the front page of the *Washington Post* proclaimed, "U.S. to Rely on Air Strikes if War Erupts." A headline in the *Los Angeles Times* asserted, "U.S. War Plan in Iraq: 'Decapitate Leadership.'" The opening paragraph of Rick Atkinson's story in the *Washington Post* read, "Dhahran, Saudi Arabia — The Joint Chiefs of Staff have concluded that U.S. military air power — including a massive bombing campaign against Baghdad that specifically targets Iraqi President Saddam Hussein — is the only effective option to force Iraqi forces from Kuwait if war erupts, according to Air Force chief of staff Gen. Michael J. Dugan." In his interview, Dugan said, "The cutting edge would be in downtown Baghdad. This [bombing] would not be nibbling at the edges." He also stated, "If I want to hurt you, it would be at home, not out in the woods someplace."[87]

The story revealed to the world the offensive planning for Desert Storm Phase I, the strategic air campaign. Atkinson reported Dugan stating that because of Iraq's armored forces and huge army, air power comprised the "only answer" to combating Iraqi aggression and avoiding excessive casualties. The CSAF supplied information on the number of aircraft deployed to the theater. He listed target sets. He characterized the targets as "somewhat conventional" and stated that Saddam Hussein "ought to be the focus of our efforts." He offered that "Israeli sources" had told him that to really affect Saddam, the United States ought to "target his family, his personal guard, and his mistress."[88]

In Riyadh Horner had heard about the front page story before he received Schwarzkopf's telephone call about it. He recalled,

> I picked up the phone and watched the wire melt. I said, "Good morning," and [the CINCCENT] was outraged. I said, "Why are you chewing me out? I'm outraged, too, because it is our airmen who are gonna die as a result of this." And *that is why it was wrong.* It was also insulting to the Army and the Navy, and it was also insulting to the Israelis.

The JFACC later mused that Dugan "doesn't say anything in there that any airmen wouldn't say about how to attack Saddam Hussein. Unfortunately, that's *THE PLAN!*"[89]

Glosson first learned of the *Washington Post* story in a telephone call from the CINCCENT's executive officer, who told him to stand by for a call from Schwarzkopf. As Glosson waited, Horner stopped by and explained the situation. Glosson then asked Deptula to call Warden, and the colonel in Checkmate read the article to him over the phone. When Schwarzkopf talked with Glosson, he conveyed intense anger and reported that Powell and others were upset. The CENTCOM commander wanted to know what Glosson had told Dugan and stated that the CSAF would probably be relieved of duty. Glosson telephoned Warden and told him that Dugan was in "deep trouble" and should immediately talk with Powell and Cheney. Schwarzkopf talked with Glosson a second time, asking him what he had briefed Dugan. Glosson again called Warden and repeated that Dugan would not last as chief.[90]

Dugan was at Homestead AFB, Florida, that Sunday morning, and Warden telephoned him about the article and inquired if he had "deliberately planted" his comments in the press. The general said no and that he felt "comfortable" with them. Warden then telephoned General Alexander who was shocked that Warden had called Dugan and said that he was "not all that concerned" about the story. After talking with the colonel, however, Alexander reread the article and called Warden back. "You know," he said, "I'm concerned."[91]

Colonel Warden requested permission to arrange a team to prepare a defense paper for Dugan, who might be fired. "What?! Fired?!" queried Alexander. They talked about the article highlighting the targeting of individuals such as Saddam's family members and mistress, and Alexander got a "little nervous." He told Warden to prepare some papers about what Dugan had said. Alexander telephoned General Loh, who said, "Ahhh, General Dugan knows what he is doing." He told Alexander to develop some material for Dugan's defense and stand by.[92]

On Monday morning, September 17, Secretary Cheney summoned General Dugan to his office, asked if the comments in the *Washington Post* and *Los Angeles Times* articles accurately reflected what Dugan had told the reporters, and then told the CSAF he was replacing him. Cheney held two press conferences that day. At the first he stated:

> First of all, let me state for the record that Mike Dugan is a fine officer with an outstanding record of service in the United States Air Force and to the nation. Relieving him is not a pleasant task, but I felt it was a necessary one. At this moment, we have over 150,000 military personnel deployed in Operation Desert Shield in the Middle East. They may be engaged in hostilities in the very near future and a very fragile, very important international coalition has been put together to halt Saddam Hussein's aggression.
>
> Under those circumstances, the conduct of U.S. national security policy is an extremely delicate task. The statements attributed to General Dugan in newspaper interviews this weekend did not, in my mind, reveal an adequate understanding of the situation or of what is expected of him as a member of the Joint Chiefs.[93]

At his second press conference, Cheney announced that General Loh would be acting CSAF and that he would recommend to the President that he nominate General Merrill A. "Tony" McPeak, the Pacific Air Forces commander, as the new Air Force leader.[94]

That Cheney fired him "amazed" Dugan. "I don't think I was 'uncareful'; maybe I was," he recollected. "I think what I told those reporters was useful to the American public, useful to the Department of Defense, useful to the President. I think I was very consistent with the President's policy at the time."[95] The general felt he referred to Saddam's mistress and wife to the reporters "on background," but "they chose not to honor that." General Adams had heard Dugan tell the reporters that the mistress should be targeted and nearly fell out of his seat at such bluntness. Dugan believed, nonetheless, that the strategic air campaign had to "take out things that were important to Saddam Hussein." As he later stated,

> I'm a civilian today because…I said to some folks that, if you have a society that is run by a dictator, and he makes all the decisions in the country, and he only gives a damn about himself, his wife, his mistress, and his palace guard, then you need to think about his regime and his structure differently than you do when you are thinking about Japan or Germany or whoever else.[96]

Dugan expressed disappointment that Powell gave speeches after his ouster stating that the United States does not target individuals. "I think when the [CJCS] is out giving these speeches, he confuses the troops," Dugan admonished. Continuing, he stated,

> The majors and the sergeants that run the intel operations function, if they find out that Saddam Hussein is in that latrine and going to be there for the next three minutes, they don't pass it on to anybody because "We don't target individuals." I don't know what opportunities came up, but

> I know that somebody out giving those kinds of speeches confuses the troops.[97]

Dugan firmly believed that targeting Saddam in wartime was legal. He explained that Powell referred to a Presidential directive which applied to assassinations and covert actions in peacetime.[98] "It's legal to shoot a commander or whomever," he asserted. "It's legal to shoot at military targets. This guy was a military target."[99] Indeed, Saddam had adopted the military rank of marshal, wore a military uniform, and exercised command and control over armed forces.[100] He functioned as a military leader and became a legal target in wartime. The unprovoked invasion of Kuwait and the subsequent air campaign against Iraq would bring on a condition of warfare and the lawful targeting of Saddam.[101]

The "Gorilla" Package and "Poobah's Party"

The publication of Dugan's interviews in major American newspapers significantly influenced Glosson's and Henry's thinking about the air campaign. They assumed that Iraqi intelligence officers had thoroughly briefed Saddam Hussein and Iraqi military leaders about the content of the news articles. Their assumptions led them to focus intently on the first huge attack in the Baghdad area by conventional, nonstealthy aircraft, scheduled for the September 9 MAP from H+0040 to H+0102. The idea for the strike originated in Checkmate, and because more than 40 aircraft would participate, planners referred to the huge wave of attackers as the *gorilla* package.[102] It would strike the major fighter base west of Baghdad, al-Taqaddum, and components of the IADS in the western sector of Baghdad. By destroying SAM radars and C^2 connectivity, the planners intended to establish a safe, medium-altitude regime for a large follow-on package of F–16s against the Baghdad area the next day — in broad daylight. To permit the vulnerable F–16s to fly beyond the range of the hundreds of AAA located in the heavily defended Baghdad area, the SAM radars had to be targeted and destroyed so F–16s could fly higher than the AAA could reach, all the while avoiding radar-guided SAMs. The gorilla package, itself consisting of nonstealthy conventional aircraft, would have to succeed in its SEAD mission so that the follow-on F–16 daylight raiders and other nonstealthy aircraft could survive the flight to Baghdad.[103]

Assessing the impact of the Dugan interviews, Glosson and Henry reasoned that if Saddam Hussein did not believe the news reporting, their plan need not be changed; if he did believe it, he could do little in response. They concluded, however, that they should exploit his expectation of a huge air strike against Baghdad. If he expected his radars to detect and track a gorilla package, they would give him something to see and fire SAMs against. They would send drones in advance of their gorilla SEAD package to activate the SAMs, and as the Iraqis turned on their radars and fired their SAMs at the drones, American aircraft would home in on and shoot HARMs against the SAM radars. The Instant Thunder plan had included HARM shooters in the large strike package, and Deptula had already added drones to the big raid, even before Dugan's front-page stories. The news articles highlighted for Glosson and Henry the necessary, urgent requirement to acquire and employ drones, especially ground-launched ones.[104]

When Glosson had talked with Warden shortly after the briefing on September 3 to Schwarzkopf, they discussed the use of drones in the strategic air campaign, but Glosson did not ask for them then. Warden also talked with Henry, who expressed disinterest:

> I cannot tell you the syndrome of the Washington experts calling in advice....Every day there was someone in Washington or somebody from somewhere. Sometimes they just showed up with the next hot widget to try, not unlike what I thought originally when Warden called me about drones.[105]

Knowing that he had Navy TALDs available for the air campaign, Henry declined Warden's offer of drones.[106]

On September 8 one of Warden's personally addressed messages for Glosson emphasized drone support. The colonel reported estimates showing that the Air Force and Navy could lose twenty or more aircraft to the dense SAM defenses in the strategic-strike areas, even when the Navy used its TALDs. Warden discussed the feasibility of using two other types of drones to generate deceptive targets: the air-launched BQM–35 and the ground-launched BQM–74.[107] When Warden telephoned Henry again and said he could acquire ground-launched drones and supporting equipment, Henry expressed interest in the idea, but he did not yet push for the drones because of their limited range.[108]

BQM–74 ground-launched drone

On September 10 Glosson and Warden again discussed the employment of drones and the need for Glosson to send a message formally from the theater requesting them. On his own initiative, Warden had begun working the issue, and the BQM–74 emerged as the drone of choice.[109] The colonel's initiative revealed his modus operandi which produced results but exasperated his superiors. On September 14 Generals Loh and Adams learned for the first time of Warden's activity to acquire the BQM–74s, not from the colonel, but through the Office of the Assistant Secretary of the Air Force for Acquisition. Assisted by other Air Staff officers from the Directorate of Operations and Training, the colonel had taken steps to acquire the drones without first discussing with and receiving authorization from his bosses to work the project and commit the Air Force to spending thousands of dollars. Air Force officials from the Secretary's Office demanded a written request for drones from CENTCOM before they proceeded to acquire any.[110]

Warden told Deptula about the need for sending the message formally from the theater stating the requirement for drones. On September 15, Deptula worked with CENTCOM staff members and helped them prepare the message for the J–3, General Moore, and Schwarzkopf. The J–3 staff relied heavily on Deptula and Checkmate to state the requirement about the number of drones, trucks, radios, and support equipment needed. On the15th, Deptula incorporated BQM–74 drones into the MAP, even though none were in theater with U.S. units. On September 20, the CINCCENT formally sent the drone requirement message to the JCS.[111]

After the Dugan interviews, the BQM–74 drones assumed greater significance for Glosson and Henry. The SEAD gorilla package, now planned from H+0050 to H+0110, incorporated the drones, and they became the generals' highest priority. Glosson gave Henry full responsibility for their acquisition and employment. As he discussed the project by telephone, Henry needed a code name for the drones. He chose Poobah's Party as the cover designation, using his nickname, or call sign, "Poobah," from the Vietnam War.[112]

On September 23, the Air Force Logistics Command received a message from the Air Force Secretariat's acquisition program directing it to obtain, modify, test, support, and prepare for deployment forty-four BQM–74C drones, eighteen launch systems, and equipment and personnel to support Desert Shield.[113] The Logistics Command conducted four BQM–74C tests, on September 28 and 29 and on October 2 and 3. The first three produced good results, but during the fourth, for unknown reasons, the drones flew far off the desired track. Adams had to determine if, based on the four test results and analysis, the decoys should be sent to theater or held back, pending further testing. He recommended deployment.[114]

Three C–5 Galaxies departed the United States on October 6 carrying the first cargo: twenty drones and ten launchers. On October 12, one C–5 and one C–141 departed with the second delivery: twenty drones and six launchers.[115] By October 22, TAC, through its DCS for operations, Brig. Gen. Michael E. Ryan, had assumed control of the drone project in the United States. TAC selected the people who would operate the systems, and it issued orders to former members of the 868th Tactical Missile Training Group, a ground-launched cruise missile unit that had disbanded in June 1990, to report for a classified mission. Thirty-seven members of the 868th assisted by two experts from the drone's manufacturer, plus a few other individuals, would form the 4468th Tactical Reconnaissance Group to operate drones in Saudi Arabia.[116]

Henry divided the 4468th into two teams to staff drone launch sites on the Saudi peninsula: one team would locate near the Saudi town of Ar Ar to operate against Baghdad and the H–2 and H–3 airfields; the second would locate near Hafar al-Batin and KKMC to launch against Basra targets.[117] Henry worked continuously with the teams. Initially, estimates of how long it would take them to set up the mobile equipment and launch was far too long for him. He recalled, "They said it will take nine and a half hours to set it up, and I said, 'We're not standing out in the open for nine and a half hours before we shoot. I want this *down*.' We got down to about an hour and thirty minutes." Driving into the desert at night, the teams practiced with night vision goggles and special flashlights.[118] Henry arranged with the Saudis to allow the teams to function without interference; acquired armed security police protection for the crews; arranged to have the drones modified to extend their range and magnification signatures; and oversaw all aspects of the preparation for effectively utilizing the drones in air combat. The first thirty-one hours of the air campaign included ten drone packages. Within the first hour the 4468th would send four packages to four target areas: Baghdad; the KTO; Kuwait and the Shaibah area south of Basra; and the H–3 area.[119]

Complaints about Intelligence Support

General Dugan's trip to the theater caused more controversy among CENTAF units than his ouster did because it revealed significant dissatisfaction with the intelligence support that CENTAF provided the wings. When Dugan's aircraft landed at Riyadh on September 11, its cargo included hundreds of pounds of targeting material and imagery which included the DIA's OSPs. As Glosson had prepared his briefing for Chairman Powell, he telephoned Warden and requested assistance in acquiring target imagery, and Warden and his staff sprung into action, acquiring the best imagery in Washington, D.C., in bulk, and loaded it on pallets on Dugan's aircraft.[120]

Adams, who had just been promoted to four-star rank and accompanied Dugan on his tour of Desert Shield bases, soon learned that wing commanders thought CENTAF/IN had failed to adequately assist them in acquiring target imagery and materials. Adams recounted, "We went over to the West Coast to Khamis Mushait..., then up at Taif with the 111s, and each of those commanders took us in and briefed us on [his] part of the plan. I became quickly attuned to the lack of intelligence support, and it was a constant complaint." Adams had facilitated the acquisition of satellite imagery from the French commercial satellite company, and he knew that TAC had sent a large amount of it to theater, so it surprised him that the units he visited had received none of the material. He also realized that CENTAF/IN had received the pallets of imagery from Dugan's aircraft and had stored bundles in a secure facility without yet breaking them apart and initiating a distribution process. Adams himself had seen and studied some of the photographs in the Pentagon and found it hard to believe that the wings executing the air campaign had not yet received them, nor had CENTAF/IN informed the commanders when to expect the information at their bases. He concluded that CENTAF/IN acted as a bottleneck for imagery from the United States to the units.[121]

On September 13, Glosson, who had received feedback from commanders about Dugan's and Adams's visit to their bases and their discussions about intelligence problems, called Colonel Leonardo to his office and told him that General Dugan thought intelligence support to the wings was "atrocious."[122] Glosson himself expressed dissatisfaction.[123] That same day, Colonel Whitley, commander of the 37th Tactical Fighter Wing, the F–117 unit at Khamis Mushait, sent a message to Glosson, bluntly stating his criticism. In part, he reported,

> Intelligence support from CENTAF has continued to be relatively nonexistent and certainly far short of what we expected or need. Support to date has been accomplished by some behind the scenes wheeling and dealing by my intelligence guys with TAC/IN. TAC/DO and TAC/IN have gone to great efforts to provide necessary target study materials to CENTAF/IN, that have never made their way to us.[124]

Whitley stated that he had sent his own intelligence officer to Riyadh to explain the requirements for maps, charts, area and target imagery, and other data, but to no avail.[125]

Whitley quoted two messages he had previously sent to Colonel Crigger specifying CENTAF/IN's lack of support for his wing, citing three complaints. First, material for the wing piled up in the CENTAF/IN classified storage facility, and when a master sergeant from the wing, a targeting specialist, arrived at CENTAF headquarters to assist in the intelligence dissemination process, CENTAF/IN ignored him.[126] Second, Whitley described as meaningless CENTAF/IN's "watered-down" and "generic" intelligence reports. He explained, "Each unit needs to have an in-depth knowledge of the threats their pilots/aircrews will face. In many cases knowing the version of airframe and the model may be very important, yet not one CENTAF intel summary goes to the depth required." The colonel reported that the wing required data on the Iraqis' electronic order of battle and marine, air, and ground orders of battle, which was not forthcoming from CENTAF/IN.[127]

Whitley's third complaint was that Leonardo had threatened to "pull the plug" on the wing's tactical electronic-intelligence processor (TEP) van, which provided his pilots crucial information for mission planning. The TEP, a data-processing and communications system, was a thirty-foot unit consisting of a satellite transceiver and an analytical processor with automatic digital-network communications capability. The TEP received near-real-time electronic intelligence from national and theater sources and produced information on the location and parameters of the enemy's radars.[128] The wing used the van to query and acquire data from a variety of sources, but Leonardo wanted all requests for intelligence data to go through CENTAF/IN. Whitley protested, "'To pull the plug' on the information that comes to that system, narrative and TAC ELINT [electronic intelligence], would put our mission planning efforts dead in the water and could jeopardize our ability to safely execute our tasking."[129]

Governing the intelligence requests of the 37th Tactical Fighter Wing were the two prime requirements of an F–117A pilot planning a mission to deliver laser-guided bombs against a target in a heavily defended area: specialized imagery with correlating target data, and abundant information about enemy radars. Whitley and Maj. Robert J. Heston, Jr., the wing intelligence officer, firmly believed the imagery and target data were essential to navigate to, acquire, designate, and hit a target's aim point. Electronic intelligence allowed a pilot to avoid high-threat areas, enabling a safer flight to and from the target.[130]

According to Major Heston, the F–117A was "imagery dependent — no radar — everything is done visually at night." Another intelligence officer at the 37th Tactical Fighter Wing, Maj. Joseph Azzato, explained that the F–117 pilot needed images of the entire route to his target, from Khamis Mushait to Baghdad, and the acquisition of such imagery was expected to take a good while, requiring a long lead-time. Even before the 37th received orders to deploy to Saudi Arabia in August 1990, it requested from the 480th Tactical Intelligence Group negatives of imagery for probable Iraqi targets. The wing preferred negatives because it had its own photo-processing equipment, and original negatives produced the clearest, best photoproducts. The request from the 37th Tactical Fighter Wing to the 480th Tactical Intelligence Group via the TAC Battle Staff became garbled, with the result that the radius of the imagery centered on the target was more than three times greater than the distance required. The 480th had to acquire imagery and build enormous mosaics and then photograph, reduce, and digitize them. Fortunately, the mistake was caught before the F–117s deployed; nonetheless, the group's precious time and capabilities had been misdirected for nearly two weeks.[131]

Data related to a target's construction had to accompany the target's image so that the 37th Tactical Fighter Wing could set the fuzes on weapons to allow for sufficient penetration. The wing did its own weaponeering and munitions effectiveness tests on the GBU–27 bomb, specially configured to fit inside the F–117. From Khamis Mushait, it sent a steady stream of questions to CENTAF/IN about the construction of assigned targets. Leonardo's staff did not promptly respond. When it failed to supply the requested data, the wing used its TEP communications equipment to acquire the requested information from the national intelligence community in Washington, D.C., via the equipment and connectivity that the wing's home base at Tonopah, Nevada, had with the national community.[132]

Whitley's message of September 13 criticized not only Colonel Leonardo, but General Horner as well — albeit gingerly:

> During Gen Horner's recent visit, it was obvious he may not have a complete appreciation for what we think it takes for us to properly mission plan. In fact he commented that CENTAF/IN would provide all the information we needed and gave the impression that he saw no need for us to have a TEP (since the 9 TIS [Tactical Intelligence Squadron] has one) and even questioned why we brought our mission planning vans. In fact when we attempted to show him our mission planning cycle, he commented that mission planning has been around a long time and saw our requirements to be nothing special vis-à-vis other units. Frankly, his statements echoed the same words we'd been hearing from CENTAF/IN since our arrival.[133]

Horner expressed an uncomplimentary view of the F–117 wing's demands, characterizing them as excessive and unnecessary:

> We also had some of the people that were unhappy about the imagery distribution because they had been spoiled in peacetime. The F–117s are the prime example. When they lived out in the desert, they got anything they wanted, and their targeting was minuscule — Nicaragua, Panama, an air field, or something like that. So they always got exactly what they wanted because they were the dream team. When Desert Storm came along, they were just regular shovel throwers like everybody. There wasn't any difference between the A–10s and the 117s. The 117s went to Baghdad, and the A–10s went to Basra. They used to complain bitterly about not getting any imagery support. We always wanted to do it better, but they got what they needed to do the job.[134]

Other commanders besides Whitley complained about CENTAF/IN, but the 37th Tactical Fighter Wing leader put his comments in writing, with copies to TAC headquarters.[135] The critical reports reached the Air Staff and prompted the assistant chief of staff for intelligence to send three colonels from the AFIA to Checkmate to discuss ways to improve targeting support for the Special Planning Group. In consultation with Colonel Cannon at CENTCOM Rear, MacDill AFB, arrangements had already been made to have Lt. Col. F. L. Talbot, a senior Air Force targeteer at the Supreme Headquarters Allied Powers, Europe, deploy to Riyadh to improve CENTAF/IN's targeting support.[136] Within days of receiving his orders, Talbot arrived in Riyadh.

Leonardo, a highly capable officer who excelled at developing communication system architectures, had led the intelligence community in reorienting itself to study Iraq as a regional threat. He defended his intelligence unit against the criticisms from the wings by explaining that he understood requirements, for photographs in particular, and did all that he could to satisfy their requests, but he depended on national overhead reconnaissance systems to provide the imagery and on DIA to analyze it and produce the targeting material from it. DIA and the office controlling reconnaissance systems did not give CENTAF's requirements the highest priority.[137] CENTAF requests competed with other requirements for images on the locations of hostages, the American embassy in Kuwait, and the deployment and disposition of Iraqi ground forces.

Leonardo emphasized that much of the imagery arriving in theater for CENTAF, including the pallet transported by Dugan's aircraft, carried a classification in SPECAT channels that required CENTCOM's authorization for its dissemination, and it required that people at the wings be indoctrinated into the SPECAT system. Leonardo believed he could not release the material to people not authorized to receive it, although they needed the material to accomplish their missions. Before distributing the imagery and data to the units, the colonel directed his staff to account for it and pull or make duplicates for CENTAF/IN's use.[138] He recalled that Horner's advice to him was to develop better public relations skills in giving the units the disappointing news that imagery was not immediately available.[139]

Leonardo's retirement date came due about September 15th, and after discussing the matter with Horner, he decided to retire. He had already initiated the paperwork to effect his retirement when Iraq invaded Kuwait, and Horner had selected his successor, Colonel Christon, in the spring of 1990. Christon had arrived at Shaw AFB in August as Leonardo deployed to the AOR, and then Christon traveled to the theater September 8–9 and waited in the wings. In mid-September Leonardo left the theater, having postponed his retirement during CENTAF's initial, hectic deployment days.[140]

Col. Christopher Christon

The problem with intelligence support was only partially traceable to CENTAF/IN, which represented only a small portion of a vast, complicated intelligence system composed of national, CENTCOM, component, and unit levels. Within a day or so of Leonardo's departure, the imagery and intelligence reports in storage at CENTAF headquarters reached the 37th Tactical Fighter Wing. The French satellite imagery, which Whitley and Heston had so desperately wanted, proved to have limited value. The broad-coverage prints provided enough clarity, but enlargements of the vertical shots produced too many data pixels which blurred the aim point and surrounding target. The need for better imagery still existed, but as Leonardo had explained, CENTAF's top-priority requirements were not necessarily those of the national intelligence community which controlled the national overhead reconnaissance systems. Christon also had trouble acquiring imagery and told Horner that CENTAF did not have high enough priority for it. CENTAF/IN would continue to have difficulty servicing the needs of the units and the Special Planning Group, and where such units had secure communication lines to units in the United States, they built their own ad hoc intelligence sources to supplement and sometimes supplant CENTAF/IN's support. A unit like the 37th Tactical Fighter Wing did not settle for receiving less intelligence in theater than it had routinely received at home.[141]

Phase I Target List Grows

Despite intelligence problems, planning for the offensive air campaign continued unabated. From early September to mid-October, the strategic target list increased by 28 percent. The target categories that expanded the most or stirred the greatest interest during this period were strategic CW; military production and storage; strategic air defense; and airfields.

The strategic CW and the military production and storage target sets included sites associated with the NBC trio of weapons of mass destruction. Initially, facilities associated with CW concerned the planners more than the BW targets, but by mid-September, BW loomed as the most difficult and frightening NBC problem confronting planners.

CW Targets

As early as April 1990, Horner and Schwarzkopf had discussed the danger posed by Iraqi CW. To deter their use, the CENTAF commander suggested holding valuable facilities in Iraq hostage and informing Saddam Hussein that if he unleashed lethal chemicals, the United States would obliterate these critical Iraqi sites.[142] The CW threat worried the generals because during the Iran-Iraq War, Iraqi forces employed CW against Iranians and Kurds. On March 16, 1988, they used blister agent mustard gas, mixed with the nerve agents sarin, tabun, and VX, against the Kurdish people in Halabja, a town of 45,000 in northern Iraq, in the largest CW attack ever against a civilian population. Five thousand people died immediately, gruesomely, and thousands more suffered short- and long-term effects, some similar to those from excessive exposure to radiation from nuclear weapons. In 1984, the Iraqis first used nerve agent gas on the battlefield against the Iranians, and by 1988 they had incorporated CW into their warfighting doctrine. They could deliver lethal gasses with spray tanks mounted on aircraft and by aerial bombs, artillery shells, and rockets.[143]

On August 6, 1990, CENTAF had issued a message from Horner's office stating, "As we continue to evaluate the threat in our area of responsibility (SWA), it becomes more evident that chemical weapons pose a definite threat to our forces. The primary chemical threat to our operating base will be the Scud missile."[144] CENTAF knew it could defend Saudi Arabia against enemy aircraft, but the Iraqi missiles posed a serious problem, which Horner had discussed with Schwarzkopf in April 1990. With the CINCCENT's encouragement, for the Internal Look exercise, Horner and Yeosock incorporated Patriot batteries into CENTCOM's air defense plans and programed them in the antimissile mode. A week after Iraq invaded Kuwait, an Iraqi official announced that Baghdad would use CW if either the United States or Israel attacked Iraq.[145]

The Checkmate planners had recognized the Iraqi CW threat and established a strategic CW target category, which included eight sites associated with CW research, production, and storage facilities. Their OPORD indicated they considered adding "chemical" airfields, those with CW storage facilities on them, and mobile Scud launchers to the strategic CW list. They also listed some CW and Scud-related targets in the military production and storage category. By September 13 Glosson had expanded the strategic CW set to sixteen targets and added the H–2 airfield and four other Scud sites to it. He expanded the military production and storage set to thirty-five targets and continued to include a few CW and Scud-related targets.[146]

The U.S. intelligence community understood more about Iraq's CW than its BW capabilities in terms of how Iraq produced, stored, weaponized, and delivered CW. Experience with CW in the American military arsenal and the study of the use of such munitions in twentieth-century combat, most recently during the Iran-Iraq War, supported the U.S. database on CW targets. Air Force officers could also consult published manuals to receive some guidance on how to strike CW, but not BW, sites.[147]

BW Targets

In August and early September 1990, the scenario of Iraq's launching BW against Coalition forces generated profound concern among the planners. Iraq's extensive BW program concentrated on the development of anthrax spores and botulinum toxin as agents. Iraq would likely deliver BW munitions by methods ranging from aerial bombs and artillery rockets to surface-to-surface missiles.[148] Instant Thunder included only one BW-related target, the Baghdad Nuclear Research Center, described as the "only nuclear/biological/chemical research center in Iraq." On September 13, the center remained the only BW target on the Special Planning Group's strategic target list.[149]

Starting in mid-September, the chief BW problem confronting planners was striking BW targets without causing unacceptably high casualties due to the release from damaged facilities of toxic organisms into the atmosphere where winds could carry them over large areas and infect thousands of people. On September 14 when CENTCOM sent a message to its component commands and the JCS announcing a joint no-fire target list for Operation Desert Shield, the first targets comprised six BW-related sites whose attack "might release deadly biological material into the atmosphere with unknown results." The BW facilities included the Salman Pak CW production and storage facility (a confirmed anthrax storage site), al-Fallujah South, and four ammunition storage depots.[150]

Even before CENTCOM issued its no-fire list, the Special Planning Group took a cautious approach to striking BW targets. Glosson had told Deptula on August 23, "Don't hit bio storage." The no-fire message indicated that national intelligence agencies continued to research confirmed and suspected BW sites. Checkmate tapped the flow of intelligence reports on BW and passed on information to the special planners. Over the next few weeks, the casualty figures projected from the unintended release of toxins into the air after strikes cracked open storage facilities loomed larger and larger. Warden explained to General Adams that Saddam had significant amounts of anthrax at Salman Pak, about twenty miles south of Baghdad. He stated, "Threat may be significant enough to make neutralization of Salman Pak a high national priority. So far, problem does not appear amenable to bombardment because of the high danger of releasing anthrax spores into the air and into the Tigris River."[151]

Horner and Glosson faced a dilemma. As they learned more about the BW threats from Iraq, the targeting priority of BW facilities rose, but the more unstrikable those targets became in terms of collateral, unintended casualties. Glosson, the special planners, and Checkmate acquired and studied numerous intelligence reports to help them understand the problems involved and determine the appropriate military action to eliminate the threat. At the end of September, Glosson chaired a meeting to consider options to safely destroy or neutralize BW sites. The planners acknowledged that using only conventional iron bombs against a BW target would probably create a toxic cloud that, blown by the wind over heavily populated areas, could possibly kill a million people, a sobering, shockingly high number. They considered unconventional methods to deal with BW facilities. Ideas fell into two categories: crack open and destroy the targets, or deny access to them. Some of the suggestions included dropping conventional munitions and huge fuel bladders to incinerate the BW material; delivering PGMs in close sequence to reduce the facilities to rubble; seeding the areas surrounding the facilities with mines; sending special forces teams to use methods to deny access to sites; and dropping a super glue on the facilities.[152]

At Glosson's meeting, an input from an intelligence agency irritated and exasperated him. In preparation for the session, Captain Glock, the targeteer, had sent a message to the agency, soliciting recommendations on how to strike BW storage bunkers. In return, he received a memorandum recommending the generation of extremely high temperatures as the only way to ensure the destruction of hazardous BW material. Glosson correctly thought that the only capability to produce sufficiently high temperatures would be "politically unthinkable."[153] In the days after the meeting, Glosson asked the agency for more options, which in turn asked for more detailed information about the quantity of biological material and its storage configurations. The planners created various scenarios for the analysts, but the analysts requested estimates on the amount of BW material for each facility. As of October 4 Glosson had no option to recommend to Horner. He lamented, "We cannot make an intelligent recommendation at this time...without more support from the, quote, 'experts.' We will be forced to rely on instincts which will be characterized as mindless military thinking by the Washington Brain Trust."[154]

From Washington the suggestion surfaced for detonating fuel-air explosive (FAE) munitions over BW targets. Checkmate personnel thought the idea had great merit. FAEs create a tremendous fireball and the sustained, crushing overpressure could pull open the hatch of an armored vehicle or tear off the roof of a building. Arrangements were made for the Los Alamos Laboratory to test an FAE to determine if heat and overpressure would kill BW agents stored in bunkers.[155] By October 2 a promising suggestion to safely strike BW targets surfaced in both Riyadh and Washington, which called for dropping a PGM on a bunker to open it and then immediately follow with a fire-sustaining munition. Planners seriously studied the tactic, but no decision was made throughout October. The BW targeting remained unresolved for many weeks.[156]

NW Targets

Iraqi nuclear warfare (NW) facilities did not worry the planners as much as the CW and BW ones because the nuclear threat was less immediate and Saddam Hussein lacked an operational nuclear capability. The Iraqis had reached the early stages for production of enriched uranium, and researchers followed multiple paths to develop such material. The Iraqis were designing, engineering, and testing to manufacture a nuclear weapon, and U.S. analysts estimated that Iraq could produce a crude nuclear explosive device within six months to a year. In 1981 the Israelis had dealt Saddam's nuclear ambitions a blow when they launched a successful aerial strike against the French-built Osirak reactor in the massive Tuwaitha complex. After that attack, the Iraqis built an air defense system around the compound's eighty buildings and began to disperse equipment and camouflage and conceal its NW facilities.[157]

Instant Thunder planners had placed on the strategic target list the Tuwaitha Nuclear Research Center, also known as the Baghdad Nuclear Research Center, located about seventeen miles south of Baghdad. By the end of August, intelligence indicated that Iraq had two known and two suspected NW facilities, including the Tuwaitha complex.[158] Glosson and Deptula learned that striking those facilities would not release massive lethal radiation into the atmosphere, so they did not worry as much about collateral casualties from the NW-related sites as from BW targets.[159] After the Gulf War, more NW-related sites were discovered in Iraq than were known of previously. The Iraqis had spent about $10 billion on their nuclear program, employing over 20,000 people.[160]

IADS Targets

From early September to mid-October, the number of targets under consideration by the planners for inclusion in the strategic air defense target category more than doubled, from 23 definite targets on September 3, to 33 definites and 16 possibles on October 13. During this time, the planners continued to learn about how the Iraqi IADS functioned and what its critical nodes were. Henry and Deptula gathered intelligence about the IADS first-hand when they found an Iraqi EWR border site near KKMC on September 17, 1990. Riding in a jeep along the Iraqi-Saudi border near KKMC with Col. Jesse Johnson, USA, the SOCCENT commander, and Lt. Col. John Turk and Captain O'Boyle, Special Planning Group members, they came upon an Iraqi EWR van about a hundred yards to their north and snapped photographs across the border berm. Their presence set off an alarm at the site which prompted them to duck below the rim and only take quick looks at the Iraqis running to man machine gun emplacements. They scrambled for their vehicle and sped off. Back in Riyadh, Glosson ordered RF–4 reconnaissance of the area because planners and intelligence officers had not known about that EWR unit and suspected more near KKMC.[161]

Henry, his aides Colonel Cunningham and Lieutenant Holdaway, and the EC staff in the basement of the RSAF building continued to expand the detailed picture of the components, functions, strengths, and weaknesses of the IADS, effectively exploiting various intelligence sources. Extremely valuable human resource intelligence expanded their understanding of the IADS, as did information from French sources involved with designing and installing the Kari system.[162]

In mid-September, Holdaway briefed Glosson and Deptula on the IADS, with the result that they placed all backup IOCs on the target list. Holdaway also explained the IADS in great detail to Horner. When the JFACC received subsequent briefings from the Navy's Strike Projection Evaluation and Anti-Air Research (SPEAR) team, part of the Navy's Operational Intelligence Center in Washington, he already had a clear, comprehensive picture of the IADS and regularly received up-to-date information on it from the CENTAF Combat Intelligence Division and the 6975th Electronic Security Squadron.[163]

Capt. Michael "Carlos" Johnson, USN, headed the SPEAR team which traveled to Riyadh, and he and Colonel Christon, Horner's new CENTAF/IN, discussed the differences in various electronic order of battle databases. The colonel recalled that "everybody was operating from a different order of battle" and he believed that CENTAF's database consistently incorporated current information while the Navy operated on data usually two to three days old.[164] To help correlate the electronic order of battle, Admiral Mauz visited Horner to discuss requirements, and he subsequently sent twenty Navy intelligence officers to CENTAF headquarters to coordinate electronic order of battle with the JFACC's experts and communicate data directly to carriers. Horner and Christon hailed the NAVCENT–CENTAF intelligence cell as a historic, effective joint innovation.[165]

Airfield Targets

Between early September and mid-October the number of targets in the airfields category more than doubled, to twenty-seven. Aircraft dispersal became a major concern for Glosson because the Iraqis deployed aircraft to a well-built network of airfields, complicating the targeting process by significantly increasing the number of sites and aim points. By the end of October, U.S. intelligence had identified twenty-five Iraqi main bases, including some in Kuwait, and fifteen dispersal fields. By the start of the air war, reports indicted twenty-four primary and thirty dispersal bases. Many of the main and minor airfields had multiple runways and taxiways and hardened fuel storage, aircraft, and personnel shelters.[166]

Aircraft shelters consisted of massively hardened bunkers with concrete walls a half meter thick. British, Belgian, French, and Yugoslav contractors had built nearly 600 hardened shelters for Saddam Hussein's air force. Iraq also trained airfield repair teams and supplied them with fast-setting concrete and appropriate equipment. An Air Staff intelligence officer in December 1990 observed that Iraq's air base system comprised the "strongest component" of the Iraqi air force. Another analyst observed, "Iraq hadn't built mere airfields, it had built fortifications."[167]

Horner and Christon believed that Saddam would send aircraft not only to the dispersal airfields, but also outside the country. Indeed, at the start of the Iran-Iraq War in 1980, Iraqi pilots flew to other Arab nations after the Iranians mounted raids on their airfields. Saddam then recalled his pilots and planes a week to ten days later. Horner instructed Glosson to plan for possible Iraqi flights to Jordan. In November, the new CSAF, General McPeak, asked Glosson what he would do if the Iraqi aircraft stayed on the ground in the hardened facilities. The planner answered that air power would destroy more than 300 shelters in three to five days.[168]

The Special Planning Group intended to employ air power against Iraqi airfields to achieve three objectives: win air supremacy, prevent Iraqi airmen from employing CW, and eliminate the Iraqi air force as a long-term military threat against neighboring countries. To prevent sortie generation, strikes would hit aircraft, C^2 facilities, storage and maintenance facilities, and personnel. To prevent CW delivery, attacks would target CW storage bunkers in addition to aircraft and airfield facilities. Although enemy pilots composed a primary target, Glosson emphasized that Coalition forces should not bomb pilots' living quarters at bases to avoid killing civilian family members who might also reside in military housing.[169]

By August 29 word had reached Glosson that in an offensive campaign the British wanted to send Tornados to attack and crater runways. On September 1 Deptula met with and formally explained the air campaign to Wing Commander Michael Richardson, RAF, and discussed with him the use of the British JP–233 weapon against airfields. The JP–233 cratered runways and spread area-denial mines around them, fuzed to detonate at random intervals to prevent the airfields' quick repair. Richardson assumed responsibility as the RAF representative to the Special Planning Group, and Deptula included British GR–1 Tornado sorties in the MAP.[170]

Horner and Glosson thought the B–52s, with their tremendous bomb-carrying capacity, could operate effectively against airfields. Deptula discussed with Captain Hawkins, the STRATFOR representative, the requirement for B–52s to deliver area-denial weapons. The bombers' conventional iron munitions, however, did not crater runways well; tests revealed that the bombs skipped off runways. Neither did the CBU–89 Gator antipersonnel-antiarmor mines close down runways. The Gators did not explode if aircraft taxied over them, and they did not cause large enough craters when they did explode.[171]

In mid-September, SAC identified a British 1,000-pound bomb as the weapon to satisfy CENTAF's airfield-denial requirement. The UK 1000 munition had a fuze that could detonate the weapon at random intervals. B–52Gs, with modified bomb racks, could deliver the weapon at low-level.[172] Over the next three months, CENTAF, STRATFOR, SAC, the Air Staff, the Oklahoma City Air Logistics Center, British officials, and contractor personnel, among others, cooperated to acquire UK 1000s for SAC's testing and training, and for operational use by B–52Gs. The first shipment of bombs arrived at Diego Garcia on December 6; a second delivery would come in early January 1991. As the air war commenced, B–52s would deliver the weapons to ensure that Iraqi aircraft from forward operating bases could not launch quick, devastating sorties against high-value assets like AWACS aircraft and tankers.[173]

Task Force Normandy

As September drew to a close and the target list continued its unrelenting growth, planners still had to address issues associated with the opening minutes of the air campaign. When Colonel Johnson, as SOCCENT commander, sent a message back to his headquarters requesting Global Positioning System (GPS) navigation equipment, radios, and vehicles for the SOF attacking two EWR sites, the message crossed Schwarzkopf's desk and made him go, as Glosson recalled, "mildly ballistic." Horner remembered that the CINCCENT "blew a gasket" when he realized that ground forces would destroy the first two targets in Desert Storm at H–0021; he did not want troops in Iraq at that early time. Horner had not realized that the CENTCOM commander did not understand that the plan called for land forces to take out the border EWR sites. On September 25 Glosson explained the air campaign once again to Schwarzkopf. The key planner noted, "I walked through the briefing another time because General 'Stormin' Norman' (as he likes to be called — when not referred to as 'Bear') now all of a sudden thinks that maybe there's some other things he doesn't know." Glosson explained the plan in "excruciating detail" to allay any concern the CINCCENT might harbor. He had no intention of withholding any aspect of the campaign from Schwarzkopf who, as he acknowledged, had the ultimate responsibility for it.[174]

Eliminating the ground troops, the CINCCENT and the planners substituted Regular Army AH–64 Apache attack helicopters, guided to the border sites by Air Force SOF MH–53J Pave Low helicopters, to execute the first strikes of the war. The Army assumed responsibility for assembling and training the Joint Task Force Normandy crews who would execute the operation to destroy the EWR sites and open a corridor in the IADS for nonstealthy aircraft to pour through. Utilizing inertial navigation, GPS, and terrain-following radar, the MH–53J helicopters would lead the Apaches to the site with exquisite accuracy, and the Army helicopters would then unleash laser-guided Hellfire missiles, rockets, and 30-mm rounds against electrical generators, C^3 vans, shelters, antennas, and radars. Col. Richard Cody, USA, 1st Battalion Commander, 101st Aviation Regiment, 101st Airborne Division, led the task force. He worked with Col. Richard Comer, USAF, who commanded the Air Force's 20th Special Operations Squadron, 1st Special Operations Wing. The helicopter crews flew their first flight rehearsals in Saudi Arabia the second week of October and continued training until the war commenced.[175]

Milestone Briefings — JCS and the President, October 10 and 11

On October 6 Powell telephoned Schwarzkopf and directed him to send a team to Washington to brief the Desert Storm plan to the JCS, SecDef, and "possibly" the President. Schwarzkopf warned Powell, "I gotta tell you, as far as a ground offensive is concerned, we've still got nothing." "Well," Powell replied, "your air offensive plan is so good that I want these people to hear it....But you can't just brief the air plan. You have to brief the ground plan too."[176] Schwarzkopf hung up the phone, "seething" because he still had no defined plan for the offensive land campaign against the massive Iraqi army. Nonetheless, he quickly complied with the request and selected Glosson to deliver the air plan, and Lt. Col. Joseph H. Purvis, USA, a graduate of the Army's School for Advanced Military Studies (SAMS) and a recent arrival in Riyadh from the Pacific Command, and General Johnston, his chief of staff, to present the ground offensive planning. Maj. Rick Francona, USAF, would deliver the CENTCOM intelligence assessment.[177] Schwarzkopf was directly responsible for the ground campaign plan because he kept for himself the role of CENTCOM's land component commander.

The officers briefed the CINCCENT and then received instructions from him. After listening to the presentations, Schwarzkopf recalled,

> I looked at each one of the men: "One of the things we have going for us is that we don't bullshit the President. You should explain our capabilities, but do not tell the President we're capable of something we're not. This is no time for a 'can do' attitude. Do not speculate when you answer questions: confine your responses strictly to what we've analyzed."[178]

The CENTCOM commander then gave Johnston a slide to display at the conclusion of their briefing in Washington. They were to say it represented the CINCCENT's assessment of planning:

Phase I, II solid and high confidence in successful execution
Phase III executable in preparation for Phase IV
Phase IV offensive ground plan not solid
We must not assume away enemy capability and willingness to fight
Present assessment — We do not have capability to attack on ground at this time
Need additional heavy corps to *guarantee* successful outcome.[179]

Although the ground offensive planning pained Schwarzkopf, he believed it offered the best option, given the forces available. The strategic air portion of Desert Storm comforted him. "By the middle of October, we had a completely robust strategic air campaign that was very executable, right down to a gnat's eyelash," he proudly recollected.[180]

Glosson, Purvis, Johnston, and Francona traveled to Washington where they briefed the SecDef and JCS on Wednesday, October 10, and the President, SecDef, and others on Thursday, October 11. Glosson's Phases I to III essentially repeated the material he had prepared for Powell in Riyadh on September 13.

The end of the session in the White House Situation Room on October 11, 1990, at which Brig. Gen. Buster C. Glosson (center rear) briefed the Desert Storm air campaign and Maj. Gen. Robert B. Johnston, USMC, and Lt. Col. Joseph H. Purvis, USA (far left), briefed the land campaign to National Security Advisor Brent Scowcroft, Chief of Staff John H. Sununu, Secretary of State James A. Baker III, and President George H. W. Bush (left to right), among others.

When he delivered it in the Tank, General Loh attended, as did Secretary Rice. Loh thought the session "went reasonably well."[181] Immediately afterward, Powell pulled Glosson aside and told him he had made the air campaign look too easy. The CJCS wanted the planner to "tone it down" and offer a more conservative estimate of outcomes. He cautioned, "Be careful over at the White House tomorrow. I don't want the President to grab onto that air campaign as a solution to everything."[182] Glosson related Powell's remarks to Secretary Rice and received from him the advice to explain the plan as the CINCCENT had approved it. The plan was not the airman's, it was the CINCCENT's. The next day, Glosson basically gave President Bush the same briefing he had delivered to the JCS, but his time for the presentation was halved; this time he had thirty minutes to present his briefing, not the hour he had been allotted the previous day.[183]

The audience for the Desert Storm briefings in the Situation Room at the White House included President Bush, Vice President Quayle, Secretaries Baker and Cheney, Chairman Powell, National Security Advisor Scowcroft, Presidential Advisor Sununu, and Deputy National Security Advisor Gates.[184] Glosson presented large charts and slides and gave an overview of the air campaign to show that he would cover the topics "Iraq Air Defense Posture," "Strategic Air Campaign," "Roll Back Air Defense," and "Attrit Enemy Ground Forces."[185]

Discussing the Iraqi IADS, he displayed illustrations of SAM and AAA threats in the H–2 and H–3 airfield areas, in Baghdad and Basra, in the Iraqi air defense sectors, and at Iraqi airfields.[186] Next came discussion of Phase I, with its centers of gravity identified as leadership, military forces, and infrastructure. He displayed a list showing 218 strategic targets:

Target Set	No. of Targets
Strategic air defense	40
Strategic CW & Scuds	20
Leadership	15
Republican Guard & Military production and storage	43
Telecommunications	27
Electricity	18
Oil	10
Railroads	12
Airfields	27
Ports	6
	218[187]

The attack plan encompassed six days and included 822 sorties occurring over the first 24 hours, divided into four periods: 265 sorties planned for the first period, the predawn hours; 266 for the second period, in the morning; 97 for the third period, the afternoon; and 194 during the night. Using six huge maps and overlays, Glosson illustrated the strikes during each of the four periods. Looking at the quiet hour preceding H-hour, he showed the CAPs and the AWACS orbits that the Iraqis would have seen for weeks on end.[188] The war plan's strategic air campaign still kept the time duration of the retaliatory air option.

The sorties planned for the second day would bomb 20 percent of the first day's targets, targets not hit during the first 24 hours, and attack sites that BDA indicated required additional strikes. The plan for the third through sixth days would send sorties against targets still requiring attacks, as determined by BDA, and hit the remainder of the targets not covered during the first two days.[189]

The LIMFACs for Phase I revolved around the 60-hour closure time required for three groups of assets: 84 KC–10 and KC–135 tankers, 1 carrier battle group (USS *Saratoga*), and 12 F–117s. The B–52s carrying CALCMs also caused concern.[190] Glosson's "Results" slide, depicted as a flow chart, asserted that Phase I would both "destroy military capability" and "disrupt government control," which would "reduce confidence in government" and then "decapitate Saddam regime," resulting in "change." Although this chart varied somewhat from the one displayed on September 13, both clearly stated that the air campaign would "decapitate Saddam regime."[191]

Glosson preceded his discussion of Phases II and III by discussing the SAM and AAA threats in the KTO. He showed four strike packages that would neutralize these threats and gain air supremacy in the KTO. Next, he looked at Phase III, split into two parts: Republican Guard and regular Iraqi army forces in Kuwait. He described three strike packages against the Guard and four against the frontline troops in Kuwait.[192] His CONOPS for Phases II and III consisted of three missions:

> Roll IADS umbrella back
>
> Fixed SAM sites
>
> Mobile SAMs, AAA
>
> Attack enemy positions
>
> Kill armor
>
> Attack C^3I/logistics base
>
> Conduct interdiction
>
> Phase I targets
>
> Expand as Phase I draws down[193]

The Phase II and Phase III strike and EC forces were 96 A–10s; 40 AV–8Bs; 132 AH–64/AH–1s; 24 F/A–18s; 12 F–4Gs; and 4 EF–111s.[194]

During and after his briefing, Glosson answered approximately two dozen questions, most of which focused on Phase I.[195] Some of the queries addressed topics such as the religious and cultural value of targets, the benefits of launching attacks from Turkish territory, the status of Saddam's regime at the end of Phase I, projected aircraft losses, and differences between air operations during the Vietnam War and those planned against Iraq.[196] In response to the President's question, "Why not do Phases I, II, and III, and then stop?" Powell interjected and gave the following answer:

> Phase I will devastate him, it will be massive; I don't know how he will deal with it. Phase II will make it more difficult for him, and Phase III will be additive — but you will have no assurance or guarantee we would get him out of Kuwait. Because we can't guarantee he'll leave Kuwait, we must be prepared to do Phase IV.[197]

The Phase I leadership target set once again raised concerns about targeting the person of Saddam Hussein.[198] Baker, Cheney, and Powell all commented on Glosson's "decapitate Saddam regime" slide. Baker thought the word *decapitate* misleading. He, Cheney, and Powell wanted to dampen expectations that the air campaign would physically eliminate Saddam, although they did not explicitly oppose that outcome.[199] After the war, Baker wrote:

> It's important to recall that, while it would have been welcome, Saddam's departure was never a stated objective of our policy. We were always very careful to negate it as a war aim or a political objective. At the same time, we never really expected him to survive a defeat of such magnitude. Perhaps we should have remembered that Saddam had always been a wily survivor, somehow finding a way to confound his enemies.[200]

Upon returning to Riyadh, Glosson rewrote the Phase I results to list new ones:

> Destroy leadership's C^2
> Disrupt and attrit Republican Guard forces
> Disrupt leadership's ability to communicate with populace
> Destroy key electrical grids and supply
> Destroy NBC capability
> Disrupt military resupply capability[201]

Glosson had handled the questions well, and the NCA thought highly of CENTAF's air campaign plan. Powell recalled, "The air plan continued to impress." The CJCS told the CINCCENT, "The White House is very comfortable with the air plan."[202]

After Glosson's session, Colonel Purvis briefed the ground attack plan, primarily based on a single Army corps option. Purvis led a handful of Army officers who arrived in theater in mid-September to prepare in great secrecy the framework of Schwarzkopf's ground assault. He explained that "taken as a whole, the air campaign crates the environment for a successful ground operation."[203] The plan's imperatives served to incorporate the counterland, airpower mission:

> Air campaign must attrit 50% of Iraqi armor and mechanized forces in theater. Of these, selected brigades must be attrited to no larger than battalion size.[204]

> Air power attriting the Iraqi forces in Phase III would result in a "more favorable ground force ratio."[205]

The CONOPS called for air strikes for two weeks against the Iraqi ground forces. No one attending the session questioned the proposition that even though air power would attrit Iraqi ground combat power to the 50 percent level, Coalition forces would still fight a "relatively unbroken enemy."[206] Phase IV would commence with Coalition attacks into southern Kuwait northeastward from the tri-border area and the Wadi al-Batin, the dry riverbed running south-southwest from Kuwait into Saudi Arabia, toward the elbow of Kuwait. Led by the 24th Infantry Division, with the 1st Cavalry Division and the 3d Armored Cavalry Regiment, the main thrust would head northeast through the Iraqis' formidable defensive line and then turn east to place Coalition troops on either side of the highway leaving Kuwait City, heading north to Basra. The assault would then continue to secure the Iraqi-Kuwaiti border and cut off the Republican Guard in Kuwait. The 82d Airborne Division would protect lines of communication while the 101st Airborne Division and the Marines would defend the rear. Coalition forces would secure the left flank of the primary offensive thrust. From the Persian Gulf, the Navy and Marines would feint amphibious landings in a grand deception scheme.[207]

After Purvis finished, General Johnston showed the slide providing the CINCCENT's assessment that the offensive ground campaign was not solid. Scowcroft and Cheney emphatically agreed with Schwarzkopf's view of Phase IV and rejected the planning for putting too much force on force, attacking into enemy strength. The ground campaign plan actually angered Scowcroft, who stated:

> I was not happy, and it sounded to me like a briefing by people who didn't want to do it. Or didn't want to undertake the operation, and that's why I was so upset. The preferred option that they presented was frankly a poor option, and my first question is, "Why don't you go round to the west?" and the answer was "Well, we don't have enough gas trucks for it, running out of gas when we're up there on the shoulder, we can't do that, it's not a feasible option...." I was pretty appalled.[208]

The CINCCENT himself later described the plan as "a straight-up-the-middle charge right into the teeth of the Iraqi defenses." He believed it would result in a "bloodbath." Purvis's team estimated that U.S. forces alone would suffer 8,000 wounded and 2,000 dead, not including the possibility of massive casualties from Iraq's use of CW. Army planners recognized that the plan was executable, but its cost in casualties, high.[209]

On October 11 dissatisfaction and controversy with the Phase IV Army plan overshadowed the acceptance of Phases II and III. Distracted by the casualty-saturated ground attack and impressed by the strength and boldness of Phase I, officials in Washington gave scant attention to air operations against the Iraqi ground forces, and no one asked about air power in Phase IV, even though by this time Colonel Crigger and the CENTAF and ARCENT staffs had worked on a CONOPS to integrate employment of A–10s and helicopters in joint air attack operations.[210] In Washington, Glosson had lost the opportunity to show how air power in Phase III would affect Phase IV. He admitted,

> You've got to understand, at this point in time, I had not requested the Checkmate guys to do the modeling for me on the specific attrition, based on our attacks of Republican Guards and other KTO units. This was October 10th. Okay?…I didn't include that as part of my briefing. In all fairness to everybody, I screwed this up.[211]

He lamented that before he briefed, he should have asked Warden and the Checkmate guys to do some war-gaming to help him explain how Phase III, an air scheme of maneuver, could influence the Army's scheme. Army planners and briefers, not Glosson, had highlighted the importance of air attriting the Iraqi forces to the 50 percent level, an airpower counterland mission.

Chapter Eight

Phases II, III, and IV

In mid-October 1990, the stinging criticism Secretary Cheney and other officials in Washington leveled against CENTCOM's land campaign planning forced General Schwarzkopf to develop another option for attacking Iraqi troops in the KTO and helped to accelerate development of Phases II and III of the air campaign. Concurrently, a study by the RAND Corporation at the request of the Secretary of the Air Force concluded that strategic air strikes were necessary but insufficient to achieve Presidential objectives vis-à-vis Iraqi aggression. Prior to this time, Glosson's Special Planning Group in Saudi Arabia and Colonel Warden's staff in the Pentagon had focused primarily on developing Phase I of the Desert Storm plan, the strategic air campaign, but now Checkmate took the lead in producing the analysis which supported Glosson's assertions that air power in Phase III could attrit the Iraqi army to the 50 percent level before the start of the ground offensive. The regular CENTAF staff in Riyadh planned the air operations for Phase IV of Desert Storm, culminating with General Horner's issuing concepts of operations for the command and control of tactical air power in support of land forces. In Washington, Air Staff officers kept the President and Secretary of Defense apprised of the air campaign planning, while Chairman Powell openly disagreed with claims of air power enthusiasts.

Ground Campaign Planning Intensifies

The criticism directed against Schwarzkopf's land campaign briefing presented on October 11 at the White House led CENTCOM to intensify its efforts to develop a Phase IV strategy that would maximize the chance of success as ground troops ejected Iraqi forces from Kuwait while minimizing the specter of Coalition forces bogging down and sustaining high casualties as they attacked Iraqi positions. Secretary Baker derided the CINCCENT's Phase IV planning:

"We called it the Washington Monument plan: straight up the middle. Our troops would have been ground up, and casualties would have been enormous."[1] President Bush recalled Schwarzkopf's caveats about his own plan: "The briefing made me realize we had a long way to go before the military was 'gung ho' and felt we had the means to accomplish our mission expeditiously, without impossible loss of life."[2] Schwarzkopf remembered, "Colin reported back to me almost immediately that the briefing on the air campaign had gone wonderfully; the briefing on the ground campaign had gone terribly."[3]

The land campaign plan so disappointed Secretary Cheney that he established his own special unit in the Pentagon, headed by a retired Army lieutenant general, to develop a ground-attack option through the western Iraqi desert. Referred to as the Western Excursion and Operation Scorpion, the concept called for airborne troops seizing the H–2 and H–3 airfields and, linking up with helicopter and armored forces, holding the fields and threatening Baghdad with an invasion down the Amman-Baghdad highway. Cheney wanted to send the message to CENTCOM planners, "Guys, get your act together and produce a plan, because if you don't produce one that I'm comfortable with, I'll impose one."[4] Schwarzkopf hated Cheney's option and intrusion into CENTCOM's war planning. When the CINCCENT's staff evaluated the SecDef's product in November, they reviewed it carefully and found many flaws. By then, Schwarzkopf had developed new, different offensive concepts. On October 15 he instructed his planners to envision a wider sweep around the Iraqi forces in the KTO and to plan for two scenarios; a one-corps and a two-corps force structure.[5]

Surprisingly, General Yeosock, the ARCENT and Third Army commander, had not participated in the ground campaign planning that culminated with the briefing by Colonel Purvis and General Johnston at the White House. In September, the Army Chief of Staff had offered to send Schwarzkopf a small group of graduates from SAMS to form a special group at CENTCOM, unencumbered by daily deployment and defensive issues, who could direct their attention solely to offensive planning. The CINCCENT, who retained for himself the responsibility as the Joint Force Land Component Commander, with its attendant obligation to devise the strategy for the ground campaign, accepted the offer. He kept the secret unit small, consisting of its leader, Colonel Purvis, and four majors, who thoroughly understood SAMS planning concepts. Periodically, specialists would assist the group.[6] It functioned under the purview of Admiral Sharp. On October 17 Purvis's unit briefed General Yeosock on the one-corps plan and the emerging two-corps option. The next day, Admiral Sharp received briefings on the plans and approved them for presentation to the CINCCENT.[7]

On October 21 the SAMS planners presented their concepts to Schwarzkopf. When he heard the idea of assigning a heavy corps the responsibility for the main attack west of the tri-border area and the Wadi al-Batin, with the XVIII Airborne Corps even farther west of the primary thrust, he became "very animated and enthusiastic about the course of action." He pointed to the map and exclaimed,

"I sit on Highway 8. I've defeated him in his mind. I've threatened his Republican Guard; now, I'll destroy it!" Schwarzkopf viewed the Republican Guard as the center of gravity in Iraq and its destruction as the objective of the invasion. He approved sending the two Army corps west of the Kuwaiti border as the main coalition thrusts. He also emphasized the destruction of the Republican Guard.[8] The option called for the XVIII Airborne Corps to move to control Highway 8 south of the Euphrates River, cutting off a major escape route, while a second Army corps, unnamed as of yet, would smash the Guard and continue northeast to secure the Kuwaiti northern border.[9]

On October 22 at CENTCOM headquarters in the MODA building, Army officers briefed Chairman Powell who had just arrived in theater for the specific purpose of discussing the land campaign with the CINCCENT. They presented both the one- and two-corps plans. Some of the topics discussed included the problems with the single corps option; the role of the Marines in the ground attack; the opportunity to maneuver provided by a second corps; and the deception plan to portray the attack exclusively into Kuwait and not through Iraq. Powell advised Schwarzkopf to identify all the forces he needed to accomplish the mission and to eschew halfway measures. The Chairman said he would request that the SecDef and the President approve sending significant numbers of additional forces and he advocated a course of action to acquire and use overwhelming U.S. force against the Iraqis.[10] Indeed, the CINCCENT and Powell would soon request Army, Air Force, Marine Corps, and Navy assets to double the size of the Desert Shield deployment.

As Army planners struggled to improve the one-corps option and devise the two-corps plan, Colonel Purvis met with General Glosson, and they discussed the extent to which air power could attrit the Iraqi army, as required in Phase III of the CINCCENT's Desert Storm plan. Purvis had already determined, working with Col. Gary Ware, USAF, Maj. James Mudd, USA, and other staff members in the CENTCOM CAG, that attriting the Iraqi forces to the 50 percent level would cause a downward shift in Iraqi combat power allowing a successful offensive assault. Ware's group of computer analysts and Purvis's special planners were "joined at the hip," and the CAG's modeling produced the 50 percent requirement. Purvis wanted to know what air power could actually achieve.[11] Glosson asked the younger officer to identify the point at which the Army considered a division no longer an effective fighting force as it took losses in combat. Glosson recalled Purvis's reply that officers at the Army War College would say anywhere between 40 and 60 percent, whereas officers at the Army Command and Staff College tended to cite the 20 to 40 percent level. Considering the range, Glosson decided that 50 percent would be an acceptable, solid figure to establish the attrition objective for Phase III to render Iraqi units ineffective.[12]

Glosson came to the 50 percent attrition figure quite differently from Colonel Ware's CAG. From the general's perspective, 50 percent emerged from considerations of unit effectiveness, specifically focusing on the division as the unit under consideration. Glosson took a micro view of the entity being attrited, and his answer emerged by examining how long a unit could effectively continue to fight as it experienced casualties and its attrition level increased. He extrapolated this percentage to the entire Iraqi army. Ware's computer analysts, in contrast, held a macro view of the entity requiring attrition, and they examined the Iraqi army as a whole, with its thousands of tanks, artillery pieces, and APCs in the aggregate. Using the TACWAR theater-level computer model, they added data to their calculations not only about the number of divisions fielded, but about the equipment deployed. Their analysis accounted for CENTCOM seeking a 3:1, 4:1, or 5:1 advantage of attacker over defender. They measured the advantage in the number of pieces of equipment each side employed. This view had entered the CENTCOM briefing that Admiral Sharp's staff had produced on September 5, 1990. The briefing stated air campaign requirements in terms of specific numbers of tanks, APCs, artillery pieces, multiple-rocket launchers, and air defense guns requiring attrition. Each number represented 50 percent of the Iraqi total for each type of weapon.[13] Although Glosson arrived at his attrition goal differently from the CENTCOM staff, his unit-effectiveness focus would also use 50 percent attrition as the objective.[14]

The time had now arrived in October for Glosson to rivet his attention on Phases II and III of the air campaign. He had to answer the questions, How long will it take air power to achieve the 50 percent attrition level? and How will air power attrit the enemy combat forces to the 50 percent level? Since the ground war would not start until the airmen achieved the 50 percent goal, the length of time required to execute Phase III directly affected the date for initiating Phase IV. To provide answers related to Phase III, the general once again turned to the Air Staff for assistance.

RAND Critique Stimulates Planning

Just as Glosson had to put more effort into Phase III planning in October, the Air Force leadership too began its focus on the airpower counterland mission. On the Air Staff, discussion of the NCA's rejection of CENTCOM's Phase IV planning stirred interest in the questions of how air power could affect the Iraqi army before the start of the Coalition's land campaign. A RAND study also called attention to the air requirement to attrit and destroy the Iraqi ground forces before a ground war began. On the afternoon of October 10, analysts from RAND briefed the SecAF, a former president of RAND, on a computerized simulation of the strategic air campaign against Iraq. Secretary Rice had requested the report on the strategic strikes at the end of September, and Checkmate personnel provided the RAND analysts with information about Instant Thunder and Phase I, including explanations from Colonel Deptula, who had returned to the Pentagon from Saudi Arabia on September 21. Attending the session in the SecAF's office were Generals Loh, Adams, Alexander, and McPeak (the latter preparing for his confirmation hearings in Congress as the new CSAF); Colonels Warden, Deptula, and Harvey; and members of the SecAF's Staff Group. David A. Ochmanek led the RAND team.[15]

RAND's presentation explained that their analysis derived from a two-sided game, Red versus Blue, representing Iraq and the United States. The objectives of the Iraqi side were survival of the Hussein regime, maintenance of Iraq's hold on Kuwait, and Iraq's ascension as a leader of Arab nations. U.S. objectives were continued access to Persian Gulf oil, deterrence of further Iraqi aggression, liberation of Kuwait, diminution of Iraq's influence on the Arab world, release of foreign nationals, and minimum loss of life and property.[16]

RAND identified Phase I, the strategic air campaign, as the Northern Strike Package and concluded that it would leave Iraq "bloodied but unbowed." It would cause no popular uprising against Saddam Hussein and leave him and his supporters in power. Iraq would view the land battle for Kuwait as more important than the strategic attacks. It would fight the war in the KTO with ground forces still "intact."[17] The RAND analysts rejected Warden's claim that the strategic air campaign by itself would force the Iraqis to leave Kuwait.

RAND's briefing addressed the need for a ground victory and affirmed the necessity for executing all of the Desert Storm phases as a "seamless web." It emphasized the importance of heavily bombing the deployed Iraqi troops.[18] It concluded that U.S. political leaders would not use force unless they firmly believed they could win a land campaign; that the strategic air campaign was necessary but insufficient to achieve national objectives; that the war required a coalition effort; and that Saddam probably did not understand the potency of air power but did recognize defeat of armies on the battlefield.[19]

Both Warden and Harvey had heard the RAND conclusions the day before and disagreed with them. Warden expressed more concern with RAND's critique of the strategic air campaign than with its discussion of the merits of counterland operations. Harvey noted, "Their presentation gives impression (strong) that war *cannot* be won w/o grnd forces engaged w/grnd forces. This conclusion is damaging and seems unsupported by internal evidence. There is a real presentation problem here that they should fix." It irritated Warden that the RAND analysts had not changed their briefing from the day before to incorporate his criticisms, which he thought highlighted RAND's narrow thinking about air power's capability, based as it was on the European war scenario of the Soviets invading through West Germany's Fulda Gap. The colonel believed RAND underestimated the importance that Saddam Hussein placed on Iraq's economy and overestimated his view of the value of the Iraqi ground forces.[20] He offered no substantial proof, however, to challenge RAND's conclusions.

In the first week of October, Warden still saw the regime of Saddam Hussein as the center of gravity in Iraq; therefore, since the strategic campaign targeted the regime, air operations had a "good chance of winning" the war. Even if they did not end the conflict on completely favorable terms, air power could still "pound Kuwait" while more ground forces deployed to the theater. Warden wrote to General Loh, "Hard to believe that anyone in Iraq has motivation to die in huge numbers in Kuwait." He told Loh that the Air Force could execute the strategic attack and should act soon for five reasons: Iraq grew stronger in Kuwait; the weather would begin to worsen in the foreseeable future; events involving Israel could crack the Coalition or deny Coalition forces the option of acting on their time schedule; Iraq's nuclear weapons program could give Saddam a credible threat; and Iraq could preempt Coalition actions by launching conventional or terrorist attacks.[21] Warden saw no value in directing air power against the Iraqi ground forces.

The RAND briefing pushed Air Force officers to analyze air power's direct role in weakening the Iraqi army and forcing it out of Kuwait. At the same time, the strong negative reaction in the Pentagon to CENTCOM's Phase IV briefing — the one-corps scenario — stirred keen interest in planning for the ground offensive, which in turn stimulated Air Force officials to clarify and explain how air power in Phase III would be executed, and to what effect. Loh turned to Warden and to Checkmate for the answers. During the next two months, the colonel emphasized Phases II and III.[22]

Checkmate's Phases II and III Analysis

On October 10 Warden reported to the Checkmate staff that General Adams directed him to determine "how much air" was required to "kill the whole Iraqi army." This remarkable question echoed Secretary Rice's to the Air Staff a week earlier: "What is joint/allied air capability against Iraqi ground forces?" Rice would emerge as a strong proponent of counterland operations. These queries caused the colonel to carefully examine Phase III of the air campaign, which, in turn, provided Glosson in Riyadh with the analysis to support his planning concepts for the phase.[23]

Warden relied on Maj. Roy Y. "Mac" Sikes to do Checkmate's analysis for the air campaign's counterland mission.[24] In August 1990, the major had supported the development of Instant Thunder by tracking the arrival of aircraft and munitions in theater to determine when forces could execute the plan. In addition, Sikes tried unsuccessfully to apply the warfare computer program widely used in theater by Instant Thunder planners to study logistics and attrition, but the model did not appropriately apply to the strategic attack scenario.[25]

During the first week of October, as RAND conducted its analysis, Warden visited Sikes in his office area in Checkmate and asked, "How do you use air power to destroy the Iraqi army in Kuwait?" His question focused on only the regular army in Kuwait and did not address the Republican Guard forces in southern Iraq or the regular army troops in Iraqi territory near the Wadi al-Batin. Warden asked the major to form and lead a team to answer the question utilizing computer-based calculations.[26]

Sikes initially thought the query unanswerable because the end result, destruction of the army in Kuwait, was unattainable. The effort to destroy the "last tank or last platoon" would be like "trying to find a needle in a haystack," he thought, especially if that tank or platoon was positioned among equipment and units already destroyed. How would pilots know what was struck previously so they did not just "throw bombs into the dirt"? Sikes had flown as a forward air controller at the Army's National Training Center and he knew the difficulty pilots experienced in finding camouflaged tanks in the desert. He understood that dropping munitions in multiple sorties against a target obscured it by stirring up sand, dirt, and debris. Sikes had familiarity with calculations in the Joint Munitions Effectiveness Manual (JMEM), but he found them only partially useful for Warden's question. Moreover, he did not know how to define the "destruction" of an army. What percent of destruction rendered an army "destroyed"? There existed no definite one-to-one correlation between, for example, the demolition of 40 percent of an army's tanks and the destruction of 40 percent of the army's combat effectiveness.[27]

Sikes concluded that he did not think it possible to satisfy the requirements of Warden's tasking. The combination of the colonel's not identifying his inquiry as a high priority, the major's belief that he could not answer the question, and the tremendous workload he and everyone else in Checkmate carried at the time led Sikes to slow roll the problem, to temporarily ignore it. He continued to track the munitions flow to and around the theater to determine the executability of Instant Thunder, and he operated under the assumption that the strategic air strikes could occur within days. The colonel's latest tasking became for him just "one more thing to do."[28]

A week later, Warden called Sikes to the main Checkmate conference room to discuss the "regular army in Kuwait issue." The major arrived accompanied by Ross Ashley, a computer software development contractor who assisted Sikes by modeling Instant Thunder logistics and munitions problems. Warden was now more clearly focused on the problem of how to use air power to destroy the Iraqi army and told the young officer that this issue had top priority. The major explained his reservations about and his inability to tackle the question without better understanding the nature of the problem. Warden set out to "simplify assumptions" for developing a strategy to analyze scenarios.[29]

He and Sikes discussed the Phase III objective of destroying the Iraqi army in Kuwait in terms of daylight bombing using iron bombs; target acquisition, discrimination, and obscuration; and airspace management. The colonel reemphasized that the regular army in Kuwait was the Phase III target. The major understood from talking with Warden that the analysis should not target the Republican Guard because, once the regular army was destroyed, the carnage would so outrage the Guard that it would revolt against Saddam Hussein and provide new leadership for the nation. The Republican Guard would lead in rebuilding postwar Iraq. Warden then explained to Sikes that, historically, when an army was attrited 20 to 40 percent, it lost effectiveness. Forty percent was the attrition goal for the desired destruction result; the colonel thought 50 percent too high. The strategic air campaign would already have been executed for six days, with about sixty sorties continuing to fly maintenance against strategic targets. Pilots would fly A–10s, F–16s, and F–15Es directly against the Iraqi army, looking out their cockpit windows during daylight and dropping unguided, dumb bombs.[30]

Warden characterized Sikes's concern about the inability of pilots to find targets in a desert environment and to discriminate between targets already struck from those not yet hit as an ordinary target acquisition problem. He told the major to assume a 95 percent target acquisition rate, which meant that 95 percent of the time the pilots would fly to the target area, look out of their cockpits and see the targets, and employ their weapons against them. Once the pilot acquired the target, the weapons effectiveness calculations in JMEM would assist Sikes in determining the percent likelihood that the weapon would actually hit the observed target. Warden wanted to know, based on a 95 percent acquisition rate, the number of sorties required to achieve a 40 percent attrition rate. Kim Campbell, an intelligence analyst from the Office of the Assistant Chief of Staff for Intelligence, joined Sikes's team and provided the data on the Iraqi army's location in Kuwait and its order of battle.[31]

Issues immediately surfaced concerning sortie rates for various types of aircraft, including Navy and Marine Corps platforms, and the munitions quantity each type carried. Sikes knew he could consult the War and Mobilization Plan rates, which would indicate for aircraft types the number of sorties per day for specified lengths of time. He knew, also, that he would have to adjust the planned sortie rates because of the tremendous distances most aircraft would have to fly from bases in Saudi Arabia to targets in Kuwait. Airspace management considerations also entered the analysis because airspace control problems affected the number of sorties.[32]

At the conclusion of his meeting with Warden, Sikes had a clearer understanding and sense of direction for accomplishing Phase III analysis. He, Ashley, Campbell, and others worked the entire weekend of October 12 to generate data. Sikes discussed with representatives from the other services in Checkmate the sortie rates for Navy and Marine Corps aircraft. He made a gentleman's agreement with them that their figures would be used only for air campaign analyses and not for Pentagon interservice budget battles.[33]

The major brought his Microsoft Excel computer software program from his home because it performed better than the programs available in Checkmate. Excel generated printouts that Sikes pieced together to form what he called larger-than-life spreadsheets to display data runs for different days of the air campaign at various levels of effectiveness. The computer calculated the number of sorties for each kind of aircraft flown and matched them with munitions availability and depletion figures, and with sortie and target acquisition rates. Sikes became a fragger, allocating weapons to targets, using his knowledge of JMEM, and matching appropriate types of aircraft and munitions to targets. His computer runs and graphics soon showed a progression of bomb damage over time, disclosing the days required for various levels of destruction, even as high as 95 percent.[34]

During the weekend, Warden peered over the shoulders of Sikes and his team as they loaded Phase III data and did spreadsheet calculations. On Sunday, October 14, Warden typed some of his ideas about the analysis. He stated, "It appears entirely feasible to destroy almost the entire Iraqi army in Kuwait from the air — with the exception of the forces in Kuwait City." He knew that attacking troops in the city, by air or house-to-house fighting, would cause many civilians to suffer. Beyond the urban area, climate and terrain allowed for the destruction of the Iraqi army in a week to ten days, with minuscule American losses.[35]

Warden had confidently told Chairman Powell on August 11 that in six to nine days strategic attacks would induce the Iraqi army to leave Kuwait. Because in his view that army was not a center of gravity, he did not target it in Instant Thunder.[36] Nonetheless, Warden had inspired the CJCS and the CINCCENT to broaden their thinking about air power to envision a conventional strategic air campaign against Iraq. The CINCCENT's Desert Storm war plan incorporated Instant Thunder, but it also demanded more of air power than just strategic attacks. The CINCCENT's war plan now required that Warden expand his thinking about air power to include the counterland mission of Phase III. Once he began to focus on the attrition of the Iraqi ground forces, Warden anticipated results for the phases as optimistic as those he had projected for Phase I. In August he saw Phase I, in a little more than a week, forcing the Iraqi army to leave Kuwait. In October he saw Phase III, in less than two weeks, destroying the Iraqi army in Kuwait.

On Monday, October 15, Sikes showed Warden his spreadsheets, delighting the colonel. Based on a 95 percent target acquisition rate, air power could destroy the Iraqi army in seven to ten days. The analysis included a one-day Phase II effort against SAM sites in Kuwait to gain the medium-altitude regime for the airmen. Having given the colonel the analysis, the major thought he could return to his old project of tracking the munitions flow to the theater, so Warden surprised him when he told him to continue refining the Phase III material and to brief General Alexander the next day. Sikes pointed out that no briefing slides existed, only the spreadsheets, to which Warden replied that he should design them. For the next three months, Sikes focused exclusively on Phases II and III analysis and briefing presentations.[37]

The next morning Warden met with Sikes and a few other members of his Checkmate staff and enthusiastically told them, "Our air-ground Kuwait study may be [the] most important work in Washington now." He explained that if air power could destroy the Iraqi army in Kuwait in seven to ten days, U.S. ground forces would not have to invade Kuwait, and approximately 30,000 ground force casualties could be avoided. During the meeting, Maj. Robert M. King noted that some decision-makers would probably suggest that if Phase III could destroy the

Iraqi army, the Coalition should first initiate and complete Phase III of the air campaign before executing Phases I and II. This echoed General Adams's suggestion in August to first attack the Iraqi army and then execute the strategic air campaign. Warden explained that the phases could not be executed out of order because Phase I achieved air superiority, without which no other air campaign objectives could be achieved.[38]

During the week of October 15–19, Warden, Sikes, and Campbell briefed the Phases II and III analysis to General Alexander on Tuesday; General Clapper and the RAND analysts on Wednesday; General Adams on Thursday; and General Loh on Friday. All recipients had questions or suggestions, but none were substantive, as Sikes recalled. He ran additional computer analyses using target acquisition rates of 75 percent and 50 percent, the worst-case scenario.[39]

The Phases II and III briefing analysis for General Adams showed six days for Phase I, with a maintenance effort continuing throughout the entire air campaign; one day for the Phase II SEAD operations, also with a maintenance effort; and approximately two weeks for Phase III, with the end of III corresponding with approximately the twentieth day of the entire air campaign. Sikes accounted for Navy, Marine Corps, and Air Force aircraft flying against Iraqi ground forces, but no other Coalition aircraft.[40] Campbell briefed the Iraqi ground order of battle in Kuwait to reveal that Iraq had twelve divisions deployed defensively. For weeks, their positions had remained basically static, and their protection consisted of only foxholes and hastily constructed berms. The Iraqi troops were neither concealed nor camouflaged at this time.[41]

Sikes and his team identified six Phase III target categories: airfield support facilities; C^2; armor and APCs; personnel; trucks; and area targets.[42] The analysts excluded artillery from the priority categories. In mid-October, no Coalition ground forces were in range of Iraqi artillery pieces, hence the low threat and priority. Artillery would assume greater importance, however, as friendly forces moved forward, and it would not be struck until approximately the seventh day of Phase III. Sikes differed from the JMEM when counting a piece of artillery as killed. The manual judged an artillery piece destroyed if its barrel was bent. The major agreed that a piece in such condition was out of commission, but so was an artillery site where the crew had been killed or the associated equipment destroyed. Sikes knew that Iraq possessed a "super gun" with a sixty-mile range, but intelligence reports had not identified its location.[43]

Personnel in infantry units also held a low priority on the target list. Checkmate staff reasoned that killing large numbers of troops in the field took a long time. If, however, personnel were left alone until air power destroyed other target sets, the troops would continue to consume food and water, not easily replenished, which would stress the Iraqi logistics system in Kuwait and deprive the ground forces of other essential supplies.[44] The analysts judged the Iraqi forces in Kuwait as destroyed (rendered ineffective) if they were attrited to between 20 and 40 percent, although Sikes also presented data for destruction levels well beyond 40 percent, to nearly 100 percent. Depending on the target acquisition rate, the Iraqi army in Kuwait was effectively destroyed in nine to twenty days. This meant that the national objectives could be achieved without committing any significant amount of U.S. ground forces. Only Kuwaiti and other Arab forces should reoccupy Kuwait.[45]

During the briefing session for Adams, some questions arose concerning the following topics: the possibility of Iraq's launching a ground offensive into Saudi Arabia shortly after the start of Phase I; Iraq's offensive air capability; the effectiveness of attacks against SAM and AAA sites; the use and effectiveness of A–10 Warthog guns; and the effectiveness of air power when used against enemy personnel. At the conclusion of the session, Adams praised the briefers' "good effort" and told Warden to present the material to General Loh the next day, send the briefing to Glosson, and give it to "someone" on the Joint Staff J–3.[46]

The Phases II and III briefing for Loh started on Friday afternoon and continued on Monday morning, October 22. Major Sikes and Campbell delivered it, with Alexander, Warden, Harvey, and others attending.[47] Loh asked questions about armor, trucks, artillery, and personnel. He complained that the briefing "makes us ten feet tall." He wanted more "What If?" scenarios addressed. What if the Iraqis used CW against Riyadh or executed successful terrorist acts against U.S. aircraft and ammunition depots? What if the Coalition lost all its F–4Gs? What if the Iranians helped the Iraqis? He requested that the planners run figures assuming a second-day loss of 100 U.S. aircraft and 20 percent of available munitions. The general noted that the modeling lacked sophistication, but Warden replied that they did not work a sophisticated problem. Loh requested that the briefing be cast in a military OPLAN format. He suggested, too, that it include historical and current photographs of targets in other countries and other geographical settings to contrast them with targets in the favorable desert environment.[48]

On October 22 Warden sent the Phases II and III analysis briefing to Glosson in Riyadh, via secure fax, and told him about the ongoing effort to produce the changes Loh suggested. The next day, Deptula, who had returned to Saudi Arabia when Secretary Rice visited the theater, telephoned Checkmate, talked with Colonel Stanfill in Warden's absence, and related that Glosson wanted to repackage and use the same material to brief Horner and Schwarzkopf. He needed, however, answers to a long list of questions, foremost of which was whether any analysis had been done for targeting the Republican Guard, to which he received a negative reply. Glosson came on the phone and discussed the requirement for targeting the Guard and said that he could not get through Schwarzkopf's door with the briefing until it addressed the elite troops.[49]

Deptula spent the afternoon of October 23 with Glosson reworking Checkmate's analysis to make it more "palatable" and "acceptable" to Horner and Schwarzkopf. Glosson thought the conclusion that the Iraqi army could be defeated by air in only a few days overly optimistic; he wanted to highlight only worst-case scenarios and conclusions. At the end of the afternoon, however, he decided to include both the best- and the worst-case scenarios for his own briefing.[50]

As Checkmate developed and revised its products, the Air Force Center for Studies and Analysis and RAND critiqued their assumptions and methodologies. Maj. William Troy of the Studies and Analysis group briefed General Adams on October 18. Five areas concerned him and formed the basis of the Studies and Analysis review.[51] Based on how Checkmate aggregated equipment, it underestimated the number of sorties required to kill tanks, APCs, and trucks. A 95 percent acquisition rate for some weapon systems was too high, and the values for friendly aircraft attrition would be higher than those modeled. Double-berming around equipment would worsen target acquisition problems, and finally, terrorist attacks had to be accounted for.

The RAND critique, presented by Ted Parker and Don Emerson to Major Sikes for seven hours on October 30, discussed Phase III. The reviewers pointed out that Checkmate lacked the intelligence to support their assumptions about known target locations and target arrays, and it did not sufficiently account for target overkills. It also overestimated the destruction of artillery as a result of damage to the trucks used to tow the guns and transport munitions, and to crews.[52] Once again, lack of intelligence weakened the planning effort, and since the intelligence picture did not quickly improve, Checkmate did not promptly and radically alter its assumptions. The RAND and Air Force studies, with the Checkmate Phase III analysis, were historically important because they illuminated problems and methodologies for planning the extraordinary air counterland mission whereby air power would directly destroy half the enemy army before friendly forces engaged it.

Revising the Analysis

On October 26, Glosson possessed a facsimile copy of the latest Checkmate Phase III briefing and told Deptula he wanted someone to hand-carry the Air Staff's spreadsheet computer runs to the theater. Warden chose Major Rogers to carry the material and to replace Deptula, who once again would return to Washington to continue working for Secretary Rice. Rogers would keep the lines of communication open with Checkmate and maintain the focus of offensive air operations on the strategic air campaign. Glosson viewed the computer printouts and briefings as analysis. He explained,

> We didn't have the *analysis* to back up our assertions. I needed to have some more analysis done to prove to Schwarzkopf and the other doubting Thomases that we were going to be able to attrit that land army down to that 50 percent level or the level where the ratios of attack were down to where they wanted it.[53]

On October 27 Rogers traveled to Riyadh on American and foreign commercial airlines carrying a duffle bag that contained the latest computer data and some intelligence reports and photographs. Checkmate had not yet studied the counterland mission against the Republican Guard. Neither had the analysts changed any Phase III assumptions to account for some intelligence studies that suggested the Iraqis were beginning to dig in, to build personnel bunkers in the Kuwaiti desert. Noting the reports, Warden bristled that it was "criminal" that Iraqi aggression had been given so much time to succeed. He did not, however, direct Sikes to rerun his calculations to account for well dug-in troops.[54] Since personnel benefited from the new bunkers, Warden may have thought that as long as tanks, artillery, and APCs were exposed, major planning adjustments for the Iraqis' digging in remained unnecessary.

On October 27 Warden telephoned Deptula and they discussed the Republican Guard, among other topics. The Checkmate leader thought striking them an unwise "diversion of effort." The focus of Phases II and III should remain on the Iraqi forces in Kuwait. "Why would the Republican Guard move into Kuwait to be killed?" Warden asked. Glosson came on the line and talked about the Guard and a few other issues. Warden stated that each Guard division that moved into Kuwait would require another day and a half to kill. He urged the general not to divide the initial effort in order to hit them. Phase IV would destroy the elite troops, if required. The planner in Riyadh explained that the CINCCENT viewed the Republican Guard as a center of gravity that sustained Saddam Hussein in power. Whenever Glosson talked about Phase I, Schwarzkopf consistently inquired about taking down those forces. Glosson therefore requested that Warden develop a module for the attacks, to occur before strikes against the regular army in Kuwait.[55]

Shortly after Rogers brought the Checkmate material to the Special Planning Group, he, Glosson, and Deptula carefully examined it, and Glosson thought the results were still overly optimistic. He directed Warden to run additional scenarios. Rogers in Riyadh and Sikes in Checkmate spent much time on the STU III discussing various assumptions and subsequent computer runs. They worked with numbers corresponding to assets already in theater. Glosson and Rogers applied the pilot's TLAR principle (that-looks-about-right) to the Phase III analysis and JMEM data. They thought the JMEM too optimistic, and they took the fighter-pilot-being-shot-at into account. They concluded that in a four-ship package, only three of the aircraft would find the target, and of those three, only two would actually strike the target. Rogers acquired some satellite photography of Iraqi artillery positions and overlaid bombing patterns on them to assist with determining kill ratios. He showed Glosson's assumptions to Colonel Purvis, who agreed with them, noting that they were, indeed, conservative. Glosson recalled later:

Discussing Desert Storm are (from left, around the room) Maj. Mark Rogers, Lt. Col. David Deptula, Capt. Douglas McNary, Brig. Gen. Buster Glosson, Brig. Gen. Patrick Caruana, Maj. John R. Turk, Maj. David Karns, and Wing Comdr. Michael Richardson.

> The final assumption said one out of every four airplanes that takes off will not get to the target. I don't care what reason we use — they just won't get there. So 25 percent of everything we launch is not going to get to the target. It had nothing to do with PK [probability of kill]; they were just not going to show up. You can imagine that didn't go over very well in the Air Force.[56]

Other assumptions Glosson incorporated into the Checkmate analysis concerned battlefield configuration and density data for Iraqi tanks, artillery, and deployed personnel.[57]

Rogers learned of the kill boxes established for CENTAF's defensive D-day ATO Bravo and requested that an F–15E pilot in the Special Planning Group extend the grid boxes over Iraq for offensive air operations. The boxes reminded Rogers of those established for armed reconnaissance in Korea, also defined by lines of latitude and longitude and given alphanumeric designators. He consulted with Colonel Welch of the TACC's BCE on kill boxes and computer model assumptions.[58]

Rogers recalled that the CENTAF intelligence unit gave minimum support to the development of the Phases II and III analysis and briefings. If he needed intelligence, he simply picked up the STU III, asked Checkmate for it, and promptly received it. He saw CENTAF/IN representatives at Glosson's morning staff meetings to brief on the current situation, but then they immediately left the Special Planning Group. If asked, they would respond, but they were not, Rogers stated, breaking down the door to help. Capt. Douglas McNary from CENTAF/IN, one of the briefers at the morning staff meetings, recalled that he was expected to deliver his briefing and answer questions, and then Glosson dismissed him. The general had formed a tightly knit, extremely secretive unit that made no effort to allow worker-bee intelligence officers like McNary access to the offensive planning, nor did it request their help on an ongoing basis. Because CENTAF/IN members were not briefed into the plan, they had difficulty knowing what intelligence was required.[59]

At the Pentagon on October 29, Checkmate's Phases II and III analysis, presented by Warden, Sikes, and others, was the first briefing General McPeak received as the new CSAF. He had already discussed the strategic air campaign with Warden and found it "not very interesting." "I mean, it wasn't that unusual," the general recalled. "That's exactly the planning approach anybody would have taken who knew anything about how to employ air, so it was, I think, routine planning." To McPeak, Instant Thunder, the basis for Phase I, was a "no-brainer, straightforward."[60] The briefing on the 29th of the campaign's other phases presented objectives, desired results, and anticipated U.S. losses. Only U.S. aircraft were modeled in Phases II and III, and Phase III addressed only the ground forces in Kuwait, not the Republican Guard in southern Iraq.

Warden's Phase III outcomes gave the Iraqis the three options the air planners had discussed in Riyadh in September: retreat north, surrender in place, or suffer annihilation, thus allowing Arab forces to reoccupy Kuwait and obviating the need for U.S. troops to join in the land campaign. Warden did not suggest that the Iraqis would attack south. Americans would lose sixty-six aircraft as they attacked the ground forces.[61] He and his planners asserted, "Iraqi troops are neither concealed nor camouflaged," a situation that would soon significantly change. They stated that fourteen Iraqi divisions held positions in Kuwait. The summary target list included artillery, armor, personnel, trucks, airfield C^2, airfield support facilities, and area targets.[62] The briefers highlighted 20 percent to 40 percent attrition as the level whereby army units historically lost combat capability and had to be withdrawn from battle. Checkmate's analysis went well beyond that range. Based on a 75 percent target acquisition rate, air power would reach a 95 percent destruction level in fifteen days.[63] The analysts did not single-mindedly focus on 50 percent as the attrition goal, as ground

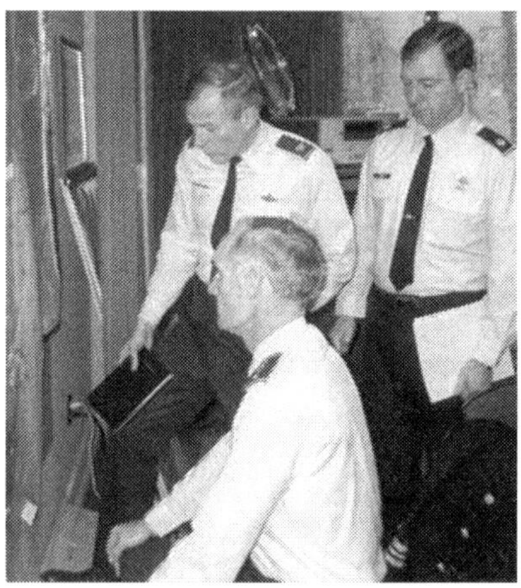

Col. John A. Warden III briefs the new Air Force Chief of Staff General Merrill A. McPeak as Maj. Roy Y. Sikes looks on.

and air planners in Riyadh did.

Warden explained to McPeak that because Schwarzkopf had insisted on destroying the Republican Guard, Checkmate had prepared an independent module to address this goal. After a preliminary SEAD effort, attacks against the elite troops would require approximately ten days.[64] To achieve a 95 percent destruction rate, planners identified four target sets and specified the length of time that would be required for their destruction: bridges, three days; artillery, nine days; armor, nine days (to achieve 88 percent destruction); and troops, nine days.[65] Little intelligence supported the Guard module. It lacked a comprehensive description of the forces (differentiating between those equipped with heavy armor and those without); the precise locations of units; and an identification and explanation of critical nodes. This boded ill for effective targeting and quick destruction of elite troops.

McPeak strongly favored destroying the Republican Guard in southern Iraq before attacking the regular army in Kuwait because he preferred to minimize damage inflicted on the small nation. The Chief did not want air power to destroy Kuwait, the prize. He questioned why planners targeted Kuwaiti airfields — they required liberation, not destruction. He saw Iraqi military equipment, tanks, and troops as the key targets.[66] After the briefing, Sikes continued to run computer calculations on attacks against the Guard. By November 2, changes in assumptions led the planners to aim for destruction levels of the elite forces and the regular army in Kuwait to only 50 percent, not 95 percent. The reduced level eased concerns about munitions shortages developing in theater, inasmuch as higher destruction objectives require greater weapons expenditures.[67]

Phase II SEAD and Air Supremacy

While Phase III dominated the discussion on the Air Staff and in the Special Planning Group at the end of October, Phase II, Air Superiority in Kuwait, developed quietly and without controversy. Consulting with the team's intelligence representative, Sikes acquired data on the Iraqi electronic order of battle, and the planners identified twenty-six radar sites in the KTO requiring destruction, not merely electronic suppression. The major assumed that Phase I would eliminate the integrated aspect of the Iraqi air defense system and that Phase II would target the system's elements that individually threatened aircraft at medium altitude. Phase II had to destroy radars, crews, and missiles at twenty-six sites capable of launching mostly SA–2s and SA–3s. The spreadsheet data suggested that air power could destroy them all in one day. Targeting the sites in and of themselves, and not eliminating them because they protected valuable fixed targets, fascinated Sikes. Before Desert Shield, he had thought of bombing radars and their SAMs only in relation to other more important targets. In Phase II, the twenty-six sites themselves comprised the primary targets. After attacks against them, the Iraqis would still possess AAA and shoulder-held, infrared, heat-seeking

SA–7s, but the medium-altitude regime would be secure.[68]

Although Horner and Glosson (and all other airmen) absolutely agreed with Schwarzkopf when he confidently lectured, "The first thing you've got to do is get air superiority!" they did not think it necessary to establish a separate Phase II to achieve command of the air in the KTO. They had designed Phase I to win air superiority at the start of the air campaign by executing counterair operations, attacking airfields, and destroying the Kari system in control of the IADS. Phase I would free up the medium altitude across the theater. Horner observed, "The whole thing *was* designed to gain control of the air. That was the first order of business."[69] Phase II would destroy SAM sites functioning autonomously, disconnected from the centralized IADS control.

Glosson repeatedly tried to convince the CINCCENT that airmen would achieve air superiority as early as possible in the air war. He explained, "I kept trying to shove Phases I and II together because I knew it was a facade. As I briefed it, I would say, 'Now, as we go to Phase II, understand that if at all possible, I'm going to do Phase II while I'm doing Phase I.'"[70] Schwarzkopf insisted on seeing an independent Phase II in each briefing he received. Describing what the commander meant by air superiority, Glosson quoted him: "I don't want anything that can even prevent a *balloon* from flying....I want such a sterile environment over the KTO that, if I want to, I can put up balloons, and they can't do anything about it."[71] The CINCCENT's vision of completely safe, benign skies at all altitudes was unattainable, given the vast number of AAA and infrared missiles the Iraqis possessed, but Glosson could provide airspace with little or no enemy interference from radar-guided SAMs and aircraft. He would give CENTCOM air supremacy in the KTO. He relied on General Henry to revise and use Checkmate's Phase II products. Rogers thought of Henry as the "Phase II guru."[72] Henry planned the hard kills of the SAM radar sites with cluster bombs and missiles. He would send F–4Gs with HARMs against the sites and would send the shorter range Shrike missiles to execute close-in hits — "stuff shots." He explained: "Now we have the upper hand. We're going to drive this down their throats. We are going to force air supremacy on them. We are going to dare them to shoot. Then when they do, we're going to pound them, and, therefore, we can roam the skies at our choosing."[73]

Increase in Desert Shield Forces

Meanwhile, back in Washington on November 8, President Bush announced his decision to significantly increase the number of Desert Shield forces. The President had made his decision in late October after conferring with Chairman Powell, who had just returned from Riyadh and extensive consultations with Schwarzkopf. Powell later offered his rationale for the increase:

> Go in big and end it quickly. We could not put the United States through another Vietnam. We could be so lavish with resources because the

> world had changed. We could now afford to pull divisions out of Germany that had been there for the past forty years to stop a Soviet offensive that was no longer coming.[74]

Powell advocated a policy of employing overwhelming force. On November 1 Schwarzkopf sent a message to his component commanders requesting that they provide him with a broad CONOPS for offensive operations against Iraq and a list of forces required to support those operations. "Assume no constraints on availability of additional forces," he directed.[75]

The next day, Horner passed a note to Glosson asking him to identify aircraft and units to deploy if, as JFACC, he were told he could have any forces he wanted. He cautioned the planner to consider theater-basing requirements for the new assets. The possibility that he could increase his air assets greatly pleased Horner, who considered that it increased his options. Glosson reacted negatively, believing that sufficient aircraft were already in the AOR and that the strategic air campaign could be launched soon, without waiting for more ground troops, which would necessitate a land war with attendant high casualties. Nonetheless, the chief planner drew up a list of aircraft. He consulted with Deptula, who immediately requested an increase in the types of platforms whose limited numbers had so sorely strained his strategic attack planning: F–117As and F–4Gs.[76] Horner and Glosson talked with General McPeak about the additional forces, and the new CSAF initially thought the overall increase in U.S. assets unnecessary. He stated:

> The decision was made fairly soon after I got here to go to Phase II of the buildup, which was to bring the armored in from Germany. I indicated at the time that I didn't think it was necessary. I thought we were ready to commence air operations by about the middle of September.... I said, "We are not going to get any style points," or something like that. I forget exactly how I put it; but, "We are making this look harder than it is," but the other Chiefs were absolutely shoulder-to-shoulder with Powell on this.[77]

The second phase of Desert Shield sent to the theater 400 Air Force aircraft; more than four Army and Marine Corps divisions, including the Army's VII Corps from Germany; and three carrier battle groups. Because it would take more than two months for the ground forces to arrive in the AOR, the estimated date for their closure, January 15, 1991, became the earliest date for when the Desert Storm offensive could commence.[78]

Horner's Recommendations

Continuing his counterland planning, on November 7 Glosson briefed the Phases II/III analysis to Horner. He prefaced his presentation by acknowledging that the Air Staff had provided the initial analytical material but that he had altered and improved it.[79] Horner responded favorably to the concepts and data, emphasizing three points. He wanted to highlight the artillery target set. He knew from attending a meeting with the CINCCENT and the CJCS on October 22 that they stressed the importance of killing artillery to prevent the Iraqis from firing CW against Coalition troops during the breaching operations. Horner already had tasked Colonel Christon to identify every artillery site in the KTO. Second, Horner urged Glosson not to "poke the Army in the eye" by overselling the effectiveness of air power in destroying the Iraqi ground forces. Third, he suggested the chief planner refer to Phase III as Preparing the Battlefield, reflecting Army terminology.[80]

To Horner and Glosson, the type of planning for Phase I of the air campaign significantly differed from that required for Phase III. Horner explained, "You don't have the collateral damage aspects, and it's open-ended. You can take as much time as you want....Hitting tanks and artillery is a level-of-effort thing."[81] Strategic targeting to achieve air superiority and to suppress the launching of CW and BW required quick strikes early in an air campaign. Strategic attacks required swift execution and had to precede the effort against the ground forces, whose destruction could unfold at a slower pace. Horner shared living quarters with General Yeosock, so the CENTAF and ARCENT commanders had an informal means to exchange ideas about the planning and coordination of the air and land campaigns. In addition, Horner regularly attended meetings with the CINCCENT, who imparted his ideas about how he envisioned the employment of air power in Desert Storm.

CINCCENT Unveils His Desert Storm Plan

On November 14 Generals Horner, Glosson, and Henry from CENTAF accompanied by other component, corps, and division commanders attended a meeting in Dhahran when Schwarzkopf delivered a rousing briefing of his Desert Storm war plan. Standing in front of a large map of Kuwait and Iraq in a rundown building converted to a dining hall, the CINCCENT, functioning also as the land component commander, addressed twenty-two generals and admirals, his senior officers. Lt. Gen. Frederick M. Franks, Jr., commander of the powerful Army VII Corps, had traveled from his headquarters in Stuttgart, Germany, to attend. He commanded the heavy corps that would execute the main thrust of the ground war. For the presentation, Schwarzkopf worked himself into a "ferocious state."[82] He believed he had to convey strength and confidence in his offensive strategy so that his subordinate commanders would accept the concepts and enthusiastically focus on common objectives. He hoped to energize them for combat and bring out the "killer instinct" in each. He wrote, "Only a few of the commanders had any idea of the plan I was about to present or of the tough assignments I was going to mete out. I needed every man in the room to embrace his mission and be breathing fire by the time he went out the door".[83] Only the

CINCCENT briefed on the 14th; it was his show alone. He emphasized the ground war, Phase IV of Desert Storm.

He gave a brief overview of his entire plan, identifying centers of gravity as Saddam Hussein, the NBC-weaponized missiles, and the Republican Guard. He highlighted three U.S. strengths: better airpower capability, superior technology, and well-trained leaders. The strengths of the Iraqis consisted of a large force structure and CW capability.[84] The CINCCENT highlighted five battlefield goals: attack Iraq's C^2 system and leadership targets; achieve and keep air superiority; sever Iraq's supply routes; destroy Iraq's NBC capability; and destroy the Republican Guard.[85] Emphasizing the fifth goal, he stated: "We need to destroy — not attack, not damage, not surround — I want you to *destroy* the Republican Guard. When you're done with them, I don't want them to be an effective fighting force anymore." He directed the commanders to have their forces ready for combat in mid-January.[86]

Schwarzkopf outlined the phases of his Desert Storm plan:

Phase I	Strategic Air Campaign
Phase II	Air Superiority in the KTO
Phase III	Preparation of the Battlefield
Phase IV	Ground Attack[87]

Although he now titled Phase III "Preparation of the Battlefield," it incorporated the same basic concept as the Phase III he had presented to Powell and Cheney in the Pentagon on August 25: Ground Combat Power Attrition, including its air counterland attrition requirement. He did not, however, explain that Phase III itself was phased, with an initial emphasis on the Republican Guard and the subsequent focus directed against Iraqi forces in Kuwait proper. During the war, Army corps commanders would fail to appreciate the CINCCENT's vision of first beating down the Guard before shifting the air level of effort against the frontline regulars.[88]

Schwarzkopf envisioned the phases occurring sequentially, not simultaneously. After the strategic attacks, Phase II had to precede Phase III to clear the skies over the KTO for fixed-wing and helicopter operations. Phase III then had to attrit the enemy army to the 50 percent level to arrive at favorable attacker-to-defender force ratios before opening Phase IV. The CINCCENT did not view the Phase III air counterland mission as rendering the Iraqi army an ineffective fighting force, which presumably it was if it experienced a 50 percent attrition level. He saw air power changing only force ratios. Phase III would prepare the battlefield, not destroy the enemy army. Armies, not air forces, defeated armies.

The CINCCENT's war strategy now included the heavily armored VII Corps moving into position to thrust into Iraq to annihilate the Republican Guard.[89] Even though the air plan had targeted the elite forces in Phases I and III, the CINCCENT believed that the VII Corps would still have to battle and destroy them. His combat experience in Vietnam may have tempered his enthusiasm for air power's ability to single-handedly destroy ground forces. In October 1990 he told a reporter that he had seen incredible air power in Vietnam. Sometimes his unit would sit outside a village while aircraft, with complete air superiority, would bomb the village and just pound it, and artillery would fire on it as well, so it was inconceivable that anyone could have survived the bombing and shelling. Once the strikes ended and Schwarzkopf's troops entered the village, however, the enemy "came right out of their holes and fought like devils."[90]

Discussing the ground attack, the CINCCENT highlighted bridges as targets. He explained that the Iraqi forces would be concentrated in the eastern portion of the battlefield, in the Kuwait area. The waters of the Persian Gulf would block their movement to the east. To the north, the Euphrates River would form a natural barrier — once the airmen had cut the spans of the bridges crossing it. The main U.S. attack would come from the west. Air strikes against the bridges would not only prevent supplies and reinforcements from moving into Kuwait, they would stop Iraqi troops from leaving. Air power would "isolate the battlefield." (Horner and Glosson had just recently added thirty bridges to the Phase I target list as interdiction targets.)[91]

The CINCCENT sketched out the broad concepts of Phase IV by explaining that he would probably send the XVIII Airborne Corps, commanded by General Luck, north to the Euphrates valley to cut off Highway 8, a possible escape route. Luck would then turn eastward and attack the Iraqi army. General Franks's VII Corps would execute the main Desert Storm attack, pushing north and then directly east, smashing into the Republican Guard.[92] To the east of the two U.S. Army corps, the U.S. Marines and Coalition forces would invade Kuwait. Two Marine divisions and a smaller Saudi force would push north, tie up Iraqi forces, and encircle Kuwait City. To their west, a pan-Arab force would attack into Kuwait to cut supply lines and then liberate Kuwait City.[93] Schwarzkopf bluntly told the ground commanders that he would not allow them to move their troops to their D-day jumping off points until the start of the air campaign. He recalled,

> I didn't want the Iraqis to learn of our battle plan and then be able to shift their defenses. I knew that once our Air Force stopped the Iraqis' reconnaissance flights, they would be blind, and even if they did finally figure out our plan, the Air Force would make it impossible for them to shift enough forces to counter it.[94]

Schwarzkopf kept the 50 percent attrition requirement embedded within Phase III even though the Desert Shield troop increases announced by President Bush on November 8 gave CENTCOM four more divisions for the ground offensive. As early as October 15, Colonel Ware's CAG had modeled offensive scenarios with a second notional corps. His group produced results by varying rates of enemy attrition attributable to air power, and a 40 percent rate seemed key to achieving success in the ground campaign. In November, Ware continued to simulate and model attacks, varying Iraqi army attrition from 15 percent to 42 percent, and then from 29 percent to 58 percent. On November 19, Saddam Hussein announced that he would reinforce troops in the KTO by 250,000 men. New Iraqi units began deploying quickly.[95] U.S. intelligence tried to track the flow of troops and supplies into the KTO and arrive at accurate numbers for the enemy forces arrayed against the Coalition, but it did so with only limited success. Nonetheless, the CAG tried to account for changes in the projected Iraqi threat and the effects of breaching operations. The group's analyses still indicated the requirement for air power to attrit the Iraqi army to the 50 percent level before initiating the ground offensive. The 50 percent requirement would permeate air and land campaign planning.[96]

On the eve of the air war, CENTCOM intelligence estimates indicated that Iraq had deployed 540,000 troops to the KTO, a figure arrived at by determining the number of divisions deployed. The total turned out to be a debated figure, however. Some postwar analysis that used information from enemy prisoner of war reports indicated that the approximately forty-three divisions were not up to full strength. While the number of units remained the same, therefore, the number of troops in undermanned units totaled only 336,000.[97]

During the coffee break at the Dhahran meeting, Maj. Gen. J. H. Binford Peay III, Commander, 101st Airborne Division, asked his fellow Army officers an unanswered, cynical, intriguing question, "If we can bomb them to 50 percent in three weeks, why don't we take another three weeks and get the other 50 percent for good measure?"[98] A few weeks earlier in theater, Secretary Rice had provided an answer. When he learned of Checkmate's Phase III analysis, he suggested to Schwarzkopf that if the counterland mission did not attrit the Iraqi army in a few days, the Phase III attacks should continue for as long as it took to eliminate Saddam Hussein's military forces. The SecAF envisioned Phase III as not inevitably leading to Phase IV, but being repeated "over and over and over" until it destroyed the enemy army. Rice reasoned that as long as the air campaign achieved desired results, it ought to continue. Only as the campaign approached the point of diminishing returns should the next phase commence.[99] Horner viewed Phase III as a level-of-effort operation which could continue indefinitely "until you get it done" — hitting tanks, APCs, and artillery. As did all commanders, Horner hoped a land war and its casualties would be unnecessary, but he knew preparations for a ground war were essential. He thought it foolish not to plan for the land campaign.[100] Glosson initially thought Phase I, if given sufficient time to play out and if the NCA remained patient, would achieve national objectives. After he began revising and developing the Phase III analysis, he concluded that Phases I and III would so weaken the Iraqi leadership and military forces that only a police action, not a full-scale ground war, could liberate Kuwait.[101]

Schwarzkopf told Horner and Glosson that the ground forces required approximately fourteen to eighteen days from the start of Phase I to move to the locations they would use as their jumping off points for D-day, the start of the invasion.[102] During this time, commanders would execute Phases I, II, and III sequentially. The first and second phases would include some maintenance strikes as the third phase unfolded. During his presentation, the CINCCENT did not attach time constraints to each phase, but from the briefings Glosson had given him in September and October, he knew that Phase I would last approximately six days. Phases II and III would therefore consume about eight to ten days. The retaliatory nature of the strategic air campaign continued to stick as the CINCCENT allowed only six days for the strategic strikes and the airmen offered no rationales to extend the length of Phase I.

As Schwarzkopf presented his strategy on November 14, the first three phases carried the war to the Iraqis while the friendly ground troops prepared themselves to deliver the primary, fatal blow to the Iraqi military forces. During the first fourteen to eighteen days of Desert Storm, the CINCCENT required air power to accomplish an astounding amount of destruction and achieve numerous objectives: attack leadership, C^2, and telecommunications sites; destroy NBC capability; prevent Scud launches; destroy the Iraqi air force and IADS to achieve air superiority; destroy key electrical grids and POL facilities; target military support and production facilities; attack individual SAM sites in the KTO; attrit the Republican Guard and then the regular army in Kuwait to the 50 percent level; conduct interdiction operations to prevent supplies and additional forces from moving into the KTO, specifically, cutting bridges to prevent reinforcements and the escape of the Republican Guard; prevent air attacks against the ground troops disembarking at ports and airfields; protect troops as they moved to and massed at staging areas, offering themselves as lucrative targets, and then concentrated at their jumping off points, and as they built huge supply bases; provide intratheater air transport for the redeploying troops; ensure the secrecy of the westward shift of two corps by stopping Iraqi reconnaissance flights; facilitate deception by not striking western targets prematurely to encourage the Iraqis to expect the main thrust to come from the south through Kuwait; execute breaching operations; prevent the Iraqis from moving to new defensive positions once they learned of the left-hook attempt to outflank them; provide continuous CAS to friendly ground troops; drop leaflets in the PSYOPS campaign; and operate C^2, intelligence-gathering, and reconnaissance platforms to provide commanders with information for targeting, operations, and BDA to aid them in keeping Coalition and civilian casualties low. The JFACC and his chief planner comfortably assumed responsibility for air power achieving the results the CINCCENT expected.

Glosson's Counterland Briefings

Four days after the meeting at Dhahran, on Sunday, November 18, Glosson attended a meeting at the MODA building with Schwarzkopf and a few land campaign planners who briefed the CINCCENT on the progress of their planning on their portions of the ground offensive. When the session ended, Major Rogers was waiting outside the conference room to meet Glosson and drive him to the RSAF building. He thought the Army planners quietly filing out of the room looked depressed. He caught the eye of Purvis, who just shook his head and walked on.[103]

Glosson held a poker face and told Rogers to walk to the car quickly, where the major burst out with, "Well, Boss, how did it go?!" Glosson beamed and replied, "Great." The CINCCENT had gone into one of his tirades against his land campaign planners. When General Yeosock told Schwarzkopf that Glosson was there to brief about what the air forces were going to do in Phase III, the CINCCENT angrily shouted,

> How the hell can any Air Force officer say he is going to stand up here and tell me that he's gonna do something to the battlefield when the ground commander doesn't even know his scheme of maneuver yet?! How can he support the scheme of maneuver if the ground commander doesn't know what the scheme of maneuver is?! What's he gonna do?! You can't possibly shape the battlefield until you know the ground commander's scheme of maneuver! Buster, what do you got?!

Glosson replied, "Sir, let me tell you about shaping the battlefield."[104] The Air Force officer then presented a short, informal briefing to the CINCCENT, showing the Phase III analysis and what the battlefield would look like after counterland air strikes, in terms of the kind of target sets and number of targets destroyed. He emphasized the conservatism of the assumptions upon which the data were based, to which Schwarzkopf replied, "Looks about right to me."[105]

The CINCCENT had raised an important point highlighting the need to coordinate air operations with the ground commanders' schemes of maneuver. Horner had already considered and knew the mechanism to satisfy the requirement. As he had with ARCENT and the XVIII Airborne Corps during peacetime exercises, he would rely on the BCE staffed by Army personnel and situated in the heart of the JFACC's TACC to provide him with the targets the corps commanders wanted struck beyond the FSCL. Presumably, the corps commanders and the ARCENT commander would prioritize and nominate targets appropriate to their plans and the CINCCENT's strategy. The JFACC placed his faith in the Army's BCE, located as close to the nerve center of the air campaign as physically possible, to receive the targets for the ground commanders' schemes of maneuver. He expected to direct air power against the targets they wanted hit, to service their targets. The Army leaders, however, did not seem to comprehend how Schwarzkopf, as theater commander *and* land component commander, would systematically employ air power to prepare the battlefield according to his Desert Storm theaterwide strategy, so their target nominations would often conflict with his. They would fail to use their BCE effectively, which existed to serve them and functioned in constant communication with the air component commander, the JFACC, and his officers in executing air operations twenty-four hours a day.

In late December, ARCENT's corps and division leaders gathered at the Eskan Village compound in Riyadh for a map exercise to review plans and iron out difficulties. Glosson delivered a formal briefing of his Phase III analysis. General Yeosock introduced him by stating that he would talk about how he "measures his approach of getting the 50 percent attrition." The airman started by reminding everyone that even before Phase III commenced, aircraft would have already bombed "the pure hell out of the Republican Guards," with 4 B–52s striking them every three hours, and 100 F–16 sorties hitting them daily.[106] "That's before we even talk about going after him seriously," Glosson confidently asserted. He explained that he based his Republican Guard calculations on 600 U.S. sorties a day, excluding A–10s, AV–8s, and helicopters, which would provide 300 sorties a day for defensive firepower in case the Iraqis attacked into Saudi Arabia. He pointed out that aircraft continued to arrive in theater and that by January 15 the Americans could fly 1,200 sorties a day, although his analysis took into account only 600. He showed the audience a gee-whiz illustration of the KTO with three huge arrows outlining aircraft streaming into the area. The aircraft types included F–111s, F–15Es, F–16s, A–6s, F/A–18s, and B–52s.[107]

Next Glosson described how the Iraqis arrayed their weapons. For armor (tanks and APCs), he explained that usually 8 to 12 pieces would occupy an area measuring 400 by 200 feet. To be as conservative as he possibly could, however, he would allow credit for killing only 3 armor pieces when an aircraft dropped munitions on such a 400- by 200-foot rectangular area. For artillery, he then stated that about 12 pieces were usually arrayed in an 800- by 400-foot area. He would only count as killed 6 pieces after aircraft struck such an array. For personnel, 90 people would usually congregate together in an area. He arbitrarily reduced that to 30 people he could claim killed from aircraft sent to attack troops. Glosson displayed a satellite photograph with outline sketches representing 400- by 200-foot areas, encompassing and highlighting deployed Iraqi armor.[108]

The general chose the dimensions for his arrays by relying, in part, on Purvis's data. For example, he chose the 800- by 400-foot dimension for an artillery configuration after he had learned that canisters of cluster bomb units, normally part of an aircraft's bomb load, covered an area 1,600 by 800 feet.[109] He then halved the area to 800 by 400 feet. He asked Purvis for information on the number of pieces of artillery that would occupy an 800- by 400-foot area in a normal battlefield configuration. The reply suggested to Glosson that 12 to 15 pieces of artillery would occupy the space. The general again reduced the number so that no one could criticize him for overestimating the expected kills per array. He followed the same logic for armor and personnel.[110] He explained:

> In other words, the Army's own doctrine said that most of the threats they faced were going to array on the battlefield in a given footprint. I

> took 50 percent of that factor and said, "No matter how effective our weapons are, I'm only going to give them credit for destroying 50 percent of what the Army's own manual says they will destroy in an area that size...." When I briefed the Chairman and the CINC, I said, "The Carlisle model uses this factor. I used this. The Carlisle model used this factor. I used this. Army doctrine says this. I used this."[111]

He next described the aircraft, their munitions, and the destruction the airmen could expect to achieve:

> 4 F–16s (8 Mavericks or 16 CBU–89s) to kill 3 tanks
> 2 F–15Es, F–111s, or A–6s (8 CBU–89s) to kill 3 tanks
> 3 F–18s (12 MK–20s) to kill 9 artillery tubes
> 3 F–16s (12 CBU–52s) to kill 10 artillery tubes
> 1 A–6, F–15E, F–16, F/A–18 or F–111 (4 to 8 CBUs or MK–20s) to kill 30-plus personnel[112]

The aircraft would carry and expend more munitions than the number shown, but the lesser quantity indicated the number attributed to the kill. Glosson highlighted that he factored in the assumption that the 600 aircraft would achieve only a 75 percent acquisition rate, so 150 would fail to identify their targets. He also assumed that the aircraft would have a mission readiness of only 80 percent.[113]

Presenting results, Glosson displayed slides showing the percent of kills graphed against time. The charts plainly revealed that air power would attrit 50 percent of the Republican Guard's armor in 4½ days. Amazingly, half of the armor would consist of "burning hulks" in that short time. In 4 days, air strikes would attrit 50 percent of the artillery; in 4½ days, attacks would kill 50 percent of the personnel.[114]

The general also explained his assumptions for counterland operations against the regular Iraqi troops in Kuwait, following the same steps and format he used in his Republican Guard analysis. He presented another satellite photo, now highlighting an 800- by 400-foot area for an artillery position, that revealed a distinct horseshoe berming pattern surrounding each piece. During these operations the CINCCENT would hold no aircraft in reserve. His charts again indicated key results in a short period of time: against armor, 9½ to 10 days to reach the 50 percent destruction level; against artillery, about 10 to 12 days; and against personnel, 12 days.[115]

Glosson told the audience that lining the phases end to end, with three to five days allowed for Phase I, indicted the air campaign would run for about twenty days. He continued by offering the airmen's gut view. He stated,

> We believe that the air war will unfold something like this. We would anticipate after about 4 days, walking on into [Phase II], going into [Phase III], and being ready at about the 14-day point. However, we can

> keep this intensity going up for 45 days if we need to, and there is no constraint for us doing that.[116]

Because the start of the ground war depended on when the air war had achieved its objectives, Glosson, in effect, told the Army corps and division commanders that they could possibly launch into battle two weeks after the beginning of the air campaign. This timetable may have accounted for some of the controversy during the war, when the corps commanders' target nominations had not been serviced even though the two-week period had expired. Although key to starting the ground war was satisfying the 50 percent attrition requirement, the ground commanders, unsure of when the land campaign would begin, grew uneasy when the air campaign continued well beyond the duration Glosson had presented, and air power had not yet pounded the frontline troops. The planner's point that the air war could continue for six weeks longer if necessary probably did not catch the Army officers' attention as much as the ground war starting two weeks after the first bombs dropped on Baghdad.

Glosson concluded by reasserting that the air campaign would attrit the enemy army to the 50 percent level, and he guaranteed those results by accepting high aircraft attrition rates. He bluntly told the commanders, "The point that I'm trying to get across is that we will attain the results that I just described to you. I guarantee you that. Like I said, we may lose three or four hundred airplanes doing it, but we will do that."[117] During the war, however, both Glosson and Horner would keep aircraft losses remarkably low by destroying the Iraqi IADS to such an extent that, as they had planned, they freed up the medium-altitude regime for pilots to fly in, beyond the lethal reach of AAA and infrared-homing SAMs. Unfortunately, flying higher than 10,000 to 15,000 feet would seriously degrade bombing accuracy.[118] Armor, APCs, and artillery would be harder to locate and hit. Even with the use of binoculars, A–10 pilots looking out their cockpit windows had trouble finding targets. When they flew lower, in the 4,000- to 7,000-foot range, they suffered increased damage from infrared SAMs, but their bombing accuracy also increased. On February 15, when the Republican Guard shot down two A–10s and damaged another, Horner pulled the Warthogs off the Republican Guard.[119] The JFACC was absolutely unwilling to take 300 or 400 aircraft losses to attrit the enemy army to the 50 percent level, despite what the chief of the Special Planning Group had promised and guaranteed, and despite the loss of bombing accuracy.

One of the major discrepancies between what Glosson told ground commanders and what actually occurred during the war concerned the types of weapons expended and the kill rates. The planner pinned great hope for tank kills on pilots flying the F–16s and delivering Maverick missiles. Few F–16 pilots, however, had trained before the war to fire the 500-pound rocket-propelled Maverick, and during Desert Storm, only 130 F–16 sorties dropped that weapon. A–10s expended most of the Mavericks, with mixed results. F–16s mainly dropped general-purpose bombs, cluster bomb units, and the older MK–20 antiarmor Rockeyes. Most cluster bomb units and Rockeyes, released at from 8,000 to 12,000 feet, were ineffective. The CBU–89 Gator mines did not do nearly as well against dug-in tanks as the CBU–87 combined effects munitions with its radar (ground-proximity) fuze, but Horner restricted use of the CBU–87 in the middle of the war to ensure that sufficient numbers were available to provide CAS during the land offensive.[120] The weather, too (regionally the worst in fourteen years), would hinder bombing effectiveness. Although Glosson had stated that by January 15 he could send 1,200 sorties a day against the Iraqi troops, he modeled only 600, which was the better figure because, on average, only 500 to 600 daily sorties flew against the Iraqi ground forces.[121]

After Glosson finished going through his slides at the map exercise, the ground commanders asked him questions about breaching, tactical air control elements, CAS, Iraqi fuel-tank farms, Saudi participation, A–10 sortie rates, and friendly-fire precautions. None of the ground commanders inquired about the coordination of fire support to ensure that procedures were in place for the Army to send attack helicopters and to launch missiles through the congested airspace beyond the FSCL. Neither did anyone suggest to Glosson that in Phase III he should make artillery a higher priority than tanks and personnel. These issues would generate controversy during and after the war, but not before it.[122]

Brig. Gen. John Stewart, Jr., the new chief intelligence officer at ARCENT headquarters, inquired about whether Glosson knew of reports indicating that at least one Republican Guard division was beginning to build two-sided and covered bunkers for its tanks. He wondered how that affected the modeling. The airman admitted that the top covering would make targeting more difficult, and he had not accounted for that type of protection. Because Glosson had used data from October, his calculations rested on the assumption that protection for the fielded forces consisted of foxholes and "hastily constructed berms." He estimated that the top covering would require three more days of air strikes. He explained that the Maverick, a "precision weapon," could "get in the slightest opening" and destroy an armor piece.[123] Stewart had raised an important issue, and the Iraqis' digging-in would emerge as a serious counterland targeting problem, not adequately accounted for in the Phase III analysis. The Iraqis would protect most of their pieces of equipment by dispersing them, digging them in, and surrounding them with berms. The Republican Guard received engineering support that was better than that received by the regular army, plus the Guard constructed better revetments and spread themselves more thinly over greater areas. Schwarzkopf later lamented, "The Republican Guard had literally gone underground. They'd built bunkers for both their men *and* their tanks." The Iraqis also employed tank decoys.[124]

Schwarzkopf had selected the U.S. Army's VII Corps to operate as the main attacking force in the ground war, with the mission to attack the Republican Guard in its sector and destroy the Guard's armored and mechanized troops. The

Corps's powerful forces would consist of the 1st and 3d Armored Divisions, the 2d Armored Cavalry Regiment, and the 1st Infantry Division. The British 1st Armoured Division, under the tactical control of the VII Corps, would also fight in the main effort. The CINCCENT would give to the Corps the theater reserve force, the 1st Cavalry Division, if it was not needed elsewhere. Throughout January, the VII Corps continued to arrive in theater from Europe. Shipping delays would prevent the 3d Armored Division from arriving at its tactical assembly area in Saudi Arabia until February 12.[125]

General Franks, the VII Corps commander, depended on the airmen to attrit the Iraqi forces to the 50 percent level. Assuming the 50 percent attrition, ARCENT calculated the force ratios that the Corps faced against Iraqi defenders. At the breach site, the Corps would outnumber the enemy by 11.5:1. En route to the Republican Guard, the ratio would be 3.8:1. At the decisive battle site, it would be 2:1. Traditionally, a favorable attacker-to-defender ratio was 3:1; ideally it was 6:1 or better at the penetration point. The ARCENT ratios, and later, similar CENTCOM ones, suggested success on the battlefield, although the VII Corps's ratios would be low at the decisive point. The Corps's fresh, powerfully equipped, three-division "fist" would compensate for the unbalanced numbers. (Postwar analysis showed the Iraqi unit strength numbers in the calculations as mistakenly inflated.) The threat of the Iraqis' using CW complicated the assessments and greatly added to the commanders' worries.[126]

CENTAF's Phase IV Planning

Glosson did not spend time planning for Phase IV; he relied instead on the regular CENTAF staff to accomplish this. The staff's Phase IV effort focused on ensuring that the TACS provided CAS and interdiction strikes for the ground forces during the land campaign.[127] The TACS supported the equivalent of five corps, which would wage the Coalition's land campaign. On the eve of the ground war, the lineup of forces from east to west positioned the Joint Forces Command–East troops, comprised of Arab forces from the six GCC states, on the right flank of the Coalition, along the coast. Immediately to the west, MARCENT's I Marine Expeditionary Force, along with the Army's Tiger Brigade from the 2d Armored Division, formed the second-corps equivalent. The Joint Forces Command–North, the majority of Arab forces, held the center position. Next came the Army's VII Corps, with the British 1st Armoured Division, to conduct the main attack. Finally, the Army's XVIII Airborne Corps, with the French 6th Light Armored Division, formed the Coalition's left flank. The Army's 1st Cavalry Division functioned as the theater reserve forces to protect against Iraq's launching an invasion down the Wadi al-Batin.[128]

Colonel Crigger, CENTAF DCS for operations, directed the planning for the employment of air power in direct support of the ground campaign and the five corps. His staff had relied on the TACS throughout Desert Shield to direct air power in defense of the Saudi kingdom, and now used the same system to prepare for the offensive war. By all accounts, Crigger had done an outstanding job on the CENTAF staff, but because he had continually interacted with officers from the other services who held general-officer rank, Horner believed that CENTAF needed a flag officer in the position the colonel held. Thus, in November, he brought Maj. Gen. John A. Corder to the theater to function as the new CENTAF director of operations. In addition to commanding the Tactical Air Warfare Center, Corder oversaw the Air Ground Operations School at Eglin AFB. He had flown the F–4D during the Vietnam War, with 100 missions over North Vietnam. Both Corder and Crigger relied on CENTAF's Lt. Col. Robert E. "Skip" Duncan to work day-to-day TACS issues, especially for providing CAS. In December 1990 Brig. Gen. Michael S. Hall of the New York Air National Guard and commander of the 174th Tactical Fighter Wing arrived at CENTAF headquarters to function as the theater air liaison officer and deal with air support to the ground forces.[129]

The primary documents encapsulating the Phase IV air planning were the JFACC's CONOPS for C² and the employment of air power in support of engaged land forces. CENTAF published four of these documents, in October, November, January, and February. The C² CONOPS issued on January 1 specifically stated that the concepts applied to both offensive and defensive operations, whereas earlier editions had referred only to the defense of Saudi Arabia. Although the C² CONOPS formed the basis of the air campaign planning for Phase IV, CENTAF did not specifically identify them as Desert Storm planning documents.[130] The CENTAF staff also developed and issued publications which provided details for executing the C² CONOPS, such as the Combat Plans Handbook and the CONOPS for the Joint Air Attack Team. The handbook provided detailed information about the ATO cycle, mission package numbers, call signs, and aerial refueling procedures. The joint team documents described procedures for the integrated employment of fighters and attack helicopters.[131]

In October 1990 the CENTAF Combat Plans Division hosted a joint conference at which four working groups discussed a variety of issues associated with executing operations. They offered suggestions about improving communications, especially against Iraqi jamming efforts; activating and using kill boxes; prioritizing immediate air requests; and integrating the Airborne Battlefield Command and Control Center (ABCCC), F–4G Wild Weasels, AC–130s, and A–10s into the TACS. Ideas and solutions to problems were discussed and incorporated into the CONOPS in November and in the January 1991 update.[132]

The C² CONOPS that Horner signed on January 1, the final set of concepts printed before the start of the air war, consisted of eleven sections and six attachments, which underwent revision even as Phases I through III unfolded. The set explained that the command arrangements for the execution of operations treated the Arab forces as corps-equivalent forces. Those in the Northern Area Command, which would form the Joint Forces Command–North, coordinated air support requirements through their own Air Support Operations Center (ASOC), while the Arab forces in the east passed their requirements through the Marine Corps's Direct Air Support Center, which also served the I Marine Expeditionary Force and functioned like an Army-corps ASOC. The concepts addressed the operations of the Marine Air-Ground Task Force to ensure the integration of Marine Corps and JFACC C^2 systems, but it did not discuss internal Marine Air-Ground Task Force procedures.[133]

The CONOPS described CAS as sorties employed short of the FSCL that required clearance by the supported ground commander before ordnance could be employed. It incorporated Horner's ideas about Push CAS, which he had explained to Schwarzkopf in April 1990 in preparation for the Internal Look exercise. Horner wanted to *push* sorties to ground commanders for use if needed, but if land operations could not employ them, the pilots were to execute preplanned interdiction missions. The ground forces received CAS as scheduled in addition to Push CAS.[134] Colonel Baptiste recalled the JFACC using a hose comparison to describe Push CAS:

> He used the analogy that it would be a hose. He could control how much was coming out the end with the ATO, and he could take that hose and point it where it needed to be. What he didn't want was a waste of air assets, by either having them sitting on the ground waiting for tasking or orbiting in the air waiting for tasking — in other words, all on call to a particular ground commander who may or may not use them. He didn't want to waste their assets that way. He wanted those assets flowing continuously into the battlefield and going wherever they were needed, and that was his guidance in setting up the Push CAS system. It was definitely a Push system rather than a Pull system.[135]

Army officers liked Push CAS.[136] After the war, General Franks wrote, "CENTAF had originated a system...whereby they would push sorties of CAS into our area without request. We could then employ them or send them to someone else. It worked well — just as CAS had worked well for us in the Blackhorse in Vietnam." He also asserted, "So far, we had plenty of close air support...as much as we wanted, and we got as much as we wanted for the rest of the war."[137]

The CONOPS discussed kill zones, which CENTAF had incorporated into its D-day ATO and ATO Bravo defensive planning. During Desert Storm, planners called the zones *kill boxes.* They based them on the RSAF's 30- by 30-nautical mile (nm) (34½- by 34½-statute mile) air-to-air grid system. The 30- by 30-nm zones could be subdivided into 15- by 15-nm (17¼- by 17¼-mile) quadrants or into 15- by 30-nm halves. CENTAF defined the zones as "fire support measures used by the TACS in the command and control of tactical support of land forces."[138] The planners defined three categories of kill boxes: open, closed, and avoidance. Pilots could expend ordnance in open boxes but not in closed ones unless they were under the control of a forward air controller who had the ground commander's approval. Avoidance boxes functioned temporarily as zones where flights were restricted for deconfliction purposes associated with artillery barrages or naval gunfire.[139]

The CONOPS stipulated that if the enemy damaged or destroyed the TACC where Horner operated, the heart of the TACS, then the ABCCC aircraft assumed combat functions for CAS, untargeted interdiction in kill boxes, and rear-area security. Responsibility for interdiction missions with preplanned targets and all offensive and defensive counterair operations would revert to the AWACS or the Control and Reporting Center.[140] Some of the topics addressed in the "mechanics" section of the CONOPS included inflight reports, scramble authority, search and rescue, and the tactical air request net.[141]

The CONOPS did not specifically address friendly fire problems, although Horner and his staff harbored great concerns about aircraft attacking Coalition forces by mistake. During the war, he tasked Lt. Col. Clyde "Joe Bob" Phillips, who had recently arrived in theater from the Fighter Weapons School, to head a team and suggest procedures to eliminate blue-on-blue strikes.[142] While aircraft flew with electronic devices that sent and received IFF signals from other aircraft, ground forces did not employ such equipment, in part from concern that if captured by the enemy, they could use the signals to pass through friendly lines. During Desert Storm, CENTCOM did rely, however, on other equipment and measures to protect against fratricide. During daylight, ground troops would display on each vehicle a 2- by 4-foot orange-red reflecting panel, recognizable from the air. They would also paint inverted Vs on their vehicles for sighting by other ground troops. For nighttime, they would display white-light chemical devices or infrared lights (rushed to the theater just at the start of the ground war) or infrared tape.[143]

The structure of the TACS itself — with the BCE operating within the TACC, air officers assigned to ground units, air- and ground-based forward air controllers, and airborne C^2 aircraft linked by radio communication networks — provided C^2 information to airmen to direct ordnance away from friendly forces and toward the enemy. Rules required that within the FSCL, where friendly troops concentrated, airmen had to coordinate with ground commanders through forward air controllers before they could release munitions. Prior to the start of Phase IV operations, the ground commanders established preplanned FSCL lines which activated by time or by troops moving to points that would trigger their activation. Horner still worried about the "next General Patton" in a tank racing beyond the FSCL into a target-rich area where pilots could strike without first checking with the forward air controllers. As Phase III operations unfolded, some F–16 pilots played the role of scout beyond the FSCL to guide other aircraft to targets within kill boxes. Horner turned these pilots into scouts to verify that tanks just beyond the FSCL were, indeed, Iraqi, and not Coalition armor.[144] Horner often told the wing and weapon system representatives in TACC to pass the word down to be careful about fratricide. He stated, "The main thing we did

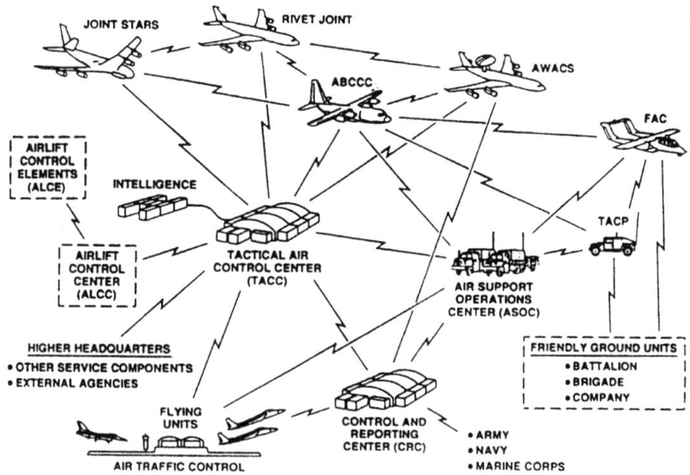

The Tactical Air Control System

was talk to the guys and say, 'If in doubt, don't drop.' That's what it amounted to. [Friendly fire is] a terrible thing."[145]

Planning for Phase IV would continue even as the air campaign commenced. The CAS and interdiction sorties in direct support of the ground war required that pilots accept risks greater than those in Phases I through III.[146] Horner urged the airmen to fly low, and pilots had to fly beneath the air sanctuary they had created at the medium-altitude level. The lives of the ground troops were now at stake, and aviators had to execute missions within the reach of AAA and infrared SAMs.

Training for Offensive Operations

Because the Desert Storm phases required that Coalition pilots execute a variety of air missions, CENTAF continued to provide training and exercises to give aviators the experience required for wartime offensive operations. Both recurring and one-time training exercises continued from October 1990 into January 1991, honing the skills of pilots and crews and testing the coordination and communication procedures for CAS, kill-box operations, interdiction, air-to-air combat, force packaging, air defense, border interception, CSAR, armor attrition, tanker and airspace control, and ATO generation and execution. Pilots practiced portions of the offensive war plan under the guise of defensive operations. Horner commented, "We practiced the strike packages, we practiced the air refueling, integration of the command and control elements…it was a very long iterative process to get the thing that we launched on the morning of the 17th of January."[147]

The largest and most publicized exercise, Imminent Thunder, November 15–21, 1990, involved more than 2,200 sorties in five phases executed by U.S.,

Saudi, British, Canadian, Kuwaiti, and French units. Newsmen covered the U.S. Marines performing an amphibious landing near Al Mish'ab, Saudi Arabia, just south of Khafji, and within visual range of Iraqi forces. Although the landing played an important part of the exercise, Schwarzkopf, since as early as August 1990, had not intended to use Marines in an amphibious assault in Desert Storm. The landing exercise was part of a deception plan.[148] Exercise Fish Barrel, January 7–9, 1991, involved most of the Coalition air forces flying in excess of 350 daytime and 200 nighttime CAS and interdiction sorties. A major objective tested C^2 procedures outlined in CENTAF's TACAIR CONOPS issued January 1 in support of Phase IV operations.[149]

Night Camel, held weekly from December 1990 to January 1991, exercised operations and procedures necessary for accomplishing Phase III of the air campaign to attrit the Iraqi army. U.S. Army fielded forces unknowingly served as guinea pigs, the simulated enemy forces. The exercise tested the ability of airmen to identify ground forces and target armor arrays at night using the F–15E LANTIRN; F–16C LANTIRN; F–111F Pave Tack; A–6E Target Recognition Acquisition Multisensor (TRAM); A–10 Pave Penny; and B–52–TR–1/U–2 ASARS. Other objectives tested tactics for each system, developed C^2 methods for communicating current target locations, tested the feasibility of using systems for BDA, and used AWACS and procedures to deconflict airspace.[150]

Night Camel introduced two innovations in altitude and targeting to pilots flying the F–15E, F–16C, and F–111F with LANTIRN or Pave Tack targeting pods. First, they flew at medium altitude instead of at lower levels, to stay in the safe altitude regime that would emerge after Phase I attacks defeated Kari and the IADS. Second, crews would acquire and target components of the enemy fielded army instead of attacking facilities deep behind enemy lines. Maj. Michael J. Bodner, an F–111F pilot, and Maj. William W. Bruner III, an F–111F weapons system officer, wrote,

> By December 1990, General Horner, General Glosson, and Maj. Gen. John Corder, General Horner's deputy for operations, had concluded that fighter aircraft equipped with new infrared (IR) targeting pods would be able to find and destroy armored vehicles from medium altitude at night. This seemingly simple idea was a radical departure from the tactics manuals, which advocated the traditional concept of low-altitude ingress against a single fixed target deep in enemy territory.

The two officers noted that crews in peacetime did not routinely fly medium-altitude nighttime sorties to kill armor and APCs.[151]

F–111 personnel, in fact, scoffed at the idea of flying medium-level sorties against an enemy fielded force. According to Bodner and Bruner,

> F–111 wing planners wanted their crews to spend as little time as possible on medium-altitude sorties during Night Camel. They preferred

> instead to train at low level, preparing for the low level war they expected to fight against the dangerous and sophisticated Iraqi Integrated Air Defense System.[152]

Wings participating in Night Camel sent copies of cockpit videotapes to Riyadh for viewing by the air commanders and planners. The effectiveness of the targeting pods in finding ground targets at night in the desert impressed the leaders. "I think we all became very enthusiastic about the night capability that we had with the LANTIRN and Pave Tack against armored vehicles," Horner stated. "The crews could become trained. They hadn't really thought about this stuff."[153]

The attitude of the F–111F pilots represented views of most airmen. In the years immediately before Desert Shield and Desert Storm, the Air Force had emphasized low-level ingress to targets, popping up to deliver ordnance, and the resumption of low-level flying. An F–16C pilot wrote:

> High-altitude tactics had been considered a relic of the Vietnam era by the majority of Air Force aviators and had been largely discarded after the mid-1970s. Survival and target acquisition in a European scenario appeared to require low flying, and training throughout the 1980s had a clear low-altitude focus. High-altitude training often met with resistance. The common attitude was that low flying is more demanding; if one can fly low, he can fly high.[154]

The Gulf War air campaign planners, in Checkmate and Riyadh, had decided early on that they would dismantle the Iraqi IADS and eliminate the effectiveness of its centrally controlled aircraft and radar-guided SAMs to create the medium-altitude sanctuary. Horner told the wing commanders that only those who could convince him that their units had to go low could do so. Col. Hal Hornburg of the 4th Tactical Fighter Wing with its F–15Es and Col. Thomas Lennon of the 48th Tactical Fighter Wing with F–111s made their case and flew at low altitudes during the first few days of the war; they then flew high.[155] Glosson expressed the view that no target was worth dying for, and during the war he ordered pilots to fly at medium altitude.[156] Before that, aviators within each unit and their commanders debated the benefits and drawbacks of low-level tactics and decided on their own flying tactics, which eventually took the crews high.[157] The air campaign Phases I to III soon produced a medium-altitude war, with minimum air attrition.

Briefings in Washington

In December, while military commanders in theater continued to develop the war plan and conduct training exercises to ensure its successful execution, President Bush and Secretary Cheney, the NCA, kept themselves informed of the progress of the planning and war readiness. On December 1, the President met with the JCS at Camp David to hear their views about military operations in the Gulf region. Bush had recently returned from his Thanksgiving visit to the AOR, meeting with the CINCCENT but not with Horner and Glosson. In preparation for the meeting, General McPeak requested briefings from Warden's Checkmate group. When Glosson had traveled to Washington at the end of November, the new CSAF also conferred with him about the air war plan.[158]

At Camp David, McPeak stressed the air campaign's probable aircrew and aircraft losses, stating that a plane or two would be lost daily. He emphasized the probable results of pilots falling into enemy hands, civilian casualties, and collateral damage. He later recalled telling the President:

> We will do well, but you have to understand the following things are going to happen. You are going to have this attrition. Half the aircrews are going to be killed. The other half are going to be walking around on television with their hands up, so you will see them parading these guys down the main street in Baghdad. You are going to kill a couple thousand people that you aren't angry with just because we make mistakes and bomb the wrong thing. We will have collateral damage, and you will see that on television; kids that have their arms blown off or something; mothers are killed.

McPeak wanted the President to understand the potential downside of a successful air campaign. "I tried to make it just a little bit darker picture than I thought it was going to be, but not terribly darker than I thought it was going to be," he stated.[159]

Early in the morning of December 11, Warden presented a briefing to Secretary Cheney that was based on the computer analysis Major Sikes had accomplished in Checkmate. The data and information that Warden presented had been generated since Glosson's Washington briefings to Cheney on October 10 and 11. Some of the others attendees in the Tank with Secretary Cheney were Generals McPeak, Carns, and Kelly and Admirals Jeremiah and McConnell.[160] The colonel provided estimates of anticipated U.S. losses: Phase I, 40 aircraft and 400 to 2,000 Iraqi civilian casualties; Phase II, 5 aircraft; Phase III, 35 aircraft; and Phase IV, 66 aircraft, maximum. Aircraft losses totaled 146.[161] Phase II would occur if Phase I did not achieve the national political objectives of forcing the Iraqis from Kuwait. It required one day, focused on the Iraqi IADS in Kuwait and southern Iraq, and concentrated on radar-guided SAMs. The phases occurred sequentially even though, in theater, the planners were on the verge of merging them because additional aircraft had arrived in the AOR as a result of the buildup for offensive operations.

Warden exuded enthusiasm about the potency of air power. He explained to Cheney that Phase III, Part A, would destroy the Republican Guard as an effective fighting force. Damaging the elite troops would significantly affect their ability to support Saddam's regime and would hurt the morale of the regular soldiers in Kuwait, probably resulting in their surrender. Phase III, Part B, directed attacks on the Iraqi forces in Kuwait proper. In Phase IV the colonel envisioned Kuwaiti and Arab forces reoccupying Kuwait and sustaining low casualties. He told Secretary Cheney that U.S. ground troops would not have to fight to liberate the country.[162] Cheney asked numerous detailed questions, noted no serious problems, and offered no significant suggestions.[163]

Airpower Enthusiasts Irritate Powell

Chairman Powell did not attend Warden's briefing to Cheney, although he was uneasy, in fact, angry, about how airpower enthusiasts in the Pentagon and Washington — Warden being the most prominent — presented the efficacy of the air campaign. At the end of October, before the President authorized the doubling of Desert Shield forces, the CJCS worried that the President would conclude that air power alone could resolve the crisis, and thus neglect the ground forces buildup. He knew that when Glosson had briefed the air plan at the White House on October 11, Bush had asked whether only Phases I to III, the portions of the war plan dominated by air power, would accomplish objectives. On October 30 Powell met with the President and recalled that after he explained the number of additional American troops necessary to execute the left-hook flanking attack — another 200,000 troops — Bush inquired, "Now Colin, you and Norm are really sure that air power alone can't do it?" Powell replied, "Mr. President, I wish to God that I could assure you that air power alone could do it, but you can't take that chance. We've got [to] take the initiative out of the enemy's hands if we're going to go to war."[164]

On December 3, the CJCS appeared before the Senate Armed Services Committee and spoke frankly about a multidimensional war plan, not just a one-dimensional — an airpower — plan:

> The mission is to take action to achieve our political objective if Saddam Hussein does not change his mind.
>
> Many experts, amateurs, and others in this town believe that this can be accomplished by such things as surgical air strikes or perhaps a sustained air strike. There are a variety of other, nice, tidy, alleged low-cost incremental, may-work options that are floated around with great regularity all over this town.
>
> The fundamental flaw in all such strategies is that it leaves the initiative in Saddam Hussein's hands. He makes the decision as to whether or not he will or will not withdraw. He decides whether he has been punished enough so that it is now necessary for him to reverse his direction and take a new political tack.[165]

Powell stated that he knew that the deserts of Kuwait and Iraq offered a better environment for air strikes than the dense vegetation of Vietnam or the forests of

Germany. He expressed full confidence that the U.S. Air Force could "inflict terrible punishment" on an opponent. He stressed, however: "One can hunker down. One can dig in. One can disperse to try to ride out such a single-dimensioned attack." After sustaining great bombardment, a defender could still make demands, decide to withstand more strikes, and continue the war indefinitely. The CJCS explained that a one-dimensional airpower attack against Iraq may win, but it did not give the assurance of victory as offered by a decisive multidimensional, combined, air-land-sea campaign.[166] On the same day on Capitol Hill in a congressional hearing, Powell explained that air power was a "supporting arm," capable of achieving effects similar to those from the economic embargo. Once air power and the sanctions had pummeled Iraq, then ground forces would move in, take over, and bring the war to a conclusion.[167]

Warden enthusiastically spread the word about the efficacy of the air weapon, even though he believed Powell opposed lobbyists for air power as a war-winning arm. The colonel explained:

> Part of this whole thing and part of the fascination of this whole business is that military plans have little to do with [the] military. I mean, that's only 5 percent of it — getting military people convinced and selling them on that. The other 95 percent is getting the civilians to sign on to it."[168]

The colonel found an ally in Secretary Rice in getting out the message about the potency of air power. Warden explained,

> Rice was invaluable....He was just wonderful, especially when Dugan left. Rice was able to do things that Loh, as a military officer, couldn't do. I mean, Loh and Rice both were four-square airpower men without any question, and Rice was willing to go out on a limb to talk to people, and we had given him the briefing pretty early on.[169]

Since neither Rice nor Warden were in the chain of command, however, the airpower views of Bush, Cheney, and Schwarzkopf (as influenced by Powell) carried the day. They relied on air power playing an important part in each of the four phases of the Desert Storm war plan, including the application of the air weapon in the counterland mission directly against the Iraqi ground forces.

Chapter Nine

Problems and Solutions

From October 1990 to January 1991, the JFACC's offensive air campaign planners struggled to solve crucial problems concerning imagery dissemination, BDA, joint and Coalition warfare, deception, PSYOPS, and target development. Concurrently Glosson and a few personnel helped to develop a bold and, as one officer described it, suicidal plan to rescue hostages in Kuwait City. By mid-October the Special Planning Group had moved from the conference room next to General Horner's office on the third floor of the RSAF building to the more secure basement of the facility. The regular CENTAF staff began to refer to the group as the Black Hole because it seemed whenever anyone entered it they were never seen again. In early December when Iraq test-launched missiles, surprised staff members scrambled to develop a "reflex" air plan to execute immediately if Iraq initiated hostilities.

Reflex Plan

On December 2, 1990, within approximately thirty minutes, the Iraqis launched three Scud missiles northwestward from a site near Basra. The Scuds landed downrange in Iraq near the H–2 and H–3 airfields. No intelligence reports had provided advance warning of the ballistic missile firings for General Horner, the AADC. Sensors detected the launches, and messages reached Riyadh, where "all hell broke loose" for air campaign planners.[1]

In response to the firings, CENTAF headquarters swiftly issued a recall of all personnel. "When they shot the test Scuds," Colonel Christon recalled, "it precipitated the fastest drive on record on my part from Eskan Village to my headquarters." At Horner's staff meeting, Captain McNary, CENTAF/IN, briefed details about the three launches, and the JFACC immediately moved to a discussion of the ramifications of the tests. After the meeting, Horner asked key staff members, Generals Olsen and Corder, and Colonels Crigger and Christon to remain behind to discuss CENTAF's options in response to an Iraqi air attack, especially a Scud attack, and a ground invasion. Glosson was in the United States at the time, so the JFACC requested that Major Rogers attend for the Special Planning Group.[2]

During the discussion, Horner tasked Rogers to work with the other officers planning the offensive air campaign to determine what air assets would be available within two hours of an Iraqi-launched Scud attack or an invasion by Iraqi ground forces into Saudi Arabia. The major rushed to his colleagues and told them to first determine the number of tankers and alert aircraft that could be airborne quickly, which soon revealed that tanker availability severely constrained the use of air power. Brig. Gen. Glenn A. Profitt II, who had replaced General Henry as the EC expert, kept the JFACC informed of the group's progress.[3] (General Henry had returned to Texas at the request of the commander of the Air Training Command to undertake planning duties there.)

A few hours later, Horner came to the Black Hole and discussed response options at great length with Rogers. (The regular CENTAF staff began to refer to the Special Planning Group as the "Black Hole" because it seemed that whenever anyone entered the basement area of the RSAF building, where the planning group was housed, they were never seen again.) Horner repeatedly returned to the question of how to strike defensively while retaining the ability to execute Phase I of the offensive plan. Similar to his merry-go-round concept for executing the D-day ATO Bravo, the JFACC wanted to use air assets against appropriate targets for initial strikes until the time of day allowed for the full initiation of strategic air operations and execution of the preplanned ATO for the first twenty-four hours of the air campaign.[4]

In the midst of the Scud response planning, General Corder gave Rogers two hours' notice that he was to brief Phases II and III of the air campaign to the new deputy CINCCENT, Lt. Gen. Calvin A. H. Waller, USA, who would be coming to the RSAF building to meet with Horner. Schwarzkopf was not in Riyadh, so Waller answered all the telephone calls from Chairman Powell about the air campaign and the options available if Iraq launched missile attacks. During the briefing for the deputy CINCCENT, the JFACC emphasized and clarified key ideas of the air campaign. Waller repeatedly asked about the response to Iraq's attacking *now.* Horner replied that if Iraq went on the offensive, the airmen would not "pussyfoot around" but would hit the aggressor with all they could. He emphasized that the planning they had accomplished that very day allowed for a transition to Phase I, and that they continued to study logistics requirements associated with the newly planned strikes. Rogers thought Horner presented a magnificent defense of the strategic air plan as the appropriate response to an Iraqi preemptive attack, with transition strikes preceding the initiation of the preplanned Phase I of the air campaign. Although some Checkmate personnel had warned Rogers that Horner neither understood nor appreciated the strategic air campaign, the young officer thought the characterization untrue as he saw and heard the JFACC and Waller vigorously discussing air power.[5]

Over the next few days, the Special Planning Group, led by Rogers, developed the plan they called the Response Flow or Attack Response Option. The major requested and received ideas for the project from Checkmate. Returning to Riyadh a couple of days later, Glosson assumed control of the plan's development and briefed the concepts to Schwarzkopf. On December 12 he discussed the transition strikes with Col. David Eberly, the deputy commander of the 4th Tactical Fighter Wing (Provisional), who suggested the name Reflex which Glosson adopted.[6] Reflex targeted Iraq's offensive capability: Scud missiles; airfields and aircraft; and NBC weapon components. Coalition aircraft included those allocated for the strategic campaign and those held in reserve, such as the A–10s, AV–8s, and attack helicopters.[7] By December 17, Glosson had approved a Reflex MAP with three package options, each correlated to the time of day of an Iraqi preemptive attack.[8]

The Navy prepared input to the Reflex plan, which the NAVCENT commander approved. Because the Navy's section did not reach Riyadh by the December 20 deadline, it was not incorporated into the main Reflex plan at that time, or later. By early January, preparation for the execution of Desert Storm Phase I dominated planners' time, and the Navy's contribution would have been a nearly exclusive use of TLAMs.[9]

Scud Problem

Reflex was not the first air plan to respond specifically to a missile attack. In mid-October, Glosson had discussed a Scud attack plan with the CENTAF commander and advocated not only strikes against the launch sites in western Iraq, but in the east, too, as well as sorties against air defense and leadership targets. "Executing an attack on Scud sites and omitting SOCs, IOCs, airfields, and leadership targets," Glosson judged, "is analogous to launching Phase IV with a ground frontal attack, against both armor and mechanized, with the 82d Airborne and using the 24th Infantry Division, Mechanized, as a reserve force." He believed that attacking only Scud sites in response to Scud attacks invited additional missile launches.[10]

Horner viewed the Scud as "militarily insignificant." "Its warhead is small," he reasoned, "less than 500 pounds. Its accuracy is horrible, and our operation will be disrupted more likely by terrorist attacks than Scud attack." He noted after the war, "Understand that I had never been in this position in war, so I am insensitive to the responsibilities I had with regard to civil defense and the impact that a Scud can have on the civilian populace." The JFACC's plan was to hit all the fixed Scud sites and fuel-related facilities. Because the liquid fuel used to propel the missiles becomes unstable after a relatively short period, it presented a vulnerable target. Attacking it could prevent some of the Iraqis' Scud launches.[11]

Planners recognized the targeting of mobile missiles as the toughest Scud problem. In late October, the DIA sent two analysts to the theater, who briefed Schwarzkopf, Horner, and Glosson, plus other CENTAF staff members, addressing Iraq's tactical Scud combat operations and the location and identification of its mobile missiles. The detailed briefing failed to alleviate Horner's concern about his inability to find and target mobile Scuds — it reinforced his concern.[12]

After the session, Horner and his staff sat in the targeteers' tent in the soccer field and tried to develop a strategy for dealing with the mobile Scuds. They identified three aspects of the problem. According to Christon: "Number 1, define the circumstances under which they can launch Scuds and don't let them mass." The planners intended to keep the number of simultaneous Scud launches down to the number that the Patriot system could handle. Second, they would prevent the Iraqis from utilizing their logistics and maintenance systems to replenish launch teams in their hidden locations, making them fight with what they had. Finally, the staff did not want the Iraqis to mate Scuds with NBC capability to create weapons of mass destruction. During the strategic campaign, strikes would hit weapon production and storage sites to prevent the enemy from drawing on stocks to arm Scuds with NBC warheads.[13]

Operation Touted Gleem comprised another initiative to assist the war fighters with understanding the mobile Scud threat. U.S. technicians and operators acquired a Scud B training missile and the MAZ–543 TEL and arranged for various types of Air Force and Navy aircraft to fly against Scud B configurations at night to determine how well pilots could identify the missile in combat situations. The Iraqis would make the task as difficult as possible, hiding their mobile missile launchers under overpasses and bridges and in culverts and by adopting "shoot-and-scoot" procedures. In less than an hour after arriving at a launch site, a crew could position the missile on the TEL, start the engines, launch the weapon, lower the launch platform, pack up, and drive away. Within minutes after firing, the Iraqis could be miles from the launch site. Checkmate kept planners in Riyadh fully apprised of Touted Gleem results, which were not good. The information they obtained led Christon to conclude that the mobile Scud threat was a "tough target to acquire." Col. Thomas Lennon, 48th Tactical Fighter Wing (Provisional) Commander at Taif, echoed Christon's assessment after his F–111 pilots flew training missions to find and target mobile missiles, with scant success.[14]

In mid-December Secretary Cheney and Chairman Powell traveled to the theater, and Horner discussed Scuds with them. He explained that Iraq had 500–700 Scud B missiles and variants, and that the Iraqi inventory included 36 mobile Scud launchers. The Iraqis had prepared locations for fixed and mobile launchers: in western Iraq, they had 64 fixed sites; in southern Iraq and Kuwait, 15 mobile launcher sites. Horner recalled, "I told Cheney that there was no way I could get them all. I can do the best I can, and we will do whatever we can, but we are going to get shot at by Scuds." The CENTAF commander assured Cheney

General Colin L. Powell, Chairman of the Joint Chiefs of Staff, and General H. Norman Schwarzkopf, Commander, U.S. Central Command.

that air power would hit fixed sites the first night but it could not strike all the mobile launchers. He could not guarantee that the Iraqis would not launch ballistic missiles.[15]

Scuds concerned Cheney because he communicated often with Israeli officials who worried about the missiles aimed at Israel from sites in western Iraq. In fact, in December, the SecDef suggested that his Western Excursion option, the airborne assault into the H–2 and H–3 airfield vicinity, could secure that area and prevent Scud launches from there. As earlier, however, CENTCOM and ARCENT planners rejected the plan. On January 2 Deputy Secretary of State Eagleburger and Under Secretary of Defense Wolfowitz traveled to Israel to reconfirm the U.S. commitment to Israel's security. President Bush authorized the establishment of a special, secure voice communication link, code-named Hammer Rick, between the Pentagon and the Israeli Ministry of Defense to permit U.S. indications and warning intelligence to pass quickly and to facilitate frequent contact between American and Israeli officials.[16] In the fall, the President had also authorized sending two Patriot air defense missile batteries to Israel, but the Israelis rejected the offer.[17] They later sent Cheney a list of Scud-related targets in Iraq, but it caused no major changes in the preplanned offensive ATO, which had already included many of the same targets.[18]

Horner grappled with the possibility that Israel, on its own in response to ballistic missile attacks, would strike against Iraq. His concepts for handling the eventuality of a third-party attack on Iraq accommodated the Israelis, either by pulling them into the strategic air campaign, with times and targets of their choosing, or by pulling back some U.S. assets during an Israeli air assault.[19] He did not foresee the Coalition collapsing if the Israelis joined the conflict. Horner explained, "It would not have bothered the Arab allies. al-Buhairi [chief of the RSAF] and I talked about that frequently. He said that was no problem."[20] After the war, Bush reported that King Fahd had indicated that if the Israelis struck Iraq, the Saudis would remain in the Coalition. Nonetheless, the United States withheld from the Israelis the IFF codes, which were necessary to avoid air fratricide, effectively keeping the Israelis out of the war.[21]

Against the possibility that Iraq would use CW or BW, delivered with or without Scuds, Horner requested that Glosson and Corder prepare a deterrence plan to retaliate against Iraq with horrific severity against unconventional targets. The deterrence campaign would attack numerous sites in Tikrit, the hometown of Saddam Hussein and the base of his political and military power; dams on the Tigris and Euphrates Rivers, which would interdict water for irrigation and hydroelectric power generation; and POL production, refining, and storage. "We went through a drill to say what we would do if he shot chemicals at us," Corder stated. "I sat down with Buster, and we came up with some of the worst stuff you can think of, like bombing the dams and flooding the whole country and a lot of other things like that. Then Buster took that and did some more work with it with his friends back in Washington." The CENTAF targeteers who had initially nominated the sites, knowing that dams not used for military purposes were not legal targets, weaponeered for strikes against them anyway. Corder never learned if the target list was passed on to the Iraqis via Tariq Aziz, as some of Glosson's planners believed it would be. It was not.[22] A letter from the President to the Iraqi foreign minister did state that if Iraq employed CW or BW, "the American people would demand the strongest possible response."[23]

In Washington in early December Chairman Powell had urged the White House to plainly communicate to Aziz the fury of the air campaign if Saddam should use CW or BW. The CJCS later recalled that on January 15 he especially worried about Iraq's use of BW, and he drafted a warning to the Iraqi leader that included a threat to attack dams on the Tigris and Euphrates Rivers, which would flood Baghdad with "horrendous consequences." He intended the statement as a bluff to worry Saddam. The war commenced, however, before the message was coordinated and approved, and it remained as a draft document.[24]

Hostage Rescue Plan

On December 6 when Saddam Hussein announced he would release the foreign nationals held hostage in Iraq and Kuwait and allow people, in both official and nonofficial status, to leave embassies, a sigh of relief swept through Washington and Riyadh. The action eliminated the anxiety about the fate of the Western foreigners once the Coalition offensive began. In August the Iraqis had let it be known that (in violation of the law of armed conflict) they placed some persons at key industrial and military sites to protect those facilities from attack. U.S. authorities knew the locations of some of the structures having human shields, but they did not know all of them. On December 13 John M. Broder of the *Los Angeles Times* reported, "Since the beginning of the crisis in August, President Bush and other senior Administration officials have said consistently that the taking of hostages and their dispersal to strategic sites would have no impact on U.S. policy or military planning." After the war, Horner privately stated, "We knew where the hostages were being kept, but even then, you cannot be blackmailed in war."[25] Glosson received no explicit guidance from Schwarzkopf and Horner and told Deptula *not* to target any site with hostages unless he had Glosson's approval.[26] The colonel identified hostage locations on the target list with a letter *P*, to indicate people, and he kept these sites off the MAP. As far as Deptula was concerned, the no-strike hostage list made little difference to Phase I planning because most of the facilities with human shields were not primary targets anyway.[27]

Schwarzkopf considered hostage rescue operations, but he ruled out any attempts to free foreigners held in Iraq, primarily because of sparse intelligence. A rescue attempt in Kuwait, however, seemed feasible. When Iraq had threatened to arrest personnel at embassies in Kuwait after August 24, 1990, the international diplomatic corps left the country. As of mid-October, only the U.S. and British embassies in Kuwait City still retained small diplomatic staffs, although the Iraqis had cut the electricity entering the foreign nationals' compounds.[28]

In late October, Glosson, Deptula, Major Oelrich (an EC specialist), and Major Rogers began planning for air support for an extremely secret Anglo-American operation, code-named Night Life (subsequently called Pacific Wind) to rescue people at the U.S. and British embassies in Kuwait City. SOCCENT functioned as the executive agent for the rescue effort. On October 24 Glosson, Deptula, and Oelrich met with SOF personnel at King Fahd International Airport and first learned details of the complicated rescue plan. The SOF planners wanted as much air support for the operation as possible. The next day back in Riyadh, Glosson and Deptula met with Maj. Gen. Wayne A. Downing, USA, Commander, Joint Special Operations Command, and discussed the rescue effort. That day Deptula began to determine assets, timing, and sequence of strikes for the rescue to occur concurrently with the Phase I attacks. Within the next few days, he placed Night Life targets into the MAP.[29] When Deptula returned to the United States on November 4, Rogers assumed responsibility for the continual development and refinement of air operations for the plan and updated the MAP accordingly. He found that SOF planners expected all available air assets to support the rescue at the expense of other air missions, including the first-wave attacks of Phase I, of which the SOF planners knew nothing.[30] He believed that they not only wanted an unreasonable number of air assets, but they would use them in a tactically unsound, even "suicidal" manner regarding, for example, ingress altitudes.[31] He would ensure planning from an airman's perspective.

Glosson and Downing would command the operation from an orbiting C–130 aircraft eighty miles off the Kuwaiti coast.[32] Strike aircraft at night — F–117s, F–111s, F–15s, and F–14s — accompanied by jamming platforms would attack two power plants to cut electricity to Kuwait City, strike the high-rise Hilton Hotel overlooking the American embassy, and hit defensive sites along roads leading to the embassies and on the beaches to the east. Helicopters entering Kuwait from a sea route would arrive at the compounds and rescue personnel at both sites, located in close proximity.[33] Glosson saw the operation as a "damned tough mission." Horner later mused, "Thank God we were never told to execute."[34]

McConnell–Glosson Link

Intelligence supported the planning of the rescue operation, just as it continued to form the basis of offensive air campaign planning. In December 1990, the flow of intelligence into the Special Planning Group increased significantly, from an unexpected source. During the first few days of December when Glosson was in the United States, Admiral McConnell, the recently promoted chief intelligence officer on the Joint Staff J–2, sought out the general, provided him with a tour of the Joint Intelligence Center (JIC) at the Pentagon, and told him the facility could serve him twenty-four-hours a day, seven days a week. McConnell had already supplied Glosson with vital intelligence since mid-October, when the planner briefed the air campaign to the JCS, but during the tour of the JIC in December, the admiral offered to exponentially increase direct support to the airman in Riyadh.[35]

Admiral McConnell knew that the JIC, which the DIA had established in the Pentagon in the fall, knocking out walls to accommodate the hundreds of people who would staff it, was "expensive baggage." It primarily served the JCS, but because it was so huge, he wanted to justify its cost, so he sought out customers, and the key air campaign planner was the ideal consumer for the intelligence support that the facility provided. Also, the admiral believed that his experience as a Navy intelligence officer imbued him with a mission to take the initiative and support decision-makers and operations on a timely basis. Indeed, in his view, Navy intelligence officers were "half operators," and he believed that if intelligence personnel could not communicate with operators and be useful to them, they would fail. McConnell would not fail, and he enthusiastically placed the Pentagon's JIC at the service of Glosson.[36]

Rear Adm. John M. McConnell

For his part, the general wished to acquire as much assistance as possible from the U.S. intelligence community in Washington. He knew that McConnell and the JIC could function as his unimpeded, direct link to the community. He later recalled, "Mike said you can have anything you want. Up until that point, I was in a position of not knowing what to ask for in some cases because I didn't know what I didn't know. All those things were laid open to me. Believe me, I asked for anything that could possibly contribute."[37] Interestingly, Glosson did not summon Colonel Christon, the chief CENTAF intelligence officer, to Washington, and arrange for him to tour the JIC and to be another recipient at CENTAF for intelligence sent from the facility to Riyadh. Neither did he exploit the opportunity for himself and Christon to discuss with McConnell and other key members of the intelligence community how to improve support to the Special Planning Group and the flying units. Glosson was satisfied that he himself was the recipient of JIC's intelligence expertise.

Military Intelligence Board Investigation

Admiral McConnell knew that in theater the CENTCOM J–2, Brig. Gen. John A. Leide, USA, could not provide Glosson with the intelligence necessary to plan and prosecute an air war because the theater J–2 himself struggled to satisfy the CINCCENT's requirements for planning the ground war. CENTCOM's confederated intelligence system did not require the CENTCOM J–2 to provide constant intelligence support to the JFACC, and neither could he, given the paucity of resources that he controlled and the great demands Schwarzkopf made for the land campaign.[38]

In November, the Military Intelligence Board (MIB), led by the director of the DIA and composed of the heads of the service intelligence organizations and the director of the NSA, formed an inspection team and sent it to the AOR to review the CINCCENT's in-theater intelligence support and to report findings and recommendations to the CINCCENT's J–2. Team members, chartered by their service intelligence chiefs to represent the services, visited each component, with some members also visiting and receiving briefings by representatives from the XVIII Airborne Corps, 1st Marine Division, 3d Marine Air Wing, and SOCCENT.[39]

The team found that imagery support for everyone proved insufficient. Everywhere the members traveled, they found too few national imagery products to support combat forces, particularly for ground operations. They expected that during the war, imagery from the United States would arrive too late, and once there, it would receive little or no analysis because of resource constraints. The inspectors recommended that CENTCOM receive a transportable satellite imagery-receive location, with attendant production and analytical capabilities. They cautioned, however, that the imagery-receive location would not solve all the problems. The AOR also lacked adequate secondary dissemination capabilities to transmit images around the theater in a timely manner.[40]

Looking ahead to combat, the team reported that wartime imagery requirements would not be met. They concluded that under the stress of the combat environment, with simultaneous military operations underway, national imagery would be inadequate. The team made the extraordinary recommendation that the SR–71 reconnaissance aircraft be reactivated to help bridge the gap between the enormous wartime requirements and a limited capability to satisfy them.[41] Although a few members of Congress also called for the reactivation of the SR–71, and associated crews and logistics, the aircraft system remained in retirement.

As a result of the MIB's prompting and the inspectors' report, the CINCCENT requested and the JCS approved a significant increase in the size of the J–2 staff. The CINCCENT's JIC at MODA headquarters began to grow in December. January 15, 1991, was the date set for having a sufficient number of analysts available to examine imagery as well as signals and human intelligence. The team surveyed the site for the downlink equipment for the imagery-receive location, and MIB facilitated the transfer of equipment from Europe to Riyadh. The imagery-receive location became fully operational on January 10. Planning began, too, for the establishment of a Joint Imagery Production Complex to produce imagery from space and air-breathing reconnaissance assets. Many other initiatives to beef up the J–2's capabilities were undertaken. The MIB team's report served as a blueprint for building the CINCCENT's J–2 capability. The report, however, had no immediate and direct impact on the ability of the CENTAF staff to support the air campaign planning process. By the start of the war, the informal conduit McConnell established with Glosson surpassed in usefulness the support that hundreds of intelligence personnel on the CENTCOM J–2 staff could or would provide Glosson, Horner, and the air campaign. The CENTCOM J–2 staff would first and foremost provide Schwarzkopf with the intelligence he personally required.[42]

Target Material Problem

In December, Colonel Christon, CENTAF/IN, still grappled with the two major problems that would inflict on him "two sucking chest wounds," as he described it: imagery dissemination and BDA. Since mid-September he had made significant progress with sending photographs of targets on the strategic list to the flying units. At the end of October, to ensure that each unit had the imagery it required to plan missions assigned in the ATO, he told his staff to poll all the wings regarding the status of their requirements. Each reported it possessed imagery for every assigned target.[43]

Christon had to monitor changes in the ATO as the strategic target list grew and then send imagery to the units accordingly. He tried to avoid the mistake of his predecessor in August and September of primarily supporting the generation of the ATO and neglecting to aid in its execution. Christon serviced the wings in addition to the CENTAF commander and TACC. He knew, too, that certain weapon systems with PGM capability — F–117A, F–15E, and F–111F — generated special imagery requirements for mission planning, and he intended to learn what the scenarios were and to facilitate the quick acquisition of imagery in meeting them. He agreed with the MIB inspection report that stated, "The Achilles heel of the theater intelligence infrastructure is communications." He relied primarily on the TDF to transmit imagery electronically to the wings, a process that required minutes for one image. Courier deliveries had to supplement and often supplanted the TDF.[44] Not only was the TDF slow in its transmissions, the quality of its output varied. Major Azzato, with the 37th Tactical Fighter Wing/Intelligence, reported, "It appeared that during the high usage times for the telephone lines in theater, the TDF quality was directly and adversely affected. By using the lines during 'slack' times, we were able to work with the system; however, this was not always possible given short notice changes."[45]

Despite Christon's best efforts and assistance from Colonel Minihan, TAC/IN, who oversaw the operation of the 480th Tactical Intelligence Group, CENTAF's imagery dissemination during Desert Shield remained a constant irritant to the wings. When Captain McNary, Horner's current intelligence briefer, traveled in late autumn with General Corder to numerous bases in the AOR, he heard abundant and sharp criticism about inadequate imagery and target materials. He came to view imagery distribution as the number one intelligence problem in Desert Shield. He observed the CENTAF/IN staff working diligently to alleviate the problem. Ironically, at the end of December, Christon again had his staff poll each flying unit, and again, each reported that it had the imagery to fly assigned missions against strategic targets. Christon believed that despite heavy criticism, the units possessed the required target materials.[46]

Anticipating wartime conditions, Christon expected new targets to appear in the MAP and ATO for which he could not rapidly provide imagery. He talked with F–15E pilots about this probable situation, asking them, "What do I need to do to get you to a point where you feel comfortable with a pop-up target, one you haven't seen before?" He recalled their reply, "The answer was 'Get us within 2 miles, and we will find it on the radar.' Well, 'get within 2 miles' — I could do that with coordinates. I don't need to get you an image to do that; so that was the going-in proposition." Christon put his faith in the proposition of relying on coordinates, because that was all he expected to have for some targets — coordinates and faith — no imagery.[47]

By December, Air Force combat wings had at least one Mission Support System II (MSS 2) computer terminal in the operations center to aid target recognition and mission planning. The MSS 2 was an "automated target folder" that displayed on a video screen satellite and airborne reconnaissance imagery, maps, terrain overviews, and threat data from several intelligence sources. This information enabled pilots to generate various perspectives on targets, study targets in relation to terrain and structures, and choose offset aim points. The system produced images on paper and target coordinate data on cartridges which pilots could load into their aircraft.[48]

In September General Henry had given Glosson and Deptula a demonstration of the MSS 2 in the EC cell, and the chief planner asked officials at TAC headquarters to acquire the equipment for wings in the AOR. When the command made little progress with the project, Glosson turned to Warden at Checkmate and asked him to "stir the pot" to have one computer system sent to each key location. As expected, the colonel sprang to action, consulting with and convincing General Loh and the director of acquisitions at the secretariat level to purchase the hardware. Soon thirty-three computers were sent to the theater, direct from the factory (seventeen were already there).[49]

By the end of October, Glosson proudly reported that Capt. Michael Cosby had taken approximately 240 targets from the strategic air campaign and programmed them into the MSS 2. The system, however, depended on analysts and intelligence officers loading timely and accurate imagery and data, just as the old, paper-target folders were as good as the intelligence and photographs placed in them manually. The MSS 2 did allow the electronic transmission of data, including imagery, across the AOR. Major Rogers reported to the Checkmate staff in December that MSS 2 was "very useful."[50]

BDA Challenges

Christon expected his other big problem would come from BDA. He was prescient. BDA estimated the effect of air attacks on targets, target sets, and the accomplishment of objectives. The Air Force's Target Intelligence Handbook in 1990 identified the key questions the assessments addressed:

> Did the strike or attack achieve the stated objective and predicted damage?
> What was the impact of the strikes on the enemy, considering the objective and targets? Should other targets be selected?
> Are additional strikes or attacks against the targets required? Should the objective be changed?
> What changes or improvements are required to better achieve the basic planned objectives?
> Were actual delivery parameters similar to those expected?
> Were there any unanticipated operational limitations?
> What were the unintended consequences of the operation?[51]

For the Desert Storm war plan, BDA posed four major, complex challenges. The first involved the requirement that it assess strikes in Phases I and II against strategic and air supremacy targets as well as strikes in Phase III against battlefield targets. The types of targets in Phases I and II, electric power plants, for example, varied greatly from those in Phase III, tanks and artillery. BDA for Phase III battlefield preparation, in particular, would frustrate the planners because there existed no standard, tested methodology for measuring air power's destruction of an enemy army and identifying when attrition reached the 50 percent level.

With Horner in complete agreement, Schwarzkopf assigned BDA for Phase III to ARCENT and MARCENT. ARCENT assumed responsibility for determining the combat effectiveness of Iraqi ground forces in the KTO, except for the Iraqi III Corps area for which MARCENT was in charge. Horner noted,

> I was not going to get involved in keeping track of the decimation of the Iraqi army in the field. One, it's something that the United States Army ought to be doing. Since they weren't fighting, they should have been doing something. Second, they were going to do it anyway, so why do I want to get crosswise of them.[52]

By the start of the air campaign, ARCENT had not yet fully devised its methodology for estimating enemy composition, disposition, and strength, nor for determining when Iraqi forces in the KTO had degenerated to 50 percent of their combat capability. The outline of ARCENT's emerging game plan indicated a deceptively simple strategy: base the assessment of combat effectiveness on the percentage of armor and artillery destroyed in comparison with a Desert Shield baseline. Originally, ARCENT did not include APCs in its calculations.[53]

CENTAF carried the primary responsibility for BDA for Phases I and II of the air campaign, including interdiction targets. (By the start of the air war and as a result of the MIB inspection report, the CENTCOM J–2 staff grew by hundreds, and some of its targeteers began to take a special interest in the progress of the strategic air campaign and produced BDA assessments at odds with CENTAF's.) Meeting with General Leide, the J–2, and the other CENTCOM component senior intelligence officers, Christon helped to sort out in-theater BDA responsibilities. He recalled,

> The basic architecture that we laid out was that…the Army was going to come up with the assessment model of ground forces, and that makes sense. They are ground forces; they understand ground.…We were going to take the strategic targets, and we were going to take the enemy air defense system and the interdiction targets, bridges or whatever.[54]

In the Special Planning Group as early as September, Glosson had assigned Major Olsen of the Marine Corps to head the BDA team. He and Deptula designed a tracking mechanism consisting of target-set grease boards and worksheets to record strike results. They initially focused on determining whether targets had to be restruck. The plan called for Christon's staff to supply the group with BDA intelligence.[55] During the war, the boards fell into disuse as assessments flowed to the planners too slowly to keep pace with Deptula as he built the daily MAP. The planners next tried using the MSS 2 computer system, but that too lacked timely feedback. Deptula came to rely on Checkmate steadily transmitting analytical reports from Washington.[56]

The second major challenge of the BDA enterprise mandated that intelligence officers satisfy the needs of customers at the national, theater, and unit levels. To service the CJCS, SecDef, CINCCENT, and, to a lesser degree, the components, the DIA established a formal BDA system to exploit the products from satellites and provide strategic BDA directed at strategic targets in Iraq. In theater, CENTCOM headquarters belatedly established a BDA capability, as each of the components had done, to track the progress of its wartime operations. CENTCOM would receive DIA's assessments and also exploit information collected by airborne reconnaissance assets, most of which would be directed against tactical targets in the KTO. In setting up CENTAF's BDA system for the strategic air campaign, Christon tapped directly into the DIA system, which consisted of three phases.[57] (BDA phases should not be confused with air campaign phases.) The first-phase analysis involved personnel in Washington, D.C., examining imagery to determine, Did the weapon hit or miss — yes or no? They telephoned CENTCOM and CENTAF with their results, which Christon referred to as the ring-down report. The analysts followed up their voice ring-down report with a textual message and copies of imagery sent electronically. The second- and third-phase analyses encompassed more detailed studies of the imagery and assessments of the impact of the strikes on the target sets and the war's objectives. Results from those phases were also sent to the theater.[58]

Christon thought the DIA's ring-down telephone call to CENTAF relaying hit-or-miss feedback on priority targets would be most useful in supplementing the mission reports the wings would send to him. He was leery of the rest of the DIA process, however. He lamented that the system was too complex: "It requires too much data to make it work, and we can't get there from here, and it diverts resources from focusing on the questions that I really would like to focus on and try to turn more quickly." Continuing, he explained,

> The problem was that the time phasing that they had, the level of detail of information that they required to implement that at the Washington level, was so horrendous a burden on the theater....It was executed totally outside of tactically relevant timelines so that it became a Washington area artifact, in our estimation. In other words, it was something that I am sure was a grand and glorious thing to do to support the Checkmate group and to support whomever in the building.[59]

In addition to answering the hit-or-miss question, Christon wanted DIA simply to answer his question, "Are we doing the damage to the target that we anticipated doing?" DIA appropriately addressed the question because it had the research tools and experience to provide the most useful, accurate analysis. Christon explained, "You simply can't, for instance, deploy the technical experts to tell you what the impact on the Tuwaitha nuclear power facility is, even if you got the ordnance there. Those judgments have to be made by folks in a rear area."[60]

DIA and CENTAF practiced using the ring-down about seven times during Desert Shield. Calls and transmissions used the DIA's National Military Intelligence Support Terminal and the Image Communications and Operators Node which terminated in a tent housing CENTAF intelligence personnel. The information could be phoned to the TACC and Special Planning Group or be taken there with a short walk from the soccer field.[61]

Christon believed it more important to send the ring-down, hit-or-miss intelligence into the TACC rather than to Glosson's planners. "Much is made about the Black Hole," he explained, "but the fact of the matter is that retasking, when you are in an operation, is done out of combat ops in the TACC; so therefore the primary focus in my architecture was for [ring-down, hit-or-miss] decisions to get the information into the TACC." His emphasis on the TACC receiving the BDA was noteworthy because the MAP was not generated in the TACC, but in Glosson's group, and without timely BDA, the planning process and ATO generation would suffer.[62] Deptula complained, "the information was provided, but not in a timely nature. It wasn't inside the planning cycle, and that was very frustrating."[63]

The number of targets tested on the ring-down, hit-or-miss circuit was quite small. Christon knew the war would generate a huge number of requirements, and last-minute changes would complicate everything. "I had told General Horner and General Glosson on several occasions prior to the war that there will be insufficient imagery BDA to support all of the things [they] would like to do. We are simply not going to get that," he stated. Although Christon felt the DIA system would basically be unresponsive, he did verbally contract with DIA representatives to send him information. He did not reciprocate and agree to send them target updates. "I didn't have the resources to notify DIA every time we changed a target — simply couldn't do it," he recalled.[64]

Christon and the CENTAF staff planned to rely on their own internal BDA system in addition to the DIA's. They would track BDA from an age-old source, aircrew mission reports, from reconnaissance imagery, and with information obtained from other sources. Knowing that the lines used for sending the crew reports as message traffic would be too slow to allow for timely assessments, the staff tried electronically to connect the computers they used to send ATOs to units with the computers they employed for tracking BDA. They failed to achieve success, however, before the war began. The colonel knew the report messages would arrive at CENTAF headquarters too late to effectively influence retargeting decisions.[65] In addition, because crew debriefings were not based on standardized procedures and often lacked essential elements of information about strike sorties, even timely reports could be useless.[66]

Christon and the CENTAF staff did not plan to use aircraft gun-camera film (cockpit videotapes) as a BDA source, though film carried by strike aircraft had been routinely exploited for BDA during the Vietnam War. By 1991 Air Force intelligence officers had come to rely on other sources for the assessments, and they viewed video recordings as merely an indicator of a successful bomb release.[67] Christon did anticipate that wing personnel would watch the videotapes and then incorporate descriptions of what they had seen into their mission reports, but he did not consider such tapes to be a reliable intelligence source. He noted, "What you see on a [videotape]...does not always correspond to actual damage to the aim point. The reason is because you have a lot of smoke, a lot of dust; it's low resolution. You never actually see the bomb damage itself."[68] To Christon's surprise, during the war, Glosson's staff would so lack responsive BDA that they would rely heavily on videotape recordings sent to CENTAF headquarters for analysis.

Christon assigned to himself, as the senior intelligence officer at CENTAF, the responsibility of daily briefing Horner on the crucially important question of how well the air war met campaign objectives.[69] He viewed his primary role as serving the intelligence requirements of the JFACC. He regarded as less important the task of supplying intelligence to the key campaign planners. While the commander could be briefed once or twice daily, with the intelligence officer generally choosing what information the JFACC should hear, the planners required constant attentiveness, and the supporting officer had to respond to specific queries. Although the customers required different kinds of service, Christon emphasized the commander.

In considering BDA and the wings, Christon considered using the TDF to electronically send poststrike photos to the units, but he decided against it. He would use the equipment to transmit only the critical, prestrike mission-planning photos. He would rely on couriers — trucks and aircraft — to transport hard-copy BDA photos to the wings. He chose this course because a TDF transmission of an image consumed so much time, and CENTAF/IN simply did not have time to electronically send BDA photographs to all units. Providing the units with images to use in their prestrike planning was itself a round-the-clock requirement, so Christon considered BDA photos as nonessential to the mission, merely "happy snaps." He did not send them over the TDF.[70]

As Christon prepared to supply BDA for the air campaign, Warden and Checkmate also geared up to provide damage assessments. When the DIA developed its three-phased BDA CONOPS, Checkmate grafted itself onto the agency's system. Warden could even claim partial credit for prodding the intelligence organization to undertake the BDA mission in support of the strategic air campaign.[71] He tasked Colonel Harvey to lead the Checkmate effort, with Lt. Col. Allan W. Howey his deputy.

The DIA's Col. Joel M. Litman welcomed Checkmate's assistance because it provided him with experts on aircraft and weapons delivery and effects. On October 29 he and a few other DIA personnel met with Warden's staff, explained the three-phased BDA process, and requested that Checkmate officers help to staff the second- and third-phase BDA cells on a twenty-four hour basis. Also accepting Checkmate support, though somewhat reluctantly, was the JCS BDA action officer, who did not understand how Checkmate fit into the chain of command, which, of course, it did not.[72] Whereas Christon was not eager to tap fully into the DIA's phased system, Warden was keen on helping to direct and then open as wide as possible the agency's BDA spigots, flowing as much intelligence into Checkmate as possible. He wanted his staff to play an important role in the system that officially would pass judgment on the effectiveness of the strategic air campaign.

The third major BDA challenge concerned imagery interpretation and judgments about bombing effectiveness. BDA was imagery-dependent, yet the craft of interpreting poststrike photographs was nearly dead throughout the intelligence community in 1990 and 1991. Not since the Vietnam War had the evaluation process attained such prominence in military operations, but few personnel, military or civilian, had experience doing damage assessments. At DIA, training in the craft during peacetime held a low priority, and officers in operational exercises routinely relegated BDA to a notional or simulated mode. Greatly complicating the challenge was the introduction into the military arsenal of penetrating weapons without the concomitant training of intelligence officers to recognize and understand the effects of penetrators on different target types. Information about the F–117A's GBU–27 laser-guided bomb was uniquely classified, which kept most targeteers and intelligence analysts ignorant of the munition, the exact people who now had to pass judgment on the weapon's effectiveness against actual targets.[73]

Key intelligence officers at DIA charged with BDA responsibilities welcomed Checkmate's assisting them in training their staffs to interpret penetrating-weapon effects. Even Checkmate, however, could not continuously supply data on Desert Storm targets in relation to the types of aircraft flown against them, nor on weapons and fuzing, aim points, target objectives, and other essential elements of information. Imagery interpretation could not occur in a vacuum. Analysts had to know the aircraft, munitions, and objectives to know what results to look for as they studied poststrike photos. A precision, penetrating GBU–27 produced a different damage pattern than an MK–84 free-fall, nonguided, general-purpose bomb. Officers had to know what type of damage effects to expect as they examined the imagery. A successful hit by a GBU–27 could produce only a small entry hole on a structure that, to the untrained eye, might pass unnoticed if the munition type were unknown. Timely, accurate BDA required unimpeded communication among planners, operators, and analysts, which did not occur during Desert Storm.[74]

Since August, DIA possessed the CENTCOM version of the target list for the strategic air campaign, which was separate from but similar to the Special Planning Group's list. DIA personnel used the CENTCOM information to prepare prestrike BDA material. With Warden's nod of approval, Colonel Harvey also supplied them with Glosson's up-to-date list. Fearing security violations and information leaks, Schwarzkopf had sternly prohibited officers in theater from sending the ATO and MAP to the DIA until the eve of the air war. The CINCCENT's directive hamstrung intelligence analysts and photo interpreters in Washington from adequately preparing for their enormous and numerous BDA tasks.[75]

Adding to the Black Hole's emphasis on targeting for effects, the stress that Deptula, Glosson, Horner, and Warden placed upon the *effects* concept further complicated the interpretation process. Eschewing analysis focusing solely on the level of physical damage inflicted on a target, they expected judgments about the ability of the target to function — how the level of damage affected its operation. They looked for an assessment of functional, not only physical or structural, damage, and they demanded that analysts view results across target sets as a whole, disclosing synergistic effects. An intelligence officer's training usually addressed the effects aspect of BDA production, but achieving this type of analysis proved more difficult than most imagined, compared with the less sophisticated approach required for the first phase of the BDA process, given the paucity of intelligence feedback on some targets.

The final challenge of the BDA process required the generation of sufficient imagery and data from satellite and aircraft collection systems.[76] The amount of usable material acquired from satellites was limited by the number of assets and the characteristics of each platform. To ensure that planners received imagery on priority targets, Glosson and McConnell worked out a deal whereby the general would receive images for a set number of targets every twenty-four hours; however, even this arrangement proved inadequate. Glosson and Christon understood that often last-minute pop-up targets would not be among the desired imagery. Glosson recalled, "I would telephone last-minute requests to McConnell. If the bird had not passed overhead he would always react. We would have been in the 'dark' 90 percent of the time without McConnell."[77]

The photographic yield from satellites did not measure up to the requirements for it. McConnell's deputy, who was sent to CENTCOM headquarters during Desert Shield, explained the high expectations–low output problem with national reconnaissance systems:

> The folks that went out and procured National Systems probably oversold the capabilities of some of those systems.... We went out to the generals or the fair-haired boys that were going to become generals, and we told them how great all these systems were, but [we] didn't say, "We can only do this once a day" or whatever, so these guys grew up through their careers, and when they go to their briefings in the Pentagon, they get all this stuff, and they see the best. They have 150 people putting together one little piece of a package. Then you come to a war, when you are trying to support the numbers of strikes that we were, monitor the size of the force that we were, and there wasn't nearly enough of that National stuff to go around.[78]

Bad weather traditionally hindered the collection of optical imagery, and Christon feared it would compound the BDA problem during Desert Storm. He knew that if weather prevented a strike against Baghdad, for example, Horner would exploit the flexibility of air power and shift sorties to other targets. Unfortunately, the collection of space-based BDA imagery lacked immediate responsiveness, constrained as it was by the physics of satellite orbits.[79] The weather during January and February would be the worst in the region in fourteen years and would affect operations, though not to the extent that it prevented achievement of campaign objectives.

The TR–1/U–2 aircraft were expected to fill some of the imaging shortfalls, but these assets were delicate platforms and pilots could not safely fly them over Iraq or the KTO until the air campaign had achieved air superiority. The RF–4 aircraft, too, depended on protective escorts or air superiority.[80] Before the start of hostilities, CENTCOM flew these tactical reconnaissance systems only on missions on the periphery of enemy-occupied territory. Even then, the command did not process and disseminate the film they obtained on a scale to satisfy wartime requirements. Neither did CENTCOM integrate Navy F–14 and British Tornado reconnaissance planes and their imagery into a smoothly operating BDA collection, production, and dissemination system. Overall, BDA for the air campaign could not keep up with the scope and pace of operations, and its processes lacked synchronization with the air war's execution.[81]

Planner–Intelligence Officer Friction

Despite Christon's diligent effort to provide targeting material and BDA for the air offensive, an extraordinary characteristic of the campaign planning process was the absence of a close working relationship between two groups: CENTAF intelligence officers and targeteers on the one hand, and Glosson and his staff in the Special Planning Group on the other. Christon described the interaction between the two units as a clear we–them situation. Horner knew that a cooperative, continuous interaction did not exist between the staffs. As he regretfully observed, "We didn't integrate intelligence into the Black Hole as much as I wanted to." The situation, however, was not unexpected. He explained: "Intel was a real problem. Christon was in a struggle from day 1. If you want to talk about a struggle, talk about Christon and Glosson. These are normal things. This is stuff you should imagine to happen, and it shouldn't surprise you when it happened."[82]

After the war Glosson described intelligence as a colossal failure for its inability to locate Saddam Hussein (so he could be targeted) and for its lack of timely BDA. He also complained that human intelligence did not locate mobile Scud launchers.[83] These were enormously difficult problems even in the best of circumstances. He concluded that the serious inadequacies stemmed from the manner in which intelligence functioned in peacetime. He stated:

> The problem is that even if they had been working for me in this war, I still would have had a difficult time because of the way that they're trained and the way they function in a peacetime environment. The problem is that we are organized too functionally in the peacetime mode, and we're not organized to be able to prosecute a war. That's where we have to solve this problem. If the Intel community was working for the operational side of the house, they would realize they are a support entity. This type of problem would then not arise during war. It's really a sad situation because in many cases, they work themselves to death to satisfy their own needs.[84]

Horner also believed that training did not prepare intelligence personnel for combat. He observed, "In peacetime we never practice wartime intelligence, so the ability to move wartime levels of targeting information is never experienced."[85]

After Desert Storm, Christon highlighted CENTAF/IN's involvement in strategic air campaign planning as an area in which intelligence did not measure up. He reported:

> Initial planning developed without effective CENTAF/IN participation due to non-availability of adequately experienced/skilled personnel. Situation improved with arrival of senior targets and collection management personnel (Oct), but the basic plan was already established, and we were consistently behind the power curve. Problem was further compounded by the physical separation of the planning cell (Black Hole) and the SCIF [Sensitive Compartmented Information Facility] which stymied close coordination. Direct Pentagon (DIA/J[oint]S[taff], Checkmate) participation in target selection at times bypassed theater intelligence functions entirely, a problem which could have been averted.[86]

Christon's postwar observation that Glosson's team "cornered the truth-and-justice market" expressed his frustration at how the Special Planning Group operated and then defended its modus operandi. He viewed the planners as steeped in "massive ignorance" about how intelligence and photographs were produced, leading them to make unreasonable demands on intelligence officers and, when the demands remained unfulfilled, to level unjust criticism.[87] The planners went a step further: when CENTAF/IN did not produce, they sought and found other sources of intelligence.

Colonel Talbot, the chief CENTAF targeteer, observed that between the target division and the Black Hole "a feeling of mutual distrust evolved which bedeviled our efforts throughout the entire period of Desert Storm."[88] He believed that the source of the friction between Glosson's group and the intelligence officers and targeteers originated with the very existence of the Special Planning Group. The group planned offensive operations in a manner unlike any operation with which Talbot had familiarity. At the end of the war, the unorthodox planning process tempered the triumph of victory for him. He stated,

> We won! Most everything that follows pales in the light of the fact that we did win. People can argue with the way its was done. I certainly did. But that does not alter the fact. The victory, however, is not so sweet as it might have been, if we had been able to prove the correctness of how we trained all these years.[89]

The situation galling the chief targeteer the most was the Checkmate–McConnell–Black Hole relationship, which he called a gigantic pain because it excluded CENTAF/IN.[90] He thought it prevented his division from doing proper target development for the air campaign. Talbot explained:

> A major factor affecting the coordination between CENTAF Targets and CENTAF Combat Plans…was the providing of intelligence directly from the Washington area into the Combat Plans function, especially to BG Glosson.…I have no problem with intelligence being provided from Washington where there is an abundance of analysts and databases galore and first-rate communication. I do, however, take exception with the manner in which it was provided to CENTAF. The intelligence should have been provided to CENTAF Intelligence so it could be examined in light of intelligence gathered within the AOR and judged in the light of the current and expected situation and the Commander's guidance. This was not the case. It completely bypassed CENTAF/IN.[91]

The officer noted that in a few cases he thought the target nominations from Washington were politically risky, at odds with the CINCCENT's guidance. Most, he thought, were based on sound analytical techniques. He primarily complained that he first learned of some intelligence sent to the Black Hole when planners asked him to clarify part of it, or provide imagery or coordinates for a target nomination. It bothered him that sometimes the planners gave *him* the imagery that he had sought from the intelligence community — the steps were backwards. He believed that any products sent to Glosson's group from Washington should have been simultaneously transmitted to CENTAF/IN. He fretted that the intelligence flowing directly to the special planners, bypassing theater intelligence officers, would establish a precedent harmful for future operations. The deleterious effect would occur because, without the direct input from targeteers and intelligence personnel in the AOR, operators and planners would not understand and follow the CINCCENT's and JFACC's guidance. That, however, did not transpire during Desert Shield or Desert Storm.

Talbot's objection to the Black Hole's existence and to its not following steps reinforced through training echoed Blackburn's exhortation at the end of August to let the system work, as he withheld target photographs from the air campaign planners. Air Staff targeteers viewed the procedures practiced in peacetime as the means to achieve objectives. Operators and planners soon found such measures to be inadequate for wartime demands, and so discarded them, substituting procedures that worked better. In theater, Christon and Talbot had a direct link to the DIA through the National Military Intelligence Support Terminal — Image Communications and Operators Node line, and if they could not exploit it to acquire intelligence on a timely basis, the fault was with the system they championed. CENTAF/IN proved incapable of meeting the planners' wartime needs, so Glosson's staff found and exploited providers who met their requirements. The operations division of CENTAF/IN had evolved into the Joint Air Intelligence Center, composed of fifty Air Force, Navy, Army, and British intelligence analysts operating on a twenty-four-hour basis, but the group could not acquire timely imagery to meet wartime planning and BDA demands.[92]

Another problem originated with the target officers' working in the tent in the soccer field rather than in the Black Hole office space within the RSAF building itself. There they might have rubbed elbows with the planners day in and day out and learned of intelligence requirements as they materialized. Talbot attended Glosson's morning staff meetings and, during Desert Shield, periodically visited the Special Planning Group, but he did not become a part of the unit because he also served the CENTAF planners in developing the defensive ATO. Besides, Glosson did not request that targeteers spend their time in the RSAF building with his personnel; he was content to leave them in the tent. Colonel Kershaw was the first CENTAF/IN officer permanently assigned from September on to the Black Hole, but he, too, spent only part of his time in the group. He could not forge, according to Christon, an effective working relationship with Glosson.[93] Deptula made numerous requests for targeteers to remain in the Black Hole, but he recalled that CENTAF/IN officers told him repeatedly the area in the RSAF building was not secure enough to house SCI, so the material used by intelligence officers and targeteers had to remain in the SCI tent.[94]

Just before he departed Riyadh in December to return to the United States, Major Rogers brought to a head the problem of dedicated intelligence support to the Black Hole. Having had the experience of updating the MAP for the strategic air campaign, refining the Phase II and III planning, and developing the Reflex plan without constant CENTAF/IN support, he went to Colonels Talbot and Meyer and pleaded for an intelligence officer to be assigned full-time to the Special Planning Group. The colonels stated that they themselves were the intelligence liaisons to the unit, with Kershaw, but Rogers pointed out that none of them was immediately available when needed. Rogers discussed his request with both Christon and Glosson. Shortly after, Talbot told Rogers that targeteer Captain Glock would be permanently assigned to the special planning unit in the RSAF building. Rogers left the AOR pleased at the boost in intelligence support, providing, for the first time, a targeteer within the Black Hole on a full-time basis to support offensive planning.[95] Within a few days, Christon and Talbot sent a second targeteer to the Black Hole for twenty-four-hour coverage.

Navy Issues

Horner tried to ameliorate the discord among his staff by controlling its intensity. He explained, "What you do is, you just manage it. You let them fight a little bit."[96] He also had to devote energy to reducing the level of friction arising from his role as the JFACC. Problems surfaced throughout the planning process involving the other services and Coalition partners, and Horner sought diligently and patiently to find solutions that would not undermine the principle of unity of command of the air campaign. The Navy pressed the air planners on five significant issues, the first concerning the location of Navy CAPs. A steady undercurrent of criticism flowed into the Black Hole that the JFACC assigned CAP stations to deliberately position Air Force CAPs in better areas than those assigned to the Navy to give Air Force pilots the advantage of being able to shoot down more Iraqi aircraft than Navy pilots could. Deptula correctly maintained, however, that the Navy CAP location accommodated Navy F–14 fueling requirements. He explained,

> Here's the map. Tabuk is just over here off this map. The Red Sea is down here. The CAP stations are located up in here. Now, it doesn't take a…brain surgeon to figure out that if both of these require air refueling, that I can keep more sorties flying F–15s out of Tabuk than I can flying F–14s out of the Red Sea.

With the eastern CAPs, Deptula lobbied Glosson and Horner hard to have the JFACC press the NAVCENT commander to move aircraft carriers farther north into the Arabian Sea so Navy pilots could be closer to forward CAPs and reduce their air refueling requirements. Eventually carriers did move into the Persian Gulf.[97]

The second issue concerned Navy A–6E Intruders attacking targets in Baghdad. The A–6 was TRAM-equipped, which included a forward-looking infrared sensor and a laser designation system. The aircraft could deliver PGMs, so planners considered it a good candidate for strikes in the Iraqi capital. When Glosson briefed President Bush on October 11, 1990, A–6s appeared in the MAP to strike two leadership targets in Baghdad. Navy officials, however, worried about the survivability of the A–6E, which lacked stealth and supersonic speed. The Navy's operational intelligence cell strongly recommended against sending the Intruders to Baghdad. When representatives from the Air Force Center for Studies and Analysis

A–6E Intruder

came to Riyadh in late October and did computer modeling of the A–6 sorties to the capital city, dismal loss rates emerged. Glosson told Major Rogers to pull the Navy aircraft off the Baghdad targets, which were soon retargeted with TLAMs.[98]

Air refueling was the next problem. When the second wave of deployment forces began to arrive in theater in late November and December, the need for aerial tanker support increased accordingly. The Navy would add three more aircraft carrier groups for a total of six, split between the Red Sea to the west and the Arabian Sea and the Persian Gulf to the east: USS *John F. Kennedy*, USS *Midway*, and USS *Saratoga*, joined by USS *Theodore Roosevelt*, USS *America*, and USS *Ranger*. The Navy "begged" for tankers to support the additional carriers en route. Again, Deptula maintained that whenever he or Rogers adjusted the MAP, they tried to equitably accommodate Navy fuel requirements. Deptula explained:

> They wanted more and more tanker support.... We promised them this tanker support, and they were going to get it. And addressing that issue, if I may, I can honestly say with a straight face, I put together the master attack plan and did it on the basis of the most effective use of assets available.[99]

The air refueling component of the air campaign was unprecedented. Air Force, Navy, and Marine Corps aircraft had to refuel, as did British, Saudi, Omani, UAE, Egyptian, Turkish, Italian, and Canadian air assets. Tankers supported every facet of Desert Storm air operations. Before the war, airmen practiced refueling maneuvers on a small scale. General Corder recalled the complexity and uncertainty of the enormous enterprise required for wartime:

> We tried to get 40 or 50 tankers airborne and get a few tracks to get the density in the track we thought we'd have in all the tracks. We tried it one time in the second week of December, and it was a major debacle, because the Saudi air traffic controllers would not let the tankers take off in short intervals. They were used to 3 or 4 minute separation between tankers, and of course you can't launch 50 tankers with 5 minute separation and get everybody there at the right time. So that was a big problem. General Horner took appropriate steps with the Saudi Air Force commander, who by the way is in charge of the air traffic control system. And when it came time for the war to go, there was no problem, and all the tankers got off at 60- to 90-second intervals. The second time we practiced it there was weather, and we had to cancel. So we didn't have real good practice on that before we went, which kind of scared me some. People knew it was going to be dense, and people knew that they had better be at the right place at the right time.[100]

Glosson wanted to fly the tankers stacked with only 500 feet of altitude separating them. "The Navy felt that was unacceptable, they couldn't handle it," he recalled. "They wanted 1,000 feet altitude separation." The general accommodated the Navy for the tanker cells naval pilots used.[101]

The fourth issue concerned the use of the Navy's TLAMs. In October, Navy officials in Washington expressed reservations about the accuracy of TLAMs targeted against power facilities. The issue surfaced because F–111Fs originally sent against electrical plants were switched to other types of targets, leaving only TLAMs and CALCMs to take down the critically important power grid. In late October, Deptula had to retarget F–111Fs as backup weapon systems to TLAMs. Right up to the start of Desert Storm, the Navy worked at solving problems with the missiles' navigational and targeting systems.[102]

The final issue engendered the most controversy of the five and focused on BVR ROE. According to Horner as the JFACC, air-to-air weapons could be used BVR only if two types of nonvisual electronic verification could be made that the bogey, the unidentified aircraft, was, indeed, a bandit, an enemy aircraft. Navy aircraft did not have onboard electronic systems to make two identifications. The F–14 Tomcats, which carried the Phoenix air-to-air missiles capable of hitting a target up to 115 miles, could only interrogate the bogey's IFF transponder; F/A–18s used another electronic means. In contrast, most Air Force fighters were equipped to use either or both methods. The JFACC issued restrictive BVR rules to avoid air-to-air fratricide in enormously congested air space. Horner explained,

> Long before the war started, we concluded we couldn't live with unrestricted BVR because it wasn't required because the Iraqis weren't going to pose that big a threat. We were going to take out their command and control and then we were going to shoot them down. So, the decision was one of practicality, not one of doctrine.[103]

In January the NAVCENT commander, Vice Adm. Stanley R. Arthur, requested that Horner loosen the ROE. The JFACC held firm, telling the admiral to elevate the decision to the CINCCENT, a rare piece of advice by the officer who loathed not settling issues among the component commanders and passing problems to Schwarzkopf. When the CINCCENT received Arthur's recommendation for less restrictive rules of engagement, he summoned Horner to explain the admiral's request. The JFACC recalled the awkward situation: "So, I was put in the position of defending Stan in front of Schwarzkopf, which I did. Then he said, 'What is the alternate argument?' I gave him my argument, and he said, 'Write me that answer, and I'll send it.'" The general replied on behalf of the CINCCENT, explaining that the risk of easing the rules outweighed the benefit. (The progress of the war would eventually allow the JFACC to give the Navy loosened BVR rules if planners knew no Coalition aircraft were in areas where Navy aircraft operated.)[104]

Marine Corps Issues

The primary issues involving the Marine Corps as Desert Storm approached were the extent to which Marine airmen would participate in the air campaign and the number of HARMs they would employ. The agreement worked out in August still held that 50 percent of the F/A–18s, all the A–6s, and no AV–8s would be available for the JFACC to task in the ATO for strategic air operations. "The Marines and the AV–8s — they never wanted the AV–8s to do anything," complained Glosson. "They wanted to sit them on the ground until the ground campaign started or when they started preparing the battlefield for the land campaign." Shortly after arriving in theater as the new CENTAF director of operations, Corder asked General Moore, the 3d Marine Air Wing commander, to put more F/A–18s into the air war. The Marine countered that his units had trouble acquiring ordnance and he had only four days' worth. Learning of the problem, Horner immediately took steps to supply Moore's pilots with all the ordnance they needed.[105]

The JFACC, however, did not provide as many HARMs as Moore wanted because the Air Force's F–4Gs could more effectively employ the radar-killing missiles than the Navy's A–6s and F/A–18s could. The Marine Corps and the Navy programmed their HARMs prior to takeoff, which limited their flexibility; in contrast, Air Force pilots flying the F–4Gs could change frequencies and locate more up-to-date and accurate data on enemy radars during a mission before they launched their HARMs. Horner gave the Marines more Shrike missiles (700) than HARMs (300). The issue went to Schwarzkopf, who decided that the Marines would receive only 300 HARMs.[106]

Army Issues

The primary Army issue that the JFACC dealt with in planning the air campaign centered on the deployment and use of the Joint Surveillance and Target Attack Radar System (JSTARS). JSTARS would greatly augment the capability of airmen flying counterland missions. In 1990 two E–8A prototype aircraft carried the radar system which enabled commanders to see the battlefield in near real-time, night or day, in all weather. The surveillance control data link connected the E–8As to ground-station modules that displayed for ground crews the same data the airborne personnel observed. These two JSTARS, reconfigured Boeing 707s developed jointly by the Army and Air Force to detect, locate, and track ground targets, provided information on moving and fixed targets. The E–8A's radome, located under the forward fuselage, housed a 24-foot, side-looking, phased-array radar antenna which functioned in two primary modes. In its first mode, the wide-area surveillance–moving target indicator covered thousands of square miles and tracked moving vehicles within that area. Its imagery displayed vehicles as yellow dots against a black background. In the second mode, the synthetic aperture radar produced photograph-like images of ground

JSTARS

terrain, installations, and fixed targets. As an Army–Air Force project, the Air Force was responsible for development of the aircraft, airborne radars, and air-to-ground communication links.[107]

In August 1990 Horner had considered advising the CINCCENT to request deployment of the E–8A, but after discussing the issue with Colonel Leonardo, who thought JSTARS just a toy, and with General Russ, commander of TAC, he recommended against it. Knowing that the system was not scheduled to become operational until 1997, Russ and Horner thought JSTARS too immature and fragile in 1990. On September 3 the CINCCENT sent a message to Chairman Powell stating that Desert Shield was neither the time nor place to introduce JSTARS.[108]

In September and October, a JSTARS field demonstration in Europe greatly impressed the Supreme Allied Commander Europe, Gen. John R. Galvin, USA, and General Franks, the VII Corps commander, who viewed JSTARS radar data both while airborne and at a ground station. At a distance of 62 miles, JSTARS disclosed the wreckage of a C–5 aircraft that had crashed at the end of a runway at Ramstein AB. During a simulated combat exercise, it showed Franks a moving "enemy" armored convoy, against which he launched helicopter gun ships, resulting in fifty-one armored vehicles "killed." The platform also conducted surveillance for several hours against a huge convoy, intermixed with civilian traffic, heading east across Germany. After seeing the battlefield through JSTARS, Galvin noted that for the previous twenty years he had been "blindfolded."[109]

In December as Franks prepared his VII Corps for deployment to Saudi Arabia, he urged the CENTCOM commander to receive a JSTARS briefing and consider having the air asset deployed to theater. The CINCCENT agreed, and Col. George K. Muellner, one of the Air Force's experts on the system, presented a series of briefings to Schwarzkopf and his component commanders and staffs. Muellner explained the JSTARS capabilities and discussed how the deployment could proceed in stages. He emphasized that the deployment would probably cost about $1 million a day. The CINCCENT replied that he did not care if it cost $1 billion a day if it added value to the ground offensive. As the colonel recalled, "It became fairly obvious early on that the briefing was almost lip service more than anything else, and the general consensus was that General Schwarzkopf really wanted to see the system deployed."[110]

Generals Horner, Russ, and McPeak did not want the deployment. "The Joint STARS had been kind of talked about, but at every opportunity the leadership of the Air Force stomped it," remembered Corder. Muellner's assurances that the JSTARS would not fail in combat alleviated Horner's concern that the deployment of such an immature asset would result in inadequate performance and lead to termination of the program. The cost of the employment also worried the JFACC. He explained, "It was going to be expensive. I think it ran about a million dollars a day, very expensive. You see, we were getting the same kind of information out of TR–1s and stuff. So JSTARS was an additive, but it wasn't filling a vacuum."[111] TR–1s carried the ASARS, which, like JSTARS, provided day and night, all-weather, near real-time radar images. It could detect armor, artillery, defensive positions, and logistics sites and feed images to a ground station.[112]

Corder strongly favored the JSTARS deployment, knowing how vigorously General Leide, CENTCOM J–2, and Franks had lobbied Schwarzkopf for it. He described his discussion with Horner:

> I go into the story with him. No. 1, it does have a decent capability, and it has been demonstrated. No. 2, the lead corps commander that is going to lead the main attack, VII Corps, has seen it, likes it, wants it, asks for it, and is begging for it. If that corps gets torn up, anything happens to that corps, guess whose fault it's going to be? It's going to be the United States Air Force's fault because they didn't bring Joint Stars over. Now Horner is in a dilemma. I said, "We have got to bring it over."[113]

Horner decided to recommend to the CINCCENT that JSTARS be deployed. Schwarzkopf, in turn, requested the deployment to Powell, who approved it.[114] The JFACC then relied on Corder to make JSTARS work effectively in theater.

The CENTAF staff scrambled to receive the two E–8A prototypes, which arrived in theater January 12 and were assigned to the 4411th JSTARS Squadron, 15th Air Division (Provisional). Personnel had to develop, coordinate, and publish the CONOPS for integrating JSTARS into the JFACC C^2 and planning processes and learn how to receive, interpret, and use JSTARS radar data. The data had great potential for assisting General Glosson in establishing target-rich kill boxes for Phase III strikes, but he and his staff were incapable of exploiting JSTARS for such purposes in December and early January. According to Muellner: "It took them an extended period…for Buster Glosson's people in the Black Hole and for Christon's people in the intel side of the house to be able to take the information and effectively exploit it. So what we tried to do, with a lot of help from Major General Corder, was 'spoon-feed' them." Muellner would eventually rely on trained Reservist augmentees to interpret JSTARS data, and he established his own joint planning and exploitation cell at CENTAF headquarters.[115]

The E–8A's arrival in theater quickly raised two employment issues. First, was the platform a corps-level or theater-level asset? The corps commanders saw it as their system; indeed, the Army supported the development of JSTARS as a corps asset. The range of the initial data link between the E–8A and the ground-station module argued for keeping the aircraft flying directly above a corps with a ground station. In contrast, Corder and Muellner saw the platform as primarily a theater-level asset which provided a commander with a view of the entire battlefield, not just allowing a corps commander a bowling-alley view of it. Because only two JSTARS aircraft were available in January 1991, the JFACC, following CINCCENT guidance, had to task the JSTARS crews to provide coverage not always in accord with the corps commanders' requests. Through the ATO, the JFACC scheduled the aircraft's flying time, identified its station and times on station, provided refueling instructions, and controlled the asset. Muellner felt the strong tension of the pull on JSTARS from all organizations with ground stations, which numbered five: ARCENT, MARCENT, VII Corps, XVIII Airborne Corps, and CENTAF. Later, a sixth ground station arrived in theater from NATO and was assigned to CENTCOM headquarters.[116]

The second JSTARS question was whether the asset should function as a surveillance and intelligence collection system, or as a targeting and operations platform. Muellner observed, "It was a battle between the intelligence community, and for lack of a better word, the targeting community. The intelligence folks wanted to use the thing primarily for intelligence....The targeting folks said, No. We're buying this thing to provide responsive targeting." When General Franks received his ground station, he assigned it to his operators to aid them in launching deep targeting strikes. In contrast, General Luck of the XVIII Airborne Corps and General Boomer of MARCENT assigned their modules to their intelligence officers who would acquire situational awareness and intelligence from the downlink data but not necessarily for near real-time targeting. Col. William P. Armstrong, the CENTCOM J–2 deputy, explained, "Killing five vehicles is important because that is a mission, but from a ground perspective, being able to see [that] the Tawakalna Division is still in place is ultimately more important to a ground commander at that given point in time." CENTAF staff tended to see JSTARS as a near real-time targeting platform.[117]

At the onset of the air war, the CINCCENT stipulated that JSTARS locate Republican Guard positions, employing the resource in a surveillance-intelligence mode. During other times, however, planners intended to send two aircraft every thirty minutes to JSTARS to receive target taskings, thus also employing it in targeting and operations, a hunter-killer mode.[118]

A second major Army issue confronting the JFACC was the use of air power to breach Iraqi obstacles on the battlefield, especially land mines. Iraqi defenses consisted of minefields nearly 250 feet wide, berms up to 10 feet high, antitank trenches, and miles of concertina wire. In November 1990, modeling and limited testing in the United States showed the Army that breaching minefields and other obstacles with current U.S. engineering equipment would result in limited success and high casualties. Ground commanders worried that the Iraqis would employ CW against the Coalition forces just as they struggled through the formidable defense barriers. Because the Saudis and Egyptians lacked breaching equipment, they looked to air power to open paths for them.[119]

In early January 1991, SAC and the Army Corps of Engineers conducted B–52 tests against barriers at the National Training Center with encouraging results, given that breaching was a new mission for the heavy bombers. In theater, Army personnel in the BCE of the TACC functioned as project officers for breaching operations and passed their test reports to ARCENT's 513th Military Intelligence Brigade. Testing in the United States and AOR continued after the air war commenced. Lacking enthusiasm for employing air power against minefields, Horner explained that air-delivered ordnance disturbed the pattern of mine emplacements and made their clearance more difficult. Marines, too, had to confront mines and tested the efficacy of FAE munitions, but the FAE overpressure of the small weapons they used lacked intensity sufficient to detonate mines.[120]

During the war, aircraft that engaged in breach operations would be B–52s dropping 750-pound unguided, general-purpose M–117s and 500-pound unguided, general-purpose MK–82s; MC–130s employing the stupendous 15,000-pound BLU–82 "daisy cutter" weapon; AV–8Bs dispensing FAEs and napalm against fire trenches; and F–117s delivering 500-pound laser-guided weapons against oil pipes and distribution points that were sending fuel into the fire trenches. ASARS radar imagery revealed to B–52 planners that Arab forces did exploit B–52 breach points. Most units still employed their countermine plows and counterobstacle equipment in areas saturated with air-delivered ordnance, and the heavy, steady rains in February helped wash away dirt and sand from mines exposed as a result of the cratering action due to aerial strikes.[121]

Coalition Issues: Saudis

In addition to addressing joint problems, the JFACC and his planners dealt with Coalition-related issues. Among the allied partners, the Saudis and British, after the Americans, carried the greatest responsibilities in the air campaign. Until late November, the Saudis had not been fully briefed on the offensive war plan, but since October, Deptula had been working with a few Saudi air officers on targets and times.[122] Glosson and Deptula included their hosts in the MAP, assigning targets suitable to their air-asset capabilities.

In late November, Brig. Gen. Prince Turki bin Nasser bin Abd al-Aziz al-Saud, RSAF commander for the Eastern Region, visited CENTAF headquarters and, during a discussion about aerial refueling operations, was mistakenly shown the offensive air campaign's ATO, a breach of security because the general had not yet been formally read into the offensive plan. Glosson was in the United States at the time, so Major Rogers had the unwelcome task of telling Horner that Prince Turki had carefully perused the ATO. "I expected to get my head ripped off," the major recalled. The JFACC told him not to worry about it. When Glosson returned in early December, he formally briefed the plan to Brig. Gen. Ahmad al-Sudari, RSAF director of operations. As Rogers reported, al-Sudari's reaction was that it was a good attack plan and the sooner executed the better.[123] The Saudis were, of course, fully apprised of the D-day plan and its ATO Bravo. General Khalid had been briefed on aspects of it on November 22, with emphasis on airfield attacks, the type of mission the Saudis would execute.[124]

At the request of CENTCOM in late October, the Saudis' CSS–2 medium-range surface-to-surface ballistic missiles obtained from China were incorporated into the MAP and tasked against three targets in Iraq. No official Saudi approval for their use, however, had been conveyed to the JFACC before the start of the air war. The missiles were controversial because China had agreed with a U.S. request that it would not sell such weapons to countries in the Middle East, to avoid starting a new arms race in the region. The transaction between the Saudis and Chinese occurred in utter secrecy, and when the world learned of the acquisition in March 1988, the United States received assurances from the Saudis that the weapons would carry only conventional warheads.[125] Due to the missiles' inaccuracy, they constituted terror weapons, and their use would probably help Saddam claim legitimacy for his Scud launches. Because the missiles lacked precision, Deptula, wary of collateral damage, selected large target areas like railroad yards, ammunition depots, and airfields for the Saudi missile strikes. Because he did not count on the missiles' being used (which they were not) or having an effective circular error probable, he tasked other weapons against the targets as well.[126] General Khalid explained the situation immediately after Iraq attacked Saudi Arabia with Scuds: "If ever there was a right moment to unleash our Chinese-built surface-to-surface missiles, this seemed to be it....But, after some anxious hours, King Fahd decided not to escalate the conflict."[127]

Coalition Issues: British

Air Chief Marshal Sir Patrick Hine commanded the British deployment to the Gulf region, Operation Granby, from his headquarters in England at High Wycombe, the RAF air base. His immediate subordinate in Saudi Arabia, Lt. Gen. Sir Peter de la Billiere, commanded all British forces in theater, with Air Vice Marshal William Wratten leading the airmen. The British had participated in the air campaign planning process since the first week of September, with Wing Commander Richardson representing the RAF in the Black Hole. Deptula raved about the cooperation Richardson provided the planners. In late November, Richardson, Corder, Rogers, and Wratten visited the British embassy in Riyadh where they received a briefing on the British version of an offensive air campaign. Corder and Rogers listened intently and, as Rogers recalled, functioned strictly as information receivers, accepting all the target materials provided them, which included excellent imagery. They did not discuss the Desert Storm plan.[128]

On December 17 an event occurred in England that embarrassed the British and jeopardized the security of the Desert Storm air campaign. A few days before the 17th, Air Chief Marshal Hine had visited the Black Hole and received a briefing on the four-phased air campaign. Back in London, he briefed the campaign to Prime Minister John Major. Immediately afterward, Hine turned his documents and laptop over to his aide, a wing commander, who decided to stop at a used car dealership instead of returning directly to High Wycombe with the Top Secret material. While the aide was shopping for an automobile, a thief broke into the trunk of the aide's vehicle and stole the computer and a briefcase containing plans and money. The thief pocketed the money, kept the computer, and threw the briefcase and papers into a trash bin in a supermarket parking lot. A physician found the items and, recognizing their importance, turned everything over to the police. At the end of December the London tabloids learned of the theft but were prevented from publishing the story by a government-imposed prohibition. The restraining order did not apply to the *Irish Times,* which published the news. Military officials worried that the computer's hard drive contained an outline of the war plan and that the thief would try to sell it, assuming he was not an Iraqi agent to start with. Glosson depended on Admiral McConnell to inform him of any intelligence revealing that the Iraqis had acquired the plan, but he never received any indication that Saddam Hussein's forces knew about the Desert Storm air campaign before its execution.[129]

Deception Options

The loss of the Desert Storm plan in Britain, plus General Dugan's revelations in American newspapers, highlighted for planners the value of security and its corollary: deception. CENTCOM had incorporated into its plans operational and tactical deception. Schwarzkopf and his staff led the Iraqis to believe two false propositions: that the bulk of the ground forces would attack Iraqi forces in Kuwait, charging directly into the most heavily defended positions, and that the U.S. Marine Corps and Navy would execute a massive amphibious landing on the east coast of Kuwait. The first of these operational deceptions concealed the real plan to attack the right flank of the Republican Guard in Iraq. It required that the two Army corps not move to their jumping-off points for D-day until the air campaign commenced, preventing Iraqi reconnaissance aircraft from seeing the great redeployment and the Americans as lucrative targets. The CINCCENT prohibited airmen from striking some targets too early to preserve the secrecy of the ground scheme of maneuver, even though that meant not hitting targets as soon as the corps commanders nominated them, a delay contributing to criticism that the JFACC was unresponsive to the land campaign's requirements. The second operational deception successfully resulted in the Iraqis' keeping at least four infantry divisions and a mechanized division oriented eastward toward beaches along the Persian Gulf for the amphibious assault force, which never came. The CINCCENT ordered amphibious landing training exercises, and the news media covered them extensively.[130]

The air campaign's primary deception operations, underway throughout Desert Shield, desensitized the Iraqis to seeing routine AWACS and Rivet Joint orbits, CAPs, and aerial refueling operations at night in a pattern similar to what they might see on their radars the night the war started. Surge operations occurred as well. As Desert Storm commenced on January 17, the great armada of strike aircraft and tankers refueled beyond the range of Iraqi EWRs so they would remain hidden from the defenders and preserve the element of surprise.[131] Tactical deception also involved the use of Navy decoys and Poobah's Party BQM–74 ground-launched drone missiles, which achieved some SEAD success. Capt. Jerrold R. Hubbard, Glosson's deception officer, solicited and developed other deception options to execute before and during the air war.

Psychological Operations

Closely related to deception operations were PSYOPS. On September 19, 1990, the CENTCOM commander approved the CENTCOM PSYOPS plan, Burning Hawk, and sent it to Chairman Powell for approval by Secretary Cheney. Schwarzkopf recommended the plan's full implementation, pointing out that Saddam Hussein currently waged a vigorous propaganda war which required that the United States not only counter it, but initiate its own comprehensive program. Schwarzkopf bluntly told Powell,

> All factors strongly suggest we have only a narrow window of opportunity remaining to get ahead in the information war before Saddam's initiatives begin to have a negative impact on our overall efforts here. Failure to act soon in a concerted manner will relegate us to a "response-only" posture.[132]

At the CINCCENT's headquarters, personnel from SOCCENT and the Army's 4th Psychological Operations Group developed Schwarzkopf's plan under the leadership of Col. Anthony Normand, commander of the psychological operations group. Checkmate planners passed PSYOPS information to the colonel, focusing on the corrupt regime of a hypocritical Saddam Hussein and on the fact that the United States had no quarrel with the Iraqi people. Burning Hawk consisted of time-sequenced campaigns containing approximately 100 specific PSYOPS actions in accordance with SecDef and JCS guidance and objectives. Radio and television broadcasts, leaflets, and other media would be the means to achieve four objectives: undermine the morale and combat effectiveness of Iraqi troops; foment desertion; educate Iraqi forces about the law of armed conflict; and encourage the overthrow of Saddam's regime.[133] The PSYOPS would primarily destroy Iraqi morale and encourage surrenders and deserters.[134]

The CJCS did not give the plan his stamp of urgency, allowing it instead to enter a multilayered bureaucratic review and action process that consumed months. Warden continually expressed frustration about the lack of progress in Washington with approval for a comprehensive PSYOPS campaign.[135]

When the director of the Joint Staff received Burning Hawk, he decided that some options fell under Executive Order 12333 and would therefore require Presidential approval. He divided the Burning Hawk package, sending a portion of it to the intelligence community, with no recommendation from the JCS or SecDef for implementation. The JCS then lost control of the approval timetable for those projects.[136]

By December the CINCCENT was frustrated at the dearth of Burning Hawk actions that had been approved. On December 5 he sent a message that referred to bureaucratic bungling to the CJCS, and he resubmitted revised Burning Hawk options. Within two weeks, DoD approved seventeen of the CINCCENT's twenty-one proposals.[137]

Horner believed that, in deference to Saudi opposition to some Burning Hawk options, the U.S. government never officially approved them. Speaking with Ambassador Freeman in October, Horner learned that propaganda calling for the overthrow of an Arab leader bothered the Saudis. They feared such an approach could backfire and be turned against King Fahd and his family. Also, they wished to see only Arabic nationals depicted in propaganda leaflets, no Americans. Horner stated, "They really had the veto on the PSYWAR [psychological warfare] campaign. It wasn't until we started the war that Schwarzkopf got tough about getting a PSYWAR campaign in place."[138]

In December intelligence officers at CENTCOM suggested strikes against two targets in Baghdad for psychological impact: the Victory Arch, representations of Saddam Hussein's hands holding crossed swords; and a 40-foot statue of Saddam Hussein. When Deptula heard of these target nominations, he scoffed because of the large number of military targets to hit. Near the end of the war, however, he convinced Glosson to strike them for their psychological impact, but objections from Pentagon officials stopped the targeting. They argued that the risk of collateral damage and subsequent international criticism so late in the war outweighed potential benefits.[139]

Horner thought that strikes against even obviously military targets produced PSYOPS gains. He explained, "The primary factor in selecting targets was military significance. Yet middle-of-the night bombings of targets in Baghdad also were intended to remind Iraqis that a war was going on and Saddam was vulnerable and unable to stop it."[140] Before the start of the war, PSYOPS primarily consisted of leaflet distribution and radio and loudspeaker broadcasts aimed at Iraqi soldiers in the KTO. Initial themes focused on peace and brotherhood. Messages encouraging desertion were later prepared for wartime dissemination. In the Black Hole, preparations were underway to drop leaflets in Baghdad and broadcast radio messages via the EC–130 Volant Solo aircraft exhorting civilians and soldiers alike to overthrow Saddam. CENTCOM neither received authorization for nor allowed execution of those plans.[141]

Leadership and C^3 Targeting Intensified

From mid-October to mid-January, planners continued to identify targets. Leadership, C^3, and BW targets received an extraordinary amount of scrutiny from the national intelligence community, which passed new information about these sets to the Black Hole, via Checkmate and Admiral McConnell, and belatedly through CENTAF/IN. In response to Warden's concern in October that the Iraqi leadership target set was not being scrubbed and worked dilligently enough, Colonel Harvey volunteered to head a study group, subsequently called the Leadership Facilities Team, which sponsored meetings with analysts from CIA and DIA, briefed them on the Instant Thunder plan, and requested of them information and imagery about leadership and C^3 targets. The nominations discussed over the next few weeks included sites in Tikrit, Saddam Hussein's hometown; leadership shelters; Saddam's movements; presidential palaces; government facilities; communications systems; and headquarters for Iraqi special security forces, the Baath Party, and the Republican Guard. The analysts provided Harvey's facilities group with valuable intelligence, which was sent to the Black Hole.[142] At a team meeting in early November, Checkmate planners learned that the Iraqi leader mostly traveled within Baghdad by automobile and had communications systems in his personal command vehicles.[143]

The Leadership Facilities Team received a mixture of information and processed intelligence about bomb shelters, which were of three types, as determined by their method of construction: Type C, F, or S. Type C shelters numbered 76; Type F numbered 10; and Type S, 24. By November 3, Harvey had learned that the Iraqis had reinforced the Type F shelters and converted them into C^3 bunkers. CIA and DIA analysts were asked to confirm the validity of these facilities as targets. In the Type S category, a 25th target was identified as probably being an alternate C^3 site. Again, inquiries to intelligence specialists requested confirmation of the "No. 25" as a valid target.[144]

On December 20 when Horner briefed Secretary Cheney, Chairman Powell, and Under Secretary Wolfowitz in Riyadh, the ten Type F shelters, described as C^3 bunkers and labeled A through J, and the No. 25 Type S shelter, carrying the description "VIP bombshelter," appeared on the air campaign leadership target list.[145] Returning to Riyadh on January 2, 1991, Deptula reviewed new overhead photos of the ten Type F structures. He was uncertain of their actual use and asked Captain Glock, the targeteer, to obtain information that would explain their function. None was available, and the absence of strong, positive intelligence indicating their use as C^3 bunkers bothered both officers. Accordingly, Deptula drew a huge Z through the ten targets on the leadership list, clearly flagging them as no-strike targets. The VIP bombshelter was not so designated, remained on the list, and was attacked by an F–117 the first night of the air campaign.[146]

During the war, one of the Type F shelters, identified as "C^3 Bunker G (al-Firdos)," was placed on the active target list, based on new intelligence associating the facility with C^3 activity. Two F–117As struck it the night of February 12/13; it then became the subject of worldwide news coverage revealing that numerous civilians had been inside and were killed in the bunker-cum-shelter.

Only about a week before the start of the air war did new intelligence reach campaign planners about Iraq's new copper telephone cables and a fiber-optic communications network. The intelligence surprised its recipients because the fiber-optic cable network was not, as originally thought, associated with oil pipeline operations but was indeed a fundamental component of Saddam's military C^2 system. A DIA analyst working with the Leadership Facilities Team broke the news to Checkmate, and Colonel Howey immediately passed it to Deptula. Meanwhile DIA began to prepare and send messages reporting the information, which carried the caveat, "not finally evaluated intelligence."[147]

When Captain Glock studied the incoming messages identifying elements and facilities associated with landline communications, he informed Glosson that he would have to consider targeting the Baghdad bridges. One message indicated that cables were attached to the underside of the roadways of two Tigris River bridges in Baghdad. Buried fiber-optic lines connected C^2 sites and the al-Rashid Hotel and linked the Iraqi capital with the KTO.[148] News reporters from around the world, including CNN, stayed at the hotel, a component of the military C^2 system.

Information on January 11 revealed new, ominous information about the fiber-optic system: it transmitted Scud launch commands.[149] Because of the association of landline communications with Scud missiles, a raw truth confronted the planners: some high-value military targets also had a clear, overt civilian function, the targeting of which could kill many noncombatants, including foreigners, generating an international outcry and undermining the Coalition's cohesion. "We weren't allowed to hit either the Babylon Hotel, which was where a lot of leadership was staying, or the al-Rashid Hotel," Deptula noted.[150] Intelligence during the war did, indeed, reveal that fiber-optic cables ran beneath bridges in Baghdad, and air strikes hit the structures to cut the C^2 landlines.[151]

BW Targeting Revisited

The most worrisome, controversial targets in mid-December remained those in the BW set. The Iraqi BW "scared the hell out of us," recollected Colonel Christon. The big question was whether BW facilities should be struck at all, given the possibility of inadvertently releasing spores and toxins into the air with the concomitant deaths of thousands of people, perhaps a million. Horner admitted, "We were in a terrible dilemma. There were two white papers — one from England and one from the United States — that said if you bomb those biological storage areas in Iraq, every living thing on the peninsula of Saudi Arabia would die."[152] General Henry remembered a report on BW at Salman Pak, quite unlike any intelligence study he had ever read:

> It talked about how many millions of casualties could result if this crap got out in the air. I thought, "Man, if we make a mistake here....This is why Horner was exactly right not to do offensive attacks until we know what the hell we're doing. If we let somebody push us into an early air campaign where we didn't sufficiently target this stuff, we could wind up as the worst guys on earth. If we bombed this stuff, didn't kill it, and it gets out in the damn air, we could wipe out half of Southern Russia and Iran."[153]

To examine Iraqi BW capabilities and facilities and make recommendations about their disposition, DIA and CIA established an Iraqi Interagency Biological Warfare Working Group. The two agencies shared the concerns of the air planners about BW agents being released into the atmosphere as a result of bombing BW facilities. In mid-December a study undertaken by BW experts reported that air strikes against BW sites could cause a range of results from no live agents being released into the atmosphere to considerable amounts entering the air and causing significant loss of life. The study highlighted one mitigating factor: ultraviolet irradiation from sunlight accelerates the breakdown of anthrax and botulinum toxin agents.[154]

For weeks, Horner agonized over the BW problem. One day in December, however, an Army major from Fort Detrick, Maryland, a germ warfare expert, showed up at Horner's office to discuss BW agents with him. The major's main point stressed that anthrax's lethality derived from the *amount* of anthrax a person was exposed to, not merely from the fact of exposure. He told the general, "The only people who die of anthrax are people who are shearing a sheep that's ill, then they will get too much of it." As Horner recalled, the major explained how chlorine and sunlight kill anthrax spores, emphasizing that sunlight has a "tremendous impact on it."[155] The expert's explanations gave the commander "a whole different outlook on hitting the bios." Horner recounted, "I don't know who sent him but he just showed up — almost like God sent him."[156]

During the December 20 briefing in Riyadh to Cheney, Powell, and Wolfowitz, a thorough discussion of BW targets ensued. Having consulted with a lawyer from the CENTAF Judge Advocate's Office, Col. Dennis E. Kansala, USAF, who placed no legal roadblocks to launching strikes against BW sites, Horner presented a statement about the law of armed conflict to Cheney and Powell pertinent to BW targeting. It asserted that BW production and storage facilities lost their protection from attack if they directly supported military operations and the attack offered the only feasible option for ending the military support. He explained that the law required that means and method of attack be chosen to minimize the incidental loss of civilian life.[157]

The JFACC explained that airmen would take precautions when attacking BW facilities. They would employ aircraft and munitions in special sequences to minimize the escape of agents into the atmosphere. He discussed tactics, timing, and munitions. From December 20 to January 17 the considerations would change, but the intent would remain: deny the Iraqis use of this material and prevent the agents from causing collateral civilian deaths. For an individual BW bunker, the plan for the first night of the war eventually required that an F–117A attack the structure with a GBU–27 PGM to penetrate and crack it open. The agents inside would be exposed first to heat and blast from the explosion and later to sunlight. An F–111F would follow two minutes after the F–117 and deliver CBU–89 antitank, antipersonnel mines to prevent the Iraqis from gaining entry to the facility. The attacks would occur close to dawn so that sunshine would destroy agents not decimated by the initial blast and heat.[158]

Horner presented reasons to Cheney, Powell, and Wolfowitz for hitting the BW targets. He remembered Cheney asking questions during the session and Powell presenting arguments against the strikes. Horner countered the CJCS's objections. He thought the turning point came when he pointed out that collateral casualties, though unintended, might serve a useful purpose. He recalled saying, "There probably will be some people in Iraq that are killed from fallout from these BW, but that isn't all bad because a nation has to know that it incurs danger, a penalty, in building and storing these horrible weapons." The JFACC remembered Schwarzkopf near the end of the discussion addressing Cheney and stating, "If it's up to me, we are going to hit the biological storage areas."[159] After the war, the CINCCENT's memoir revealed that he had confidence in Horner's timing and sequence of attacks to minimize collateral casualties. He reasoned that by not destroying BWs, the United States could not guarantee that the Iraqis would not use them against U.S. troops — "an unforgivable sin."[160]

As far as Horner was concerned, the decision to strike BW targets was made at the December 20 meeting in Riyadh. Back in Washington, the interagency working group provided new intelligence to support this decision by downplaying the earlier dire predictions of horrendously high collateral deaths. The group ruled out any danger from strikes to Coalition troops and generally reduced the probable Iraqi casualties from the thousands to the hundreds, calculated on a bunker-by-bunker basis.[161] On January 13, 1991, Chairman Powell discussed with President Bush air strikes against BW-related facilities and gave him "our best military judgment." The CJCS stated that attacks would probably destroy the biological agents. There existed the possibility that some deadly toxins would be released. He told Bush the strikes were a gamble, but they had to be executed.[162] The President's position was that "we had to get rid of Saddam's nuclear and biological weapons capabilities."[163] The air campaign did target BW sites the first night of the war.

On January 11 Admiral McConnell sent Glosson BW-related intelligence material, which included information on the Abu Ghraib Infant Formula Plant. It identified the area of the plant that should be struck to destroy production capability.[164] This "Baghdad baby milk factory" had been first pinpointed as a potential biological site in 1983. The factory was surrounded by a nine-foot fence with a guarded gate and was located next to a major military post. In December the Iraqis painted mottled camouflage on two confirmed BW facilities — and on the "baby milk factory." The latter structure was eventually added to the target list and struck.[165]

Joint Task Force Proven Force

In January 1991, the activation of the Joint Task Force Proven Force gave a tremendous boost to the hitherto remote possibility that aircraft would fly from Turkey to strike at Iraq in offensive air operations, complicating Iraq's defense problems. As early as August 1990, air campaign planners in Checkmate and then the Black Hole had considered the option of sending aircraft from Turkey against sites in northern Iraq because, otherwise, Coalition aircraft flying the great distance from Saudi Arabia would require numerous, vulnerable tankers overflying the Iraqi airspace to support them. Despite the risks, Glosson planned to send tankers into Iraqi airspace once air supremacy was achieved.[166]

On December 27, 1990, the U.S. Air Forces in Europe Commander appointed Maj. Gen. James L. Jamerson, USAF, to be the Commander of the Joint Task Force Proven Force, and he in turn activated Proven Force at Ramstein AB, Germany, effective January 7, 1991. The task force's purpose stated: "Develop a substantial joint and combined combat capability in Turkey to deter hostilities in SWA. In the event of hostilities and with permission of [the] Turkish government, coordinate and conduct military operations in response to mission tasking from USCINCCENT." The task force was organized as a modified joint staff organization, with functions J–1 through J–6, and Jamerson had three component commanders: Commander Air Force Forces, Commander Joint Special Operations Task Force, and Commander Army Forces.[167]

Brig. Gen. Lee A. Downer, USAF, became Commander Air Force Forces and its 7440th Composite Wing (Provisional), the latter activated at Incirlik AB, Turkey, January 16, 1991. The 7440th was a composite wing, meaning it included various types of aircraft: fighter, bomber, EC, tanker, reconnaissance, and C^3. The 7440th included F–15Cs, F–16Cs, F–16Ds, F–111Es, EF–111As, F–4Gs, RF–4s, KC–135s, E–3A AWACS, and an EC–130. The wing, however, had no aircraft that delivered PGMs.[168] During the war, B–52 bombers from England and Spain flew on missions with the wing's support, but they were not assigned to the 7440th.

On January 3 in Riyadh, Horner met with Jamerson, who had been one of Horner's wing commanders years earlier, and they discussed the relationship between Proven Force and the JFACC.[169] They assigned the wing a geographic area in Iraq above the 35th parallel, which included about one-third of the country. Glosson had favored this dividing line just north of Tikrit and south of Kirkuk. After the execution of the first two days of Desert Storm operations, for which the JFACC had already generated ATOs, Proven Force would then produce its own ATOs, on the basis of the targets and times-over-targets selected in the Black Hole to optimize the impact of strikes all across Iraq. Hotline telephone links connected Proven Force with both Glosson's planners and the TACC.[170]

Although Horner incorporated Proven Force sorties into the air campaign's planning, it was unclear to the airmen if the Turkish government would allow offensive air operations from Turkish soil. On January 12, U.S. Secretary of State Baker and Turkey's President Turgut Ozal met in Ankara, and Baker found Ozal "as solid as ever." On November 7, however, the Turkish president had thought economic sanctions were working and said he was unsure if he could approve aircraft flying from Turkey to attack Iraq. Planners in Riyadh believed they had sufficient air power to conduct a successful air campaign even without Proven Force sorties.[171] Not until the war commenced did the Turkish government approve the use of the task force's assets.

Chapter Ten

Gulf War Air Campaign Plan

On December 20, 1990 in Riyadh, General Horner explained to Secretary Cheney, Chairman Powell, and General Schwarzkopf the four phases of the Gulf War air campaign and described how the Coalition would wage air warfare against Iraq. In the same month, Horner also reorganized CENTAF in two fundamental ways, each having a direct, significant impact on the air campaign's planning and execution. The arrival of additional aircraft in theater drastically intensified the planning effort in early January and resulted in the merging of the campaign's phases. Then, unexpectedly, two days before the start of Desert Storm, Schwarzkopf exploded in anger at the airmen for what he thought were serious flaws in the air plan, only to have the JFACC calm and convince the CINCCENT to stay the course.

Gulf War Air Campaign

On December 20, 1990, General Horner explained to Secretary Cheney, Under Secretary Wolfowitz, Chairman Powell, and General Schwarzkopf the four phases of the Gulf War air campaign, uniting in a single presentation the planning of General Glosson's staff for Phases I through III and that of General Corder and Colonels Crigger and Baptiste's staff for Phase IV. He briefed the theater campaign spread over approximately thirty-two days: Phase I, Strategic Air Campaign, lasting six days; Phase II, KTO Air Supremacy, needing one day; Phase IIIA, Battlefield Preparation–Republican Guard, five days; Phase IIIB, Battlefield Preparation–Kuwait, six days; and Phase IV, Ground Attack, eighteen days. He emphasized that the timing for all phases represented only estimates, not precise schedules. He had directed Glosson to "scallop the edges" on the time bars on the chart showing the phase durations to indicate that the times were only approximations.[1]

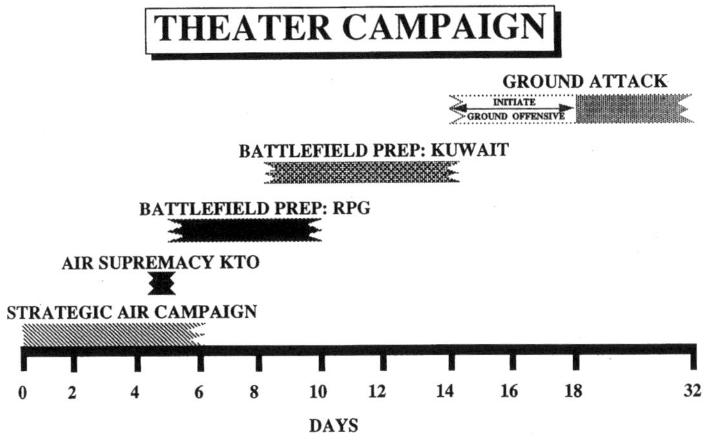

The air campaign's strike forces available by January 15 totaled 1,316 aircraft: 73 F–5s; 98 F–14s; 133 F–15Cs; 48 F–15Es; 210 F–16s; 162 F/A–18s; 64 F–111s; 36 F–117s; 105 A–6Es; 22 A–7s; 60 AV–8Bs; 144 A–10s; 42 B–52s; 53 Tornados; 28 Jaguars; 12 Mirage 2000s; 8 Mirage F1s; and 18 CF–18s.[2]

Horner presented 11 target categories, comparing the increase in number of targets in each group with the original Instant Thunder list of 84 and an early CENTCOM list of 171. The December 18 list totaled 238 targets:

Target Category	No. of Targets
Strategic air defense	28
CW and Scuds	25
Leadership	32
Republican Guard	11
C^3	26
Electricity	16
Oil	7
Railroads and bridges	28
Airfields	28
Ports	4
Military support, production, and storage	33
Total:	238[3]

Discussing strikes in the strategic air campaign, Horner highlighted airfields, the air defense environment, SAM and AAA defenses, the Scud threat, and problems associated with hitting BW production and storage facilities.[4] Cheney, who worried about Scuds against Israel, directed the airmen to "hit the Scuds first." The most intense and prolonged discussion centered on the Iraqi BW weapons.[5]

Horner cited six results expected from the Phase I strategic air campaign: destroy the regime's military C^2; destroy Iraq's ability to produce and deliver its NBC weapons; disrupt and attrit the Republican Guard; disrupt the regime's communications with the Iraqi people; destroy priority electrical power and oil storage facilities; and limit the regime's ability to replenish deployed forces.[6]

Moving to Phase II, the JFACC presented the objectives as establishing air supremacy in the KTO and creating conditions for effective attacks against ground forces.[7] The SAM-AAA threat in the KTO derived from 3,520 missiles and 1,224 guns.[8] The aircraft associated with the second phase comprised F–4Gs, F/A–18s, F–16s, F–15Es, F–111Fs, EF–111s, and EA–6Bs. The expected Phase II results would destroy all radar-directed SAM threats and achieve air supremacy in the KTO.[9]

Horner described Phase III as "shaping the battlefield" and as "battlefield preparation."[10] He explained the "level of effort" of the air campaign by highlighting three broad target categories: Iraqi air defenses, strategic targets, and targets in the KTO. Strikes would occur against air defenses and strategic facilities during Phases I and II and then continue at a reduced level of effort as the primary focus of the air campaign shifted to attacks in the KTO. The general felt more comfortable describing the air operations as a shifting level of effort than as a series of four distinct segments. About the phases, he observed,

> We had [them], but they had no meaning other than emphasis on where we were going to put our effort. We [were] going to put our effort at gaining control of the air and trying to get into the targets like biological weapons storage areas. Then we turned our full attention toward destroying things military.[11]

Horner relied on the Glosson–Checkmate computations and briefing charts to explain the effort against armor, artillery, and personnel, which stated that the Republican Guard would be attrited to the 50 percent level in those three categories by the fifth day of Phase III, and by the tenth day, the attrition rate would reach 95 percent. He noted the conservative assumptions the planners applied, that 25 percent of the aircraft in each 24-hour period would not acquire their targets.[12]

Likewise, against the armor, artillery, and personnel of the regular Iraqi army in the KTO, based on a 75 percent acquisition rate, 50 percent of the Iraqi forces would be attrited in twelve days, and 95 percent, in eighteen days.[13] Horner emphasized that the figures derived from Glosson's methodology and JMEM calculations — data from books and weapons testing, with the computer churning out numbers. Horner shared with Cheney and Powell his gut feeling that it would probably take longer to get 50 percent of the tanks and artillery than the computer printouts indicated, probably twice as long. "Cheney understands...when you talk to him like that," Horner commented. "You don't try to pull the wool over his eyes." Later in the session, Cheney asked point-blank if air power could take the Republican Guard down to the 50 percent level. Schwarzkopf said it could, but the attempt made him "nervous" because it had "never been done before."[14] (Postwar analysis indicated that air power did not reduce the Republican Guard to the 50 percent level; it did, however, sufficiently degrade the Guard's warfighting effectiveness.[15]) Horner summarized the results of the battlefield preparation phase: prepare the KTO for the offensive land war to liberate Kuwait and achieve Presidential objectives while keeping casualties to a minimum.[16]

For the land campaign in Phase IV, Horner described the air power level of effort on a round-the-clock basis. For day and night CAS in the first twenty-four hours, A–10s, AV–8Bs, F–16s, and F–5s would fly 830 sorties; for nighttime interdiction, F–111s, F–117s, A–6s, F–15Es, F–16s, and Tornados would fly 465 sorties; and for daylight interdiction, F–16s, F/A–18s, B–52s, and Jaguars would fly 735 sorties.[17] Phase IV provided both preplanned CAS and interdiction sorties. If ground commanders required unplanned CAS, interdiction sorties would be diverted. On the basis of urgency and priority, even preplanned CAS would be redirected. Horner outlined seven primary results of the entire air campaign:

- Establish air superiority over Iraq
  - Prevent air attack
  - Preclude Scud attack
- Destroy leadership communication
  - With military
  - With populace
- Destroy NBC research, production, and storage
- Destroy transportation nodes that resupply Iraqi forces in Kuwait
- Destroy 50 percent of Republican Guard's armor, artillery, and personnel
- Shape battlefield for ground forces
- Provide constant firepower for ground forces[18]

As a final briefing topic, the CENTAF commander discussed the timing of the air campaign in terms of weather and periods of available moonlight. He presented cloud ceiling and visibility information for January and February and illumination data for the weeks of Phases I–IV. He also gave the moonlight preferences for air and ground forces. The optimum period for the start of the air campaign was January 15–21.[19] Later in the session, Schwarzkopf stated that the earliest date for initiating the ground campaign was February 15, but he could not guarantee that date. The Army forces might need until March 1.[20]

Aside from the discussion on BW, Cheney and Powell had no significant questions and raised no objections to CENTCOM's air campaign plan. Although pilot casualties greatly concerned Secretary Cheney, he did not inquire about expected losses. The briefing he had received from Colonel Warden nine days earlier may have answered his concerns about attrition. In preparation for his trip to Riyadh, Cheney had visited Checkmate, and the colonel briefed him on air operations in the KTO. Warden provided anticipated U.S. aircraft losses for each of the air campaign's four phases: Phase I, 40 aircraft lost and 400 to 2,000 Iraqi civilian casualties; Phase II, 5 aircraft lost; Phase IIIA, against the Republican Guard, 35 aircraft lost; Phase IIIB, against the regular army in Kuwait, 66 aircraft lost; and Phase IV, an "unknown" number of planes shot down. Phases I to III would claim a total of 146 U.S. aircraft.[21]

CENTAF Command and Headquarters Reorganizations

With his offensive planning in good shape, Horner turned his attention to the campaign's execution, and to facilitate direction of it, he reorganized both his command and headquarters staff. In December he approved two significant changes. The first established two additional provisional air divisions within CENTAF, increasing their number from two to four and cutting his direct span of control over seventeen operational units. On December 5 he established the 14th Air Division (Provisional) to provide OPCON over ten tactical fighter wings. He appointed General Glosson the commander. He also established the 15th Air Division (Provisional) to provide OPCON of EC, reconnaissance, and C^2 aircraft, as well as miscellaneous units. The JFACC selected as this division commander General Profitt, who had arrived in theater in early November, replacing General Henry. The two other divisions were the 17th Air Division (Provisional), established on August 24, 1990, under the command of General Caruana and assigned tankers and B–52s, and the 1610th Airlift Division (Provisional), established October 31, 1990, and led by Brig. Gen. Edwin E. Tonoso.[22]

As soon as Horner appointed Glosson the commander of the 14th Air Division (Provisional), the brigadier general visited his fighter wings and flew familiarization flights in the F–15E Strike Eagle. As both the director of the planning effort and the commander of the division, he now had considerable power to ensure that the wings executed operations as he had planned them. Upon returning to Riyadh, he reported to Horner that the crews were combat-ready.[23] The JFACC wryly told him, "It will be interesting to me to see if you believe this plan is as good as you thought it was before you owned all the airplanes and all these aircrews." Shortly thereafter, Glosson tasked Lt. Col. Richard B. Lewis, USAF, who had arrived in theater in early January to be the general's special assistant and troubleshooter, to carefully review the campaign as if he were flying each mission, to discover problems. The chief planner also met with other pilots, sitting around a table to desk-fly the air plan and look for flaws. He found none of consequence.[24]

Horner's second organizational change merged the offensive and defensive air campaign planning staffs at CENTAF headquarters. He joined the Black Hole with the regular, augmented CENTAF staff that produced the ATOs.[25] The reorganization established a Directorate of Campaign Plans with Glosson in charge. The directorate consisted of four divisions: the Guidance, Apportionment, and

Targeting (GAT), ATO, ACE, and Liaison Component Divisions.[26] The GAT, headed by Col. Anthony Tolin, included the Iraqi Planning Cell headed by Colonel Deptula; the KTO Planning Cell, led by Colonel Baptiste; and six support cells: Airfields/Aircraft, CSAR, IADS, NBC, Republican Guard/Artillery, and Scuds. Col. Richard B. Bennett directed the ATO Division; Col. Mark A. Winstel headed the ACE Division; and Col. Joseph W. Robben, USMC, was in charge of the Liaison Component Division, with Capt. Lyle Bien representing the Navy.[27]

General Corder remained the CENTAF director of operations. Under the traditional CENTAF organizational structure, the director of operations was in charge of combat plans and combat operations in the TACC. On paper, Corder supervised Glosson, the director of campaign plans; however, the latter's unrestricted access to Horner and his dual hat as 14th Air Division (Provisional) commander, created an unusual chain of command in CENTAF headquarters. Glosson and Corder sometimes gave Baptiste in the KTO Cell conflicting guidance. Corder outranked Glosson, but it was not always clear to Baptiste to whom he answered. Horner knew of the fuzzy lines of authority, but believed people just had to live with it.[28]

The JFACC intended that the reorganization break the isolation of the Black Hole, bring Glosson's planners into contact with the CENTAF ATO builders, and result in a fast, frictionless generation of daily ATOs for the offensive air campaign. Majors Waterstreet and Sweeney had already prepared ATOs for the first two days of the offensive operations, but Horner's realignment would meet the requirements of a month-long campaign and the production of numerous ATOs. The changes, however, failed to eliminate the segregation of Glosson's staff and to blend the offensive and defensive planners into a smoothly operating group. After the reorganization, only a few more CENTAF staff were read into the Desert Storm plan. The vast majority of the CENTAF regulars at the headquarters, normally responsible for planning and executing air operations, remained ignorant of the offensive plan until just before the start of the air war. Secrecy still shrouded the Desert Storm planners, segregating them from the remainder of the CENTAF organization even during the war. An armed guard still barred entrance to their work area.[29] Colonel Muellner, who came to the headquarters in December to work JSTARS issues, quickly observed the isolation of Glosson's people and planning:

> I think that total isolation...probably is a good idea back in the very early stages...when you need to remain very, very covert with what your overall strategy is. Once you start executing, I think that approach is dysfunctional to efficient execution. I really do. That was always a joke to me. Of course, I had the ability to go in and out of there....But the folks in the TACC...they couldn't even get in there some of them. And I don't mean to overplay it.[30]

CENTAF staff members, who generated daily, training ATOs and produced the defensive tasking orders for Desert Shield, had forged a cooperative organization, which efficiently created the ATOs. Some of those staff members disliked the establishment of the Directorate of Campaign Plans under Glosson and the establishment of the GAT and ATO Divisions. Before the reorganization, Glosson functioned as Horner's special assistant and his Black Hole staff of about thirty kept themselves separated from the TACC and combat operations planning staff.[31] The CENTAF commander knew about the attitudinal split in his organization, but his management and leadership style was to work around it. He explained, "So we started integrating these two staffs. That was not easy. There was a lot of friction, and sometimes I would beat up on everybody then everybody would calm down. Sometimes I would let them beat up on me. It was just a way of handling people."[32]

The TACC operated at one end of the basement of the RSAF building; the GAT and Glosson's people occupied the other end; and the ATO builders and their CAFMS equipment worked in the center.[33] The reorganization involved a physical relocation of the TACC from the bubble-tent behind the RSAF building to the basement, where the Black Hole had moved in October. As Col. Allan M. Doman of the TACC explained:

> We were in the bubble for almost all of Desert Shield,...screaming bloody murder about the vulnerability of that location in the parking lot, with all the high-rises surrounding us that could lob shells in and kill us and take out the equipment, it was only when the Saudis finally recognized that we were really going to go to war that just prior to Christmas they allowed us to move into the basement.[34]

Deptula bemoaned, "I mean, it just got crazy," describing the beginning of January with the reorganization underway and people pulling down walls and rebuilding them, boxing and carrying files, and moving office and computer equipment, all the while he was updating the MAP to incorporate additional aircraft as they arrived in theater. Those days were "very hectic," he recalled.[35]

Iraqi–Strategic Targeting Cell

As head of the Iraqi Planning Cell, Deptula met with his staff on January 6 and exhorted them to understand the significance of the impending air campaign. When he began to address the group, he referred to the "big adventure" ahead, and the members applauded, cheered, and whistled. Calming them, he said:

> Now, obviously, I don't need to give everybody a pep talk, but one of the things I wanted to do in this meeting is ensure that everybody's got the proper focus. And on a serious note, if you haven't thought about it, we are about to embark on an event that is going to make airpower

> history. It's going to be unprecedented in the history of air power and for that matter it's going to be unprecedented in military history, and it's serious as well. You know as well as I do that your [buddies] and mine have got their lives out there on the line, and what we need to do is ensure that whatever we do helps save the maximum amount of U.S. and allied lives possible. We can do that by ensuring the success of the strategic air campaign.[36]

Deptula riveted his attention on the strategic operations. In fact, he referred to his cell as the Strategic Targeting Cell rather than the Iraqi Cell, because in planning strikes, he would send sorties to Kuwait, not just to Iraq, to hit strategic targets such as the Kari SOC at al-Salem.[37]

Because the reorganization was meant to bring Glosson's planners into closer cooperation with Colonel Bennett's and Lt. Col. Jeffrey S. Feinstein's ATO builders, Deptula devised charts to illustrate the relationship between the MAP and the ATO and how the interaction would unfold. A "dynamic planning process" would occur over 72 hours, a 3-day period. On day 1, the GAT Division would produce the MAP and guidance letters and translate these into target sheets, a format familiar to the CENTAF staff. On day 2, the ATO Division would use the sheets to generate the ATO, with appropriate data on airspace deconfliction, tanker tracks, and SPINS, and transmit the ATO to the units. On day 3, the ACE Division and the TACC would oversee and facilitate the execution of the tasking order.[38]

Various members of the CENTAF staff had differing opinions about the value of Deptula's MAP. For years, Feinstein had generated an ATO without a MAP, so he denigrated the importance of the innovation, saying it was neither *master* nor a *plan.*[39] Because Deptula had designed a way to make the MAP look like the normal input received to build an ATO — target-planning worksheets — Feinstein may not have understood that the MAP generated the sheets. Colonel Doman in the TACC, however, saw value in the document:

> The Master Attack Plan was, as a piece of paper, a lifesaver to me in combat operations because it went the next step beyond the Guidance and Apportionment Letter in telling me what the target set was of critical importance to that day's ATO....I thought it was a wonderful piece of paper, very effective, very efficient.[40]

Horner asked Deptula to do a dry run of the briefing process he would use to apprise Schwarzkopf of the progress of strikes planned by the Iraqi–Strategic Cell. In preparing the presentation, Deptula and Feinstein discussed the term *strategic,* which the Black Hole planner favored as a mission category, but Feinstein rejected, noting that *strategic* was not used in CENTAF's ATO format. Deptula showed him a copy of Air Force Manual 1–1 that identified the airpower role as *strategic* aerospace offense. Deptula did not want to push CENTAF too hard so he listed interdiction and strategic offense as a single mission category in briefings and the air guidance letters. He later regretted that he did not insist that *interdiction* missions be counted and briefed separately from *strategic* strikes.[41]

ATO Production Test

On January 11 and 12, Glosson tested the GAT and ATO Divisions to see how well the GAT could produce the MAP and target worksheets and pass them to the ATO builders for use in generating the ATO and other essential data. Unbeknownst to the ATO production staff, Deptula used the MAP for the third day of the air campaign as the test material. The targets, attack times, and sorties were real. Glosson, however, did not send the ATO to the units as part of the test. Until now, Horner had not allowed his staff to create an ATO for the third day of the air campaign, fearing that too much prewar planning would impose unacceptable rigidity on operations. He reasoned, "I didn't let them do the first 2½ or 3 days because I didn't want to become a slave to a 10- or 20-day ATO because we wouldn't have any flexibility. War is chaos, managing chaos."[42] The JFACC, however, did not foresee how smoothly, all in all, the first two days would unfold, and under those circumstances it would have helped to have had basic, preplanned ATOs to execute, with modifications made as BDA, weather, and contingencies required. The TLAMs required a few days to program their guidance systems, and more preplanned ATOs would have facilitated Navy planning. Deptula still developed the MAP manually and gave the data to a clerk to input into a word-processing program. During Desert Shield he had tried to get help in designing an interactive database to accommodate the information, coordinating with a computer-literate officer from the Judge Advocate's Office, but they never developed a workable program. In the evaluation of the ATO generation exercise, the most sweeping and ominous of the recommendations stated, "Simplify tanker planning to speed overall ATO process."[43] The CENTAF organization could have used many more days to practice generating an ATO to launch the maximum possible number of sorties.

By the start of the air war, the GAT and ATO Divisions had not crafted procedures to generate on schedule an ATO that compared in length and intricacy to the first day's document. The main problem revealed itself during the scheduling of aerial refueling and tanker operations. After Deptula and his staff produced the MAP and target worksheets and Feinstein's group (the fraggers) built their portion of the ATO, the document passed to the STRATFOR planners in the ATO Division to identify the tanker tracks (areas, orbits, and altitudes) and refueling schedules. At that point, the complexity of the tasking order and the vast number of sorties required more time for planning than the war allowed. General Corder explained the tanking design for the first two days of the air war:

> The first two-day plan was a thing of exquisite beauty, in terms of integration and coordination, especially with the tankers, because we wanted to get every possible bomb up there we could, at the right time

> and right coordinates to take advantage of every advantage we could take. Consequently, sometimes to make a change it would take a week. For example, if you wanted to take one flight of four, it might take a week to get the change done because that would impact on tankers, the tankers would impact on something else, and it involved a tremendous coordination process to decide how to do that.

The general then described what happened during the war in trying to generate the third day's ATO:

> Then they gave the whole thing to the tanker guys about 4 hours before the ATO was due to be published, and it was absolute chaos! The tanker guys would get up to about 40 or 45 of these packages, and they would run out of tankers because they didn't have time to do the exquisite planning that had been done on the first two days which had gone on for weeks and weeks before. So the…day's ATO was a shambles, it was only about a 45 or 50 percent ATO, the first 12 to 13 hours (of a 24-hour plan).[44]

CENTAF sent the ATOs to the wings late for days 3, 4, and 5, and included fewer sorties in them than Glosson expected; the daily shortage of sorties was about 50 or 60. Bad weather led to multiple, cascading changes in the document. Too few airborne tankers, or those in the wrong place, caused many sortie cancellations. At this point, Glosson immersed himself in the effort to improve the aerial refueling procedures. He huddled with Corder; General Caruana, STRATFOR commander; Major Hente, a tanker planner; and Major Sweeney, an ATO builder. Relying on his experience with tanking operations during the Vietnam War, Glosson helped resolve the problem by establishing two tanker tracks to operate 24 hours a day. He telephoned the F–111, F–15E, and A–10 wings and told them to refuel at those new tracks anytime, day or night, which simplified the planning requirements and shortened the time necessary to complete the ATO. Corder and Caruana agreed not to task all the tankers, but to leave some unscheduled for flexibility in meeting unanticipated requirements.[45]

Merging Campaign Phases

From Glosson's perspective, the most significant change to the air campaign plan from October 11, when he briefed the plan for President Bush, to January 17, when the war started, was the merging of the campaign's phases. The increase in the number of aircraft, resulting from the President's November 8 order to double the size of the Desert Shield forces, allowed, indeed, required, that Deptula and Rogers in the Iraqi–Strategic Cell and Baptiste in the KTO Cell plan strikes against targets across the target categories identified for Phases I through III. An additional fourteen fighter squadrons, two bomber squadrons, and eleven squadrons of airlift and tanker aircraft arrived in theater.[46]

Corder's lobbying to increase the intensity of the SEAD campaign contributed to the merging process. As soon as the general came to Riyadh in November, he carefully reviewed the air plan and generously praised it.[47] He did see, however, one aspect that needed improvement: SEAD. He thought a greater effort should go into actually bombing and destroying all components of SAM sites, not just launching HARMs against radars. He asked why A–10s and F/A–18s sat idle the first night. When told that they were reserve aircraft, Corder vigorously disagreed. He did not concur with all aircraft not joining the fight against the chance that the Iraqis would launch a ground attack. He remembered his angry retort:

> That is a bunch of baloney. That is the biggest bunch of baloney I ever heard. We have got to go talk to Horner and Schwarzkopf. You don't hold airplanes in reserve; you go jump on them. If they attack, fine. Let them attack. We will just redirect the forces. With a telephone call, we can have them go do close air support. It's like holding artillery in reserve; you don't hold any of that stuff in reserve.[48]

According to Glosson, the CINCCENT prohibited the employment of aircraft associated with CAS, such as A–10s, too early in the campaign for fear the Iraqis would attrit them too heavily before they could perform their dedicated mission.[49] Instant Thunder had originally held the Warthogs in reserve to satisfy concerns that if the Iraqis invaded Saudi Arabia in August or September, the A–10s and other aircraft would strike them as Instant Thunder was executed. Colonel Warden's book, *The Air Campaign*, devoted an entire chapter to discussing the importance of holding aircraft in reserve.[50] Besides, A–10s would not fly deep into Iraq and conduct strategic attacks, so they might as well be called reserves as they sat idle. Explaining his and Horner's view, General Henry recalled, "Well, our thoughts also were that if we were to initiate air operations against the north, we should always have in reserve holding down here sufficient forces to deal with an invasion."[51] Corder's view highlighted the speed, flexibility, and range of air power to negate the value of reserves. Employed aircraft, if needed, could perform the missions assigned to reserve aircraft; otherwise those assets ought to contribute to the active, massive use of fire power. Corder's view was not unlike Horner's idea on Push CAS: do not waste air power by having it sit idly on alert when it could be employed on preplanned missions and then diverted elsewhere as urgently needed.

In January Horner "broke loose" the A–10s and gave them to Glosson to use at the start of the air war. The freeing of the Warthogs pleased the commander of the 14th Air Division (Provisional) who now owned the aircraft. He recounted, "I couldn't live with myself having those kids sitting on the ground doing nothing."[52] Planners put the A–10s into the MAP and ATO for the first twenty-four hours to hit EWR sites and the Nukhayb IOC (which F–117s would strike earlier); to attack ground forces in the tri-border area; and to stand continuous alert,

A–10 Thunderbolt II

starting at H-hour, to attack specified Iraqi ground forces, as directed by the Marine Corps's Direct Air Support Center via the 354th Tactical Fighter Wing.[53]

Colonel Sawyer, the commander of the 23d Tactical Fighter Wing (Provisional) which flew A–10s, welcomed the Warthogs in the first day's MAP. He told Horner during the conflict,

> When we were all anticipating this war, the A–10 was envisioned as a classic CAS asset, working the forward edges of an advancing force of enemy armor. When we went offensive, I was delighted the A–10s had a role. It made sense for us to take out the lightly defended EWR/GCI sites along the southern Iraqi border and to introduce the frontline Iraqi divisions to the violence of warfare.[54]

To plan strikes for the A–10s and numerous other aircraft that had arrived in theater as a result of the Desert Shield second-wave deployment, Deptula relied on Baptiste in the KTO Cell to share the tasking workload. He handed over A–10s, B–52s, and F–16s used against the Republican Guard and targets in the KTO not associated with the strategic campaign.[55]

The merging of the three phases became more noticeable as the increase in forces allowed for the scheduling of additional sorties. In the initial twenty-four hours of the air war, during the original Phase I time frame, A–10s hitting KTO radar sites would strike Phase II targets, and Warthogs attacking troops in the tri-border area would bomb Phase IIIB targets. F–16s would strike Phase II SAM sites in Phase I. As the allies joined the air campaign, some of their aircraft, like the Saudi F–5s, Bahranian F–16s, and French Jaguars, were short-legged, unable to fly deep to hit Phase I facilities in Iraq, so they flew their first sorties against Phases II and III KTO targets. If Iraqi artillery fired on Coalition forces during Phase I, Marine Corps aircraft would immediately attack these Phase III targets.

Shortly before the air war started, Glosson called the CINCCENT's attention to the phase-merging process. He remembered:

> We're sitting there with General Schwarzkopf in his command post, which he called his war room. He asked me a question. I said, "Sir, Phases I, II, and III are going to occur simultaneously. That's the way you must think." I said, "Don't misunderstand me, I know we have Phases I, II, and III. We are doing Phases I, II, and III simultaneously." He laughed and said, "Well, Buster, you finally got your way." I said, "No, Sir, we have a four-phase operation here, but we are going to do the first three phases simultaneously."[56]

From the perspective of the KTO Cell, Baptiste clearly saw the phases meld.[57] He agreed with Horner's view that the execution should occur as the level of effort shifted. Deptula noted the phase-merging and tried to ensure that the air campaign planners kept some pressure on Phase I targets throughout the war, even as the phases blended and the intensity moved to Phase III. His ace in the Black Hole for doing this was to continue to task the PGM systems almost exclusively against Phase I sites. Although the Coalition had far fewer PGM-capable aircraft in theater than it had conventional assets, PGMs served as force multipliers.[58]

Even with additional aircraft, Deptula generally kept intact his targeting-for-effects methodology with respect to the use of F–117As against high-value targets. More Nighthawks arrived in theater in December, but the planner immediately tasked those platforms against other critical facilities. He did not systematically use them to restrike sites for which stealth attacks were already planned.[59] He did add a second F–117 to fly against the Iraqi air defense headquarters building, one of the most important targets associated with the IADS. Deptula — and Glosson — depended totally on the skill of two pilots and the accuracy of only two GBU–27 laser-guided weapons to hit the nerve center of the Iraqi air defense system.[60]

KTO Cell

Horner and Glosson chose Colonel Baptiste to head the KTO Cell because Baptiste had been intimately involved with building the defensive ATOs and had focused on Iraqi army targets throughout Desert Shield. From Horner's perspective, once the Black Hole developed the Reflex plan, the JFACC would no longer execute ATO Bravo if the Iraqis attacked Saudi Arabia; instead, Reflex would initially answer the invasion, followed by the Desert Storm offensive air campaign. Baptiste was now free to work in the KTO Cell.

Horner thought of Phase III analysis as something the computer produced, based on Glosson's assumptions, JMEM data, and sortie rates. "It had nothing to do with the Army," he observed, meaning that up to that point, ARCENT and the

Lt. Col. William G. Welch

Corps commanders had not influenced the analytical process to show how air power would meet the 50 percent attrition requirement. To acquire target nominations from the ground commanders, the JFACC directed Baptiste to work closely with the Army's representative in the TACC, Colonel Welch, and his BCE. Welch had already extensively collaborated with Baptiste and the CENTAF staff throughout Desert Shield to produce the D-day and the D-day Bravo ATOs.[61] Surprisingly, two days before the start of the air campaign, ARCENT Commander General Yeosock thought the head of the BCE required more rank, so he sent Col. David A. Schulte, USA, to the TACC to head the element. Welch stayed on and worked the night shift. Schulte had to hastily and swiftly familiarize himself with the BCE, the TACC, the ATO process, and the air war plan. He would coordinate closely with the ARCENT Deep Operations Cell, which the Third Army had just established. According to Welch, "The [ARCENT] cell wasn't fully manned until just before Desert Storm, which didn't allow the new personnel enough time to train for their mission."[62]

Horner wanted the KTO Cell to rely on the Army, through the BCE, to nominate targets, just as he wanted ARCENT to track the BDA for Phase III. "I'm not going to pick which Army target gets hit," he asserted, "because I knew we were going to hit them all." Baptiste, indeed, relied heavily on Army target lists. He recalled, "Let's face it, most of the targets in the KTO we were working on came from Army nominations, although the Marines nominated some in and around Kuwait, Kuwait City in there, especially when they started thinking about whether they were going to do an amphibious landing or not."[63] Heavy reliance on the BCE for Army target nominations accorded with CENTAF's standard operating procedures. CENTAF Regulation 55–45 stated "[The BCE] maintains a continuous dialog with ARCENT and the Army Corps on the status of the current battle to include updating the Army's prioritized interdiction target listing."[64]

The head of the ARCENT Deep Operations Cell, Lt. Col. Bart Engram, USA, passed on to CENTAF the targeting objectives the Army wanted hit prior to the start of Phase IV, G-day, and two days hence, on G+2. These comprised general target categories and desired effects. For the pre-G-day Phase III, the Army asked for strikes against Iraqi C^3; Iraqi deep-strike capability from fixed and rotary-wing aircraft and from Scud and Frog missiles; combat forces; intelligence systems; and logistics.[65]

Although not noticeable at first, a problem with the telephone line from the ARCENT Deep Operations Cell into the BCE would exacerbate communication problems between Army commanders and the JFACC's staff. Only a single, regular telephone line connected the cell and the BCE, and the Deep Operations Mission Manager at ARCENT headquarters had to compete with others for switch time on the totally inadequate phone connection. A postwar Army report concluded:

> The Mission Manager was unable to respond effectively to the corps or the ARCENT commander when there was a requirement to divert aircraft from one target to another, or to change the FSCL....This limitation was both a hindrance to operations and a danger to friendly troops on the ground. During this war, many opportunities to strike the enemy a devastating blow were lost because the Mission Manager was unable to talk directly to the BCE when the telephone switch was tied up. The Deep Operations Mission Manager must be able to transmit and receive secure real-time data from both the BCE and the commands subordinate to ARCENT.[66]

Colonel Christon had provided intelligence for the development of the defensive air planning, and he now continued to assist Baptiste with KTO targeting. ARCENT sent representatives to Christon's staff to assist the airmen.[67] The Marine Corps representative, Major Olsen, moved from the Black Hole to the KTO Cell to assist with Marine targeting.[68]

For the defensive ATOs, Baptiste had worked with an informal, joint targeting board, whose members consisted of component liaison officers (captains, majors, and lieutenant colonels) at CENTAF headquarters. He continued to work with the board within the KTO Cell, and, as time wore on, more informally with individual members, not the board per se.[69] He relied on the officers to prioritize target nomination lists from MARCENT, ARCENT, and the Arab forces, and he relied on them at times when the BCE failed to provide enough valid targets or failed to prioritize their nominations. Before the war, Schwarzkopf had not convened a formal Joint Targets Coordination Board of senior component representatives at CENTCOM headquarters. Over the years, by an informal, evolutionary process during training exercises, the joint targeting board had come to consist of junior officers, with a CENTAF representative acting as chair, and it met at the JFACC level.[70] The board's sitting at CENTAF, instead of at CENTCOM, was a peacetime development untested by the stress of war. During Desert Storm in February, the CINCCENT's new deputy, General Waller, would chair a board that produced a prioritized target list. Baptiste welcomed valid Army target nominations from any source.

The KTO Cell planned to do direct and indirect targeting. The former involved identifying specific targets and assigning sorties against them in the ATO. Indirect targeting sent airborne pilots to second parties such as ABCCC or JSTARS for instructions, or to kill boxes where aviators hit either targets of opportunity or those assigned. Having incorporated kill boxes into the defensive ATOs and Phase IV, Baptiste used the concept in the KTO Cell.[71] During the war, innovations that the planners did not foresee included F–16s flying scout missions and F–111Fs, F–15Es, and A–6Es expending laser-guided munitions against tanks, artillery, and APCs in "tank-plinking" strikes. From Horner's perspective, overseeing Baptiste's KTO Cell and Deptula's Iraqi–Strategic Cell, he saw significantly different targeting processes at work. Referring to the cells' targets and procedures, he explained:

> You don't have the collateral damage aspects [in the KTO], and it's open-ended. You can take as much time as you want. [In contrast], you've got to get control of the air very quickly. You've got to get the biological, chemical, and nuclear sites hit very quickly. You've got to get the Scud fixed launchers hit very quickly, so all these point targets have to be done very quickly. Hitting tanks and artillery is a level of effort thing. You also are just going to do it until you get it done.[72]

The Iraqi Cell transferred all of its Phase II and III analysis to the KTO Cell, but Baptiste soon had to solve problems not thoroughly addressed, such as the Iraqi berms and revetments for armor and equipment and an acute shortage of EC assets for KTO operations. In solving the latter problem, Baptiste would provide areawide electronic jamming for multiple sortie packages instead of building mission packages with self-contained jamming support. F–4Gs flew as "Weasel Police," providing presence and protecting aircraft in their sector.[73]

Two conditions beyond the control of Baptiste and his unit threatened to confuse air operations in the KTO, once they began. First, a disconnect loomed

Planning Phase III targeting in the KTO Cell are (from left to right around the table) Brig. Gen. Glenn A. Profitt, Lt. Col. Richard Lewis, Brig. Gen. Buster Glosson, and Col. Anthony Tolin.

between the Corps's and the CINCCENT's targeting emphasis. On the surface, the Corps commanders and Schwarzkopf should have been in harmony regarding the level of effort against targets in the air campaign's Phase IIIA, the Republican Guard, and those in its Phase IIIB, the regular Iraqi army. Serious fissures, however, had already occurred between the Corps commanders' and the CINCCENT's perspectives. On November 14 during Schwarzkopf's initial briefing of his four-phase Desert Storm plan to his ground commanders, General Franks of the VII Corps openly disagreed with his commander about the number of ground forces allocated to him to achieve his assigned objective. Franks and the CENTCOM commander did not see the big picture from the same viewpoint. The CINCCENT, like the JFACC, thought in terms of the entire theater as his AOR, but the Corps tactical commanders viewed the battlefield more narrowly, focusing on their own, individual sectors.[74] Schwarzkopf would basically target the theater from north to south, from the Republican Guard to the frontline troops in Phases IIIA and IIIB. The Corps commanders' nominations reflected a south-to-north emphasis, their great concern being targets immediately in front of them.[75] Different outlooks produced different priorities. Baptiste in the KTO Cell would receive sets of target nominations from the ground commanders, and another set, in terms of expressed level of effort, from the CINCCENT. The KTO Cell and the JFACC would be caught in the middle. The CINCCENT's directives would prevail, but misunderstanding about the CENTAF commander's responsiveness to the Corps would develop.

After the war, Horner and Christon commented on the KTO Cell targeting process in the context of the CENTCOM war plan. The JFAAC explained:

> The thing that really messes it up is you have this planning process for doing the KTO, and you go to the Army and say, "What do you want? What do you think is most important?" They tell you, then you take it down to Schwarzkopf and he says, "That's all bullshit. Here is what I want you to do." You just get a pencil and paper and listen.[76]

Christon's view echoed that of his boss:

> Quite honestly a lot of problems with Army targeting, when you hear the guys at the divisions and the corps complaining about it, had absolutely nothing to do with the Air Force. They had to do with the United States Army and the fact that their priorities didn't match up necessarily with the priorities of their next upper echelon, and ultimately with General Schwarzkopf's priorities. And *that* is where a lot of the disconnect happened, not between the Army and the Air Force, although we get tarred with that brush, and that is very unfair tarring.[77]

Baptiste recalled his frustrating wartime experience of receiving Army target nominations not in accord with the CINCCENT's targeting priorities:

> I would get guidance back from General Glosson from the evening CINCCENT's meeting on the effort that we wanted to do day after tomorrow. As an example I think of, the CINCCENT was still wanting to put pressure on the Republican Guards, and I would get specific guidance on what weight of effort to put on, say, Medina and Tawakalna, the two we were going to concentrate on that day. So that is the guidance I would leave my night guys.
>
> Well, the word wasn't getting down through General Yeosock and the ARCENT channels to their targeting function, who provided the Army inputs to the prioritized target lists. As a result, we would get a prioritized target list that had most of the targets on the infantry units down on the border. Now, the two didn't match up.[78]

The second major problem concerned the shift in level of effort from Phase IIIA to Phase IIIB, which depended on BDA results, as did the shift to Phase IV. The changes in emphasis would occur as the CINCCENT saw that air power had met his 50 percent attrition goal. ARCENT and MARCENT held responsibility for the BDA, but neither component had ever undertaken the task of tracking air power's systematic destruction of a fielded army through air counterland operations. If they failed to accurately discern the progress of the air campaign, the entire war effort could be thrown off.

During the conflict, CENTCOM's JIC developed its own BDA reporting system, based on inputs from MARCENT and ARCENT, on the number of tanks, APCs, and artillery pieces destroyed, and on consideration of bridges destroyed, communications degraded, supplies interdicted, and troop morale.[79] The staff displayed results on charts marked with red, green, or yellow disks for each Iraqi division, indicating the level of attrition achieved: 0–25 percent showed red; 25–50 percent, yellow; and 50 percent and greater, green.[80] Once Schwarzkopf saw a green disk telling him that the unit had been sufficiently degraded and an attack against it could proceed, he did not want the airmen to hit the unit anymore, despite requests by the Corps commanders.[81]

Neither should the aviators strike targets in western Iraq too early in the campaign so as not to alert the Iraqis of the shift of thousands of ground troops and trucks secretly moving westward for the CINCCENT's grand flanking strategy. He wanted the Iraqis to continue thinking that the main ground attack would come from Kuwait or up the Wadi al-Batin, definitely not from western Iraq.[82] If Corps commanders' target nominations interfered with Schwarzkopf's deception plans, the targets were not hit when requested, contributing to perceptions that the JFACC ignored Army inputs. In addition, General Corder noted that the CINCCENT wanted to ensure that the Saudi, Syrian, and Egyptian sector received sufficient air power to facilitate the Arab forces' attack through heavy Iraqi defenses. General Khalid al-Saud bluntly told Schwarzkopf that his troops would not budge an inch until a "satisfactory ratio between attacking and defending forces" was achieved, which meant that air strikes had to attrit to the 50 percent level the Iraqi tanks and guns opposite the Arab forces.[83]

Weather diversions, bombing inaccuracies, and outdated, invalid Army nominations would also result in Corps commanders' thinking that airmen were not servicing their target lists. "Horner's F–16 pilots used Stewart's [ARCENT G–2] six-digit locations to set their inertial guidance systems to fly to the targets," reported an Army publication after the war, "only to find nothing and then divert to secondary targets less important to corps commanders' desires."[84] A B–52 target planner recalled, "The Army supplied intelligence information that was not helpful from the Air Force point of view. The coordinates were erratic, usually a mile off, or even as much as ten miles off. At times, the information was weeks old."[85] When the JFACC had to divert aircraft to the enormous Scud-hunting enterprise, even fewer Coalition aircraft were available to strike KTO targets. During the war, Colonel Schulte, the BCE head, also found a problem, the unsatisfactory "5-3-2-2" process, which contributed to the Corps commanders' frustration and derived from ARCENT and Army procedures. After visiting ARCENT headquarters, he recorded in his notes on February 20, 1991:

> Given permission by G–3 [Brig. Gen. Steve Arnold of ARCENT]. I am to go into his Deep Operations shop and make recommendations to him on how to improve their operations. I spend about 5 hours there, observing the development of the ARCENT target list....I find that Cpt..., OIC [officer in charge] for the target list development, is using a standard 5, 3, 2, 2 rotating target nomination acceptance standard for ARCENT, VII Corps, 18 ABC [Airborne Corps], and NAC [Northern Area Command (Arabic)] submitted targets. That is, he simply puts on the ARCENT list in priority order the first 5 from the ARCENT G–2 list, the first 3 from the VII Corps list, the first 2 from the 18 ABC list, and the first 2 from the NAC list. Then he goes on with the next 5 from the ARCENT G–2 list, etc. I asked if this changed daily, and he said no. I asked if this was approved by the G–3; answer, no. (Looks like an Iron Captain has made a command decision.) I submitted a handwritten report to the G–3 and then got back to the BCE.[86]

Finally, another aspect of misunderstanding between the ground and air leaders stemmed from the CINCCENT not assigning a date for the start of Phase IV. The beginning of the land campaign would depend on the progress of the air operations and the degradation of the enemy army to a level sufficient to guarantee victory on the ground with a minimum of casualties. On November 14 in Dhahran, the CINCCENT had suggested that the air campaign would be completed within three weeks. When Glosson briefed the Phase III counterland operations to the ground commanders at Eskan Village at the end of December, he stated that the air campaign's Phases I through III could be completed in as little as two weeks. By the end of January, therefore, the Corps commanders may have misjudged the imminence of the ground war and become angry when their target nominations were not immediately hit, blaming the JFACC for not adequately preparing the battlefield for them.[87] Despite the commanders' discomfort, Schwarzkopf and Horner would effectively wield the air weapon in the KTO and send more than 35,000 sorties there. A report by the VII Corps after the war spoke of air power's effectiveness: "With hindsight, it appears that targets key to Corps plan were ultimately hit (222 targets) — over time — but not as fast as Corps expected....Bottom line is that the effect of air-delivered fires did clearly set the stage for minimum exploitation."[88]

Bridges and the Republican Guard comprised target sets in both Phases I and III. Deptula, who worked cordially and well with Baptiste, assumed responsibility for the bridges. "He fragged a lot of bridges up on the river," recalled Baptiste. "Actually, that is what we said was the northern border of the KTO Cell, but either one of us could have fragged those. I think he kept fragging the bridges up until the end."[89] Deptula gave Baptiste's KTO Cell responsibility for the Republican Guard as well as the B–52s allocated to strike Guard targets.[90]

Schwarzkopf "was always terrified that the Republican Guard was going to escape and that they were going to get up into Iraq," recalled Horner. The CINCCENT feared they would decamp and move into Baghdad, or simply disperse. At the meeting in Dhahran on November 14, the CINCCENT had, indeed, explained that he wanted the airmen to destroy bridges to seal off the Republican Guard's escape routes and to attrit the elite forces by air.[91] Members of STRATFOR, Captain Hawkins, Capt. Richard Cleary, and Capt. James Wright, planned B–52 strikes, and Hawkins and Cleary moved into the KTO Cell. They believed that Schwarzkopf had specifically asked for B–52 strikes against the Guard. Indeed, during the Internal Look exercise in July 1990, the CINCCENT had requested massive B–52 raids against Iraqi troop concentrations. (The CINCCENT and JFACC had OPCON of the B–52s.) Black Hole planners had intended to use the massive bombers against the Republican Guard, but not until Iraqi air defenses had been sufficiently degraded to allow the vulnerable old aircraft to fly in the KTO.[92]

The MAP revealed that the first B–52 strikes against Republican Guard targets would occur in the first 24-hour period of the air campaign. At 2100, three B–52s, accompanied by four F–4Gs for SEAD and four F–15Cs in a protective sweep, would hit the Tawakalna Mechanized Infantry Division. In the second 24-hour period, at 0100–0115 and at 0250–0300, B–52 packages would again hit the Tawakalna. After these initial strikes, the Guard would come under attack by three B–52s every three hours for the remainder of the war.[93]

The Republican Guard in the KTO consisted of three heavy and five infantry divisions, including special forces. The heavy armored, mechanized divisions — the Tawakalna, Hammurabi, and Medina — all positioned themselves in Iraq along the Iraqi-Kuwaiti border. Newly formed Guard units also held positions in northern Iraq, and aircraft flying from Incirlik in Turkey would hit them, but these forces ranked lower than C^3, weapons production and storage, electricity, oil, airfields, and aircraft on the Proven Force target list.[94]

The Guard formed part of the Iraqi three-tiered KTO theater defense. First, on the Kuwaiti-Saudi border and along the Gulf coast, regular army infantry divisions occupied positions behind extensive, formidable barriers, dubbed the Saddam Line. Artillery units supporting them held lines farther back. In the second tier, armored and mechanized troops of the regular army held areas behind the artillery. These were the troops that would launch counterattacks against advancing Coalition forces. Finally, the Republican Guard located along the Iraqi-Kuwaiti border functioned as the reserve force.[95]

The Guard posed formidable challenges for the B–52s. STRATFOR planners actually preferred not to use the heavy bombers against them and thought these aircraft should strike targets more suitable to their capabilities, such as sprawling petroleum facilities, huge ammunition storage depots, logistics bases, and sites like the Taji military complex, packed with factories, barracks, and bunkers over several square miles. Because the CINCCENT insisted that the B–52s attack the dispersed elite forces, STRATFOR planners confronted the problem of targeting moving ground forces. Even if the Guard remained stationary, the planners lacked imagery revealing the locations of the troops. By late October, the STRATFOR planners had submitted formal requests through intelligence channels for photographs, but they never arrived at the Black Hole. In November, knowing that accurate coordinates from imagery were essential for effective targeting, Captain Hawkins began shopping around for an aircraft platform to supply timely images and coordinates. He considered four systems and, after investigating each, decided that the TR–1's ASARS looked promising.[96]

During his research with Captains Cleary and Wright, they learned that the Army operated an ASARS van near CENTAF headquarters which received real-time radar imagery and precise coordinates (coordinates more accurate than JSTARS provided, the officers would later learn).[97] The ASARS downlink would enable planners to "see" Republican Guard units on radar, day or night, in all weather, and obtain coordinates that they could send to B–52 crews, either on the ground or airborne. Horner and Corder approved the captains' plan to test their ASARS proposal, and in December during the Night Camel exercises their "dynamic targeting" concept showed good results. Corder enthusiastically pushed use of ASARS targeting procedures.[98]

Unbeknownst to anyone before the war, ASARS-derived targeting coordinates were in error. The relative location of the TR–1 aircraft to the ASARS downlink van and the pointing angle of the ASARS sensor determined a target's coordinates. Unfortunately, contractors had entered into the new ASARS computer system incorrect coordinates denoting the exact position of the van in the soccer field. The discrepancy arose because of confusion between coordinates expressed in degrees–minutes–seconds and those given in degrees–minutes–decimal minutes. As a result, the coordinates for the van were incorrect by nearly 700 yards. Since the B–52s had radar-controlled bombsights and the radar navigator could drop bombs based on radar returns, the coordinate error did not necessarily matter. The navigator could "roll the ball," move the radar crosshair, and search for the target. This error could affect bombing accuracy, however, when the faulty target coordinates were used with offset bombing procedures. (F–15s, F–16s, and F–111s flying against fielded forces were also given ASARS-derived coordinates.) Captain Cleary discovered the error and corrected it on February 18.[99]

STRATFOR planners in the KTO Cell repeatedly had difficulties with the intelligence community's routine use of degrees–minutes–seconds coordinates, whereas the B–52's avionics system and the ASARS used the degrees–minutes–decimal minutes format. A variety of mapping systems complicated the coordinate problem. Materials produced by the DMAAC were in World Geodetic System 84 and World Geodetic System 72, and target nominations came to the STRATFOR planners based on geographic, geodetic, and Army grid systems, all of which slowed the planning process in a fast-paced war as coordinate systems had to be identified and converted.[100]

Accurate bombing by the B–52s also posed a challenge because Horner and Glosson had determined that once the radar-guided SAM threat was lessened, aircraft would fly at medium or high altitude to avoid the AAA and infrared-homing SAMs. During peacetime, however, SAC's B–52s practiced at low altitudes. B–52s crews had to make adjustments to their tactics and equipment when flying at the higher altitudes. B–52 mission planners and crews had a variety of weapons and fuzes to mate for appropriate effects, but no peacetime training against dug-in troops had validated the best combinations. Prompt BDA feedback to planners and crews would assist them in adjusting their tactics, but assessments would arrive slowly, if at all. About the time the ASARS coordinate error was discovered, SAC sent to the theater the test results of B–52s flying at higher altitudes on U.S. test ranges. The data led all B–52 units to make allowances for consistent errors of 400 to 600 feet when selecting their DMPIs for high-level bombing. Pilots of other aircraft slated as the workhorses against the Republican Guard — A–10s and F–16s — would also have to change tactics and adjust their equipment to accommodate sorties flown at altitudes higher than those at which they had practiced in peacetime.[101]

B–52s in three-ship cells hitting the Republican Guard every three hours involved bombers using the Jeddah New airfield, the only base in the AOR to accept the B–52s. General Henry personally knew Brig. Gen. Prince Mansour bin Bandar bin Abd al-Aziz al-Saud, who was in charge at Jeddah, and visited the prince to persuade him to convince higher Saudi officials to accept the massive bombers. The general recalled telling him, "Sir, if you'll let us do this, we can bring one here at night and taxi it around to see if it will work, with no munitions on it. We've got the munitions out here in ships." The Saudis only allowed CENTAF to grade out a weapons storage area. Glosson worked out calculations and numbers of sorties, and as Henry departed Riyadh to meet with Prince Mansour, Glosson told him that by using Jeddah New, B–52s in three-ship cells could hit the Republican Guard every three hours throughout the war. The Saudis, however, did not want the Cold War nuclear bombers on their soil, especially near Mecca. They feared the negative image that such a presence might produce throughout the Arab world. Horner broached the subject with General Khalid, explaining that he could send far more B–52 sorties against the Guard if he could base the aircraft closer to the KTO. The two reached an agreement whereby, after the war commenced, the first B–52s hitting targets in Iraq could recover at Jeddah New and then operate from there for the rest of the conflict. The accord emphasized that when Desert Storm ended, the bombers would immediately depart the Saudi kingdom. B–52s would also fly combat missions from RAF Fairford, England; Moron, Spain; and Diego Garcia.[102]

F–117 Jamming Support Revisited

During the first week of January, Colonel Whitley, commander of the 37th Tactical Fighter Wing which flew F–117A Nighthawks, again raised the controversial issue of electronic jamming support for his stealthy aircraft. He sent Glosson a message requesting slight adjustments in the EF–111 EC missions during the first twenty-four hours so that the F–117s could take advantage of the EF–111 jamming for nonstealthy aircraft flying in the general vicinity of the Nighthawks.[103] For the second and third 24-hour periods, Whitley requested retasking the EF–111s to cover F–117 missions, or else simply repositioning the jammers already on SEAD sorties to provide additional coverage for the Nighthawks. He related that EF–111 mission planners indicated that most if not all of the 37th Tactical Fighter Wing requests could be met by the EF–111 aircraft.[104]

On January 5 Glosson approved the electronic jamming as suggested by Whitley for the first twenty-four hours, but he disapproved it for the second and third days of the air campaign. The general visited Khamis Mushait shortly thereafter and discussed the issue with the wing commander and pilots, who favored EF–111 support. They reached a compromise whereby the 37th was given latitude to plan missions to take advantage of jamming in direct support of nonstealthy mission packages.[105]

International and National Perspectives

Everyone in Riyadh paid close attention to CNN coverage of the meeting in Geneva, Switzerland, on January 9, 1991, between U.S. Secretary of State Baker and Iraqi Foreign Minister Aziz. The diplomats attempted to find a peaceful resolution to the Persian Gulf crisis. Baker wanted the option of conveying to Aziz in no uncertain terms the devastating blows Iraq would experience if war commenced. While preparing for the conference, Baker directed his aide to prepare an unclassified briefing on the war plan, accompanied by satellite imagery of potential air targets in Baghdad. He believed that the Iraqis needed to understand that they could not fight a war of attrition as they had against Iran and that the Coalition would set the pace and conditions of the deadly conflict. The day before the meeting, however, Secretary Cheney and Chairman Powell advised Baker not to discuss the offensive planning. Secretary Baker recalled, "Powell in particular was concerned that if we talked too much about the air war, the Iraqis would simply hunker down, which would make our task of destroying their troop concentrations more difficult and extend the length of the war." He changed the war scenario briefing and kept it as an option to respond to Aziz's bombast, if needed.[106]

Attending the session with the foreign minister was Barzan Ibrahim al-Hasan al-Takriti, Saddam Hussein's half brother, who, Baker surmised, reported to the Iraqi leader as a check on Aziz's account of the meeting. Secretary Baker presented Aziz with a letter from President Bush and, at the behest of Chairman Powell, warned the Iraqis that if they used CW or BW, the American people would demand "vengeance," and the Coalition would extract it. The letter emphasized the same point. Baker later wrote, "In hopes of persuading them to consider more soberly the folly of war, I purposely left the impression that the use of chemical or biological agents by Iraq could invite tactical nuclear retaliation." (This was a diplomatic bluff, however, because, in December, the President had ruled out the use of retaliatory nuclear or chemical weapons.) During the nearly seven-hour meeting, the two diplomats could not reach agreement. Afterward, Aziz told reporters that if Iraq were attacked, it would strike at Israel.[107]

On January 12, the U.S. Congress voted to give President Bush authority to wage war against Iraq in accordance with U.N. Security Council Resolution 678, which authorized member nations to use "all necessary means" to force Iraq to withdraw from Kuwait if it had not done so by January 15, 1991. The House voted 250 to 183, while the Senate passed the joint resolution 52 to 47. The President had telephoned and visited with many members to ensure affirmative votes. Even if the results had gone the other way, he would have taken the nation to war, believing he had the Constitutional authority to do so.[108]

On January 14, out of view of the news media, General McPeak, the CSAF, lunched at the White House with Bush, Secretary Cheney, and National Security Advisor Scowcroft. Their meeting was informal. "It was just four guys sitting around having a hamburger," McPeak related. The general had just returned from a visit to the Gulf region during which he met with the air campaign planners and flew the F–15 in training sorties.[109] His main message to the President was, "Hey, we are ready to go." He described the missions he flew and the morale of the fliers. "They have been doing wind sprints and pushups now for six months, so don't delay." McPeak knew of the January 15 U.N.-imposed deadline and had read in the press some recommendations to delay military action for another thirty days.

He advised against delay: "The impact on morale, the psychological thing, would be severe, I think, because on the air side we have been ready to go for some time, and we have just been waiting for the nod. If you put it off, everybody is going to go to bed with a mild case of the blahs." Bush told him, "Don't worry about it." The night before, the President had approved the execution of the Desert Storm air campaign, with H-hour as 0300 Baghdad time, January 17, 1991.[110]

The next day, early in the morning, the President took a solitary walk around the White House, consumed by thoughts of the impending war and the awesome power of aerial warfare. He entered his office at 0645 and dictated some of his thoughts into a tape recorder:

> I have trouble with how this ends. Say the air attack is devastating and Saddam gets done in by his own people. How do they stop? How do we keep from having overkill? Most people don't see that as a scenario because they are convinced it will be long and drawn out with numerous body bags on the U.S. side. But I want to be sure we are not there pounding people. I think we need to watch and see when our military objectives are taken care of in Baghdad and Iraq.[111]

Bush may also have been thinking about General McPeak's warning to him on December 1 at Camp David: "You are going to kill a couple of thousand people that you aren't angry with just because we make mistakes and bomb the wrong thing." The concern about loss of life had influenced the planning for the air campaign from the very beginning in August 1990 and would continue to do so throughout the war.[112]

On January 15 Bush signed NSD 54, whereby he authorized military actions against Iraq for the following purposes:

> To effect the immediate, complete and unconditional withdrawal of all Iraqi forces from Kuwait
> To restore Kuwait's legitimate government
> To protect the lives of American citizens abroad
> To promote the security and the stability of the Persian Gulf

The President had repeated the objectives he gave to the nation on August 8, 1990, to explain the Desert Shield deployment. He tied his decision to terminate the military action to the accomplishment of those goals.[113]

He indicated that the United States would dissuade Israel from initiating or joining any military actions. If Israel were attacked, the United States would respond against Iraq and discourage Israel from joining the battle.[114] He included a strong statement about Iraq's possible use of NBC weapons and the unleashing of terrorism. Should Iraq undertake such actions, the United States would make it an "explicit objective" to "replace the current leadership of Iraq."[115]

Admiral McConnell telephoned Glosson and read the NSD 54 text to him. They discussed several points, especially those addressing CW and BW. The general felt comfortable that the air campaign accorded with the President's guidelines.[116] He would soon learn that Schwarzkopf, however, had qualms about the air plan.

CINCCENT's Explosion and OPORD & OPLAN

On January 15 Schwarzkopf visited Horner and his CENTAF staff at the RSAF headquarters building, specifically to tour and receive a briefing in the GAT Division. In preparation for the event, Glosson and Deptula placed a huge sign in the Iraqi–Strategic Cell to reassure the CENTCOM commander that the airmen understood and had planned according to his objectives. The banner proclaimed:

CINC Guidance
1. Strategic Air Campaign
2. Republican Guards
    a. Isolate
    b. Annihilate
3. KTO Artillery

Deptula wanted Schwarzkopf to know, "We're paying attention to you."[117]

The CINCCENT arrived on the afternoon of the 15th, preceded by his armed Delta Force bodyguards who conducted a security sweep through the areas the general would visit. He stopped first in the NBC unit and then moved to the Iraqi–Strategic Cell where Horner, Glosson, and Deptula would present the first twenty-four hours of the air campaign. Generals Olsen, Corder, and Caruana, Colonels Tolin, Lewis, and Greenawalt, and Major Rogers attended, with a few others. Someone took photographs. "The guys were all pumped up. They were ready to go to war. They have got their stuff together and everything," recalled Horner.[118]

Deptula began the briefing by showing the first attack wave on a huge wall map. As he explained the subsequent strikes, the CINCCENT asked about attacks against the Republican Guard. Deptula stated that they would come later, near the end of the first 24-hour period, after they had suppressed the SA–6 missile threat. Schwarzkopf "exploded" at hearing this. He wanted the Guard hit at the first hour and stated that he had repeatedly told the airmen he wanted them struck at the earliest possible time. He saw that only twenty-four F–16s would hit Guard command posts from 0905 to 0920 local time.[119]

"You guys have lied to me!" he shouted. "Where are the B–52s?" He saw that at 0355 to 0410, starting within the first hour of the campaign, thirteen of the massive bombers would hit Iraqi air bases at forward locations, which were not heavily defended and filled with fighter aircraft, but he did not see any B–52s simultaneously striking ground troops. Horner joined in to explain that before the vulnerable aircraft could overfly the Republican Guard, the formidable air

On January 15, 1991, Lt. Col. David A. Deptula explains the first 24 hours of the air campaign to General H. Norman Schwarzkopf, minutes before Schwarzkopf explodes in anger for not seeing B–52s used during the initial hour of the air campaign. Looking on (left to right) are Maj. Gen. Thomas R. Olsen, Lt. Gen. Charles A. Horner, and Brig. Gen. Buster C. Glosson.

defenses had to be struck. He pointed out that the concept of Phase II was to gain air superiority over the battlefield and that the phase now merged with the first. The two phases would be executed simultaneously, and after that, B–52s could hit the elite forces. Glosson pointed out that the B–52s would hit the Tawakalna Division at 2100, but the CINCCENT yelled that he didn't care about the Tawakalna. What about the Hammurabi and Medina Divisions? The Tawakalna was, indeed, one of the heavy units, a mechanized infantry division, while the other two were armored divisions. Horner assured the CINCCENT those units would be struck.[120]

The CINCCENT seethed as Glosson stepped in and continued the briefing. At the point he showed the A–10s striking lightly defended EWR sites at the border area, Schwarzkopf again exploded, "Who authorized you to use A–10s there? Who told you to use the A–10s there??!" Horner responded, "I did." The CINCCENT now saw that the JFACC had, just within the last few days as more aircraft arrived in theater, broken loose and employed the A–10 "reserve" force. The CINCCENT turned on Horner, and as Rogers recalled, shouted, "I'm the only one giving directions, and if you people aren't listening to me I'll replace you!!" Horner recalled Schwarzkopf telling him, "I could fire you!," and his response, "I know you can." Deptula recalled, "He went on and on and on, started yelling and ranting and raving at General Horner."[121] All in the area froze in disbelief and amazement at the CINCCENT's tirade. Major Rogers thought, ironically, "This is going well."[122]

Schwarzkopf continued his tour through the basement areas of the building before he and Horner were to end their visit by meeting alone in the JFACC's office.[123] In the meantime, Glosson and Deptula had raced to Horner's office to set up the original briefing charts with Republican Guard attacks marked. They passed a note to Horner while he was still escorting the CINCCENT, telling him the charts were in his office. Deptula was on pins and needles. To significantly change the plan now would force cascading changes throughout the entire first MAP and ATO, especially coordinating SEAD and tanker support, with a new ATO having to be sent to all units at this late date.[124]

Horner showed Schwarzkopf the charts and tried to allay his fears that the Republican Guard would run and that the A–10s would be used — and lost — prematurely. He calmed the CINCCENT, and the plan did not change in deference to Schwarzkopf's apprehensions.[125] After the war, General de la Billiere, commander of the British forces, commented on the CINCCENT's temper tantrums: "Like everyone else, he had failings, among them the quick temper which gave him his nickname, 'Stormin' Norman.' He could certainly flare up — or, as his staff described it, 'go ballistic' — and when he did so, he became very frightening."[126]

The day after his memorable visit to the JFACC headquarters, Schwarzkopf issued his USCINCCENT OPORD 91–001 for Operation Desert Storm. It contained no surprises for the airmen. The air, naval, and ground offensive would consist of four phases to eliminate Iraq's ability to manufacture and use NBC weapons, destroy Iraq as a regional offensive threat, force the Iraqis from Kuwait, and restore Kuwait's government. The length of Phase I was to be 6 to 9 days; Phase II, 1 to 4 days; Phase III, 6 to 8 days; and Phase IV, yet to be determined. The OPORD's estimates suggested that with the start of the air war on January 17, the earliest completion date of Phases I through III would be January 30, the latest, February 7. Phase III was to reduce "Iraqi combat effectiveness in the KTO by at least 50 percent prior to the ground offensive," to shift "combat force ratios in favor of friendly forces."[127]

CENTCOM and the Saudi Joint Forces–Theater Operations had already issued a combined OPLAN to eject Iraqi forces from Kuwait. It stated that the combined offensive operations would counter Iraqi aggression, secure Kuwait, and provide the establishment of a legitimate government in Kuwait.[128] The OPLAN identified three enemy centers of gravity: C^2 and leadership; NBC capability; and forces of the Republican Guard. The OPLAN indicated that the offensive campaign would focus on the destruction, neutralization, elimination, or degradation of the centers of gravity. The length of each phase was slightly shorter than the periods provided for in the OPORD. A matrix disclosed operational objectives targeted during each phase:

Operational Campaign Objective	Phase I: 3–6 Days	Phase II: 1–2 Days	Phase III: 5–8 Days	Phase IV: Days TBD
Military capability to wage war	X	X	X	X
Air supremacy	X	X		
Cut supply lines	X	X	X	X
Destroy Republican Guard Forces	X		X	X
Liberate Kuwait City				X

Phase III, Battlefield Preparation would include PSYOPS, deception, and Special Operations activities.

Although the Desert Storm OPORD and OPLAN were ambiguous about the specific outcome desired against the Iraqi political and military leadership per se, planners developed the air campaign to attack leadership, C^3, and telecommunications targets, while maintaining compliance with the general and specific parameters of the Desert Storm OPORD and OPLAN.

The Calm before the Storm

In the remaining days before the air campaign, Glosson visited units and discussed with air crews their role in the impending offensive. His bottom line for the upcoming operations asserted, "The pride and confidence of our nation rests squarely upon your shoulders." He proclaimed to the troops: "The quickest way home is through Baghdad."[129] While with F–15C wings, he emphasized that Eagle pilots could deliberately run out of fuel on two priority missions. First, if the AWACS used the code words, "Horner's Buster," and vectored them to an enemy aircraft, they should do everything possible to shoot the plane down (even if it meant flaming out) because the aircraft carried Saddam Hussein. Second, if they chased a plane south into Saudi Arabian airspace, they were cleared to expend all fuel as they pursued the enemy over Saudi soil.[130]

Two days before the war, Horner and Glosson sat in the TACC, and the chief planner quietly asked his boss what he thought the attrition would be. The JFACC jotted down "39" and passed the slip of paper to the planner. Horner believed the figure to be a good estimate for U.S. Air Force losses. He thought the number for the entire Coalition would be nearly 100. Six weeks later when the war ended, Coalition aircraft combat losses totaled 38.[131]

On January 16, 0600 Riyadh time, Horner, as CENTAF Commander, with authorization from the CINCCENT, sent the message, "Wolfpack Warning Order," to all units scheduled to fly in the air campaign during the first nine hours. (Glosson had chosen the Wolfpack code name after his alma mater, North Carolina State University.) The message warned units to be ready to execute "subject strategic air campaign," heed operations security, and anticipate an execute order within eighteen hours from the time the warning message was sent.[132]

Six and one-half hours later on January 16, Horner issued the "Wolfpack Execute Order." It referenced a JCS execute order and directed all tasked units to execute Wolfpack in accordance with USCENTAF ATO-1M, with changes 1 and 2, 110104Z January 1991. The order declared H-hour as 0000 Zulu time, January 17, 1991.[133] (Zulu is the military term for Greenwich mean time; local time in the theater for H-hour was three hours later than Zulu time, making H-hour 0300 in Riyadh and Baghdad. The local time in Washington for the Desert Storm H-hour was 1900 on January 16th.) Air campaign planners had selected this time as H-hour in August, after they had eliminated the two attack waves of the first night and opted for initial strikes when most Iraqis would be asleep. Planners wanted to hit the Iraqis when they would be most disoriented and groggy, awakened from their slumber.

At midnight in Riyadh on January 16/17 the J–3 at CENTCOM issued the message, "Execute Order — USCINCCENT OPORD 001 for Desert Storm." The message began: "The President of the United States has directed execution of Operation Desert Storm."[134]

NCA and military officials in Washington would follow the course of the air strikes by reading the MAP. Officials at the White House, in Secretary Cheney's office, in Chairman Powell's office, and in Checkmate would study Deptula's MAP. They also watched CNN television to follow the news coverage.[135] Cheney spent the night at his office, worrying about losing aviators. He had learned well the numbers and strength of the Iraqi air force and air defense system and knew that in the first hours, pilots flew against the undamaged, full-up systems. He expected the highest number of casualties the first night of the air war.[136]

Baptiste had foreknowledge of the date and hour of the first attacks because Glosson had pulled him aside and whispered the time to him. The KTO Cell leader withheld the information from all but a few of his staff, waiting until just hours before H-hour to explain the offensive campaign to his cell.[137]

Glosson resisted second-guessing himself and the plan at this late date. He telephoned all his fighter wing commanders and told them that, during the war, they should report all incidents to him, good and bad. At about 2200 on the 16th he placed a few "political" phone calls to officials in Gulf countries, telling them that the war would start that night.[138]

Deptula spent the last day before the attacks accomplishing last-minute coordination with the flying units and planning for the next series of strikes and how to streamline the BDA process to give the planners the earliest news possible. He finished a project Glosson had given him a few days earlier, when the general plunked a stack of computer printouts in front of him, told him to prioritize the targets listed, and within an hour, send the first set of fifty to an office in Washington. These would become the priority list for overhead imagery and reveal the first BDA for Desert Storm. By cross-referencing the Basic Encyclopedia numbers to the Deptula numbers on his master target list, and knowing the rationale for each of the targets selected, he accomplished the first stage of the project before its deadline, and then kept working the task.[139] The master target list he would refer to as he built the wartime MAPs now included 375 targets in 13 categories.

At about 2100 in Riyadh on January 16, General Corder introduced Major Rogers to the personnel in the TACC, where he briefed everyone on the start of the air campaign. Three hours earlier, Rogers had presented the plan to the CENTAF colonels. Some officers in the TACC expressed amazement that they were not told of the offensive operation until now even though they would monitor and facilitate the execution of the plan that very night.[140]

General Henry, the EC expert, watched CNN at the home of the commander of the Air Training Command at Randolph AFB, Texas. Having worked on the air campaign for four months before departing the theater, Henry knew the plan intimately, and the sequence of strikes. He especially anticipated the launch of the drones in his Poobah's Party and the giant SEAD raid in the area west of Baghdad.[141]

In the darkness as H-hour neared, when targeteer Captain Glock walked from the RSAF building to the targeteers' tent in the soccer field, the distant, continuous roar of jet engines from Riyadh AB drowned out other sounds, as tanker after tanker rumbled down the runways and lifted off into the darkness. He recalled that everyone now knew what was happening, was "pumped up," and was thinking "Yes!" Glock was both proud of the planning and fearful it would all be wrong.[142]

Colonel Tolin, GAT division head, flew as the airborne mission director on the lead AWACS the first night. He would spend eighteen hours in the aircraft and monitor the first twelve hours of the campaign. Although he had just recently arrived in theater, he had talked extensively with the planners, studied and memorized the MAP and ATO, and repeatedly ran a computer simulation of the first strikes. Recollecting those initial attacks, he mused, "At that point, we had no idea if we were going to lose a whole lot of airplanes or lose none at all."[143]

After midnight, Deptula walked upstairs to Horner's office and met him just as the JFACC walked out. They shook hands, and the young planner wished the CENTAF commander good luck. They rode down the elevator together and the general said that Schwarzkopf had apologized for his outburst. Deptula thanked him for convincing the CINCCENT not to change anything in the plan because at that late date it would have resulted in chaos and lessened the anticipated effectiveness of the coordinated attacks. As they reached the basement, others joined them as they walked into the TACC.[144]

Horner spent the night in the TACC. "We knew it was going to kick off at 3:00 or 4:00 in the morning," he recalled, "so you wanted to get all rested up because you know you are not going to get much sleep. Well, try going to sleep! Finally you get up, shower, put on clean clothes because you know you are going to live in your clothes for a while. I went in about 1:00. Buster was in there, John Corder was in there, Crigger was in there...Christon, all the guys. You had

Rattan, the head Frenchman, Bahairi [al-Buhairi]. We are all in there."[145] When a message alerted Horner that the Navy had launched the TLAMs, everyone knew the war was inevitable, after months of planning and anticipation, because there was no recalling the missiles.[146]

Horner watched two screens side by side in the TACC: the Rivet Joint downlink displayed aircraft and near real-time fused intelligence about Iraqi air defense radars and missiles, and the AWACS link showed air activity over Saudi Arabia and Iraq. On the AWACS screen, he watched as aircraft formed a great armada and headed north. He turned to Rogers and asked him to go upstairs to his office, watch the television, and report any significant news. When the major arrived on the third floor, people had already crowded into the office to watch the set, waiting intently for information on the first air strikes.[147] Downstairs Horner thought of Vietnam, the conflict that had made him a warrior, and he remembered the pilots and crews shot down and killed or taken prisoner and paraded through the streets of the enemy's capital. He felt a despair and despondency and wanted desperately not to "screw it up just like we did in Vietnam." He worried about friendly casualties. He wondered if the technology would work. "We had a lot of technical data about stealth technology, but I had no way of knowing that we wouldn't lose the entire fleet the first night." He wondered about the effectiveness of ECM, which were never practiced in peacetime to the extent necessary now. He thought about the human toll on himself and many others. "You know in your soul you are involved in the business of taking human life, and there is nothing nice about that. You know you may be condemned for that." He thought, "we know we are about to lose friends, and people are depending upon us to protect their lives."[148]

A key moment signaling the campaign's initial success was the timing of the call Horner received from Rogers. Hanging up the receiver, the general announced that CNN had just gone off the air. Deptula looked at his watch and let out a cheer. General Olsen asked what that meant. The news clearly revealed that the plan was working, the F–117s had gotten through and hit their H-hour targets in Baghdad. Deptula, MAP in hand, spent the next several hours answering questions as the air campaign proceeded.[149]

People crowded into Checkmate that night, jammed into the former lounge area to watch CNN. Colonel Howey held the MAP and tried to do crude BDA as the reporters described where explosions had occurred. Officers consulted their watches and did mental calculations to convert Baghdad time to eastern standard time and noted the progress of the attacks. They cheered with every bomb strike. At 1950, Colonel Warden, Secretary Rice, General Adams, Colonel Blackburn, and others walked over to the small room where a screen displayed the Rivet Joint downlink and watched symbols present periodic snapshots of Coalition aircraft and the radar threats they flew against. At about 2000 General McPeak joined the group.[150]

From the headquarters in the MODA building in Riyadh, General Schwarzkopf released a message to the men and women of Central Command, announcing the start of Operation Desert Storm to enforce U.N. resolutions and force Iraq from Kuwait.[151] He told the troops that the President, the American people, and, indeed, the world supported them. Their force was massive, their readiness at its peak, their determination fierce to get the job done quickly, and their cause just. The CINCCENT had total confidence in them. He exhorted, "Now you must be the lightning and thunder of Desert Storm."

Epilogue

The Execution and Key Aspects

The first twenty-four hours of the air war unfolded largely according to plan and seized the initiative in the forty-three-day conflict.[1] Repetitive nighttime flying by Coalition personnel had desensitized Iraqi air defenders to seeing AWACS, tanker, and CAP flights on their radarscopes each night. In the early hours of January 17, however, most Coalition aircraft flew beyond the range of the enemy's radars, so the Iraqis could not detect the 160 tankers, AWACS and command aircraft, and strike aircraft that were marshaling and topping off their fuel tanks. Darkness shrouded the first three hours of the air campaign, hiding helicopters skimming along the desert floor in western Iraq. At 0238, one minute early, Joint Task Force Normandy, consisting of Army AH–64 Apache helicopter gunships led to their targets by Air Force Special Operations MH–53J Pave Low III Pathfinders, shot off Hellfire missiles, Hydra rockets, and 30-mm cannons and destroyed two EWR sites that reported to the Nukhayb IOC.[2] At one of the remote sites, someone got off a message to higher command sounding the alert that the war was underway, which led the Iraqi defenders in Baghdad to set off a horrific barrage of AAA.[3] F–117As flew in Iraqi airspace at the time, but not near Baghdad. After a few minutes, the artillery fire stopped and the capital was quiet again. The AAA debris falling back to earth probably damaged buildings in the city. At 0251, nine minutes before H-hour, two F–117s simultaneously hit the Nukhayb IOC, about fifty miles inside western Iraq. The pilots then flew through heavy AAA flak to the H–3 airfield to strike the SOC. They missed the targets there; nonetheless, throughout the war, the Iraqis did not use this facility as an active component of the IADS.[4]

H-hour, the time the first bombs fell on Baghdad, came at 0300 as two F–117As delivered GBU–27 laser-guided penetrating bombs into two targets: the so-called AT&T building and the Baghdad Telecommunications Center. These strikes abruptly cut off telephone reporting by NBC and ABC news correspondents to their parent television stations. CNN reporters, however, maintained their live telephone connectivity to Atlanta and provided vivid verbal descriptions of the city under bombardment to CNN viewers across the United States.[5] The F–117s each dropped one weapon, and the pilots then flew on to release their second PGMs against targets west and north of the city, scoring two more hits.[6] These two Nighthawk airmen had received quite a shock as they approached Baghdad when the night sky over the city lit up with AAA for the second time that night, as millions of television viewers heard reporters describing the lethal fireworks.[7] The aviators had expected to reach the capital stealthily, bomb, and egress before the Iraqis responded. Instead, they had to acquire and hit their targets amidst terrible artillery fire, which did not have the range to reach the altitudes where they flew. A few SAMs did sail by them, but they lacked a radar lock-on to the aircraft. The electronic jamming from EF–111As for the first wave of six F–117s, heading toward Baghdad and two SOCs for strikes five minutes after H-hour, probably caused the barrage. The area-jamming may have tipped off the enemy that aircraft were approaching; however, all F–117As made it safely to and from Baghdad protected by 552 missiles and 1,267 AAA guns. The H+0005 strikes, at 0305 local time, represented the only time the EF–111s flew sorties to deliver direct jamming support exclusively for F–117s. Throughout the war, the F–117 Nighthawks flying against the most heavily defended areas received neither dedicated EC support nor fighter cover.[8]

The strikes preceding H-hour against the two EWR stations and the Nukhayb IOC created a safe-passage corridor through the IADS. Into the breach flew 20 F–15Cs to sweep and patrol airfields where Iraqi pilots sat on alert in western Iraq; F–14s to fly CAPs; the large F–15E package heading to blast the western Scud sites; and SEAD aircraft, including three EF–111As, to jam for the anti-Scud package and the F–117 strikes in Baghdad at 0305. Protecting the Strike Eagle mission in the west, F–15Cs could fire freely BVR and kill anything lifting off Iraqi airfields. They had to intimidate and overpower Iraqi pilots, which they did as they downed five aircraft in their initial sweeps and patrols that night.[9] The nineteen F–15E Strike Eagles flew low with terrain-following radar, and at 0305 they hit fixed Scud sites in the vicinity of the H–2 airfield to prevent retaliatory Scud launches against Israel, dropping MK–20 Rockeyes — free-fall, unguided, cluster munitions. The F–15Es lacked LANTIRN targeting pods, which were still undergoing testing and evaluation in the United States, but a half dozen would soon arrive in theater.[10]

At 0305, four F–117s hit more targets in Baghdad: two strikes against the air defense headquarters building (no hits), a restrike against the AT&T building (hit), and an attack against the Abu Ghurayb presidential palace (hit). Two other 117s sent weapons into the SOC at Taji (hit), just north of Baghdad, and the SOC at Tallil (hit), near Basra in southern Iraq. The Nighthawk pilots then flew on to drop PGMs against air defense and C³ targets.[11]

Immediately after the F–117s, from 0306 to 0311, the Navy TLAMs arrived at Baghdad, hitting electric power plants and transformer facilities, the Baath

Party Headquarters, and the Baghdad presidential office complex. The Aegis cruiser USS *San Jacinto* in the Red Sea had fired the first missiles at 0130; they flew at 100 to 300 feet for more than ninety minutes, relying on their inertial navigation systems, updated by terrain contour-matching guidance and the Digital Scene Matching Area Correlation systems.[12]

Planners heavily targeted Scud-related facilities the first night. At 0330, twenty more TLAMs pounded the Scud support facility at Taji. Next, a big raid preceded by drones hit Scud storage facilities at two air bases in the Kuwaiti area with subsequent missions to Tallil and three other bases, to destroy more Scud storage shelters. Two raids hit the fiber-optic repeater stations that intelligence had recently shown carried Scud C^2 communications. From H-hour through the next twenty-four hours, F–15Es sat alert to immediately react to mobile Scud launches by trying to locate and attack the sites of the missiles' origin. During the initial twelve-hour period, if no word came to scramble, the aircraft attacked preassigned Scud sites.[13]

A–10s also sat alert during the first twenty-four hours to hit Iraqi artillery in the KTO if fired against the Marines, who worried about the employment of CW. The Marine's Direct Air Support Center had the authority to launch the Warthogs.[14]

From 0340 to 0420 U.S. Air Force, U.S. Navy, U.S. Marine Corps, Saudi, and British pilots flew air superiority missions throughout Iraq against aircraft, runways, and SAMs. The attacks included those occurring from 0348 to 0415 with Poobah's Party drones, which supported SEAD attacks in the western Baghdad area, and strikes against the huge al-Taqaddum AB west of the capital. By 0348, the Iraqis knew without doubt that the Coalition had started the air war. The Instant Thunder planners had reasoned that now was the time to send in the gorilla SEAD package to beat down the IADS system in the Baghdad area and to free up the medium-altitude range for nonstealthy aircraft. In September, Generals Glosson and Henry had determined that Colonel Warden's offer of the BQM–74 drones was opportune because the Iraqis would have their radars operating to detect large strike packages against the capital, as General Dugan had discussed with newspaper reporters.

An Air Force package from the south and two packages from Navy carriers in the Red Sea, with British Tornados joining in, would execute the SEAD operations west of Baghdad. In its first package, the Navy sent EA–6 jammers, F–14 escorts, KA–6 tankers, and HARM shooters: F/A–18s, A–6s, and A–7s. The second package, a few minutes later than the first, consisted of eight Navy A–6s and four British GR–1 Tornados, and they would attack facilities and runways at al-Taqaddum. Some of the A–6s fired TALDs. From Saudi Arabia in the south, the BQM–74 ground-launched drones reached the Baghdad airspace shortly before the TALDs were fired, revealing to the Iraqis what looked like a massive bombing raid. The drones flew in a pattern over Baghdad until they expended their fuel and crashed or were shot down. As the Iraqis wasted effort trying to track and kill drones and TALDs, Air Force EF–111 electronic jammers forced the radar operators to turn their equipment to full power to see through the electronic clutter and static. Then the Air Force F–4G HARM shooters arrived and began launching missiles to destroy the full-up ground radars, as did the Navy HARM shooters. The missiles not only destroyed radars, they intimidated the surviving Iraqi operators to keep their radars off or to turn them on only momentarily, blinking them on and off, while trying to acquire aircraft.[15] Simultaneously, two other waves of aircraft with drone, TALD, and SEAD support hit the H–3 airfield in the west and the Shaibah airfield in the Kuwaiti area. Navy A–6 pilots struck hangars, runways, and ramps at Shaibah, with Saudis targeting runways, to preclude aircraft and helicopters from shooting Exocet antiship missiles at Coalition naval vessels.[16]

As the SEAD mission west of Baghdad was underway, from 0355 to 0410, low-flying B–52s from Diego Garcia arrived at five forward operating bases and delivered UK 1000 runway-cratering weapons, timed to go off at various intervals; CBU–58s, each with 650 bomblets; and CBU–89 Gator mines for runway denial. British Tornados dropping their specialty JP–233 cratering munitions and F–15Es also joined the effort against Iraqi forward operations locations, which were generally positioned along a line running through southwestern and southern Iraq near the Saudi border. Strikes against these forward locations insured that Iraqi aircraft could not take off and quickly bear down on high-value assets like AWACS or tankers, which was Horner's primary concern because, if he were in command of the Iraqi air force, those were the targets he would have destroyed first. Six of the B–52s landed at Jeddah New and, accompanied by other, later arriving B–52s, would fly combat missions from there for the remainder of the war.[17] Major air bases, like Tallil and Balad Southeast, also received heavy assaults.

At 0420, on the heels of the SEAD attack against the capital and taking advantage of the chaos it created, more F–117s arrived over Baghdad and delivered munitions against the city's primary television transmitter (no hit); two international radio transmitters (no hits); three telephone exchanges at Maiden Square (hit), Jenoub (no hit), and Gharb (no hit); the Abu Ghurayb presidential bunker (no hit); the Baghdad presidential bunker and residence (hit); an I-Hawk missile site (no hit) (weapons seized during the assault into Kuwait); the air force headquarters building near the Baghdad/Muthenna airfield (hit); and the Baghdad Telecommunications Center (no hit) (second attack of the night). Other Nighthawks struck IADS targets in central (hit), western (hit), and southern Iraq (no hit). Poor weather obscured visibility and caused some pilots to refrain from dropping their weapons. Clouds and fog prevented aviators from acquiring and laser-designating their targets.[18]

At 0500, one hour before sunrise, F–117As were to blast open twelve BW bunkers, exposing their contents to the initial heat and explosion of the GBU–27s and then allowing sunlight to stream into the damaged, penetrated portions of the structures. Within minutes, F–111Fs would drop CBU–89 Gator mines around the facilities to deny entrance to salvage BW.[19] Sunlight streaming through the wrecked facilities and reaching anthrax would cause the spores to steadily deteriorate. That morning, however, fog enveloped many of the bunkers, and the pilots had difficulty acquiring their targets, with most not hitting their targets.[20]

The Navy executed the last strikes of the first night at 0525 as A–6s from the USS *Ranger* hit Umm Qasr naval port facilities. During the first three hours of the air campaign, the Coalition lost one aviator, a Navy F/A–18 pilot from the USS *Saratoga* flying in the gorilla SEAD attack against Baghdad who was likely brought down by a MiG–25.[21]

The sun rose at about 0600, and at 0700 a Navy E–2C Hawkeye airborne early warning and C^2 aircraft, capable of surface surveillance coordination, and four F–14s from the USS *John F. Kennedy* patrolled the skies near the H–3 airfield in western Iraq. Their presence was meant to reassure the Israelis that Scud launches from that region concerned the Coalition. A similar package would fly at 1100. The first TLAMs to arrive in daylight hit the Shaibah airfield helicopter ramp from 0700 to 0800 to again deny the Iraqis the use of their Exocet missiles. From 0730 to 0740, F–16s made their first daylight raid at As Samawah, against the first oil refinery to be targeted, followed by more F–16s hitting a microwave antenna and other communications targets from 0800 to 0820.[22]

The air campaign's Phase II targeting occurred from 0810 until 1130 as twenty-four A–10 Warthogs flew against lightly defended border EWR sites. These attacks had angered Schwarzkopf when he learned of them on January 15, but he nonetheless sanctioned them. Later in the war, A–10s taking out radar sites earned the nickname Wart Weasels, a variant on the traditional SEAD mission performed by the F-4G Wild Weasels. Phase II attacks also unfolded from 0835 to 0850 as thirty-six F–16s hit SA–2, –3, and –6 SAM sites in the Kuwaiti area. Other F–16s hit Scud missile sites in the KTO.[23]

The first of seven B–52Gs, in flight for seventeen hours, now arrived in theater and at 0830, for the first time in combat, fired AGM–86C CALCMs. The previous day at 0635 CST the B–52Gs began taking off from Barksdale AFB, Louisiana, and pilots timed their flights to reach Saudi Arabia during daylight of the first morning of the air war. As they arrived in theater, they positioned themselves beyond the range of Iraqi radars and launched thirty-five CALCMs against two hard-to-reach electrical power plants in northern Iraq and one south of Baghdad, and against communications sites in high-threat areas. At least twenty-eight missiles hit their targets. When the Instant Thunder planners had originally inserted these weapons into the planning, they called them long-range bombs, an informal code name for the highly classified CALCMs, conventional variants of the AGM–86B nuclear weapon, and that designator remained unchanged in the MAP. Four of the missiles did not actually launch from the B–52s, and of those that did, all successfully transitioned to cruise flight, guided by GPS and inertial navigation systems. The overhead location of the satellites defined the CALCMs' launch window. Without landing, the intercontinental bombers returned to Louisiana, completing the longest combat sorties in history up to that time.[24]

Though the B–52 CALCM mission had been planned since August, the sorties that twelve French Jaguar pilots flew at 0855 against Scud shelters and facilities at Al Jaber airfield in Kuwait had been planned only within the last twenty-four hours, when the government in Paris agreed to let pilots fly before the start of the ground war.[25] Horner gave them a target close to Qatar to accommodate the distances the Jaguars could fly without refueling.

Assisted by BQM–74 drones, F–16s from 0905 to 0920 hit three Republican Guard command posts in the Kuwaiti area. Starting at 0920 and lasting through the day until 1800, eight A–10s working together would strike Iraqi army forces in the tri-border area, executing Phase III targeting.[26]

Throughout the day from 0930 to 1645, Coalition aircraft continued to pound the defenders, hitting a variety of targets: air defense and SAM sites; airfield runways, buildings, and CW and Scud facilities; and a petroleum pumping station. More TLAMs arrived from 1000 to 1500 crashing into three CW sites, two electrical power facilities, and an oil pumping station and manifold. Ten TLAMs hit one target: the Ministry of Defense, the army headquarters in Baghdad. These Tomahawk attacks reflected Horner's admonition on August 27 to Glosson to keep the pressure on the Iraqis twenty-four hours a day. TLAMs functioned as ideal daylight weapons in high-threat areas. Weather caused the cancellation of a large Navy F/A–18 package planned for 1400–1410 against a railroad yard and IOC in the al-Zubayr area near Kuwait. Instead, the force hit Iraqi patrol boats.[27]

The Poobah's Party drones, Navy TALDs, and SEAD operations west of Baghdad the preceding night enabled forty F–16s flying at medium altitude, with drones, EF–111 jamming, and F–15C escorts, to strike the al-Taqaddum airfield and nearby Habbaniyah petroleum storage facility in daylight from 1700 to 1715. No aircraft were lost in this large raid into densely defended central Iraq.[28]

Twelve F–111Fs accomplished the first evening raid of the first twenty-four hours when they attacked three airfields from 1830 to 1915. Darkness settled in at 1830. At 2000 Navy F–14s and A–6s hit Silkworm missile sites in the Kuwaiti area. Forty minutes later, four F–111Fs hit Saddam Hussein's residence in Tikrit in northern Iraq while two B–52s struck the al-Sahra undergraduate pilot training base near Tikrit, the hometown of Saddam's clan.[29] The planners wanted the Tikritis to feel the power of the allied air weapon early in the conflict.

The darkness at 2015 brought nine F–117s back to Baghdad, hitting leadership targets — the Ministry of Defense National Computer Center (hit), a VIP bunker (no hit), and the Iraqi intelligence service headquarters (hit). Two stealth aircraft targeted an NW-related site for the first time, the Tuwaitha nuclear research center, but bad weather prevented the weapon drops. Other Nighthawks flew against two IOCs, with no hits. The F–117s flew to secondary targets, with varied results.[30]

From 2100 to 2115 three B–52s hit Republican Guard troops in the Tawakalna Division, and this commenced a minicampaign that would soon send three of the massive bombers against Guard targets every three hours throughout the war. Schwarzkopf had feared the elite forces would decamp with the first air attacks against Iraq, but they stayed in place, and tactical reconnaissance aircraft which Horner kept airborne all day confirmed it.[31]

From 2227 to 2320 three large packages of U.S. Air Force, Navy, and Marine Corps and British aircraft flew in the Basra area near Kuwait and struck oil, railroad, airfield, and electrical power targets. At the far western regions of Iraq, Coalition aircraft returned to attack airfields, Scud sites, and a petroleum pumping station, to again establish a presence in western Iraq so the Israelis could see it on their radarscopes. From 2330 to 0010 on January 18, British GR–1s flew low and dropped their JP–233s at Mudaysis and Wadi al-Khir airfields.[32]

At 0100 January 18, two TLAMs hit the Baghdad government control center which constituted the final strike of the first MAP, except for recurring B–52 visits against the Republican Guard. Planners had expected the Navy to send six F/A–18s from a Red Sea carrier to launch standoff, land-attack missiles against the Salman Pak air defense site, but the mission was canceled.[33]

At the end of the first twenty-four hours, the Coalition had downed eight Iraqi aircraft: three MiG–29s, three F1 Mirages, and two MiG–21s. The Coalition lost six: a U.S. Navy F/A–18, probably downed by a Mig–25; a British GR–1, a Kuwaiti A–4, and a Navy A–6E, all lost to SAMs; and an Air Force F–15E and a British GR–1, hit by AAA. The Coalition's losses were light, given the thick, lethal, integrated air defenses controlled by the computerized Kari system.[34] Reaching their targets at scheduled times, Coalition aviators significantly damaged the enemy IADS and made great headway in establishing the medium-altitude regime for the air war's combat missions. The first day's results thrilled the planners as they saw 5½ months of effort pay off in a big way — few Coalition casualties, little collateral damage, and the functions at major targets systems disrupted. At his 1700 staff meeting in the TACC, Horner tried to focus everyone and place the campaign in perspective. He observed, "We are at Day 1 of a thirty- to forty-day war."[35]

The two mission-package cancellations during the first twenty-four hours not occasioned by weather were the attacks into the Mosul-Kirkuk areas of northern Iraq by aircraft flying from the NATO base at Incirlik, Turkey, and the Saudi Arabian CSS–2 missile attacks against an Iraqi railroad station, ammunition depot, and airfield. In the first, permission from the government at Ankara to fly offensive missions from Turkish soil only arrived in time for sorties to fly the evening of January 18, when F–111s dropped cluster bombs on EWR sites, opening a second front of the air war and compounding the Iraqis' air defense problems. In the second, the Saudis did not launch their imprecise CSS–2 missiles because King Fahd withheld his permission, and he did not authorize the missile's use throughout the conflict, even when Iraqi Scuds hit the Saudi kingdom.

Airpower Advantage

The worsening weather over Iraq posed the first problem for planners after the initial day of air operations. On January 18/19, nearly two of every three planned strikes by the F–117As either missed their targets or did not drop their weapons as a result of miserable weather. The situation did not improve, and the months of January and February 1991 offered some of the worst weather the region had seen in more than fourteen years, the period for which DoD had climatological data. The lack of timely BDAs compounded the difficulties caused by persistent cloud cover. Overcast skies prevented optical reconnaissance from producing usable BDA imagery. Not until January 21 were images acquired for most strategic targets. Even with clear photographs, the interpretation of the images and the assessment of effects proved difficult and contentious.[36]

The Iraqis retaliated against the air bombardment by firing missiles. On the morning of January 18, starting at 0259 and lasting for nearly thirty minutes, they sent eight Scuds against Israel, none of which carried CW or BW warheads or caused serious physical damage upon landing. Their psychological impact, however, was severe. Horner and Glosson riveted their attention on additional ways to curtail and stop additional firings. At 0938 Glosson reported, "CINC is getting a lot of calls from Washington about the Scuds."[37] Finding and killing mobile Scud launchers emerged as the air war's first major planning priority in the 43-day conflict.

Key Aspects of the Planning

JFACC Produced the Plan for the CINCCENT's Air Campaign

In retrospect, key aspects of the Gulf War air campaign plan and planning process emerge. Clearly, Schwarzkopf fulfilled his responsibilities as both a U.S. and Coalition commander. A few days before the ground war commenced in February 1991, the CINCCENT displayed his authority, reinforced by the Goldwater-Nichols Act, when he met with his subordinate commanders to discuss the land offensive. General Horner explained his Push CAS modus of flowing airplanes to the battlefield twenty-four hours a day (rather than keeping them idle while sitting alert). When General Franks ignored what Horner had said and demanded that VII Corps be allotted hundreds of CAS sorties per day (whether needed or not), the airman angrily disputed the allocation of air power in that manner and reiterated his Push CAS procedures. Horner believed it important for unity of command to let his anger show as he vehemently rejected Franks's claim for so much unfocused air power. He remembered his outburst having no effect: "Everyone looked at me and said, 'Well, he fell on his sword; isn't that quaint.'" General Boomer jumped in and requested as many dedicated sorties for his Marines, and General Luck joined the "run on the bank" and demanded as many CAS flights for his XVIII Corps. The ground commanders argued for *their* sorties, but after a while Schwarzkopf called a halt to the debate, reminding all present, "You people don't understand. It's *all my air,* and I'll use it any way I please." "That ended the argument," Horner recalled, "and we maintained a centralized command."[38] The CINCCENT depended upon his JFACC to ensure that all the ground commanders received adequate air support.

The air campaign plan was not an Air Force, Navy, Marine Corps, or Army plan; it was the CINCCENT's plan. After the war, Horner summarized Schwarzkopf's control of air power: "The CINC owns it all. As soon as you understand that, then everything falls into place."[39] Horner understood the implications of the Goldwater-Nichols Act and the power of the combatant commander and visited Schwarzkopf at MacDill AFB in April 1990 to explain how he would wield the air weapon — on behalf of the joint force commander. He wanted to discuss aerial warfare with Schwarzkopf and receive his blessing for CENTAF's method of employing air power in executing CENTCOM's OPLAN 1002–90. Schwarzkopf agreed with the key concepts of Horner's briefing.

The CINCCENT appointed Horner his JFACC, AADC, and ACA. As JFACC, Horner strove diligently to establish the centralized control of air, fostering a concentration of purpose. He had a theaterwide perspective on the war, similar to the CINCCENT's and broader than the corps commanders' sector-oriented outlook. Horner insisted on deconflicting air throughout the theater by time and the ATO, and he rejected the route package system of the Vietnam War when the Navy and Air Force essentially fought two separate, uncoordinated air wars. He would have resigned rather than divide the airspace by Navy and Air Force geographic or service-specific sectors. Horner got most of what he needed, but he was not dogmatic and adapted to a decentralized control of air assets, as when Army helicopters flying interdiction missions beyond the FSCL remained apart from the ATO, or when Proven Force assets flying from Turkey had their own ATO, sanctioned by the JFACC.

Horner brought other lessons from Vietnam into the Gulf War planning: plan and pick targets in theater, work with allies respectfully, conduct operations with no pauses to disallow the enemy time to regroup and rebuild, secure the medium-altitude regime, and do not waste air assets by not flying them. The powerful effects of strategic bombing accomplished in Linebacker II impressed him, but he applied that lesson sparingly before April 1990, giving the CINCCENT a means to prevent the use of CW by threatening Saddam Hussein with destruction of his high-value strategic targets. When Schwarzkopf asked about the apportionment and allocation of air assets, Horner explained that a better way to think about using air power was by objectives and targets sets. The CINCCENT would explain his goals; the JFACC would then assign assets based on mission and aircraft capabilities. Horner wanted his fellow component commanders to tell him not *which* airplanes to employ, but *what* they wanted air power to accomplish.

The CINCCENT imposed his vision and CONOPS on the offensive war plan. Chairman Powell requested that Schwarzkopf brief his ideas at the Pentagon on August 25, before departing for Saudi Arabia. The CINCCENT called his plan Desert Storm, and it consisted of four phases:

Phase I	Strategic Air Campaign
Phase II	Kuwait Air Campaign
Phase III	Ground Combat Power Attrition
Phase IV	Ground Attack.

The CINCCENT always assumed that a ground invasion would have to expel the Iraqis from Kuwait, so Phase III would "prepare the battlefield" and attrit the Iraqi army to the 50 percent level. Phase II would gain control of the skies over the KTO so helicopters and B–52s and other fixed wing aircraft could accomplish Phase III. After the war, Horner explained, "The 50 percent armored and artillery came directly from Schwarzkopf. The 'gain control of the air in the Kuwaiti theater of operations' came directly from Schwarzkopf."[40] The CINCCENT saw U.S. air power as a dominant strength over Iraq, with its million-man army, so air power dominated his war plan.

Horner and Glosson were never comfortable with Schwarzkopf's four phases, especially when they saw *air superiority* listed explicitly in his Phase II. They would gain air superiority in Phase I with the attacks on the Iraqi IADS controlling aircraft, missiles, and AAA. Glosson often tried to compress Phases I and II, but Schwarzkopf always objected. Horner thought of the air campaign simply in terms of gaining air superiority, quickly striking the Scuds and NBC capability, isolating and preparing the battlefield, and supporting the ground invasion to liberate Kuwait. By January 17 the CINCCENT's phases had become:

Phase I	Strategic Air Campaign
Phase II	Air Supremacy in the KTO
Phase III	Battlefield Preparation
Part A	Republican Guard
Phase III	Battlefield Preparation
Part B	Regular Iraqi Fielded Forces
Phase IV	Ground Attack

Glosson's Black Hole planned Phases I through III, and the regular CENTAF staff (with augmentation) planned the air portion of Phase IV. Representatives from the other services and the Coalition assisted both enterprises. When executed, the phases would then merge.

No Off-the-Shelf Offensive Plan

The offensive air campaign planning began in August 1990 after Iraq invaded Kuwait, lasted the entire 5½ months of Desert Shield, and continued into Desert Storm. The suppression of mobile Scud launches was the major new wartime planning initiative. No off-the-shelf offensive plan existed prior to August. The Joint Operational Planning and Execution System had produced the incomplete CENTCOM OPLAN 1002–90 to defend Saudi Arabia against an Iraqi attack. It was primarily a deployment — not employment — plan, and defensive — not offensive — in character. The OPLAN consisted of three phases: deterrence, defense, and counterattack. It did not include a strategic air campaign. It did require that air power attrit the Iraqi ground troops in the second phase to a level of strength favorable to a counterattack by friendly forces, a counterland mission which would undergird Desert Storm Phase III.

When he left Horner in Saudi Arabia on August 7 as the CENTCOM Forward commander, Schwarzkopf expected Horner to protect Saudi Arabia while preparing the way for a massive deployment. The CINCCENT at that time did not order Horner to plan an offensive campaign. Planning for the defensive D-day ATO and ATO Bravo produced concepts that the JFACC would incorporate into Desert Storm, such as kill boxes and EC techniques. Schwarzkopf initially looked elsewhere for his offensive air campaign plan.

Instant Thunder as the Basis of Phase I

The Air Staff's Instant Thunder plan served as the basis for the development of the Desert Storm Phase I Strategic Air Campaign. Colonel Warden, the architect of Instant Thunder, helped Schwarzkopf consider the use of conventional strategic air power and convinced him of its potency, leading the CINCCENT to incorporate the strategic air campaign into his offensive war planning. Schwarzkopf originally telephoned the Air Staff on August 8, 1990 for a response option to use if Saddam Hussein committed heinous acts, such as murdering hostages. The planning task went to Warden and his staff in the Deputy Directorate for Warfighting Concepts, and the colonel used his five strategic rings model to select target sets. Instant Thunder identified eighty-four sites in Iraq and did not employ air power directly against the Republican Guard forces nor the Iraqi troops occupying Kuwait, despite the fact that fielded forces constituted the fifth strategic ring in Warden's model. The Instant Thunder sets under the fielded forces category consisted of only strategic air defense targets and strategic air offensive targets (bombers and missiles). Warden placed Iraqi soldiers in Kuwait as a fourth-ring population target set to be subjected to nonlethal PSYOPS. He wrote, "The essence of war is applying pressure against the enemy's innermost strategic ring — its command structure. Military forces are a means to an end. It is pointless to deal with enemy military forces if they can be bypassed, by strategy or technology, either in the defense or offense."[41]

On August 8, Warden had begun to use his five *operational* rings model dealing with enemy forces, but soon discarded it to concentrate solely on the *strategic* ring model. When the CJCS told the Air Staff briefers to kill tanks, a few officers in Checkmate sketched out concepts for using air power directly against the Iraqi army. Warden expressed contempt for this planning and dismissed it. He held some air power in reserve to attack the Iraqi ground troops if they invaded Saudi Arabia in response to the initiation of Instant Thunder. To Warden, diverting air power to the KTO could seriously weaken Instant Thunder, his aerial Schlieffen plan. The CINCCENT had asked for a *strategic* air plan on August 8, and Warden gave him that aspect of air power.

Schwarzkopf liked Instant Thunder partly because it served his purpose as a retaliation option. He sent it to Horner in Riyadh with instructions to turn it into a real-world plan. In the meantime, he also incorporated it into his offensive war plan that would culminate with a ground attack to expel the Iraqis from Kuwait. By August 25, when the CINCCENT briefed his four-phased Desert Storm plan to the SecDef and CJCS, Warden was still advocating only the Instant Thunder strategic air campaign, eighty-four targets in Iraq struck in six days, as the independent, stand-alone campaign plan that would induce the Iraqis to leave Kuwait.

Warden explained Instant Thunder to Horner, just as he had to Schwarzkopf and Powell. The JFACC, then acting as CENTCOM Forward commander, rejected the colonel's assertion that six days of strategic bombing would force the Iraqis from Kuwait. Horner did not believe that the strategic attacks would paralyze Iraq and prevent it from launching an invasion of Saudi Arabia. He believed that the execution of the plan could provoke the Iraqis to invade the Saudi kingdom, and he wanted the Army's 24th Infantry Division, Mechanized, in place to halt the Iraqi assault. When Horner learned of the CINCCENT's four phases, he changed the name of the strategic air campaign from Instant Thunder to Offensive Campaign Phase I. The JFACC relied on General Glosson to turn the plan quickly into an executable ATO, in case an air option against Iraq was needed, and to further develop it as Phase I of the CINCCENT's four-phased war plan.

Retaliation Option

Instant Thunder started as a retaliation plan, but it became so imbedded in the CINCCENT's offensive war planning that, by December, it lost its retaliatory character. On August 5, Horner's staff at Shaw AFB had tried to produce a punishment ATO as a response if Saddam committed some further aggression or atrocity. The start of the Desert Shield deployment on August 7, however, cut short the CENTAF planning effort. Schwarzkopf called the Air Staff for a retaliation option on August 8, resulting in Instant Thunder. By December, the Phase I strategic air campaign was pegged to predawn execution times. Its 0300 H-hour facilitated surprise, its darkness exploited the advantages of the stealthy F–117A Nighthawks and LANTIRN and Pave Tack systems, and its sunrise strikes against BW storage bunkers allowed a full day of sunlight to stream into the penetrated, damaged structures. When the Iraqis, however, test-fired their Scud missiles on December 2, CENTCOM and the CJCS wanted a retaliatory option ready for execution within two hours of an Iraqi provocation, regardless of the time of day. The Reflex plan then emerged as the quick-response option, and its MAP eventually included three parts, with various weapons packages suitable for nighttime or daylight response. Reflex attacks were a stopgap until the preplanned Desert Storm Phase I strikes could be executed. In December, therefore, Reflex planners frantically worked on a retaliatory option, just as they had done in August.

Phases Merged

During execution, the air campaign phases merged. By January 17, 1991, the JFACC had so many aircraft in theater that he used them simultaneously, causing the campaign segments to blend. He thought it more accurate to describe the execution not by distinct, sequential phases but as a shifting of weight and level of effort over time. Even during the lightest level of effort in a particular phase, some targets specified for it were still struck. The heaviest weight for Phase I occurred from January 17 to 27, when the CINCCENT declared air *supremacy* and more strike sorties shifted to the Republican Guard. The Scud attacks against Israel during this time led to the great Scud hunt for mobile missiles and launchers, which diverted aircraft from planned missions and targets. Much later, the strategic strikes against the Al Firdos bunker in Iraq, February 12/13, killing 200 civilians, caused Powell and Schwarzkopf to carefully review all attacks in central Baghdad, and the event reemphasized the importance of minimizing civilian casualties.[42]

The greatest level of effort in Phase II also occurred January 17 to 27. Its emphasis on SEAD helped gain medium-altitude air supremacy, not just air superiority, in the KTO. The main attrition effort against the Republican Guard in Phase III Part A lasted from approximately January 27 to February 14 and saw the initiation of tank-plinking. The Iraqi-launched ground offensive against Khafji, January 29 to 31, was halted in part by air strikes. The primary effort against the frontline regular army troops in Phase III Part B lasted from February 14 to 24 and included PSYOPS.[43] Phase IV, February 24 to 28, involved breaching, CAS, and interdiction operations, while some fleeing Republican Guard forces escaped to Basra and its suburbs, and then farther northward. During the air and ground offensive operations in the final phase, lasting only 100 hours, the Iraqi army in the KTO withdrew, surrendered, or were killed or wounded, and Kuwait was liberated.

Strategic Air Campaign

From January 17 to February 28, 1991, the Coalition made 11,610 strikes against twelve strategic target sets, excluding the Republican Guard:

Target Set	No. of Strikes
Leadership	260
Electric power	280
Naval targets	370
Oil	540
Telecommunications and C^3	580

IADS and Kari	630
Military industry	970
NBC	990
LOCs	1,170
SAMs	1,370
Scuds	1,460
Airfields	2,990
Total	11,610[44]

The most immediately successful results stemmed from the strategic target sets hit to gain and maintain air supremacy. Strikes against electrical power plants and telecommunications and C^3 contributed to destroying the effectiveness of Kari, the computerized brain of the IADS. The attacks gained air superiority in the first hours of the air campaign, and on January 27 Schwarzkopf declared that the Coalition had achieved air supremacy.[45]

Before the war, the most worrisome targets were those related to BW. Planners feared that strikes on BW research, production, and storage facilities would inadvertently kill an enormous number of civilians by causing the release of toxic spores and agents into the atmosphere. As the weeks wore on and the DIA and other agencies studied the problem, results indicated that the expected collateral casualties would not outweigh the benefit of preventing Saddam from using BW against the Coalition. The airmen planned strikes against BW storage bunkers during the first twenty-four hours of the campaign and they took special precautions to prevent the spread of toxic material. After the war, the United Nations Special Commission learned conclusively that Iraq had undertaken a military biological research program. In August 1995, Saddam's son-in-law, Lt. Gen. Hussein Kamel Hasan al-Majid, defected. He had firsthand, detailed knowledge of Iraq's NBC programs and disclosed that Iraq had actually weaponized biological agents before the war. No credible evidence surfaced to reveal that Desert Storm air strikes had caused the release of BW agents and the deaths of civilians.

After the war, electrical power plants emerged as the most controversial strategic target set. Planners in Washington and Riyadh consistently had seen electricity-producing installations as military targets because they powered the IADS, C^2 systems, weapon production sites, and refrigerated bunkers. Shutting down electrical facilities would create confusion and temporarily blind the IADS if backup power generators did not immediately activate. By "turning out the lights in Baghdad," and elsewhere, the attacks might also send a political message to the Iraqi people that the war was on, thanks to the reckless, brutal leadership of Saddam Hussein. The planners' intent was to strike elements of the power plants most easily replaceable, permitting a rapid regeneration of electricity once the war ended. If the conflict led to Saddam Hussein's ouster, the new leadership in Baghdad could win the goodwill of the people by restoring power quickly. The ATOs sent to units during Desert Storm, however, neglected to identify aim points that would permit timely restoration of the electric grid. Wing personnel, therefore, selected DMPIs on the basis of standard targeting guidance; thus they often selected for destruction generators that were difficult to replace. Given the postwar objectives of rapidly returning electricity to the nation, the appropriate aim points were transformers, switching yards, and control buildings, not generators.[46]

Shutting down electric power plants shut down water purification and sewage treatment facilities, causing disease levels to rise, especially among infants and children. Before Desert Storm, planners had not accounted for the connection between electrical power facilities and clean water and sewage treatment. They did not think in terms of preventing the spread of cholera, typhoid, and gastroenteritis, nor did they think of disease as collateral damage. "Turning out the lights in Baghdad" served as the explanation for the major anticipated result afflicting the civilians, not the elimination of their clean water supply. Saddam Hussein remained in control after the war, and his lack of cooperation with U.N. inspection teams kept economic sanctions on his country, preventing the replacement of damaged equipment. Saddam callously allowed his people to suffer and die unnecessarily while using mortality data as propaganda.[47] Despite the Iraqi leadership's role in contributing to civilian deaths, some DoD officials had second thoughts about electrical plants as targets and believed they required the closest scrutiny to determine how best to eliminate the military benefits of power generation while not affecting civil life-support systems. After the war, Secretary Rice observed:

> I think we need to think through with some care how we handle the targets that are dual-purpose, that not only support the war-making potential but also have significant effects on the civil population — the things that affect electricity and water supply....It might turn out that we would go and do the same thing again because the effect on the war-making capability was so great. But, my guess is we would modulate that, the attacks on that set of targets in some ways, if we had it to do again.[48]

The need existed for ambitious intelligence collection and the most rigorous analysis of data to determine critical nodes and strike effects against national electrical power grids.

Missing from the strategic air campaign was strategic surprise. U.N. Security Council Resolution 678, passed on November 29, 1990, threatened to expel the Iraqis from Kuwait, using "all necessary means," unless Iraq unconditionally withdrew its troops from Kuwait by midnight, January 15, 1991. This deadline gave the Iraqis six additional weeks to dismantle, disperse, bury, and conceal key components of their NBC capabilities.[49] After the Israeli attack against the Osirak nuclear reactor in 1981, the Iraqis adopted a strategy of dispersing their nuclear production systems, and they continued to do so before and during Desert Storm.[50] If NBC scientists and technicians dispersed as well, a likely probability, the objective of destroying them all would be unachievable unless they were targeted while in conference, an improbable scenario.[51]

In September 1990 the revelations about the air campaign in the *Washington Post* and *Los Angeles Times,* emphasizing strategic strikes, probably reinforced Saddam Hussein's extreme anxiety and sense of vulnerability to attack if he stayed in official buildings and bunkers during the war.[52] A civilian analyst who visited Baghdad in 1991 and 1993 to study the effects of the bombing campaign concluded, "There is no concrete evidence that any Baghdad leadership target was actually in use at the time of attack. Ministers and key staff evacuated buildings before January 17, removing with them equipment and files."[53] During the war, the Soviet foreign minister, Yevgeny M. Primakov, and the CNN reporter, Peter Arnett, met with Saddam Hussein in a modest home in a residential neighborhood, away from a government facility.[54] At the operational level, the airmen did achieve surprise by preventing Iraqi reconnaissance from seeing the preparations for the left-hook flanking attack on the ground. The airmen also achieved tactical surprise by preventing the Iraqis from seeing the air armada forming just beyond their radar range the night the war started.[55]

Air Superiority and the Medium Altitude

Desert Storm seriously damaged the Iraqi IADS, whose Kari network linked radars, aircraft, and missiles. The objective was to create a safe flying regime at medium altitude, out of the range of infrared-guided SAMs and AAA. Because enemy aircraft and radar-guided SAMs threatened aircraft flying at medium altitude, Coalition aviators also had to intimidate Iraqi pilots and SAM radar operators by destroying their aircraft and defensive equipment.

Kari and its key nodes (the ADOC, the SOCs, and the IOCs) had to be struck to destroy the integration of the defense network. Shooting down enemy aircraft and cratering runways or hitting hardened aircraft shelters and airplanes parked in the open would further degrade the effectiveness of the Iraqi air force. Electronic jamming, destruction of radars with homing missiles, and the bombing of radar sites would force missile sites to operate autonomously and launch ballistically. Coalition pilots would still see AAA barrage firings and infrared-homing SAMs, but they could fly above the weapons' ranges.

After the first days of the air campaign until the start of the ground war, most pilots flew their missions at medium altitude. At this height, however, their bombing accuracy was compromised. At the end of January, to improve the pace of the destruction of tanks and artillery in the KTO, Horner told the A–10 pilots to decrease their altitude to the 4,000- to 7,000-foot range, and in February he directed F–16s working with scout pilots also to drop their weapons at lower altitudes.[56] Once Phase IV commenced and the airmen had to provide CAS for friendly ground forces, the JFACC told pilots to fly as low as necessary to acquire and hit targets.

A remarkable effect of defeating the IADS and the Iraqi air force it controlled was to provide magnificent protection for two Army corps shifting west to their jumping-off points for the start of Phase IV, the ground invasion. The American troops, supplies, and equipment were lucrative targets, but the Iraqi air force could not effectively respond. After the war, an official U.S. Army history explained:

> If an Iraqi pilot had managed to penetrate the air space over the border area during the great shift west, he would have been stunned by the panorama below. It was "mile after mile of tank transporters, gasoline tankers, troop and ammunition carriers," while "overhead was the continuous clatter of C–130 transport planes and cargo helicopters." Occasionally, a truck pulled into one of the rest stops along the twelve-to-fourteen-hour ride from the ports to the assembly areas. If any proof of allied air supremacy was necessary, this was it: "I shudder to think," an American observer wrote, "what a couple of Iraqi planes could have done to that column on a strafing and bombing run."[57]

Air superiority prevented Iraqi air power from decimating the massed and moving XVIII Airborne Corps and VII Corps, just as planners had anticipated.

Counterland Operations

The Coalition's ground offensive, Desert Storm Phase IV, would not commence until air power had attrited the enemy army to the 50 percent level. This attrition would achieve a favorable force ratio for Coalition attackers against Iraqi defenders and ensure success while keeping the Coalition casualties low. The air counterland mission to change ground-force ratios originated in CENTCOM OPLAN 1002–90. CENTCOM's CAG supplied the specific attrition percentage, based on the TACWAR computer-simulation scenarios, and analyses focused on deployed tanks, artillery pieces, and APCs.

General Glosson and Checkmate viewed the 50 percent goal differently than the CENTCOM commander did. They thought in terms of unit effectiveness and level of attrition required to cause a unit to lose its combat capability. Schwarzkopf, however, persisted in seeing the 50 percent in terms of force ratios and deployed troops in the aggregate. As early as August 4, 1990, at Camp David, he told the NCA that to wage a successful offensive and achieve favorable attacker-to-defender force ratios, air power must heavily attrit the enemy. At the White House on October 11, Schwarzkopf's CENTCOM briefers explained the ground campaign and told the President that air power had to attrit 50 percent of the Iraqi armor and mechanized forces in theater. On January 16, 1991, the CINCCENT's OPORD for Desert Storm bluntly stated that the objective of Phase III was to "reduce Iraq's capability in the KTO by at least 50 percent prior to the ground offensive" and to shift "combat ratios in favor of friendly forces."

In his televised briefing on February 27, 1991, in Riyadh, Schwarzkopf explained to reporters his color-coded charts showing the attrition level of Iraqi divisions. He explained, "Green represents units that have been attrited below 50 percent strength. The yellow are units that are between 50 and 75 percent strength, and, of course, the red are units that are over 75 percent strength."[58] He talked about attacker-to-defender ratios and pointed out the Iraqis numerical advantage. He lectured:

> I think any student of military strategy would tell you that in order to attack a position you should have a ratio of approximately three-to-one in favor of the attacker. In order to attack a position that is heavily dug in and barricaded such as the one we had here, you should have a ratio of five-to-one in the way of troops in favor of the attacker.

He then revealed how he solved the problem of the Iraqi forces' numerical superiority: "What we did, of course, was start an extensive air campaign."[59]

The responsibility for tracking and measuring counterland attrition originally fell to ARCENT and MARCENT. Producing BDAs for the air counterland mission generated much controversy. The CINCCENT's JIC developed its own BDA system, counting tanks, artillery pieces, and APCs killed, and assessing the destruction of bridges, the interdiction of supplies, the degradation of communications, and the level of troop morale. Approximately two-thirds of Desert Storm sorties flew against Phase III targets, prompting Colonel Deptula to conclude, "We are not *'preparing* the battlefield,' we are *destroying* it!"[60]

Missing from Phase III counterland campaign planning was the approach Warden had used with the strategic plan: a model to help identify and prioritize target sets. By August 10, 1990, the colonel had dropped his five operational rings from the planning process, and the model was not resurrected. Horner expected the BCE to supply the JFACC with target nominations from the Army, and airmen would service them. During the war, when the BCE failed to deliver valid nominations, kill boxes assumed greater importance for designating areas where pilots could search for targets of opportunity. The CINCCENT's directions to achieve the 50 percent attrition against the Republican Guard and then against the regular army units drove the wartime targeting process.

Parallel Warfare and Targeting for Effects

After the war, Warden and officers from Checkmate tried to create a concise, memorable term to describe Deptula's targeting-for-effects strategy and his emphasis on precisely hitting as many Phase I targets as possible during the first days of the air campaign and thereby seize the initiative and paralyze the Iraqi war machine. Linked to that strategy was Glosson's and Deptula's adherence to Horner's directive to apply pressure twenty-four hours a day so the enemy could not repair damaged target sets and improve defenses — no bombing pauses as in the Vietnam War. Deptula called the intense tempo and numerous targets *simultaneity*.[61] In Checkmate Lt. Col. T. K. Kearney suggested the descriptive *hyper-*

war to describe the unrelenting, fast-paced conflict. Warden liked the new term even though some on his staff thought it suggested hyperactivity and was associated with frenetic, unfocused actions, especially those of schoolchildren.[62] General Dugan, now retired, visited Checkmate, discussed the war with Warden, and wrote an article on Desert Storm for *U.S. News and World Report,* where the word *hyperwar* appeared in print.[63] Warden delivered a paper at Tufts University in May 1991 and emphasized the concept. He lectured:

> The Gulf conflict was also the first example of "hyperwar" — one that capitalizes on high technology, unprecedented accuracy, operational and strategic surprise through stealth, and the ability to bring all of an enemy's key operational and strategic nodes under near-simultaneous attack.[64]

In a January 1993 briefing at the Air Command and Staff College, Maxwell AFB, Deptula presented a slide, "Parallel Warfare: What Is It?"[65] He linked the concept to his targeting-for-effects strategy and reliance on stealth technology during Desert Storm. He credited Warden's Deputy Directorate for Warfighting Concepts for coining the terms *parallel* and *serial* warfare based on analogies from parallel and serial electrical circuitry.[66] He expounded on the concepts in two articles in 1995 and 1996. He wrote: "Simultaneous application of force (time) across each level of war uninhibited by geography (space) describes the conduct of parallel warfare."[67] In 1990 Deptula had envisioned parallel operations in terms of simultaneous attacks across the strategic target sets in Desert Storm Phase I. As the execution of the air plan merged the phases, he could see that simultaneous attacks actually encompassed targets in Iraq and the KTO, Phase I through Phase III targets. Air power operated across the spectrum of phases and targets, simultaneously on the strategic, operational, and tactical levels of warfare.

In 1992 Warden became the commandant at the Air Command and Staff College. He emphasized topics emerging from the Gulf War — centers of gravity, the revolution in military affairs, information warfare, the ring models, and parallel warfare. He encouraged the college faculty and students to analyze planning and operational requirements suggested by these concepts. In 1994, articles published by a faculty member and a student focused on parallel warfare, and in the same publication an article by Warden likened parallel strategic attacks on Iraq to death by a "thousand cuts."[68] This new analogy of death by a thousand cuts had taken Warden far from his tightly focused targeting advocacy in 1990 when he wrote:

> We may not have to find and destroy thirty thousand tanks if we can destroy the few hundred fuel or ammunition distribution points. We may not have to destroy the few hundred fuel distribution points if we can immobilize an entire society by destroying dozens of electrical gen-

eration systems. And we may not need to destroy dozens of electrical generation systems if we can capture or kill the enemy leader.[69]

In 1997, Air Force doctrine subsumed the parallel warfare concept under the *versatility* tenet of air power:

> Air and space attacks can be simultaneous and continuous against a broad spectrum of targets and with sufficient force to overwhelm the enemy. The versatility of air and space power, properly executed in parallel attacks, can attain parallel effects which present the enemy with multiple crises occurring so quickly that there is no way to respond to all or, in some cases, any of them. Such a strategy places maximum stress on both enemy defenses and the enemy society as a whole. Parallel operations can be conducted at the strategic, operational, and tactical levels of war and symmetrically against the adversary's air and space forces or asymmetrically against the enemy's surface forces — often simultaneously.[70]

In 1998 the Air Force's new Strategic Attack doctrine devoted a section to "parallel application."[71] This doctrine omitted Deptula's targeting-for-effects idea — strike facilities to affect their function and not necessarily to destroy their physical structure — and emphasized his concept of simultaneity — hit targets from all the sets to inflict on the enemy strategic and operational paralysis.

After the war, the targeting-for-effects concept assumed a life of its own with its emphasis on PGMs, weapons in use since the Vietnam War but only catching the world's attention in 1991. Postwar critiques of BDA highlighted the differences between physical and functional damage to targets and target systems, and in 1993 the second volume in the Gulf War Air Power Survey stressed the difference between *effects* and *effectiveness* and put the problem in historical context. Deptula popularized the concept in the pamphlet, "Firing for Effect," published by the Aerospace Education Foundation in 1995 and updated in 2001 as "Effects-Based Operations."[72] In 1996 the Quadrennial Defense Review kept the idea alive, the Air University included it in the subject matter appropriate for research reports and theses, and civilian and military analysts expounded on the concept. In 1998, Maj. Gen. Charles D. Link, USAF (Ret.), used a version of the term, effects-based warfare, when he criticized the TACWAR model.[73] In answering critics in 1999 who claimed that the air war over Kosovo was ineffective during Operation Allied Force, airmen defended their operations using a targeting-for-effects rationale. Speaking about the conflict, the commander of the U.S. Air Forces in Europe, General John P. Jumper, explained, "Effects-based targeting has to be the objective of the air campaign planners, as opposed to campaigns by target-list management."[74] In the years 2000 and 2001, the concept labeled "effects-based operations" was widely written about and debated.

Intelligence Support

General Horner summed up the role of intelligence in the Gulf War air campaign: "It all starts and ends with intelligence."[75] Supporting decision-making at the strategic, operational, and tactical levels of warfare, this function aided the President in considering the threat Iraq posed to regional stability, assisted planners with target selection and BDA, and guided the wings' mission planning. In August 1990, CENTCOM's intelligence organization was unprepared and incapable of adequately supporting an offensive war against Iraq. CENTAF's intelligence function was also unprepared for extensive offensive combat. It lacked, for example, on-line connectivity with some of the intelligence community's basic tools for target selection. A young targeteer in Riyadh complained that had he returned to Omaha, Nebraska, to use the resources and equipment at SAC headquarters, he could have provided better assistance for Glosson's Special Planning Group from thousands of miles away than he provided from the targeteers' tent. Horner concluded that CENTAF/IN's unpreparedness stemmed from training exercises within his command that failed to require intelligence personnel to participate in realistic ways and to be graded on their performance in the fashion that operational flying personnel were. The entire intelligence community had to participate more significantly in military training exercises.

Even had CENTAF/IN been more integrated into operations and training, the targeting databases it depended on in 1990 would still have been inadequate because the U.S. intelligence community had not yet completed reorienting its focus from the USSR and Warsaw Pact countries to post–Cold War regional threats. In fact, CENTAF had moved ahead of the rest of the community as it developed its targeting list to support CENTCOM OPLAN 1002–90 to defend the Saudi kingdom from Iraqi aggression.

Compared with other wars and other nations, the support the intelligence community provided for the planning and execution of Desert Storm contributed enormously to setting and achieving national and military objectives. Many airmen, however, expressed dissatisfaction with intelligence support. Some of the frustration originated with decisions people made and initiatives they failed to take. When some intelligence officers heeded admonitions to "operate by the book" and "function as trained," their performance proved inadequate. Consequently, planners improvised and became dependent on Checkmate or the Joint Staff J–2, who espoused the principle "act now, fix the system later." CENTAF/IN had access to the DIA's National Military Intelligence Support Terminal satellite link, but sophisticated hardware alone could not make timely reports flow to the theater as well as Checkmate could, using an overworked, but secure, fax machine. The segregation of the targeteers in the tent away from the Black Hole exacerbated the inability of officers to anticipate requirements and then to satisfy them. The stacking of imagery in piles at headquarters instead of sending the photos to the wings impeded mission planning. The officer withholding valuable information on the IADS until planners asked for it in a *pull* mode contrasted starkly with Checkmate personnel selecting and *pushing* information to the Black Hole.

Equipment limitations, too, hindered the work of intelligence officers. Although unprecedented in technological sophistication, hardware could not keep up with demands for intelligence and imagery: the TDF machine took too long to send a single photo, some reconnaissance systems could not see through rain clouds and sandstorms, Iraqi communications security thwarted information collection, and aircraft could not overfly Iraq and take photos until the war had begun. The level of satisfaction that operators expressed for the intelligence function in peacetime could not be achieved in wartime because hardware could not generate products quickly enough to keep pace with continuous strike, parallel warfare.

The system itself proved inadequate to the task. The intelligence community's lack of emphasis on wartime BDA prevented photo interpreters from understanding and practicing the production of BDA for missions that delivered penetrating PGMs. Furthermore, the requirement to track air power's destruction of an enemy army had no standardized measurement, the concern for secrecy overrode need-to-know as a criterion for disseminating target material, and the lack of effective collection against Iraqi NBC production and delivery systems kept some of those facilities off the target list.

For all its imperfections, the intelligence community acquired, analyzed, and disseminated enough worthwhile reports and imagery to allow the effective prosecution of the war. The DoD rightly told Congress after Desert Storm, "Perhaps in no other conflict in American history have tactical commanders — corps-level and below — been able to call on as capable an intelligence system as in the Gulf War."[76] The information Checkmate sent to the theater came from the intelligence organizations in Washington. Admiral McConnell, whom Glosson praised so highly, was a key figure in the intelligence community, a system that was less stovepiped than operating as a pipe organ. Sometimes intelligence officers expressed as much frustration with the "system" as the operators did.

Short Duration Expected

The six-day duration of Instant Thunder transferred to the planning for Phase I of the offensive plan. Warden had limited his plan to six days so he could sell it to Schwarzkopf, who believed that about six days would be all the time CENTCOM would have to execute a retaliatory air option. On December 20, Horner told Cheney and Powell that the Phase I Strategic Air Campaign would last six days; Phase II KTO Air Supremacy would take one day; Phase III, Part A, Republican Guard would require five days; and Phase III, Part B, KTO Forces would need six days. Horner presented a chart, with the time bars showing scalloped ends to indicate approximations, and explained that the Phase III estimates derived from computer calculations, but his gut feeling was that the KTO strikes would take twice as long, meaning ten days to destroy 50 percent of the Republican Guard, and twelve days to effect the same result against the regular forces in Kuwait.

The short time, six days, allotted to the strategic air operations did not bother the JFACC, even though the duration originated with Instant Thunder striking only 84 targets, and by December 18 the strike list included 238 targets. The number of targets would increase during the war so that by February 26, 1991, the eight core strategic sets encompassed 531 targets.[77] President Bush had doubled the assets for the offensive war, but the number of targets outpaced the increase in aircraft. Horner simply believed that the CINCCENT and the NCA would allow him time to hit all targets necessary to meet the objectives. For Phase III he thought air power would continue to attack the enemy army until all targets were hit, but he did not account for Soviet and Iraqi diplomatic maneuvering and the NCA anxious for a ground war to begin sooner rather than later. After the war, Bush explained the view he held on February 3:

> At the meeting Powell explained that Schwarzkopf was anticipating at least another two weeks plus for the air campaign before a ground attack would begin. The news concerned me, for I thought this would give Saddam more time to wriggle out of his predicament with a cease-fire offer of some kind. We had to balance this danger against our own readiness and make a decision on when to go.[78]

The President wanted to eliminate Iraq as a military threat to the region, and he was never to have as good an opportunity as the one in Desert Storm.[79] He wanted a ground offensive to end the conflict before the air campaign destroyed the Coalition from having killed too many civilians.[80]

While the air campaign's Phase III analysis from Checkmate heavily emphasized determining the time required to achieve objectives, no comparable analysis was done for hitting Phase I targets. For the strategic campaign, no one tried to account for the cumulative effects of weather and mission diversions, acquisition rates, nonexistent BDA, and enemy countermeasures, such as emptying buildings and dispersing components of target sets. The Phase III analysis itself was deficient by not accounting for dug-in, bermed, and camouflaged forces, with the tanks and artillery of the Republican Guard especially well protected from aircraft flying at medium altitude and dropping munitions less effective than CBU–87s and laser-guided bombs.

The CINCCENT's vision of when the land war would commence complicated consideration of how long the air campaign would last. He depended on the aviators to destroy a significant portion of the enemy ground forces before the Coalition invaded Kuwait and Iraq. In addition, he took into account the time required for two Army corps to move to their jumping-off points for D-day. Once they arrived and their support areas were established, they could attack. Their move to their assigned D-day zones required about the same amount of time as the airmen said Phase III would take — less than two weeks. Horner had told Schwarzkopf, Cheney, and Powell on December 20 that the overlapping Phases I through III would last about fourteen days. The CINCCENT liked what he heard because it coincided with when the ground war would be ready to launch.

During Desert Storm, Phases I to III lasted thirty-nine days, and the VII Corps needed that time to prepare for G-day, the start of the ground war. On February 23, the CINCCENT's BDA indicated that air had destroyed 1,688 tanks (a 39 percent kill rate), 1,452 artillery pieces (47 percent destroyed), and 929 (32 percent) of enemy APCs.[81] Schwarzkopf's color-coded charts showed almost all Iraqi frontline divisions at less than 50 percent effectiveness, while the rear divisions, including the Republican Guard, were at above the 75 percent level. Even though the 50 percent goal had not been consistently achieved, the ground war launched the next day. The Coalition troops were in place and ready to move, the air war had gone on for more than twice as long as planners' estimates, the air campaign had significantly destroyed the deployed enemy forces, Soviet diplomats were trying to broker a peace to spare the Iraqi army further destruction, and the President pressed to start the land offensive.

Throughout Desert Storm, prewar planning directed the course and focus of the air operations, and aviators executed all four phases of the campaign according to a shifting level of emphasis. The CINCCENT based his strategy on the employment of air power at the strategic, operational, and tactical levels of warfare, and the JFACC employed that power through a plan crafted in a long, complex process. Early on, the CINCCENT and his airmen had recognized the strength and versatility of the aerial weapon, and they fully exploited the Coalition's airpower advantage.

Glossary

AAA	antiaircraft artillery
AADC	Area Air Defense Commander
AB	Air Base
ABCCC	Airborne Battlefield Command and Control Center
ACA	Airspace Control Authority
ACE	airborne combat element
ACTS	Air Corps Tactical School
ADOC	air defense operations center
AFB	Air Force Base
AFIA	Air Force Intelligence Agency
ALARM	air-launched antiradiation missile
AOR	area of responsibility
APC	armored personnel carrier
ARCENT	U.S. Army Forces Central Command
ARS	Air Rescue Service
ASARS	Advanced Synthetic Aperture Radar System
ASOC	Air Support Operations Center
ATO	air tasking order
ATTG	Automated Tactical Target Graphics
AWACS	Airborne Warning and Control System
BAI	battlefield air interdiction
BCE	battlefield coordination element
BDA	battle damage assessment; bomb damage assessment
BTG	basic target graphics
BVR	beyond visual range
BW	biological warfare; biological weapons
C^2	command and control
C^3	command, control, and communications
C^3I	command, control, communications, and intelligence
CADS	Combat Airspace Deconfliction System
CAFMS	Computer-Assisted Force Management System
CAG	Combat Analysis Group
CALCM	conventional air-launched cruise missile
CAP	combat air patrol
CAS	close air support
CENTAF	U.S. Central Command Air Forces
CENTCOM	U.S. Central Command

CIA	Central Intelligence Agency
CINC	commander in chief (of a unified or specified command)
CINCCENT	Commander, U.S. Central Command
CINCSAC	Commander, Strategic Air Command
CJCS	Chairman of the Joint Chiefs of Staff
CNO	Chief of Naval Operations
CONOPS	concept of operations
CSAF	U.S. Air Force Chief of Staff
CSAR	combat search and rescue
CTG	contingency target graphics
CW	chemical warfare; chemical weapons
DCS	deputy chief of staff
D-day	the day designated for the initiation of military operations
DIA	Defense Intelligence Agency
DMAAC	Defense Mapping Agency Aerospace Center
DMPI	desired mean point of impact
/DO	Directorate of Operations
DoD	Department of Defense
EC	electronic combat
ECM	electronic countermeasures
EWR	early warning radar
FAE	fuel-air explosive
FM	Field Manual
FSCL	fire support coordination line
G–2	director of intelligence (General Staff)
G–3	director of operations and plans (General Staff)
GAT	Guidance, Apportionment, and Targeting
GCC	Gulf Cooperation Council
GCI	ground-controlled interception
G-day	the beginning day of the ground campaign
GPS	Global Positioning System
HARM	high-speed antiradiation missile
H-hour	the moment the strategic air campaign began
IADS	integrated air defense system
IFF	identification – friend-or-foe
/IN	Directorate of Intelligence
IOC	intercept operations center
J–2	director of intelligence (Joint Staff)
J–3	director of operations (Joint Staff)
J–4	director of logistics (Joint Staff)
J–5	director of plans/strategic plans and policy (Joint Staff)
JCS	Joint Chiefs of Staff
JEWC	Joint Electronic Warfare Center

JFACC	Joint Force Air Component Commander
JFC	Joint Force Commander
JFLCC	joint force land component commander
JIC	Joint Intelligence Center
JMEM	Joint Munitions Effectiveness Manual
JRCC	Joint Rescue Coordinating Center
JSTARS	Joint Surveillance and Target Attack Radar System
JTFME	Joint Task Force Middle East
KKMC	King Khalid Military City
KTO	Kuwaiti Theater of Operations
LANTIRN	low-altitude navigation and targeting infrared for night
LIMFAC	limiting factor
LOC	lines of communication
MAC	Military Airlift Command
MAP	master attack plan
MARCENT	U.S. Marine Forces Central Command
MIB	Military Intelligence Board
MODA	Ministry of Defense and Aviation
MSS 2	Mission Support System II
NAVCENT	U.S. Naval Forces Central Command
NBC	nuclear, biological, and chemical
NCA	National Command Authorities
NSA	National Security Agency
NSC	National Security Council
NSD	National Security Directive
NW	nuclear warfare
OPCON	operational control
OPLAN	operation plan
OPORD	operation order
OSP	operational support package
PGM	precision-guided munition/missile/weapon
POL	petroleum, oil, and lubricant
PSYOPS	psychological operations
RAF	Royal Air Force
RAND	RAND Corporation
ROE	rules of engagement
RSAF	Royal Saudi Air Force
SAC	Strategic Air Command
SAM	surface-to-air missile
SAMS	School for Advanced Military Studies (U.S. Army)
SAR	search and rescue
SCI	sensitive compartmented information
SEAD	suppression of enemy air defenses

SecAF	Secretary of the Air Force
SecDef	Secretary of Defense
SIDS	secondary image dissemination system
SIOP	Single Integrated Operations Plan
SOC	sector operations center
SOCCENT	Special Operations Command Central Command
SOF	special operations forces
SPEAR	Strike Projection Evaluation and Anti-Air Research
SPECAT	special category
SPINS	special instructions
STRATFOR	Strategic Forces
STU III	Secure Telephone Unit (third generation)
SWA	Southwest Asia
TAC	Tactical Air Command
TACAIR	tactical aircraft
TACC	Tactical Air Control Center
TACS	Tactical Air Control System
TACWAR	tactical warfare
TALD	tactical air-launched decoy
TDF	Tactical Digital Facsimile
TEL	transporter-erector-launcher
TEP	tactical electronic-intelligence processor
TLAM	Tomahawk land-attack missile
TRAM	Target Recognition Acquisition Multisensor
UAE	United Arab Emirates
USA	United States Army
USAF	United States Air Force
USMC	United States Marine Corps
USMTM	U.S. Military Training Mission
USN	United States Navy
WSO	weapon systems officer

Bibliography

Interviews

For some interviews, more than one version exists because of editing stages and security classification.

Adams, Gen Jimmie V., by Lt Col Richard Reynolds and Lt Col Suzanne Gehri, Feb 3, 1992, CADRE (College of Aerospace Doctrine, Research, and Education), Air University (AU). Transcript.

Alexander, Lt Gen Robert M., by Lt Col Suzanne Gehri, Lt Col Richard Reynolds, and Lt Col Edward Mann, May 30, 1991, and Jun 3, 1992, CADRE, AU. Tape and transcript.

——— by Diane T. Putney, Nov 26, 1993, Office of Air Force History (AFHSO). Tape.

Armstrong, Col William P., by Lt Col Richard Reynolds, Oct 23, 1991, CADRE, AU. Transcript. See Moore interview.

Baptiste, Lt Col Samuel J., by Perry D. Jamieson and Barry Barlow, Mar 3, 1992, AFHSO. Tape.

——— by Diane T. Putney and Lt Col Richard Reynolds, Sep 24, 1992, AFHSO. Tape.

Bettinger, Col Alexander, by Lt Col Suzanne Gehri and Lt Col Richard Reynolds, Sep 26, 1991, CADRE, AU. Transcript. See Griffith interview.

Blackburn, Col James R., by Diane T. Putney, Feb 12 and 19, 1992, AFHSO. Tape.

——— by Lt Col Edward Mann, Lt Col Richard Reynolds, and Lt Col Suzanne Gehri, Apr 21, 1993, CADRE, AU. Transcript.

Bruner, Maj William, by Diane T. Putney, Jul 14, 1993, AFHSO. Tape.

Caruana, Brig Gen Patrick P., by Lt Col Edward Mann, Aug 19, 1991, CADRE, AU. Transcript.

Casey, Lt Cdr Michael, by Lt Col Richard Reynolds, Oct 21, 1991, CADRE, AU. Transcript.

Christian, Maj Mark, by Diane T. Putney, Apr 23, 1992, AFHSO. Tape.

Christon, Col Christopher, by Richard G. Davis and Barry Barlow, Mar 4, 1992, AFHSO. Tape.

——— by Diane T. Putney, Apr 25–26, 1994, AFHSO. Tape.

Corder, Maj Gen John A., by Robert L. Mandler, Dec 21, 1991, USAF Air Warfare Center History Office. Transcript.

——— by Lt Col Richard T. Reynolds and Lt Col Suzanne Gehri, Feb 4, 1992, CADRE, AU. Transcript.

Cox, Col George W., by Robert L. Mandler, Dec 21, 1991, USAF Air Warfare Center History Office. Transcript.

Creech, General Wilbur L., by Hugh N. Ahmann, Jun 1992, Air Force Historical Research Agency (AFHRA).Transcript.

Crigger, Col James, by Lt Col Suzanne Gehri and Lt Col Richard Reynolds, Dec 2–4, 1991, CADRE, AU. Transcript.

Deptula, Lt Col David A., by TSgt Theodore J. Turner, Nov 1, 1990, AFHRA. Transcript.

——— by Richard G. Davis, Nov 20, 1991; by Davis, Perry D. Jamieson, and Diane T. Putney, Nov 29, 1991, and Jan 8, 1992; by Putney and Davis, Dec 12, 1992; and by Putney, Feb 14, 1994, and Apr 11, 1994, AFHSO. Tape and transcript.

——— by Lt Col Richard Reynolds and Lt Col Edward Mann, Dec 10, 1991; and by Reynolds, Mann, and Lt Col Suzanne Gehri, Jul 23–24, 1992, CADRE, AU. Tape and transcript.

Doman, Col Al, by Lt Col Richard Reynolds and Lt Col Edward Mann, May 28, 1993, CADRE, AU. Transcript.

Dugan, Gen Michael J., USAF (Ret), by Lt Col Richard Reynolds, Aug 15, 1991, CADRE, AU. Transcript.

Eskridge, Maj Robert, by TSgt Theodore Turner, Mar 3, 1991, Gulf War file, TAC/HO, Langley AFB. Tape.

——— by Richard G. Davis, Mar 19, 1992, AFHSO. Tape.

Feinstein, Lt Col Jeffrey S., by Richard G. Davis, Perry D. Jamieson, and Barry Barlow, Mar 3, 1992, AFHSO. Tape.

Gain, Col Tony, by Lt Col Richard Reynolds, Oct 21, 1991, CADRE, AU. Transcript.

Getchell, Col George, by Richard G. Davis, Mar 2, 1992, AFHSO. Tape.

Getchell, Maj Ralph W., by MSgt Barry Spink, May 1992, AFHRA. Tape.

Glock, Capt John R., by Diane T. Putney and Richard Davis, Aug 27, 1992; and by Putney, Oct 26, 1992 , AFHSO. Tape.

Glosson, Brig Gen Buster C., by TSgt Theodore J. Turner, Oct 17–27, 1990; and by MSgt Theodore J. Turner, Mar 6, 1991, AFHRA. Transcript.

Glosson, Maj Gen Buster C., by Richard G. Davis, Perry D. Jamieson, and Diane T. Putney, Dec 12, 1991; and by Putney, Aug 30, 1993, AFHSO. Tape and transcript.

——— by Lt Col Richard Reynolds, Lt Col Suzanne Gehri, and Lt Col Edward Mann, May 29, 1991, and Jun 4, 1992, CADRE, AU. Transcript.

Glosson, Lt Gen Buster C. by Diane T. Putney, Aug 30, 1993, AFHSO. Tape.

Glosson, Lt Gen Buster C. (Ret), Maj Gen Larry L. Henry (Ret), and Col Richard Lewis by Diane T. Putney, May 20, 1997. Tape.

Griffith, Brig Gen Thomas R., by Lt Col Suzanne Gehri and Lt Col Richard Reynolds, Sep 26, 1991, CADRE, AU. Transcript.

Harvey, Lt Col Bernard E., by Diane T. Putney and Richard G. Davis, Dec 7, 1992, and Jan 7 and 14, 1993, AFHSO. Tape.

Heintzelman, Maj Harry L., by TSgt Scott A. Saluda, Mar 14, 1991, AFHRA. Transcript.

Henry, Brig Gen Larry L., by Lt Col Suzanne Gehri, Lt Col Edward Mann, and Lt Col Richard Reynolds, [Jun 2, 1992], CADRE, AU. Transcript.

Henry, Maj Gen Larry L. (Ret), by Diane T. Putney, Jul 3, 1997. Transcript and tape.

Hente, Lt Col Scott, by Richard G. Davis, Oct 4, 1993, AFHSO. Tape.

Heston, Maj Robert J., by Mark D. Mandeles and Lt Col Sanford S. Terry, Oct 16 and 19, 1992, Mark Mandeles file, GWAPS, AFHRA. Transcript.

Horner, Lt Gen Charles A., by CMSgt John R. Burton, Mar 10, 1991, Gulf War file, TAC/HO, Langley AFB. Transcript.

——— by Lt Col Suzanne Gehri and Lt Col Richard Reynolds, Dec 2, 1991, CADRE, AU. Tape and transcript.

——— by Richard G. Davis, Perry D. Jamieson, and Barry Barlow, Mar 4, 1992, AFHSO. Tape and transcript.

Horner, Gen Charles A., by Diane T. Putney and George W. Bradley III, Apr 26, 1994, AFHSO. Tape and trasnscript.

Horner, Gen Charles A. (Ret), in response to questions sent by Diane T. Putney, Nov 30, 1996, AFHSO. Tape.

Hoyes, Maj Michael B. by Donna Clark, Mar 29, 1991, USAF Tactical Fighter Weapons Center History Office. Transcript

Jamerson, Maj Gen James L., by CMSgt Jerome E. Schroeder, Mar 27, 1991, United States Air Forces in Europe History Office. Transcript.

Krieger, Col Clifford R., by Diane T. Putney, Jan 12, 1994, AFHSO. Tape.

Leonardo, Col John (Ret), by Diane T. Putney, Jan 4–5, 1994, AFHSO. Telecon notes.

Loh, Gen John M., by Lt Col Suzanne Gehri and Lt Col Richard Reynolds, Sep 19, 1991, [Sep 26, 1991], CADRE, AU. Tape and transcript.

McConnell, Rear Adm John M., by Diane T. Putney and Ronald H. Cole, Feb 5 and 14, 1992, JCS/HO. Tape.

McNary, Capt Douglas, by Diane T. Putney, Aug 9, 1994, Oct 20, 1994, and Nov 4, 1994, AFHSO. Tape.

McPeak, Gen Merrill A., by Lt Col Suzanne Gehri, Lt Col Edward Mann, and Lt Col Richard Reynolds, Nov 5, 1992, CADRE, AU. Transcript.

McSwain, Cdr Donald W., by Richard G. Davis, Apr 7, 1992, AFHSO. Tape.

——— by Mark D. Mandeles and Maj Sanford S. Terry, Apr 21, 1992, Mark Mandeles file, GWAPS, AFHRA. Transcript.

Marion, Lt Col Bobby, by Diane T. Putney, Jun 4, 1992, AFHSO. Tape.

Meullner, Brig Gen George K. by Thomas C. Hone, Anne Leary, and Mark Mandeles, Apr 16, 1992, NA 257, GWAPS, AFHRA. Transcript.

Moore, Maj Gen Burton R., by Lt Col Richard Reynolds, Oct 23, 1991, and Reynolds, Lt Col Suzanne Gehri, and Lt Col Ed Mann, Sep 21, 1992, CADRE, AU. Tape and transcript.

Olsen, Maj Gen Thomas R., by MSgt Theodore J. Turner, Sep–Nov 1990, Gulf War file, TAC/HO, Langley AFB. Transcript.

——— by Richard G. Davis, Perry D. Jamieson, and Barry Barlow, Mar 5, 1992, AFHSO. Tape.

Rice, The Honorable Donald B., by Lt Col Richard Reynolds, Lt Col Suzanne Gehri, and Lt Col Edward Mann, Dec 11, 1991, NA 234, GWAPS, AFHRA. Transcript.

Rogers, Maj Mark B., by Lt. Col Suzanne Gehri, Lt Col Ed Mann, and Lt Col Richard Reynolds, Jun 3–4, 1991, CADRE. AU. Tape and transcript.

Rogers, Lt Col Mark B., by Lt Col Alan Howey, Feb 19, 1992, NA 174, GWAPS, AFHRA. Transcript.

Rogers, Col Mark B., by Diane T. Putney, Sep 18, 1994, AFHSO. Tape.

Roman, Lt Col Ronald V., by Diane T. Putney, Jun 9, 1992, AFHSO. Tape.

Russ, Gen Robert D., by Lt Col Suzanne Gehri, Lt Col Richard Reynolds, and Lt Col Edward Mann, Dec 9, 1991, CADRE, AU. Transcript.

Ryan, Maj Gen Michael E., by Lt Col Suzanne Gehri and Lt. Col Richard Reynolds, Sep 4, 1992, CADRE, AU. Tape and transcript.

Sawyer, Col David A., by TSgt Gary S. Trice, Oct 31, 1990, Gulf War file, TAC/HO, Langley AFB. Transcript.

Schwarzkopf, General H. Norman, by Diane T. Putney, May 5, 1992, AFHSO. Telecon notes.

Setnor, Maj Michael P., by Richard G. Davis, May 5, 1992, AFHSO. Tape.

Sharpe, Col Ervin C., by Lt Col Suzanne Gehri, Lt Col Edward Mann, and Lt Col Richard Reynolds, Nov 1, 1991, CADRE, AU. Transcript.

Sikes, Maj Roy "Mac," by Diane T. Putney, Apr 7, 1993, AFHSO. Tape.

Thomits, Lt Col, by Kent Beck, Jul 3, 1991, SAC/HO. Transcript.

Tolin, Brig Gen Anthony, by Joe Guilmartin, Jan 30, 1992, GWAPS, AFHRA. Transcript.

——— by Richard G. Davis, Nov 23, 1993, and Jan 7, 1994, AFHSO. Tape.

Warden, Col John A. III, by Lt Col Suzanne Gehri, Oct 22, 1991, CADRE, AU. Transcript.

——— by Lt Col Suzanne Gehri, Lt Col Ed Mann, and Lt Col Richard Reynolds, May 30, 1992, CADRE, AU. Transcript. See also "May 1992" transcript.

——— by Diane Putney, Richard Davis, Perry Jamieson, and Richard Hallion, Feb 6, 1992; and by Richard Davis, Mar 2, 1993, AFHSO. Tape.

Ware, Col Gary R., by Diane T. Putney, Mar 28, 1994. AFHSO. Telecon notes.

——— by Barry Watts, Feb 26, 1992, GWAPS. Telecon notes.

Waterstreet, Lt Col David L., by Richard G. Davis, Mar 6, 1992, AFHSO. Tape.

Welch, Lt Col William G., by MSgt Theodore J. Turner, Mar 4, 1991, Gulf War file, TAC/HO, Langley AFB. Tape.

Wilson, Col Steve, by Lt Col Suzanne Gehri, Lt Col Edward Mann, and Lt Col Richard Reynolds, Dec 11, 1991, CADRE, AU. Transcript.

Congressional Documents

U.S. Congress. House. Committee on Armed Services. Subcommittee on Oversight and Investigations. *Intelligence Successes and Failures in Operations Desert Shield/Storm.* 103d Cong., 1st sess., August 16, 1993.

——— Senate. Committee on Armed Services. *Crisis in the Persian Gulf Region: U.S. Policy Options and Implications.* 101st Cong., 2d sess., December 1990.

——— Senate. Committee on Armed Services. Hearings. 102d Cong., 1st sess., May 21, 1991.

——— Senate. Subcommittee of the Committee on Appropriations. *DoD Appropriations for Fiscal Year 1991.* 101st Cong., 2d sess., March 6, 1990.

Books

Allen, Charles. *Thunder and Lightning: The RA in the Gulf: Personal Experiences of War*. London: Her Majesty's Stationery Office, 1991.

Anderegg, C. R. *Sierra Hotel: Flying Air Force Fighters in the Decade After Vietnam.* Washington: Air Force History & Museums Program, 2001.

Andrews, William F. *Airpower against an Army: Challenge and Response in CENTAF's Duel with the Republican Guard.* Maxwell AFB, Ala.: Air University Press, 1998.

Association of the U.S. Army. *Personal Perspectives of the Gulf War.* Arlington, Va.: Institute of Land Warfare, 1993.

Atkinson, Rick. *Crusade: The Untold Story of the Persian Gulf War.* Boston: Houghton Mifflin, 1993.

Baker, James A. III, and Thomas M. DeFrank. *The Politics of Diplomacy: Revolution, War, and Peace, 1989–1992.* New York: G.P. Putnam's Sons, 1995.

Ball, Desmond. *The Intelligence War in the Gulf.* Canberra: Australian National University, 1991.

Bassford, Christopher. *Clausewitz in English: The Reception of Clausewitz In Britain and America 1815–1945.* New York: Oxford University Press, 1994.

Berquist, Ronald E. *The Role of Airpower in the Iran-Iraq War*. Maxwell AFB, Ala.: Air University Press, 1988.

Blackwell, James. *Thunder in the Desert: The Strategy and Tactics of the Persian Gulf War.* New York: Bantam Books, 1991.

Borowski, Harry R., ed. *Military Planning in the Twentieth Century:Proceedings of the Eleventh Military History Symposium 10–12 October 1984.* Washington: Office of Air Force History, 1986.

Boyne, Walter J. *Beyond the Wild Blue: A History of the United States Air Force 1947–1997.* New York: St. Martin's Press, 1997.

Bush, George, and Brent Scowcroft. *A World Transformed.* New York: Alfred A. Knopf, 1998.

Campen, Alan D., ed. *The First Information War: The Story of Communications, Computers, and Intellience Systems in the Persian Gulf War.* Fairfax, Va.: AFCEA International Press, 1992.

Cardwell, Thomas A. III. *Airland Combat: An Organization for Joint Warfare.* Maxwell AFB, Ala.: Air University Press, 1992.

——— *Command Structure for Theater Warfare: The Quest for Unity of Command.* Maxwell AFB, Ala.: Air University Press, 1984.

Clancy, Tom, with Fred Franks, Jr. *Into the Storm: A Study in Command.* New York: G.P. Putnam's Sons, 1997.

——— with Chuck Horner. *Every Man a Tiger.* New York: G.P. Putnam's Sons, 1999.

Clausewitz, Carl von. *On War.* Translated and edited by Michael Howard and Peter Paret. Princeton, N.J.: Princeton University Press, 1976 and 1989.

Clodfelter, Mark. *The Limits of Air Power: The American Bombing of North Vietnam.* New York: Free Press, 1989.

Cordesman, Anthony H., and Abraham R. Wagner. *The Iran-Iraq War.* Vol. 2 of *The Lessons of Modern War.* Boulder, Colo.: Westview Press, 1990.

Creech, Bill. *The Five Pillars of TQM: How to Make Total Quality Management Work for You.* New York: Truman Talley Books/Dutton, 1994.

Crowe, William J., with David Chanoff. *The Line of Fire: From Washington to the Gulf, the Politics and Battles of the New Military.* New York: Simon & Schuster, 1993.

Davis, Richard G. *The 31 Initiatives: A Study in Air Force–Army Cooperation.* Washington: Office of Air Force History, 1987.

——— *On Target: Organizing and Executing the Strategic Air Campaign against Iraq.* Washington: Air Force History & Museums Program, 2002.

De la Billiere, Sir Peter. *Storm Command: A Personal Account of the Gulf War.* London: Motivate, 1992.

Defense Intelligence Agency. *A Chronology of Defense Intelligence in the Gulf War: A Research Aid for Analysts.* Bolling AFB, D.C.: DIA History Office, 1997.

Dunnigan, James F. and Austin Bay. *From Shield to Storm: High Tech Weapons, Military Strategy, and Coalition Warfare in the Persian Gulf.* New York: William Morrow, 1992.

Finney, Robert T. *History of the Air Corps Tactical School 1920–1940.* Washington: Center for Air Force History, 1992.

Finnie, David H. *Shifting Lines in the Sand: Kuwait's Elusive Frontier with Iraq.* Cambridge, Mass.: Harvard University Press, 1992.

Francona, Rick. *Ally to Adversary: An Eyewitness Account of Iraq's Fall from Grace.* Annapolis, Md.: Naval Institute Press, 1999.

Freedman, Lawrence and Efraim Karsh. *The Gulf Conflict, 1990–1991: Diplomacy and War in the New Wold Order.* Princeton, N.J.: Princeton University Press, 1993.

Friedman, Norman. *Desert Victory: The War for Kuwait.* Annapolis, Md.: Naval Institute Press, 1991.

Frostic, Fred. *Air Campaign Against the Iraqi Army in the Kuwaiti Theater of Operations.* Santa Monica, Calif.: RAND, 1994.

Fuller, J.F.C. *The Generalship of Alexander the Great.* New Brunswick, N.J.: Rutgers University Press, 1960; reprint, New York: Da Capo Press, 1989.

Futrell, Robert Frank. *Ideas, Concepts, Doctrine.* 2 vols. Maxwell AFB, Ala.: Air University Press, 1989.

Gentile, Gian P. *How Effective Is Strategic Bombing: Lessons Learned from World War II to Kosovo.* New York: New York University Press, 2001.

Gordon, Michael R., and Bernard E. Trainor. *The Generals' War: The Inside Story of the Conflict in the Gulf.* Boston: Little, Brown, 1995.

Hallion, Richard P. *Storm over Iraq: Air Power and the Gulf War.* Washington: Smithsonian Institution Press, 1992.

Hansell, Haywood S. Jr. *The Air Plan that Defeated Hitler.* Atlanta, Ga.: Higgins-McArthur/Longino & Porter, 1972.

Head, William, and Earl H. Tilford, Jr. *The Eagle in the Desert: Looking Back on U.S. Involvement in the Persian Gulf War.* Westport, Conn.: Praeger, 1996.

Hosmer, Stephen T. *Psychological Effects of U.S. Air Operations in Four Wars, 1941–1991: Lessons for U.S. Commanders.* Santa Monica: Calif.: RAND, 1996.

Hourani, Albert. *A History of the Arab Peoples.* New York: Warner Books, 1991.

Howard, Michael. *Clausewitz.* New York: Oxford University Press, 1983, reprint 1990.

Jamieson, Perry D. *Lucrative Targets: The U.S. Air Force in the Kuwaiti Theater of Operations.* Washington: Air Force History and Museums Program, 2001.

Kearns, Doris. *Lyndon Johnson and the American Dream.* New York: Harper & Row, 1976.

Khaled bin Sultan, with Patrick Seal. *Desert Warrior: A Personal View of the Gulf War by the Joint Forces Commander.* New York: Harper Collins, 1995.

LeMay, General Curtis E. and MacKinley Kantor. *Mission with LeMay: My Story.* Garden City, N.Y.: Doubleday, 1965.

Liddell Hart, B.H. *Scipio Africanus Greater than Napoleon.* 1926. Reprint, Navato, Calif.: Presidio Press, 1992.

Liddell Hart, B.H. *Strategy.* 2d revised ed. New York: Meridian, 1991.

Luttwak, Edward. *Coup D'état: A Practical Handbook.* New York: Alfred A. Knopf, 1969

McNamara, Stephen J. *Air Power's Gordian Knot: Centralized versus Organic Control.* Maxwell AFB, Ala.: Air University Press, 1994.

Magyar, Karl P., Maris McCrabb, Albert U. Mitchum, Jr., and Lewis B. Ware, eds. *Challenge and Response: Anticipating U.S. Military Security Concerns.* Maxwell AFB, Ala.: Air University Press, 1994.

Mann, Col Edward C. III. *Thunder and Lightning: Desert Storm and the Airpower Debates.* Maxwell AFB, Ala.: Air University Press, 1995.

Marolda, Edward J., and Robert J. Schneller, Jr. *Shield and Sword: the United States Navy and the Persian Gulf War.* Washington: Naval Historical Center, 1998.

Mathews, Jay and Cora J. Holt. *So Many, So Much, So Far, So Fast: United States Strategic Deployment for Operations Desert Shield/Desert Storm.* Washington: Research Center, U.S. Transportation Command and Joint History Office, 1996.

Makiya, Kanan. *Republic of Fear: The Politics of Modern Iraq*. Rev. ed. with new intro. Berkeley, Calif.: University of California Press, 1998.

Mets, David R. *The Air Campaign: John Warden and the Classical Airpower Theorists.* Maxwell AFB, Ala.: Air University Press, 1998.

Miller, Judith and Laurie Mylroie. *Saddam Hussein and the Crisis in the Gulf.* New York: Times Books, 1990.

Mitchell, William. *Skyways: A Book on Modern Aeronautics.* Philadelphia: J.B. Lippincott, 1930.

——— *Winged Defense: The Development and Possibilities of Modern Air Power—Economic and Military.* New York: G.P. Putnam's Sons, 1925.

Pagonis, William G., with Jeffrey L. Cruikshank. *Moving Mountains: Lessons in Leadership and Logistics from the Gulf War.* Boston: Harvard Business School Press, 1992.

Palmer, Michael A. *On Course to Desert Storm: The United States Navy and the Persian Gulf.* Washington: Naval Historical Center, 1992.

——— *Guardians of the Gulf: A History of America's Expanding Role in the Persian Gulf, 1833–1992.* New York: Free Press, 1992.

Pape, Robert A. *Bombing to Win: Air Power and Coercion in War*. Itahaca, N.Y.: Cornell University Press, 1996.

Pergamon-Brassey's. *Five War Zones: The Views of Local Military Leaders*. Washington: Pergamon-Brasseys's International Defense Publications, 1986.

Pokrant, Marvin. *Desert Shield at Sea: What the Navy Really Did.* Westport, Conn.: Greenwood Press, 1999.

Powell, Colin L., with Joseph E. Persico. *My American Journey: An Autobiography.* New York: Random House, 1995.

Quayle, Dan. *Standing Firm: A Vice-Presidential Memoir.* New York: Harper Paperback, 1995.

Quilter, Charles J. III. *U.S. Marines in the Persian Gulf, 1990–1991: With the I Marine Expeditionary Force in Desert Shield and Desert Storm.* Washington: Marine Corps History and Museum Division, 1993.

Record, Jeffrey. *Hollow Victory: A Contrary View of the Gulf War.* Washington: Brassey's, 1993.

Reynolds, Col Richard T. *Heart of the Storm: The Genesis of the Air Campaign against Iraq.* Maxwell AFB, Ala.: Air University Press, 1995.

Ritter, Gerhard. *The Schlieffen Plan: Critique of a Myth.* 1958. Reprint, Westport, Conn.: Greenwood Press, 1979.

Romjue, John L. *From Active Defense to AirLand Battle: The Development of Army Doctrine 1973–1982.* Fort Monroe, Va.: U.S. TRADOC Historical Office, 1984.

Santoli, Al, ed. *Leading the Way: How Vietnam Veterans Rebuilt the U.S. Military—An Oral History.* New York: Ballantine Books, 1993.

Scales, Robert H., Jr., et al. *Certain Victory: The U.S. Army in the Gulf War.* Washington: Office of the Chief of Staff, U.S. Army, 1993.

Schneider, Barry R. and Lawrence E. Grinter. *Battlefield of the Future: 21st Century Warfare Issues.* Maxwell AFB, Ala.: Air University Press, 1995.

Schubert, Frank N., and Theresa L. Kraus, eds. *The Whirlwind War: The United States Army in Operations Desert Shield and Desert Storm.* Washington: Center of Military History, 1995.

Schwarzkopf, General H. Norman, with Peter Petre. *The Autobiography: It Doesn't Take a Hero.* New York: Linda Grey Bantam Books, 1992.

Shultz, Richard H. Jr., and Robert L. Pfaltzgraff, Jr., eds. *The Future of Air Power in the Aftermath of the Gulf War.* Maxwell AFB, Ala.: Air University Press, 1992.

Sifry, Micah L., and Christopher Cerf, eds. *The Gulf War Reader.* New York: Random House Times Books, 1991.

Smallwood, William L. *Warthog: Flying the A–10 in the Gulf War.* Washington: Brassey's, 1993.

Summers, Harry G., Jr. *On Strategy II: A Critical Analysis of the Gulf War.* New York: Dell, 1992.

Swain, Richard W. *"Lucky War": Third Army in Desert Storm.* Fort Leavenworth, Kans.: U.S. Army Command and General Staff College Press, 1994.

Thompson, Warren E. *Bandits over Baghdad: Personal Stories of Flying the F–117 over Iraq.* North Branch, Minn.: Specialty Press, 2000.

Triumph Without Victory: The Unreported History of the Persian Gulf War/U.S. News & World Report. New York: Times Books, 1992.

United States. Department of the Air Force. *Gulf War Air Power Survey.* 5 vols. Washington: Government Printing Office, 1993.

United States. Department of Defense. *Conduct of the Persian Gulf War: Pursuant to Title V....* April 1992. Washington: Government Printing Office, 1992.

United States. Department of State. *Iraqi Weapons of Mass Destruction Programs.* U.S. Government White Paper, February 13, 1998. Washington: Government Printing Office, 1998.

Vriesenga, Capt Michael P., ed. *From the Line in the Sand: Accounts of USAF Company Grade Officers in Support of Desert Shield/Desert Storm.* Maxwell AFB, Ala.: Air University Press, 1994.

Warden, John A. III. *The Air Campaign: Planning for Combat.* Washington: National Defense University Press, 1988.

Waters, Gary. *Gulf Lesson One — The Value of Air Power: Doctrinal Lessons for Australia.* Fairbairn, Australia: Air Power Studies Centre, 1992.
Watson, Bruce W., ed. *Military Lessons of the Gulf War*. Novato, Calif.: Presidio Press, 1991.
Winnefeld, James A., and Dana J. Johnson. *Joint Air Operations: Pursuit of Unity in Command and Control, 1942–1991.* Annapolis, Md.: Naval Institute Press, 1993.
———, Preston Niblack, and Dana J. Johnson. *A League of Airmen: U.S. Air Power in the Gulf War.* Santa Monica, Calif.: RAND, 1994.
Witt, Randy. *The Desert Shield/Desert Storm Comm Story: Air Force Tactical Communications in War.* Riyadh, Saudi Arabia: Headquarters United States Central Command Air Forces, 1991.
Woodward, Bob. *The Commanders*. New York: Simon & Schuster, 1991.

Articles

Albright, Joseph. "'I am not...going to waste American lives.' An Interview with Gen H. Norman Schwarzkopf." *Atlanta Journal and Constitution*, 28 October 1990, 12.
Alexander, Maj Gen Robert M. "World Is Rapidly Changing and AF Must Keep Up." *Air Force Times,* February 11, 1991, 23.
Allen, Charles E. "Warning and Iraq's Invasion of Kuwait: A Retrospective Look." *Defense Intelligence Journal* 7 (Fall 1998):33–44.
Arkin, William M. "Baghdad: The Urban Sanctuary in Desert Storm?" *Airpower Journal* 11 (Spring 1997): 4–20.
Atkinson, Rick. "U.S. to Rely on Air Strikes if War Erupts." *The Washington Post,* September 16, 1990, 1(A).
——— "The Chief Who Said Too Much." *The Washington Post* September 23, 1990, 1–2(B).
Aviation Week & Space Technology (27 April 1992): 20. S.v. "BQM–74 Drones Operated by Former GLCM Unit..."
Belote, Howard D. "Warden and the Air Corps Tactical School: What Goes Around Comes Around." *Airpower Journal* 13 (Fall 1999): 39–47.
Biddle, Stephen. "Victory Misunderstood: What the Gulf War Tells Us about the Future of Conflict." *International Security* 21 (Fall 1996): 139–179.
Bien, Lyle G. "Desert Storm: From the Strike Cell," *U.S. Naval Institute Proceedings* 117 (June 1991): 58–60.
Bird, Julie. "Horner: Further AF Role in Gulf Not Needed." *Air Force Times,* March 18, 1991, 8.
——— "Air War Legacy." *Air Force Times,* January 6, 1992, 12, 30.
Bodner, Maj Michael J., and Maj William W. Bruner III. "Tank Plinking." *Air Force Magazine* 76 (October 1993): 28–31.

Broder, John M. "With Its Hostages Out, U.S. Revises List of Iraqi Targets." *Los Angeles Times*, December 13, 1990, 1+.

Centner, Christopher M. "Ignorance Is Risk: The Big Lesson from Desert Storm Air Base Attacks." *Airpower Journal* 6 (Winter 1992): 25–33.

Chain, John T. "Strategic Bombers in Conventional Warfare." *Strategic Review* 16 (Spring 1988): 23–32.

Cigar, Norman. "Iraq's Strategic Mindset after the Gulf War: Blueprint for Defeat." *Journal of Strategic Studies* 15 (March 1992): 1–29.

Clodfelter, Mark. "Of Demons, Storms, and Thunder: A Preliminary Look at Vietnam's Impact on the Persian Gulf Air Campaign." *Airpower Journal* 5 (Winter 1991): 17–32.

——— "Pinpointing Devastation: American Air Campaign Planning before Pearl Harbor." *Journal of Military History* 58 (January 1991): 75–101.

Coakley, Paul. "Tomahawk Weapon System Imagery Support to Mission/Strike Planning." *American Intelligence Journal* (Winter/Spring 1992): 69–74.

Cohen, Eliot A. "The Mystique of U.S. Air Power." *Foreign Affairs* 73 (January 1994): 109–124.

Deptula, David A. "Firing for Effect: Change in the Nature of Warfare." Pamphlet in the Defense and Airpower Series. Arlington, Va.: Aerospace Education Foundation, 1995. Updated as "Effects-Based Operations" in 2001.

——— "Firing for Effects." *Air Force Magazine* 84 (April 2001): 46–53.

——— "Parallel Warfare: What Is It? Where Did It Come From? Why Is It Important?" In *The Eagle in the Desert: Looking Back on U.S. Involvement in the Persian Gulf War,* William Head and Earl H. Tilford, Jr., eds. (Westport Conn.: Praeger, 1996): 127–156.

Dinges, Edward A., and Richard H. Sinnreich. "Battlefield Interdiction: Old Term, New Problem." *Field Artillery Journal* 48 (January–February 1980): 14–17.

Donnelly, Tom. "The Generals' War: How Commanders Fought the Iraqis." *Army Times.* Desert Storm After-Action Review, March 2, 1992.

Franks, Gen Frederick M., Jr., and Col Gary B. Griffin. "The Army's View of Joint." *U.S. Naval Institute Proceedings* 119 (May 1993): 54–60.

Fulghum, David. "Secret Carbon-Fibre Warheads Blinded Iraqi Air Defenses." *Aviation Week & Space Technology,* April 27, 1992, 18–20.

Gershanoff, Hal. "EC in the Gulf War: An Exclusive JED Interview with the Director of Air Operations for Desert Storm." *Journal of Electronic Defense* 14 (May 1991): 37–48.

Glosson, Buster C. "The Impact of Precision Weapons on Air Combat Operations." *Airpower Journal* 7 (Summer 1993): 4–10.

Goodman, Glenn W., Jr. "JSTARS Flies European Demonstrations; House Reverses Cancellation Vote." *Armed Forces Journal International* 128 (November 1990): 21.

——— and John G. Roos. "An Exclusive AFJI Interview with Lt Gen Walter E. Boomer, USMC." *Armed Forces Journal International* 130 (August 1992): 38–41.

Grier, Peter. "Joint STARS Does Its Stuff." *Air Force Magazine* 74 (June 1991): 38–42.

Hammick, Murray. "Iraq Obstacles and Defensive Positions." *International Defense Review* 24 (September 1991): 989–991.

Hardy, Stephen M. "Planning and Rehearsing the Future." *Journal of Electronic Defense* 15 (November 1992): 48–53.

Hattendorf, John B. "The Evolution of the Maritme Strategy: 1977–1987." *Naval War College Review* 41 (Summer 1988): 7–28.

Herskovitz, Sheldon B. "High Marks for Military Radar: The Patriot Missile System." *Journal of Electronic Defense* 14 (May 1991): 55–59.

Hertberg, Rob. "Beyond the Fire Support Coordination Line (FSCL): Contact the Killer Scouts." *USAF Fighter Weapons Review* 40 (Spring 1992): 12–17.

Hine, Sir Patrick. "Air Operations in the Gulf War." In *The War in the Air 1914–1994: The Proceedings of Conference Held by the Royal Australian Air Force in Canberra, March 1944*, ed. Alan Stephens, 303–320. Fairbairn, Australia: RAAF Air Power Studies Centre, 1994

Hopkins, Robert S., III. "Ears of the Storm." *Air Force Magazine* 75 (February 1992): 38–43.

Horner, Charles A. "The Air Campaign." *Military Review* 71 (September 1991): 16–27.

——— "New Era Warfare." In *The War in the Air 1914–1994: The Proceedings of Conference Held by the Royal Australian Air Force in Canberra, March 1994,* edited by Alan Stephens. Fairbairn, Australia: RAAF Air Power Studies Centre,1994.

——— "Air Power: Growing Beyond Desert Storm." *Aviation Week and Space Technology,* April 16, 1997, 70–73.

——— "What We Should Have Learned in Desert Storm but Didn't." *Air Force Magazine* 79 (December 1996): 52–56.

Humphries, John G. "Operations Law and the Rules of Engagement in Operations Desert Shield and Desert Storm." *Airpower Journal* 6 (Fall 1992): 25–41.

Hurley, Matthew M. "Saddam Hussein and Iraqi Air Power: Just Having an Air Force Isn't Enough." *Airpower Journal* 6 (Winter 1992): 4–16.

Kay, David. "Denial and Deception: Iraq and Beyond." *American Intelligence Journal* (Spring/Summer 1995): 79–88.

Keaney, Thomas A. "Surveying Gulf War Air Power." *Joint Forces Quarterly* (Autumn 1993): 25–36.

Kessel, Richard M. "Parallel Warfare: Anticipating the Enemy's Response." In *Challenge and Response: Anticipating U.S. Military Security Concerns*, ed. Karl P. Magyar *et al.,* 297–310. Maxwell AFB, Ala.: Air University Press, 1994.

Kindsvatter, Peter S. "VII Corps in the Gulf War: Ground Offensive." *Military Review* 72 (February 1992): 16–37.

Kuehl, Daniel T. "Airpower vs. Electricity: Electric Power as a Target for Strategic Air Operations." In *Airpower: Theory and Practice*, edited by John Gooch, 237–266. London: Frank Cass, 1995.

Lewis, Richard B.H. "JFACC Problems Associated with Battlefield Preparation in Desert Storm." *Airpower Journal* 8 (Spring 1994): 4–21.

Lind, William S. "If We Fight This War, Can We Win?" *The Washington Post*, August 19, 1990, 2.

Lohide, Kurtis. "Desert Storm's Siren Song." *Airpower Journal* 9 (Winter 1995): 100–110.

McCarthy, James P. "SAC Looks to the Future." http://www.cdsar.af.mil/aureview/1987/mccarthy.html, 1–6.

Mackenzie, Richard. "A Conversation with Chuck Horner." *Air Force Magazine* 74 (June 1991): 57–64.

——— "Apache Attack." *Air Force Magazine*, 74 (October 1991): 54–60.

MacNamara, Steve. "Assessing Airpower's Importance: Will the QDR Debate Falter for Lack of Proper Analytic Tools? *Armed Forces Journal International* 134 (March 1997): 36–37.

Mann, Edward. "One Target, One Bomb: Is the Principle of Mass Dead"? *Airpower Journal* 7 (Spring 1993): 35–43.

Meilinger, Phillip S. "The Problem with Our Air Power Doctrine." *Airpower Journal* 6 (Spring 1992): 24–31.

——— "Winged Defense: Air War, the Law, and Morality." *Armed Forces and Society* 20 (Fall 1993): 103–123.

Mitchell, William. "Let the Air Service Crash!" *Liberty* 2 (January30, 1926): 43–46.

Mixson, Riley D. "Where We Must Do Better." *U.S. Naval Institute Proceedings* 117 (August 1991): 38–39.

Moore, Lt Gen Royal, Jr., USMC. "Marine Air There When Needed." *U.S. Naval Institute Proceedings* 117 (November 1991): 63–70.

Morrocco, John D. "Allied Strategists Altered Battle Plan to Components for Dugan's Comments." *Aviation Week and Space Technology,* July 22, 1991, 60–61.

Muir, Cdr Daniel J. "A View from the Black Hole." *U.S. Naval Institute Proceedings* 117 (October 1991): 85–86.

Munk, Erika. "Witness in Baghdad: The New Face of Techno-War." *The Nation.* 252 (May 6, 1991): 583–586.

Murphy, Timothy G. "A Critique of *The Air Campaign*." *Airpower Journal* 8 (Spring 1994): 63–74.

Norwell, Bruce D. "Electronic Warfare Played Greater Role in Desert Storm than Any Conflict." *Aviation Week and Space Technology,* April 22, 1991, 68–69.

Pardo, John R., Jr. "Parallel Warfare: Its Nature and Application." In *Challenge and Response: Anticipating U.S. Military Security Concerns*, ed. Karl P. Magyar *et al.*, 277–296. Maxwell AFB, Ala.: Air University Press, 1994.

Parks, W. Hays. "Air War and the Law of War." *Air Force Law Review* 32 (1990): 1–225.

Parks, W. H. "Rules of Engagement: No More Vietnams." *U.S. Naval Institute Proceedings* 117 (March 1991): 27–28.

Pickett, Jr., George E. "The High Stakes Game of Competitive Strategies." *Army* 38 (November 1988): 22–25.

Polmar, Norman, and Scott C. Truver. "The Maritime Strategy." *Air Force Magazine* 70 (November 1987): 70–79.

Press, Daryl G. "What If Saddam Hadn't Stopped? The Myth of Coalition Vulnerability in the Early Days of Desert Shield."*Breakthroughs* (Spring 1994): 5–11.

Price, Alfred. "Tornado in the Desert." *Air Force Magazine* 75 (December 1992): 42–46.

Putney, Diane T. "From Instant Thunder to Desert Storm: Developing the Gulf War Air Campaign's Phases." *Air Power History* 41 (Fall 1994): 38–50.

Ross, Bruce A. "The Case for Targeting Leadership in War." *Naval War College Review* 46 (Winer 1993): 73–93.

Rowen, Henry S. "Inchon in the Desert: My Rejected Plan." *The National Interest* 40 (Summer 1995): 34–39.

Russ, General Robert D. "An Open Letter on Tacair Support." *Armor* (May–June 1988): 45.

——— "The Air Force, the Army, and the Battlefield of the 1990s." *Defense 88,* July/August 1988, 13–17.

Schemmer, Benjamin F. "No USAF Combat Rescue Aircraft in Gulf; It Took 72 Hours to Launch One Rescue." *Armed Forces Journal International* 128 (July 1991): 37–38.

Stambaugh, Jeffrey E. "JFACC: Key to Organizing Your Air Assets for Victory." *Parameters: US Army War College Quarterly* 24 (Summer 1994): 98–110.

Stanik, Joseph L. "Welcome to El Dorado Canyon." *U.S. Naval Institute Proceedings* 122 (April 1996): 57–62.

Starry, Donn A. "Extending the Battlefield." *Military Review* 61 (March 1981): 31–50.

——— "Keynote Address." *Armor* 87 (July–August 1978): 32–36.

——— "A Tactical Evolution—FM 100–5." *Military Review* 58 (August 1978): 2–11.

——— "To Change an Army." *Military Review* 63 (March 1983): 20–27.

Swain, Richard M. "Reflections on the Revisionist Critique: Grand Operations in the Gulf War." *Army* 46 (August 1996): 24–31.

Szafranski, Richard. "Parallel War: Promise, Problems." *U.S. Naval Institute Proceedings* 121 (August 1995): 57–61.

Thompson, Wayne W. "After Al Firdos: The Last Two Weeks of Strategic Bombing in DESERT STORM." *Air Power History* 43 (Summer 1996): 48–65.

Valliere, John E. "Stop Quibling: Win the War." *U.S. Naval Institute Proceedings* 116 (December 1990): 38–45.

Warden, John A. III. "Air Theory for the Twenty-first Century." In *Challenge and Response: Anticipating U.S. Military Security Concerns,* ed. Karl P. Magyar *et al*, 311–332. Maxwell AFB, Ala.: Air University Press, 1994.

——— "Centers of Gravity—The Key to Success in War." In *Proceedings: A Mini-Symposium on Operational Art and Analysis,* March 6–9, 1990, National Defense University. Alexandria, Va.: Military Operations Research Society, n.d.

——— "Employing Air Power in the Twenty-first Century." In *The Future of Air Power in the Aftermath of the Gulf War*, Richard H. Shultz, Jr., and Robert L. Pfaltzgraff, Jr., eds., 57–82. Maxwell AFB, Ala.: Air University Press, 1992.

——— "The Enemy as a System." *Airpower Journal* 9 (Spring 1995): 40–55.

——— "Planning to Win." *Air University Review* 34 (Mar–Apr 1983): 94–97.

——— "Planning to Win." Paper delivered at RAAF Air Power Conference, "Testing the Limits," Mar 30–31, 1998, at www.defence.gov.au/aerospacecentre/publish/download/paper66.rtf.

——— "Success in Modern War: A Response to Robert Pape's *Bombing to Win.*" *Security Studies* 7 (Winter 1997/98): 172–190.

Ware, Lewis. "Ware on Warden: Some Observations of the Enemy as a System." *Airpower Journal* 9 (Winter 1995): 87–93.

Welch, William G. "Notes from the BCE: Observations on Joint Combat Operations at Echelon above Corps." *Field Artillery,* June 1992, 16–21.

Werrell, Kenneth P. "Air War Victorious: The Gulf War vs. Vietnam." *Parameters: U.S. Army War College Quarterly* 22 (Summer 1992): 41–54.

Winton, Harold R. "Partnership and Tension: The Army and Air Force Between Vietnam and Desert Shield." *Parameters: US Army War College Quarterly* 26 (Spring 1996): 100–119.

Yeosock, Lt Gen John J. "Army Operations in the Gulf Theater." *Military Review* 71 (September 1991): 2–15.

Theses and Reports

Alonzo, Rod A. "Blinded by Speed, Inexperience, Disagreement, and Clouds: Battle Damage Assessment in Desert Storm." Master's thesis, Defense Intelligence Agency College, 1993.

Barlow, Jason B. "Strategic Paralysis: An Airpower Theory for the Present," Master's thesis, Air University Press, 1994.

Beagle, T. W., Jr. "Effects-Based Targeting: Another Empty Promise?" Master's thesis, Air University Press, 2001.

Brungress, James R. "Setting the Context: Suppression of Enemy Air Defenses and Joint War Fighting in an Uncertain World." Maxwell AFB, Ala.: Air University Press, 1994.

Buchanan, Thomas H. "The Tactical Air Control System: Its Evolution and Its Need for Battle Managers." Research report, Air University Press, 1987.

Carpenter, P. Mason. "Joint Operations in the Gulf War: An Allison Analysis." Master's thesis, Air University Press, 1994.

Fadok, David S. "John Boyd and John Warden: Air Power's Quest for Strategic Paralysis." Master's thesis, Air University Press, 1994.

Griffith, Thomas E., Jr. "Strategic Attacks of National Electrical Systems." Master's thesis, Air University Press, 1994.

Kreighbaum, Jay M. "Force Application Planning: A Systems-and-Effects-Based Approach." Master's thesis, Air University Press, 1998.

Nowland, Mark C. "Eliminating the Rhetoric: An Evaluation of the Halt-Phase Strategy." Master's thesis, Air University Press, 2001.

Runge, Thomas G. "Firepower and Follow-On Forces Atack: Making Every Round Count." Research report, Air University Press, 1991.

Smith, Kevin W. "Cockpit Video: A Low Cost BDA Source." Research report, Air University Press, 1993.

Tillotson, David III. "Restructuring the Air Operations Center: A Defense of Orthodoxy." Research report, Air University Press, 1993.

Walker, Scott G. "Targeting for Effect: Analytical Framework for Counterland Operations." Master's thesis, Air University Press, 1998.

Warden, John Ashley III. "The Grand Alliance: Strategy and Decision." Master's thesis, Texas Tech University, 1975.

West, Scott D. "Warden and the Air Corps Tactical School: Deja Vu?" Master's thesis, Air University Press, 1999.

Notes

All material acquired by the author in preparation of this volume was retired to the Air Force Historical Research Agency, Maxwell AFB,

Chapter 1

1. Biographical sheet, Lt Gen Charles A. Horner, SAF/PA, Jan 1989; Tom Clancy with General Chuck Horner, USAF (Ret), *Every Man a Tiger* (New York: G.P. Putnam's Sons, 1999), 55.

2. Public Law 99–433 [H.R. 3622], "Goldwater-Nichols Department of Defense Reorganization Act of 1986," Oct 1, 1996, 100 Stat., 992–1075a; Intvw tape, Lt Gen Charles A. Horner by Lt Col Suzanne Gehri and Lt Col Richard Reynolds, Dec 2, 1991, College of Aerospace Doctrine, Research, and Education (CADRE), Air University (AU), Air Force Historical Research Agency (AFHRA), Maxwell AFB, Ala.; Lt Col Thomas T. LoPresti, USA, "The JCS System before and after Goldwater-Nichols," U.S. Military Studies Program Paper (Carlisle Barracks, Pa.: U.S. Army War College, 1991), 16–19.

3. CENTCOM Regulation 10–3, "Organization and Functions, Terms of Reference for Component Commanders," 1989; Hist, SMSgt Charles E. Arnold, Ninth Air Force/CENTAF, Jan–Dec 1989, vol I-A, frame 952, reel 27048, 5–8. The JCS defined OPCON as the "transferable command authority which may be exercised by commanders at any echelon at or below the level of combatant command. Operational control is inherent in combatant command (command authority) and is the authority to perform those functions of command over subordinate forces involving organizing and employing commands and forces, assigning tasks, designating objectives, and gaining authoritative direction necessary to accomplish the mission." COCOM was the "nontransferable command authority,...exercised only by commanders of unified or specified combatant commands." See also Department of Defense (DoD), *Conduct of the Persian Gulf War: Final Report to Congress* (Washington, D.C.: April 1992), 548.

4. Intvw tape, Gen Charles A. Horner, USAF (Ret), by Diane T. Putney, Nov 30, 1996, Air Force History Support Office (AFHSO), Bolling AFB, D.C.

5. Hist, CENTCOM, 1989, 1–10, CENTCOM/HO, MacDill AFB, Fla. The CENTCOM AOR included Afghanistan, Bahrain, Djibouti, Egypt, Ethiopia, Iran, Iraq, Jordan, Kenya, Kuwait, Oman, Pakistan, Peoples Democratic Republic of Yemen, Qatar, Saudi Arabia, Somalia, Sudan, United Arab Emirates, and Yemen Arab Republic, and the Persian Gulf and Red Sea.

6. In speeches and interviews, Horner stated that his first meeting with Schwarzkopf occurred in November 1989; however, records at CENTAF headquarters indicate that the CINCCENT visited Shaw AFB in February and August 1989, not in November.

7. During interviews, the author often heard Horner described as in control of his emotions and calm during stressful events, although he did use sarcasm and cursed. The general attributed his self-discipline to the example set by Gen Wilbur L. Creech, former TAC commander. See drft intvw trnscrpt, Gen Charles A. Horner by Diane T. Putney and George W. Bradley III, Apr 26, 1994, 97, AFHSO. Numerous written accounts about Schwarzkopf have vividly

described his angry outbursts.

8. Comment, Horner on draft manuscript, Putney, "Airpower Advantage."

9. Intvw tape, Horner by Putney, Nov 30, 1996; Drft intvw trnscrpt, Horner by Putney and Bradley, Apr 26, 1994, 20.

10. Jeffrey E. Stambaugh, "JFACC: Key to Organizing Your Air Assets for Victory," *Parameters: U.S. Army War College Quarterly* 24 (Summer 1994): 104. The JCS had only recently codified the JFACC concept in doctrine in their Joint Publication 25, issued in 1986. For a lengthy discussion of the JFACC role, see *Gulf War Air Power Survey* (*GWAPS*), vol 1, part 2, *Command and Control* (Washington: Government Printing Office, 1993). Although the JFACC concept had been operational since World War II, the Gulf War was the first regional conflict in which the JFACC was formally established. See DoD, *Conduct of the Persian Gulf War*, 101.

11. AFM 1–3, "Doctrine and Procedures for Airspace Control in the Combat Zone," Dec 1, 1975, 2-1; AFM 2–14/Army FM 100–42, "Airspace Management in an Area of Operations," Nov 1, 1976, 1-1; AFM 1–1, "Basic Aerospace Doctrine of the United States Air Force," Jan 5, 1984, 2-20; USCENTAF Reg 55–45, "Air Employment Planning Process," Jun 27, 1990, 2-1.

12. Intvw tape, Horner by Putney, Nov 30, 1996; Intvw trnscrpt, Horner by Gehri and Reynolds, Dec 2, 1991, 48; John L. Romjue, *From Active Defense to AirLand Battle: The Development of Army Doctrine, 1973–1982* (Fort Monroe, Va.: TRADOC Historical Office, 1984), doc 6, 100–108; Richard G. Davis, *The 31 Initiatives: A Study in Air Force–Army Cooperation* (Washington: Office of Air Force History, 1987), 31; AFM 1–1, Jan 5, 1984, 2-18.

13. See Joint Pub 1–02, *Department of Defense Dictionary of Military and Associated Terms,* Dec 1, 1989.

14. The ground commander established the fire support coordination line (FSCL), after coordinating with the air component commander. Air and ground commanders coordinated air strikes behind the line.

15. Intvw tape, Horner by Putney, Nov 30, 1996; Intvw trnscrpt, Horner by Gehri and Reynolds, Dec 2, 1991, 48 (quote).

16. Drft intvw trnscrpt, Horner by Putney and Bradley, Apr 26, 1994, 80. For an account of the President choosing targets in the White House see Doris Kearns, *Lyndon Johnson and the American Dream* (New York: Harper & Row, 1976), 269–270. Even in 1999 Horner remained embittered about target selection and mission planning during the Vietnam War. See Clancy with Horner, *Every Man a Tiger*, 95–99.

17. Intvw tape, Horner by Putney, Nov 30, 1996; Drft intvw trnscrpt, Horner by Putney and Bradley, Apr 26, 1994, 20.

18. Hist, Arnold, 9AF/CENTAF, 1989, 34.

19. Maj Thomas H. Buchanan, *The Tactical Air Control System: Its Evolution and Its Need for Battle Managers* (Maxwell AFB, Ala.: AU Press, 1987), 30–35.

20. Drft intvw trnscrpt, Horner by Putney and Bradley, Apr 26, 1994, 15–16, 18–19; Intvw trnscrpt, Lt Gen Charles A. Horner by CMSgt John R. Burton, Mar 10, 1991, 11–12, 20–22, Gulf War file, TAC/HO, Langley AFB, Va.; Intvw trnscrpt, Gen Jack Chain by Lt Col Edward Mann, Aug 12, 1991, 1–2, 6–9, CADRE, AU, AFHRA; Study, "Organizing for War: SAC Command Relations and Organization in Operation Desert Shield/Desert Storm," SAC/HO, 1–2, NA 89, GWAPS, AFHRA.

21. Study, "Organizing for War," 3, NA 89, GWAPS, AFHRA.

22. USCENTAF Reg 55–45, "Air Employment Planning Process," Jun 27, 1990, 2–5; Lt Col Robert J. Blunden, *Tailoring the Tactical Air Control System for Contingencies* (Maxwell AFB, Ala.: AU Press, 1992), 8, 12.

23. Msg, USCENTAF/SC/DO to CDR COMB ARMS CBTDEW ACTV, 021402 May 90, subj: Battlefield Coordination Element (BCE), frame 971, reel 26563, in Hist, David L. Rosmer and Barry R. Barlow, Ninth Air Force/USCENTAF, Jan–Dec 1990, AFHRA; USCENTAF Reg 55–45, Jun 27, 1990, 3–12; Ed drft intvw trnscrpt, Lt Gen Charles A. Horner by Richard G. Davis, Perry D. Jamieson, and Barry R. Barlow,

Mar 4, 1992, 51, AFHSO; Richard M. Swain, *"Lucky War": Third Army in Desert Storm* (Ft. Leavenworth, Kans.: U.S. Army Command and General Staff College Press, 1991), xvi; David Tillotson III, *Restructuring the Air Operations Center: A Defense of Orthodoxy* (Maxwell AFB, Ala.: AU Press, 1993), 44.

24. According to FM 100–5, Aug 20, 1982, the strategic level applied force or the threat of force to achieve national policy objectives and set the fundamental conditions for operations. The operational level pertained to a theater of war, employed military assets to attain strategic objectives, and encompassed campaign planning and execution. The tactical level comprised the techniques used to win battles and engagements to achieve operational goals.

25. Donn A. Starry, "An Organization for Theater Operations: From a Commander's Perspective," in Col Thomas A. Cardwell, USAF, *Command Structure for Theater Warfare: The Quest for Unity of Command* (Maxwell AFB, Ala.: AU Press, 1984), 137–143. For the evolution of the AirLand Battle doctrine, see Romjue, *From Active Defense.* For a critique of Air Force doctrine, see Harold R. Winton, "Partnership and Tension: The Army and Air Force between Vietnam and Desert Shield," *Parameters: U.S. Army War College Quarterly* 26 (Spring 1996): 100–119.

26. FM 100–5, May 5, 1986, 29 (quote), 47–50, 179–180. See also AFM 1–1, Jan 5, 1984, 2-12 to 2-15, 3-3 to 3-5.

27. USAF oral history intvw trnscrpt, Gen Wilbur L. Creech, K239.0512–2050, 72 (quote) 77, 81, 220–222, 230, 252, AFHRA; Davis, *31 Initiatives,* 16.

28. Robert T. Russ, "The Air Force, the Army, and the Battlefield of the 1990s," *Defense 88* (July–August 1988): 13.

29. Drft intvw trnscrpt, Horner by Putney and Bradley, Apr 26, 1994, 12, 19–20; Intvw tape, Horner by Putney, Nov 30, 1996; E-Mail msg, Gen Charles A. Horner, USAF (Ret), to Diane Putney, Aug 19, 1997.

30. Intvw tape, Col Clifford Krieger, USAF, by Diane T. Putney, Jan 12, 1994, AFHSO; General H. Norman Schwarzkopf with Peter Petre, *The Autobiography: It Doesn't Take a Hero* (New York: Linda Grey Bantam Books, 1992), 269–270, 287; Comment, Horner on draft manuscript, Putney, "Airpower Advantage"; Gen. Charles A. Horner, "Banquet Address," in *Seeing Off the Bear: Anglo-American Air Power Cooperation during the Cold War, Proceedings, Joint Meeting of the Royal Air Force Historical Society and the Air Force Historical Foundation,* ed. Roger G. Miller (Washington: Air Force History & Museums Program, 1995), 140; Adm William J. Crowe, Jr., with David Chanoff, *The Line of Fire: From Washington to the Gulf, the Politics and Battles of the New Military* (New York: Simon & Schuster, 1993), 271–298.

31. The Berlin Wall came down in November 1989.

32. Goldwater-Nichols Act, sec. 3, ch 4(2), para 134; DoD, *Conduct of the Persian Gulf War*, 349; Schwarzkopf, *It Doesn't Take a Hero,* 286; Rpt, Rear Adm Grant Sharp, USN (Ret), CENTCOM J–5, "Planning for the Gulf War," 2–4, JCS/HO, Pentagon, Washington, D.C.

33. Hist, Arnold, 9AF/CENTAF, 1989, 67; *GWAPS,* vol 1, part 1, *Planning,* 20–21. See also DoD, *Conduct of the Persian Gulf War*, 32, 350–351, for the development of OPLAN 1002–90, "Defense of the Arabian Peninsula," from a concept outline plan, which was not a standard joint planning document but was unique to CENTCOM.

34. Drft outline plan, USCINCCENT OPLAN 1002–90, Apr 6, 1990, frame 1456, reel 26572, 5–7, 17–21; Rpt, Sharp, "Planning for the Gulf War," 13.

35. The author of this volume uses the unfamiliar but appropriate term *counterland* to describe the mission of air power to directly attack the enemy army and substantially attrit and destroy it. In this context, counterland sorties against enemy ground forces are analogous to counterair sorties against the enemy air force. In 1990 the Air Force's basic doctrine manual, AFM 1–1, did not identify *counterland* as an air mission. Neither did the term enter the revision of the manual in March 1992. This volume's author first heard the term used in a different

context by Maj Gen Charles D. Link, HQ USAF/QR, in his briefings on the "decisive halt" of invading forces by air power. The USAF incorporated the counterland term into its doctrine in September 1997 in Doctrine Document 1, stating that counterland involved "those operations conducted to attain and maintain a desired degree of superiority over surface operations by the destruction or neutralization of enemy surface forces." Interdiction and close air support were the specific traditional functions associated with counterland.

36. Rpt, Sharp, "Planning for the Gulf War," 5; Rpt, USCENTCOM, "Security Environment 2000: A CENTCOM View," May 21, 1990, III-2 to III-3; Congress, Senate, Subcommittee of the Committee on Appropriations, "DoD Appropriations for Fiscal Year 1991," 101st Cong., 2d sess., Mar 6, 1990, 137 (quote).

37. Visitor folder, USCENTAF Southwest Asia Symposium, Feb 28–Mar 1, 1990, 1 (quote), Shaw AFB, CHSH 51-39, GWAPS, AFHRA.

38. Horner, "Banquet Address," 141; Comment, Horner on draft manuscript, Putney, "Airpower Advantage"; Memoir excerpt, Col Randy Witt, ch 1, "Gearing Up," 2, AFHSO.

39. Drft msg, USCENTAF/DOX to 314 TAW et al., subj: Disclosure Guidance for USCENTCOM/USCENTAF Planning Information, in Hist, Rosmer and Barlow, 9AF/CENTAF, 1990, frame 903, reel 26567, AFHRA.

40. James A. Baker III with Thomas M. DeFrank, *The Politics of Diplomacy: Revolution, War, and Peace, 1989–1992* (New York: G.P. Putnam's Sons, 1995), 261–264, 267 (quote). See NSD 26, "U.S. Policy toward the Persian Gulf," at the Bush Presidential Library at http://bushlibrary.tamu.edu/research/nsd/NSD/NSD%2026/0001.pdf.

41. Rpt, USCENTCOM, "Security Environment 2000: A CENTCOM View," May 21, 1990, IV-4.

42. Drft outline plan, USCINCCENT OPLAN 1002–90, Apr 6, 1990, 22; Intvw trnscrpt, Horner by Burton, Mar 10, 1991, 8–9; Intvw trnscrpt, Horner by Gehri and Reynolds, Dec 2, 1991, 1–4.

43. Bahrain, Kuwait, Oman, Qatar, Saudi Arabia, and the UAE formed the GCC.

44. Brfg, OPLAN 1002–90 Air Operations, [Lt Gen Horner], [Apr 1990], 1–17.

45. Ibid., 18–24; Intvw trnscrpt, Horner by Gehri and Reynolds, Dec 2, 1991, 1–2.

46. Drft intvw trnscrpt, Horner by Putney and Bradley, Apr 26, 1994, 7; Horner, "Banquet Address," 141; Brfg, OPLAN 1002–90 Air Operations, 25–26. The U.S. intelligence community had also identified a second Scud B variant, the Al Abbas, having a range of approximately 485 nautical miles.

47. Sheldon B. Herskovitz, "High Marks for Military Radar: The Patriot Missile System," *Journal of Electronic Defense* 14 (May 1991): 55. Five basic elements comprised a Patriot fire unit: engagement control station; eight or more launching stations; radar set; electrical power plant; and antenna mast group.

48. Brfg, OPLAN 1002–90 Air Operations, 27–32.

49. Ibid., 33–34; Drft intvw trnscrpt, Horner by Putney and Bradley, Apr 26, 1994, 12, 14 (quote). The briefing did not specifically list the thirteen targets; it identified them only generically on a map.

50. Drft intvw trnscrpt, Horner by Putney and Bradley, Apr 26, 1994, 12, 19–20, 84; Intvw tape Horner by Putney, Nov 30, 1996. Horner referred to "punishment targets" in reference to his CW deterrence plan. Horner thought "strategic" was too closely identified with "nuclear" forces and, with the SAC-dominated Air Force, "strategic" had come to mean "More important than tactical."

51. Drft intvw trnscrpt, Horner by Putney and Bradley, Apr 26, 1994, 15, 32 (quote).

52. Ibid., 15; Intvw trnscrpt, Horner by Burton, Mar 10, 1991, 9.

53. Horner's biographer also concluded that this discussion of *strategic* targets was only "peripherally related to the plan to attack that later was to emerge in August and September of 1990." See Clancy with Horner, *Every Man a Tiger,* 248.

54. Brfg, OPLAN 1002–90 Air Operations, 35–38; 43–51, 51 (quote); Drft intvw trnscrpt, Horner by Putney and Bradley, Apr 26, 1994, 2–4; Intvw trnscrpt, Lt Col Sam Baptiste by Diane Putney and Lt Col Richard Reynolds, Sep 24, 1992, 11–12, CADRE, AU, AFHRA. Others used the air hose analogy, as well, including Gen Larry D. Welch, CSAF, 1986–1990.

55. Drft intvw trnscrpt, Horner by Putney and Bradley, Apr 26, 1994, 2–3.

56. Ibid., 3.

57. Ibid., 12; Intvw tape, Horner by Putney, Nov 30, 1996.

58. Second drft plan, USCINCCENT OPLAN 1002–90, Jul 18, 1990, i–xii, GWAPS, AFHRA.

59. Ibid., 4–5.

60. Ibid., iv–vii, 20–26. In Appendix 15 to Annex C of OPLAN 1002–90, a statement indicated that the commanders of ARCENT and MARCENT would plan and execute interdiction in their respective AORs. Horner, however, explained that Schwarzkopf agreed that the JFACC would plan and execute all air interdiction operations in cooperation with ARCENT and MARCENT. The CINCCENT deferred to his JFACC. See Comment, Horner on draft manuscript, Putney, "Airpower Advantage."

61. Second drft plan, USCINCCENT OPLAN 1002–90, v; FM 100–5, Jul 1, 1976, 3-4; Telecon notes, Barry Watts and Col Gary Ware, USAF (Ret), Feb 26, 1992, GWAPS, frame 1193, reel 27584, AFHRA. See also DoD, *Conduct of the Persian Gulf War,* 350, which described war gaming and OPLAN 1002–90 development.

62. Second drft plan, USCINCCENT OPLAN 1002–90, Jul 18, 1990, 19.

63. Ibid., B-4–b-1.

64. Ibid., Tab A to Appendix 4 to Annex B; Memo, Maj Heidrick, 9AIS/INT, to L. Greenberg, GWAPS, May 4, 1992, frame 741, reel 27564, 1–2, AFHRA. The Joint Target List supported the offensive counterair and interdiction operations to restore the status quo antebellum and was not described as supporting strategic attacks or a strategic air campaign with a major objective to reduce Iraq's ability to threaten its neighbors. It was a list with no categories or systems identified or rationales provided for selecting targets.

65. Msg, HQ SAC/DOO to 8AF/DO et al., 182202Z Jun 90, subj: SAC Participation in Internal Look (IL) 90, SAC/HO; Proposed planning directive, "USCENTCOM Proposed Exercise Planning Directive for Internal Look 90," HQ USCENTCOM, SAC/HO.

66. Memo, Maj Heidrick, 9AIS/INT, to L. Greenberg, GWAPS, May 4, 1992, 1–3; Telecon notes, Col John Leonardo, USAF (Ret), with Diane T. Putney, Jan 4, 1994, AFHSO; Study, OPLAN 1002–90 Targeting Study, 9AF/IN file, AFHSO; Study, Iraqi Targeting Study, 9TIS/INT, Jun 15, 1990, atch in paper by Capt John R. Glock, GWAPS, AFHRA. The author of this volume did not incorporate the category *air defense,* including 17 ADOC, SOC, and FOP-IOC sites, because this category was added to the 9TIS/INT list at a later date than June 1990. The Al Jahrah FOP-IOC and GCI site was on the list, but the Iraqis did not establish it until after they invaded Kuwait in August 1990. In addition, its label is not consistent with the other target category labels, and the target study bibliography contained two sources published after June 1990.

67. Thomas A. Keaney, Notes, CENTAF Visit, 8–9 Mar 92, GWAPS, frame 1495, reel 27583, AFHRA; Memo, Maj Heidrick, 9AIS/INT, to L. Greenberg, GWAPS, May 4, 1992, 3; Memo, Internal Look 90 COMUSCENTAF Air Guidance Letter, subj: ATO Planning Guidance for D+18, Jul 26, 1990—Change 1, Jul 24, 1990; Comment, Horner on draft manuscript, Putney, "Airpower Advantage" (quote). Major Heidrick provided the general description of the cross-border targets; a list of the specific targets could not be found.

68. Brig Gen Robert H. Scales Jr., et al., *Certain Victory: The U.S. Army in the Gulf War* (Washington: Office of the Chief of Staff, 1993), 43, 44 (quote).

69. Lt Col Steve McNamara, "Assessing Airpower's Importance: Will the QDR Debate Falter for Lack of Proper Analytic Tools?" www.afji.com/mags/1997/Mar/assess.

html, and Mark C. Nowland, "Eliminating the Rhetoric: An Evaluation of the Halt-Phase Strategy" (master's thesis, AU, 2001).

70. Baker, *Politics of Diplomacy*, 271 (quotes); *GWAPS,* vol 1, part 1, *Planning,* 56, 58; DoD, *Conduct of the Persian Gulf War,* 5; Executive Summary, U.S. Central Command Operations Desert Shield/Desert Storm, Jul 11, 1991, 3, NA 131, GWAPS, AFHRA.

71. Executive Summary, U.S. Central Command Operations Desert Shield/Desert Storm, Jul 11, 1991, 2–3; Rpt, "Operations Desert Shield and Desert Storm Bomber Story," SAC/DO, Sep 18, 1991, 7, SAC/HO; Schwarzkopf, *It Doesn't Take a Hero*, 292–293; *GWAPS,* vol 1, part 1, *Planning,* 58–59; Chronology, OSD Public Affairs, "Operation Desert Shield," 1, CHSH 48-4, GWAPS, AFHRA.

72. Saddam Hussein must have noted, too, that within a few months of the terrorist attack against the Marine barracks in Beirut in October 1983, the National Command Authorities pulled U.S. forces from war-torn Lebanon without their "peacekeeping" mission being accomplished.

73. Msg, AMEMBASSY Baghdad to SECSTATE, 251528Z Jul 90, subj: Saddam's Message of Friendship to President Bush; Baker, *Politics of Diplomacy,* 271–272.

74. Khaled bin Sultan with Patrick Seale, *Desert Warrior: A Personal View of the Gulf War by the Joint Forces Commander* (New York: Harper Collins, 1995), 176–178; *GWAPS,* vol 1, part 1, *Planning*, 59. *GWAPS* included a fourth demand, access to Bubiyan and Warba Islands. An examination of Iraq's historical claims to the territory of Kuwait found them to be without merit. See David H. Finnie, *Shifting Lines in the Sand: Kuwait's Elusive Frontier with Iraq* (Cambridge: Harvard University Press, 1992).

75. Colin L. Powell with Joseph E. Persico, *My American Journey* (New York: Random House, 1995), 460; Schwarzkopf, *It Doesn't Take a Hero*, 269; Msg, USCINCCENT to JCS, 292100Z Jul 90, subj: UAE Request for Extension of U.S.-UAE Joint Exercise...," frame 1241, reel 26569, AFHRA.

76. Powell, *My American Journey,* 461; Intvw trnscrpt, Maj Gen Burton R. Moore by Lt Col Suzanne Gehri, Lt Col Richard Reynolds, and Lt Col Edward Mann, Sep 21, 1992, 20–22, CADRE, AU, AFHRA. The author has a photocopy of a list of 23 political, economic, and military targets from a packet of briefing slides labeled, "USCENTCOM Preliminary Planning 2–6 Aug 90."

77. Schwarzkopf, *It Doesn't Take a Hero,* 294, 295 (quote); Intvw trnscrpt, Moore by Gehri, Reynolds, and Mann, Sep 21, 1992, 28; Powell, *My American Journey*, 461. The author searched for the slides but could not be certain that those she found were those briefed.

78. DoD, *Conduct of the Persian Gulf War*, 3.

79. Originally sent to the Persian Gulf during Earnest Will, the JTFME consisted of five frigates, a cruiser, a destroyer, and the flagship USS *LaSalle.*

80. Msg, CJCS to USCINCCENT, 020602Z Aug 90, subj: Deployord, SAC/HO.

81. Rivet Joint is a reconnaissance aircraft.

82. Msg, CJCS to USCINCCENT, 020759Z Aug 90, subj: Warning Order, SAC/HO; Summary, COMUSCENTAF Rapid Reaction Plan 1307–88, Dec 1, 1988, SAC/HO.

83. Msg, CJCS to USCINCCENT, 020759Z Aug 90, subj: Warning Order, SAC/HO; Msg, USCINCCENT to COMUSCENTAF, 021130Z Aug 90, subj: [Warnord], SAC/HO; William T. Y'Blood, *The Eagle and the Scorpion: The USAF and the Desert Shield First-Phase Deployment, 7 August–8 November 1990* (Washington: Center for Air Force History, 1992), 26–27.

84. DoD, *Conduct of the Persian Gulf War,* 19–20; Powell, *My American Journey,* 462–463; Schwarzkopf, *It Doesn't Take a Hero,* 297–298; George Bush and Brent Scowcroft, *A World Transformed,* (New York: Alfred A. Knopf, 1998), 314–318.

85. Bush and Scowcroft, *World Transformed,* 314, 316–317; Schwarzkopf, *It Doesn't Take a Hero,* 298 (quote).

86. Bush and Scowcroft, *World Transformed*, 316; Schwarzkopf, *It Doesn't Take a Hero,* 298.

87. Bob Woodward, *The Commanders* (New York: Simon & Schuster, 1991), 230 (quotes are Woodward's). The author of this volume believes Woodward presented reliable information because his text generally accords with the notes of participants, briefing slides, or interviews. In his book, *Standing Firm: A Vice-Presidential Memoir* (New York: Harper Paperback, 1995), Dan Quayle stated that Cheney talked extensively with Woodward.

88. Handwritten copy, Lt Gen Thomas W. Kelly's notes, August 1, 2, and 3, 1990, JCS/HO, Pentagon; Powell, *My American Journey,* 460–468; Bush and Scowcroft, *World Transformed*, 318, 319 (quote). The JCS historian, Wayne D. Dzwonchyk, had access to Kelly's notes and handcopied them.

89. Handwritten copy, General Kelly's notes, Aug 2, 1990 ("hurt" quote); Woodward, *Commanders*, 232, 233 ("pinprick" quote), 234. The quoted material is as written, not necessarily as actually spoken, because no one tape-recorded the meeting. Powell's version of his reprimand by Cheney occurred on August 3 (incorrect). See Powell, *My American Journey,* 465–466.

90. Handwritten copy, General Kelly's notes, Aug 3, 1990, 0700. The quotation marks indicate exactly how Kelly (and presumably the copier) wrote the comment, not necessarily how Powell stated it.

91. *Punish,* as written by Kelly, was a word used loosely, informally, as decisionmakers groped for options early in the crisis and contemplated the scenario of Iraq's murdering hostages. *Punishment* in not an official term within the DoD, nor is it suitable as an official planning objective.

92. Bush and Scowcroft, *World Transformed*, 322–323, 324 (quote); Woodward, *Commanders*, 238.

93. Further discussion of these weapon systems occurs in later chapters of this volume. For Cheney's involvement with this planning, see Woodward, *Commanders*, 234–235, 238–239.

94. Background paper, Capt Hawkins, DOOQ, Apr 4, 1991, SAC/HO, frame 620, reel 27576, AFHRA; Special study, Kent Beck, Edward W. Gale, and Robert de V. Brunkow, "'Black' Weapon, Covert Mission: The Conventional ALCM, Desert Shield and Desert Storm, 1986–1991," 17, SAC/HO, NA 311, GWAPS, AFHRA; Intvw trnscrpt, Lt Gen Charles A. May, Jr., by Lt Col Richard Reynolds, Aug 21, 1992, 1–4, CADRE, AU, AFHRA.

95. DoD, *Conduct of the Persian Gulf War,* 787; Summary, Lt Col David Bina, XOXOC-COB, Aug 2, 1990, CHSH 29-147, GWAPS, AFHRA; Second drft plan, USCINCCENT OPLAN 1002–90, Jul 18, 1990, Targeting section, C-15-1, GWAPS, AFHRA; Slide, JTFME, in packet, "USCENTCOM Preliminary Planning 2–6 Aug 90," GWAPS, AFHRA.

96. Schwarzkopf, *It Doesn't Take a Hero*, 299.

97. Intvw trnscrpt, Moore by Gehri, Reynolds, and Mann, Sep 21, 1992, 33, 38–39.

98. Intvw trnscrpt, Horner by Gehri and Reynolds, Dec 2, 1991, 8–12; Intvw trnscrpt, Moore by Gehri, Reynolds, and Mann, Sep 21, 1992, 28–45; Intvw trnscrpt, Col James Crigger by Lt Col Suzanne Gehri and Lt Col Richard Reynolds, Dec 2–4, 1991, 5–10, CADRE, AU, AFHRA; Intvw trnscrpt, Horner by Burton, Mar 1991, 1–2.

99. Handwritten copy, General Kelly's notes, Aug 4, 1990, Camp David; Bush and Scowcroft, *World Transformed,* 327–329; Quayle, *Standing Firm*, 225–227.

100. Handwritten copy, General Kelly's notes, Aug 4, 1990, Camp David; Schwarzkopf, *It Doesn't Take a Hero*, 299–301; Woodward, *Commanders,* 247–251; Quayle, *Standing Firm*, 225–226; Powell, *My American Journey,* 466. The packet of hardcopy slides, "USCENTCOM Preliminary Planning 2–6 Aug 90," contains slides which, matched against General Kelly's notes and the published memoir accounts of the Camp David meeting, indicate that they are, in part, the slides the CINCCENT briefed on August 4. The package contains additional unidentified slides. See slides, "USCENTCOM

Preliminary Planning 2–6 Aug 90," GWAPS, AFHRA.

101. Schwarzkopf, *It Doesn't Take a Hero,* 301; Slide with first words, "Home Forces," in packet of hardcopy slides, "USCENTCOM Preliminary Planning 2–6 Aug 90," Desert Shield, GWAPS, AFHRA.

102. Ibid. In his autobiography as he discussed the slide, Schwarzkopf did not include the statement about air power. See *It Doesn't Take a Hero*, 301.

103. Intvw trnscrpt, Horner by Gehri and Reynolds, Dec 2, 1991, 13.

104. Ibid., 13–14.

105. Intvw trnscrpt, Horner by Burton, Mar 1991, 2. Horner has provided various answers to questions concerning his briefing at Camp David on August 4, 1990. Based on a letter from him on January 10, 1998, to the author of this volume and numerous accounts of the meeting, the author has concluded that Horner did brief the slides titled, "U.S. Air Campaign Plan," faxed by Horner to Lt Col Guillette, CENTAF, Aug 4, 1990, 03:13. The slides addressed "punitive air strikes against Iraq."

106. Memo for record, Col Douglas C. Roach, USAF, Dep Asst Dir for Jt and NSC Matters, Aug 4, 1990, subj: Camp David Discussion Re: Iraq, Saturday 4 Aug 90, Checkmate, Pentagon; Handwritten copy, General Kelly's notes, Aug 4, 1990, 0800 Camp David; Bush and Scowcroft, *World Transformed*, 327–328.

107. Handwritten copy, General Kelly's notes, Aug 4, 1990, 0800 Camp David; Bush and Scowcroft, *World Transformed,* 328–330; Intvw trnscrpt, Horner by Gehri and Reynolds, Dec 2, 1991, 15. Of the various accounts of the meeting, some quite detailed, Horner is the only one who remembered Bush talking about minimizing loss of life.

108. Drft intvw trnscrpt, Horner by Putney and Bradley, Apr 26, 1994, 24–27; Woodward, *Commanders,* 266; Trnscrpt, DoD News Brfg, Sec Cheney and Chairman Powell, Aug 8, 1990–1:00 p.m., JCS/HO, Pentagon; Cheney interview, www/pbs.org/wgbh/pages/frontline/gulf/oral/decision.html.

109. Intvw trnscrpt, Horner by Gehri and Reynolds, Dec 2, 1991, 20 (quotes); Trnscrpt, DoD News Brfg, Sec Cheney and Chairman Powell, Aug 8, 1990–1:00 p.m., 2, JCS/HO, Pentagon. For the Saudi perspective on why the king invited the Americans and united with Egypt and Syria to form the "Arab axis" of the coalition against Iraq, see Khaled, *Desert Warrior,* 168–174.

110. Intvw trnscrpt, Horner by Gehri and Reynolds, Dec 2, 1991, 20–21.

111. Communication between the JCS and CENTCOM produced the names, "Peninsula Shield" and "Crescent Shield" before "Desert Shield" was suggested and approved by Secretary Cheney. See handwritten copy, General Kelly's notes, Aug 8, 1990, and Powell, *My American Journey*, 471–472.

Chapter 2

1. Intvw trnscrpt, Horner by Gehri and Reynolds, Dec 2, 1991, 17; Intvw trnscrpt, Crigger by Gehri and Reynolds, Dec 2–4, 1991, 7–10; Memo, [Col James Crigger to Diane T. Putney], subj: Air Campaign Planning for Desert Storm…, Mar 1, 1993, AFHSO; Intvw trnscrpt, Baptiste by Putney and Reynolds, Sep 24, 1992, 15, 19–20, 25; Telecon notes, Col John Leonardo, USAF (Ret), with Diane T. Putney, Jan 4, 1994, AFHSO; Memo, Maj Heidrick, 9AIS/INT, to L. Greenberg, GWAPS, May 4, 1992, 4. Horner remembers his April 1990 chemical deterrence targets as the "punishment" list, but his staff referred to their efforts to produce the Iraqi list and ATO August 4–7 as the "Punishment ATO," even though they did not complete the ATO. See Comment, Horner on draft manuscript, Putney, "Airpower Advantage." In interviews and speeches, Horner did not discuss the instructions he gave his staff on August 4 and 5, but staff members clearly remember those he issued. Horner probably learned of the requirement levied by Secretary Cheney for a "serious air campaign to punish" Iraq while at CENT-

COM headquarters the afternoon and night of August 3, which prompted his directing the CENTAF staff to prepare the "political, economic, and military" list, which would have been based on his April 1990 one.

2. Intvw trnscrpt, Col James Crigger by Lt Col Suzanne Gehri and Lt Col Richard Reynolds, Dec 2–4, 1991, 17; List, "Targets for Proposed Punishment Campaign," 9TIS, Aug 8, 1990, NA 168, GWAPS; Rpt, "Target Intelligence Support during Desert Shield and Storm," [Capt John Glock for GWAPS], 8, Tab 3, GWAPS, AFHRA; Telecon note, Lt Col John Sweeney by Diane T. Putney, Sep 3, 1993, AFHSO. Since the specific, not generic, list of Horner's chemical deterrent, "strategic" targets from April 1990 has not been found, a comparison cannot be made with the "political, economic, and military" list prepared August 4–7, but they would be very similar. Likewise, only a generic description of cross-border targets exists for the Internal Look exercise, so no detailed comparisons can be made with the August list. The CENTAF staff did use the "Iraqi Target Study," 9TIS/INT, June 15, 1990, prepared for Internal Look, to develop the Punishment ATO list.

3. Telecon notes, Gen H. Norman Schwarzkopf by Diane T. Putney, May 5, 1992, AFHSO; Intvw trnscrpt, Horner by Gehri and Reynolds, Dec 2, 1991, 33; Ed drft intvw trnscrpt, Horner by Davis, Jamieson, and Barlow, Mar 4, 1992, 13, AFHSO.

4. Intvw trnscrpt, Horner by Burton, March 1991, 9; Excerpts, intvw, Lt Gen Horner by Maj Terry New, XOXWD, Mar 28, 1991, frame 831, reel 27400, AFHRA; Intvw trnscrpt, Horner by Gehri and Reynolds, Dec 2, 1991, 33.

5. Telecon notes, Gen H. Norman Schwarzkopf by Diane T. Putney, May 5, 1992, AFHSO; Schwarzkopf, *It Doesn't Take a Hero*, 320; Intvw trnscrpt, Horner by Gehri and Reynolds, Dec 2, 1991, 33; Ed drft intvw trnscrpt, Horner by Davis, Jamieson, and Barlow, Mar 4, 1992, 13, AFHSO. Schwarzkopf's account in his memoir of Horner turning "furious" about involving people in Washington amuses Horner in light of the CINCCENT's many documented tantrums. The JFACC displayed a controlled anger. (Comment on draft manuscript, Putney, "Airpower Advantage.")

6. Intvw trnscrpt, Gen John M. "Mike" Loh by Lt Col Suzanne Gehri and Lt Col Richard Reynolds, Sep 19 [26], 1991, 1, 6, CADRE, AU, AFHRA. Neither the JCS nor CENTCOM history offices have accounts of the CINCCENT-CJCS telephone call, so reconstructing it and related discussions within the JCS is difficult. Schwarzkopf told the author that he talked with Powell about involving the Air Staff and he would not have made the call without first discussing the action with the CJCS. See Telecon notes, Gen H. Norman Schwarzkopf and Diane T. Putney, May 5, 1992, AFHSO. Horner remembers Schwarzkopf saying at Jeddah that he would call the Joint Staff, not the Air Staff. Horner also remembered the purpose of Schwarzkopf's call was to request preparation of a list of "strategic" targets, which reminded him of the list he briefed to Schwarzkopf in April 1990 to deter Saddam's use of chemical weapons; it did not remind him of the list his staff prepared August 4–7. Even if Horner had explained to Schwarzkopf that his staff was already preparing a "Punishment ATO," the CENTCOM commander knew that the CENTAF staff was about to be stretched to its limits just with the basing of troops and defensive planning.

7. Intvw trnscrpt, Loh by Gehri and Reynolds, Sep 19 [26], 1991, 1–2, 3 (quoted sentence), 4–5, 7–8 (quoted phrases) CADRE, AU, AFHRA; Telecon notes, Gen H. Norman Schwarzkopf and Diane T. Putney, May 5, 1992, AFHSO; Notes, Lt Col Bernard E. Harvey, HQ USAF/XOXWS, Aug 10, 1990/0830, GWAPS, AFHRA; DoD, *Conduct of the Persian Gulf War*, 65; Schwarzkopf, *It Doesn't Take a Hero*, 313 (quote), 318 (quote), and 319 (quote). Loh did not make detailed notes about Schwarzkopf's call during or immediately after it, so Loh later struggled to recall his exact words and ideas. Loh remembered Schwarzkopf explaining that within CENTCOM, unspecified planners could not do strategic targeting, the "broader planning" required for a set of

strategic targets because they lacked the experience with them. The author interprets Loh's recollection to refer to Schwarzkopf's CENTCOM staff at MacDill AFB, not Horner's CENTAF staff.

8. Schwarzkopf, *It Doesn't Take a Hero*, 313. The date in the book is incorrect; he called the Air Staff on August 8. See also Schwarzkopf's interview, www.pbs.org/wgbh/pages/frontline/gulf/oral/Schwarzkopf, pp 1–2 of 10.

9. Intvw trnscrpt, Loh by Gehri and Reynolds, Sep 19, 1991, 1–2.

10. Ibid., 3.

11. Ibid., 1–2, 4, 6, 8.

12. Ibid., 8–9, 11–12.

13. Ibid., 6, 7 (1st quote); Discussion, Col John A. Warden III, USAF (Ret), and Diane T. Putney, Sep 28, 2001, Montgomery, Ala.; Intvw trnscrpt, Warden by Gehri, Reynolds, and Mann, May 1991, 117 (2d quote).

14. Warden encouraged his staff to question assumptions and interpretations of data in intelligence reports. See Intvw tape, Warden by Putney et al., Feb 6, 1992, AFHSO.

15. Intvw tape, Warden by Davis, Mar 2, 1993, AFHSO; Intvw trnscrpt, Warden by Gehri, Reynolds, and Mann, May 1991, 48–50, 87.

16. Brfg notes by Putney, Col John A. Warden III to AF/HO and CAFH staff, Feb 6, 1992, AFHSO; Org chart, HQ USAF, DCS/Plans and Ops, Sep 1, 1990; Intvw trnscrpt, Col John A. Warden III by Lt Col Gehri, Oct 22, 1991, 15–18 CADRE, AU; Intvw trnscrpt, Warden by Gehri, Reynolds, and Mann, May 1991, 62–63.

17. In his thesis, Warden highlighted the divergent thinking undergirding the strategy and decision-making of President Roosevelt and Prime Minister Churchill as allies in World War II, which led to compromises and a failure to integrate military and political objectives into an effective grand strategy which addressed the postwar problems posed by the Soviet Union. See John Ashley Warden III, "The Grand Alliance: Strategy and Decision" (master's thesis, Texas Tech University, 1975).

18. Carl von Clausewitz, *On War*, ed. and trans. Michael Howard and Peter Paret (Princeton, N.J.: Princeton University Press, 1976 and 1989). For an explanation of how Clausewitzian studies permeated the military service schools in the late 1970s and 1980s and Army doctrine, see Harry G. Summers, Jr., *On Strategy II: A Critical Analysis of the Gulf War* (New York: Dell, 1992), 126–135.

19. Intvw trnscrpt, Warden by Gehri, Mann, and Reynolds, May 30, 1991, 13. While at Texas Tech, Warden also read extensively about General Douglas MacArthur's island-hopping strategy in the Southwest Pacific theater.

20. B. H. Liddell Hart, *Strategy* (1954; reprint 1967 2d revised ed., New York: Penguin Books–Meridian, 1991). Liddell Hart influenced airpower theorists at the Air Corps Tactical School in the 1920s and 1930s, so Warden encountered Liddell Hart's thinking indirectly through his study of the Air Corps Tactical School and directly through his reading the British theorist while researching his thesis. See Wesley Frank Craven and James Lea Cate, eds. *Plans and Early Operations, January 1939 to August 1942,* The Army Air Forces in World War II, vol 1 (1948; reprint Washington: Office of Air Force History, 1983), 51.

21. For Warden's view on waging war to shape the postwar peace, see Lt Col John A. Warden III, "Planning to Win," *Air University Review* 34 (Mar–Apr 1983): 94–97.

22. Liddell Hart, *Strategy*, 204.

23. The Air Force doctrine manual did not address operational art at the time, but the new version of the Army's operations field manual highlighted the topic and stated, "Operational art is the employment of military forces to attain strategic goals in a theater of war or theater of operations through the design, organization, and conduct of campaigns and major operations." Army FM 100–5, May 5, 1986, 10.

24. John A. Warden III, *The Air Campaign: Planning for Combat* (Washington: National Defense University Press, 1988), 3–4. Curiously, Warden did not define *campaign* in his book, but a draft of a revision of the Air Force doctrine manual, prepared

under his tutelage in 1990, explained, "A campaign is a series of related military operations aimed to accomplish a strategic or operational objective within a given time and space. A major operation is simply a shorter term, more limited version of the same thing." See Drft AFM 1–1, "Employing Aerospace Power," May 25, 1990, 13.

25. AFM 1–1, "Basic Aerospace Doctrine of the United States," Jan 5, 1984, 2:12.

26. Warden, *Air Campaign*, 153.

27 Ibid., 160.

28. Warden defined distant interdiction as "an attack against the source of men and materiel, or, in the case of a warring party that has no industry, the ports or airfields where materiel provided from outside enters the country." Ibid., 94.

29. Ibid., 9.

30. Clausewitz, *On War* (1989), 619.

31. Warden, *Air Campaign*, 10. The eminent historian and expert on Clausewitz, Michael Howard, noted that airpower theorists have often drawn ideas from *On War*. He wrote, "The major strategic innovation of the interwar years was the development of air power. The theorists who pressed for its development used Clausewitzian arguments, but few mentioned his name. They started with his concept of 'the centre of gravity.'" See Michael Howard, *Clausewitz* (New York: Oxford University Press, 1983; reprint 1990), 68. Christopher Bassford diligently hunted for direct references to Clausewitz in the writings of airpower theorists. He concluded, "It is in fact difficult to find any positive reference — or, for that matter, any reference at all — to Clausewitz in the works of any of the major interwar air power writers in either Britain or the United States." See Christopher Bassford, *Clausewitz in English: The Reception of Clausewitz in Britain and America 1815–1945* (New York: Oxford University Press, 1994), 150. Airpower theorists at the Air Corps Tactical School in the 1930s did cite Clausewitz in their lectures. See Haywood S. Hansell, Jr., *The Air Plan that Defeated Hitler* (Atlanta, Ga.: Higgins-McArthur/Longino & Porter, 1972), 30–40.

32. Clausewitz, *On War* (1976), 485. This identification appears in the chapter, "Defense of a Theater of Operations."

33. Ibid., *On War*, 595–596.

34. Warden, *Air Campaign,* 147–148. For a review of Warden's book, see Lt Col Timothy G. Murphy, USAF, "A Critique of *The Air Campaign*" at www.airpower.maxwell.af.mil/airchronicles/apj/Apr94/murphy.html, pp 1–12.

35. Intvw trnscrpt, Warden by Gehri, Mann, and Reynolds, May 30, 1991, 33.

36. Intvw trnscrpt, Warden by Gehri, Oct 22, 1991, 21 (1st quote), 28 (2d quote). Two key projects XOXW undertook from 1988 to 1990 involved revising AFM 1–1 and suggesting revisions to the Air War College curriculum. See intvw trnscrpt, Warden by Gehri, Reynolds, and Mann, May 1991, 91.

37. Essay, Col John A. Warden III, "Centers of Gravity—The Key to Success in War," [Mar 1990], 1, Historical Advisor's (HA) file, GWAPS, AFHRA. (The essay's date derives from a "For Public Release" stamp on the document.) Since 1988, Warden had been talking and writing about the rings, and in December 1989, at a retreat at Airlie House in Virginia, Col Emery M. Kiraly, Warden's deputy in XOXW, submitted and discussed his written critique of the rings. See GWAPS HA file, AFHRA. The ring model Warden used after the war at Air University differed from his model in 1990. Compare the rings in his essay in 1990 with the model described in David S. Fadok, "John Boyd and John Warden: Air Power's Quest for Strategic Paralysis" (master's thesis: AU, 1995), 24–25. In March 1990 at a symposium sponsored by the Military Operations Research Society (MORS), Warden delivered his "centers of gravity" paper with only slight modifications to the version he submitted to the USAF public affairs office for policy review. See Col John A. Warden, USAF, "Centers of Gravity—The Key to Success in War," I-18–22 in *Proceedings,* MORS Mini-Symposium on Operational Art and Analysis, Mar 6–9, 1990, National Defense University (Alexandria, Va.: MORS, n.d.).

38. Essay, Warden, "Centers of Gravity," 4, 6–7 (quote); John A. Warden III, *The Air Campaign: Planning for Combat* (Washing-

ton: National Defense University Press, 1988). In his essay, Warden repeated from his book the emphasis on targeting command functions. In his book, he had written, "Command is a true center of gravity and worth attack in any circumstance in which it can be reached." See Warden, *Air Campaign*, 53.

39. Intvw trnscrpt, Warden by Gehri, Oct 22, 1991, 3. See also J.F.C. Fuller, *The Generalship of Alexander the Great* (New Brunswick, N.J.: Rutgers University Press, 1960; reprint, New York: Da Capo Press, 1989), 163–180.

40. Intvw trnscrpt, Warden by Gehri, Oct 22, 1991, 59; Discussion, Col Emery M. Kiraly and Diane T. Putney, Sep 3, 1992. For discussion of conflicting views about the effects of Linebacker II, see *GWAPS,* vol 2, part 2, *Effects and Effectiveness*, 63–67. Qaddafi spoke less publicly about terrorism, but he did not disavow it and continued to support it. See Joseph L. Stanik, USN (Ret), "Welcome to El Dorado Canyon," *U.S. Naval Institute Proceedings* 122 (April 1996): 61.

41. Essay, Warden, "Centers of Gravity," 3–5.

42. Ibid., 5.

43. Ibid., 5.

44. Ibid., 5–6.

45. Brfg notes by Putney, Warden to AF/HO and CAFH staff, Feb 6, 1992, AFHSO.

46. Essay, Warden, "Centers of Gravity," 6–7.

47. Ibid., 7.

48. Ibid., 8.

49. Ibid., 8–9. Warden referred to a report his staff had prepared, "Soviet Operational Level Fuel Depot Interdiction Study," which focused on the vulnerability and importance of petroleum, oil, and lubricants (POL) depots in East Germany and how crippling them could slow or stop a Soviet invasion through the German northern plain. He explained that logistics supporting POL requirements for a major offensive required complex and difficult operations, rendering them an excellent center of gravity for targeting, resulting in a decisive outcome. Study, Checkmate, Dec 30, 1989, subj: Soviet Operational Level Fuel Depot Interdiction Study, HA file, GWAPS, AFHRA.

50. Essay, Warden, "Centers of Gravity," 9.

51. Ibid., 10.

52. Brfg notes by Putney, Warden to AF/HO and CAFH staff, Feb 6, 1992, AFHSO.

53. Gen William Mitchell, *Skyways: A Book on Modern Aeronautics* (Philadelphia: J.B. Lippincott, 1930), 255–256. See also William Mitchell, *Winged Defense: the Development and Possibilities of Modern Air Power — Economic and Military* (New York: G.P. Putnam's Sons, 1925), 126–127.

54. Brfg notes by Putney, Warden to AF/HO and CAFH staff, Feb 6, 1992, AFHSO; Robert T. Finney, *History of the Air Corps Tactical School 1920–1940* (Washington: Center for Air Force History, 1992), 61–78. One of the ways Warden learned of Air Corps Tactical School concepts was through Hansell, *Air Plan That Defeated Hitler*, which he used when writing his master's thesis.

55. Hansell, *Air Plan That Defeated Hitler*, 10–11, 28, 32–33, 36, 40, 42, 45.

56. *GWAPS,* vol 1, part 1, *Planning*, 109 n. 11; Org charts, HQ USAF, Directorate of Plans, Aug 1, 1988 and HQ USAF, DCS/Plans and Ops, Sep 1, 1990, HA file, GWAPS, AFHRA; Paper, Lt Col L. Dixon, AF/XOOIR, Aug 17, 1981, subj: Checkmate, HA file, GWAPS, AFHRA.

57. Thompson, "Checkmate" section in draft rpt, GWAPS, "Planning," 3:80–81.

58. Ibid., 3:78.

59. Ibid., 3:82–83; Brfg, [Col Warden, 1990], subj: The Air Option, HA file, GWAPS, AFHRA (quotes). Warden did not present proofs that the air option could be brief and limit casualties, and this assertion contradicted statements in his book. See Warden, *Air Campaign,* 147–148.

60. Intvw trnscrpt, Warden by Gehri, Oct 22, 1991, 22, 36–38, 43–44.

61. Brfg notes, by Putney, Warden to AF/HO and CAFH staff, Feb 6, 1992, AFHSO; Memo, Lt Col David A. Deptula to Secretary Rice, Aug 8, 1990, subj: Air Campaign Plan Against Iraq, Deptula/Rice folder, GWAPS, AFHRA; Telecon, Wayne W. Thompson,

Checkmate historian, and Diane T. Putney, Feb 19, 1993; Discussion, Col Emery M. Kiraly and Diane T. Putney, Sep 3, 1992.

62. The official date and time for the start of the deployment was 1700Z August 7, 1990.

63. Brfg notes by Putney, Warden to AF/HO and CAFH staff, Feb 6, 1992, AFHSO; Harvey notes, Aug 6–8, 1990; Intvw notes by Thompson, Col John A. Warden III by Wayne W. Thompson, Aug 18, 1991, HA file, GWAPS, AFHRA; Intvw notes by Thompson, Col Emery M. Kiraly by Wayne W. Thompson, Feb 26, 1992, HA file, GWAPS, AFHRA.

64. In the afternoon of August 7, Lt Col Harvey and his staff in the Strategy Division had prepared a think-piece for Warden presenting air options and critiquing the JCS time-phased force and deployment list. See Memo, Col Ben Harvey to Col Rich Reynolds, subj: Comments on March 1994 draft manuscript, "Heart of the Storm," Jun 2, 1994, CADRE, AU, AFHRA.

65. Intvw tape, Lt Col David A. Deptula by TSgt Theodore Turner, Nov 1, 1990, AFHSO.

66. CENTCOM had planned for B–52s to operate from Diego Garcia, but at this early time, the deployment flow had not included them. They had participated in Internal Look and other CENTCOM exercises.

67. Memo, Lt Col David A. Deptula to Secretary Rice, Aug 8, 1990, subj: Air Campaign Plan Against Iraq, Deptula/Rice folder, GWAPS, AFHRA.

68. Harvey notes, Aug 8, 1990; Brfg, [HQ USAF/XOXW, Aug 8, 1990], subj: Iraqi Air Campaign, CHSH 7-11, GWAPS, AFHRA.

69. Brfg slides, Aug 8, 1990, subj: Iraqi Air Campaign, 2–3.

70. Ibid., 4.

71. Ibid., 5.

72 Ibid., 6–7.

73. Planners did not have time to create a new operational column chart, so they used the strategic one for the operational target sets. See Ibid., 8–9.

74. Ibid., 11.

75. Intvw trnscrpt, Warden by Gehri, Oct 22, 1991, 42, 49 (quote).

76. Harvey notes, Aug 8, 1990.

77. Study, SAC/XPA, [Apr–May 1991], subj: Air Staff/Desert Shield Planning, SAC/HO; Intvw trnscrpt, Lt Col Thomits by Kent Beck, Jul 3, 1991, SAC/HO; Intvw trnscrpt, Loh by Gehri and Reynolds, Sep 19, 1991, 8–10; Harvey notes, Aug 10, 1990/0830.

78. Intvw trnscrpt, Lt Gen Robert M. Alexander by Lt Col Suzanne Gehri, Lt Col Rich Reynolds, and Lt Col Ed Mann, May 30, 1991, CADRE, AU, AFHRA; Memo, Lt Gen James R. Clapper, Jr., to Secretary of the Air Force (Office for Security Review), subj: Comments on Security Review of Referenced Manuscript, May 31, 1994, CADRE, AU, AFHRA. Clapper wrote the memo as a negative review of how Reynolds portrayed his phone conversation with Alexander in the book, Richard T. Reynolds, *Heart of the Storm: The Genesis of the Air Campaign against Iraq* (Maxwell AFB, Ala.: AU Press, 1995), 31–32, based solely on Alexander's account. In 1994 when Clapper wrote to Alexander asking for clarification about their conflicting versions of the phone call and its aftermath, Alexander expressed his policy of declining all comments about Desert Shield and Storm. Clapper's memo did include the sentence, "I might add General Alexander later sent me a note of apology for having misunderstood me, and his mischaracterizing to General Loh my support, or lack thereof — a class act in my view." The apology strongly suggests that miscommunication and misunderstanding led to Alexander's complaint and not Clapper's refusal to support Loh and Warden.

79. Memo, Lt Gen James R. Clapper, Jr., to Secretary of the Air Force (Office for Security Review), subj: Comments on Security Review of Referenced Manuscript, May 31, 1994, CADRE, AU AFHRA. According to AFP 200–17, "An Introduction to Air Force Targeting," June 23, 1989, 8, the targeteer is "an expert on the application of aerospace forces. A targeteer's knowledge should encompass the intelligence and operations disciplines."

80. Intvw tape, Blackburn by Putney, Feb 12, 1992; Intvw tape, Lt Col David A.

Deptula by Lt Col Richard Reynolds, Lt Col Suzanne Gehri, and Lt Col Edward Mann, Jul 24, 1992, CADRE, AU, AFHRA. The author cites August 9 as the start date because this is what Blackburn told the CINCCENT a week later.

81. AFM 1–1, Jan 5, 1984, 3-2; AFP 200–17, "An Introduction to Air Force Targeting," Jun 23, 1989; Intvw tape, Blackburn by Putney, Feb 12, 1992.

82. AFP 200–17, "An Introduction to Air Force Targeting," June 23, 1989, 21; Intvw tape, Blackburn by Putney, Feb 19, 1992.

83. AFP 200–17, June 23, 1989, 9–13.

84. AFP 200–18, "Target Intelligence Handbook," Oct 1, 1990, 59; Intvw tape, Blackburn by Putney, Feb 12, 1992; Memo for record, Col James R. Blackburn, Jr., Oct 17, 1990, subj: USAF/INT Targeting/MC&G Support to Desert Shield.

85. Intvw tapes, Blackburn by Putney, Feb 12 and 19, 1992.

86. Intvw tapes, Blackburn by Putney, Feb 12 and 19, 1992 (quote); Intvw tape, Lt Col Bobby Marion by Diane T. Putney, Jun 4, 1992, AFHSO.

87. Intvw tape, Warden by Putney et al., Feb 6, 1992; Brfg, Col James R. Blackburn, Jr., USAF Targeteers Conference, Oct 31–Nov 1, 1991, videotape in AFISA/INT.

88. Intvw tape, Blackburn by Putney, Feb 12, 1992; AFP 200–18, Oct 1, 1990, 64.

89. Intvw tape, Blackburn by Putney, Feb 12, 1992.

90. Ibid; Memo for record, Col James R. Blackburn, Jr., Oct 17, 1990, subj: USAF/INT Targeting/MC&G Support to Desert Shield; AFP 200–17, June 23, 1989, 21.

91. Intvw tape, Blackburn by Putney, Feb 12, 1992; Intvw trnscrpt, Warden by Gehri, Oct 22, 1991, 55 (quote).

92. Intvw tape, Blackburn by Putney, Feb 12, 1992; AFP 200–17, June 23, 1989, 17.

93. Harvey notes, Aug 10, 1990/0830.

94. Brfg slides, "Instant Thunder: A Strategic Air Campaign Proposal for CINCCENT," [Aug 10, 1990], 1, CHSH 7-6, GWAPS, AFHRA. Lt. Col. T. K. Kierney recounted that while in Checkmate, he and Warden stood by the grease board displaying the ring categories, and from the group of about a dozen officers discussing the air campaign, someone suggested a gradual approach, and Kierney emphatically, negatively spoke against another "Rolling Thunder." The discussion focused on a violent, quick approach. Warden interjected that the campaign should be "Instant Thunder," and the phrase persisted, moving from a descriptive characteristic to the plan's title. See telecon notes, Col T. K. Kierney and Diane T. Putney, Mar 30, 1993, AFHSO.

95. Mark Clodfelter, *The Limits of Air Power: The American Bombing of North Vietnam* (New York: Free Press, 1989), xi, 118.

96. Brfg Slides, "Instant Thunder," [Aug 10, 1990].

97. Ibid.

98. Ibid., 3.

99. Ibid., 5.

100. Ibid., 6.

101. DoD, *Conduct of the Persian Gulf War,* 611–617. See also AFP 200–17, "An Introduction to Air Force Targeting," June 23, 1989, 37.

102. Brfg slides, "Instant Thunder," [Aug 10, 1990], 6; Intvw trnscrpt, Warden by Gehri, Oct 22, 1991, 1–2; J.F.C. Fuller, *The Generalship of Alexander the Great* (New Brunswick, N.J.: Rutgers University Press, 1960; reprint, New York: Da Capo Press, 1989), 264–280.

103. Brfg slides, "Instant Thunder," [Aug 10, 1990], 12.

104. Intvw trnscrpt, Alexander by Gehri, Reynolds, and Mann, May 30, 1991, 12. In postwar lectures, Warden restored the five concentric rings to his Instant Thunder/Desert Storm briefing.

105. Intvw trnscrpt, Alexander by Gehri, Reynolds, and Mann, May 30, 1991, 9; Intvw trnscrpt, Lt Col David A. Deptula by Richard Davis, Perry Jamieson, and Diane Putney, Jan 8, 1992, 38, AFHSO.

106. Brfg slides, "Instant Thunder," [Aug 10, 1990], 9.

107. Ibid.

108. Ibid.

109. Ibid.

110. Ibid., 11, 22.

111. Ibid., 21.

112. Ibid., 19–20.

113. Ibid., 2.

114. Ibid., 22.

115. Ibid., 23–25.

116. Ibid., 26. Later versions of the plan would complete the campaign in only six days.

117. Ibid., 27–29.

118. Harvey notes, Aug 10, 1990/0853; Intvw trnscrpt, Dugan by Reynolds, Aug 15, 1991, 3, 10; Intvw trnscrpt, Loh by Gehri and Reynolds, Sep 19, 1991, pp 13–14.

119. Intvw trnscrpt, Gen Robert D. Russ by Lt Col Suzanne Gehri, Lt Col Richard Reynolds, and Lt Col Edward Mann, Dec 9, 1991, 20–21, 67 (quote), CADRE, AU. For detailed studies of TAC opposition to Instant Thunder and Air Staff involvement in CENTCOM planning, see Reynolds, *Heart of the Storm,* and Col. Edward C. Mann III, USAF, *Thunder and Lightning: Desert Storm and the Airpower Debates* (Maxwell AFB, Ala.: AU Press, 1995).

120. Intvw trnscrpt, Russ by Gehri, Reynolds, and Mann, Dec 9, 1991, 23.

121. Intvw trnscrpt, Russ by Gehri, Reynolds, and Mann, Dec 9, 1991, 21. See later chapters in this volume for Henry's role in defeating the Iraqi air defense system. Russ had other comments about the plan, including that it was "too violent."

122. Memo for record, Lt Col Bernard E. Harvey, Aug 10, 1990, subj: "Instant Thunder" briefing to USCINCCENT, 10 August/ 1320–1400/HQ CENTCOM/J3 Office/MacDill AFB Fla., Lt Col Stanfill files, GWAPS, AFHRA.

123. The quoted material derives from notes taken during the briefing; the quotes are the exact words in the notes, but not necessarily the precise words spoken by the commander because no one tape-recorded the meeting. See Harvey notes appended to and written on Instant Thunder brfg slides, [Aug 10, 1990], 22, CHSH 7-6, GWAPS, AFHRA. See also Intvw trnscrpts, Alexander by Gehri, Reynolds, and Mann, May 30, 1991, and June 3, 1992, and Intvw tape, Moore by Gehri, Reynolds, and Mann, Sep 21, 1992.

124. Harvey notes appended to and written on Instant Thunder brfg slides, [Aug 10, 1990], 10, 16, CHSH 7-6, GWAPS, AFHRA; Memo for record, Col John A. Warden III, Aug 10, 1990, subj: "Instant Thunder" Briefing to USCINCCENT, 10 August/ 1320–1400/HQ CENTCOM/J–3 Office/ MacDill AFB Fla., Gen Alexander file, CHSH 14, GWAPS, AFHRA.

125. Harvey memo for record, Aug 10, 1990; Harvey notes appended to Instant Thunder brfg slides, [Aug 10, 1990]. It is unclear from Harvey's material to what the CINCCENT was referring when he talked about his confidence being restored. Schwarzkopf was probably referring to SAC's lack of confidence in its air-launched cruise missiles and its advice about not sending B–52s to targets without extensive electronic combat support.

126. Harvey notes appended to Instant Thunder brfg slides, [Aug 10, 1990]; Harvey memo for record, Aug 10, 1990; Warden memo for record, Aug 10, 1990.

127. Harvey notes appended to Instant Thunder brfg slides, [Aug 10, 1990]; Harvey memo for record, Aug 10, 1990.

128. Harvey notes appended to Instant Thunder brfg slides, [Aug 10, 1990]; Harvey memo for record, Aug 10, 1990.

129. Harvey notes appended to Instant Thunder brfg slides, [Aug 10, 1990].

130. Ibid.; Intvw trnscrpt, Warden by Gehri, Oct 22, 1991, 95–96 (quote). See also Intvw tape, Lt Col Bernard E. Harvey by Diane T. Putney and Richard G. Davis, Jan 14, 1993, AFHSO; Intvw trnscrpt, Alexander by Gehri and Reynolds, May 30, 1991, 15, CADRE, AU, GWAPS.

131. Intvw trnscrpt, Maj Gen Burton R. Moore by Lt Col Richard Reynolds, Oct 23, 1991, 17, CADRE, AU, AFHRA; Intvw trnscrpt, Moore by Gehri, Reynolds, and Mann, Sep 21, 1992, 48.

132. Harvey notes, Aug 10, 1990/1405.

133. Ibid., Aug 10, 1990/1515/1930.

134. Ibid., Aug 11, 1990/0810.

135. Intvw trnscrpt, Warden by Gehri, Oct 22, 1991, 74.

136. Brfg slide, "Instant Thunder," [Aug 11, 1990], CHSH 7-5, GWAPS, AFHRA.

137. Brfg slides, "CENTCOM Air Cam-

paign Plan," with fax cover sheet, Brig Gen Griffith, TAC/XP, to Maj Gen Alexander, AF/XOX, Aug 11, 1990, 0001, CHSH 14, GWAPS, AFHRA.

138. Intvw trnscrpt, Russ by Gehri, Reynolds, and Mann, Dec 9, 1991, 21–22.

139. Brfg slides, "CENTCOM Air Campaign Plan," [Aug 11, 1990], CHSH 14, GWAPS, AFHRA.

140. Ibid., 8.

141. Ibid., 10–11.

142. Ibid., 12.

143. Intvw trnscrpt, Griffith by Gehri and Reynolds, Sep 26, 1991, 10–11.

144. Brfg slides, "CENTCOM Air Campaign Plan," [Aug 11, 1990], 13–14, CHSH 14, GWAPS, AFHRA.

145. Ibid., 15.

146. Ibid., 16.

147. After the war, Loh could not remember Alexander giving him a copy of the plan, nor could he recall reading it. He seemed to have just learned about it in September 1991. See Intvw trnscrpt, Loh by Gehri and Reynolds, Sep 19, 1991 [Sep 26, 1991].

148. Brfg slides, "Iraqi Air Campaign Instant Thunder," [Aug 17, 1990], 1, Checkmate/Deptula 7/Theater Campaign Slide Brfg.

149. Intvw trnscrpt, Loh by Gehri and Reynolds, Sep 19, 1991 [Sep 26, 1991], 15–18.

150. Powell, *My American Journey,* 473.

151. Harvey notes, Aug 11, 1990/0924. See also Notes, Maj Steve Cullen, XOXWS, Aug 11, 1990, subj: Notes from 1030, Saturday, 11 Aug 1990, Air Campaign Working Group, Led by Col Warden, XOXW, CHSH 14, GWAPS, AFHRA. Events moved so quickly that Warden did not return to brief Powell a second time the week of August 11–17, 1990. The quotes represent words as Lt Col Harvey wrote them and may not be the exact words Powell used because no one tape-recorded the meeting.

152. Harvey notes, Aug 11, 1990/0924.

153. Ibid.

154. Intvw trnscrpt, Warden by Gehri, Oct 22, 1991, 71 (quote). See also intvw tape, Warden by Putney et al., Feb 6, 1992, AFHSO; Discussion, Warden and Putney, Sep 28, 2001.

155. Intvw trnscrpt, Alexander by Gehri, Reynolds, and Mann, Jun 3, 1992, 14. See Loh's comments on Instant Thunder being "totally decisive" in intvw trnscrpt, Loh by Gehri and Reynolds, Sep 19, 1991 [Sep 26, 1991], 26.

156. Memo for record, Lt Col Bernard E. Harvey, Aug 11, 1990, subj: "Instant Thunder" briefing to CJCS, 11 August/0924…, CHSH 14, GWAPS, AFHRA (quote). (This is Harvey's typed, edited transcript of his handwritten notes.)

157. Ibid. (quote); Intvw trnscrpt, Alexander by Gehri, Reynolds, and Mann, Jun 3, 1992, 14; Intvw tape, Warden by Putney et al., Feb 6, 1992. See also Powell, *My American Journey*, 472–473.

158. Harvey memo for record, Aug 11, 1990 (quotes); Harvey notes, Aug 11, 1990/0924.

159. Ed drft intvw trnscrpt, Lt Gen Robert M. Alexander by Lt Col Suzanne Gehri, Lt Col Rich Reynolds, and Lt Col Ed Mann, June 3, 1992, 14, CADRE, AU.

160. Schwarzkopf, *It Doesn't Take a Hero,* 301; Powell, *My American Journey,* 473 (1st quote), 476–477, 479 (2d quote); Powell's Frontline interview, www.pbs.org/wgbh/pages/frontline/gulf/oral, pp 2–3 of 6.

161. Targeteers are intelligence officers, but Checkmate also needed experts on Iraq, order of battle, photo interpretation, intelligence communication systems, and bomb damage assessment.

162. Org chart, "Campaign Plans and Applications Organization," [Aug 1990], HA file, GWAPS, AFHRA; Intvw tape, Deptula by Davis, Jamieson, and Putney, Jan 8, 1992; Harvey notes, Aug 11, 1990/1240; Lt Col Daniel Kuehl, "Notes on Instant Thunder…", Sep 1990, 2, box 5, Kurt Guthe file, GWAPS, AFHRA.

163. Intvw tape, Deptula by Gehri, Reynolds, and Mann, Jul 23, 1992; Lt Col Daniel Kuehl, "Notes on Instant Thunder…," box 5, Kurt Guthe file, GWAPS, AFHRA.

164. Dr. Wayne W. Thompson performed the duties as the Checkmate historian.

Chapter 3

1. Intvw trnscrpt, Adams by Gehri and Reynolds, Feb 3, 1992, 5–6, 12–14, 19, 24; Intvw trnscrpt, Lt Gen Charles A. May, Jr., USAF (Ret), by Lt Col Rich Reynolds, Aug 21, 1992, 18–23. Adams's recollection of the dates for initial events, as related to Gehri and Reynolds, is off by one week according to when Schwarzkopf telephoned Loh on August 8, 1990.

2. Intvw trnscrpt, Adams by Gehri and Reynolds, Feb 3, 1992, 19–20.

3. Ibid., 1–19; Ed drft intvw trnscrpt, Alexander by Gehri, Reynolds, and Mann, June 3, 1992, 34–35; Intvw trnscrpt, Loh by Gehri and Reynolds, Sep 19, 1991 [Sep 26, 1991], 13, 21–24.

4. Intvw trnscrpt, Adams by Gehri and Reynolds, Feb 3, 1992, 2, 5 (quote), 9–11.

5. Intvw trnscrpt, Loh by Gehri and Reynolds, Sep 19, 1991 [Sep 26, 1991], 22.

6. Intvw trnscrpt, Adams by Gehri and Reynolds, Feb 3, 1992, 2–3, 6, 17. Lt Gen Carns, JCS Director, had discussed the J–3 for Air idea at General Loh's breakfast meeting, and probably suggested it to General Kelly. By this time, representatives from the other services were already in Checkmate.

7. Intvw trnscrpt, Warden by Gehri, Oct 22, 1991, 77.

8. Ibid., 76–77; Harvey notes, Aug 11, 1990/0810, Aug 12, 1990 0715/1035; Intvw trnscrpt, Adams by Gehri and Reynolds, Feb 3, 1992, 9–10, 20. Harvey's notes reveal that Adams raised the issue of targeting and weaponeering with General Alexander at 0715 and with Warden at 1035.

9. Intvw trnscrpt, Adams by Gehri and Reynolds, Feb 3, 1992, 24; Harvey notes, Aug 12, 1990/1035.

10. Intvw trnscrpt, Warden by Gehri, Oct 22, 1991, 19–20, 30; Brfg tape, Warden to AF/HO and CAFH staffs, Feb 6, 1992, AFHSO; Intvw tape, Col John A. Warden III by Richard G. Davis, Mar 2, 1993, AFHSO.

11. Intvw trnscrpt, Adams by Gehri and Reynolds, Feb 3, 1992, 13.

12. Adams had earlier told Alexander that the plan reminded him of the unfulfilled promises of the Vietnam War.

13. Harvey notes, Aug 12, 1990/0715, 1035 (Warden and Adams quotes). The quoted material is written as Harvey recorded the comments and may not represent the exact words spoken because the session was not tape-recorded.

14. Harvey notes, Aug 12, 1990/1035 (quotes).

15. Brfg slides, Instant Thunder, [Aug 13, 1990], 35–45, Warden file, GWAPS, AFHRA; Intvw notes Col Emery M. Kiraly by Wayne W. Thompson, Feb 26, 1992, HA file, GWAPS, AFHRA.

16. Discussion notes, Col Emery M. Kiraly and Diane T. Putney, Jan 22, 1993, AFHSO. Warden also thought Powell's directive reflected a "parochial" interest. See intvw trnscrpt, Warden by Gehri, May 1991, 111.

17. Lt Col Daniel Kuehl, "Notes on Instant Thunder…," Sep 1990, 2, box 5, Kurt Guthe file, GWAPS, AFHRA.

18. Memo, Col Ben Harvey to Col Rich Reynolds, June 2, 1993, subj: Comments on March 1994 Draft, "Heart of the Storm," 6, in ltr with atch, Col Ben Harvey to Lt Gen Jay W. Kelley, Aug 3, 1994, AU, AFHRA.

19. In October 1990, Warden joined the effort to plan for air power in the counterland mission, attacking the stationary Iraqi army, but in August he focused on the strategic air campaign.

20. Intvw trnscrpt, Warden by Gehri, Oct 22, 1991, 58.

21. Ibid. During Warden's briefing to the CINCCENT on Aug 17, 1990, the colonel did state that Instant Thunder would inflict "paralysis and shock" upon the Iraqis. For antecedents to Warden's concepts, see B.H. Liddell Hart, *Strategy* (1954; reprint 1967 2d revised ed., New York: Penguin Books-Meridian, 1991), 212; Haywood S. Hansell, Jr., *The Air Plan that Defeated Hitler* (Atlanta, Ga.: Higgins-McArthur/Longino & Porter, 1972), 9; William Mitchell, "Let the Air Service Crash!" *Liberty* 2 (January 30, 1926): 43; William Mitchell, *Winged Defense*, 16–17, 126–127; and William Mitchell, *Skyways,* 8, 255. For more discussion of "strate-

gic paralysis" and air power, see the theses Jason B. Barlow, "Strategic Paralysis: An Airpower Theory for the Present" (master's thesis, Air University, 1994), and Fadok, "John Boyd and John Warden."

22. Intvw tape, Warden by Davis, Mar 2, 1993, AFHSO.

23. Intvw trnscrpt, Warden by Gehri, Oct 22, 1991, 71. During the war, Warden conceived and advocated the idea of supplying the Iraqi conscript frontline troops with USAF C–130 airlift flights, so they could overfly the Republican Guard to their rear and reach Baghdad where they could replace the regime. See intvw tape, Warden by Davis, Mar 2, 1993, AFHSO. The colonel seemed to have struggled for a marketable idea that would enable the Coalition to use the enemy forces, as his hero, Alexander the Great, had consistently done in his campaigns in the ancient world, and which the modern military strategist, J.F.C. Fuller, claimed was appropriate in the modern world. See Fuller, *Generalship of Alexander*, 5, 264–280, 306–314; Intvw trnscrpt, Warden by Gehri, Oct 22, 1991, 1–2.

24. Notes, Lt Col Phillip S. Meilinger, "Thoughts on Instant Thunder...," Sep 1990, 2, box 5, Kurt Guthe file, GWAPS, AFHRA; Telecon notes, Col Phillip S. Meilinger and Diane T. Putney, Jan 11, 1994, AFHSO.

25. Intvw trnscept, Warden by Gehri, Oct 22, 1991, 97. See also Gerhard Ritter, *The Schlieffen Plan: Critique of a Myth* (1958; reprint, Westport, Conn.: Greenwood Press, 1979).

26. Warden had written about the idea of holding aircraft in reserve in his book, *Air Campaign*, 115–127.

27. Harvey notes, Aug 14, 1990/1040.

28. Intvw trnscrpt, Adams by Gehri and Reynolds, Feb 2, 1992, 10.

29. Ibid., 10, 24, 28.

30. Brfg slides, "Iraqi Air Campaign Instant Thunder," Deptula file, Checkmate, Pentagon (hereafter cited as IT Brfg slides), 25. After the war, Warden defended his confidence in his reserve air forces by referring to a study done for him by Richard P. Hallion, an air power historian; the published works of Trevor DuPuy, military analyst; and computer simulations run by the Air Force Center for Studies and Analysis. See intvw tape, Warden by Davis, Mar 2, 1993, AFHSO. The author of this volume located the Hallion study, but it was dated after the second briefing to Schwarzkopf on August 17 and the briefing to Horner on August 20. Colonel Kiraly told the author he remembered serious discussions in Checkmate before the 20th of the probable routes of attack that the Iraqis would follow and the conclusions that available air power would, indeed, halt the Iraqi invasion of the kingdom. Kiraly believed that confidence in the reserve air force was justified through those discussions. Checkmate had done a study, the results shown to General Adams on August 13 in the Instant Thunder Phase II briefing segment, that focused on 96 A–10s with AGM–65D and MK–20 munitions employed against only Iraqi tanks and APCs traveling at a maximum rate of advance of 100 kilometers a day. See Instant Thunder brfg slides, [briefed to AF/XO, 13 Aug/1330], 62–64, "Col Warden's Notes," GWAPS, AFHRA.

31. IT Brfg slides, 25.

32. For both his master's thesis and book, Warden referred to the published works of Haywood Hansell and agreed with his judgment that the diversions of the strategic air campaign in Europe were mistakes. See Hansell, *Air Plan that Defeated Hitler,* 251; intvw trnscrpt, Warden by Gehri, Reynolds, and Mann, May 1991, 102; and intvw trnscrpt, Warden by Gehri, Oct 22, 1991, 72.

33. Warden, *Air Campaign*, 115–127.

34. Intvw trnscrpt, Griffith by Gehri and Reynolds, Sep 26, 1991, 15.

35. Ibid., 25.

36. Intvw trnscrpt, Warden by Gehri, Oct 22, 1991, 73.

37. Warden wanted a "near term," "surprise" execution. He believed time worked against the United States in the region, and it was "important to strike before Hussein acts." See intvw trnscrpt, Warden by Gehri, Oct 22, 1991, 99; Brfg slides, "Instant Thunder," [Aug 10, 1990], 2.

38. Intvw tape, Warden by Putney et al.,

Feb 6, 1992; Telecon, Wayne Thompson and Diane T. Putney, Jul 2, 1992. Majors Dan Farley and Tom Odom represented the Army in Checkmate. See Scales, *Certain Victory*, 176.

39. Telecon log, Checkmate, Aug 11, 1990/1700L, CHSH 22, GWAPS, AFHRA; Harvey notes, Aug 11, 1990/1800 and Aug 12, 1990/1035/1705.

40. Intvw trnscrpt, Dugan by Reynolds, Aug 15, 1991, 5.

41. Harvey notes, Aug 14, 1990/1630; Intvw trnscrpt, Warden by Gehri, Oct 22, 1991, 87.

42. Harvey notes, Aug 15, 1990/1327 (quote); Intvw tape, Warden by Putney et al., Feb 6, 1992.

43. Intvw trnscrpts, Alexander by Gehri, Reynolds, and Mann, May 30, 1991, 14, and Jun 3, 1992, 60–61.

44. Harvey notes, Aug 10, 1990/1030 and Aug 14, 1990/1040; Intvw tape, Warden by Putney et al., Feb 6, 1992, AFHSO; Brfg slide, "CSAF Notes 14 Aug," Lt Col Ronnie Stanfill file, GWAPS, AFHRA; Intvw trnscrpt, Dugan by Reynolds, Aug 15, 1991, 11.

45. Harvey notes, Aug 14, 1990/1040; Brfg slide, "CSAF Notes 14 Aug."

46. Ibid., 1990/1745/1905.

47. Ibid., Aug 15, 1990/0802; Handwritten note on memo, Lt Col David A. Deptula, SAF/OSX, to Secretary Rice, Aug 8, 1990, subj: Air Campaign Plan against Iraq, Deptula-Rice folder, GWAPS, AFHRA.

48. Telecons, Wayne Dzwonchyk, JCS/HO, and Diane T. Putney, May 4 and 5, 1992; Kelly notes, Aug 11, 1990; Brfg slides, "Campaign Objectives," CHSH 5-16, GWAPS, AFHRA; Stanfill notes, Aug–Sep, 2, GWAPS, AFHRA; Intvw tape, Lt Col Bernard E. Harvey by Diane T. Putney and Richard G. Davis, Dec 7, 1992, AFHSO; Intvw tape, Warden by Davis, Mar 2, 1993, AFHSO.

49. Intvw trnscrpt, Donald B. Rice, Secretary of the Air Force, by Lt Col Richard Reynolds, Lt Col Suzanne Gehri, and Lt Col Edward Mann, Dec 11, 1991, 4, New Acquisitions (NA) 234, GWAPS, AFHRA.

50. "Remarks to Department of Defense Employees," Aug 15, 1990, *Weekly Compilation of Presidential Documents*, Aug 20, 1990, vol 26, 1255.

51. Harvey notes, Aug 15, 1990/1710/1800/1910.

52. Msg, USCINCCENT to JCS/J3-JOD et al., 162005Z Aug 90, subj: USCENTCOM Target List for Operation Desert Shield, CHSH 7, GWAPS, AFHRA.

53. Brfg paper, USCENTCOM CCJ3-PT, fax date Aug 12, 1990, subj: Strategic Targeting Considerations, CHSH 17, GWAPS, AFHRA; Telecon log, Checkmate, Aug 11, 1990; Intvw tape, Maj Mark Christian by Diane T. Putney, Apr 23, 1992, AFHSO.

54. Telecon log, Checkmate, Aug 11–12, 1990.

55. Slide, "Targeting," in brfg by Maj Lou Harvey, USAF Targets Conference, Oct 31–Nov 1, 1991, subj: USCENTCOM CCJ2 Desert Shield/Desert Storm Targeting, Conference file, AFISA/INT, Bolling AFB.

56. Msg, USCINCCENT/CCJ2-P to JCS/J3-JOD et al., 162005Z Aug 90 subj: USCENTCOM Target List for Operation Desert Shield, CHSH 7, GWAPS, AFHRA; Intvw tape, Christian by Putney, Apr 23, 1992.

57. Msg, USCINCCENT/CCJ2-P to JCS/J3-JOD et al., 162005Z Aug 90, subj: USCENTCOM Target List for Operation Desert Shield, CHSH 7, GWAPS, AFHRA; Intvw tape, Blackburn by Putney, Feb 19, 1992.

58. Memo, Col James R. Blackburn, Jr., Oct 17, 1990, subj: USAF/INT Targeting/MC&G Support to Desert Shield, Blackburn file, AFISA/INT.

59. Ibid.; Intvw tape, Blackburn by Putney, Feb 19, 1992, AFHSO.

60. Intvw tape, Blackburn by Putney, Feb 19, 1992; Harvey notes, Aug 16, 1990/1630/2100.

61. OPORD, "Instant Thunder MCMXC," CHSH 1-8, GWAPS, AFHRA (hereafter cited as IT OPORD); IT Brfg slides.

62. IT OPORD, 1.

63. Ibid.

64. IT Brfg slides, 6, 10; IT OPORD, 17.

65. IT OPORD, 8, 17–30. When briefing the CINCCENT on August 17, 1990, discus-

sion at one point focused on a single "ground to air assets" site in Kuwait, which was probably the newly installed Iraqi air defense sector operations center.

66. IT Brfg slides, 10, 12.

67. IT OPORD, 7; IT Brfg slides, 14; Draft worksheet, "Sortie Availability," [David A. Deptula], Aug 13, 1990, CHSH 18, GWAPS, AFHRA.

68. IT OPORD, 8, 69.

69. IT Brfg slides, 29.

70. IT OPORD, 19, 28–29.

71. IT Brfg slides, 13, 19; IT OPORD, 8.

72. IT OPORD, 44–49; IT Brfg slides, 22.

73. IT OPORD, 44–49.

74. IT Brfg slides, 27.

75. Ibid., 29; IT OPORD, 63–67, 159.

76. IT OPORD, 160.

77. Ibid.

78. Harvey notes, Aug 17, 1990/0900; Intvw trnscrpt, Warden by Gehri, Oct 22, 1991, 93.

79. Harvey notes, Aug 17, 1990/1006, 1.

80. Notes, Lt Col Ronnie Stanfill, Aug 17, 1990/1006, 1, CHP folder, GWAPS, AFHRA; Harvey notes, Aug 17, 1990/1006, 1. The quoted phrase indicates exactly how each notetaker wrote the words; it does not necessarily repeat the exact words spoken because no one tape-recorded the meeting.

81. Harvey notes, Aug 17, 1990/1006, 1–3; IT OPORD, 23, 37.

82. Harvey notes, Aug 17, 1990/1006, 3.

83. Intvw trnscrpt, Col James R. Blackburn by Lt Col Edward Mann, Lt Col Richard Reynolds, and Lt Col Suzanne Gehri, Apr 21, 1993, 79–80, CADRE, AU.

84. Ibid., 95; Harvey notes, Aug 17, 1990/1006, 3; Intvw tape, Blackburn by Putney, Feb 19, 1992; Memo for record, Col Blackburn, Oct 17, 1990.

85. Harvey notes, Aug 17, 1990/1006, 3.

86. Ibid., 3, 4 (quotes).

87. IT Brfg slide, 23.

88. Harvey notes, Aug 17, 1990/1006, 5 (quotes).

89. Ibid., 5–6.

90. Ibid., 6–9.

91. Stanfill notes, Aug 17, 1990/1006, 11; Harvey notes, Aug 17, 1990/1006, 9.

92. Harvey notes, Aug 17, 1990/1006, 9. During Desert Shield and Desert Storm, 262 KC–135s and 46 KC–10s supported the theater, a total of 308 tankers.

93. Draft report, Capt Johnson (J–3/JOD EC/CC) to J–31, n.d., subj: CINCCENT Trip Report, 2–3, JCS/HO.

94. Harvey notes, Aug 17, 1990/1006, 11–12.

95. Intvw trnscrpt, Warden by Gehri, Oct 22, 1991, 78, 100, 101 (quote).

96. Harvey notes, Aug 17, 1990/1006, 12.

97. Ibid., 17–18.

98. Ibid., Aug 17, 1990/1730; Intvw trnscrpt, Warden by Gehri, Oct 22, 1991, 105.

99. Memo for record, Col Blackburn, Oct 17, 1990; Intvw tape, Blackburn by Putney, Feb 19, 1992 (quote); Intvw tape, Christian by Putney, Apr 23, 1992.

100. Memo for record, Col Blackburn, Oct 17, 1990; Intvw, Blackburn by Putney, Feb 19, 1990; Msg, DMAAC/SDFP to USCINCCENT/CCJ2-P et al., 270138Z Aug 90, subj: Desert Shield Point Mensurations—Msg 2, 92-XOXWF-027, GWAPS, AFHRA.

101. Telecon notes, Gen H. Norman Schwarzkopf and Diane T. Putney, May 5, 1992, AFHSO.

102. Schwarzkopf's Frontline interview, www.pbs.org/wgbh/pages/frontline/gulf/oral/schwarzkopf, p 3 of 10.

103. Drft brfg slides, "Offensive Campaign [Desert Storm]," [24 Aug 90], 15–18, 27 (hereafter cited as DS brfg slides). With these slides, "Desert Storm" was penned on the title page, as was the date. The CENTCOM emblem appears on all pages. Col Robert J. Martinelli, CENTCOM CCJ1, Oct 21, 1993, sent a copy of these slides to Putney at CAFH (later AFHSO). GWAPS researchers also obtained a copy. The "USCINCCENT's Intent," page 5, matches exactly the statement of intent in DoD, *Conduct of the Persian Gulf War,* 66. See also a similar set of slides, with different pagination, "Offensive Campaign Desert Storm," without the CENTCOM emblem but with the date "24 Aug 90" penned on the title page, with other notations. This too was sent

from Col Martinelli to Putney, and the GWAPS researchers obtained a copy. Martinelli also sent a set of very different slides, "Offensive Campaign Concept of Operations Outline," and on the title page was penned, "Schwarzkopf Brief to CJCS/SECDEF" and the date "26 Aug 90." Referring to the penned material, Col Clint Williams, CENTCOM staff, wrote on the title page, "This is wrong! This is the earliest J5 effort, not the version (24 Aug) given to CJCS on 25 Aug/to President on 26th of Aug." The CENTCOM historian, Hans Pawlisch, Dec 15, 1993, identified Col Williams as the author of the corrective note. In *It Doesn't Take a Hero*, 318–321, Schwarzkopf states that he showed Warden the four phases on August 17 at the second Instant Thunder briefing. Warden told the author of this volume that he has no recollection of this. Schwarzkopf provided an incorrect date and time for the second briefing, and there are other discrepancies with his account compared with notes taken during the meeting by officers in attendance, summary reports written shortly after the meeting by officers who attended, and oral history interviews of officers who attended. Also, Schwarzkopf's account given telephonically to the author of this volume is at odds with the book, but consistent with the notes, reports, and interviews. The autobiography, co-written with Peter Petre, seems to have compressed discussions the commander had about the phases at other meetings held within 24 hours of the second Air Staff briefing. See also Memo, GTR to RMT, subj: Planning for DS/DS, 250700 Nov 91, with atch, Drft study, "Planning for the Gulf War," [by Rear Adm USN (Ret) Grant Sharp, CENTCOM J–5], 12/3/91 version, 28–30, JCS/HO, Pentagon and drft brfg, "Conceptual Scheme of Maneuver that Has Not Been Analytically Validated," CENTCOM, Kurt Guthe file, GWAPS, AFHRA. According to Sharp's study, 28, CENTCOM developed the "Conceptual Scheme" briefing about August 10, 1990. See also intvw trnscrpt, Lt Col Richard Reynolds and CENTCOM staff, Oct 21–22, 1991, 107–113, CADRE, AU, AFHRA.

104. Schwarzkopf, *It Doesn't Take a Hero*, 313. See also Schwarzkopf's Frontline interview www.pbs.org/wgbh/pages/frontline/gulf/oral/Schwarzkopf, p 3 of 10.

105. Intvw notes, Lt Gen Robert B. Johnson by Ron Cole, May 6, 1992, JCS/HO. See also Powell, *My American Journey,* 473.

106. Powell, *My American Journey*, 472 (quote); DoD, *Conduct of the Persian Gulf War,* 66; Schwarzkopf, *It Doesn't Take a Hero,* 326–327.

107. DS brfg slides, 5; DoD, *Conduct of the Persian Gulf War,* 66.

108. DS brfg slides, 10, 12.

109. Ibid., 15.

110. Ibid.

111. Ibid., 13.

112. Ibid., 28.

113. Ibid., 16. Phase II reflected thinking in the Army's FM 100–5 Operations doctrine, "Active Defense," which identified the Air Force's first contribution to the AirLand Battle: "Drive enemy air forces from the battlefield so that Army forces can exploit their mobility and mass at the critical places and times." See FM 100–5, Jul 1, 1976, 8-2, which provided a clearer statement about the airspace above the battlefield than the version of FM 100–5 published in 1982, the famous AirLand Battle doctrine. Phase II of the draft outline for CENTCOM OPLAN 1002–90 required airmen to conduct air operations and an interdiction campaign designed, among other objectives, to "gain control of the air environment." General Horner, too, talked about air superiority with Schwarzkopf at every opportunity. Warden's Instant Thunder Phase II contained a statement about air superiority over Kuwait, but the colonel did not discuss the plan with the CINCCENT on August 17, mentioning it to him only briefly. Schwarzkopf was especially concerned with air superiority over Kuwait so Army helicopters could fly without being attacked and destroyed by the Iraqi air force. By August 10, Iraq's "robust, overlapping air defenses" in Kuwait especially concerned CENTCOM planners. See drft brfg, "Conceptual Scheme of Maneuver That Has Not Been Analytically Validated," CENTCOM, 6, Kurt Guthe file, GWAPS, AFHRA. Horner recalled after the war, "The 'gain

control of the air in the Kuwaiti theater of operations' came directly from Schwarzkopf." See intvw trnscrpt, Horner by Gehri and Reynolds, Dec 2, 1991, 54.

114. DS brfg slides, 17.

115. Ibid., 18.

116. Ibid., 25.

117. Schwarzkopf, *It Doesn't Take a Hero*, 319 (1st quote), 320 (2d quote).

118. The commander's presentation showed that 6¹/₃ U.S. divisions would have to battle 12 Iraqi divisions in Kuwait and southern Iraq, or in a worst-case scenario, 17 divisions. See DS Brfg slides, 2, 3. Air power would offset the imbalance.

119. Rpt, Combat Analysis Chronology of Significant Events, Operations Desert Shield and Desert Storm, 1, frame 781, reel 27576, GWAPS, AFHRA; Rpt, Combat Analysis Group After Action Report, Col Gary R. Ware, USAF, Chief, CAG, 4, frame 758, reel 27576, GWAPS, AFHRA; Telecon notes, Barry Watts and Gary Ware, Feb 26, 1992, GWAPS, AFHRA; DoD, *Conduct of the Persian Gulf War*, 350–351.

Chapter 4

1. Since 1951 the USMTM had assisted the Saudis in modernizing their military forces.

2. Intvw trnscrpt, Horner by Burton, Mar 1991, 3; Intvw trnscrpt, Horner by Gehri and Reynolds, Dec 2, 1991, 20; Brfg, DoD News Brfg, SECDEF and CJCS, Aug 8, 1990, 1 P.M., OSD/PA, Pentagon 1–5; Rpt, Sharp, "Planning for the Gulf War," 16.

3. Intvw trnscrpt, Horner by Gehri and Reynolds, Dec 2, 1991, 20–21.

4. Intvw trnscrpt, Horner by Burton, Mar 1991, 3.

5. Quoted in Richard Mackenzie, "A Conversation with Chuck Horner," *Air Force Magazine* 74 (June 1991): 57.

6. Intvw trnscrpt, Horner by Gehri and Reynolds, Dec 2, 1991, 20.

7. Ibid., 21–23.

8. Intvw trnscrpt, Horner by Burton, Mar 1991, 24; Intvw trnscrpt, Horner by Gehri and Reynolds, Dec 2, 1991, 23–25.

9. Khaled, *Desert Warrior*, 12. The British spelling "Khaled" differs from the American version "Khalid."

10. Ibid., 137–150, 217–265.

11. Intvw tape, Horner by Putney, Nov 30, 1996; Comment, Horner on draft manuscript, Putney, "Airpower Advantage."

12. Msg, USCINCCENT to Joint Staff et al., 101100Z Aug 90, subj: Operation Desert Shield, Checkmate file, GWAPS, AFHRA.

13. Ibid.

14. Ibid.

15. Ibid.

16. Ibid.

17. Joint Pub 1–02, *Department of Defense Dictionary of Military and Associated Terms,* Dec 1, 1989.

18. Msg, USCINCCENT to Joint Staff et al., 101100Z Aug 90, subj: Operation Desert Shield, Checkmate file, GWAPS, AFHRA; Rpt, "Organizing for War," 1–6, NA 89, GWAPS; After Action Rpt, "Operation Desert Shield/Storm Historical Summary," Desert Shield/Storm file, SAC/HO.

19. Rpt, "Organizing for War," NA 89, GWAPS, AFHRA; Msg, SAC/CAT to USCENTCOM/J–3, 162331Z Aug 90, subj: OPCON of B–52 Aircraft, frame 1789, reel 23628, AFHRA.

20. Intvw trnscrpt, Olsen by Turner, Sep–Nov 1990, 63, 64, 72, 78; Rpt, "Desert Shield/Desert Storm Bomber Story," SAC/DO, Sep 18, 1991, 4, NA 91, GWAPS, AFHRA; Msg, CINCSAC to CJCS, 021500Z Apr 91, subj: Preliminary Report on Lessons Learned in Operation Desert Shield and Desert Storm, Checkmate Lessons file, GWAPS, AFHRA.

21. Rpt, "Desert Shield/Desert Storm Bomber Story," 5, NA 91, GWAPS, AFHRA; Msg, CINCSAC to JCS/CAT, 130430Z Aug 90, subj: CINCSAC SITREP, frame c. 1668, reel 23628, AFHRA.

22. Rpt, "Organizing for War," 4–5, 11, NA 89, GWAPS, AFHRA.

23. For discussion of the deployment,

see Y'Blood, *Eagle and Scorpion*.

24. Intvw trnscrpt, Maj Gen Michael E. Ryan by Lt Col Suzanne Gehri and Lt Col Richard Reynolds, Sep 4, 1992, 29, CADRE, AU, AFHRA.

25. Intvw trnscrpt, Olsen by Turner, Sep–Nov 1990, 3–4, 22; Speech trnscrpt, Lt Gen Charles A. Horner to Dadaelians, Sep 11, 1992, 2, folder 17, Deptula file, GWAPS, AFHRA; Intvw tape, Col George L. Getchell by Richard G. Davis, Mar 1992, AFHSO; Memo, Col James C. Crigger, Jr., [c. Mar 1, 1993], subj: Air Campaign Planning for Desert Storm…, Crigger's HQ NORAD/IGD file, Peterson AFB; Intvw tape, Maj Gen Thomas R. Olsen by Richard G. Davis, Perry D. Jamieson, and Barry Barlow, Mar 5, 1992, AFHSO; Draft intvw trnscrpt, Lt Gen Charles A. Horner by [CMSgt John R. Burton], Mar 10, 1991, 5, CENTAF Gulf War file, TAC/HO.

26. Speech trnscrpt, Reuter, Lt Gen Charles A. Horner to Business Executives for National Security Education Fund, May 8, 1991, 3, AFHSO.

27. Intvw trnscrpt, Olsen by Turner, Sep–Nov 1990, 5–7; Intvw tape, Olsen by Davis, Jamieson, and Barlow, Mar 5, 1992; Ltr, USCENTAF/DCP to CC/COMALF et al., Aug 10, 1990, subj: ATO Planning Guidance for C+5, 11 August 90 and C+6, 12 August 90, frame 1299, reel 23977, AFHRA; Ltr, USCENTAF/DCP to CC/COMALF et al., Aug 12, 1990, subj: ATO Planning Guidance for C+7 (corrected), 14 August 90, frame 1283, reel 23977, AFHRA.

28. Intvw trnscrpt, Baptiste by Putney and Reynolds, Sep 24, 1992, 30.

29. Intvw trnscrpt, Olsen by Turner, Sep–Nov 1990, 31; Intvw tape, Baptiste by Putney and Reynolds, Sep 24, 1992; Tactical Analysis Bulletin, USAF Tactical Fighter Weapons Center, Jul 1991, vol 91-2, 1–3, NA 83, GWAPS, AFHRA.

30. Intvw trnscrpt, Caruana by Mann, Aug 19, 1991, 12.

31. Drft intvw trnscrpt, Horner by Putney and Bradley, Apr 26, 1994, 28.

32. Draft intvw trnscrpt, Horner by Davis, Jamieson, and Barlow, Mar 4, 1992, 9; Intvw tape, Olsen by Davis, Jamieson, and Barlow, Mar 5, 1992.

33. Intvw tape, Horner by Davis, Jamieson, and Barlow, Mar 4, 1992; Intvw tape, Baptiste by Putney and Reynolds, Sep 24, 1992; Intvw tape, Olsen by Davis, Jamieson, and Barlow, Mar 5, 1992; Intvw trnscrpt, Horner by Gehri and Reynolds, Dec 2, 1991, 105.

34. Intvw trnscrpt, Olsen by Turner, Sep–Nov 1990, 12; P. J. Quaintmere, "Airspace Control for Operation Desert Shield/Storm," in *The Desert Shield/Desert Storm Comm Story: Air Force Tactical Communications in War* (Riyadh, Saudi Arabia: HQ USCENTCOM, 1991), ed. Col [Buford R.] Randy Witt, 58–59.

35. Intvw tape, Lt Col Jeffrey S. Feinstein by Richard G. Davis, Perry D. Jamieson, and Barry Barlow, Mar 3, 1992, AFHSO; Msg, USCENTAF/DO to USCENTAF Rear, 051800Z Nov 90, subj: Additional Templar Work Stations for Desert Shield, frame 871, reel 23969, AFHRA.

36. Intvw trnscrpt, Olsen by Turner, Sep–Nov 1990, 16; Notes, Lt Col Bernard E. Harvey, HQ USAF/XOXWS, Aug 27, 1990, GWAPS, AFHRA; Quaintmere, "Airspace Control for Operation Desert Shield/Storm," 59, and Capt Lee Patton, "Getting the Air Tasking Order (ATO) to the Navy," 30, in *Desert Shield/Desert Storm Comm Story*, ed. Col Witt; Brfg slides, "Air Tasking Order (ATO) Preparation and Composite Force Packaging," 7, HQ 9AF/DOOW, Langley AFB.

37. Intvw tape, Feinstein by Davis, Jamieson, and Barlow, Mar 3, 1992; Patton, "Getting the Air Tasking Order (ATO) to the Navy," 30.

38. Patton, "Getting the Air Tasking Order (ATO) to the Navy," 30; After Action Rpt, "Operation Desert Shield/Storm Historical Summary," Desert Shield/Storm file, SAC/HO; Intvw tape, Feinstein by Davis, Jamieson, and Barlow, Mar 3, 1992; Lt Mike Pervere, "Mini-ATO Distribution System (MADS)," in *Desert Shield/Desert Storm Comm Story*, ed. Col Witt, 28.

39. Intvw trnscrpt, Lt Col Sam Baptiste by Diane Putney and Lt Col Richard Reynolds, Sep 24, 1992, 20–22, 32, 36–37; Tele-

con notes, Maj Clinton D. Null, Apr 2, 1993, by Diane T. Putney, AFHSO; Fax rpt, Maj John Heidrick, 9AIS/INT, to L. Greenberg, "9TIS/INT Planning Procedures...," May 4, 1992, 4–6, Greenberg file, GWAPS, AFHRA; Rpt, Capt John Glock, "Target Intelligence Support during Desert Shield and Storm," 6–8, GWAPS, AFHRA. *GWAPS* erroneously reports that the D-day ATO was the same as the ATO Bravo. *GWAPS,* vol 1, part 1, *Planning,* 136–139. Also, *GWAPS* erroneously states that CENTAF began the Punishment ATO on August 8 (p 140).

40. Fax rpt, Maj John Heidrick, 9AIS/INT to L. Greenberg, GWAPS, "9 TIS/INT Planning Procedures...," May 4, 1992, 5, Greenberg file, GWAPS, AFHRA.

41. Brfg slides, "D-day Game Plan," frame 964, reel 23969, AFHRA; Intvw trnscrpt, Olsen by Turner, Sep–Nov 1990, 37; Telecon notes, Maj Clinton D. Null by Diane T. Putney, Apr 2, 1993, AFHSO.

42. Brfg, "D-day Game Plan," frame 964, reel 23969, AFHRA; *GWAPS,* vol 1, part 1, *Planning,* 136 n. 67. Scales reported that in August "rectangular kill boxes" were drawn to correspond to the Saudi air defense and control grid, but Captain Glock disassociated the D-day boxes from the Saudi structure and illustrated them in his rpt, "Targeting Intelligence Support during Desert Shield and Storm," 6–8, GWAPS, AFHRA. See Scales, *Certain Victory*, 85. The Saudi grid system was used later in Desert Shield.

43. Intvw trnscrpt, Olsen by Turner, Sep–Nov 1990, 24; Telecon notes, Null by Putney, Apr 2, 1993; Notes, Aug 10, 1990, "Lt Gen Horner's Visit," frame 1045, reel 23969, AFHRA.

44. Drft intvw trnscrpt, Horner by Putney and Bradley, 26 Apr 1994, 29.

45. During the Iran-Iraq war, the GCC states contributed the Peninsula Shield forces, based in Saudi Arabia, to respond to threats in the Gulf region. As the Joint Forces Command commander in Desert Shield, Khalid transferred the troops to their various national contingents. See Khaled, *Desert Warrior,* 248.

46. Scales, *Certain Victory*, 82–86; Khaled, *Desert Warrior,* 9, 11. For a discussion of the different views on where and how to defend on the ground against an Iraqi invasion, see Scales, 94, and Khaled, 15–16.

47. From November 6, 1990, to January 15, 1991, the XVIII Airborne Corps swapped M1 tanks with 105-mm guns for the newer M1A1 models with 120-mm guns and other improvements sent from Europe to ensure superiority over Iraq's advanced T–72 tanks. See Scales, *Certain Victory,* 79, 88.

48. Scales, *Certain Victory,* 87–88, 90–93; 392; Drft intvw trnscrpt, Horner by Putney and Bradley, Apr 26, 1994, 30; Intvw trnscrpt, Horner by Burton, Mar 1991, 6.

49. Telecon notes, Gary Ware, Col. USAF (Ret), with Barry Watts, GWAPS, Feb 26, 1992, frame 1193, reel 27584, AFHRA; Telecon notes, Gary R. Ware, Col, USAF (Ret), with Diane T. Putney, Mar 28, 1994, AFHSO; Rpt, Combat Analysis Group After Action Report, frame 758, reel 27576, 1–2, 4, AFHRA.

50. Fax rpt, Capt John Heidrick to L. Greenberg, GWAPS, "9TIS/INT Planning Procedures...," May 4, 1992, 4–5, Greenberg file, GWAPS, AFHRA; Memo for record, Capt Heidrick, 9TIS/INT to Lt Col Combs, AF/DOJ, May 21, 1991, subj: Composition of Joint Target Coordination Board (JTCB) during Operations Desert Shield/Storm, Kurt Guthe file, GWAPS, AFHRA.

51. Edited intvw trnscrpt, Baptiste by Putney and Reynolds, Sep 24, 1992, 21, AFHRA ("frag" corrected to "Frog"); Discussion, Capt John R. Glock and Diane T. Putney, Mar 31, 1995; Msg, USCINCCENT to Joint Staff et al., 101100Z Aug 90, subj: Operation Desert Shield, Checkmate, GWAPS, AFHRA. See target materials throughout reel 10215, AFHRA.

52. Telecon notes, Maj Clinton D. Null by Diane T. Putney, Apr 2, 1993, AFHSO.

53. Memo for record, Aug 25, 1990, subj: Captain Kniffen's Meeting with Target Analysts, frame 275, reel 10203, AFHRA.

54. Brfg, D-day (24 hours) Bravo, Sep 14, 1990, frame 165, reel 23969, AFHRA.

55. Fax rpt, Maj John Heidrick to L. Greenberg, GWAPS, "9TIS/INT Planning Procedures...," May 4, 1992, 2, 4–5, Green-

berg file, GWAPS, AFHRA; Telecon notes, Null by Putney, Apr 2, 1993; Brfg, "Follow-On D-day 'ATO Bravo,'" 5–6, Lt Col Sam Baptiste, in Desert Shield brfg, Dec 11, 1990, Checkmate, GWAPS, AFHRA.

56. Telecon notes, Maj Clinton D. Null, CENTAF, by Diane T. Putney, Apr 2, 1993, AFHSO; Fax rpt, Maj John Heidrick, 9TIS/INT to L. Greenberg, GWAPS, "9 TIS/INT Planning Procedures…," May 4, 1992, 6, Greenberg file, GWAPS, AFHRA.

57. Intvw tape, Cdr Donald W. McSwain by Richard G. Davis, Apr 7, 1992, AFHSO.

58. Electronic combat, a broad concept, encompasses electronic warfare, to prevent enemy use of the electromagnetic spectrum while ensuring friendly use of the same; electronic countermeasures, to protect friendly C^3 while degrading or destroying enemy C^3; and the electronic suppression of enemy air defenses. See AFM 1–1, Jan 5, 1984, 3-6/7.

59. Intvw tape, Maj Gen Larry L. Henry, USAF (Ret), by Diane T. Putney, Jul 3, 1997, AFHSO; Bio sheet, Brig Gen Larry L. Henry, SAF/PA, May 1991.

60. SEAD comprised neutralizing, degrading, or destroying enemy air defense systems to gain freedom of action for pursuit of air missions. See AFM 1–1, Jan 5, 1984, 3-7.

61. Intvw tape, Horner by Putney, Nov 30, 1997; E-Mail msg, Gen Charles A. Horner, USAF (Ret), to D Putney, subj: Gulf War Manuscript, Oct 28, 1997; Rpt, Capt Melvin F. Porter, "Air Tactics against NVN Air/Ground Defenses," Feb 27, 1967, Hq PACAF, Contemporary Historical Evaluation of Combat Operations (CHECO) series, 11–14, AFHRA; Wayne Thompson, *To Hanoi and Back: The United States Air Force and North Vietnam, 1966–1973* (Washington: Air Force History and Museums Program, 2000), 36.

62. The altitudes pilots flew in Desert Storm varied by aircraft, mission, location, and date. AAA was most lethal up to 5,000 feet, but it could reach and be effective up to 15,000 feet. Some Gulf War interviewees identified 10,000 feet as the altitude where risk was acceptable, which they referred to as "medium altitude." "Medium-altitude bombing" was defined as "horizontal bombing with the height of release between 9,000 and 14,000 feet." See Air Force Pamphlet 14–210, "U.S. Intelligence Targeting Guide," Feb 1, 1998, 121. See also *GWAPS,* vol 2, part 2, *Effects and Effectiveness*, 99; William F. Andrews, *Airpower against an Army: Challenge and Response in CENTAF's Duel with the Republican Guard* (Maxwell AFB, Ala.: AU Press, 1998), 35; Perry D. Jamieson, *Lucrative Targets: The U.S. Air Force in the Kuwaiti Theater of Operations* (Washington: Air Force History and Museums Program, 2001), 94.

63. Intvw tape, Henry by Putney, Jul 3, 1997; Intvw tape, Horner by Putney, Nov 30, 1997; E-Mail msg, Gen Charles A. Horner, USAF (Ret), to D Putney, subj: Gulf War Manuscript, Oct 28, 1997. For comments about how General Creech tried to change the "go-low"mentality at TAC from 1978 to 1984, which involved acquiring new weapon systems, see USAF oral history intvw trnscrpt, General Wilbur L. Creech, K239.0512–2050, 225–229, AFHRA. For a discussion of the pros and cons of low altitude, see C. R. Anderegg, *Sierra Hotel: Flying Air Force Fighters in the Decade after Vietnam* (Washington: Air Force History & Museums Program, 2001), 60–62, 99, 126–134.

64. Intvw tape, Henry by Putney, Jul 3, 1997; Lt Col James R. Brungress, USAF, *Setting the Context: Suppression of Enemy Air Defenses and Joint War Fighting in an Uncertain World* (Maxwell AFB, Ala.: AU Press, 1994), 16–25.

65. Intvw tape, Henry by Putney, Jul 3, 1997.

66. Ibid.; Brfg, "Electronic Combat: An Airman's Perspective," Maj Gen Larry L. Henry, USAF (Ret), Lockheed-Martin, slides 2054/15–16.

67. Intvw tape, Lt Gen Buster C. Glosson, USAF (Ret), Maj Gen Larry L. Henry, USAF (Ret), and Col Rick Lewis, USAF, by Diane T. Putney, May 20, 1997, AFHSO.

68. Intvw tape, Henry by Putney, Jul 3, 1997; Brfg, "Electronic Combat: An Airman's Perspective," Maj Gen Larry L. Henry, USAF (Ret), Lockheed-Martin, slides 2054/17–26.

69. Msg, COMUSCENTAF FWD to USCINCCENT FWD et al., 211800L Aug 90, subj: Joint Electronic Warfare Campaign (EWC)."

70. Intvw tape, Henry by Putney, Jul 3, 1997; Msg, COMUSCENTAF FWD to USCINCCENT FWD, 211800L Aug 90, subj: Joint Electronic Warfare Campaign.

71. Intvw tape, Henry by Putney, Jul 3, 1997; Msg, COMUSCENTAF FWD to USCINCCENT FWD, 211800L Aug 90, subj: Joint Electronic Warfare Campaign; Intvw trnscrpt, Henry by Gehri, Mann, and Reynolds, [Jun 2, 1992], 154.

72. Intvw tape, Henry by Putney, Jul 3, 1997; Brfg, "Electronic Combat: An Airman's Perspective," Maj Gen Larry L. Henry, USAF (Ret), Lockheed-Martin, slide 2054/12.

73. Intvw tape, Henry by Putney, Jul 3, 1997; Brfg, "Electronic Combat: An Airman's Perspective," Maj Gen Larry L. Henry, USAF (Ret), Lockheed-Martin, slides 2054/15–17.

74. Intvw tape, Henry by Putney, Jul 3, 1997.

75. Ibid.

76. Intvw tape, Henry by Putney, Jul 3, 1997; Brfg, "Electronic Combat: An Airman's Perspective," Maj Gen Larry L. Henry, USAF (Ret), slide 2054/6.

77. Intvw tape, Henry by Putney, Jul 3, 1997; Brfg, "Electronic Combat: An Airman's Perspective," Maj Gen Larry L. Henry, USAF (Ret), slide 2054/6.

78. *GWAPS,* vol 1, part 2, *Command and Control*, 121–122; Msg, DIA/JS1-6A to DIA CURINTEL list, 122340Z Aug 90, subj: Iraq-Kuwait Situation Update, microfilm frame 327, reel 23629, AFHRA; Memo, USAF/DCS Operations to Director, Joint Staff, Apr 22, 1991, subj: Joint Assessment Report, Checkmate JCS Lessons file, GWAPS, AFHRA.

79. Tactical Analysis Bulletin, USAF Fighter Weapons Center, Jul 1991, vol 91-2, 1–5, NA 83, GWAPS, AFHRA; *GWAPS,* vol 5, part 1, *A Statistical Compendium,* 151.

80. Rules of engagement placed units on weapons "tight" status, meaning they could engage only targets "positively identified as hostile," or on weapons "hold," meaning they could not engage any aircraft unless self-defense criteria were met. See Msg, USCINCCENT to JCS et al., 191200Z Jan 91, subj: COMUSCENTAF Wartime Rules of Engagement: Desert Shield, para 4c.

81. Intvw trnscrpt, Crigger by Gehri and Reynolds, Dec 2–4, 1991, 105–106. *GWAPS* stated that slow communications forced the restrictions on the missile firings, but Horner stated that he relied on aircraft to counter aircraft, not missiles. See drft intvw trnscrpt, Horner by Putney and Bradley, Apr 26, 1994, 41; *GWAPS,* vol 1, part 2, *Command and Control*, 122.

82. Rpt, "Notes from the AD Fact-Finding Trip [Oct 9–12, 1990]," AFHSO; Intvw trnscrpt, Crigger by Gehri and Reynolds, Dec 2–4, 1991, 105; Drft intvw trnscrpt, Horner by Putney and Bradley, Apr 26, 1994, 42; Khaled, *Desert Warrior,* 233–234.

83. Intvw trnscrpt, Olsen by Turner, Sep–Nov 1990, 15, 18, 20.

84. DoD, *Conduct of the Persian Gulf War,* 13–14, 82; *GWAPS,* vol 4, part 1, *Weapons, Tactics, and Training,* 30, 278, 281.

85. DoD, *Conduct of the Persian Gulf War,* 168, 339, 574; *GWAPS,* vol 4, part 1, *Weapons, Tactics, and Training*, 280–281; *GWAPS,* vol 1, part 2, *Command and Control*, 246, 248–249; Alan D. Campden, ed. *The First Information War: The Story of Communications, Computers, and Intelligence Systems in the Persian Gulf War* (Fairfax, Va.: AFCEA International Press, 1992), 129; Sheldon B. Herskovitz, "High Marks for Military Radar: The Patriot Missile System," *Journal of Electronic Defense* (May 1991): 55. For additional information about the Scud net, see Hist, George W. Bradley III, Richard S. Eckert, and Rick W. Sturdevant, "AFSPACECOM Support to Operations Desert Shield/Desert Storm," Apr 1993, 19–22, AFSPACECOM/HO, Peterson AFB, Colo.; Annex B of Atch 1 to Ltr, ND to SAG/OSG, Jul 13, 1991, subj: Operation Desert Storm/Shield After Action Information…, NA 328, GWAPS, AFHRA.

86. Intvw trnscrpt, Maj Harry L. Heintzelman by TSgt Scott A. Saluda, Mar 14, 1991, 1–2, AFHSO; Intvw trnscrpt, Olsen by

Turner, Sep–Nov 1990, 5.

87. Msg, CJCS to USCINCCENT/CAT, 091330Z Aug 90, subj: ROE Authorization SO/SAR, frame 112, reel 10203, AFHRA.

88. Msg, USCENTAF/DO to USCENTAF FWD/CC et al., 160100Z Aug 90, subj: Transition Rules of Engagement (ROE) Operation Desert Shield, frame 1287, reel 23629, AFHRA.

89. Ibid.

90. Intvw trnscrpt, Heintzelman by Saluda, Mar 14, 1991, 2–3; Agreement, Peacetime Rules of Engagement, Sep 2, 1990, frame 309, reel 10203, AFHRA.

91. Proceedings trnscrpt, "Operations Law Session," Maj Harry L. Heintzelman IV, 3–5, NA 68, GWAPS, AFHRA.

92. Maj Tony Culp, "Saudi Arabian Air Traffic Control System," in *Desert Shield/Desert Storm Comm Story*, ed. Col Witt, 45; Khaled, *Desert Warrior,* 239.

93. Capt Bob Peacock, "Combat Airspace Management," in *Desert Shield/Desert Storm Comm Story*, ed. Col Witt, 47–48; *GWAPS,* vol 5, part 1, *Statistical Compendium*, 133–135.

94. Intvw trnscrpt, Olsen by Turner, Sep–Nov 1990, 9.

95. Ibid., 9, 24, 26; Brfg slides, [Apr 1990], "OPLAN 1002 Air Operations," AFHSO.

96. No author, "Air Traffic Control and Airspace Management," 43, and Capt Kevin Beebe, "Air Traffic Control Manning," 56 in *Desert Shield/Desert Storm Comm Story*, ed. Col Witt.

97. Pt paper, Aug 6, 1990, LTC Guy Chabot, XOXOC-COB, CHSH 29-145, GWAPS, AFHRA; Norman Friedman, *Desert Victory: The War for Kuwait* (Annapolis, Md.: Naval Institute Press, 1991), 69–70; James F. Dunnigan and Austin Bay, *From Shield to Storm: High Tech Weapons, Military Strategy, and Coalition Warfare in the Persian Gulf* (New York: William Morrow, 1992), 34.

98. Msg, CJCS to USCINCCENT et al., 111700Z Aug 90, subj: Operation Desert Shield, JCS file, Checkmate file, GWAPS, AFHRA; James Blackwell, *Thunder in the Desert: The Strategy and Tactics of the Persian Gulf War* (New York: Bantam Books, 1991), 95.

99. DoD, *Conduct of the Persian Gulf War*, 552–553; Intvw trnscrpt, Olsen by Turner, Sep–Nov 1990, 2.

100. Drft intvw trnscrpt, Horner by Putney and Bradley, Apr 26, 1994, 33; Intvw response no. 13, Adm Henry H. Mauz, Jr., USN (Ret), to Edward Marolda, Jun 12, 1996, Center for Naval History, Washington, DC; Horner quote as recalled by Mauz in Edward J. Marolda and Robert John Schneller, *Shield and Sword: The United States Navy and the Persian Gulf War* (Washington: Naval Historical Center, 1998), 114.

101. Schwarzkopf, *It Doesn't Take a Hero*, 321–322; Intvw notes, Maj John Harris, USMC, by Edward J. Mirolda, Aug 28, 1990, frame 549, reel 23628, AFHRA; Intvw trnscrpt, Col Ervin S. (Sandy) Sharpe by TSgt Gary S. Trice, Oct 31, 1990 (quotes), AFHSO.

102. Schwarzkopf, *It Doesn't Take a Hero*, 322; Dunnigan and Bay, *From Shield to Storm*, 35.

103. Intvw trnscrpt, Olsen by Turner, Sep–Nov 1990, 35, 37–38, 50.

104. In November Rear Adm Conrad C. Lautenbacher replaced Wright.

105. Intvw trnscrpt, Olsen by Turner, Sep–Nov 1990, 23–24, 29, 31, 46; After action rpt, Lt W. J. Campbell, USN, Mar 8 1991, and Trip rpt, Maj Rich King to XOXW-G et al., May 28, 1991, folder 36c, Deptula file, GWAPS, AFHRA.

106. Col Charles J. Quilter II, USMCR, *U.S. Marines in the Persian Gulf, 1990–1991: With the I Marine Expeditionary Force in Desert Shield and Desert Storm* (Washington: Marine Corps History and Museum Division, 1993), 1, 8–9.

107. Glen W. Goodman, Jr., and John G. Roos, "An Exclusive AFJI Interview with Lt Gen Walter E. Boomer, USMC," *Armed Forces Journal International* (Aug 1992): 41 (quotes); Memo for record, Wayne Thompson, GWAPS historian, "Lt Gen Walter Boomer's Views," Feb 19, 1992, NA 159, GWAPS, AFHRA; Intvw notes, Lt Gen Walter E. Boomer, USMC, by Eliot A. Cohen et al., Feb 18, 1992, NA 142,

GWAPS, AFHRA; Draft intvw trnscrpt, Horner by Davis, Jamieson, and Barlow, Mar 4, 1992, 65–66.

108. Intvw trnscrpt, Olsen by Turner, Sep–Nov 1991, 14, 25; USCENTAF Reg 55–45, "United States Central Command Air Forces Air Employment Planning Process," Jun 27, 1990, 3–12; Drft intvw trnscrpt, Horner by Putney and Bradley, April 26, 1994, 39.

109. Intvw trnscrpt, Horner by Davis, Jamieson, and Barlow, Mar 4, 1992, 79.

110. Ibid., 79–80.

111. Msg, USCINCCENT to Joint Staff, 101100 Aug 90, subj: Operation Desert Storm, Checkmate file, GWAPS, AFHRA; DoD, *Conduct of the Persian Gulf War*, 523–525; Plan, "Operation Desert Shield Combat Search and Rescue Plan," Nov 1, 1990, 1, Lt Col Hampton file, Air Force Rescue Coordination Center (AFRCC), Scott AFB, Ill.

112. DoD, *Conduct of the Persian Gulf War*, 531, 534; Plan, "Operation Desert Shield Combat Search and Rescue Plan," Nov 1, 1990, 11, Lt Col Hampton file, AFRCC; Telecon notes, Lt Col Joseph Hampton and Diane T. Putney, Jun 22, 1993, AFHSO; Telecon notes, Maj Thomas J. Stilwell and Diane T. Putney, Jun 22–23, 1993, AFHSO.

113. Telecon notes, Maj Thomas J. Stilwell and Diane T. Putney, Jun 22–23, 1993, AFHSO; Telecon notes, Lt Col Joseph Hampton and Diane T. Putney, Jun 23, 1993, AFHSO; Intvw tape, Horner by Davis, Jamieson, and Barlow, Mar 4, 1992; Rpt, Desert Storm Lessons Learned, CENTAF/JRCC JULLS inputs, JULLS 14951-37900 (4), Lt Col Hampton file, AFRCC.

114. Msg, USCENTAF FWD/DO to COMUSNAVCENT, 280001Z Aug 90, subj: Joint Rescue Coordination Center (JRCC) Augmentation, frame 996, reel 23628, AFHRA; Telecon notes, Maj Thomas J. Stilwell and Diane T. Putney, June 22–23, 1993, AFHSO.

115. Benjamin F. Schemmer, "No USAF Combat Rescue Aircraft in Gulf; It Took 72 Hours to Launch One Rescue," *Armed Forces Journal International* (July 1991): 37–38; Telecon notes, Maj Thomas J. Stilwell and Diane T. Putney, Jun 22–23, 1993, AFHSO; Rpt, Desert Storm Lessons Learned, CENTAF/JRCC JULLS inputs, JULLS 14955-37100 (7), Lt Col Hampton file, AFRCC.

116. Plan, "Operation Desert Shield Combat Search and Rescue Plan," Lt Col Hampton file, AFRCC; Telecon notes, Hampton by Putney, June 22, 1993.

117. Intvw trnscrpt, Col David A. Sawyer by TSgt Gary S. Trice, Oct 31, 1990, 25–26, Gulf War file, TAC/HO; Intvw tape, Baptiste by Putney and Reynolds, Sep 24, 1992.

118. Intvw trnscrpt, Olsen by Turner, Sep–Nov 1990, 22, 26, 33; Intvw tape, Baptiste by Jamieson, Mar 3, 1992.

119. Intvw trnscrpt, Olsen by Turner, Sep–Nov 1992, 49; Memo for record, Lt Col Robert S. Coombs, CENTAF, Mar 20, 1991, subj: Desert Shield Training Exercises, NA 342, GWAPS; Tactical Analysis Bulletin, USAF Tactical Fighter Weapons Center, Jul 1991, vol 91-2, 1–3, NA 83, GWAPS, AFHRA. Since September 18, AFSOC's AC–130s, under OPCON of SOCCENT, had been using live ordnance in exercises; see *GWAPS,* vol 5, part 1, *Statistical Compendium* 173.

120. Y'Blood, *Eagle and Scorpion*, 111, 132; Rpt, "Desert Shield/Desert Storm Bomber Story," 22.

Chapter 5

1. Harvey notes, Aug 19, 1990; Intvw tape, Harvey by Putney and Davis, Dec 7, 1992; Trnscrpt of dictation notes on tape, Lt Col David A. Deptula, n.d., subj: Instant Thunder Presentation to CENTAF Aug 20, 1990, Kurt Guthe file, GWAPS, AFHRA; Discussion notes, Col E. Michael Kiraly and Diane T. Putney, Sep 3, 1992, AFHSO.

2. Harvey notes, Aug 19, 1990/2230L, 1; Trnscrpt of Deptula dictation notes on

tape, "Instant Thunder Presentation…," 1–2.

3. Intvw trnscrpt, Brig Gen Patrick P. Caruana by Lt Col Edward Mann, Aug 19, 1991, 14–15, CADRE, AU; Intvw trnscrpt, Baptiste by Putney and Reynolds, Sep 24, 1992, 24, 27; Intvw trnscrpt, Adams by Reynolds and Gehri, Feb 3, 1992, 14 (quote), CADRE, AU; Telecon notes, Col John Leonardo, USAF (Ret), with Diane T. Putney, Jan 4, 1994, AFHSO.

4. Harvey notes, Aug 19, 1990/2230L, 1. The account of the August 19 Instant Thunder briefing, reconstructed primarily from Lt Col Harvey's notes, highlights key issues and is organized and written according to attendees and their comments, rather than as a chronological statement-by-statement reconstruction of the briefing. The author has chosen this form of presentation to emphasize the substance and ideas of the meeting, not the chronological, somewhat disjointed flow of the session. The quotation marks represent the words as written by those in attendance taking notes and do not necessarily represent the exact words as spoken. The leaner sets of notes by Deptula and Stanfill are cited as cross-references.

5. The author of this volume could not find the CIA and DIA assessments done before or after August 19, 1990, that focused on Instant Thunder's reserve aircraft stopping an Iraqi invasion. Wayne Thompson, the Air Force historian assigned to Checkmate and who arrived August 15, could not recall CIA and DIA assessments addressing the issue before August 19, and he preserved none in the Checkmate files. Checkmate did analyze the effects of A–10s against invading Iraqi troops. See Instant Thunder brfg slides, [Briefed to AF/XO, 13 Aug/1330], 62–64, "Col Warden's Notes," GWAPS, AFHRA. Colonel Kiraly stated that he participated in discussions in Checkmate earlier than August 19, and the consensus was that, given the possible routes of attack into Saudi Arabia, air power, notably from B–52s and A–10s, could "handle" an invasion. The Iraqis, it was believed, might have reached Khafji, but would have gotten no farther. Discussion notes Col Emery M. Kiraly and Diane T. Putney, Mar 18, 1993, AFHSO.

6. Harvey notes, Aug 19, 1990/2230L, 2, 4; Notes, Lt Col Ronnie Stanfill, Aug 19, 1990/2350, 1, 3, CHP folder 27, GWAPS, AFHRA; Trnscrpt of Deptula dictation notes on tape, "Instant Thunder Presentation…," 2–3.

7. Harvey notes, Aug 19, 1990/2230L, 3–4, 6.

8. While Powell and Schwarzkopf approved of Instant Thunder, they did not see it as a stand-alone war plan, but as a retaliation plan. They both anticipated that air power would have to destroy deployed enemy ground forces during offensive operations to liberate Kuwait.

9. Harvey notes, Aug 19, 1990/2230L, 9; Stanfill notes Aug 19, 1990/2250, 5.

10. Harvey notes, Aug 19, 1990/2230L, 8–10; Trnscrpt of Deptula dictation notes on tape, "Instant Thunder Presentation…," 2.

11. Harvey notes, Aug 19, 1990/2230L, 5; Trnscrpt of Deptula dictation notes on tape, "Instant Thunder Presentation…," 2; Stanfill notes, Aug 19, 1990/2250, 3.

12. Harvey notes, Aug 19, 1990/2230L, 5–6.

13. Ibid., 7–8, 10–11; Trnscrpt of Deptula dictation notes on tape, "Instant Thunder Presentation…," 2 (quotes), 2–3; Stanfill notes, Aug 19, 1990/2250, 2, 4–5.

14. Trnscrpt of Deptula dictation notes on tape, "Instant Thunder Presentation…," 3; Intvw tape, Harvey by Putney and Davis, Dec 7, 1992.

15. Intvw trnscrpt, Wilson by Gehri, Mann, and Reynolds, Dec 11, 1991, 15–16.

16. Ibid. 16, 27; Intvw trnscrpt, Baptiste by Putney and Reynolds, Sep 24, 1992, 27; Drft intvw trnscrpt, Deptula by Davis, Nov 20, 1991, 6.

17. Trnscrpt of Deptula dictation notes on tape, "Instant Thunder Presentation…," 3 (quote), 4.

18. Intvw trnscrpt, Wilson by Gehri, Mann, and Reynolds, Dec 11, 1991, 25.

19. Intvw trnscrpt, Warden by Gehri, Oct 22, 1991, 106.

20. Harvey notes, Aug 20, 1990/1055, 1–2.

21. Ibid., 2–3.

22. Trnscrpt of Deptula dictation notes on tape, "Instant Thunder Presentation…," 4.

23. Ibid.; Harvey notes, Aug 20, 19990/1320.

24. Intvw trnscrpt, Horner by Reynolds and Gehri, Dec 2, 1991, 30–31; Msg, TACOPS/XP to COMUSCENTAF, 100145Z Aug 90, subj: Air Campaign Briefing, Deptula file, GWAPS, AFHRA (Horner's comment in margin); Intvw tape, Baptiste by Putney and Reynolds, Sep 24, 1992; Intvw tape, Lt Gen Buster C. Glosson by Diane T. Putney, Aug 30, 1993, AFHSO; Schwarzkopf, *It Doesn't Take a Hero*, 320; Intvw trnscrpt, Wilson by Gehri, Mann, and Reynolds, Dec 11, 1991, 15–18.

25. Harvey notes, Aug 20, 1990/1355, 1; Trnscrpt of Deptula dictation notes on tape, "Instant Thunder Presentation...," 8; Stanfill notes, Aug 20, 1990/1400, 1.

26. Intvw trnscrpt, Warden by Gehri, Oct 22, 1991, 102–103, 107–108.

27. Intvw tape, Warden by Putney et al., Feb 6, 1992.

28. Horner's anger expressed directly to Schwarzkopf on August 7 and in his lecture about Air Staff interference to Lt Col Steven Wilson, his discarding the TAC plan, his postwar interviews, and his autobiography continually repeat the complaint that air war planning should be done by the airmen in theater who had to execute the plan. For discussion of the low-level mission in July 1965, see Thompson, *To Hanoi and Back*, 36.

29. Drft intvw trnscrpt, Horner by Putney and Bradley, Apr 26, 1994, 77, 80–81; E-Mail msg, Gen Horner to Diane Putney, Sep 17, 1997, subj: Gulf War Manuscript; Comment, Horner on draft manuscript, Putney, "Airpower Advantage."

30. Trnscrpt of Deptula dictation notes on tape, "Instant Thunder Presentation...," 5 (1st quote); Memo, Col Ben Harvey to Col Rich Reynolds, Jun 2, 1994, subj: Comments on March 1994 Draft, "Heart of the Storm," 17–18, AU, AFHRA. Acknowledging it was a minor point, Harvey wanted to "set the record straight" and stressed that boxes of candy were on the table while the bag of sundry items remained on the floor. Adams had mentioned in passing a shortage of certain items in theater, and it was Warden's idea to buy the items and take them to Horner. See intvw trnscrpt, Adams by Gehri and Reynolds, Feb 3, 1992, 15; Intvw trnscrpt, Warden by Gehri, Oct 22, 1991, 108; Discussion, Warden and Putney, Sep 28, 2001.

31. Intvw trnscrpt, Warden by Gehri, Oct 22, 1991, 108.

32. Trnscrpt of Deptula dictation notes on tape, "Instant Thunder Presentation...," 5. For accounts of the now legendary briefing on August 20th, from Horner's perspective, see Clancy with Horner, *Every Man a Tiger,* 259–265, and from a Warden admirer's view, see Reynolds, *Heart of the Storm,* 120–130, the latter of which has been on the reading list recommended by the Air Force Chief of Staff. Both books indicate that serious friction and strong emotions saturated the session. Horner's version referred to "sharp words," "choking" on some assumptions, the "debate" going "downhill," Horner treated like a "boob," "personal arrogance," "he seemed certain I was too stupid to grasp his central concept," and "in love with his own thinking." Reynolds's account included the phrases "Horner's face twisted into a sneer," "grimacing," "rudeness or vulgarity," "impatient and visibly frustrated," "waving his hand in disgust," "anger ebbed from his eyes," "made Warden angry," and "stared daggers at the colonel."

33. Trnscrpt of Deptula dictation notes on tape, "Instant Thunder Presentation...," 5. The account of the Warden/Horner briefing in this chapter is structured chronologically and walks the reader entirely through the discussion. The quotation marks represent the words as written by those in attendance taking notes, the words of Deptula as recorded on tape after the briefing, and the interview recollections of persons in attendance. They do not necessarily represent the exact words used because no one tape-recorded the meeting.

34. Memo, Col Ben Harvey to Col Rich Reynolds, Jun 2, 1994, subj: Comments on March 1994 Draft, "Heart of the Storm," 18, AU, AFHRA.

35. Intvw trnscrpt, Henry by Reynolds, Mann, and Gehri, [Jun 2, 1992], 32, 37, 51.

36. For Horner's recollection of the ring model, see E-Mail msg, Gen Horner to Diane Putney, Sep 17, 1997, subj: Gulf War Manuscript, and drft intvw trnscrpt, Horner by Davis, Jamieson, and Barlow, Mar 4, 1992, 20.

37. Trnscrpt of Deptula's dictation notes on tape, "Instant Thunder Presentation…," 5; Harvey notes, Aug 20, 1990/1355, 1.

38. Trnscrpt of Deptula dictation notes on tape, "Instant Thunder Presentation…," 5; Harvey notes, Aug 20, 1990/1355, 1–2; Stanfill notes, Aug 20, 1990/1400, 1. The documents do not indicate why Horner thought it was a "poor way."

39. Harvey notes, Aug 20, 1990/1355, 2–3. See also trnscrpt of Deptula dictation notes on tape, "Instant Thunder Presentation…," 5; Intvw trnscrpt, Wilson by Gehri, Mann, and Reynolds, Dec 11, 1991, 37–38; Stanfill notes, Aug 20, 1990/1400, 1–2.

40. Trnscrpt of Deptula dictation notes on tape, "Instant Thunder Presentation…," 5.

41. Stanfill notes, Aug 20, 1990/1400, 2.

42. Harvey notes, Aug 20, 1990/1355, 3.

43. Ibid.

44. Ibid.

45. Trnscrpt of Deptula dictation notes on tape, "Instant Thunder Presentation…," 6; Stanfill notes, Aug 2, 1990/1400, 3. At this point in the briefing, Harvey wrote in his notes that Horner asked "general questions," but it is unclear if Harvey recorded all of the queries. Henry, who did not take notes during the session, many months later recalled Horner inquiring about munitions and sustainability; bad weather allowing Iraq to recover from initial strategic strikes and to invade Saudi Arabia; and Scuds launched against Israel. None of those at the meeting who took notes recorded these concerns. See intvw tape, Henry by Putney, Jul 3, 1997, AFHSO.

46. Harvey notes, Aug 20, 1990/1355, 4.

47. Ibid.; Trnscrpt of Deptula dictation notes on tape, "Instant Thunder Presentation…," 6 (quote); Stanfill notes, Aug 20, 1990/1400, 3.

48. Harvey notes, Aug 20, 1990/1355, 4; Stanfill notes, Aug 20, 1990/1400, 3.

49. Trnscrpt of Deptula dictation notes on tape, "Instant Thunder Presentation…," 7. See also Stanfill notes, Aug 20, 1990/1400, 4.

50. Harvey notes, Aug 20, 1990/1355, 5.

51. Ibid.

52. Ibid., 6.

53. Ibid.

54. Stanfill notes, Aug 20, 1990/1400, 5.

55. Ibid.

56. Trnscrpt of Deptula dictation of notes on tape, "Instant Thunder Presentation…," 7.

57. Harvey notes, Aug 20, 1990/1355, 6; Stanfill notes, Aug 20, 1990/1400, 5–6; Trnscrpt of Deptula dictation notes on tape, "Instant Thunder Presentation…," 7.

58. Harvey notes, Aug 20, 1990/1355, 6; Trnscrpt of Deptula dictation of notes on tape, "Instant Thunder Presentation…," 7.

59. Harvey notes, Aug 20, 1990/1355, 7; Trnscrpt of Deptula dictation notes on tape, "Instant Thunder Presentation…," 7.

60. Harvey notes, Aug 20, 1990/1355, 7.

61. Ibid. See also Trnscrpt of Deptula dictation notes on tape, "Instant Thunder Presentation…," 8.

62. Harvey notes, Aug 20, 1990/1355, 8.

63. Trnscrpt of Deptula dictation of notes on tape, "Instant Thunder Presentation…," 8.

64. Stanfill notes, Aug 20, 1990/1400, 5 (quote), 6.

65. Harvey notes, Aug 20, 1990/1355, 8; Trnscrpt of Deptula dictation of notes on tape, "Instant Thunder Presentation…," 8.

66. Harvey notes, Aug 20, 1990/1355, 8.

67. Ibid.

68. Ibid., 9.

69. Ibid.

70. Ibid. See also trnscrpt of Deptula dictation notes on tape, "Instant Thunder Presentation…," 8.

71. Trnscrpt of Deptula dictation notes on tape, "Instant Thunder Presentation…," 8. The first units of the 24th Infantry Division, Mechanized, departed the United States August 13, but major combat elements did not arrive in theater until September 12.

72. Comment, Horner on draft manuscript, Putney, "Airpower Advantage."

73. Ibid.

74. Brfg slides, "Iraqi Air Campaign Instant Thunder," 25, Deptula file, Checkmate, Pentagon. Deptula told the author that Warden initially briefed the slide, but it was very near the end of his initial presentation (the slide's position was close to the bottom of the package). Deptula thought that Horner's strong impressions of Instant Thunder had congealed by this time: the strategic air campaign did not address the use of air power against the Iraqi army. Telecon notes, Col David A. Deptula and Diane T. Putney, Aug 30, 1993, AFHSO.

75. Intvw trnscrpt, Warden by Gehri, Oct 22, 1991, 73.

76. Ibid., 108. Neither Deptula's nor Harvey's notes included Horner, at this point, saying that he could look out his window and see Iraqi tanks rolling into Riyadh. Warden and Harvey, however, in postwar interviews remembered the general saying this, which Warden thought absurd. The morning of August 20, Major Roehler from the CENTAF staff told them that CENTAF estimated the Iraqis could probably travel 20 to 30 kilometers a day, at best.

77. Essay, Warden, "Centers of Gravity," [Mar 1990], 6–7.

78. Ibid., 4.

79. Notes, Lt Col Ronnie Stanfill, Aug 17, 1990/1006, 1, CHP folder, GWAPS, AFHRA.

80. Essay, "Centers of Gravity," [Mar 1990], 4.

81. Intvw trnscrpt, Warden by Gehri, Oct 22, 1991, 73. Although Warden said this after the war, the author of this volume believes it also reflects his thinking in August 1990.

82. Harvey notes, Aug 20, 1990/1355, 9–10.

83. Trnscrpt of Deptula dictation notes on tape, "Instant Thunder Presentation…," 8.

84. Harvey notes, Aug 20, 1990/1355, 10; Trnscrpt of Deptula dictation notes on tape, "Instant Thunder Presentation…," 7. Harvey's notes contain a line, which seems to be an insert, stating that Horner "demands" an apology, but neither Deptula nor Stanfill noted the demand, and Horner did not recall asking for the apology.

85. Horner specifically singled out General Adams, XO, as someone who should know better than to plan the war from Washington. See Harvey notes, Aug 20, 1990/1355, 10. In *Heart of the Storm,* Reynolds's account of the briefing included an exchange between Horner and Henry. The latter explained that his remarks occurred that evening at dinner with Horner, not at the briefing. See comment by Henry on draft manuscript, Putney, "Airpower Advantage."

86. Stanfill notes, Aug 20, 1990/1400, 7.

87. Harvey notes, Aug 20, 1990/1355, 10; Trnscrpt of Deptula dictation notes on tape, "Instant Thunder Presentation…," 8.

88. Harvey notes, Aug 20, 1990/1915. Horner's overt anger expressed to Generals Glosson and Henry during their briefing to him on August 26 will far surpass his displeasure and criticism directed toward Warden on August 20.

89. Harvey notes, Aug 20, 1990/1600.

90. Ibid.

91. Ibid.

92. Ibid; Stanfill notes, Aug 20, 1990/1600.

93. Brfg, "CJCS and CINC's Conference," National Defense University, Washington, Aug 20–21, 1990, Checkmate file, GWAPS, AFHRA. The 197th Infantry Brigade substituted for the 48th Infantry Brigade of the Georgia National Guard, the "roundout" brigade for the 24th Infantry Division, Mechanized. See Scales, *Certain Victory*, 52–53.

94. Drft intvw trnscrpt, Horner by Davis, Jamieson, and Barlow, Mar 4, 1992, 20. Horner probably remembered the five strategic rings in bulls-eye format in the package of slides that Lt Col Steven Wilson presented August 15, unless Warden presented the ring graphic to Horner — even though he did not brief it to Schwarzkopf on August 17.

95. Ed drft intvw trnscrpt, Horner by Davis, Jamieson, and Barlow, Mar 4, 1992, 13.

96. Speech trnscrpt, Reuters, Lt Gen Charles A. Horner to Business Executives for National Security Education Fund, May

8, 1991, 3, AFHSO.

97. Ed drft intvw trnscrpt, Horner by Davis, Jamieson, and Barlow, Mar 4, 1992, 18, AFHSO.

98. Ibid., 29 (quotes).

99. Intvw trnscrpt, Horner by Reynolds and Gehri, Dec 2, 1991, 54.

100. Ibid., 34–35.

101. Drft intvw trnscrpt, Horner by Putney and Bradley, Apr 26, 1994, 97.

102. Harvey notes, Aug 20, 1990/1915.

103. Ibid., Aug 21, 1990/0900; Intvw tape, Harvey by Putney and Davis, Jan 7, 1993.

104. Intvw trnscrpt, Henry by Reynolds, Mann, and Gehri, [Jun 2, 1992], 51.

105. Drft intvw trnscrpt, Henry by Putney, Jul 3, 1997, 44–45; Drft intvw trnscrpt, Horner by Putney and Bradley, Apr 26, 1994, 77, 97; Intvw trnscrpt, Horner by Gehri and Reynolds, Dec 2, 1991, 37; Comment, Glosson on draft manuscript, Putney, "Airpower Advantage."

106. Intvw tape, Harvey by Putney and Davis, Jan 7, 1993.

107. Brfg, Lt Col David A. Deptula to AF/HO and CAFH staff, Jan 8, 1992; Intvw tape, Deptula by Putney and Davis, Dec 12, 1992; Intvw trnscrpt, Deptula by Turner, Nov 1, 1990, 8–9.

108. Intvw trnscrpt, Wilson by Gehri, Mann, and Reynolds, Dec 11, 1991, 19; Intvw trnscrpt, Lt Col David A. Deptula by Lt Col Richard Reynolds and Lt Col Edward Mann, Dec 10, 1991, 16–17, CADRE, AU; Intvw tape, Harvey by Putney and Davis, Jan 7, 1993.

109. Intvw tape, Deptula by Reynolds, Gehri, and Mann, Jul 24, 1992; Org chart, [Instant Thunder] Planning Group Det 1, Aug 21, 1990, Deptula file, GWAPS, AFHRA; Harvey notes, Aug 21, 1990/0900; Intvw trnscrpt, Deptula by Reynolds and Mann, Dec 10, 1991, 12–13.

110. Intvw tape, Glock by Putney and Davis, Aug 27, 1993; Intvw tape, Lt Col David L. Waterstreet by Richard G. Davis, Mar 6, 1992, AFHSO.

111. Drft intvw trnscrpt, Deptula by Davis, Nov 20, 1991, 6.

112. Intvw tape, Waterstreet by Davis, Mar 6, 1992.

113. Harvey notes, Aug 21, 1990/1100.

114. Intvw trnscrpt, Deptula by Reynolds and Mann, Dec 10, 1991, 18–19.

115. Comment, Deptula on draft manuscript, Putney, "Airpower Advantage."

116. Telecon notes, Leonardo by Putney, Jan 5, 1994, AFHSO; Harvey notes with note within, Aug 21, 1990/1130; Stanfill notes, Aug 21, 1990; Intvw trnscrpt, Blackburn by Reynolds, Gehri, and Mann, Apr 21, 1993, 85.

117. Stanfill notes, Aug 21, 1990.

118. Intvw trnscrpt, Blackburn by Gehri, Reynolds, and Mann, Apr 21, 1993, 108.

119. The targeteers were Capts Jay Bachhuber, Timothy Carver, Thomas Clements, John Glock, and John Heidrick.

120. Discussion notes, Capt John R. Glock and Diane T. Putney, Jan 29, 1992, AFHSO.

121. Intvw tape, Glock by Putney and Davis, Aug 27, 1992; Intvw tape, Glock by Putney, Oct 26, 1992. Horner told the author of this volume that he did not want to keep the Air Staff officers in theater too long because they were not assigned to him. The day before, Harvey noted that Horner had referred to them as "worker bees," implying that the general wanted them to augment his growing but still small CENTAF staff.

122. Intvw tape, Glock by Putney and Davis, Aug 27, 1992.

123. Ibid.; Telecon notes, Capt John R. Glock and Diane T. Putney, Sep 20, 1993, AFHSO; Intvw tape, Glock by Putney, Oct 26, 1992.

124. Intvw tape, Glock by Putney and Davis, Aug 27, 1992; Intvw tape, Glock by Putney, Oct 26, 1992.

125. Captain Glock has extensively criticized Instant Thunder, especially in terms of the relationship between its target sets and objectives. Much of his analysis and articulation of it occurred after August 21, 1990, and during his work with the postwar GWAPS. See intvw tapes, Capt John R. Glock by Diane T. Putney and Richard G. Davis, Aug 27, 1992, and by Putney, Oct 26, 1992, AFHSO. See also his working paper, Capt John R. Glock, "Target Intelligence

Support during Desert Shield and Storm," Glock file, GWAPS, AFHRA.

126. Intvw tape, Glock by Putney and Davis, Aug 27, 1992; Intvw tape, Deptula by Gehri, Reynolds, and Mann, Jul 24, 1992; Brfg notes, Capt John R. Glock to GWAPS staff, Jan 21, 1992; Comment, Deptula on draft manuscript, Putney, "Airpower Advantage." The targeteer later regretted that he told Deptula he did not provide maps.

127. Deptula's view of Glock would turn positive during Desert Storm.

128. Harvey notes, Aug 22, 1990/1030–1050.

129. Memo, Lt Col Harvey to [Checkmate], Aug 22, 1990/1208, n.s., CHSH 22, GWAPS, AFHRA.

130. Intvw trnscrpt, Horner by Gehri and Reynolds, Dec 2, 1991, 35. General Olsen's notes indicate that Horner initially called the effort the "Special Planning Project."

131. Drft intvw trnscrpt, Maj Gen Buster C. Glosson by Richard G. Davis, Perry D. Jamieson, and Diane T. Putney, Dec 12, 1991, 3, AFHSO; Bio sheet, Lt Gen Charles A. Horner, SAF/PA, Jan 1989; Intvw trnscrpt, Glosson by Mann and Gehri, May 29, 1991, 46.

132. Intvw tape, Glosson, Henry, and Lewis by Putney, May 20, 1997; Intvw trnscrpt, Maj Gen Buster Glosson, by Lt Col Edward Mann and Lt Col Richard Reynolds, May 29, 1991, 19–22.

133. Intvw trnscrpt, Maj Gen Buster C. Glosson by Lt Col Richard Reynolds, Lt Col Edward Mann, and Lt Col Suzanne Gehri, Jun 4, 1992, 52, CADRE, AU; Notes, Brig Gen Buster C. Glosson, "Arrival in Riyadh," Aug 21, 1990/1745, given by Glosson to Diane T. Putney, during intvw, Glosson, Henry, and Lewis by Putney, May 20, 1997. The quotes represent the words as Glosson wrote them, not necessarily Horner's exact words.

134. Comment, Horner on draft manuscript, Putney, "Airpower Advantage" ("sheet" quote); Intvw tape, Glosson, Henry, and Lewis by Putney, May 20, 1997 ("constraint" quote).

135. Intvw trnscrpt, Horner by Reynolds and Gehri, Dec 2, 1991, 39.

136. Notes, Glosson, "Arrival in Riyadh," Aug 21, 1990/1745.

137. Notes, Brig Gen Buster C. Glosson, "Riyadh [to] *LaSalle*," Aug 22, 1990/2115, given by Glosson to Diane T. Putney, during intvw, Glosson, Henry, and Lewis by Putney, May 20, 1997.

138. Stanfill notes, Aug 22, 1990/1430; Harvey notes Aug 22, 1990/1400 and 1420–1545 (quotes); Chronology, "Chronology/Overview of In-Theater Events," Lt Col David A. Deptula, [Sep 24, 1990], Deptula/Rice folder, Checkmate, GWAPS, AFHRA.

139. Intvw trnscrpt, Deptula by Reynolds and Mann, Dec 10, 1991, 5; Chronology, "Chronology/Overview of In-Theater Events," Lt Col David A. Deptula, [Sep 24, 1990], Deptula/Rice folder, GWAPS, AFHRA.

140. Intvw trnscrpt, Brig Gen Buster C. Glosson by TSgt Theodore J. Turner, Oct 27, 1990, 28, AFHSO; Drft intvw trnscrpt, Lt Col David A. Deptula by Richard G. Davis, Perry D. Jamieson, and Diane T. Putney, Nov 29, 1991, 82, AFHSO; Harvey notes, Aug 22, 1990/1920–1945.

141. Notes, Brig Gen Buster C. Glosson, "Telecon CINC," Aug 22, 2310, given by Glosson to Diane T. Putney, during intvw, Glosson, Henry, and Lewis by Putney, May 20, 1997. The quotes are words as Glosson wrote them and not necessarily the CINCCENT's exact words.

142. Intvw tape, Glosson, Henry, and Lewis by Putney, May 20, 1997.

143. Notes, Glosson, "Telecon CINC," Aug 22, 1990/2310.

144. Intvw trnscrpt, Glosson by Turner, Oct 17, 1990, 3 (quote); Drft intvw trnscrpt, Glosson by Reynolds, Gehri, and Mann, Jun 4, 1992, 51; Intvw trnscrpt, Deptula by Reynolds and Mann, Dec 10, 1991, 26.

145. Intvw trnscrpt, Glosson by Turner, Oct 17, 1990, 3.

146. Harvey notes, Aug 22, 1990/1400, Aug 24, 1990/0925, and Aug 25, 1990/2015.

147. List, "Black Hole," Strategic Air Campaign Planners, n.d., Deptula file, GWAPS, AFHRA.

148. Ibid.

149. Sensitive compartmented information (SCI) differed from special category (SPECAT) material. The SCI required stor-

age in a highly secure SCI facility (SCIF), which could also house SPECAT.

150. Harvey notes, Aug 23/1990/2000; Working paper, Capt John R. Glock, "Target Intelligence Support during Desert Shield and Storm," 11, GWAPS, AFHRA; Intvw tape, Glock by Putney and Davis, Aug 27, 1992; Intvw tape, Glock by Putney, Oct 26, 1992.

151. Harvey notes, Aug 23, 1990/1620 and 2200.

152. Intvw trnscrpt, Glosson by Turner, Oct 17, 1990, 3.

153. Intvw tape, Waterstreet by Davis, Mar 6, 1992; Drft intvw trnscrpt, Deptula by Davis, Nov 20, 1991, 6, AFHRA.

154. Intvw tape, Waterstreet by Davis, Mar 6, 1992; Drft intvw trnscrpt, Deptula by Davis, Nov 20, 1991, 18.

155. Intvw trnscrpt, Baptiste by Putney and Reynolds, Sep 24, 1992, 55–56.

156. Campaign flow sheet, Aug 18, 1990/1230L, Black Hole folder 1-1-1, GWAPS, AFHRA; Worksheet, "Sortie Availability," Aug 23, 1990, Black Hole folder 1-1-3, GWAPS, AFHRA. See also other Deptula flow sheets in Black Hole folders 1-1-1 and 1-1-3, GWAPS, AFHRA.

157. Intvw trnscrpt, Deptula by Reynolds and Mann, Dec 10, 1991, 24; Comment, Deptula on draft manuscript, Putney, "Airpower Advantage."

158. Instant Thunder OPORD, Aug 17, 1990, Annex C, 7, CHSH 1-8, GWAPS, AFHRA; Harvey notes, Aug 19, 1990/2230L, and Aug 24, 1990/1050; Intvw tape, Lt Col David A. Deptula by Diane T. Putney and Richard G. Davis, Dec 12, 1992, AFHSO; Stanfill notes, Aug 22, 1990/1430; Chronology, "Chronology/Overview of In-Theater Events," Lt Col David A. Deptula, [Sep 24, 1990], Deptula/Rice folder, Checkmate, GWAPS, AFHRA.

159. Intvw trnscrpt, Crigger by Gehri and Reynolds, Dec 2–4, 1991, 26.

160. Trnscrpt of dictation notes on tape, Lt Col David A. Deptula, n.d., subject: Instant Thunder Presentation to CENTAF 20 Aug 90, Kurt Guthie file, GWAPS, AFHRA; Discussion notes, Col David A. Deptula and Diane T. Putney, Dec 10, 1993, AFHSO.

161. Harvey notes, Aug 24, 1990/1050; Ed drft intvw trnscrpt, Horner by Davis, Jamieson, and Barlow, Mar 4, 1992, 75; Stanfill notes, Aug 24, 1990/1100.

162. Memo for record, "Answers to Questions…," Col James C. Crigger, Jr., Feb 25, 1993.

163. Harvey's notes, Aug 24, 1990/1050.

164. Intvw trnscrpt, Olsen by Turner, Oct 20, 1990, 53; OPORD, COMUSCENTAF Operations Order Offensive Campaign—Phase I, Sep 2, 1990, B–2, Black Hole file, GWAPS, AFHRA.

165. Harvey notes, Aug 24, 1990/1425; Memo and atch, [Col Crigger] to [Diane Putney], Mar 1, [1993]. Crigger was unaware of the Checkmate authorship of the plan titled, "Instant Thunder Phase II, An Operational Air Campaign against Iraqi Forces in Kuwait."

166. Harvey notes, Aug 24, 1990/1425, 2330 and Aug 25, 1990/0630.

167. Drft intvw trnscrpt, Deptula by Davis, Nov 20, 1991, 7; Intvw tape, Harvey by Putney and Davis, Jan 7, 1993; Comment, Glosson on draft manuscript, Putney, "Airpower Advantage"; Notes, Brig Gen Buster C. Glosson, "Telecon CINC," Aug 22, 2310, given by Glosson to Putney during intvw, Glosson, Henry, and Lewis by Putney, May 20, 1997.

168. Intvw tape, Deptula by Putney and Davis, Dec 12, 1992; Harvey notes, Aug 26, 1990/0530; Drft intvw trnscrpt, Deptula by Davis, Jamieson, and Putney, Nov 29, 1991, 47–48; Discussion notes, Col David A. Deptula with Diane T. Putney, Dec 10, 1993, AFHSO; Deptula notes, Aug 26, 1990, Deptula custody.

169. Intvw trnscrpt, Horner by [Burton], [Mar 1991], 10.

170. Intvw tape, Glosson, Henry, and Lewis by Putney, May 20, 1997.

171. Intvw trnscrpt, Glosson by Reynolds, Gehri, and Mann, May 29, 1991, 47 (quote). The quote sometimes has been attributed to Glosson, but both he and Henry agree that Henry provided the description. See intvw tape, Glosson, Henry, and Lewis by Putney, May 20, 1997.

172. Intvw trnscrpt, Horner by Gehri and

Reynolds, Dec 2, 1991, 40.

173. Ibid.

174. Intvw trnscrpt, Glosson by Mann, Gehri, and Reynolds, May 29, 1991, 47.

175. Brfg slides, "Instant Thunder Concept of Operations and Execution," Aug 26, 1990, CHP folder 3, GWAPS, AFHRA; Drft intvw trnscrpt, Deptula by Davis, Jamieson, and Putney, Nov 29, 1991, 47.

176. DoD, *Conduct of the Persian Gulf War*, 66.

177. Brfg slides, "Offensive Campaign Concept of Operations Outline," Aug 26, 1990, Warden file, Checkmate, GWAPS, AFHRA; Harvey notes, Aug 26, 1990/0925; Drft intvw trnscrpt, Deptula by Davis, Jamieson, and Putney, Nov 29, 1991, 47–48; Ltr and atch, Col Robert J. Martinelli, CENTCOM, to Diane T. Putney, subj: General Schwarzkopf's Briefing Slides from Operations Desert Shield/Desert Storm, Oct 21, 1993.

178. Drft intvw trnscrpt, Deptula by Davis, Jamieson, and Putney, Nov 29, 1991, 48; Harvey notes, Aug 26, 1990/2100; Intvw tape, Col David A. Deptula by Diane T. Putney, Apr 11, 1994, AFHSO.

179. Deptula notes, Aug 26, 1990.

180. Harvey notes, Aug 26, 1990/2100 (1st quote); Stanfill notes, [Aug 26, 1990] (2d quote); Drft intvw trnscrpt, Deptula by Davis, Nov 20, 1991, 10; Intvw tape, Deptula by Putney and Davis, Dec 12, 1992; Intvw tape, Col David A. Deptula by Diane T. Putney, Feb 14, 1994, AFHSO.

181. Ed drft intvw trnscrpt, Horner by Davis, Jamieson, and Barlow, Mar 4, 1992, 15 (quote); Intvw trnscrpt, Glosson by Reynolds, Mann, and Gehri, May 29, 1991, 47.

182. Deptula notes, Aug 26, 1990/1640.

183. Brfg slides, "Offensive Campaign Phase I," Aug 27, 1990, CHP folder 3, GWAPS, AFHRA. See comment, Horner on draft manuscript, Putney, "Airpower Advantage."

184. Brfg slides, "Offensive Campaign Phase I," Aug 27, 1990, CHP folder 3, GWAPS, AFHRA; Drft flow chart, by Glosson in Barry Watts file, GWAPS, AFHRA.

185. Brfg slides, "Offensive Campaign Phase I," Aug 27, 1990, CHP folder 3, GWAPS, AFHRA.

186. Ibid.

187. Ibid; Chart, with Deptula explanatory note, "Attack Flow (Intensity)," folder 19D, Deptula file, GWAPS, AFHRA; Discussion, Col David A. Deptula and Diane T. Putney, Jul 15, 1994; Drft intvw trnscrpt, Deptula by Davis, Jamieson, and Putney, Jan 8, 1992, 28. Air Force doctrine urged, "Attack the enemy relentlessly." See AFM 1–1, Jan 5, 1984, 2-13.

188. Brfg slides, "Offensive Campaign Phase I," Aug 27, 1990, CHP folder 3, GWAPS, AFHRA.

189. Harvey notes, Aug 26, 1990/1730.

Chapter 6

1. Bush and Scowcroft, *World Transformed,* 349–350.

2. Harvey notes, Aug 27, 1990/0945 and Aug 28, 1990/1610. The quoted material is as Harvey wrote it, not necessarily as Glosson precisely spoke it.

3. Harvey notes, Aug 21, 1990/1130, Aug 23, 1990/2200, and Aug 26, 1990/2205L; Intvw tape, Blackburn by Putney, Feb 19, 1992; Intvw trnscrpt, Deptula by Turner, Nov 1, 1990, 10–11; Intvw tape, Capt John R. Glock and Diane T. Putney, May 26, 1992, AFHSO. Harvey knew that the DMAAC would send the mensurated coordinates after hearing this from Blackburn in Checkmate.

4. Intvw trnscrpt, Blackburn by Gehri, Reynolds, and Mann, Apr 21, 1993, 101–106.

5. Intvw trnscrpt, Deptula by Turner, Nov 1, 1990, 10–11.

6. Intvw tape, Deptula by Gehri, Reynolds, and Mann, Jul 24, 1992.

7. Discussion notes Capt John R. Glock and Diane T. Putney, Jul 17, 1992, AFHSO.

8. Intvw tape, Blackburn by Putney, Feb 19, 1992.

9. Intvw tape, Blackburn by Putney,

Feb 19, 1992; Intvw trnscrpt, Blackburn by Gehri, Reynolds, and Mann, Apr 21, 1993, 84–85, 87–88, 101–103.

10. Intvw tapes, Blackburn by Putney, Feb 12 and 19, 1992; Intvw trnscrpt, Blackburn by Gehri, Reynolds, and Mann, Apr 21, 1993, 91–93, 100.

11. Intvw tapes, Blackburn by Putney, Feb 12 and 19, 1992; Intvw trnscrpt, Blackburn by Gehri, Reynolds, and Mann, Apr 21, 1993, 94–95, 101–103, 111–115.

12. Intvw tape, Blackburn by Putney, Feb 19, 1992; Intvw trnscrpt, Blackburn by Gehri, Reynolds, and Mann, Apr 21, 1993, 87, 102–103, 106. See also Msg, DMAAC to USCENTCOM REAR/CCJ2-PT et al., 270138Z Aug 90, subj: Desert Shield Point Mensurations, GWAPS, AFHRA.

13. Msg, DMAAC/SDFP to USCINCCENT/CCJ2-PT et al., 270138Z Aug 90, subj: Desert Shield Point Mensurations, GWAPS, AFHRA.

14. Telecon notes, Capt John R. Glock and Diane T. Putney, May 26, 1992, AFHSO; Brfg notes, Capt John R. Glock to GWAPS staff, Jan 21, 1992; Intvw trnscrpt, Blackburn by Gehri, Reynolds, and Mann, Apr 21, 1993, 107–109.

15. Intvw trnscrpt, Blackburn by Gehri, Reynolds, and Mann, Apr 21, 1993, 103–105, 109, 110 (quote); Intvw tape, Blackburn by Putney, Feb 19, 1992.

16. A target folder consisted of "a file of assembled target intelligence about a specific geographic area." See Joint Pub 1–02, *Department of Defense Dictionary of Military and Associated Terms,* Dec 1, 1989. Intvw trnscrpt, Blackburn by Gehri, Reynolds, and Mann, Apr 21, 1993, 107, 109.

17. Intvw trnscrpt, Blackburn by Gehri, Reynolds, and Mann, Apr 21, 1993, 103–104 (quotes), 110, 112 (quotes), 114 (quote).

18. Ibid., 109 (quote), 111 (quotes). The author of this volume used the phrase "make the system work" to describe Blackburn's view.

19. Intvw tape, Blackburn by Putney, Feb 19, 1992.

20. Intvw trnscrpt, Blackburn by Gehri, Reynolds, and Mann, Apr 21, 1993, 109 (quote), 111, 112 (quotes).

21. Intvw tape, Warden to Putney et al., Feb 6, 1992.

22. See Joint Pub 1–02, *Department of Defense Dictionary of Military and Associated Terms*, Dec 1, 1989.

23. Intvw tape, Col Christopher L. Christon by Richard G. Davis and Barry Barlow, Mar 4, 1992, AFHSO.

24. JULLS Long Rpt, "Concept of Operations for Intelligence," JULLS No. 41846-19500 (00038), AF/INDDA, 05/09/91, Lessons-Intel, Checkmate, GWAPS, AFHRA; Rpt, Secretary, Joint Staff Directive on Joint Assessment Report, Apr 23, 1991, C-12, Lessons-JCS/CINC folder, Checkmate file, GWAPS, AFHRA.

25. Intvw trnscrpt, Col Armstrong by Lt Col Richard Reynolds, Oct 23, 1991, 34–35, CADRE, AU.

26. Working Papers, "Defense Intelligence Team Report Operation Desert Shield," Nov 25, 1990, 2, NA 187, GWAPS, AFHRA.

27. Intvw trnscrpt, Armstrong by Reynolds, Oct 23, 1991, 10. See also Intvw trnscrpt, Adm Taylor, COMNAVCENT by Ed Marolda, Mar 1992, Navy Historical Center, Washington.

28. CINCCENT's input with Memo, Chairman Powell to Secretary of Defense, subj: Preliminary Report on Lessons Learned in Operations Desert Shield and Desert Storm, Apr 12, 1991, Lessons-JCS/CINCs, Checkmate file, GWAPS, AFHRA.

29. DoD, *Conduct of the Persian Gulf War,* 337; Brfg, Air Force Council, Nov–Dec 1990, Capt Kelly file, HQ USAF/INX, Pentagon.

30. Msg, CENTAF/IN to TAC/IN, 110915Z Apr 1991, subj: Assessment of Desert Storm Intelligence Operations," Gulf War file, TAC/HO.

31. Intvw tape, Christon by Davis and Barlow, Mar 4, 1992.

32. Ibid.

33. Drft intvw trnscrpt, Horner by Putney and Bradley, Apr 26, 1994, 128.

34. Intvw tape, Deptula by Gehri, Reynolds, and Mann, Jul 24, 1992. See also intvw tape, Harvey by Putney and Davis, Jan 7, 1993.

35. Brfg notes, Capt John R. Glock to GWAPS staff, Jan 21, 1992; Intvw tape, Glock by Putney and Davis, Aug 27, 1992; Intvw tape, Glock by Putney, Oct 26, 1992.

36. Pamphlet, AFP 200–18, vol 1, "Target Intelligence Handbook Unclassified Targeting Principles," Oct 1, 1990; Intvw tape, Glock by Putney and Davis, Aug 27, 1992.

37. Rpt, Maj John Heidrick, "9 TIS/INT Planning Procedures for Internal Look—90 and Operation Desert Shield…," May 4, 1992, Larry Greenberg file, GWAPS, AFHRA; Intvw tape, Glock by Putney and Davis, Aug 27, 1992.

38. Pamphlet, AFP 200–18, vol 1, "Target Intelligence Handbook Unclassified Targeting Principles," Oct 1, 1990, 64.

39. Rpt, Maj John Heidrick, "9 TIS/INT Planning Procedures for Internal Look 90 and Operation Desert Shield…," May 4, 1992, Larry Greenberg file, GWAPS, AFHRA.

40. Working paper, Capt John R. Glock, "Target Intelligence Support during Desert Shield and Storm," 4, Glock file, GWAPS, AFHRA.

41. Brfg, "Operation Desert Shield TAF Intelligence Support," [TAC/IN], [c. Nov 90], Col Souza file, HQ USAF/INX; Telecon notes, Capt John R. Glock and Diane T. Putney, May 26, 1992, AFHSO.

42. Brfg notes, Capt John R. Glock to GWAPS staff, Jan 21, 1992; Harvey notes, Sep 8, 1990/1200 and Oct 12, 1990/1530–1630; Brfg, "Operational Support for Targeting: The Role of the Office of Imagery Exploitation," DIA/ODX-7B; Discussion notes, Capt John R. Glock and Diane T. Putney, Jan 29, 1992, AFHSO.

43. Pamphlet, AFP 200–18, vol 1, "Target Intelligence Handbook Unclassified Targeting Principles,: Oct 1, 1990, 64; Brfg, "Air Force Intelligence: Present and Future," Briefing to Air Force Council, c. Nov–Dec 1990.

44. Brfg, "Operation Desert Shield TAF Intelligence Support," [TAC/IN], [c. Nov 1990], Col Souza file, HQ USAF/INX; Intvw tape, Glock by Putney and Davis, Aug 27, 1992; Brfg, "Intel Systems Support to Desert Shield," HQ TAC/INYS, slide: "Tactical Digital Facsimile," CHSH 91-1, GWAPS, AFHRA; Intvw tape, Christon by Davis and Barlow, Mar 4, 1992; Telecon notes, Capt John R. Glock and Diane T. Putney, May 26, 1992, AFHSO.

45. Intvw tape, Christon by Davis and Barlow, Mar 4, 1992 (quote); Intvw trnscrpt, Armstrong by Reynolds, Oct 23, 1991, 17–18.

46. Intvw tape, Glock by Putney and Davis, Aug 27, 1992; Telecon notes, Capt John R. Glock and Diane T. Putney, May 26, 1992, AFHSO; Discussion notes, Capt John R. Glock and Diane T. Putney, Oct 26, 1992, AFHSO.

47. Intvw tape, Glock by Putney and Davis, Aug 27, 1992; Telecon notes by Putney, Capt John R. Glock and Diane T. Putney, May 26, 1992, AFHSO.

48. Brfg notes, Capt John R. Glock to GWAPS staff, Jan 21, 1992; Intvw tape, Glock by Putney and Davis, Aug 27, 1992.

49. Brfg, Capt John R. Glock to GWAPS staff, Jan 21, 1992; Intvw tape, Glock by Putney and Davis, Aug 27, 1992; Discussion notes, Capt John R. Glock and Capt William Bruner with Diane T. Putney, Jan 29, 1992, AFHSO.

50. Harvey notes, Aug 27, 1990/0945.

51. After the war, Glosson explained that he had directed that someone from the SCI tent and CENTAF/IN in the RSAF building attend every one of the meetings of the group, but, even issuing threats at least four times, his directives were not fulfilled. (Comment, Glosson on draft manuscript, Putney, "Airpower Advantage.") He did not indicate, however, that he took action to resolve the matter of inadequate intelligence representation. Captain Glock explained that word never reached the targeteers about when Glosson's staff meetings would occur. See fax, Glock to Putney, Dec 26, 2000.

52. Working paper, Capt John Glock, "Target Intelligence Support during Desert Shield and Storm," 11, Glock file, GWAPS, AFHRA; Brfg, Capt John Glock, HQ SAC/INT, "Targeting and the Black Hole," in "Target Director's Update," Aug 1991, No. 15, folder 18A, Deptula file, GWAPS, AFHRA.

53. Brfg, Capt John R. Glock, "Targeting and the Black Hole," in "Target Director's Update," Aug 1991, No. 15, folder 18A, Deptula file, GWAPS, AFHRA; Intvw tape, Harvey by Putney and Davis, Jan 7, 1993; Intvw tape, Glock by Putney, Oct 26, 1992.

54. Intvw tape, Deptula by Gehri, Reynolds, and Mann, Jul 24, 1992.

55. Harvey notes, Aug 28, 1990/2100 [Aug 29, 1990/0035–0115].

56. Intvw tape, Harvey by Putney and Davis, Jan 7, 1993. See also Harvey notes, [Aug 29, 1990]/0035–0115.

57. Stanfill notes, [Aug 29, 1990].

58. Intvw tape, Glock by Putney, Oct 26, 1992; Harvey notes, Aug 29, 1990/1325; Intvw tape, Deptula by Gehri, Reynolds, and Mann, Jul 24, 1992.

59. Harvey notes, Aug 29, 1990/1325.

60. Intvw tape, Deptula by Davis, Jamieson, and Putney, Jan 8, 1992; Intvw tape, Deptula by Gehri, Reynolds, and Mann, Jul 24, 1992; Intvw tape, Glock by Putney and Davis, Aug 27, 1992.

61. Intvw tape, Glock by Putney and Davis, Aug 27, 1992; Intvw tape, Glock by Putney, Oct 26, 1992.

62. Intvw tape, Deptula by Gehri, Reynolds, and Mann, Jul 24, 1992.

63. Drft intvw trnscrpt, Deptula by Davis, Nov 20, 1991, 17; Intvw trnscrpt, Deptula by Turner, Nov 1, 1990, 11; Intvw tape, Blackburn by Putney, Feb 12, 1992.

64. Paper, Capt John Glock, "Targeting and the Black Hole," in "Target Director's Update," Aug 1991, No. 15, folder 18A, Deptula file, GWAPS, AFHRA; Intvw tape, Glock by Putney and Davis, Aug 27, 1992.

65. Intvw tape, Deptula by Gehri, Reynolds, and Mann, Jul 24, 1992; Intvw tape, Glock by Putney and Davis, Aug 27, 1992; Deptula notes, Aug 28, 1990, (quote), in Deptula's custody.

66. Intvw tape, Glock by Putney and Davis, Aug 27, 1992; Intvw tape, Glock by Putney, Oct 26, 1992.

67. Intvw tape, Deptula by Gehri, Reynolds, and Mann, Jul 24, 1992; Intvw tape, Glock by Putney and Davis, Aug 27, 1992; Intvw tape, Glock by Putney, Oct 26, 1992; Brfg trnscrpt, Capt John Glock, USAF Targeteers Conference, Oct 31–Nov 1, 1991, AFISA/INT.

68. Ed drft intvw trnscrpt, Deptula by Davis, Jamieson, and Putney, Nov 29, 1991, 81; Intvw tape, Glock by Davis and Putney, Aug 27, 1992; Intvw tape, Glock by Putney, Oct 26, 1992; Discussion notes, Capt John R. Glock and Diane T. Putney, Jan 29, 1992, AFHSO.

69. Pamphlet, AFP 200–17, "An Introduction to Air Force Targeting," Jun 23, 1989, 15.

70. Ibid., 21.

71. Intvw tape, Glock by Putney and Davis, Aug 27, 1992; Discussion notes, Capt John R. Glock and Diane T. Putney, Jan 29, 1992 and Sep 24, 1996, AFHSO.

72. Eighteen more F–117As arrived in the AOR on Dec 1, 1990, and another six on Jan 26, 1991, for a total of 42.

73. Ed drft intvw trnscrpt, Deptula by Davis, Jamieson and Putney, Nov 29, 1991, 81 (quote), 83; Drft intvw trnscrpt, Deptula by Davis, Jamieson, and Putney, Jan 8, 1992, 21–22; Chronology, SMSgt Harold P. Myers, USAF (Ret), "Nighthawks over Iraq: A Chronology of the F–117A Stealth Fighter in Operations Desert Shield and Desert Storm," 5, TAC/HO, Langley AFB. The Instant Thunder slides and OPORD do not provide persuasive evidence to show that "targeting for effects" originated with the Air Staff instead of with Deptula in theater.

74. Brfg notes, Lt Col David A. Deptula to GWAPS staff, Nov 26, 1991; Intvw tape, Deptula by Gehri, Reynolds, and Mann, Jul 24, 1992; Drft intvw trnscrpt, Deptula by Davis, Nov 20, 1991, 10–11; Ed drft intvw trnscrpt, Deptula by Davis, Jamieson, and Putney, Nov 29, 1991 (atch to intvw Nov 20, 1991), 82; Intvw tape, Deptula by Davis, Jamieson, and Putney, Jan 8, 1992. The "targeting for effects" concept occurred to Deptula in theater, not earlier in the Pentagon.

75. Drft intvw trnscrpt, Deptula by Davis, Nov 20, 1991, 11. See also David A. Deptula, "Parallel Warfare: What Is It? Where Did It Come From? Why Is It Important?" in *The Eagle in the Desert: Looking Back on U.S. Involvement in the Persian Gulf War*, ed. William Head and Earl H. Til-

ford, Jr. (Westport, Conn.: Praeger, 1996) and Col David A. Deptula, "Firing for Effect: Change in the Nature of Warfare," (Arlington, Va.: Aerospace Education Foundation, 1995).

76. Ed drft intvw trnscrpt, Deptula by Davis, Jamieson, and Putney, Nov 29, 1991, 82.

77. Intvw tape, Deptula by Putney and Davis, Dec 12, 1992.

78. Drft intvw trnscrpt, Deptula by Davis, Nov 20, 1991, 31.

79. Intvw trnscrpt, Deptula by Turner, Nov 1, 1990, 9; Ed drft intvw trnscrpt, Deptula by Davis, Jamieson, and Putney, Nov 29, 1991 (atch to intvw, Nov 20, 1991), 82.

80. Air Force targeting instructional material offered options such as degrade, neutralize, and disrupt as well as destroy. Target system analysis determined what effects would likely be achieved against target systems and their activities, and critical node analysis focused on the enemy activities to be affected, not on the characteristics of individual targets. See AF Pamphlet 200–17, "An Introduction to Air Force Targeting," Jun 23, 1989, 9–10, 20.

81. Brfg notes, Lt Col David A. Deptula to GWAPS staff, Nov 26, 1991.

82. Drft intvw trnscrpt, Deptula by Davis, Nov 20, 1991, 13.

83. Other aircraft also delivered laser-guided weapons, but the airframes were all nonstealthy.

84. Intvw tape, Deptula by Putney and Davis, Dec 12, 1992. The data did not, however, account for wartime conditions, such as flak turbulence.

85. Ed drft intvw trnscrpt, Deptula by Davis, Jamieson, and Putney, Nov 29, 1991, 118–119 (quote); Drft intvw trnscrpt, Deptula by Davis, Nov 20, 1991, 11; Pt paper, "F–117 Attack on Iraqi Air Defense Command HQ," Maj Mike Ritchey, XOOTT, Aug 12, 1990, CHSH 95-50, GWAPS, AFHRA.

86. The GBU–10s and GBU–24s, mostly delivered by F–111Fs, were also penetrator weapons.

87. Intvw tape, Glock by Putney, Oct 26, 1992; Extract, Capt Jeffery A. Paulk, 50 TFW, "Unguided BLU–109/B," Hotline sheets, USAF Fighter Weapons Review, 32–34, n. d.

88. Intvw tape, Glock by Putney, Oct 26, 1992; Brfg notes, Capt John R. Glock to GWAPS staff, Jan 21, 1992; Discussion notes, Capt John R. Glock and Diane T. Putney, Jan 29, 1992, AFHSO; Fax, Glock to Putney, Dec 26, 2000.

89. Drft paper, Lt Col David A. Deptula, "Observations on the Air Campaign against Iraq Aug 90–Mar 91," Mar 29, 1991, 3, Deptula file, GWAPS, AFHRA.

90. Ibid., 2.

91. Brfg, Lt Col David A. Deptula to AF/HO and CAFH staff, Jan 8, 1992.

92. Drft paper, Deptula, "Observations on the Air Campaign against Iraq," Mar 29, 1991, 2.

93. Intvw tape, Glosson, Henry, and Lewis by Putney, May 20, 1997, (quotes), AFHSO; Ed drft intvw trnscrpt, Deptula by Davis, Jamieson, and Putney, Nov 29, 1991 (atch to intvw Nov 20, 1991), 83.

94. Intvw tape, Glosson, Henry, and Lewis by Putney, May 20, 1997, AFHSO; Comments, Glosson and Howey on draft manuscript, Putney, "Airpower Advantage"; Ed drft intvw trnscrpt, Deptula by Davis, Nov 20, 1991, 41–42; Ed drft intvw trnscrpt, Deptula by Davis, Jamieson, and Putney, Nov 29, 1991 (atch to intvw Nov 20, 1991), 74–75; Article, Capt John R. Glock, HQ SAC/INAT, "Targeting and the Black Hole," in Target Director's Update No. 15, Aug 1991, 8–11, folder 18A, Deptula file, GWAPS, AFHRA; Discussion, Wayne Thompson, Checkmate historian during Desert Shield/Storm, and Diane Putney, Mar 25, 1998. See Warren E. Thompson, *Bandits over Baghdad: Personal Stories of Flying the F–117 over Iraq* (North Branch, Minn.: Specialty Press, 2000), 165–167, for a discussion of F–117 pilots sometimes flying simultaneous, multiship attacks involving as many as sixteen aircraft against single targets, with bomb impacts within 1.5 seconds.

95. Drft intvw trnscrpt, Deptula by Davis, Jamieson, and Putney, Jan 8, 1992, 48.

96. Memo, Cdr Jack P. Hassinger, Jr., USN, OIC, JEWC LO EUR, to Director of

Operations, Aug 16, 1990, subj: Proud Flame..., folder 4, Deptula binder, Black Hole file, GWAPS, AFHRA; Drft intvw trnscrpt, Deptula by Davis, Jamieson, and Putney, Jan 8, 1992, 48.

97. Memo, Cdr Jack P. Hassinger, Jr., USN, OIC, JEWC LO EUR, to Director of Operations, Aug 16, 1990, subj: Proud Flame..., folder 4, Deptula binder, Black Hole file, GWAPS, AFHRA; Drft intvw trnscrpt, Deptula by Davis, Jamieson, and Putney, Jan 8, 1992, 48; DoD, *Conduct of the Persian Gulf War,* 12, 96, 114–117, 129–130, 154, 162, 177; Rpt, U.S. General Accounting Office, "Operation Desert Storm Evaluation of the Air Campaign," GAO/NSIAD-97-134, June 1997, www.fas.org/man/gao/nsiad97134/app-06.htm.

98. Intvw tape, Deptula by Putney, Feb 14, 1994; Drft intvw trnscrpt, Deptula by Davis, Jamieson, and Putney, Jan 8, 1992, 48.

99. Ed drft intvw trnscrpt, Deptula by Davis, Jamieson, and Putney, Nov 29, 1991, 91. Intelligence officers giving planners every bit of intelligence pertinent to a campaign, however, would overwhelm them with information. The right balance had to be struck.

100. Rpt, "Proud Flame...," Proud Flame Division, Operations Directorate, Joint Electronic Warfare Center, 7, frame 775, reel 0269521, AFHRA; Harvey notes, Sep 19, 1990/0950.

101. Ed drft intvw trnscrpt, Glosson by Davis, Jamieson, and Putney, Dec 12, 1991, 12–13.

102. Ibid., 13–15.

103. Ibid., 33 (quote), 33–34.

104. Comment, Glosson on draft manuscript, Putney, "Airpower Advantage."

105. Intvw tape, Glock by Putney, Oct 26, 1992; Intvw notes, Gen Glosson by Alexander Cochran and GWAPS staff, Apr 9, 1992, 13, Alexander Cochran file, GWAPS.

106. Study, Kent M. Beck, Edward W. Gale, and Robert de V. Brunkow, "'Black' Weapon, Covert Mission: The Conventional ALCM, Desert Shield and Desert Storm, 1986–1991," SAC/HO, May 29, 1992, 20–21, NA 311, GWAPS, AFHRA.

107. Ed drft intvw trnscrpt, Glosson by Davis, Jamieson, and Putney, Dec 12, 1991, 32–33.

108. Ibid., 32.

109. Intvw notes, Gen Glosson by Alexander Cochran and GWAPS staff, Apr 9, 1992, Alexander Cochran file, GWAPS, AFHRA; Intvw tape, Glosson by Putney, Aug 30, 1993.

110. Intvw tape, Glosson by Davis, Jamieson, and Putney, Dec 12, 1991.

111. Ltr, Lt Col John D. Sweeney, 9CPS/CXEF, to Diane T. Putney, Aug 25, 1993; Intvw tape, Waterstreet by Davis, Mar 6, 1992.

112. Ltr, Lt Col John D. Sweeney, 9CPS/CXEF, to Diane T. Putney, Aug 25, 1993 (quotes); Drft intvw trnscrpt, Deptula by Davis, Nov 20, 1991, 15–17.

113. Ed drft intvw trnscrpt, Deptula by Davis, Nov 20, 1991, 27–28.

114. Intvw trnscrpt, Deptula by Turner, Nov 1, 1990, 11; Brfg notes, Lt Col David A. Deptula to GWAPS staff, Nov 26, 1991; Intvw tape, Deptula by Putney, Apr 11, 1994; Drft intvw trnscrpt, Deptula by Davis, Jamieson, and Putney, Nov 29, 1991, 65.

115. Ed drft intvw trnscrpt, Deptula by Davis, Nov 20, 1991, 39.

116. Air Force targeteers did understand "force application planning," to apply forces and weapons effectively and economically to achieve desired objectives, based on a modeling process weighted toward determining levels of "damage expectancy" and an "estimate of the percentage of the total value of the target that would be destroyed by each increment of force." Force application differed from force packaging. See Pamphlet, AFP 200–18, vol 1, "Target Intelligence Handbook Unclassified Targeting Principles," Oct 1, 1990, 26–29. The handbook did not address aircraft force packaging. Lt Col Baptiste explained after the war that the CENTAF force packaging process did involve considerations of target characteristics, level of threat, and asset capabilities. See brfg, Lt Col Baptiste, "ATO Prep/Composite Force Packaging," Jan 1992, 17, HQ 9AF/DOOW.

117. Drft intvw trnscrpt, Deptula by Da-

vis, Nov 20, 1991, 12.

118. Intvw tape, Deptula by Davis, Nov 20, 1991; Comment, Glosson on draft manuscript, Putney, "Airpower Advantage."

119. Intvw tape, Glosson by Davis, Jamieson, and Putney, Dec 12, 1991. A major aspect of the ATO that required far more skill than Glosson and Deptula acknowledged focused on air refueling requirements, which would distress Glosson on days 3 through 6 of Desert Storm.

120. Ed drft intvw trnscrpt, Glosson by Davis, Jamieson, and Putney, Dec 12, 1991, 99.

121. Comment, Glosson on draft manuscript, Putney, "Airpower Advantage."

122. Intvw trnscrpt, Deptula by Turner, Nov 1, 1990, 12–13; Drft intvw trnscrpt, Deptula by Davis, Nov 20, 1991, 8, 14.

123. Discussion, Capt John R. Glock and Diane T. Putney, Jan 23, 1992; Intvw tape, Maj Michael P. Setnor by Richard G. Davis, May 5, 1992, AFHSO.

124. Intvw tape, Deptula by Davis, Jamieson, and Putney, Jan 8, 1992.

125. Drft intvw trnscrpt, Horner by Davis, Jamieson, and Barlow, Mar 4, 1992, 36.

126. Ltr, Lt Col John D. Sweeney, 9CPS/CXEF, to Diane T. Putney, Aug 25, 1993.

127. Ibid.

128. Ibid.

129. Intvw trnscrpt, Glosson by Turner, Oct 20, 1990, 25–26.

130. Harvey notes, Aug 28, 1990/1610.

131. Ibid.

132. Intvw tape, Deptula by Reynolds, Mann, and Gehri, Jul 23, 1992; Ed drft intvw tape, Deptula by Davis, Nov 20, 1991, 15; Harvey notes, Aug 29, 1990/0245; Deptula notes, Aug 28, 1990/1615, in Deptula's custody.

133. Ltr, Brig Gen Buster C. Glosson to 4TFW/CC, subj: Offensive Air Campaign (Desert Storm), Aug 29, 1990, folder 8, box 4, Black Hole file, GWAPS, AFHRA. See also Intvw trnscrpt, Deptula by Turner, Nov 1, 1990, 13.

134. Intvw trnscrpt, Wilson by Gehri, Mann, and Reynolds, Dec 11, 1991, 52–55; Intvw trnscrpt, Deptula by Turner, Nov 1, 1990, 13; Chronology, "Chronology/Overview of In-Theater Events," Lt Col David A. Deptula, c. Sep 24, 1990, Deptula-Rice folder, Checkmate file, GWAPS, AFHRA.

135. Chronology, "Chronology/Overview of In-Theater Events," Lt Col David A. Deptula, c. Sep 24, 1990, Deptula-Rice folder, Checkmate file, GWAPS, AFHRA; Stanfill notes, Aug 23, 1990/1330–1500.

136. Deptula notes, Aug 30, 1990/1520. The quoted material represents words taken directly from Deptula's notes and may not be the precise words Moore used.

137. Deptula notes, Aug 30, 1990/1520; Intvw tape, Deptula by Putney and Davis, Dec 12, 1992.

138. Intvw tape, Deptula by Putney and Davis, Dec 12, 1992 (quote as Deptula remembered it); Deptula by Reynolds and Mann, Dec 10, 1991, 30; Discussion notes, Col David A. Deptula and Diane T. Putney, Mar 27, 1998.

139. Ed drft intvw trnscrpt, Deptula by Davis, Jamieson, and Putney, Nov 29, 1991, 104.

140. Deptula notes, Sep 7, 1990/0900; Intvw tape, Deptula by Putney and Davis, Dec 12, 1992; Lt Gen Royal N. Moore, Jr., USMC, "Marine Air: There When Needed," intvw with Moore, *Proceedings* (Nov 1991): 64; Intvw tape, Glosson, Henry, and Lewis by Putney, May 20, 1997.

141. The arrival of 12 more F–117s in theater was a planning LIMFAC, requiring more than 48 hours' notice before the aircraft landed in the AOR.

142. Intvw tape, Deptula by Putney and Davis, Dec 12, 1992; Lt Col Ralph W. Getchell, "Stealth in the Storm: Sorting the Facts from the Fiction," quoted in Michael R. Gordon and Gen Bernard E. Trainor, *The Generals' War: The Inside Story of the Conflict in the Gulf*, (Boston: Little, Brown, 1995), 487 n 7; Deptula notes, Sep 26, 1990. See MAPs in folders 1-1-2 and 1-1-3, Black Hole, GWAPS, AFHRA.

143. Intvw tape, Maj Robert Eskridge by TSgt Theodore J. Turner, Mar 3, 1991, Gulf War file, TAC/HO.

144. Getchell, quoted in Gordon and Trainor, *Generals' War*, 487 n 7; Intvw tape, Maj Ralph W. Getchell by MSgt Barry

Spink, May 1992, AFHRA.

145. Gordon and Trainor, *Generals' War,* 487 n. 7 (quote); Intvw tape, Setnor by Davis, May 5, 1992.

146. Ed drft intvw trnscrpt, Glosson by Davis, Jamieson, and Putney, Dec 12, 1991, 62–64; Intvw tape, Glosson by Reynolds, Mann, and Gehri, Jun 4, 1992 (quote).

147. Intvw tape, Glosson by Davis, Jamieson, and Putney, Dec 12, 1991; Intvw tape, Deptula by Davis, Jamieson, and Putney, Jan 8, 1992.

148. Drft intvw trnscrpt, Horner by Putney and Bradley, Apr 26, 1994, 74.

149. Intvw trnscrpt, Henry by Gehri, Mann, and Reynolds, [Jun 2, 1992], 63.

150. Ed drft intvw trnscrpt, Glosson by Davis, Jamieson, and Putney, Dec 12, 1992, 62.

151. Intvw trnscrpt, Henry by Gehri, Mann, and Reynolds, [Jun 2, 1992], 63.

Chapter 7

1. Schwarzkopf, *It Doesn't Take a Hero*, 329–334.

2. Intvw tape, Horner by Gehri and Reynolds, Dec 2, 1991.

3. DoD, *Conduct of the Persian Gulf War*, 92–94; Deptula notes, Aug 31, 1990/2010.

4. DoD, *Conduct of the Persian Gulf War,* 10.

5. Brfg, "Instant Thunder Concept of Operations and Execution," Aug 26, 1990, 34, CHP folder 3, GWAPS, AFHRA; Drft memo, "Desert Storm Phase I," [Aug 28, 1990], folder 6, Deptula file, GWAPS, AFHRA.

6. Deptula notes, Aug 31, 1990/2010; MAP, Aug 29, 1990/0945, CHSH 20-13, GWAPS, AFHRA; MAP, Aug 31, 1990/1630, "Evolution of 1st 24 hours" folder, box 4, Deptula papers, Deptula custody.

7. Deptula notes, Aug 31, 1990 (quote), Sep 1, 1990, and Sep 2, 1990/2115; Intvw tape, Deptula by Putney and Davis, Dec 12, 1992; Diagram, Lt Col Deptula, Sep 2, 1990, folder 19E, Deptula file, GWAPS, AFHRA; OPORD, "COMUSCENTAF Operations Order Offensive Campaign—Phase I," Sep 2, 1990, C-2-4, "Other Documents" folder, Black Hole, GWAPS, AFHRA; Brfg, "Offensive Campaign Phase I," Sep 3, 1990, CHP 3, GWAPS, AFHRA.

8. Msg, HQ USAF/XOXW to USCENTAF/DO, Personal for Brig Gen Glosson, 062332Z Sep 90, subj: Targeting Iraq's Republican Guard Army, Out-msg folder, Checkmate, GWAPS, AFHRA.

9. For the Republican Guard targeting changes in the MAPs, see "Evolution of 1st 24 hours" folder, box 4, Deptula papers, Deptula custody.

10. Deptula notes, Sep 2, 1990/2115 and 2245.

11. Drft transcript of dictation notes on tape, Deptula, [1991], Aug 24, 1990, 50; Deptula notes, Sep 2, 1990/2300 and Sep 3, 1990; MAP, Sep 3, 1990/1000, folder 8, box 4, Black Hole, GWAPS, AFHRA; MAP, "Evolution of the 1st 24 hours" folder, box 4, Deptula papers, Deptula custody; Harvey notes, Sep 8, 1990/1705; Stanfill notes, Sep 5, 1990. The Instant Thunder OPORD had stated about the F–15Es, "Eagles don't plan on going into Baghdad SAM rings or north of Baghdad." See also Jennifer Palmer, "Missile Protection to Improve for F–15E," *Air Force Times,* Dec 28, 1998, 9.

12. Khaled, *Desert Warrior,* 175, 181.

13. Deptula notes, Aug 31, 1990. See MAPs in folder "Evolution of 1st 24 hours," folder, box 4, Deptula papers, Deptula custody.

14. Intvw tape, Deptula by Putney, Feb 14, 1994.

15. Deptula notes, Sep 1, 1990, [1315]; Drft trnscrpt of dictation notes on tape, Deptula, [1991], Sep 1, 1990, 79–81.

16. List, "Phase II and III Attrition Goals [Approximate] (As of 30 Aug 90)," CENTCOM J–5 After Action Rpt, vol 1, Tab R, Guthe file, GWAPS, AFHRA; Brfg, War Plans Briefing, Sep 5, 1990, CENTCOM J–5, 15, in CENTCOM J–5 After Action Rpt,

vol 6, Tab A, Guthe file, GWAPS, AFHRA; Drft trnscrpt of dictation notes, Deptula, [1991], Sep 1, 1990, 80.

17. Deptula notes, Sep 2, 1990, 1000; Drft trnscrpt of dictation notes on tape, Deptula, [1991], Sep 2, 1990, 82.

18. Deptula notes, Sep 3, 1990/1600; Memo for record, "Answers to Questions in Letter—Reference Planning for Phase II/ Phase III," Feb 25, 1993, Crigger file, HQ NORAD/IGD, Peterson AFB, Colo. (Crigger quote).

19. Comment, Horner on draft manuscript, Putney, "Airpower Advantage."

20. Intvw tape, Deptula by Putney, Feb 14, 1994.

21. Ibid.

22. Brfgs, "Offensive Campaign Phase I," Sep 3 and Aug 27, 1990, CHP 3, GWAPS, AFHRA.

23. Ibid., Sep 3, 1990. Although the Target List briefing slide showed 171 as the total for the CENTCOM and CENTAF list, the correct sum was 174.

24. Ibid.

25. Comment, Horner on draft manuscript, Putney, "Airpower Advantage."

26. Brfg, "Offensive Campaign Phase I," Sep 3, 1990, CHP 3, GWAPS, AFHRA; DoD, *Conduct of the Persian Gulf War*, 28.

27. Brfg, "Offensive Campaign Phase I," Sep 3, 1990, CHP 3, GWAPS, AFHRA.

28. Intvw tape, Deptula by Putney, Feb 14, 1994.

29. Msg, USCENTAF REAR to CJCS, subj: Response Time Reevaluation, 201325 Sep 90.

30. OPORD, COMUSCENTAF Operations Order Offensive Campaign—Phase I, Sep 2, 1990, B-1 to B-5, "Other Documents" folder, Black Hole file, GWAPS, AFHRA.

31. Ibid., 2.

32. Ibid., C-5-1; Brfg, Offensive Campaign Phase I, Sep 3, 1990, CHP 3, GWAPS, AFHRA.

33. Stanfill notes, Sep 4, 1990.

34. Schwarzkopf, *It Doesn't Take a Hero*, 353–354.

35. Intvw trnscrpt, Gen H. Norman Schwarzkopf, USA (Ret), for "The Gulf War," Frontline, WGBH Educational Foundation, Public Broadcasting Service, www.pbs.org/wgbh/pages/frontline/gulf/oral/schwarzkopf/4.html.

36. Intvw tape, Deptula by Putney and Davis, Dec 12, 1992; Stanfill notes, Sep 4, 1990.

37. Intvw tape, Deptula by Putney, Feb 14, 1994; Deptula notes, Sep 3, 1990 (quote).

38. Deptula notes, Sep 3, 1990.

39. Comment, Horner on draft manuscript, Putney, "Airpower Advantage"; Drft trnscrpt of dictation notes, Deptula, [1991], Sep 3, 1990, 87.

40. Deptula notes, Sep 3, 1990/2015; Intvw tape, Deptula by Putney, Feb 14, 1994.

41. Comment, Horner on draft manuscript, Putney, "Airpower Advantage."

42. Notes, Col Phillip Meilinger, Sep 1990, Kurt Guthe file, GWAPS, AFHRA; Harvey notes, Aug 29, 1990/1345; Msg, USAF/XOXW to USCENTAF/DO, Pass to Lt Col Harvey, 282006Z Aug 90, subj: Counterair Campaign, and Msg, USAF/XOXW to USCENTAF/DO, Pass to Lt Col Harvey, 282011Z Aug 90, subj: Multinational Force (MNF) Participation, both in folder 5, box 7, Black Hole file, GWAPS, AFHRA; Drft intvw trnscrpt, Deptula by Davis, Nov 20, 1991, 7 (quote); Brfg, Lt Col David A. Deptula to AF/HO and CAFH staff, Jan 8, 1992; Msg, USAF/XOXW to USCENTAF/DO, Personal for Brig Gen Glosson, 012012Z Sep 90, subj: OCA–Airfield Attack, Msg, USAF/XOXW to USCENTAF/DO, Personal for Brig Gen Glosson, 012015Z Sep 90, subj: LIMFAC for Rapid Execution of Instant Thunder, Msg, USAF/XOXW to USCENTAF/DO, Personal for Brig Gen Glosson, 012035Z Sep 90, subj: Status of Additional GBU–15, and Msg, USAF/XOXW to USCENTAF/DO, Personal for Brig Gen Glosson, 012100Z Sep 90, subj: SRBM Threat, all four in folder 5, box 7, Black Hole file, GWAPS, AFHRA:.

43. Stanfill notes, Sep 4 and 5, 1990; Harvey notes, Sep 5, 1990/1600, and Sep 6, 1990/0730; Intvw trnscrpt, Adams by Gehri and Reynolds, Feb 3, 1992, 22 (quote).

44. The seven messages from Warden to Glosson are in folder 5, box 7, Black Hole file, GWAPS, AFHRA.

45. Stanfill notes, Sep 8, 1990.

46. Intvw trnscrpt, Alexander by Gehri and Reynolds, May 30, 1991, 40, 43; Discussion notes, Col Emery M. Kiraly and Diane T. Putney, Sep 3, 1992, AFHSO; Paper, XOXW to XOXWF, Sep 16, 1990, NA 247, GWAPS, AFHRA.

47. Warden requested and received assistance from Dr. Richard P. Hallion, an aerospace historian, SAF/OSX, who received the Instant Thunder briefing and who, on August 24, 1990, provided the colonel with the study, "Expectations of Success of Iraqi Forces during a Coastal Drive from Kuwait in Light of Historical Experience," HQ USAF/HO.

48. Drft intvw trnscrpt, Deptula by Davis, Jamieson, and Putney, Nov 29, 1991, 66 (1st quote); Intvw trnscrpt, Adams by Gehri and Reynolds, Feb 3, 1992, 22 (2d quote); Intvw tape, Alexander by Putney, Nov 26, 1993; Intvw trnscrpt, Warden by Gehri, Reynolds, and Mann, May [n.d.] 1991, 107; Intvw tape, Warden by Putney et al., Feb 6, 1992; Brfg notes by Putney, Warden to AF/HO and CAFH, Feb 6, 1992; Thompson notes, Oct 27, 1990.

49. Intvw trnscrpt, Alexander by Gehri, Reynolds, and Mann, Jun 3, 1992, 29, 47.

50. Stanfill notes, Sep 8, 1990; Deptula notes, Sep 9, 1990.

51. Comment, Horner on draft manuscript, Putney, "Airpower Advantage."

52. Deptula notes, Sep 9, 1990; Talking notes, Instant Thunder (Offensive Campaign Phase I) Planning Assessment—24 Sep 90, Lt Col David A. Deptula, Deptula/Rice folder, Checkmate, GWAPS, AFHRA; Drft trnscrpt of dictation notes on tape, Deptula, [1991], Sep 6 and 9, 1990, 93, 96, 100–101, 103.

53. Deptula notes, Sep 6, 1990; Drft intvw trnscrpt, Horner by Putney and Bradley, Apr 26, 1994, 49; Horner, "Air Power Growing Beyond Desert Storm," 70; Intvw tape, Glosson, Henry, and Lewis by Putney, May 20, 1997.

54. Msg, COMUSCENTAF FWD to USCINCCENT FWD, 211800 Aug 90, subj: Joint Electronic Warfare Campaign.

55. Intvw tape, Henry by Putney, Feb 18, 1998; Intvw tape, Henry by Putney, Jul 3, 1997; Comment, Glosson on draft manuscript, Putney, "Airpower Advantage"; Drft intvw trnscrpt, Horner by Putney and Bradley, Apr 26, 1994, 49–50.

56. For Adnan 1 and Baghdad 1 targeting, see Deptula notes, Sep 4, 1990; MAP, Sep 6, 1990 and MAP, Oct 7, 1990, in "Evolution of 1st 24 hours" folder, box 4, Deptula papers, Deptula custody; Memo with atch, Lt Gen Jimmie V. Adams to XOXW, n.s., Nov 1, 1990, CHSH 95-20, GWAPS, AFHRA; Intvw tape, Deptula by Putney, Apr 11, 1994.

57. Deptula notes, Sep 6–11, 1990; MAPs, Sep 6–11, 1990, folder 1-1-2, Black Hole, GWAPS, AFHRA; Intvw tape, Getchell by Spink, May 1992; Intvw tape, Deptula by Putney, Apr 11, 1994.

58. For evidence that the border EW sites at H–21 and SAD21 target at H–09 were struck, in part, in relationship to the EF–111 jamming for F–117s, see Deptula notes, Sep 9, 1990; Intvw tape, Deptula by Putney, Apr 11, 1994; DoD, *Conduct of the Persian Gulf War*, 115.

59. Intvw trnscrpt, Henry by Gehri, Mann, and Reynolds, Jun 2, 1992, 84–85 (quotes), 87–89.

60. Memo, Wayne Thompson, AFHSO, former Checkmate historian, to Diane Putney, Mar 31, 1994; Discussion, Wayne Thompson and Diane Putney, Mar 31, 1994; Comment Glock on draft manuscript, Putney, "Airpower Advantage."

61. Memo, Maj Buck Rogers, XOXWF, to BG Glosson, subj: Iraqi Telecommunication Vulnerability, Oct 10, 1990, (quote), box 11c, Black Hole file, GWAPS, AFHRA; Ed drft intvw trnscrpt, Deptula by Davis, Jamieson, and Putney, Jan 8, 1992, 192.

62. Harvey notes, Sept 10, 19, 21, 23, and Oct 25, 1990; Deptula notes, Oct 25, 1990; Pt paper, Col Warden, XOXW, "Working Group Liaison Activity," Sep 10, 1990, CC folder 58, Checkmate file, GWAPS, AFHRA; Working paper, "Defense Intelligence Team Report Operation Desert

Shield," Nov 25, 1990, 5, NA 187, GWAPS, AFHRA.

63. Drft intvw trnscrpt, Christon by Putney, Apr 25, 1994, 99.

64. MAP, Oct 25, 1990, folder 1-1-4, Black Hole, GWAPS, AFHRA; Study, DIA, "Desert Storm BDA Imagery Review," DDX-2900-489-91 vol 4, 40, DIA.

65. MAP, Jan 10, 1991/2200 with changes 1, 2, 3, Jan 16, 1991/2121, folder 3, box 1, Black Hole file, GWAPS, AFHRA.

66. Drft transcript of dictation notes on tape, Deptula, [1991], Sep 6, 1990, 96; *GWAPS,* vol 2, part 1, *Operations*, 119; Notes, Black Hole planner, Sep 23, 1990, Deptula custody.

67. Memo for record, Answers to Questions in Letter—Reference Planning for Phase II/Phase III, Col James C. Crigger, Jr., Feb 25, 1993, Crigger file, HQ NORAD/IGD, Peterson AFB, Colo.

68. Intvw trnscrpt, Deptula by Turner, Nov 1, 1990, 15; Deptula notes, Sep 12, 1990; Intvw tape, Deptula by Gehri, Reynolds, and Mann, Jul 23, 1992.

69. Deptula notes, Sep 12 and 13, 1990; Memo, Lt Col David A. Deptula to Secretary Rice, Oct 9, 1990, Deptula file, GWAPS, AFHRA.

70. Deptula notes, Sep 13, 1990.

71. Intvw trnscrpt, Deptula by Turner, Nov 1, 1990, 16–17.

72. Ibid., 17.

73. Ibid., 18 (quote); Deptula notes, Sep 12, 1990; Drft trnscrpt of dictation notes on tape, Deptula, [1991], Sep 12, 1990, 109–110.

74. Intvw tape, Moore by Reynolds, Gehri, and Mann, Sep 21, 1992; Intvw tape, Deptula by Putney and Davis, Dec 12, 1992.

75. Brfgs, Offensive Campaign Phase I, Sep 13 and Sep 3, 1990, CHP 3, GWAPS, AFHRA.

76. Intvw trnscrpt, Horner by Gehri and Reynolds, Dec 2, 1991, 42–43.

77. Brfg, Offensive Campaign Phase I, Sep 13, 1990, CHP 3, GWAPS, AFHRA.

78. Ibid.

79. Deptula notes, Sep 13, 1990/0947.

80. Ibid. (1st quote); Schwarzkopf Frontline intvw, www.pbs.org/wgbh/pages/frontline/gulf/oral/schwarzkopf/2.html (2d quote).

81. Brfg, Offensive Campaign Phase I, Sep 13, 1990, CHP 3, GWAPS, AFHRA.

82. Intvw trnscrpt, Adams by Gehri and Reynolds, Feb 3, 1992, 26.

83. Ibid. (quote); Rick Atkinson, "The Chief Who Said Too Much," *Washington Post*, Sep 23, 1990, 1–2(B).

84. Atkinson, "Chief Who Said Too Much," 1(B); Intvw trnscrpt, Adams by Gehri and Reynolds, Feb 3, 1992, 27.

85. Intvw trnscrpt, Olsen by Turner, Sep 30–Nov 16, 1990, 107; Intvw trnscrpt, Adams by Gehri and Reynolds, Feb 3, 1992, 26; Comment, Horner on draft manuscript, Putney, "Airpower Advantage."

86. Atkinson, "Chief Who Said Too Much," 2(B) (quotes).

87. Rick Atkinson, "U.S. to Rely on Air Strikes If War Erupts," *Washington Post*, Sep 16, 1990, 1(A).

88. Ibid.

89. Drft intvw trnscrpt, Horner by Putney and Bradley, Apr 26, 1994, 70 (2d quote) and 72 (1st quote).

90. Intvw tape, Glosson, Henry, and Lewis by Putney, May 20, 1997.

91. Intvw trnscrpt, Alexander by Gehri, Reynolds, and Mann, May 30, 1991, 47.

92. Ibid., 47–49 (quotes).

93. Statement, "Secretary of Defense Richard Cheney Meets with Regional Reporters," Sep 17, 1990 in *Public Statements of Richard B. Cheney, Secretary of Defense*, vol 4, 1990, Historical Office, Office of the Secretary of Defense.

94. Statement and Q&A, "Secretary of Defense Richard B. Cheney Press Briefing for Reporters Covering the Defense Department…," Sep 17, 1990, in *Public Statements of Richard B. Cheney, Secretary of Defense*, vol 4, 1990, Historical Office, Office of the Secretary of Defense.

95. Drft intvw trnscrpt, Dugan by Reynolds, Aug 15, 1991, 25.

96. Ibid., 11, 26; Intvw trnscrpt, Adams by Gehri and Reynolds, Feb 3, 1992, 35.

97. Drft intvw trnscrpt, Dugan by Reynolds, Aug 15, 1991, 31–32 (quote). For the CJCS's view of Dugan's ouster, see Powell, *My American Journey,* 476–478.

98. President Ford issued Executive Order 11905 on February 18, 1976, which prohibited political assassination, and President Reagan signed Executive Order 12333 on December 4, 1981, which tightened such restrictions.

99. Drft intvw trnscrpt, Dugan by Reynolds, Aug 15, 1991, 32.

100. *GWAPS,* vol 4, part 1, *Weapons, Tactics, and Training*, 2.

101. The targeting of individuals, nonetheless, was not U.S. *policy*, despite its legality in wartime circumstances.

102. For a description and sketch of a "gorilla" package, see *GWAPS,* vol 4, part 1, *Weapons, Tactics, and Training*, 162–165.

103. Comments, Glosson on draft manuscript, Putney, "Airpower Advantage"; MAP, Sep 9, 1990, Black Hole folder 1-1-2, GWAPS, AFHRA; Drft trnscrpt of dictation notes on tape, Deptula, [1991], Sep 5 and 11, 1990, 78, 90, 106; Deptula notes, Sep 6, 1990.

104. Comments, Glosson on draft manuscript, Putney, "Airpower Advantage"; Ed drft intvw trnscrpt, Deptula by Davis, Jamieson, and Putney, Jan 8, 1992, 136–138; Intvw tape, Glosson by Davis, Jamieson, and Putney, Dec 12, 1991; Stanfill notes, Sep 17, 1990/1540L; Intvw trnscrpt, Henry by Reynolds, Gehri, and Mann, Jun 2, 1992, 68–69, 84–85; Memo, Warden to Gen Adams, n. s., n.d., CHSH 84-1, GWAPS, AFHRA; OPLAN, Instant Thunder MCMXC, Aug 17, 1990, 105–106, CHSH 1-8, GWAPS.

105. Intvw trnscrpt, Henry by Gehri, Mann, and Reynolds, Jun 2, 1992, 97.

106. Drft intvw trnscrpt, Henry by Putney, Jul 3, 1997, 53–54; Discussion, Warden and Putney, Sep 28, 2001.

107. Msg, USAF/XOXW to USCENTAF FWD/DO, 080103Z Sep 90, subj: DSFIT, GWAPS, AFHRA.

108. Drft intvw trnscrpt, Henry by Putney, Jul 3, 1997, 54.

109. Harvey notes, Sep 6, 1990/0730 and Sep 10, 1990/1145 and 1205; Intvw trnscrpt, Henry by Reynolds, Gehri, and Mann, Jun 2, 1992, 68–70; Msg, USAF/XOXW to USCENTAF FWD/DO, 080103Z Sep 90, subj: DSFIT, GWAPS, AFHRA; Memo, Maj Buck Rogers, XOXWF, to XO, Oct 4, 1990, subj: Drone Support for CENTCOM (Scathe Mean), CHSH 84-1, GWAPS, AFHRA.

110. Harvey notes, Sep 14, 1990/1215 and Sep 21, 1990/1820; Intvw tape, Deptula by Davis, Jamieson, and Putney, Jan 8, 1992; Note, Maj Bill Holway to Col Warden, n.s., n.d., CHSH 84-1, GWAPS, AFHRA.

111. Deptula notes, Sep 13, 15, 16, and 18, 1990; MAP, Sep 15, 1990/1500, folder 8 box 4, Black Hole, GWAPS, AFHRA; Msg, USCINCCENT to Joint Staff, 200800Z Sep 90, n.s., SCATHE MEAN file, GWAPS, AFHRA.

112. Comments, Glosson on draft manuscript, Putney, "Airpower Advantage"; Drft intvw trnscrpt, Henry by Putney, Jul 3, 1997, 53–54; Intvw trnscrpt, Henry by Gehri, Mann, and Reynolds, Jun 2, 1992, 73, 74,

113. Msg, SAF/AQL to HQ AFLC/AZ, 242130Z Sep 90, n.s., Scathe Mean file, GWAPS, AFHRA.

114. Brfg sheet, Test Results, n.d., CHSH 84-1, GWAPS, AFHRA; Memo, Maj Buck Rogers, XOXWF, to XO, Oct 4, 1990, subj: Drone Support for CENTCOM (Scathe Mean), CHSH 84-1, GWAPS, AFHRA; Stanfill notes, Oct 4, 1990.

115. Staff summary sheet, Maj Bill Holway, XOXW, Scathe Mean Update, Oct 22, 1990, CHSH 84-1, GWAPS, AFHRA.

116. Ibid.; "BQM–74 Drones Operated by Former GLCM Unit…," *Aviation Week & Space Technology* (Apr 27, 1992): 20; Capt Phil Smith, "Tactical Deception in the Desert—Scathe Mean," in Capt Michael P. Vriesenga, ed., *From the Line in the Sand: Accounts of USAF Company Grade Officers in Support of Desert Shield/Desert Storm* (Maxwell AFB, Ala.: AU Press, 1994), 93–101; Intvw trnscrpt, Ryan by Gehri and Reynolds, Sep 4, 1992, 29–30.

117. "BQM–74 Drones Operated by Former GLCM Unit…," 20; Intvw trnscrpt, Henry by Gehri, Reynolds, and Mann, Jun 2, 1992, 69.

118. Intvw trnscrpt, Henry by Gehri, Reynolds, and Mann, Jun 2, 1992, 75; "BQM–74 Drones Operated by Former GLCM Unit…," 20.

119. Drft intvw trnscrpt, Henry by Putney,

Jul 3, 1997, 54–63; Msg, AFEWC/CC to SAF/AQP, 182100Z Sep 91, subj: Constant Light Report No. 11—Air Force Unmanned Aerial Vehicle (UAV) Effectiveness, NA 245, GWAPS, AFHRA.

120. Pt paper, Col Warden, XOXW, "Working Group Liaison Activities," Sep 10, 1990, folder 5, box 7, Black Hole file, GWAPS, AFHRA; Intvw tape, Glosson by Reynolds, Gehri, and Mann, Jun 4, 1992; Harvey notes, Sep 8, 1990/1705; Intvw tape, Glock by Putney, Oct 26, 1992.

121. Intvw trnscrpt, Adams by Gehri and Reynolds, Feb 3, 1992, 32.

122. Deptula notes, Sep 13, 1990.

123. Comment, Glosson on draft manuscript, Putney, "Airpower Advantage."

124. Msg, 37TFW (Deployed)/CC to USCENTAF HQ ELEM FWD/XX, Personal for BG Glosson, 131400Z Sep 90, subj: Intelligence Support, folder 18E, Deptula file, GWAPS, AFHRA.

125. Ibid.; Drft intvw trnscrpt, Maj Robert J. Heston by Mark D. Mandeles and Lt Col Sanford S. Terry, Oct 16 and 19, 1992, 19–20.

126. Msg, 37TFW (Deployed)/CC to USCENTAF HQ ELEM FWD/XX, Personal for BG Glosson, 131400Z Sep 90, subj: Intelligence Support, folder 18E, Deptula file, GWAPS, AFHRA.

127. Ibid.

128. Ibid.; Brfg, Intel Systems Support to Desert Shield, HQ TAC/INYS, CHSH 91-1, GWAPS, AFHRA; Brfg, Air Force Intelligence: Present and Future, Col George Souza file, HQ USAF/INX; Statement, Maj Gen Richard E. Hawley, Director of Operations, HQ USAF, "Tactical Intelligence and Related Activities," Apr 16, 1991, Checkmate Read file, GWAPS, AFHRA.

129. Msg, 37 TFW (Deployed)/CC to USCENTAF HQ ELEM FWD/XX, Personal for BG Glosson, 131400Z Sep 90, subj: Intelligence Support, folder 18E, Deptula file, GWAPS, AFHRA; Deptula notes, Sep 12, 1990.

130. Drft intvw trnscrpt, Heston by Mandeles and Terry, Oct 16 and 19, 1992, 1–48.

131. Ibid., 2, 15–18; Brfg on video, Maj Joe Azzato to Air Force Targeting Conference, Oct 31–Nov 1, 1991, AFIA/INT, Bolling AFB, D.C.

132. Drft intvw trnscrpt, Heston by Mandeles and Terry, Oct 16 and 19, 1992, 13–20.

133. Msg, 37TFW (Deployed)/CC to USCENTAF HQ ELEM FWD/XX, Personal for BG Glosson, 131400 Sep 90, subj: Intelligence Support, folder 18E, Deptula file, GWAPS, AFHRA.

134. Drft intvw trnscrpt, Horner by Putney and Bradley, Apr 26, 1994, 73.

135. Drft intvw trnscrpt, Heston by Mandeles and Terry, Oct 16 and 19, 1992, 19; Intvw tape, Deptula by Reynolds, Gehri, and Mann, Jul 24, 1992.

136. Harvey notes, Sep 14, 1990/1630 and Sep 15, 1990/1015; Deptula notes, Sep 16, 1990.

137. Telecon notes, Col John Leonardo, USAF (Ret), with Diane T. Putney, Jan 5, 1994, AFHSO.

138. Ibid.; Deptula notes, Sep 12, 1990; Harvey notes, Sep 8, 1990/1200; Intvw tape, Glock by Putney and Davis, Aug 27, 1992.

139. Telecon notes, Col John Leonardo, USAF (Ret), with Diane T. Putney, Jan 5, 1994; Drft intvw trnscrpt, Horner by Putney and Bradley, Apr 26, 1994, 75.

140. Drft intvw trnscrpt, Horner by Putney and Bradley, Apr 26, 1994, 75; Intvw trnscrpt, Olsen by Turner, Sep 30–Nov 16, 1990, 112.

141. Drft intvw trnscrpt, Heston by Mandeles and Terry, Oct 16 and 19, 1992, 15, 18; Comment, CMSgt John Burton on draft manuscript, Putney, "Airpower Advantage."

142. Drft intvw trnscrpt, Horner by Putney and Bradley, Apr 26, 1994, 12, 14.

143. Rpt, Defense Intelligence Memorandum, DIM 3–91, subj: IAFCTDCW, Jan 1991, 2–3; DoD, *Conduct of the Persian Gulf War*, 15; Msg, DIA to DIACURINTEL et al., subj: ICABWC, Aug 16, 1990, frame 360, reel 23629, AFHRA; Christine Gosden, "Why I Went, What I Saw," *Washington Post*, Mar 11, 1998, A19. Iran also acquired chemical weapons and used them a few times against Iraq in 1987 and 1988. See Anthony H. Cordesman and Abraham R. Wagner, *The Iran-Iraq War*, The Lessons of Modern War Series (Boulder, Colo.: West-

view Press, 1990), 513.

144. Msg, USCENTAF/CC to HQ TAC/DO/LG, 061400Z Aug 90, subj: Chemical Warfare Defense Requirements, CHSH 100-33, GWAPS, AFHRA.

145. Msg, HQ SAC/INOO to AIG 7858 et al., 100718Z Aug 90, subj: Iraq-Kuwait Update…," CHSH 119-57, GWAPS, AFHRA.

146. Master target list, Sep 13, 1990, folder 6, box 4, Black Hole file, GWAPS, AFHRA.

147. DoD, *Conduct of the Persian Gulf War*, 640; Congress, House, Committee on Armed Services, Subcommittee on Oversight and Investigations, "Intelligence Successes and Failures in Operations Desert Shield/Storm," 103d Cong., 1st sess., Aug 1993, report issued with press release, 35; Rpt, Defense Intelligence Memorandum, DIM 3-91, subj: IAFCTDCW, Jan 1991, 7; Intvw tape, Lt Col Bobby Marion by Diane T. Putney, Jun 4, 1992, AFHSO; Bill McAllister and Dana Priest, "CIA Knew in '84 of Iraq Poison Gas," *Washington Post,* A–1, A–29.

148. DoD, *Conduct of the Persian Gulf War,* 15. See also msg, DIA to DIACURINTEL, subj: ICABWC, Aug 16, 1990, frame 360, reel 23629, AFHRA.

149. OPORD, Instant Thunder MCMXC, Aug 17, 1990, p 19, CHSH 1-8, GWAPS, AFHRA; Master target list, Sep 13, 1990, folder 6, box 4, Black Hole file, GWAPS, AFHRA.

150. Msg, USCINCCENT/CCCS to JCS/J–3-JOD/JSJ, 141736Z Sep 90, subj: USCINCCENT Joint No-Fire Target List 'JNFTL' for Operation Desert Shield," CHSH 100-26, GWAPS, AFHRA.

151. Memo, Warden to General Adams, n.s., Sep 24, 1990, NA 526, GWAPS, AFHRA.

152. Ed drft intvw trnscrpt, Deptula by Davis, Jamieson, and Putney, Nov 29, 1991, 75–78; Intvw tape, Glock by Putney and Davis, Aug 27, 1992; Harvey notes, Oct 2, 1990.

153. Intvw tape, Glock by Putney and Davis, Aug 27, 1992; Memo, B Gen Glosson to USCENTAF/CC, subj: Update on BW, [Oct 4, 1990], folder 19G, Deptula file, GWAPS, AFHRA.

154. Memo, B Gen Glosson to USCENTAF/CC, subj: Update on BW, [Oct 4, 1990], folder 19G, Deptula file, GWAPS, AFHRA.

155. Drft memo and atch, Maj Gen James R. Clapper, Jr., to AF/CC, subj: Iraqi Tactics Analysis Team, [c. Nov 1, 1990], CHSH 95-20, GWAPS, AFHRA; Pt paper, subj: TIBWC, [c. Oct 6, 1990], CHSH 100-16, GWAPS, AFHRA. While FAE offered a promising solution for BW, the realization that Iraq possessed FAE munitions in its active inventory posed a new problem for planners: Iraq's using FAEs against Coalition forces. Officers worried that if the Iraqis launched fifty aircraft against Riyadh, a few could get through to deliver FAEs with devastating results. See Harvey notes, Oct 5, 1990/1830; Thompson notes, Oct 19, 1990.

156. Harvey notes, Oct 2, 1990; Deptula notes, Oct 2, 1990.

157. *GWAPS,* vol 2, part 2, *Effects and Effectiveness,* 54–55; DoD, *Conduct of the Persian Gulf War,* 15–16.

158. Paper, OPLAN, Instant Thunder MCMXC, Aug 17, 1990, 19, CHSH 1-18, GWAPS, AFHRA; Thomas A. Keaney and Eliot A. Cohen, *Gulf War Air Power Survey Summary Report* (Washington: Office of the Secretary of the Air Force, 1993), 123.

159. Harvey notes, Sep 1, 1990/0845; Deptula notes, Sep 1, 1990. For a postwar assessment of Iraq's prewar nuclear weapons production capability, see David Kay, "Denial and Deception: Iraq and Beyond," *American Intelligence Journal* (Spring/Summer 1995): 79–88.

160. *GWAPS,* vol 2, part 2, *Effects and Effectiveness,* 316–317; [David Kay], "Q&A: David Kay, Former U.N. Chief Weapons Inspector" in *Desert Shield/Desert Storm: The 10th Anniversary of the Gulf War*, U.S. Central Command (Tampa, Fla.: Faircourt LLC, 2001), 174–175), 208.

161. Deptula notes, Sep 17, 1990; Drft trnscrpt of dictation notes on tape, Deptula, [1991], Sep 16/17 and 18, 1990, 121, 122.

162. *GWAPS,* vol 2, part 2, *Effects and Effectiveness,* 131; Ltr and atch, Capt Eric J. Holdaway, 6975 ESCS, Provisional, to CENTAF/EC, "Iraqi Air Defense Threat As-

sessment—After Action Report," Mar 1, 1991; Intvw tape, Glosson, Henry, and Lewis, by Putney, May 20, 1997.

163. Ltr and atch, Capt Eric J. Holdaway, 6975 ESCS, Provisional, to CENTAF/EC, "Iraqi Air Defense Threat Assessment—After Action Report," Mar 1, 1991, 4; Intvw tape, Glosson by Davis, Jamieson, and Putney, Dec 12, 1991; Intvw trnscrpt, Horner by Gehri and Reynolds, Dec 2, 1991, 54; Intvw tape, Deptula by Davis, Jamieson, and Putney, Jan 8, 1992; Trnscrpt of dictation notes on tape, Deptula, [1991], Sep 18, 1990. SPEAR shared its studies with Checkmate, which passed them to the Special Planning Group. See Gordon and Trainor, *Generals' War,* 106–107.

164. Drft intvw trnscrpt, Christon by Putney, Apr 25, 1994, 115–116.

165. Ibid., 116; Intvw tape, Horner by Davis, Jamieson, and Bradley, Mar 4, 1992.

166. Memo, B Gen Buster C. Glosson to USCENTAF/CC, subj: Eager Anvil Assessment, n.d., Maj Rogers Envelope, Oct–Dec 90, GWAPS; Memo for record and slides, Brig Gen Buster C. Glosson, "Presidential Briefing Slides," folder 12, Deptula file, GWAPS, AFHRA; Rpt, "The Kuwait Air Campaign: An Assessment Prepared for the Chief of Staff," HQ USAF Director of Plans, [Oct 29, 1990], 144–145, CHSH 6-15, GWAPS, AFHRA; DoD, *Conduct of the Persian Gulf War*, 12, 114 map.

167. Christopher M. Centner, "Ignorance Is Risk: The Big Lesson from Desert Storm Air Base Attacks," *Airpower Journal* 6 (Winter 1992): 26, 27 (quotes).

168. Intvw tape, Horner by Gehri and Reynolds, Dec 2, 1991; Intvw tape, Christon by Davis and Barlow, Mar 4, 1992; Harvey notes, Nov 30, 1990/1100.

169. Centner, "Ignorance Is Risk," 25; OPLAN, Instant Thunder MCMXC, Aug 17, 1990, pp 19, 26, CHSH 1-18, GWAPS, AFHRA; DoD, *Conduct of the Persian Gulf War*, 96–97; MAP, Oct 11, 1990/0800, "Evolution of 1st 24 hours" folder, box 4, Deptula papers, Deptula custody; Comment, Glosson on draft manuscript, Putney, "Airpower Advantage."

170. Deptula notes, Sep 1, 1990; Trnscrpt of dictation notes on tape, Deptula, [1991], Sep 1, 1990; Intvw tape, Deptula by Reynolds, Gehri, and Mann, Jul 23, 1992; Alfred Price, "Tornado in the Desert," *Air Force Magazine* (December 1992): 43.

171. Pt paper, Maj Earnhart, XOOSS, Sep 13, 1990, NA 652, GWAPS, AFHRA; Telecon notes, Capt John R. Glock and Diane T. Putney, May 27, 1994, AFHSO; Rpt, "Desert Shield and Desert Storm Bomber Story," HQ SAC/DO, Sep 18, 1991, 13, NA 91, GWAPS, AFHRA; Intvw tape, Deptula by Putney and Davis, Dec 12, 1992; Msg, USCENTAF FWD/STRATFOR to HQ SAC/DO/SBS, 101400 Sep 90, subj: Area Denial Munition Requirement, NA 652, GWAPS, AFHRA.

172. Msg, USCENTAF FWD/STRATFOR to HQ SAC/DO/SBS, 101400Z Sep 90, subj: Area Denial Munition Requirement, NA 652, GWAPS, AFHRA; Msg, HQ SAC/XRH to HQ USAF/XOOSS/LEYY, 132140Z Sep 90, subj: B–52 Class V Modification for Multi-Function Bomb Fuze (MFBF), NA 652, GWAPS, AFHRA; Rpt, "Desert Shield and Desert Storm Bomber Story," HQ SAC/DO, Sep 18, 1991, 13, NA 91, GWAPS, AFHRA.

173. Rpt, "Desert Shield and Desert Shield Bomber Story," HQ SAC/DO, Sep 18, 1991, 13–14, NA 91, GWAPS, AFHRA.

174. Intvw trnscrpt, Glosson by Turner, Oct 18, 1990, 15–16 (quotes); Ed drft intvw trnscrpt, Glosson by Davis, Jamieson, and Barlow, Mar 4, 1992, 68 (quote); Deptula notes, Sep 25, 1990 and Oct 26, 1990; Harvey notes, Sep 27, 1990/1715.

175. Intvw tape, Deptula by Putney and Davis, Dec 12, 1992; Richard Mackenzie, "Apache Attack," *Air Force Magazine* 74 (October 1991): 54–60; Hist, TSgt Randy G. Bergeron, USAF, *Desert Shield/Desert Storm: Air Force Special Operations Command in the Gulf War,* HQ AFSOC/HO, Jan 1997, 80–90.

176. Schwarzkopf, *It Doesn't Take a Hero*, 358 (quotes).

177. Ibid., 358–359; Rick Francona, *Ally to Adversary: An Eyewitness Account of Iraq's Fall from Grace* (Annapolis, Md.: Naval Institute Press, 1999), 71–76.

178. Schwarzkopf, *It Doesn't Take a Hero*, 359 (quote). See also Francona, *Ally to Adversary,* 71–76.

179. Brfg, CENTCOM Offensive Campaign, Oct 11, 1990, in CENTCOM J–5 After Action Report and Supporting Documents, NA 259, GWAPS, AFHRA.

180. Scales, *Certain Victory,* 126; Intvw, General C. Norman Schwarzkopf by Dean Fischer, *Time,* Mar 11, 1991, 27 (quote).

181. Intvw trnscrpt, Loh by Gehri and Reynolds, Sep 19, 1991, 38.

182. Intvw trnscrpt, Glosson by Mann, Gehri, and Reynolds, May 29, 1991, 67 (quote); Intvw, Horner by Gehri and Reynolds, Dec 2, 1991, 45 ("tone it down" reference); Ed drft intvw trnscrpt, Horner by Davis, Jamieson and Barlow, Mar 4, 1992, 15 ("tone it down" reference).

183. Comment, Glosson on draft manuscript, Putney, "Airpower Advantage"; Intvw trnscrpt, Loh by Gehri and Reynolds, Sep 19, 1991, 38; Stanfill notes, Oct 10, 1990; Thompson notes, Oct 10, 1990; Intvw notes (by Cochran), Glosson by Alexander Cochran and GWAPS staff, Apr 9, 1992, 16, GWAPS, AFHRA; Intvw trnscrpt, Warden by Gehri, Reynolds, and Mann, May, n.d., 1991, 99. Loh remembered counseling Glosson how to brief the CINCCENT's plan, whereas Glosson recalled the advice coming from Rice. Gordon and Trainor related that after the briefing, the CINCCENT telephonically told Glosson to "just stick to the facts." See Gordon and Trainor, *Generals' War,* 135.

184. Schwarzkopf, *It Doesn't Take a Hero*, 361.

185. Memo for record and slides, Brig Gen Buster C. Glosson, "Presidential Briefing Slides," folder 12, Deptula file, Checkmate, GWAPS, AFHRA.

186. Ibid.

187. Ibid.

188. Ibid.

189. Ibid.

190. Ibid.

191. Ibid. On or after October 13 in Riyadh, Glosson and Deptula assembled the October 10 and 11 briefing material, and Glosson preserved them with a memo for record stating, "The attached slides were used during the briefing to the President on 11 Oct 90." Missing from the package, though, was the "Decapitate Saddam Regime" sheet, which had raised concerns during the briefing from Baker, Cheney, and Powell. A set of briefing slides identified as "CENTAF Late Sep 90" and "11 Oct 90—Brig Gen Glosson briefed to Pres.," preserved by the Checkmate historian, Dr Wayne Thompson, did include the "Decapitate Saddam Regime" slide, as cited in the text above. What seemed to have happened was that Glosson changed the "Decapitate" slide to respond to the concerns expressed at the White House, and he substituted in the memo for record package a new "Results" slide, in a new format, which eliminated the troublesome "decapitate" phrase.

192. Ibid.

193. Ibid.

194. Ibid.

195. As Deptula accompanied Glosson on the aircraft returning to Riyadh on October 12, the general recounted to him in great detail the briefing presented to the President, including questions and answers. Deptula took notes as Glosson spoke. He later arranged and transcribed the questions and answers and typed them as a memo for record. Glosson reviewed and signed the "memo for record and slides."

196. Memo for record with atch, Brig Gen Buster C. Glosson, "Q&A During Presidential Briefing," folder 12, Deptula file, Checkmate, GWAPS, AFHRA.

197. Notes attached to questions, "Questions for President's Briefing," President folder, GWAPS; Notes, Lt Col Deptula, "Brig Gen Glosson debriefed on his briefing to Pres.," President folder, GWAPS, AFHRA. The quotation marks signify the questions and answers as Glosson remembered and told them to Deptula, who wrote them down.

198. Colonel Blackburn and Generals Horner and Dugan raised questions about targeting Saddam Hussein.

199. Memo for record with atch, Brig Gen Buster C. Glosson, "Q&A During Presidential Briefing," folder 12, Deptula file, Checkmate, GWAPS, AFHRA.

200. Baker, *Politics of Diplomacy,* 442.

201. Memo for record and slides, Brig Gen Buster C. Glosson, "Presidential Briefing Slides," folder 12, Deptula files, Checkmate records, GWAPS, AFHRA; Intvw tape, Deptula by Putney, Apr 11, 1994, 100; Rpt, Desert Storm BDA Imagery Review, Defense Intelligence Agency (DIA), Apr 1991, vol 1, 10, DIA.

202. Powell, *My American Journey,* 485 (1st quote); Schwarzkopf, *It Doesn't Take a Hero*, 361 (2d quote).

203. Drft working papers, "Grd Campaign Concept of Operations," Oct 14, 1990, 1–2, in excerpts from CENTCOM J–5 Plans, Augmentation Cell, After Action Report, vol 9, SAMS, frame 787, reel 27576, AFHRA.

204. Brfg, "CENTCOM Offensive Campaign," "Imperatives," in excerpt from CENTCOM J–5 Plans, Augmentation Cell, After Action Report, vol 9, SAMS, frame 787, reel 27576, AFHRA.

205. Drft working papers, "Grd Campaign Concept of Operations," Oct 14, 1990, 2, excerpts from CENTCOM J–5 Plans, Augmentation Cell, After Action Report, vol 9, SAMS, frame 787, reel 27576, AFHRA. See also Scales, *Certain Victory,* 125.

206. Scales, *Certain Victory,* 126 (quote).

207. Ibid., 126–127.

208. Intvw trnscrpt, Brent Scowcroft, National Security Advisor, for "The Gulf War," Frontline, WGBH, www.pbs.org/wgbh/pages/frontline/gulf/oral/scowcroft/1.html.

209. Schwarzkopf, *It Doesn't Take a Hero*, 356 (quote), 358 (quote); Scales, *Certain Victory*, 126. Col. Tony Gain from CENTCOM noted that on the basis of terrain and Iraqi defenses, planners did try to attack west of the main Iraqi force; it was not a "hey diddle diddle, straight up the middle" offensive. See Intvw tape, Colonel Gain by Reynolds, Oct 21, 1991. Noteworthy, too, was Glosson's comment: "Remember, I thought the air campaign would make the straight-ahead land maneuver okay." See Intvw trnscrpt, Glosson by Mann, Gehri, and Reynolds, May 29, 1991, 61.

210. See for example, Drft CONOPS, USCENTAF/USARCENT JAAT Concept of Operations, Oct 16, 1990, CENTAF file, AFHRA.

211. Intvw trnscrpt, Glosson by Mann, Gehri, and Reynolds, May 29, 1991, 63.

Chapter 8

1. Baker, *Politics of Diplomacy,* 409.

2. Bush and Scowcroft, *World Transformed*, 381.

3. Schwarzkopf Frontline interview, www.pbs.org/wgbh/pages/frontline/gulf/oral/schwarzkopf, p 5 of 10.

4. Cheney Frontline interview, www.pbs.org/wgbh/pages/frontline/gulf/oral/cheney, p 6 of 11.

5. Schwarzkopf, *It Doesn't Take a Hero,* 368–369; Memo with atch, Harry Rowan to Cochran, [May 1992], Cochran files, GWAPS, AFHRA; DoD, *Conduct of the Persian Gulf War,* 67.

6. Scales, *Certain Victory*, 109.

7. Chronology, Diary of Joseph H. Purvis, Sep 7, 1990–Feb 24, 1991, Oct 17–18 entries, Scales Collection, U.S. Army Command and General Staff College, Ft. Leavenworth, Kans.; Scales, *Certain Victory*, 128–129. This group was informally known as the Jedi Knights, after the warrior heroes of the "Star Wars" movies.

8. Hist, Col Richard M. Swain, ARCENT Historian, *Operational Narrative: Operations Desert Shield–Desert Storm*, Sep 24, 1991, 43, HQ USCENTCOM/CCHO (quotes). See also Chronology, Purvis diary, Oct 21 entry; Scales, *Certain Victory*, 129.

9. Scales, *Certain Victory,* 129–130.

10. Powell quote cited from Chronology, Purvis diary, Sep 7, 1990–Feb 24, 1991, 5; DoD, *Conduct of the Persian Gulf War*, 68; Notes by Lt Gen Charles A. Horner, "Oct Mtg with CJCS," Horner's Desert Shield file, HQ USCENTAF, Shaw AFB.

11. Scales, *Certain Victory,* 125; Intvw tape, Glosson by Putney, Aug 30, 1990; Telecon notes, Col Gary R. Ware, USAF (Ret), by Diane Putney, Mar 28, 1994, AFHSO

(quote); Telecon notes, Barry Watts and Gary Ware, Feb 26, 1992, GWAPS, AFHRA; Rpt, Combat Analysis Group After Action Report, 5, frame 758, reel 27576, GWAPS, AFHRA. Maj James Mudd of the Combat Analysis Group was a "semipermanent" member of the Purvis group. See Swain, *"Lucky War,"* 77.

12. Intvw tape, Glosson by Putney, Aug 30, 1990; Intvw notes, Glosson by Cochran and GWAPS personnel, Apr 9, 1992, 15, 18, GWAPS, AFHRA; Intvw tape, Glosson, Henry, and Lewis by Putney, May 20, 1997. Scales wrote, "The traditional rule of thumb says that if a unit suffers 30 percent casualties in close combat it is no longer combat-effective. On the other hand, a first-rate unit with high morale and good leadership can reconstitute its fighting strength if the destruction occurs gradually through attrition rather than suddenly through decisive, unrelenting close-in combat." See Scales, *Certain Victory*, 368. "Combat effectiveness" described "abilities and the fighting quality of a unit." For a discussion of tangible and intangible factors affecting combat effectiveness, see the U.S. Army Field Manual 34–3, "Intelligence Analysis," Mar 1990, 3-5, 3-28, and appendix D.

13. Rpt, Combat Analysis Group After Action Report, 1–6, frame 758, reel 27576, GWAPS, AFHRA; Telecon notes, Gary Ware and Barry Watts, Feb 26, 1992, GWAPS, AFHRA; Telecon notes, Col Gary R. Ware, USAF (Ret), and Diane T. Putney, Mar 28, 1994, AFHSO; Brfg, War Plans Briefing, Sep 5, 1990, CENTCOM J–5, Guthe file, GWAPS, AFHRA; Swain, *"Lucky War,"* 78; Scales, *Certain Victory*, 122, 128–129; DoD, *Conduct of the Persian Gulf War*, 75. For Schwarzkopf's clear force ratio aggregate view, see CENTCOM News Briefing, Gen H. Norman Schwarzkopf, Riyadh, Feb 27, 1991, 1–2, Checkmate/Desert Storm/Rep Guard, GWAPS, AFHRA.

14. Intvw notes, Glosson by Cochran and GWAPS personnel, Apr 9, 1992, 18, GWAPS, AFHRA.

15. Harvey notes, Oct 10, 1990/1710; Deptula notes, Sep 25 and Oct 10, 1990.

16. Brfg, "Gulf Crisis Analysis," Project Air Force, [RAND], Oct 6, 1990, HQ USAF/XOXP.

17. Ibid., 17.

18. Ibid., 20.

19. Ibid., 24–25.

20. Harvey quote in Harvey notes, Oct 9, 1990/1340; Thompson notes, Oct 9, 1990/1345 FA and Oct 10, 1990/1900 FA; Intvw tape, Warden by Putney et al., Feb 6, 1992, AFHSO.

21. Memo, Warden to Gen Loh, c. Oct 10, 1990, n.s., Historian file, GWAPS, AFHRA.

22. Intvw tape, Harvey by Putney and Davis, Jan 14, 1993, AFHSO; DoD, *Conduct of the Persian Gulf War*, 67; Intvw trnscrpt, Warden by Gehri, Oct 22, 1991, 88; Intvw tape, Warden by Putney et al., Feb 6, 1992, AFHSO; Memo, Warden to Gen Adams, Sep 24, 1990, n.s., NA 526, GWAPS, AFHRA; Memo, Wayne Thompson to Kurt Guthe, Apr 6, 1992, subj: Phase III, Kurt Guthe file, GWAPS, AFHRA.

23. Thompson notes, Oct 10, 1990/1900 FA; Secretary's question in Harvey notes, Oct 3, 1990/1400; Intvw tape, Glosson by Putney, Aug 30, 1993.

24. Sikes, a pilot experienced in the O–2, F–4E, and F–16, had been assigned to the 527th Aggressor Squadron at Alconbury, England, immediately before his arrival at the Air Staff in late 1989.

25. Intvw tape, Maj Roy "Mac" Sikes by Diane T. Putney, Apr 7, 1993, AFHSO.

26. Ibid.

27. Ibid.

28. Ibid.

29. Ibid.

30. Ibid.; Intvw tape, Col Mark B. "Buck" Rogers by Diane T. Putney, Sep 18, 1994, AFHSO.

31. Intvw tape, Sikes by Putney, Apr 7, 1993.

32. Ibid.

33. Ibid.

34. Ibid.; Brfg, [Phase III Analysis], Oct 18, 1990, Sikes file, Checkmate, Pentagon (identified by Sikes to Putney).

35. Notes, [Warden], Oct 14, 1990, subj: Modeling Methodology, NA 526, GWAPS, AFHRA.

36. This is the original Instant Thunder. Powell had directed Warden to "kill tanks" which led to the development of Instant Thunder Phase II—ignored by Warden as unimportant.

37. Intvw tape, Sikes by Putney, Apr 7, 1990; Harvey notes, Oct 16, 1990/0955 and 1620; Notes, [Warden], Oct 14, 1990, subj: Modeling Methodology, NA 526, GWAPS, AFHRA; Thompson notes, Oct 25, 1990/0850 FA.

38. Thompson notes, Oct 16, 1990/1000 FA (quote); Memo, Wayne Thompson to Kurt Guthe, Apr 6, 1992, subj: Phase III, Historian file, GWAPS, AFHRA; Harvey notes, Oct 16, 1990/0955 and 1600.

39. Intvw tape, Sikes by Putney, Apr 7, 1993; Thompson notes, Oct 17, 1990/0843 FA; Brfg, [Phase III Analysis], Oct 18, 1990.

40. Brfg, [Phase III Analysis], Oct 18, 1990; Intvw tape, Sikes by Putney, Apr 7, 1993.

41. Brfg, [Phase III Analysis], Oct 18, 1990.

42. Ibid.

43. Intvw tape, Sikes by Putney, Apr 7, 1993. The gun was designed by the Canadian, Gerald Bull, and his Brussels-based firm.

44. Ibid.

45. Brfg, [Phase III Analysis], Oct 18, 1990.

46. Notes by Lt Col Autry, "Phase III Briefing to XO," Oct 18, 1990/1000, Sikes file, Checkmate, Pentagon.

47. Harvey notes, Oct 22, 1990/1100.

48. Ibid.; Thompson notes, Oct 22, 1990/1545 and Oct 27, 1990/0945 FA.

49. Thompson notes, Oct 23, 1990/0820 and 0915; Harvey notes, Oct 23, 1990/0915.

50. Deptula notes, Oct 23, 1990/1230–1540 and Oct 24, 1990.

51. Pt paper, Maj Troy, SAGF, "Observations of Phase 3 of the Plan," Oct 24, 1990, CC72 folder, GWAPS, AFHRA.

52. Memo, Ted Parker to Natalie Crawford, Oct 31, 1990, subj: 10/30/90 Visit to AF/XOXWF (Checkmate), CHSH 6-7, GWAPS, AFHRA.

53. Deptula notes, Oct 26, 1990; Intvw tape, Deptula by Putney and Davis, Dec 12, 1992; Thompson notes, Oct 27, 1990/0945 FA; Glosson quote in intvw tape, Glosson by Putney, Aug 30, 1993.

54. Thompson notes, Oct 27, 1990/1530 FA; Discussion, Wayne W. Thompson with Diane T. Putney, Jan 9, 1995.

55. Intvw tape, Rogers by Putney, Sep 18, 1994; Thompson notes, Oct 27, 1990/0945 FA and 1030 FA. In Checkmate, Wayne Thompson took notes as Warden talked on the telephone, and he continued to take notes after the phone call as Warden met with his staff and discussed the call. See also Harvey notes, Oct 29, 1990/1000.

56. Intvw tape, Rogers by Putney, Sep 18, 1994; Ed drft intvw trnscrpt, Glosson by Davis, Jamieson, and Putney, Dec 12, 1991, 35–37 (quote). JMEM's standard was a 75 percent target acquisition rate, but the Checkmate analysts had used a 95 percent rate, taking into account the desert environment. See *GWAPS,* vol 1, part 1, *Planning,* 172.

57. Intvw trnscrpt, Glosson by Mann, Gehri, and Reynolds, May 29, 1991, 66.

58. Intvw tape, Rogers by Putney, Sep 18, 1994.

59. Ibid.; Intvw tape, Capt Douglas McNary by Diane T. Putney, Aug 9, 1994, AFHSO.

60. Drft intvw trnscrpt, Gen Merrill A. McPeak by Lt Col Suzanne Gehri, Lt Col Edward Mann, and Lt Col Richard Reynolds, Nov 5, 1992, 2 (quotes), CADRE, AU.

61. Brfg, "The Kuwait Air Campaign: An Assessment Prepared for the Chief of Staff," HQ USAF/XOX, [Oct 29, 1990], CHSH 6-15, GWAPS, AFHRA; Harvey notes, Oct 29, 1990/1000.

62. Brfg, "Kuwait Air Campaign," [Oct 29, 1990].

63. Ibid.

64. Harvey notes, Oct 29, 1990/1000; Brfg, "Kuwait Air Campaign," [Oct 29, 1990].

65. Brfg, "Kuwait Air Campaign," [Oct 29, 1990].

66. Harvey notes, Oct 29, 1990/1000; Thompson notes, Oct 29, 1990/1300 FA.

67. Thompson notes, Oct 31, 1990/0943 FA and Nov 1, 1990/0910 FA.

68. Intvw tape, Sikes by Putney, Apr 7,

1993.

69. Drft intvw trnscrpt, Horner by Putney and Bradley, April 26, 1994, 53 (Schwarzkopf's quote); Intvw trnscrpt, Horner by Davis, Jamieson, and Barlow, Mar 4, 1992, 16 (Horner's quote).

70. Intvw trnscrpt, Glosson by Mann, Gehri, and Reynolds, May 29, 1991, 52–53.

71. Intvw tape, Glosson by Putney, Aug 30, 1993 (quote).

72. Intvw tape, Rogers by Putney, Sep 18, 1994.

73. Drft intvw trnscrpt, Henry by Putney, Jul 3, 1997, 82.

74. Powell, *My American Journey,* 487.

75. Congress, Senate, Armed Services Committee, "Crisis in the Persian Gulf Region: U.S. Policy Options and Implications," 101st Cong., 2d sess., 1990, 693–694; Msg, USCINCCENT/CCCC to COMUSNAVCENT et al., 011030Z Nov 90, subj: Campaign Requirements, folder 9, Deptula file, GWAPS, AFHRA (quote); Note, Horner to Buster, n.d., n.s., folder 9, Deptula file, GWAPS, AFHRA; Intvw trnscrpt, Horner by [Burton], [Mar 1991], 7. For a discussion of Powell's view of overwhelming force, see Gordon and Trainor, *Generals' War,* viii–ix.

76. Drft trnscrpt of dictation notes on tape, Deptula, [1991], Nov 2, 1990, 185; Comment, Horner on draft manuscript, Putney, "Airpower Advantage"; Memo, Lt Col David A. Deptula to CENTAF/XX, Nov 2, 1990, subj: Force Structure Changes, folder 1, box 12, Deptula file, GWAPS, AFHRA.

77. Draft intvw trnscrpt, McPeak by Gehri, Mann, and Reynolds, Nov 5, 1992, 13.

78. Frank N. Schubert and Theresa L. Kraus, eds., *The Whirlwind War: The United States Army in Operations Desert Shield and Desert Storm* (Washington: Center of Military History, 1995), 108, 115.

79. Deptula notes, Nov 7, 1990; Thompson notes, Nov 8, 1990/0845 FA; Intvw trnscrpt, Horner by Gehri and Reynolds, Dec 2, 1991, 57.

80. Drft intvw trnscrpt, Col Christopher L. Christon by Diane T. Putney, Apr 25, 1994, 69, AFHSO; Ed drft intvw trnscrpt, Horner by Davis, Jamieson, and Barlow, Mar 4, 1992, 17, AFHSO; Harvey notes, Nov 8, 1990/0730; Deptula notes, Nov 7, 1990. Horner had seen the phrase "preparing the battlefield" in the first version of CENTCOM's four-phased Desert Storm briefing he received in August 1990.

81. Drft intvw trnscrpt, Horner by Putney and Bradley, Apr 26, 1994, 61.

82. Schwarzkopf, *It Doesn't Take a Hero*, 380.

83. Ibid., 384 (1st quote), 380 (2d quote).

84. Notes, by Lt Gen Charles A. Horner, "Dhahran Mtg," Nov 1990, HQ 9AF/CC files, Shaw AFB,

85. Ibid.; Schwarzkopf, *It Doesn't Take a Hero*, 381.

86. Schwarzkopf, *It Doesn't Take a Hero*, 381 (quote); DoD, *Conduct of the Persian Gulf Campaign,* 69.

87. Notes, by Lt Gen Charles A. Horner, "Dhahran Mtg," Nov 1990, HQ 9AF/CC files, Shaw AFB.

88. Swain, *"Lucky War,"* 128; Scales, *Certain Victory,* 180.

89. DoD, *Conduct of the Persian Gulf War,* 69; Schwarzkopf, *It Doesn't Take a Hero,* 383.

90. Joseph Albright, "I Am Not... Going to Waste American Lives," intvw with Gen H. Norman Schwarzkopf, *Atlanta Journal-Constitution*, Oct 28, 1990, 12 (quote).

91. Schwarzkopf, *It Doesn't Take a Hero*, 382; Intvw trnscrpt, Horner by Davis, Jamieson, and Barlow, Mar 4, 1992, 57 (quote); Thompson notes, Oct 26, 1990/1730 FA.

92. Schwarzkopf, *It Doesn't Take a Hero*, 382–383, 453.

93. Ibid., 382–383.

94. Ibid., 383. Iraqi air reconnaissance assets produced imagery and signals intelligence.

95. DoD, *Conduct of the Persian Gulf War,* 78; *GWAPS,* vol 1, part 1, *Planning*, 67–68.

96. Rpt, Combat Analysis Group After Action Report, 5–6, 9, frame 758, reel 27576, GWAPS, AFHRA; DoD, *Conduct of the Persian Gulf War*, 100–101; *GWAPS,* vol 1, part 1, *Planning*, 170 n 85. For discussion of the 50 percent level and force ratio pro-

jections by ARCENT planners in December, see Swain, *"Lucky War,"* 106, and for the CINCCENT's explanation, see CENTCOM news brfg trnscrpt, Gen H. Norman Schwarzkopf, Riyadh, Feb 27, 1991, 1–2. For correlation of forces by axes of attack, see DoD, *Conduct of the Persian Gulf War,* 84.

97. At the start of the ground war, CENTCOM estimated that 450,000 Iraqi troops were in the KTO. See DoD, *Conduct of the Persian Gulf War,* 83, 85, 254. For an explanation of the 336,000 figure, see *GWAPS,* vol 2, part 2, *Effects and Effectiveness*, 162–169.

98. Peay quote in Tom Donnelly, "The Generals War: How Commanders Fought the Iraqis," *Army Times,* Desert Storm After-Action Review," Mar 2, 1992, 14.

99. Deptula notes, Nov 5, 1990; Intvw tape, Deptula by Putney and Davis, Dec 12, 1991; Intvw tape, Sikes by Putney, Apr 8, 1993.

100. Drft intvw trnscrpt, Horner by Putney and Bradley, Apr 26, 1994, 61 (quote), 62; Intvw trnscrpt, Horner by Gehri and Reynolds, Dec 2, 1991, 57.

101. See the different views in intvw trnscrpt, Glosson and Turner, Oct 18, 1990, 12–13, and intvw tape, Glosson by Putney, Aug 30, 1993.

102. Drft trnscrpt of taped dictation notes, Deptula, [1991], Nov 15, 1990, 197.

103. Intvw tape, Rogers by Putney, Sept 18, 1994.

104. The commander's questions were as Rogers remembered Glosson recalling them in intvw tape, Rogers by Putney, Sep 18, 1994.

105. CINCCENT's remark of agreement as remembered by Glosson in intvw tape, Glosson by Putney, Aug 30, 1993; Drft trnscrpt of taped dictation notes, Deptula, [1991], Nov 19, 1990, 199.

106. Later, the plan called for 3 B–52s, not 4, every three hours.

107. Swain, *"Lucky War,"* 110; Brfg trnscrpt, MAPEX, tape D, DRS 15, [Dec 1990], [Brig Gen Buster C. Glosson], 2 (quote), 3, 4, Center for Army Lessons Learned, Ft. Leavenworth; Brfg slides, Theater Campaign, [Dec 1, 1990], 34–35, 40, CHP folder 3, GWAPS, AFHRA. Deptula wrote on the cover sheet that this set of slides was briefed to Schwarzkopf, and research has shown that Glosson gave him the Phase III briefing on November 18, not December 1. The slides generally correlate with the transcript of Glosson's taped remarks at the MAPEX. The author of this volume could not find a package of slides specifically identified as that which Glosson briefed at the MAPEX. She did examine and match the set Deptula dated "Dec 1" with another set he annotated: brfg slides, "Offensive Air Campaign," [Horner to SECDEF], [Dec 20, 1990], CHP folder 3, GWAPS, AFHRA.

108. Brfg trnscrpt, MAPEX, tape D, DRS 15, [Dec 1990], [Brig Gen Buster C. Glosson], 4–6, Center for Army Lessons Learned, Ft. Leavenworth; brfg slides, Theater Campaign, [Dec 1, 1990], 38–39, CHP folder 3, GWAPS, AFHRA.

109. Intvw trnscrpt, Glosson by Mann, Gehri, and Reynolds, May 29, 1991, 66. Unfortunately, Glosson relied on his memory during this interview and did not refer to nor provide slides or notes as he cited exact numbers and weapon types. In the interview, he discussed using the CBU–87 against artillery, but according to the slides dated Dec 1 and Dec 20, he planned to employ CBU–52s against artillery. Glosson's interview statements are important because they provide insight into the thought processes and rationale supporting his conclusions.

110. Intvw trnscrpt, Glosson by Mann, Gehri, and Reynolds, May 29, 1991, 66. As he spoke during the MAPEX, Glosson referred to 6 pieces of artillery for the Republican Guard, but his slides credited 9, and 10 tubes of artillery killed after being hit with 12 MK 20s and 12 CBU–52s, respectively. See brfg trnscrpt, MAPEX, tape D, DRS 15, [Dec 1990], [Brig Gen Buster C. Glosson], 4–5, Center for Army Lessons Learned, Ft. Leavenworth, and brfg slides, Theater Campaign, [Dec 1, 1990], "Friendly Force Assumptions: Phase III Republican Guards," CHP folder 3, GWAPS, AFHRA. See also brfg slides, "Offensive Air Campaign," [Horner to SECDEF], [Dec 20,

1990], 40, CHP folder 3, GWAPS, AFHRA.

111. Intvw trnscrpt, Glosson by Mann, Gehri, and Reynolds, May 29, 1991, 66.

112. Brfg slides, Theater Campaign, [Dec 1, 1990], 40, CHP folder 3, GWAPS, AFHRA. See also brfg slides, "Offensive Air Campaign," [Horner to SECDEF], [Dec 20, 1990], "Friendly Force Assumptions Republican Guards," CHP folder 3, GWAPS, AFHRA.

113. Brfg trnscrpt, MAPEX, tape D, DRS 15, [Dec 1990], [Brig Gen Buster C. Glosson], 5–6, Center for Army Lessons Learned, Ft. Leavenworth.

114. Ibid., 6 (quote); brfg slides, Theater Campaign, [Dec 1, 1990], 42–45, CHP Folder 3, GWAPS, AFHRA. See also brfg slides, "Offensive Air Campaign," [Horner to SECDEF], [Dec 20, 1990], "Results Republican Guards," CHP folder 3, GWAPS, AFHRA.

115. Brfg trnscrpt, MAPEX, tape D, DRS 15, [Dec 1990], [Brig Gen Buster C. Glosson], 8–9, 12, Center for Army Lessons Learned, Ft. Leavenworth; brfg slides, Theater Campaign, [Dec 1, 1990], 47–56, CHP folder 3, GWAPS, AFHRA.

116. Brfg trnscrpt, MAPEX, tape D, DRS 15, [Dec 1990], [Brig Gen Buster C. Glosson], 13, Center for Army Lessons Learned, Ft. Leavenworth.

117. Ibid.

118. *GWAPS,* vol 2 part 1, *Operations*, 155. PGMs were less affected than non-PGMs. Definitions of the medium altitude range vary from 10,000 ft. to 12,000–15,000 ft. See DoD, *Conduct of the Persian Gulf War,* 126, 154, 178.

119. *GWAPS,* vol 2, part 1, *Operations*, 279–280.

120. *GWAPS,* vol 2, part 1, *Operations*, 261; *GWAPS,* vol 2, part 2, *Effects and Effectiveness*, 205–207; Eliot A. Cohen, "The Mystique of U.S. Air Power," *Foreign Affairs* 73 (Jan–Feb): 115–116; Andrews, *Airpower against an Army*, 36.

121. *GWAPS,* vol 2, part 2, *Effects and Effectiveness*, 202–203.

122. *GWAPS,* vol 2, part 1, *Operations*, 285; Brfg trnscrpt, MAPEX, tape D, DRS 15, [Dec 1990], [Brig Gen Buster C. Glosson], 10–12, 14–24, Center for Army Lessons Learned, Ft. Leavenworth. Swain wrote that Glosson lost the trust of the Army commanders at the MAPEX; the transcript of the meeting fails to convey that result. See Swain, *"Lucky War,"* 182. The attrition goal for artillery at the breach sites would soon be 90 percent.

123. Brfg trnscrpt, MAPEX, tape D, DRS 15, [Dec 1990], [Brig Gen Buster C. Glosson], 7–8, Center for Army Lessons Learned, Ft. Leavenworth.

124. Schwarzkopf, *It Doesn't Take a Hero,* 431 (quote); DoD, *Conduct of the Persian Gulf War,* 138; *GWAPS,* vol 2, part 1, *Operations,* 319; *GWAPS,* vol 2, part 2, *Effects and Effectiveness*, 217. For a first-hand description of the Guard's use of dispersal, revetments, decoys, and camouflage, see Andrews, *Airpower Against an Army*, 15, 41, 44, 46–49, 58–59.

125. Swain, *"Lucky War,"* 103–105.

126. Ibid., 106; Scales, *Certain Victory*, 122. For the numbers of Iraqi troops, see *GWAPS,* vol 2, part 2, *Effects and Effectiveness*, 162–169. For additional attacker to defender ratios see DoD, *Conduct of the Persian Gulf War*, 84.

127. *GWAPS,* vol 1, part 2, *Command and Control,* 65–130.

128. DoD, *Conduct of the Persian Gulf War*, 257–263, 493. The JFC–E was associated with the Eastern Area Command (EAC), and the JFC–N, with the Northern Area Command (NAC).

129. Intvw tape, Horner by Davis, Jamieson, and Barlow, Mar 4, 1992; Intvw tape, Corder by Gehri and Reynolds, Feb 4, 1992; Bio sheet, Maj Gen John A. Corder, May 1991, USAF Public Affairs; Bio sheet, Maj Gen Michael S. Hall, Adjutant General, New York National Guard, March 1994, National Guard Bureau.

130. CONOPS, "Concept of Operations Tactical Air Request Net, CAS, Interdiction, and ABCCC, Desert Shield," Oct 5, 1990, frame 990, reel 10264, AFHRA; CONOPS, "Concept of Operations CAS, Interdiction and the TACS, Desert Shield," Change 1, Nov 22, 1990, frame c. 600, reel 10264, AFHRA; CONOPS, "Concept of Operations

for Command and Control of TACAIR in Support of Land Forces, Desert Shield," Jan 1, 1991, frame 642, reel 10264, AFHRA; CONOPS, "Concept of Operations for Command and Control of TACAIR in Support of Land Forces," Feb 22, 1991, frame 738, reel 10264, AFHRA.

131. Handbook, "USCENTAF Combat Plans Handbook," Aug 25, 1990, frame 462, reel 10264, AFHRA; Handout, "Desert Shield Combat Plans Handout," October 1990, frame 398, reel 10264, AFHRA; Handout, Desert Shield Combat Plans Handout, January 1991, frame 808, reel 10211, AFHRA; CONOPS, "USCENTAF/USARCENT JAAT Concept of Operations, Desert Shield," Nov 30, 1990, frame 881, reel 10264, AFHRA.

132. Ltr, Lt Col Robert E. Duncan, Combat Plans, TACS Division, to USCENTAF/DO, Nov 7, 1990, subj: Command, Control, and Employment Conference Report, frame c. 600, reel 10264, AFHRA.

133. CONOPS, "Concept of Operations for Command and Control of TACAIR in Support of Land Forces, Desert Shield," Jan 1, 1991, 1–2, frame 642, reel 10264, AFHRA.

134. Ibid., 2–6.

135. Intvw trnscrpt, Baptiste by Putney and Reynolds, Sep 24, 1992, 11–12.

136. Scales, *Certain Victory,* 189; Swain, *"Lucky War,"* 186.

137. Tom Clancy with General Fred Franks, Jr., USA (Ret), *Into the Storm: A Study in Command* (New York: Putnam's Sons, 1997), 347 (1st quote), 340 (2d quote).

138. CONOPS, "Concept of Operations for Command and Control of TACAIR in Support of Land Forces, Desert Shield," Jan 1, 1991, 18 (quote), 19, frame 642, reel 10264, AFHRA.

139. Ibid., atch 2, i–ii.

140. Ibid., 11–12.

141. Ibid., 12–14.

142. Ed drft intvw, Horner by Davis, Jamieson, and Barlow, Mar 4, 1992, 49–50.

143. Stewart M. Powell, "Friendly Fire," *Air Force Magazine* (December 1991): 61; Zachary A. Lum, "My Brother's Keeper: Technology Tackles Fratricide Problem," *Journal of Electronic Defense,* Aug 1993, 49; Brfg trnscrpt, MAPEX, tape D, DRS 15, [Dec 1990], [Brig Gen Buster C. Glosson], 24, Center for Army Lessons Learned, Ft. Leavenworth. See also msg, USCINCCENT/CCJ6 to COMUSARCENT Main/G2/G3/G6, 131304Z Jan 1991, subj: Antifratricide Measures for Coalition Forces, frame 861, reel 10264, AFHRA; DoD, *Conduct of the Persian Gulf War,* 589–597.

144. Intvw tape, Horner by Davis, Jamieson, and Barlow, Mar 4, 1992; Drft intvw trnscrpt, Horner by Putney and Bradley, Apr 26, 1994, 102; Fred Frostic, *Air Campaign Against the Iraqi Army in the Kuwaiti Theater of Operations* (Santa Monica, Calif.: RAND, 1994), 42 (quote).

145. Mackenzie, "Conversation with Chuck Horner," 63.

146. Andrews, *Airpower Against an Army,* 63; *GWAPS,* vol 2, part 1, *Operations*, 284–285.

147. Intvw trnscrpt, Horner by [Burton], [Mar 1991], 11, (quote); Intvw tape, Deptula by Putney and Davis, Dec 12, 1992, AFHSO. For comprehensive discussion of Desert Shield training, see *GWAPS,* vol 4, part 1, *Weapons, Tactics, and Training*, 343–358, 391–453, and William T. Y'Blood, *Sharpening the Eagle's Talons: The USAF and the Desert Shield Second-Phase Deployment November 9, 1990–January 17, 1991* (Washington: CAFH, 1993), 117–132.

148. Y'Blood, *Sharpening the Eagle's Talons*, 122–126; *GWAPS,* vol 4, part 1, *Weapons, Tactics, and Training*, 411–412; Brfg, Gen H Norman Schwarzkopf, HQ USCENTCOM, Feb 27, 1991, ABC video; Trnscrpt, news brfg, Gen H Norman Schwarzkopf, Riyadh, Saudi Arabia, Feb 27 1991, 1:00 p.m. (EST), Checkmate file, GWAPS, AFHRA.

149. *GWAPS,* vol 4, part 1, *Weapons, Tactics, and Training*, 414–415.

150. Memo for record, Lt Col Robert S. Coombs, USCENTAF, Mar 20, 1991, subj: Desert Shield Training and Exercises; Chart, "Exercise Night Camel (Night AI Trng)," No. 30, AFHSO; Intvw notes, Capt Rich Cleary and Capt Jim Wright by Lt Col Sandy Terry et al., Sep 1–2, 1992, NA 517, GWAPS, AFHRA. Sometimes the nighttime

exercises were called Night Cannon.

151. Maj Michael J. Bodner and Maj William W. Bruner III, "Tank Plinking," *Air Force Magazine* 76 (October 1993): 29–30.

152. Bodner and Bruner, "Tank Plinking," 30.

153. Ibid.; Drft intvw trnscrpt, Horner by Putney and Bradley, Apr 26, 1994, 52 (quote).

154. Andrews, *Airpower Against an Army*, 33.

155. Intvw tape, Horner by Putney, Nov 30, 1996.

156. Andrews, *Airpower Against an Army*, 34; Keaney and Cohen, *Gulf War Air Power Survey Summary Report,* 62; Santoli, ed., *Leading the Way*, 194–195.

157. Andrews, *Airpower Against an Army,* 33–35.

158. Drft intvw trnscrpt, McPeak by Gehri, Mann, and Reynolds, Nov 5, 1992, 20; Intvw trnscrpt, Warden by Gehri and Reynolds, May 1991, 91, 93; Deptula notes, Nov 29 and 30, 1990.

159. Drft intvw trnscrpt, McPeak by Gehri, Mann, and Reynolds, Nov 5, 1992, 17 (1st quote), 18 (2d quote), 20. McPeak's civilian casualty estimates derived from a study of noncombatant casualties by the Human Systems Division of the Air Force Systems Command. See *GWAPS,* vol 1, part 2, *Command and Control*, 377–378 and memo, Col John A. Warden III to Gen Glosson, [Oct 1990], Checkmate, CHSH 46-5, GWAPS, AFHRA.

160. Brfg, "An Analysis of Joint Air Power Capability in the KTO," Dec 11, 1990, CHSH 6, GWAPS, AFHRA; Harvey notes, Dec 11, 1990/0740 and 1100; Thompson notes, Dec 11, 1990.

161. Brfg, "An Analysis of Joint Air Power Capability in the KTO," 5–8, CHSH 6, GWAPS, AFHRA.

162. Ibid., 6–9, 15.

163. After the session, Warden met with officers in Checkmate and debriefed them, and Harvey took notes. See Harvey notes, Dec 11, 1990/0930.

164. The Bush and Powell quotations are as Powell remembered them in Powell Frontline intvw, www.pbs.org/wgbh/pages/frontline/gulf/oral/decision/html, p 2 of 10. See also Powell, *My American Journey,* 487–489.

165. Congress, Senate, Armed Services Committee, "Crisis in the Persian Gulf Region: U.S. Policy Options and Implications," 101st Cong., 2d sess., 1990, 662–663.

166. Ibid., 663.

167. Ibid., 719–720. Initial TACWAR modeling at CENTCOM provided a figure of 25,000 to 30,000 casualties for the ground war. The Center for Strategic and International Studies estimated 30,000. Later TACWAR modeling suggested 9,000 to 10,000 casualties. At the White House on October 11, Lt Col Purvis stated casualties of 8,000 wounded and 2,000 dead. Powell rejected the high estimates believing them to be based on outdated Cold War gaming. He focused on air power attriting the enemy forces and fast-paced ground maneuver and concluded that an estimate of 3,000 casualties was reasonable for killed, wounded, and missing. See telecon notes, Barry Watts and Gary Ware, Feb 26, 1992, p 3, frame 1193, reel 27584, GWAPS, AFHRA; Blackwell, *Thunder in the Desert*, 106–107; Schwarzkopf, *It Doesn't Take a Hero*, 356; Powell, *My American Journey,* 498–499.

168. Intvw trnscrpt, Warden by Gehri and Reynolds, May 1991, 97.

169. Ibid., 106–107.

Chapter 9

1. Msg, CINCCENT to SSO DIA et al., 021843Z Dec 90, subj: WWIMS Warning Report 90–01/12 for Iraq Region—IZXXX, CIS folder 2, GWAPS, AFHRA; Intvw tape, Rogers by Putney, Sep 18, 1994 (quote); General Sir Peter de la Billiere, *Storm Command: A Personal Account of the Gulf War* (London: Motivate, 1992), 130; Pt paper, "Desert Shield Support," Maj Luchte, n.d., CHSH 28-61, GWAPS, AFHRA.

2. Intvw tape, McNary by Putney, Nov 4, 1994; Drft intvw trnscrpt, Christon by Putney, Apr 25, 1994, 101 (quote); Calendar notes, Maj Mark B. "Buck" Rogers, Dec 2, 1990 entry, Rogers file, GWAPS, AFHRA; Intvw tape, Rogers by Putney, Sep 18, 1994.

3. Intvw tape, Rogers by Putney, Sep 18, 1994; Rpt, "Desert Shield/Storm—After Action Report," Lt Col Rogers file, GWAPS, AFHRA.

4. Intvw tape, Rogers by Putney, Sep 18, 1994.

5. Ibid.; Rpt, "Desert Shield/Storm After Action Report," Lt Col Rogers, Rogers file, GWAPS, AFHRA.

6. Intvw tape, Rogers by Putney, Sep 18, 1994; Harvey notes, Dec 4, 1990/1030.

7. Intvw trnscrpt, Lt Col Buck Rogers by Lt Col [Allan W.] Howey, Feb 19, 1992, NA 174, GWAPS, AFHRA.

8. MAP, "Phase I Master Attack Plan Addendum: Modified for Standing Start Two Hours Notification to Take-Off," Dec 17, 1990/1700, folder 7, box 4, Black Hole file, GWAPS, AFHRA.

9. Rpt, Cdr Smith and Cdr McSwain, "Operation Desert Storm," 8.

10. Memo, Brig Gen Buster C. Glosson to CENTAF/CC, Oct 16, 1990, subj: Scud Attacks, folder 30, Deptula file, GWAPS, AFHRA.

11. Drft intvw trnscrpt, Horner by Putney and Bradley, Apr 26, 1994, 43–44 (quotes).

12. Discussion, Kurt Guthe, GWAPS Task Force V, with Diane T. Putney, Sep 3 and 15, 1992; Telecon notes, Capt John R. Glock and Diane T. Putney, Dec 7, 1992, AFHSO; Rpt, DIA, "Iraqi Mobile SRBM Developments," DDX-1040-18-90, Dec 1990, DIA/HO.

13. Drft intvw trnscrpt, Christon by Putney, Apr 25, 1994, 104 (quote); Intvw tape, Christon by Davis and Barlow, Mar 4, 1992.

14. DoD, *Conduct of the Persian Gulf War,* 167; *GWAPS,* vol 2, part 2, *Effects and Effectiveness,* 335; *GWAPS,* vol 1, part 2, *Command and Control*, 247; Memo, Maj King to XO, "Project Touted Gleem," Nov 2, 1990, CHSH 115-5, GWAPS, AFHRA; Drft intvw trnscrpt, Christon by Putney, Apr 25, 1994, 102, AFHSO; Conversation, Brig Gen Thomas J. Lennon with Diane Putney, Apr 19, 1995, Massachusetts Institute of Technology, Mass. See also msg, Joint Staff/CAT/J3/J2 to USCINCCENT/CCJ3/CCJ2, 311846Z Oct 90, subj: Project Touted Gleem, CHSH 115-5, GWAPS, AFHRA; Memo, Col Dave Wells/LCDR Mart Luethemeyer, "Initial Results of Touted Gleem Exploitation," CHSH 115-5, GWAPS, AFHRA. The Iraqis also employed crude and sophisticated mobile Scud decoys.

15. Drft intvw trnscrpt, Horner by Putney and Bradley, Apr 26, 1994, 44 (quote); Ed drft intvw trnscrpt, Horner by Davis, Jamieson, and Barlow, Mar 4, 1992, 39; Brfg, "Offensive Air Campaign," Dec 20, 1990, 9, CHP 3, GWAPS, AFHRA.

16. Harvey notes, Dec 11, 1990/1400; Intvw trnscrpt, Horner by Gehri and Reynolds, Dec 2, 1991, 58; Diary, Joseph H. Purvis, Dec 10–11, 1990, entry, Scales Collection, Library, U.S. Army Command and Staff College, Ft. Leavenworth, Kans.; Rpt, "Combat Analysis Group After Action Report," Mar 21, 1991, 7, NA 259, GWAPS, AFHRA; Intvw tape, Olsen by Davis, Jamieson, and Barlow, Mar 5, 1992; Intvw tape, McConnell by Putney and Cole, Feb 14, 1992; DoD, *Conduct of the Persian Gulf War*, 25–26.

17. DoD, *Conduct of the Persian Gulf War,* 26; Cheney Frontline intvw, www.pbs.org/wgbh/pages/frontline/gulf/oral/Cheney, p 10 of 11.

18. Schwarzkopf, *It Doesn't Take a Hero,* 418; Intvw tape, Deptula by Reynolds, Gehri, and Mann, Jul 23, 1992, CADRE, AFHRA.

19. Brfg excerpt, "Third Party Attack on Iraq," Brfg for Sec of State, folder 7, box 3, Black Hole file, GWAPS, AFHRA.

20. Ed drft intvw trnscrpt, Horner by Davis, Jamieson, and Barlow, Mar 4, 1992, 37.

21. Bush and Scowcroft, *World Transformed,* 402–403. For the IFF codes and an account of the tense U.S.-Israeli discussions, see Baker, *Politics of Diplomacy*, 385–390.

22. Comment, Glosson on draft manuscript, Putney, "Airpower Advantage."

23. Brfg, "Chem/Bio Deterrence," Brfg

for Sec of State, folder 7, box 3, Black Hole file, GWAPS, AFHRA; Intvw trnscrpt, Corder by Reynolds and Gehri, Feb 4, 1992, 198 (Corder quote); Intvw tape, Glock by Putney, Oct 26, 1992; Schwarzkopf, *It Doesn't Take a Hero*, 389–390; Bush and Scowcroft, *World Transformed,* 442 (Bush quote).

24. Powell, *My American Journey*, 504.

25. Intvw trnscrpt, Horner by [Burton], [March 1991], 28.

26. Intvw tape, Glosson, Henry, and Lewis by Putney, 20 May 1997.

27. Drft intvw trnscrpt, Deptula by Davis, Jamieson, and Putney, Jan 12, 1992, 49–50. See also intvw tape, McConnell by Putney and Cole, Feb 5, 1992; John M. Broder, "With Its Hostages Out, U.S. Revises List of Iraqi Targets," *Los Angeles Times*, Dec 13, 1990, 1+; Telecon notes, Lt Col David A. Deptula and Wayne W. Thompson, AFHSO, Sep 13, 1991; Drft intvw trnscrpt, Deptula by Davis, Jamieson, and Putney, Jan 12, 1992, 49–50; DoD, *Conduct of the Persian Gulf War*, 28–29.

28. Schwarzkopf, *It Doesn't Take a Hero,* 326; Bush and Scowcroft, *World Transformed,* 351, 407; De la Billiere, *Storm Command*, 185.

29. Deptula notes, Oct 24 and 25, 1990, Deptula custody; Intvw tape, Deptula by Putney, Feb 14, 1994.

30. Intvw tape, Rogers by Putney, Sep 18, 1994.

31. Ibid.; Intvw tape, Deptula by Putney, Feb 14, 1994.

32. Intvw tape, Glosson, Henry, and Lewis by Putney, May 20, 1997.

33. Rick Atkinson, *Crusade: The Untold Story of the Persian Gulf War* (Boston: Houghton Mifflin, 1993), 141.

34. Comments, Glosson and Horner, on draft manuscript, Putney, "Airpower Advantage."

35. Intvw tape, McConnell by Putney and Cole, Feb 5, 1992; Intvw trnscrpt, Brig Gen Buster C. Glosson by TSgt Theodore J. Turner, Oct 27, 1990, 31–32.

36. Intvw tape, McConnell by Putney and Cole, Feb 5, 1992.

37. Drft edited intvw, Glosson by Davis, Jamieson, and Putney, Dec 12, 1992, 59.

38. Intvw tape, McConnell by Putney and Cole, Feb 5, 1992.

39. Rpt, "Defense Intelligence Team Report: Operation Desert Shield," Nov 25, 1990, 1, NA 187, GWAPS, AFHRA; DoD, *Conduct of the Persian Gulf War*, 336.

40. Rpt, Defense Intelligence Team Report, Nov 25, 1990, 2-3; DoD, *Conduct of the Persian Gulf War*, 339.

41. Rpt, Defense Intelligence Team Report, Nov 25, 1990, 4.

42. Ibid., 4-10; Brfg, Col Walter J. Whitman, USAF, "Perspective on the Joint Imagery Production Complex (JIPC)."

43. Drft intvw trnscrpt, Christon by Putney, Apr 25, 1994, 36, 60; Ltr, Christopher L. Christon, Ass't CS/Intelligence, Hq AFSPACECOM, to Natalie W. Crawford, RAND, Nov 17, 1992, Christon files, HQ AFSPACECOM.

44. Intvw tape, Christon by Putney, Apr 25, 1994; Intvw tape, Christon by Davis and Barlow, Mar 4, 1992; Rpt, Defense Intelligence Team Report, Nov 25, 1990, 9, NA-187, GWAPS, AFHRA.

45. Rpt, Maj Azzato, 37 TFW/INT, "Lessons Learned—Intelligence," Capt John R. Glock file, ACC/INAA.

46. Intvw tape, Christon by Putney, Apr 25, 1994; Intvw tape, McNary by Putney, Nov 4, 1994.

47. Drft intvw trnscrpt, Christon by Putney, Apr 25, 1994, 61 (quote), 131.

48. Stephen M. Hardy, "Planning and Rehearsing the Future," *Journal of Electronic Defense* 15 (November 1992): 50.

49. Intvw tape, Glosson by Davis, Jamieson, and Putney, Dec 12, 1991; Brfg, "Desert Storm Lessons Learned," HQ TAC/DO, Jul 12, 1991.

50. Intvw trnscrpt, Glosson by Turner, Oct 27, 1990, 30; Drft rpt, "Desert Storm/Desert Shield: Preliminary Report on Air Force Lessons Learned," 38, AFHSO; Harvey notes, Dec 14, 1990/1700.

51. Pamphlet, AFP 200–18, vol 1, "Target Intelligence Handbook Unclassified Targeting Principles," Oct 1, 1990, 31.

52. DoD, *Conduct of the Persian Gulf War*, 344; Drft intvw trnscrpt, Horner by Da-

vis, Jamieson, and Barlow, Mar 4, 1992, 40–41.

53. DoD, *Conduct of the Persian Gulf War*, 344. For discussion of Phase III BDA controversy, see Jamieson, *Lucrative Targets*, 94–97.

54. Drft intvw trnscrpt, Christon by Putney, Apr 25, 1994, 8 (quote), 9–10, 12–13.

55. Brfg notes, Capt John R. Glock to GWAPS staff, Jan 29, 1992; Brfg notes, Lt Col David A. Deptula to GWAPS staff, Nov 26, 1991; Brfg notes, Deptula to AF/HO and CAFH staff, Jan 8, 1992.

56. Drft intvw trnscrpt, Deptula by Davis, Nov 20, 1991, 45.

57. Drft intvw trnscrpt, Christon by Putney, Apr 25, 1994, 4–26; Brfg, "DIA's Battle Damage Assessment (BDA) Process," Lt Col Ben Harvey's file, Checkmate, AFHRA.

58. Drft intvw trnscrpt, Christon by Putney, Apr 25, 1994, 4–26; DoD, *Conduct of the Persian Gulf War,* 335–336; *GWAPS,* vol 1, part 2, *Command and Control*, 289; Rod A. Alonzo, "Blinded by Speed, Inexperience, Disagreement, and Clouds: Battle Damage Assessment in Desert Storm" (master's thesis, Defense Intelligence Agency College, 1993), 36–37, 71, 74.

59. Drft intvw trnscrpt, Christon by Putney, Apr 25, 1994, 7, 18 (1st quote), 11–12 (2d quote).

60. Ibid., 6.

61. Ibid., 23–26, 42; DoD, *Conduct of the Persian Gulf War,* 335; DIA, "A Chronology of Defense Intelligence in the Gulf War: A Research Aid for Analysts," DIA History Office, June 1997, 12, 15, 25–28, 32–33 at www.dia.mil/History/Chronologies/Gulf/index.html.

62. Drft intvw trnscrpt, Christon by Putney, Apr 25, 1994, 25.

63. Intvw trnscrpt, Deptula by Davis, Nov 20, 1991, 44.

64. Drft intvw trnscrpt, Christon by Putney, Apr 25, 1994, 36 (1st quote), 19 (2d quote).

65. Ibid., 1–4, 37–38.

66. Rpt, CENTAF/INO, "Desert Shield/Desert Storm Lessons Learned," Mar 13, 1991, entry no. 10, "Training-Units," Capt John R. Glock file, ACC/INAA; DoD, *Conduct of the Persian Gulf War,* 175, 341–342, 344; Kevin W. Smith, *Cockpit Video: A Low Cost BDA Source* (Maxwell AFB, Ala.: AU Press, 1993), 11–13, 37, 39–40, 51.

67. Smith, *Cockpit Video*, 33.

68. Drft intvw trnscrpt, Christon by Putney, Apr 25, 1994, 16. Not all aircraft carried cockpit video: F–117s, F–15Es, and A–6s did.

69. Drft intvw trnscrpt, Christon by Putney, Apr 25, 1994, 5.

70. Ibid., 39 (quote); Intvw tape, Christon by Davis and Barlow, Mar 4, 1992.

71. Memo, Col Warden to General Adams, n.s., Sep 24, 1990, NA 526, GWAPS, AFHRA.

72. Harvey notes, Oct 29, 1990/1300, Oct 31, 1990/1100, Nov 26, 1990/1030–1135, Dec 7, 1990/1130–1215, Dec 12, 1990/1600–1650.

73. Brfg, R.M.O. Weber, DIA/ODX-7B, "Battle Damage Assessment (BDA) Training: An Imagery Perspective"; DoD, *Conduct of the Persian Gulf War*, 343; Intvw tape, Warden to AF/HO and CAFH staff, Feb 6, 1992, AFHSO.

74. Intvw notes, Stacey Gardner, NPIC, by Diane T. Putney, Mar 2, 1992, AFHSO; Harvey notes, Nov 21, 1990/0930, Dec 12, 1990/1330–1530, Dec 14, 1990/0754; DoD, *Conduct of the Persian Gulf War,* 343.

75. Harvey notes, Nov 16, 1990/0910, Nov 19, 1990/1000, Dec 12, 1990/1330–1530; Drft intvw trnscrpt, Christon by Putney, Apr 25, 1994, 19–21; Brfg, R.M.O. Weber, DIA/ODX-7B, "Battle Damage Assessment (BDA) Training: An Imagery Perspective."

76. Drft rpt, "Desert Storm/Desert Shield: Preliminary Report on Air Force Lessons Learned," 38, Desert Storm Lessons Learned file, Checkmate file, Pentagon; Congress, House, Committee on Armed Services, Oversight and Investigative Subcommittee, "Intelligence Successes and Failures in Operations Desert Shield/Storm," 103d Cong., 1st sess., Aug 16, 1993, 4.

77. Drft intvw trnscrpt, Christon by Putney, Apr 25, 1994, 27–28; Intvw tape, Christon by Davis and Barlow, Mar 4, 1992; Comment, Glosson on draft manuscript, Put-

ney, "Airpower Advantage."

78. Intvw trnscrpt, Armstrong by Reynolds, Oct 23, 1991, 17–18.

79. Drft intvw trnscrpt, Christon by Putney, Apr 25, 1994, 32.

80. Ibid.,33–34, 42–43.

81. DoD, *Conduct of the Persian Gulf War*, 175.

82. Intvw tape, Christon by Davis and Barlow, Mar 4, 1992; Drft intvw trnscrpt, Horner by Putney and Bradley, Apr 26, 1994, 96 (1st quote), 129 (2d quote).

83. Ed drft intvw trnscrpt, Glosson by Davis, Jamieson, and Putney, Dec 12, 1991, 57–59.

84. Intvw trnscrpt, Glosson by Turner, Mar 6, 1991, 20.

85. Drft intvw trnscrpt, Horner by Putney and Bradley, Apr 26, 1994, 72.

86. Msg, CENTAF FWD/IN to TAC/IN, 110915Z Apr 1991, subj: Assessment of Desert Storm Intelligence Operations.

87. Intvw tape, Christon by Davis and Barlow, Mar 4, 1992.

88. Rpt, CENTAF Intelligence Targets Division After War Report, Mar 18, 1991, 3, "Geographic Separation of Targets and Combat Plans Function," Lt Col F. L. Talbot, USAF, box 5, Kurt Guthe file, GWAPS, AFHRA.

89. Rpt, CENTAF Intelligence Targets Division After War Report, Mar 18, 1991, 2, [Introduction], box 5, Kurt Guthe file, GWAPS, AFHRA.

90. Videotape brfg, Lt Col Ronald Talbot, SHAPE/IN, "Desert Shield/Storm 1990–91," Target Intelligence Conference, Goodfellow AFB, Oct 31, 1991, AFIA/INT, Bolling AFB.

91. Rpt, CENTAF Intelligence Targets Division After War Report, Mar 18, 1991, 12–13, "Dissemination of Intelligence from Washington Directly to the Combat Planning Function," Lt Col F. L. Talbot, USAF, box 5, Kurt Guthe file, GWAPS, AFHRA.

92. Rpt, CENTAF/INO, "Desert Shield/ Desert Storm Lessons Learned," Mar 13, 1991, 1, 4, ACC/INAA, Langley AFB.

93. Rpt, After Action Report—INT, [Lt Col Ronald Talbot], entry II, 6A, Capt John R. Glock file, ACC/INAA; Drft intvw trnscrpt, Christon by Putney, Apr 25, 1994, 81.

94. Comment, Deptula on draft manuscript, Putney, "Airpower Advantage."

95. Intvw tape, Rogers by Putney, Sep 18, 1994.

96. Drft intvw trnscrpt, Horner by Putney and Bradley, Apr 26, 1994, 129.

97. Drft intvw trnscrpt, Deptula by Davis, Jamieson, and Putney, Nov 29, 1991, 57. For a map showing locations of ships in the Persian Gulf, see Marolda and Schneller, *Shield and Sword*, 177.

98. Intvw tape, Rogers by Putney, Sep 18, 1994; Rpt, "Desert Storm BDA Imagery Review," Defense Imagery Reference Series, vol 1, Apr 1991, 4–7; Drft intvw trnscrpt, Deptula by Davis, Jamieson, and Putney, Jan 8, 1992, 52–53; Rpt, Maj Frederick T. Case, USAF Studies and Analysis Agency, "Analysis of Air Operations during Desert Shield/Desert Storm," Nov 1991, 8.

99. Deptula notes, Nov 28, 1990; Drft intvw trnscrpt, Deptula by Davis, Jamieson, and Putney, Nov 29, 1991, 57; Ltr to editor, Cdr Maurice Smith, USN (Ret), *Proceedings* (Feb 1995): 15.

100. Intvw trnscrpt, Maj Gen John A. Corder by Robert L. Mandler, Dec 21, 1991, 97, USAFAWC/HO.

101. Edited drft intvw trnscrpt, Glosson by Davis, Jamieson, and Putney, Dec 12, 1991, 74.

102. Rpt, "Conventional Land Attack Tomahawk," Technical Description Document (T2D2 for TLAM C and D), Revision A, June 1992, EX-2, NA 374, GWAPS, AFHRA; Memo, Lt Col David A. Deptula to Secretary Rice, Oct 9, 1990, Deptula file, GWAPS, AFHRA; Harvey notes, Oct 29, 1990; Deptula notes, Sep 9, 1990; Marolda and Schneller, *Shield and Sword,* 145.

103. P. Mason Carpenter, "Joint Operations in the Gulf War: An Allison Analysis" (master's thesis, AU, 1994), 22–24, 23 (Horner quote), 24.

104. Ibid., 25 (Horner quote), 26; Speech trnscrpt, Horner to Daedalians, Sep 11, 1991, 8; Ed drft intvw trnscrpt, Horner by Davis, Jamieson, and Barlow, Mar 4, 1992, 22; Marolda and Schneller, *Shield and Sword*, 180–181

105. Moore, "Marine Air: There When Needed," 64; Drft intvw trnscrpt, Glosson by Davis, Jamieson, and Putney, Dec 12, 1991, 78 (quote); Intvw trnscrpt, Corder by Gehri and Reynolds, Feb 4, 1992, 173–174.

106. Drft rpt, "Desert Storm/Desert Shield: Preliminary Report on Air Force Lessons Learned," 35, Lessons Learned File, Checkmate files, Pentagon; Intvw trnscrpt, Corder by Gehri and Reynolds, Feb 4, 1992, 173–174.

107. DoD, *Conduct of the Persian Gulf War*, 709; Intvw trnscrpt, Col George W. Cox by Robert L. Mandler, Dec 21, 1991, 7, USAFAWC/HO; Peter Grier, "Joint STARS Does Its Stuff," *Air Force Magazine* 74 (June 1991): 39, 41; Brochure, Northrop Grumman, "Unmasking the Stage," 3–4, an excerpt from "The Northrop Grumman Review," Issue 3, 1995.

108. Telecon notes, Col John Leonardo, USAF (Ret), with Diane T. Putney, Jan 5, 1994, AFHSO; Ed drft intvw trnscrpt, Horner by Davis, Jamieson, and Barlow, Mar 4, 1992, 33; Msg, Joint Staff to USCINCCENT, 192205Z Oct 90, subj: High Leverage Technology Support to Operations Desert Shield [references the Sep 3 msg], NA 523, GWAPS, AFHRA.

109. Ed drft intvw trnscrpt, Horner by Davis, Jamieson, and Barlow, Mar 4, 1992, 33–34; "Two Joint STARS Aircraft to Support Allied Operations in Persian Gulf Region," *Aviation Week & Space Technology* (January 14, 1991): 24 (quote); Glenn W. Goodman, Jr., "JSTARS Flies European Demonstrations; House Reverses Cancellation Vote," *Armed Forces Journal International* 128 (November 1990): 21.

110. Intvw trnscrpt, Brig Gen George K. Muellner by Thomas C. Hone, Anne Leary, and Mark Mandeles, Apr 16, 1992, 3–4, 4 (quote), NA 257, GWAPS, AFHRA.

111. Comment, Horner on draft manuscript, Putney, "Airpower Advantage"; Ed drft intvw trnscrpt, Horner by Davis, Jamieson, and Barlow, Mar 4, 1992, 34 (quote).

112. Thomas G. Runge, Lt Col, USAF, *Firepower and Follow-On Forces Attack: Making Every Round Count* (Maxwell AFB, Ala.: AU Press, 1991), 53–54.

113. Intvw trnscrpt, Corder by Gehri and Reynolds, Feb 4, 1992, 52, 54–55 (quote).

114. Intvw trnscrpt, Muellner by Hone, Leary, and Mandeles, Apr 16, 1992, 6.

115. Special Order, GB–21, HQ TAC/DCS Plans, Jan 10, 1991; Intvw trnscrpt, Muellner by Hone, Leary, and Mandeles, Apr 16, 1992, 11; Intvw trnscrpt, Cox by Mandler, Dec 21, 1991, 23.

116. Intvw trnscrpt, Muellner by Hone, Leary, and Mandeles, Apr 16, 1992, 7–8, 13–14, 17–18.

117. Ibid., 15 (Muellner quote); Intvw trnscrpt, Armstrong by Reynolds, Oct 23, 1991, 15–16 (Armstrong quote); Intvw trnscrpt, Corder by Mandler, Dec 21, 1991, 19–20.

118. Intvw trnscrpt, Corder by Mandler, Dec 21, 1991, 20; Intvw trnscrpt, Muellner by Hone, Leary, and Mandeles, Apr 16, 1992, 12; Intvw trnscrpt, Cox by Mandler, Dec 21, 1991, 18.

119. Staff summary sheet, Lt Col Thomits, SAC/DOOB, c. Dec 20, 1990, "Complex Obstacle Breach," working file, SAC/HO; Msg, CDRUSAEC to HQ SAC/DO, 031121Z Dec 90, subj: Joint Obstacle Breaching, working file, SAC/HO.

120. Drft rpt, SAC/DO, "Desert Shield and Desert Storm Bomber Story," HQ SAC, Omaha, Nebr., 34, NA 91, GWAPS, AFHRA; staff summary sheet, Lt Col Thomits, SAC/DOOB, "Complex Obstacle Breach," c. Dec 20, 1990, working file, SAC/HO; drft intvw trnscrpt, Horner by Putney and Bradley, Apr 26, 1994, 16; Quilter, *With the I Marine Expeditionary Force,* 38.

121. Rpt, SAC/DO, "Desert Shield and Desert Storm Bomber Story," Sep 18, 1991, HQ SAC, Omaha, Nebr., 33–34, NA 91, GWAPS, AFHRA; DoD, *Conduct of the Persian Gulf War,* 146–147; *GWAPS,* vol 2. part 2, *Effects and Effectiveness*, 301 n. 73.

122. Khaled, *Desert Warrior,* 318; Comment, Deptula on draft manuscript, Putney, "Airpower Advantage."

123. Intvw tape, Rogers by Putney, Sep 18, 1994.

124. Brfg, "Air Force Briefings to His Royal Highness Lt Gen Khalid," Nov 22, 1990, AFHSO.

125. For an account of the acquisition of

the Chinese missiles see Khaled, *Desert Warrior,* 130–152.

126. Deptula notes, Oct 28, 1990; Intvw tape, Deptula by Putney, Apr 11, 1994; Intvw tape, Christon by Putney, Apr 23, 1992; Congress, Subcommittee of the Committee on Appropriations, "DoD Appropriations for Fiscal Year 1991," 101st Cong., 2d sess., Mar 6, 1990, 167, 177.

127. Khaled, *Desert Warrior*, 350.

128. Intvw tape, Rogers by Putney, Sep 18, 1994.

129. Ibid.; De la Billiere, *Storm Command*, 175–178; Powell, *My American Journey*, 499–500; Schwarzkopf, *It Doesn't Take a Hero, 401, 403;* Intvw tape, Glosson, Henry, and Lewis by Putney, May 20, 1997.

130. Memo, Colin L. Powell, CJCS, to Sec of Defense, Apr 12, 1991, CM-830-91, subj: Preliminary Report on Lessons Learned in Operations Desert Shield and Desert Storm, Desert Storm Lessons—JCS/CINC folder, Checkmate file, Pentagon; videotape, news briefing, Gen H Norman Schwarzkopf, Feb 27, 1991, 1:00 p.m. EST., Riyadh; Scales, *Certain Victory,* 128, 133; Swain, *"Lucky War,"* 89; DoD, *Conduct of the Persian Gulf War*, 254.

131. Drft intvw tape, Deptula by Davis, Jamieson, and Putney, Jan 12, 1992, 12; Brfg, "USAF Tactical Deception Program," NA 64, GWAPS, AFHRA; DoD, *Conduct of the Persian Gulf War,* 105, 107.

132. Memo and Atchs, CJCS to Sec of Defense, subj: USCINCCENT Psychological Operations Campaign Plan—Burning Hawk, n.d., CHSH 134-12, GWAPS, AFHRA; DoD, *Conduct of the Persian Gulf War,* 537; Memo, Gen H Norman Schwarzkopf to CJCS, subj: Psychological Operations Campaign Plan—Burning Hawk, (quote), CHSH 134-12, GWAPS, AFHRA.

133. DoD, *Conduct of the Persian Gulf War*, 537; Harvey notes, Sep 7, 1990/0900 and 0945; Discussion, Wayne W. Thompson, Checkmate and GWAPS historian, with Diane T. Putney, Jan 6, 1995; Memo and Atch, Col Tony Normand to CINCCENTCOM, Sep 13, 1990, subj: PSYOP Campaign Plan Burning Hawk, CHSH 134-12, GWAPS, AFHRA; Memo and Atch, Deputy Under Secretary of Defense Craig Alderman, Jr., to CJCS et al., Nov 15, 1991, subj: Review of DOD Psychological Operations Process in Light of Operation Desert Storm, Checkmate file, Pentagon; Msg, USAF/XOXW to CENTAF/DO, 080125Z Sep 90, subj: PSYOP Objectives to Support the Air Campaign, folder 19J, Deptula file, GWAPS, AFHRA.

134. DoD, *Conduct of the Persian Gulf War,* 536.

135. Harvey notes, Nov 15, 1900/1500; Discussion, Wayne W. Thompson, Checkmate and GWAPS historian, with Diane T. Putney, Jan 6, 1995.

136. Memo, Deputy Under Secretary of Defense (Security Policy) to CJCS et al., Nov 15, 1991, subj: Review of DOD Psychological Operations Process in Light of Operation Desert Storm, 4, Checkmate file, Pentagon.

137. Msg, USCINCCENT to CJCS, 051300Z Dec 90, subj: Psychological Operations (PSYOP) in Support of Operation Desert Shield, NA 376, GWAPS, AFHRA; Memo, Deputy Under Secretary of Defense (Security Policy) to CJCS et al., Nov 15, 1991, subj: Review of DOD Psychological Operations Process in Light of Operation Desert Storm, 4, Checkmate file, Pentagon.

138. Intvw trnscrpt, Horner by Gehri and Reynolds, Dec 2, 1991, 42 (quote); Ed drft intvw trnscrpt, Horner by Davis, Jamieson, and Barlow, Mar 4, 1992, 7–8. See also Khaled, *Desert Warrior,* 395–396 and De la Billiere, *Storm Command,* 121–122; *GWAPS,* vol 2, part 1, *Operations*, 246.

139. Intvw tape, Deptula by Putney and Davis, Dec 12, 1992; Intvw tape, Deptula by Reynolds, Gehri, and Mann, Jul 24, 1992; Intvw trnscrpt, Deptula by Gehri, Mann, and Reynolds, May 23, 1991, 94–98; Schwarzkopf, *It Doesn't Take a Hero*, 455, 457, 468; Speech trnscrpt, Reuters, Lt Gen Charles Horner to Business Executives, May 8, 1991, 14; Intvw trnscrpt, Horner by Gehri and Reynolds, Dec 2, 1991, 55; Comment, Deptula on draft manuscript, Putney, "Airpower Advantage." According to Wayne W. Thompson, the Checkmate historian, the Pentagon officials who objected were lawyers, but their arguments were not on legal

grounds.

140. Julie Bird, "Horner: Further AF Role in Gulf Not Needed," *Air Force Times*, Mar 18, 1991, 8.

141. DoD, *Conduct of the Persian Gulf War*, 537–538; Scales, *Certain Victory*, 196–197.

142. Harvey notes, Oct 13, 1990/1615 and Oct 23, 1990/1610; Memo for record, Lt Col Bondzeleske, XOXWD, Oct 19, 1990, subj: CIA/DIA/Leadership Facilities Team (LEFT) Meeting Concerning Leadership Targets, Warden's Notes file, GWAPS, AFHRA; Memo for record, Capt Leeper, XOXWF, Nov 5, 1990, subj: Imagery Questions with CIA/DIA, CHSH 109-17, GWAPS, AFHRA.

143. Memo for record, Capt Leeper, XO-XWF, Nov 6, 1990, subj: Imagery Questions with CIA/DIA, CHSH 109-17, GWAPS, AFHRA.

144. List, "Leadership Facilities Targets," [Lt Col Ben] Harvey, Nov 3, 1990/1300, Warden's Notes file, GWAPS, AFHRA.

145. Brfg, "Offensive Air Campaign," Dec 20, 1990, 48 (5F), CHP 3, GWAPS, AF-HRA.

146. Intvw tape, Glock by Putney, Oct 26, 1992; Discussion, Capt John R. Glock and Diane T. Putney, Feb 7, 1995; Tgt list, "Leadership," 2/1/91, Leadership BDA-Setnor file, folder 2, box 7, Black Hole file, GWAPS, AFHRA; Comment, Deptula on draft manuscript, Putney, "Airpower Advantage." The attacking F–117 did not actually hit the VIP bunker the first night.

147. Drft intvw trnscrpt, Deptula by Davis, Jamieson, and Putney, Jan 8, 1992, 23, AFHSO; Discussion, Wayne W. Thompson, AFHSO, Checkmate and GWAPS historian, and Diane T. Putney, Mar 4, 1992; DoD, *Conduct of the Persian Gulf War,* 613.

148. DoD, *Conduct of the Persian Gulf War*, 137; *GWAPS,* vol 4, part 1, *Weapons, Tactics, and Training*, 2; *GWAPS,* vol 2, part 2, *Effects and Effectiveness*, 277, 287–288. According to Atkinson, after the Gulf War, Western correspondents toured the "bowels" of the Al Rashid Hotel and found "nothing more sinister than a laundry." In contrast, Francona wrote that when he stayed at the hotel as a guest of the Iraqi military during the Iran-Iraq war, a "malfunctioning elevator" took him to the basement where he saw "numerous racks of sophisticated communications gear." Francona believed the basement housed a "large bunker/bomb shelter complex." One of the CNN correspondents the night the war started went to look for a bomb shelter in the hotel. See Atkinson, *Crusade*, 295; Francona, *Ally to Adversary*, 14; and CNN film, "CNN Gulf War Coverage," Jan 16, 1991, Library of Congress, Washington, D.C.

149. *GWAPS,* vol 2, part 2, *Effects and Effectiveness*, 287–290; *GWAPS,* vol 4, part 1, *Weapons, Tactics, and Training*, 280.

150. Drft intvw trnscrpt, Deptula by Davis, Jamieson, and Putney, Jan 8, 1992, 23, 40 (quote); MAP with 3 changes, Jan 16, 1991, 21:21, AFHRA.

151. Brfg, Glock to GWAPS staff, Jan 21, 1992; Intvw tape, Glock by Putney, Oct 26, 1992.

152. Intvw tape, Christon by Davis and Barlow, Mar 4, 1992; General Charles A. Horner, "New Era Warfare," in *The War in the Air 1914–1994: The Proceedings of a Conference Held by the Royal Australian Air Force in Canberra, March 1994*, ed. Alan Stephens (Fairbairn, Australia: RAAF Air Power Studies Centre, 1994), 327.

153. Intvw trnscrpt, Henry by Gehri, Mann, and Reynolds, [Jun 2, 1992], 117–118 (quote).

154. Office of the Assistant for Gulf War Illness, Information Paper, "The Use of Modeling and Simulation in the Planning of Attacks on Iraqi Chemical and Biological Warfare Targets," www.gulflink.osd.mil/air-campaign/, pp 1–2 Summary, p 2 of Section 3, and p 1 of Conclusion; DoD, *Conduct of the Persian Gulf War*, 154.

155. Horner recalled the major's words in intvw trnscrpt, Horner by Gehri and Reynolds, Dec 2, 1991, 60.

156. Speech trnscrpt, Horner to Daedalians, Sep 11, 1991, 4–5; Horner's Frontline intvw, www.pbs.org/wgbh/pages/frontline/gulf/oral/horner, pp 9–10 of 11.

157. Brfg, "Offensive Air Campaign," Dec 20, 1990, CHP 3, 15, GWAPS, AFHRA.

158. To compare the sequence of attacks

against BW targets as briefed on December 20, 1990, and in operations on January 17, 1991, see the following: brfg, "Offensive Air Campaign," Dec 20, 1990, 16, CHP 3, GWAPS, AFHRA; Drft intvw trnscrpt, Deptula by Davis, Putney, and Jamieson, Jan 8, 1992, 164–165; *GWAPS,* vol 4, part 1, *Weapons, Tactics, and Training*, 179; "Master Attack Plan for First Twenty-four Hours," Jan 10, 1991/2200 w changes Jan 16, 1991/ 21:21, AFHRA.

159. Intvw trnscrpt, Horner by Gehri and Reynolds, Dec 2, 1991, 60–61.

160. Schwarzkopf, *It Doesn't Take a Hero*, 390.

161. Intvw trnscrpt, Horner by Gehri and Reynolds, Dec 2, 1991, 61; Memo, Iraq Interagency BW Working Group, Fusion Committee to Distribution List, Jan 9, 1991, subj: Estimate of Casualties Resulting from Coalition Air Strikes on Iraqi BW Related Facilities, DIA/HO.

162. Powell, *My American Journey,* 503.

163. Bush and Scowcroft, *World Transformed*, 447.

164. Rpt with note, Adm McConnell to B Gen B.C. Glosson, "Intelligence Judgments and Implications for Attacking Iraqi Biological Warfare Facilities," Jan 11, 1991, folder 19G, Deptula file, GWAPS, AFHRA.

165. Congress, House, Committee on Armed Services, Subcommittee on Oversight and Investigations, "Intelligence Successes and Failures in Operations Desert Shield/Storm," Aug 16, 1993, 103d Cong., 1st sess., 25–26. In 1998, a commentary about the factory, supported by the *Washington Post,* stated that based on information provided by Saddam Hussein's son-in-law after he defected, U.N. inspectors and U.S. intelligence analysts concluded that the Abu Ghraib facility did not produce BW-related material. See "Fog of War," at www.washingtonpost.com/wp-srv/inatl/longterm/fogofwar/vignettes/v4.htm. Bush's memoir suggests that it was a dual-use installation and that "the suspicion was that the plant might have been used for filling biological munitions." See Bush and Scowcroft, *World Transformed,* 458.

166. Drft intvw trnscrpt, Deptula by Davis, Jamieson, and Putney, Nov 29, 1991, 59–60.

167. Hist, CMSgt Jerome E. Schroeder and SMSgt Thomas L. Raab, *History of Joint Task Force (JTF) Proven Force*, 5–7, HQ USAFE/HO; *GWAPS,* vol 1, part 2, *Command and Control*, 391.

168. Hist, Schroeder and Raab, *History of JTF Proven Force*, 7, 30.

169. Intvw tape, Horner by Davis, Jamieson, and Putney, Mar 4, 1992.

170. Drft intvw trnscrpt, Deptula by Davis, Jamieson, and Putney, Nov 29, 1991, 60; Hist, Schroeder and Raab, *History of JTF Proven Force*, 49; Intvw trnscrpt, Rogers by Howey, Feb 19, 1992, 6.

171. Drft intvw trnscrpt, Deptula by Davis, Jamieson, and Putney, Nov 29, 1991, 59–60; Baker, *Politics of Diplomacy*, 283–285, 309, 377. The Proven Force aircraft flew their first sorties on January 18, 1991.

Chapter 10

1. Brfg, Offensive Air Campaign, [Dec 20, 1990], [Gen Horner brief to SECDEF], 2, 27, 29, CHP folder 3, GWAPS, AFHRA; Intvw trnscrpt, Horner by Gehri and Reynolds, Dec 2, 1991, 56–57.

2. Brfg, Offensive Air Campaign, Dec 20, 1990, 3.

3. Ibid., 5.

4. Ibid., 6–17.

5. Intvw trnscrpt, Horner by Gehri and Reynolds, Dec 2, 1991, 56 (Horner's paraphrase of Cheney's directive); Ed drft intvw trnscrpt, Horner by Davis, Jamieson, and Barlow, Mar 4, 1992, 30–33.

6. Brfg, Offensive Air Campaign, Dec 20, 1990, 18.

7. Air *superiority* meant that Coalition aircraft flew in enemy airspace without prohibitive interference, while air *supremacy* indicated that the enemy air force was no longer effective. See *GWAPS,* vol 2, part 2, *Effects and Effectiveness*, 153 n 95.

8. Brfg, Offensive Air Campaign, Dec 20, 1990, 18(19), 19(20).
9. Ibid., 20(21), 21(22).
10. Ibid., 22(23), 23(24).
11. Ibid., [25]; Drft speech trnscrpt, Lt Gen Charles A. Horner, Banquet address, Anglo-American Symposium, Air Force Historical Foundation, Bolling AFB, Sep 1993, 14 (quote).
12. Brfg, Offensive Air Campaign, Dec 20, 1990, 25(27), 27(28).
13. Ibid., 28(29), 29(30).
14. Intvw trnscrpt, Horner by Gehri and Reynolds, Dec 2, 1991, 57, 58 (Horner quote); Notes, Lt Gen Charles A. Horner, Mtg with SecDef & CJCS, Dec 20, 1990, Desert Storm file, HQ 9AF/CC (CINCCENT comment as written by Horner).
15. *GWAPS,* vol 2, part 2, *Effects and Effectiveness*, 202–226.
16. Brfg, Offensive Air Campaign, Dec 20, 1990, 30(31).
17. Ibid., 32(33).
18. Ibid., 35(36).
19. Ibid., 36(37), 39(40).
20. Notes, Lt Gen Charles A. Horner, Mtg with SecDef & CJCS, Dec 20, 1990, Desert Storm file, HQ 9AF/CC file.
21. Brfg, "An Analysis of Joint Air Power Capability in the KTO," AF/XOXW, 5–9, CHSH folder 6, Checkmate file, GWAPS, AFHRA. The colonel did not discuss Coalition losses, expected to be lower than those for the Americans.
22. Msg, USCENTAF/CV to USCENTAF REAR/BS-XP, 220930Z Nov 90, subj: Establishment of Provisional Air Divisions for Desert Shield; Msg, COMUSCENTAF to AIG 10322/CC et al., 120600Z Dec 90, subj: USCENTAF Organization Structure; Intvw trnscrpt, Corder by Gehri and Reynolds, Feb 4, 1992, 91–92.
23. Ed drft intvw trnscrpt, Horner by Davis, Jamieson, and Barlow, Mar 4, 1992, 28, 127. Horner directed that none of the general officers from headquarters fly in combat; their capture would be too great "a plum" for the Iraqis.
24. Comment, Glosson on draft manuscript, Putney, "Airpower Advantage"; Drft edited trnscrpt, Glosson by Davis, Jamieson, and Putney, Dec 12, 1991, 19 (Glosson paraphrases Horner).
25. Drft intvw trnscrpt, Horner by Putney and Bradley, Apr 26, 1994, 57–58.
26. Org chart, Campaign Planning, Dec 31, 1990, folder 3B, Deptula file, GWAPS, AFHRA; Chart, Organization: Directorate for Campaign Plans, folder 3B, Deptula file, GWAPS, AFHRA.
27. Org chart, GAT, Jan 2, 1991, folder 3B, Deptula file, GWAPS, AFHRA; Org chart, Campaign Planning, Dec 31, 1990, folder 3B, Deptula file, GWAPS, AFHRA; Org chart, [GAT, ATO, ACE], Jan 91, folder 3B, Deptula file, GWAPS, AFHRA; Marolda and Schneller, *Sword and Shield*, 186.
28. Intvw trnscrpt, Baptiste by Putney and Reynolds, Sep 24, 1992, 33; Drft intvw trnscrpt, Horner by Putney and Bradley, Apr 26, 1994, 95.
29. Discussion, MSgt Theodore J. Turner, a CENTAF historian, and Diane T. Putney, Mar 18, 1992; Intvw tape, Christon by Davis and Barlow, Mar 4, 1992.
30. Intvw trnscrpt, Muellner by Hone, Leary, and Mandeles, Apr 16, 1992, 30 (quote).
31. Intvw tape, Waterstreet by Davis, Mar 6, 1992; Intvw tape, Baptiste by Putney and Reynolds, Sep 24, 1992.
32. Drft intvw trnscrpt, Horner by Putney and Bradley, Apr 26, 1994, 59 (quote); Ed drft intvw trnscrpt, Horner by Davis, Jamieson, and Barlow, Mar 4, 1992, 27.
33. Intvw trnscrpt, Corder by Mandler, Dec 21, 1991, 91; Layout graphic, in brfg, Desert Shield/Storm Air Targeting Campaign, [Lt Col Bob Kershaw], 9TIS/DO, AFIA/INT, Bolling AFB.
34. Intvw trnscrpt, Doman by Reynolds and Mann, May 28, 1993, 30 (quote).
35. Drft intvw trnscrpt, Deptula by Davis, Nov 20, 1991, 14.
36. Trnscrpt of tape recording of meeting, Jan 6, 1991, Iraqi/Strategic Planning Cell, 1, AFHSO.
37. Intvw tape, Deptula by Davis, Jamieson, and Putney, Jan 12, 1992.
38. Chart, Offensive Air Campaign Phase I Dynamic Planning Process (Day 3+), Jan 4, 1991, Other documents folder 2,

Black Hole file, GWAPS, AFHRA (quote); Chart, Organization: Directorate for Campaign Plans, folder 3B, Deptula file, GWAPS, AFHRA; Brfg, Lt Col David A. Deptula to GWAPS staff, Nov 26, 1991.

39. Intvw tape, Feinstein by Davis, Jamieson, and Barlow, Mar 3, 1992.

40. Intvw trnscrpt, Doman by Reynolds and Mann, May 28, 1993, 38–39 (quote).

41. Intvw tape, Deptula by Reynolds, Mann, and Gehri, Jul 24, 1992; Letter formats, ATO Planning Guidance, box 1, Deptula papers, Deptula custody.

42. Drft intvw trnscrpt, Horner by Putney and Bradley, Apr 26, 1994, 58.

43. Intvw trnscrpt, Baptiste by Putney and Reynolds, Sep 24, 1992, 34–35; Intvw tape, Deptula by Davis, Jamieson, and Putney, Jan 12, 1992; Exercise sheet, ATO Exercise, Jan 12, 1991, folder 3, box 8, Deptula file, GWAPS, AFHRA.

44. Intvw trnscrpt, Corder by Mandler, Dec 21, 1991, 15–17. By about day 6, the ATO process had improved considerably.

45. Intvw trnscrpt, Glosson by Gehri, Reynolds, and Mann, June 4, 1992, 112–113; Comment, Glosson on draft manuscript, Putney, "Airpower Advantage"; *GWAPS,* vol 1, part 2, *Command and Control*, 213–214; *GWAPS,* vol 2, part 1, *Operations,* 161–162.

46. Intvw tape, Glosson by Putney, Aug 30, 1993; Congress, Senate, Armed Services Committee, *Crisis in the Persian Gulf Region: U.S. Policy Options and Implications*, 101st Cong., 2d sess., Dec 1990, 676.

47. Intvw trnscrpt, Corder by Mandler, Dec 21, 1991, 83.

48. Intvw trnscrpt, Corder by Gehri and Reynolds, Feb 4, 1992, 9–10 (10 quote).

49. Drft intvw trnscrpt, Glosson by Davis, Jamieson, and Putney, Dec 12, 1991, 77.

50. Warden, *Air Campaign*, 115–127.

51. Intvw trnscrpt, Henry by Gehri, Mann, and Reynolds, [Jun 2, 1992], 51.

52. Intvw trnscrpt, Corder by Gehri and Reynolds, Feb 4, 1992, 92 (quotes); Drft intvw trnscrpt, Glosson by Davis, Jamieson, and Putney, Dec 12, 1991, 77–78 (quote); Intvw tape, Deptula by Davis, Jamieson, and Putney, Jan 8, 1992.

53. MAP, Jan 10, 1991/1220 with changes 1–3, Jan 16, 1991/21:21, AFHRA; Brfg notes, Lt Col David A. Deptula to ACE Mission Directors, folder 7, Deptula file, GWAPS, AFHRA; Intvw tape, Deptula by Putney, Apr 11, 1994. This also references the "broke loose" quote.

54. Ltr, Col David A. Sawyer, 23 TFW(P)/CC, to Lt Gen Charles A. Horner, subj: Yr 151930Z Msg, Aircraft Losses, Feb 16, 1991.

55. Ed drft intvw trnscrpt, Deptula by Reynolds and Mann, Dec 10, 1991, 28 insert A-1.

56. Drft intvw trnscrpt, Glosson by Davis, Jamieson, and Putney, Dec 12, 1991, 24 (quote).

57. Intvw trnscrpt, Baptiste by Putney and Reynolds, Sep 24, 1992, 38.

58. Drft intvw trnscrpt, Deptula by Reynolds and Mann, Dec 10, 1991, 28 insert A-2.

59. Drft intvw trnscrpt, Deptula by Davis, Jamieson, and Putney, Jan 8, 1992, 21–22.

60. MAP, Jan 10, 1991/1220 with changes 1–3, Jan 16, 1991/21:21, AFHRA. On the first night, the pilots will not hit the air defense target. See hit/no hit data in spreadsheet, [Barry D. Watts, GWAPS], "F-117 Master [List]," GWAPS, AFHRA. "No hit" occurred because a bomb missed its target or was not dropped because of poor weather or other problems.

61. Drft intvw trnscrpt, Horner by Putney and Bradley, Apr 26, 1994, 59 (quote); Intvw trnscrpt, Horner by Reynolds, Mann, and Gehri, Dec 2, 1991, 57.

62. Lt Col William G. Welch, "Notes from the BCE: Observations on Joint Combat Operations at Echelon Above Corps," *Field Artillery,* June 1992, 18.

63. Intvw trnscrpt, Horner by Reynolds and Gehri, Dec 2, 1991, 62 (1st quote); Intvw trnscrpt, Baptiste by Putney and Reynolds, Sep 24, 1992, 44 (2d quote).

64. USCENTAF Reg 55–45, "United States Central Command Air Forces Air Employment Planning Process," June 27, 1990, 3–12, Desert Shield/Storm file, TAC/HO.

65. Brfg trnscrpt, MAPEX, DRS14, Lt Col Engram, G3—Deep Operations Targets,

Center for Army Lessons Learned, Ft. Leavenworth.

66. Rpt, "Operation Desert Storm Lessons Learned" vol. 3, Operational, III-3 to III-7, HQDA, ADCSOPS-FD, Center for Army Lessons Learned, Ft. Leavenworth.

67. Drft intvw trnscrpt, Christon by Putney, Apr 25, 1994, 71.

68. Intvw trnscrpt, Baptiste by Putney and Reynolds, Sep 24, 1992, 58.

69. Ibid., 57–58.

70. Intvw tape, Baptiste by Jamieson and Barlow, Mar 3, 1992; Discussion, Capt John R. Glock and Diane T. Putney, Mar 31, 1995.

71. Brfg, Air Tasking Order (ATO) Preparation and Composite Force Packaging, Lt Col Sam Baptiste, HQ 9AF/DOOW.

72. Drft intvw trnscrpt, Horner by Putney and Bradley, Apr 26, 1994, 61.

73. Intvw trnscrpt, Baptiste by Putney and Reynolds, 59–61; *GWAPS,* vol 4, part 1, *Weapons, Tactics, and Training*, 93 (as quoted in). For references to Iraqis being dug-in and using berms and revetments, see *GWAPS,* vol 2, part 1, *Operations* 205, 271, and vol 2, part 2, *Effects and Effectiveness,* 35, 210.

74. For Franks's emphasis on his sector, see Clancy with Franks, *Into the Storm,* 256, 267–268, 271, 315, 332, 341, 368, 371, 409.

75. Scales, *Certain Victory,* 180; DoD, *Conduct of the Persian Gulf War,* 248.

76. Drft intvw trnscrpt, Horner by Putney and Bradley, Apr 26, 1994, 61–62.

77. Drft intvw trnscrpt, Christon by Putney, Apr 25, 1994, 71–72.

78. Intvw trnscrpt, Baptiste by Putney and Reynolds, Sep 24, 1992, 9–10.

79. DoD, *Conduct of the Persian Gulf War*, 113.

80. Trnscrpt, News Brfg, Gen H. Norman Schwarzkopf, Riyadh, Saudi Arabia, Wed, Feb 27, 91, 1:00 p.m. (EST); *GWAPS,* vol 2, part 2, *Effects and Effectiveness*, 211–212.

81. Col. Richard B. H. Lewis, "JFACC Problems Associated with Battlefield Preparation in Desert Storm," *Airpower Journal* 8 (Spring 1994): 12.

82. Intvw, Horner by Gehri and Reynolds, Dec 2, 1991, 56; Swain, *"Lucky War,"* 185.

83. Intvw trnscrpt, Corder by Gehri and Reynolds, Feb 21, 1992; Khaled, *Desert Warrior,* 322.

84. Scales, *Certain Victory,* 181.

85. Intvw summary, Capt J. Hawkins by K. M. Beck, Apr 30, 1991, 4.

86. Notes, Col David A. Schulte, 0730, 20 Feb 91, Center for Army Lessons Learned, Ft. Leavenworth.

87. Swain, *"Lucky War,"* 185; Scales, *Certain Victory,* 180.

88. Memo, Hq VII Corps, AETSFA-FSE, subj: Corps Fires After-Action Report, 15 Mar 1991, 5, quoted in Swain, *"Lucky War,"* 216 n 36.

89. Intvw trnscrpt, Baptiste by Putney and Reynolds, Sep 24, 1992, 40 (quote).

90. Intvw trnscrpt, Deptula by Reynolds and Mann, Dec 10, 1991, 32 insert.

91. Ed drft intvw trnscrpt, Horner by Davis, Jamieson, and Barlow, Mar 4, 1992, 57; Richard MacKenzie, "A Conversation with Chuck Horner," *Air Force Magazine* 74 (June 1991): 60.

92. Intvw notes, Capt Rich Cleary and Capt Jim Wright by Col Frank Goldstein et al, GWAPS, Sep 1–2, 1992, 2, NA 517, GWAPS, AFHRA; Msg, STRATFOR/CC to HQ SAC/DO, 272100Z Jul 90, subj: Quick Look—Exercise Internal Look 90; MFR, K. M. Beck, historian, Talk by Maj D. Karns, SAC/DOO, [Reflections on STRATFOR Role in Persian Gulf War], to SAC Bomb-Nav Conference, Apr 23, 1991, i, working file, SAC/HO; Intvw trnscrpt, Deptula by Reynolds and Mann, Dec 10, 1991, 29. Army planners at CENTAF headquarters often referred to the B–52 strikes against ground forces as Arc Light attacks, a reference to the heavy bomber operations against Viet Cong troops and their base camps in South Vietnam. During the war in Southeast Asia, a three-ship cell of B–52s disgorging three hundred 500- and 750-pound bombs created a terrifying "man-made maelstrom" of continuous explosions, concussions, and shock waves covering an area 2 by 1 kilometers. See John L. Plaster, *SOG: The Secret Wars of America's Commandos in Vietnam* (New York: Penguin/Putnam Paperback,

1998), 50; Comment, Thompson on draft manuscript, Putney, "Airpower Advantage."

93. MAP, Dec 21, 1990/0900 and Jan 3, 1990/0900, Deptula papers, Deptula custody; MAP, Jan 10, 1990/2200 with changes 1–3, Jan 16, 1991/21:21, AFHRA; Drft intvw trnscrpt, Deptula by Davis, Jamieson, and Putney, Jan 8, 1992, 30.

94. *GWAPS,* vol 2, part 2, *Effects and Effectiveness*, 374–375; Ibid., vol 1, part 1, *Planning*, 204–205; Ibid., vol 2, part 1, *Operations*, 234.

95. *GWAPS,* vol 2, part 1, *Operations*, 251.

96. Intvw summary, Capt J. Hawkins by K. M. Beck, Apr 30, 1991, 3–4.

97. Intvw notes, Capt Rich Cleary and Capt Jim Wright by Col Frank Goldstein et al., GWAPS, Sep 1–2, 1992, 1, NA–517, GWAPS, AFHRA.

98. Ibid., 1–2; After action rpt, Operation Desert Shield/Storm, [c. Apr 9, 1991], Lessons Learned para 10, working file, SAC/HO; Intvw trnscrpt, Corder by Mandler, Dec 21, 1991, 87–91.

99. Drft rpt, RAND Corp, Maj Thomas A. Marshall, USAF, "Strategic Air Command Bomber and Tanker Operations in Desert Storm," Sep 1991, RAND WD(L)-5608-AF, 13; Rpt, "Desert Shield/Storm USCENTAF/STRATFOR After Action Report," [c. Apr 9, 1991], Lessons Learned paras 10–17, working file, SAC/HO; Ltr with Atch, HQ SAC/DOO to 8AF/DO and 15AF/DO, Jun 19, 1991, subj: Operation Desert Storm Bombing and Navigation Conference After Action Report, working file, SAC/HO; Rpt, After action rpt—executive ed, Operation Desert Shield/Storm, HQ SAC DCS/Intelligence, Aug 30,1991, 27, NA 349, GWAPS, AFHRA; Intvw tape, Baptiste by Jamieson and Barlow, Mar 2, 1992; Telecon notes, Lt Col Bryan "Buck" Rogers, ACC, Langley AFB, and Diane T. Putney, Feb 2, 1995, AFHSO; Intvw summary, Capt J. Hawkins by K. M. Beck, Apr 30, 1991, 2.

100. Ed drft intvw trnscrpt, Horner by Davis, Jamieson, and Barlow, Mar 4, 1992, 73; Ltr w Atch, HQ SAC/DOO to 8AF/DO and 15AF/DO, Jun 19, 1991, subj: Operation Desert Storm Bombing and Navigation Conference After Action Report, working file, SAC/HO; Telecon notes, Lt Col Bryan Rogers, ACC, Langley AFB, and Diane T. Putney, Feb 2, 1995, AFHSO.

101. Msg, 3909 SAES/CC to HQ SAC/DO et al., 011400Z Apr 91, subj: SAC Participation in Desert Storm, working file, SAC/HO; Drft rpt, RAND, Maj Thomas A. Marshall, "Strategic Air Command Bomber and Tanker Operations in Desert Storm," RAND WD(L)-5608-AF, 18; Ltr, HQ SAC/DOO to 8AF/DO and 15AF/DO, Operation Desert Storm Bombing and Navigation Conference After-action Report, working file, SAC/HO; Intvw summary, Capt J. Hawkins by K. M. Beck, Apr 30, 1991, 2

102. Intvw trnscrpt, Henry by Gehri, Mann, and Reynolds, [Jun 2, 1992], 133 (quote); Khaled, *Desert Warrior,* 264.

103. Msg, 37 TFW Provisional/CC to 14AD/CC et al., [no date/time] Z Jan 91, subj: RFEFJS, folder 2, box 11c, Black Hole file, GWAPS, AFHRA.

104. Ibid.

105. See Glosson's handwritten comments on Ibid.; Intvw tape, Glosson by Reynolds, Gehri, and Mann, Jun 4, 1992; Intvw tape, Deptula by Putney and Davis, Dec 12, 1992; Intvw tape, Brig Gen Anthony "Tony" Tolin by Richard G. Davis, AFHSO, Nov 23, 1993.

106. Baker, *Politics of Diplomacy,* 355–365 (355 quote).

107. Baker, *Politics of Diplomacy,* 359 (quote); Bush and Scowcroft, *World Transformed,* 441–443. For a copy of the President's letter, see "The Letter to Saddam," January 9, 1991, in Micah L. Sifry and Christopher Cerf, eds., *The Gulf War Reader* (New York: Random House Times Books, 1991), 178–179.

108. Bush and Scowcroft, *World Transformed,* 443–446.

109. Drft intvw trnscrpt, McPeak by Gehri, Mann, and Reynolds, Nov 5, 1992, 24 (quote), 23–25.

110. Ibid., 23 (quotes); Bush and Scowcroft, *World Transformed*, 447.

111. Bush and Scowcroft, *World Transformed,* 448.

112. The postwar Greenpeace estimate of Iraqi civilian casualties during the war was 2,278 dead and 5,976 injured by Coalition bombing nationwide, as cited in *GWAPS*. For a discussion of the vast number of civilian deaths which occurred after the war, see *GWAPS,* vol 2, part 2, *Effects and Effectiveness*, 304–305.

113. NSD 54, Memo for Vice President et al., "Responding to Iraqi Aggression in the Gulf," Jan 15, 1991, 2–3, Bush Presidential Library at http://bushlibrary.tamu.edu/research/nsd/NSD/NSD%2054/0001.pdf.

114. NSD 54, Jan 15, 1991, 3.

115. Ibid.

116. Comment, Glosson on draft manuscript, Putney, "Airpower Advantage."

117. Drft intvw trnscrpt, Deptula by Davis, Jamieson, and Putney, Nov 29, 1991, 50; Intvw tape, Deptula by Putney, Apr 11, 1994, (quote).

118. Intvw tape, Rogers by Putney, Sep 18, 1994; Drft intvw trnscrpt, Horner by Putney and Bradley, Apr 26, 1994, 98 (quote); Discussion, Capt John R. Glock and Diane T. Putney, Feb 7, 1995.

119. Notes, Maj Mark "Buck" Rogers, 1620/Gen Schwarzkopf, [Jan 15, 1991], Rogers file, GWAPS, AFHRA; Intvw tape, Rogers by Putney, Sep 18, 1994; Notes, Lt Col David A. Deptula, "Wartime Significance Events Outline," c. Mar 2, 1991, Deptula file, GWAPS, AFHRA; Intvw tape, Deptula by Putney, Apr 11, 1994; MAP, Jan 10, 1991/2200 with changes 1–3, Jan 16, 1991/21:21, box 1, folder 3, Black Hole file, GWAPS, AFHRA.

120. Notes, Maj "Buck" Rogers, 1620/Gen Schwarzkopf, [Jan 15, 1990], Rogers file, AFHRA; Intvw trnscrpt, Corder by Gehri and Reynolds, Feb 4, 1992, 79. MAP, Jan 10, 1991/2200 with changes 1–3, Jan 16, 1991/21:21, box 1, folder 3, Black Hole file, GWAPS, AFHRA. Corder had left the briefing before the "explosion," but he heard of it and remembered the CINCCENT's complaint about being lied to.

121. Rogers notes, 1620/Gen Schwarzkopf, [Jan 15, 1991]; Intvw tape, Deptula by Putney, Apr 11, 1994; Drft intvw trnscrpt, Deptula by Davis, Jamieson, and Putney, Jan 8, 1992, 31 (quote).

122. Intvw tape, Rogers by Putney, Sep 18, 1994, AFHSO; Intvw trnscrpt, Corder by Gehri and Reynolds, Feb 4, 1992, 79.

123. Capt Glock was in the NBC Cell and heard CINCCENT angrily pound on the wall between the NBC and BCE Cells. He recalled Schwarzkopf shouting in the BCE Cell, "You lied to me!" Discussion, Capt John R. Glock and Diane T. Putney, Feb 7, 1995.

124. Intvw tape, Rogers by Putney, Sep 18, 1994; Drft intvw trnscrpt, Horner by Putney and Bradley, Apr 26, 1994, 99; Intvw tape, Deptula by Putney and Davis, Dec 12, 1992.

125. Drft intvw trnscrpt, Horner by Putney and Bradley, Apr 26, 1994, 99; Intvw tape, Deptula by Putney, Apr 11, 1994.

126. De la Billiere, *Storm Command*, 40.

127. Msg, USCINCCENT/CCCC to JCS/CJCS, 161735Z Jan 91, subj: USCINCCENT OPORD 91–001 for Operation Desert Storm, NA 351, GWAPS, AFHRA.

128. OPLAN, Combined Operations Plan for Offensive Operations to Eject Iraqi Forces from Kuwait, USCENTCOM and JF/Theater of Operations, Dec 30, 1990, folder 57, box 1, Task Force 5, GWAPS, AFHRA.

129. Brfg, "Your Role in the Offensive Air Campaign," 6–8, folder 12, Deptula file, GWAPS, AFHRA.

130. Rpt, "Air to Air Analysis in Desert Storm," 30–31, frames 811–812, in Misc-85, GWAPS, reel 27744, AFHRA.

131. Speech trnscrpt, Horner to Business Executives, May 8, 1991, 5; *GWAPS,* vol 5, part 1, *Statistical Compendium,* 641.

132. Signed drft msg, COMUSCENTAF to 1TFW et al., 160300Z Jan 91, subj: Wolfpack Warning Order, folder 10, Deptula file, GWAPS, AFHRA; Comment, Glosson on draft manuscript, Putney, "Airpower Advantage."

133. Signed drft msg, COMUSCENTAF to 1TFW et al., 160930Z Jan 91, subj: Wolfpack Execute Order, folder 11, Deptula file, GWAPS, AFHRA. Within the execute message was ATO information which comprised the third change to ATO-1M.

134. Msg, USCINCCENT/CCJ3 to SEC-

DEF et al., 162100Z Jan 91, subj: Execute Order—USCINCCENT OPORD 001 for Desert Storm, in NA 357, GWAPS, AFHRA.

135. Intvw tape, Deptula by Reynolds, Mann, and Gehri, July 23, 1992. When Horner returned home after the war, he was amazed at how well-informed the American public was about the war—he joked that some people were more informed than he. "They had CNN, and I had intelligence officers," he good-naturedly observed. See Speech trnscrpt, Horner to Daedalians, Sep 11, 1991, 12.

136. Cheney Frontline interview, www.pbs.org/wgbh/pages/frontline/gulf/oral/cheney, p 1 of 11.

137. Intvw tape, Baptiste by Putney and Reynolds, Sep 24, 1992.

138. Intvw tape, Glosson, Henry, and Lewis by Putney, May 20, 1997.

139. Intvw tape, Deptula by Davis, Jamieson, and Putney, Jan 8, 1992; Comment, Deptula on draft manuscript, Putney, "Airpower Advantage."

140. Intvw tape, Rogers by Putney, Sep 18, 1994; Intvw tape, Eskridge by Davis, Mar 19, 1992.

141. Drft intvw trnscrpt, Henry by Putney, Jul 3, 1997, 84–85.

142. Discussion, Capt John R. Glock and Diane T. Putney, Feb 8, 1995.

143. Intvw tape, Tolin by Davis, Nov 23, 1993.

144. Comment, Deptula on draft manuscript, Putney, "Airpower Advantage."

145. Drft intvw trnscrpt, Horner by Putney and Bradley, Apr 26, 1994, 110–111.

146. Intvw tape, McNary by Putney, Aug 9, 1994.

147. Ibid; Intvw tape, Rogers by Putney, Sep 18, 1994.

148. Intvw trnscrpt, Horner by Reynolds and Gehri, Dec 2, 1991, 49 (1st quote) and 50 (3d quote); Speech trnscrpt, Horner to Business Executives, May 8, 1991, 5 (2d quote); Drft intvw trnscrpt, Horner by Putney and Bradley, Apr 26, 1994, 111 (4th quote).

149. Comment, Deptula on draft manuscript, Putney, "Airpower Advantage."

150. Intvw trnscrpt, Hoyes by Clark, Mar 29, 1991, 10; Discussion, Wayne W. Thompson, Checkmate and GWAPS historian, and Diane T. Putney, Feb 16, 1991, AFHSO.

151. Schwarzkopf, *It Doesn't Take a Hero*, 413.

Epilogue

1. The basic source for reconstructing the strikes over the first 24 hours is the MAP, "Master Attack Plan First Twenty-four Hours," Jan 10, 1991/2200, with changes 1–3, Jan 16, 1991/21:21, AFHRA, as explained in drft intvw trnscrpt, Deptula by Davis, Putney, and Jamieson, Jan 8, 1992, and intvw tape, Deptula by Putney, Apr 11, 1994. See also *GWAPS,* vol 2, part 1, *Operations* and Richard G. Davis, *On Target: Organizing and Executing the Strategic Air Campaign* (Washington, D.C.: Air Force History & Museums Program, 2002). For a comprehensive analysis of the results of air campaign strikes, see *GWAPS,* vol 2, part 2, *Effects and Effectiveness.*

2. DoD, *Conduct of the Persian Gulf War,* 114–116. Detailed Army and Air Force SOF sources pinpoint the start of the attack at 0238, one minute before the MAP indicated. See Scales, *Certain Victory,* 159, and Hist, Randy G. Bergeron, *Desert Shield/Desert Storm: Air Force Special Operations Command in the Gulf War,* 89, AFSOC/HO, Jan 1997, AFHRA.

3. *GWAPS,* vol 2, part 1, *Operations,* 126. At 0200 a group of Iraqi border guards heard the sound of Task Force Normandy helicopters 50 feet over their heads. Evidence does not seem to exist, however, to indicate if, when, how, and to whom, around 0200, the border guards sent warning messages about the helicopters. It is probable that they did report on the task force's flight, so the warning from the early-warning radar site may have been the second warning within the hour. See Scales, *Certain Victory,* 157, and Richard Cody, "Task Force Normandy,"

in *Leading the Way*, ed. Al Santoli (New York: Ballantine Books, 1993), 235–241.

4. *GWAPS,* vol 2, part 1, *Operations*, 137.

5. Howard Kurtz, "On Television, Gunfire Is Heard, but Not Seen," *Washington Post*, Jan 17, 1991, A28; James F. Clarity, "From T.V. Reporters in Iraq, News an Attack Has Begun," *New York Times,* Jan 17, 1991, A15; Walter Goodman, "On Television, The Theater of War," *New York Times,* Jan 17, 1991, A19; CNN film, "CNN Gulf War Coverage," Jan 16, 1991, Library of Congress, Washington, D.C. News reporters from ABC and NBC had relied on hotel telephone lines to call in their stories; CNN reporters, John Holliman, Bernard Shaw, and Peter Arnett, used a special international line not requiring a switchboard. See the Kurtz article.

6. Hit/no hit data from spreadsheet, [Barry D. Watts, GWAPS], "F–117 Master [List]," GWAPS, AFHRA. In this document, Watts recorded each F–117 strike by day, indicated hits, and provided reasons for no hits, including weather-related no-drops.

7. That the Iraqis fired the AAA at 2:58 A.M. local time, see *GWAPS,* vol 2, part 1, *Operations,* 121; Gordan and Trainor, *Generals' War,* 215.

8. Rpt, "F–117s and Electronic Combat Support during the War," [Lt Col David A. Deptula], Nov 1991, AFHRA. One of the three EF–111s departed its station early because of an Iraqi fighter attack. This November 1991 report also suggests that the EF–111s were probably positioned too far west of Baghdad to have significantly assisted the F–117s striking targets in Baghdad. See also discussion in *GWAPS,* vol 2, part 1, *Operations*, 120–124. For missiles and guns, see DoD, *Conduct of the Persian Gulf War*, 177.

9. *GWAPS,* vol 4, part 1, *Weapons, Tactics, and Training*, 192, 194.

10. Ibid., 88, 173; DoD, *Conduct of the Persian Gulf War*, 119. Twenty-two F–15s were scheduled, but three aborted.

11. Hit/no hit data from spreadsheet, [Barry D. Watts, GWAPS], "F–117 Master [List]," GWAPS, AFHRA. A "no hit" occurred with a miss or a bomb not dropped because of weather or other problems.

12 Marolda and Schneller, *Shield and Sword,* 170.

13. MAP, "Master Attack Plan First Twenty-four Hours," Jan 10, 1991/2200 with changes 1–3, Jan 16, 1991/21:21, AFHRA.

14. Ibid.

15. *GWAPS,* vol 2, part 1, *Operations*, 126–133.

16. MAP, "Master Attack Plan First Twenty-four Hours," Jan 10, 1991/2200 with changes 1–3, Jan 16, 1991/21:21, AFHRA.

17. Hist, John W.B. Masotti, Col., "Operation Desert Shield and Desert Storm Bomber Story," 30, SAC/DOBX, NA 91, GWAPS, AFHRA; *GWAPS,* vol 2, part 1, *Operations*, 123 (map), 135; Intvw trnscrpt, Horner by Putney, Nov 30, 1996, 57.

18. MAP, "Master Attack Plan First Twenty-four Hours," Jan 10, 1991/2200 with changes 1–3, Jan 16, 1991/21:21, AFHRA. Hit/no hit data from spreadsheet, [Barry D Watts, GWAPS], "F–117 Master [List]," GWAPS, AFHRA.

19. Although the MAP indicates a mixture of BW and CW targets hit by F–117s at 0200–0213Z, all of the sites were considered BW targets; *CW* was a typing error. See intvw tape, Deptula by Putney, Apr 11, 1994. In addition, the planners had earlier considered dropping incendiaries after the initial blast which cracked open the bunkers; however, the weapons in the early morning of January 17 did not include incendiaries. The planners believed that the morning sunlight would cause spores to deteriorate, while the mines kept Iraqis from entering the facilities to remove and preserve the biological agents. See MAP and drft intvw trnscrpt, Deptula by Davis, Putney, and Jamieson, Jan 8, 1992, 166.

20. In 1995 Gordon and Trainor wrote, "Iraq had a biological warfare program, but the UN inspectors found no evidence that it had turned its biological agents into actual weapons." *Generals' War,* 183. In 1993 the GWAPS team reported, "UN inspectors were unable to confirm after the war that the Iraqis had actually produced any biological weapons prior to 17 January 1991." See

GWAPS, vol 2, part 2, *Effects and Effectiveness*, 327. In 1995, however, after the defection of Lt Gen Hussein Kamel Majid, Saddam's son-in-law who had knowledge of Iraq's weapons of mass destruction, Iraq turned over documents to UNSCOM which revealed that Iraq *had* weaponized biological agents before the Persian Gulf War. In 1998 the State Department reported that Iraqi officials "admitted preparing BW-filled munitions—including 25 Scud missile warheads (five anthrax, sixteen botulinum toxin, and four aflatoxin), aerial bombs (157), and aerial dispensers—during the Gulf War, although it did not use them." See U.S. Government White Paper, "Iraqi Weapons of Mass Destruction," www.state.gov/www/regions/nea/iraq_white_paper.html, 3 of 11.

21. For a discussion of the shootdown of Lt Cmdr Michael S. Speicher, see *GWAPS,* vol 2, part 1, *Operations*, 136, 136 n 87; Gordon and Trainor, *Generals' War,* 219. For an early discussion of Speicher possibly surviving the crash, see Tom Weiner, "Gulf War's First U.S. Casualty Leaves Lasting Trail of Mystery," *New York Times,* Dec 7, 1997, A1, A6.

22. MAP, "Master Attack Plan First Twenty-four Hours," Jan 10, 1991/2200 with changes 1–3, Jan 16, 1991/21:21, AFHRA.

23. Ibid.

24. DoD, *Conduct of the Persian Gulf War*, 773; *GWAPS,* vol 4, part 1, *Weapons, Tactics, and Training*, 50, 78; *GWAPS,* vol 2, part 1, *Operations,* 138. B–2s flying missions to Afghanistan in Operation Enduring Freedom flew longer sorties.

25. MAP, "Master Attack Plan First Twenty-four Hours," Jan 10, 1991/2200 with changes 1–3, Jan 16, 1991/21:21, AFHRA; Gordon and Trainor, *Generals' War,* 221.

26. MAP, "Master Attack Plan First Twenty-four Hours," Jan 10, 1991/2200 with changes 1–3, Jan 16, 1991/21:21, AFHRA.

27. Ibid., with notation.

28. Ibid. The Baghdad air defenses were not de-fanged as 72 F–16 pilots, supported by F–4Gs and EF–111s, would learn on the third day of the air campaign, when their Package Q mission, the largest of the war, met stiff, deadly resistance, and many had to jettison fuel tanks and bombs to survive radar-guided SAMs, which downed two F–16s. See *GWAPS,* vol 2, part 1, *Operations*, 105–110; 171–177.

29. MAP, "Master Attack Plan First Twenty-four Hours," Jan 10, 1991/2200 with changes 1–3, Jan 16, 1991/21:21, AFHRA.

30. Ibid.; Hit/no hit data from spreadsheet, [Barry D. Watts, GWAPS], "F–117 Master [List]," GWAPS, AFHRA.

31. MAP, "Master Attack Plan First Twenty-four Hours," Jan 10, 1991/2200 with changes 1–3, Jan 16, 1991/21:21, AFHRA.

32. Ibid.

33. Ibid.

34. *GWAPS,* vol 2, part 1, *Operations*, 145–146, and vol 5, part 1, *Statistical Compendium,* 642–643.

35. Quoted in Ibid., 138.

36. Ibid., 146–147, 163; DoD, *Conduct of the Persian Gulf War*, 254–256; Keaney and Cohen, *Gulf War Air Power Survey Summary Report,* 140.

37. *GWAPS,* vol 2, part 1, *Operations*, 184.

38. Horner, "Banquet Address," in *Seeing Off the Bear*, ed. Miller, 142 (1st and 3d quotes); drft intvw trnscrpt, Horner by Putney and Bradley, Apr 26, 1994, 4 (2d quote).

39. Intvw trnscrpt, Horner by Gehri and Reynolds, Dec 2, 1991, 66.

40. Ibid., 54.

41. Essay, Warden, "Centers of Gravity," 6–7.

42. Powell, *My American Journey,* 513. Atkinson reported that the Iraqi government told the UN Human Rights Commission that 204 people died in the Al Firdos bunker. See Atkinson, *Crusade,* 286.

43. DoD, *Conduct of the Persian Gulf War*, 130, 141–142.

44. *GWAPS,* vol 2, part 2, *Effects and Effectiveness*, 148. Watts explained that *strikes* referred to "occasions on which an aircraft released air-to-ground ordnance against a discrete target." Numbers vary slightly between *GWAPS* editions.

45. DoD, *Conduct of the Persian Gulf War*, 124, 126; *GWAPS,* vol 2, part 1, *Operations*, 337; *GWAPS,* vol 2, part 2, *Effects*

and Effectiveness, 105, 266.

46. The "appropriate" aim points are those Glosson identified in a back-dated wartime memo, as planners tried to redirect strikes away from generator halls. See memo, [CENTAF] INT to All Plans Offices, Jan 12, 1991 [Feb 5, 1991], subj: Target Guidance, Deptula folder 19c, GWAPS, AFHRA. The postwar controversy involved a Harvard Study Team reporting on mortality rates. For a discussion of the issues and a defense of power plants as military targets, see *GWAPS,* vol 2, part 2, *Effects and Effectiveness*, 290–312.

47. *GWAPS,* vol 2, part 2, *Effects and Effectiveness*, 307–308.

48. Intvw trnscrpt, Dr Rice, Secretary of the Air Force, by Lt Col Richard Reynolds, Lt Col Suzanne Gehri, and Lt Col Edward Mann, Dec 11, 1991, 15 (quote), NA 234, GWAPS, AFHRA. Postwar intelligence studies revealed that simultaneously striking as few as three major power plants in Iraq would have caused the Iraqi electric grid to shut down. See *GWAPS,* vol 2, part 2, *Effects and Effectiveness*, 294 n 58. For short histories of U.S. attacks against electric power targets see Thomas E. Griffith, Jr., "Strategic Attacks of National Electrical Systems" (master's thesis, AU, 1994) and Daniel T. Kuehl, "Airpower vs. Electricity: Electric Power as a Target for Strategic Air Operations," in *Airpower: Theory and Practice*, ed. John Gooch (London: Frank Cass, 1995), 237–266.

49. That the Iraqis undertook such activity, see *GWAPS,* vol 1, part 1, *Planning*, 69; *GWAPS,* vol 2, part 2, *Effects and Effectiveness*, 50; DoD, *Conduct of the Persian Gulf War,* 155. For UNSCR 678, see www.state.gov/documents/organization/18076.pdf, p 1 of 2.

50. *GWAPS,* vol 2, part 2, *Effects and Effectiveness*, 54–57, 315, 365–366.

51. House, Committee on Oversight and Investigations Subcommittee of the Committee on Armed Services: "Intelligence Successes and Failures in Operations Desert Shield/Storm," 103d Cong., 1st sess., August 16, 1993, 24.

52. *GWAPS,* vol 1, part 1, *Planning*, 68–69.

53. William M. Arkin, "The Urban Sanctuary in Desert Storm?" at www. airpower.maxwell.af.airchronicles/apj/spr97/arkin.html, p 10 of 18.

54. Ibid.

55. DoD, *Conduct of the Persian Gulf War,* 105, 107.

56. *GWAPS,* vol 2, part 2, *Effects and Effectiveness*, 208.

57. Schubert and Kraus, eds, *Whirlwind War,* 158.

58. Trnscrpt, News brfg, Gen H. Norman Schwarzkopf, Riyadh, Saudi Arabia, Feb 27, 1991, 1:00 p.m. (EST), 1–2. See also DoD, *Conduct of the Persian Gulf War*, chart, 101, and maps, 255, 256.

59. Trnscrpt, News brfg, Gen H. Norman Schwarzkopf, Riyadh, Saudi Arabia, Feb 27, 1991, 1:00 p.m. (EST), 2 (quotes).

60. As quoted in Richard P. Hallion, *Storm over Iraq: Air Power and the Gulf War* (Washington: Smithsonian Press,1992), 209.

61. Ed drft intvw trnscrpt, Deptula by Davis, Jamieson, and Putney, Jan 8, 1992, 162.

62. Intvw, Warden by Gehri, Mann, and Reynolds, May 30, 1991, 64–66.

63. Gen Michael Dugan, USAF (Ret), "First Lessons of Victory," *U.S. News & World Report*, 18 March 1991, 36. Dugan, however, applied the word *hyperwar* to the ground attack, as a term to replace *blitzkrieg*.

64. Richard H. Shultz, Jr., and Robert L. Pfaltzgraff, Jr., eds, *The Future of Air Power in the Aftermath of the Gulf War* (Maxwell AFB, Ala.: AU Press, 1992), 79.

65. Karl P. Magyar, Maris McCrabb, Albert U. Mitchum, Jr., and Lewis B. Ware, *Challenge and Response: Anticipating U.S. Military Security Concerns* (Maxwell AFB, Ala.: AU Press, 1994), 296 n 10.

66. David A. Deptula, "Parallel Warfare: What Is It? Where Did It Come From? Why Is It Important?" in William Head and Earl H. Tilford, Jr., ed., *The Eagle in the Desert: Looking Back on U.S. Involvement in the Persian Gulf War* (Westport, Conn.: Praeger, 1996), 152 n 5. Warden stated that he used the term *parallel* during the war or right after, but did not use *serial* nor the analogy

of electrical circuitry at that time. Discussion, Warden and Putney, Sep 28, 2001.

67. Deptula, "Parallel Warfare," 127–156; David A. Deptula, "Firing for Effect: Change in the Nature of Warfare," pamphlet in Defense and Airpower Series (Arlington, Va.: Aerospace Education Foundation, 1995), 5 (quote).

68. Maj Richard M. Kessel, USAF, "Parallel Warfare: Anticipating the Enemy's Response," Maj John R. Pardo, Jr., USAF, "Parallel Warfare: Its Nature and Application," and Col John A. Warden III, USAF, "Air Theory for the Twenty-first Century," in *Challenge and Response*, ed. Magyar et al., 277–332 (324 quote). See also Richard Szafranski, "Parallel Warfare: Promise, Problems," *U.S. Naval Institute Proceedings* 121 (August 1995): 57–61.

69. Essay, Warden, "Centers of Gravity," 10.

70. AFDD 1, "Air Force Basic Doctrine," September 1997, 24.

71. AFDD 2–1.2, "Strategic Attack," May 20, 1998, 31–32.

72. David A. Deptula, "Firing for Effect: Change in the Nature of Warfare," Pamphlet in the Defense and Airpower Series (Arlington, Va.: Aerospace Education Foundation, 1995).

73. Charles A. Link, "Thoughts on the Nature of Future War," Briefing, HQ USAF, Nov 1998, CD-ROM.

74. As quoted in T.W. Beagle, Jr., "Effects-Based Targeting: Another Empty Promise?" (master's thesis, AU, 2001), 1.

75. Gen Charles A. Horner, USAF (Ret), "Air Power: Growing Beyond Desert Storm," *Aviation Week & Space Technology,* Apr 16, 1997, 74.

76. DoD, *Conduct of the Persian Gulf War*, 340.

77. *GWAPS,* vol 2, part 2, *Effects and Effectiveness*, 266.

78. Bush and Scowcroft, *World Transformed*, 466.

79. Ibid., 477–478. See also Powell, *My American Journey,* 499, and Schwarzkopf, *It Doesn't Take a Hero,* 436, 443–445.

80. Bush and Scowcroft, *World Transformed,* 466–467; 469–470. See also Powell, *My American Journey*, 513.

81. *GWAPS,* vol 2, part 2, *Effects and Effectiveness*, 207–226, 259–264. After the war, GWAPS concluded that air power destroyed fewer tanks and artillery pieces than CENTCOM indicated, but since the command had overestimated its baseline figure, its destruction percentages were fairly accurate. GWAPS figures for air power destruction rates by February 24 were 40% for tanks; 30% for APCs; and 47% for artillery.

Index

Boldface numbers indicate a photograph only on that page.